BritSlang

Other titles by Ray Puxley (also published by Robson Books)

Cockney Rabbit: A Dick 'n' 'Arry of Rhyming Slang
More Cockney Rabbit: Contemporary Rhyming Slang

RAY PUXLEY

BritSlang

An uncensored **A-Z** of the people's
language including rhyming slang

ROBSON BOOKS

First published in paperback in Great Britain in 2004 by Robson Books,
The Chrysalis Building, Bramley Road, London W10 6SP

A member of **Chrysalis** Books plc

British Library Cataloguing in Publication Data
A catalogue record for this title is available from the British Library.

ISBN 1 86105 728 8

Typeset by SX Composing DTP, Rayleigh, Essex
Printed by Creative Print & Design (Wales), Ebbw Vale

Acknowledgements

Thanks to Chris, without whose computer and lessons in its use, this book would never have been started; also to Jeannie for her support and strength when I was going through a mid-book crisis.

Thanks also to my old man, Bert, for not using my first two books as coasters, and my sister, Joy, for constantly telling me she has a talented brother. Funny I've never met him. A special thank you to my editor at Robson Books, Jane Donovan.

Finally, thanks to Scobie for being, for 15½ years, the best little dog in Dagenham. Now watering the trees of doggy Heaven.

Ray Puxley

Dedicated to the memory of
Harry Wiseman –
A Good 'Un.

Introduction

It is generally reckoned to be very non-PC these days to talk about British history. What previous generations of school children were taught to be proud of and to wave flags at, today's kids are told to regard with disdain and to shake their fists at. And while it remains a contentious issue as to whether or not the world benefited from the intervention of this little island during the days of colonialism and empire, the one thing nobody can argue with is that Britain left its mark on half the world in the form of a language.

If Britain and America are two nations divided by a common language, then what unites them is slang, the language of the street, the bar, the underworld, the gutter. This is also true of the rest of the English-speaking world. Australia, Canada, Ireland, New Zealand and South Africa all have flourishing 'slanguages' and many compilers down the years have encapsulated all these into impressive dictionaries. But does the average Briton really care what name sheep shearers deep within the Australian bush give to a kangaroo's tail? No, I don't think so either. Nor do I think he gives a monkey's what fish gutters in the Northern Territories of Canada call their snowshoes. It's far more relevant to know what they call them in Grimsby. It's for this reason then that I have compiled a book of British slang, with just the odd piece from the colonies creeping in.

Elements of slang can be traced back to the Middle Ages; Chaucer spiced up his Canterbury Tales with it, and Shakespeare wasn't averse to covering up a taboo word with a choice phrase or two. Ever since, the dialogue of countless novels, plays, comedies and films has been enriched and enlivened by its use. That said, I don't pretend to be any kind of slang historian, I leave that to the professional lexicographer who has the time, resources and inclination to peer into the mouth that has for so long housed the 'vulgar tongue'. I am therefore released from the constraints of conformity in that I do not have to produce a conventional dictionary. For me, slang is a subject for humour, something not to be taken too seriously, which is how I hope my non-academic approach comes across to the reader.

Slang is the scruffy, irreverent younger brother of language, the impoverished embarrassment who comes in, pulls up a chair and puts his feet on the table. He is the drunken, chauvinistic racist who knows a thousand ways to order a drink and insult his fellow man and woman. He knows a superabundance of ways to describe their private parts and the functions they perform. What he doesn't know about man's lavatorial needs and what they produce isn't worth knowing, and he'll tell you about them in a multitude of ways. He's the foul-mouthed yob who breaks wind at the dinner table and then asks, 'Yeah, but don't you just love me?' And apart from the devotees of his big brother, yes. We do.

Much of the content of this book is new to print and so I owe an enormous debt of gratitude to everyone who has made a verbal contribution.

My mother was a fountain of weird and wonderful phrases and sayings, as was her sister, my aunt Kate. Much of what they said had come from their mother, who was skilled in the ways of backslang and not averse to using a choice bit of East End 'Langwidge' when the need arose, so you will find a lot of unrecorded material from the 19th century.

My grandad, a soldier of the queen during the Boer War and who later served in India, brought back to Blighty, along with his campaign medals, a smattering of early soldier slang.

My dad, a docker by day and an ace tic-tac man at various dog tracks by night, introduced me to the slang of the river and the racecourse. My journey through life has taken me down some diverse side roads as far as employment has been concerned and I've picked up some terms of each trade I've been involved in.

So to everyone I have met, and everyone I have not, including the wits, the wags, the comedians, the scriptwriters, the journalists et al, who have helped to swell the pages of this book.

To my toppo-oppos Weaver, Roderick, Jamoe, Cyril, Ted, Smiffy, Big Dave, the Lucas and Skeels brothers, Stick, Al the actor and Lachiko. Also various in-laws, nephews and nieces – too many to name – all of whom have added a word or a phrase to BritSlang.

To all of them I offer my sincere gratitude. I certainly won't be offering any money!

Ray Puxley

A

A Spit and a Gob		Not far away; very close. How a cab driver will describe the distance between two points. ·
A to Z	*Shed*	Probably after the roadmap people; like you'd need a map to find the bottom of the garden.
ACAB		Typical knuckle tatoo among the police-hating fraternities meaning 'All Coppers are Bastards'.
Abdul		A World War One term for a Turk, later to become a derogatory name for an Arab as well.
Abe/Abie		A very old term for a Jew from the typical Jewish name, Abraham.
Abel & Cain	*Rain*	The biblical brothers get together to blight the English summer.
Aberdeen(s)	*Bean(s)*	Mainly applies to baked beans. Also serves as a Spoonerism of 'ad a bean', whereby the hungry may moan 'I'm starving, I haven't Aberdeen all day.' Also, what the skint may not have.
Abergavenny	*Penny*	An old term that originally applied to the pre-decimal penny, but can relate to the present one.
About Done/ Right		A couple of terms for being drunk but not excessively so. When someone's 'about right' he may inform his drinking pals: 'Right I'm about done, time I was leaving.'
Abraham	*Sham*	Pronounced 'Abram', this applies to getting out of

something by feigning illness. Many have gone on the 'Abram' by phoning in sick, only to be seen at a televised race meeting, grinning like a gom (qv) behind John McCrirrick.

Abraham's Willing *Shilling*
A piece that was defunct long before Britain's previous currency was.

Abroad
19th-century criminal parlance. 'Where's Dick?' 'Oh he's abroad somewhere.' He's out thieving.

Abso-one-hundred-per-cent-lutely
A dopey expression for 'absolutely' at it's most definite.

Abyssinia
Pun for goodbye, 'I'll be seein' ya.'

AC/DC
Based on the two different types of electrical current, alternating and direct, a well-known expression for a bisexual person, the male of the species having both a plug and a socket.

Acca
A shortening of accumulator, a bet of at least four selections. One loser and you've had it.

Accident
Roguespeak for an occupational hazard. 'I had an accident' translates to 'I was arrested.'

Ace
a) Originally an American but now a universal term for excellent, the best, an expert.
b) The anus. Closely resembling the one-spot card and the word 'arse'.
c) A single pill of whatever in the drugs world.
d) To kill. An American term included for it's common usage in films.

Ace of Spades
a) The female pubic area, after the colour and shape.
b) The very definition of blackness, 'as black as the ace of spades'.

Ace of Spades *Aids*
The traditional card of misfortune is said to have been drawn by those unfortunate enough to contract this disease.

Ace of Trumps
The highest card in the pack represents a first-class person. 'A diamond geezer.'

Ache & Pain *Rain*
If you've ever thought that a wet weekend was an arsehole-ache or a pain in the butt you'll see how apt this is.

Acid
Drugs. Originally LSD but later came to mean Ecstasy.

Acid Drops
Barbed or caustic comments. The title of a book by Kenneth Williams (1926–87), the master of the put-down.

Acid Freak/Head
A brace of terms for a frequent user of LSD.

Acid House
A youth cult, that had it's beginnings in the 1980s, which mainly involves getting out of your nut on

drugs and leaping up and down to loud synthetic noises known as house music.

Acker Bilk   *Milk*   A 1960s piece based on a British jazz clarinetist, a regular chart entrant at the time. In a coffee bar, when asked if he wanted his coffee black or white, an Irishman replied, 'Black please, with drop of Acker.'

Ackers   Money. A World War One term first coined by British soldiers serving in Egypt, where they came across a coin called an akka.

Acorn   a) An old term for the head, an extension of 'nut' (qv, a).

b) The head of an erect penis, from its accordant appearance. A fact endorsed by the similarity of it's medical term, 'glans penis', and the Latin name for an acorn, *glans*.

Acorn in a Bird's Nest   Man's genitalia as seen by a character from TV's *Til Death Us Do Part*.

Acorns   An obvious parity with 'nuts' (qv, a), relating to the testicles.

Actor   An underworld term for a good liar or con artist. Commonly used of 'diving' footballers.

Actual   Money, but hard cash rather than a cheque or credit card.

Adam & Eve   a) *Believe*   A common piece of RS, often the start of a piece of gossip: 'You won't Adam and Eve this but . . .'

b) *Leave*   Older than (a) though not as familiar. When it's time to go, it's 'time you were Adam and Eving'.

Adam & Eve's Togs   When all you've got on is your nude, this is what you are wearing.

Adam Ants   *Pants*   A term from the 1980s when this British singer was frequently in the charts. His trademark was his flamboyant dress. We can only wonder at the state of his 'Adams'.

Adam Faith   *Safe*   A piece employed by betting-shop managers of the 1960s based on the late chart-topping singer and actor (1940–2003). He later became a financial expert, no doubt with an 'Adam' of his own.

Addled   Muddled, puddled and befuddled by the effects of alcohol. An ancient term for being drunk.

Adolph   A vibrator, from the bomb-like shape. Wartime films often showed a Berlin-bound bomb, being loaded on to a Lancaster, with the words 'This one's for you Adolph' scrawled on the side of it.

Aeroplane Blonde   A woman who is not a natural blonde. She'll have a black 'box'. *See* BOX (d).

African Lager		Guinness, black nectar as opposed to that amber stuff.
African Queen		A black homosexual male or a white one with leanings towards black partners.
African Woodbine		A marijuana or cannabis cigarette, first rolled in the 1970s.
After Eight Mint	*Skint*	What the after-dinner bachelor is by Monday morning.
Afterglow		The winding down period following lovemaking, often the bit before getting up to go home.
Afternoon Delight		Sex between meals.
Afters		An old expression for staying in a pub for an after-hours drinking session. A time-honoured cause of marital disharmony. *See also* LOCK-IN.
Ag		To annoy or bother. A shortening of aggravate or aggravation: 'Don't give me any ag.'
Against the Clock		What you are said to be when time is short and you're in a hurry.
Against the Wind		Running, kicking, fighting or pissing against the wind signifies a struggle or an uphill task.
Aggie Eyes		The eyes of those who haven't had enough sleep. Don't know who Aggie was, maybe a lazy version of 'baggy', but those with their 'eyeballs on their cheeks' are said to be 'aggie eyed'.
Aggravation	*Station*	A term from the 1920s that suggests that the pain of rail travel is nothing new.
Aggro		A 1960s term associated with violence for violence's sake, often at a football ground.
Aginner		Somebody against or 'agin' something. A dissenter.
Ah-Ahs		Defecation, what small children sit on their potties for.
Ain't it a Treat	*Street*	A 19th-century term that was probably used ironically of a slum. More chance of seeing a bottle of salad cream in *Coronation Street* than hearing it now.
Ain't She Sweet	*Seat*	Before it became a sexist thing to do, men used to give up their 'ain't she's' to standing women.
Air Guitar		An imaginary instrument played by would-be guitar heroes.
Air One's Tongue		To talk. Gossips and informers will 'open their traps and give their tongues an airing'.
Air-Dance		The final cocking of the legs of a hanging victim.
Airhead		A dolt with an empty space where his brain should be.
Airs & Graces	*a) Braces*	Support for this term was suspended with the popularity of the belt.
	b) Faces	If there's some dodgy looking 'airs and graces' in the pub, go somewhere else.
	c) Races	An old term that's no longer in the running.

Airsick Pigeon		Symbol of uselessness: 'You're as much use as an...'
Aitch Dropper		Chiefly a cockney, but basically anyone what don't talk proper. According to our 'betters' that is.
Ajax	*Tax*	Based on the name of an ancient Greek warrior who later became a scouring powder and a Dutch football team. Now he is seen in the shape of a disc on a car windscreen, or should be.
Al Capone	*Phone*	An old, never-popular piece, that's probably as dead as this American gangster (1899–1947).
Alabama	*Hammer*	Heard on a 1990s building site as an 'Ala'.
Alabaster	*Plaster*	Always said as 'ala', this is the bottom rung of the most convoluted piece of RS. When you get to the top you'll be at the bottom. *See* PLASTER OF PARIS.
Aladdin's Cave		Thief's stash-point for stolen goods.
Alan Border	*Order*	Based on an Australian cricket captain whose success depressed many an Englishman. He now frustrates many more at closing time with the cry of 'Last Alan Borders'. He's also at the crease when anything or anybody is 'out of order'.
Alan Ladd	*Sad*	Often used in relation to an 'anorak' (qv). Anyone who, by choice, knows the difference in widths of any two given railway tracks in the world is laughed off as being 'a bit Alan Ladd really'. Based on a US film star (1913–64).
Alan Minter	*Splinter*	Based on the Crawley-born boxer who in 1980 became world middleweight champion, this was used briefly by woodworkers with small slivers of tree in their fingers, thumbs, ears, etc.
Alan Whicker	*Nicker (£1)*	1990s youthspeak based on an English TV personality.
Alan Whickers	*Knickers*	An example of early middle class RS dating from the late 1960s. Usually dropped to 'Alans'.
Albert Hall	*Wall*	Harrassed parents may be driven up the 'Albert' by troublesome offspring.
Alderman's Nail	*Tail*	A very old term for an animal's tail, particularly the wagpiece of a dog. 'Nail' is a 19c term for an arrest, so could a bent official of yore be in the frame here?
Aldershot Whore	*Four*	Probably from a squaddies bingo game, where 44 was known as Aldershot Ladies. Situated in Hampshire, Aldershot has been an army training centre since 1854.
Aldgate East	*Priest*	It matters not if he's Catholic or Anglican, he's still an 'Aldgate'. Or 'Allgit' in proper cockney.
Aldgate Pump	*Hump*	To be displeased or fed up is to have 'the right Aldgate' (pronounced 'Allgit'). After an ancient water pump that is no longer in use and now a landmark in the City of London.

Aled Up		Drunk, an old term for being out of the game through beer.
Alf Garnet	*Barnet (Hair)*	Actor Warren Mitchell's alter ego provides us with an example of how, when a term becomes as common as 'barnet', it acquires a piece of RS of it's own. *See* BARNET FAIR.
Alfie Bass	*Gas*	A forgotten term from the early 1960s, when this British comedy actor (1920–87) was the star of TV sitcoms, *The Army Game* and *Bootsie and Snudge*.
Alfred the Great	*Weight*	Always reduced to 'Alfred' by those seeking to reduce their 'Alfred'. Based on the old king of Wessex (849–899) who was famous for burning cakes, not calories. May also be used for what's lifted.
Algernon/Algy		A young upper-class male, a name seen to represent such an animal.
Ali Baba		An alibi, as used by forty punning thieves?
Ali G	*Pee/Wee*	This recent term sees people nipping for an 'Ali'. Based on the comic creation of British comedian Sacha Baron Cohen.
Ali Oop	*Poop (Excrement)*	*See* ALLEZ OOP.
Alight		Drunk. Famously 'well alight'.
Alive		a) When a person has money he is said to be 'alive'. When he's skint he goes back to being a dead-beat. b) To be aware of a situation or scheme, especially a dishonest one.
Alive or Dead	*Head*	A 19th-century piece that was kicked into obsolescence years ago.
All Afloat	*Coat*	A 19th-century term long consigned to the ragbag of discarded RS. It may have lasted longer had it applied to a boat.
All Arms & Legs		Weak beer. A pint with no body to it.
All Beer & Skittles		An easy life, how a would-be 19th-century hedonist envisaged a life of leisure. Times and people change, only slang terms remain the same.
All Behind	*Blind*	Applies sympathetically to those who can't see but angrily to those who can but don't. 'What d'you mean you didn't see me, what are you, all behind?'
All Behind Like a Cat's Arse/ Dog's Tail		A couple of expressions for being behind schedule or running late.
All Come on Top		When a boss tumbles to a fiddle or the police are waiting at a crime scene, for the perpetrators, it's 'all come on top'. Another version of 'when the roof caves in'.

All Complain	*Rain*	Appropriate since wet weather brings out the moaner in all of us. On the plus side though, it does keep the squeegee pests away from traffic lights.
All Dayer		A day-long drinking session. A cause of many a week-long blanking session from the wife.
All Forlorn	*Horn (Erection)*	The dictionary defines 'forlorn' as sad, abandoned and lonely, so the term may relate to waking up with an 'allfor' and having no-one to share it with.
All Mouth & Trousers		One who talks a good battle but shits himself at the first sign of trouble, he therefore has a load of mouth and a plentiful supply of trousers.
All Night Rave	*Shave*	A modern piece used by today's young shavers.
All On Top		Not the genuine article. From the person with champagne taste and brown ale money to the shiny car that hides a dodgy engine, i.e., all show and no substance. Superficial.
All Piss & Wind		Someone who promises the Earth and delivers dirt.
All Quiet on the Western Front	*Cunt*	An overlong term used when Mr unpopular, possibly an officer, is about to join the group: 'Look out. All quiet.'
All Rounder		A bisexual. Based on the cricketing term for someone who can 'bat and bowl' (qv) well.
All Sir Garnet		All's well. After Sir Garnet Wolseley (1833–1913), soldier and later commander-in-chief of the British army, who was known to be a meticulous planner. Sometimes said as 'All Sigarneo'.
All Snot & Tears		Sorry, remorseful, mournful: 'Two faced mare, she didn't have a kind word to say about him when he was alive, now she's all snot and tears.'
All the Georgie		A 1960s way of saying 'All the Best'. *See* GEORGIE BEST.
All the Jollys		An alternative to 'cheers' when glasses are raised.
All There with His/Her Coughdrops		Usually said of an old person whose mind is particularly alert.
All Tits & Teeth		A woman who gets on by using her physical assets rather than her brain. A put down, often by the brainy woman who didn't get the job.
All to Bollocks		Said of something that's gone wrong. Sometimes 'All gone to bollocks'. Often 'A bollocks-up'.
All to Buggery		Said of something that's gone wrong.
All to Cock		Said of something that's gone wrong. Sometimes 'All gone to cock'. Often 'A cock-up'.
All to Fuck		Said of something that's gone wrong. Sometimes 'All gone to fuck'. Often 'A fuck-up'.

All Wind & Water		Someone big on talk but small on action, one who makes empty promises. Sometimes said as 'All blow and splash'.
Allez Oop	*Poop (Excrement)*	The phrase, normally used by stage acrobats at the performance of a feat, may be used when a piece of hard-baked excrement is finally ejected.
Allied Irish Bank	*Wank*	A 1990s term that's generally reduced to an 'Allied Irish'.
Alligator	*Later*	A 1950s piece based on the rock 'n' roll record 'See You Later Alligator'.
Almond Rock	*Cock (Penis)*	The male member is well represented in the world of RS and many, like this one, take the form of long, suckable confectionary.
Almond Rocks	*Socks*	Old, common and always worn as 'almonds'.
Alphabet Boys		The sanctioning bodies of boxing responsible for the ridiculous number of 'world' champions in the sport today. The IBF, WBA, WBC, WBO plus eight more with varying initials give us over 200 world title holders when there should be just seventeen.
Alphonse	*Ponce*	Applies not only to a pimp but to a sponger in general, one who deliberately goes out with nuppence in his pocket and exploits the generosity of others.
Alsatian's Arsehole		What people with bad breath are said to have a mouth like.
Ambidextrous		One who can write equally well with either hand represents one who dips his nib in different inkwells, a bisexual.
Amidships		A naval term for the stomach, often relating to where a punch was landed.
Amos & Andy	*a) Brandy*	A term based on an American radio and TV series which was to political correctness what Vlad the Impaler was to humanitarianism. A & A were two black men played by white actors.
	b) Shandy	After the introduction of the breathalyser, shandies became a common member of a round of drinks and the term began it's confusing merger with (a).
Amscray		A well-known piece of pig Latin for scram – get lost!
Amsterdam	*Jam*	No matter what fruit it's made from, it's all 'amster'.
Anchor		a) A juror who has been bribed in order to influence fellow members to vote for an acquittal. b) A brake applied to a death sentence, a stay of execution. c) An old navvies' term for a pick-axe.
Anchors		Brakes. It is common to slam on the 'anchors'.

Anchors Away	*Gay*	One of a kotchel of terms that have sprung up since 'gay' became the widely accepted word for homosexuality. This may be a term among sailors.
Andy Cain	*Rain*	A 19th-century piece that has disappeared down the drain.
Andy Capp	*a) Crap*	One of many terms for defecation. Also, anyone 'spoutin' a load of Andy' is talking rubbish.
	b) Tap (Borrow)	Fittingly based on the cartoon-strip character who is always skint and therefore 'on the tap'.
Andy McNish	*Fish*	Applies mainly to fish in it's role as food.
Andy Pandy	*a) Brandy*	As watched with mother and drank with father.
	b) Shandy	Based on the TV puppet that everyone watched with mother, a pint of 'Andy Pandy' is a common order from those with a driving license to protect.
Angel		a) One who provides financial backing for a crime or a theatrical production, which sometimes amounts to the same thing.
		b) A passive homosexual, a term from the gay community.
		c) A sandwich-board man. A man sandwiched between two wings.
		d) A prostitute, originally one who worked around the Angel, Islington, North London.
		e) A common expression for a nurse. If you can find one.
Angel Dust		The drug PCP, phencyclidine.
Angle of Dangle		The degree of an erection depending on how sexually stimulated a man is by any given woman: 'What's her angle of dangle?' If she's a full 90-degree job she's one sexy lady.
Animal		a) A crude, obnoxious, ultra-violent slob. Can't relate this discription to any animal but man.
		b) An ugly woman, often seen on the arm of a 'Doctor Dolittle' (qv).
		c) A policeman, before he became a 'pig'.
Ankle		A name given to a rough place, a dive, somewhere seen as a 'low joint'.
Ankle Biter		A small child, or a little nipper.
Anna Maria	*Fire*	Applies to a domestic fire rather than anything a fireman would be interested in. 'Maria' is pronounced as a rhyme for fire.
Anna May Wong	*Pong*	Stunted at 'Anna May', this is an old piece based on a Chinese-American film actress (1907–61) who may or may not have had a 'Pit' problem. *See* PIT (b).
Annanab		A banana, a slice of backslang from the fruit market

Annie		A lorry, an example from World War Two for a three tonner, formed on the song 'Annie Laurie'.
Anorak		A boring, studious type, typically a trainspotter who would wear this type of warm hooded jacket. 'Anoraks' are those most likely to be told to get a life or to 'put a different coat on'.
Another Day Another Crap		A cynic's version of 'Another Day Another Dollar'.
Anthea Turner	*Earner*	After a TV personality, an 'Anthea' represents wages, usually for a cash-in-hand job.
Antifreeze		Strong drink, typically whisky or brandy, that keeps out the cold.
Ant's Bollock on a Beach		A colourful alternative to the cliched 'needle in a haystack'. Something that's equally impossible to find.
Antsy		Restless or agitated, a 1960s term aimed at those deemed to have 'ants in their pants'.
Anyhow		To feel 'anyhow' is to feel out of sorts.
Ape		A crude, brutish man, often a minder or enforcer. Probably an insult to an ape.
Apeshit		An extension of going 'ape', also meaning to go 'bananas'. *See* GO APE.
Applause		A venereal disease, a pun on 'clap'. A 'round of applause' you don't want.
Apple		The head. This is seldom used, but then green heads are seldom seen.
Apple & Pip	*Sip*	An uncommon example of a piece of RS for a term of backslang. 'Sip' is a back formation of piss, hence 'to go for an apple' is to urinate.
Apple Cider	*Spider*	The only multilegged 'apple' you'll ever see. Unless it's a crab apple.
Apple Core	*Score (£20)*	Shortened to an 'apple', but not very often.
Apple Dealer/ Monger		An old pair of pimps, dealers in 'Apples' (qv).
Apple Fritter	*Bitter (Ale)*	The oldest term of RS for this type of larynx lubricant.
Apple Pie	*Sky*	It's a nice day when there 'ain't a Turin in the apple pie'. *See* TURIN SHROUD.
Apple Pip(s)	*Lip(s)*	Nice to kiss but a trappy (qv) person may be told to watch his 'apple'.
Apple Polisher		The toady, can't do enough for a good guv'nor, type. 'Apple polish' – to seek favour, to crawl.
Apple Sauce	*Horse*	Often a racehorse that trails in last or 'ran like a pig'. Hence apple sauce?
Apple Shiner		Someone who keeps the guv'nor's pippins in pristine condition, a creep. 'Apple Shine' – to crawl.

Apple Tart	*Fart*	A disgusting stench often follows a dropped 'apple'.
Applejack	*Crack*	A 1980s term for this form of cocaine.
Apples		A win double in the 'what men like to nibble' stakes, breasts.
Apples & Pears	*Stairs*	Probably the one piece of RS that everybody knows. And one that hardly anyone uses.
Apples & Rice	*Nice*	Generally shortened to the first element when describing something pleasant, a sunny day may be 'apples'. But used in full when used ironically, 'Oh, that's very apples and rice' means it isn't.
Apricot & Peach	*Beach*	A trip to the 'apricot' to soak up the 'currant' may prove treble fruitful if you manage to pull a 'lemon'. *See* CURRANT BUN *and* LEMON CURD.
April Fool	*a) Stool*	Most commonly applies to a bar stool.
	b) Tool	Originally referred to a tool of the burglary trade but later evolved to cover any tool of any trade.
April Fool(s)	*(Football) Pools*	In pre-National Lottery days it was everybody's dream to win the 'Aprils', but only a fool ever dreamed he would.
April in Paris	*Aris*	A piece that is three times removed from it's meaning. Aris (Aristotle) – bottle; bottle and glass – arse. *See both.* Formed on a famous song title.
April Shower(s)	*Flower(s)*	One of the most common terms to pass between two lips. Also applies to this brand of beer as a pint of 'April'.
Arab/Ayrab		a) An urchin, a 19th-century term, when the poverty-ridden streets were running alive with 'scruffy little Arabs'.
		b) A Muslim, a piece that lumps together everybody from all the world's Islamic states.
Arabber/ Ayrabber		An urchin. At a time when Arabs and street kids were perceived as being rogues and thieves, getting up to no good was 'arabbing'.
Arbuckle		A fat person, after arguably the most famous fat man ever, the silent film comedian Roscoe 'Fatty' Arbuckle (1887–1933).
Archbishop Laud	*Fraud*	A piece from a fictional underworld (Cook's *The Crust on its Uppers*, 1962) based on William Laud (1573–1645), an Archbishop of Canterbury.
Archer		£2000, the amount paid by former Tory MP Jeffrey Archer to a prostitute to enable her to go abroad, thus avoiding a scandal. Since a scandal ensued, it can hardly be considered money well spent.
Arctic Explorer		A cocaine user, someone who gets through a lot of 'snow'.

Are Rabbis Jewish?/Yiddish?		A reply to a question that demands an answer in the affirmative.
Argie		An Argentinian. A piece that was not heard before the Falklands War of 1982, and which was a product of the *Sun* newspaper's headline writers.
Argument Ender		A fist, one that puts a nose-crunching end to a war of words.
Argy-Bargy		A 19th-century term for a bit of pushing and shoving, a row that falls short of a battle.
Aristotle	*Bottle*	Always reduced to 'Aris', this applies to any bottle but is mainly heard as a slang for slang reference to the backside. *See* BOTTLE & GLASS.
Arm & Leg	*Egg*	What a chocolate one costs at Easter.
Army & Navy	*Gravy*	An example that was first dished up in World War One field kitchens.
Army Rocks	*Socks*	World War One version of 'almond rocks' (qv).
Army Tank	*Yank*	A World War Two term for an American.
Arnold Palmers	*Farmers*	A piece of twice-removed slang based on the legendary American golfer. 'Farmers' is short for 'Farmer Giles' – piles, so if your 'grapes' are the size of golf balls, you've got 'Arnolds' or 'Arnies'.
Arnold Schwartzenegger	*Begger*	A 21st-century example that relates to beggers who ride the London Underground looking for hand-outs, Arnies would appear to be the male counter-parts of 'Samanthas'. *See* SAMANTHA EGGAR. Based on the giant Austrian actor, action hero of many a Hollywood movie.
Around the World		Body licking that takes in every nook and cranny, including the back of beyond.
Arrivederci Roma	*Coma*	An underworld term from the 1950s, based on a popular song title, which was used in connection with rendering someone unconscious. The victim was knocked into an 'arrivederci', which is Italian for 'goodbye'.
Arrows		A game of 'arrers' is a game of darts.
Arse/Ass		a) The buttocks. Not really slang any more but I suppose it needs to be here. b) A fool, famously a 'silly arse'. c) A woman seen in a sexual context, i.e., 'a piece of arse.' d) The back end of a vehicle, to reverse into a gap is to go in 'arse first'. Also Arse End.
Arse About/ Around		To mess about, muck around and generally play the fool.
Arse About Face		Anything round the wrong way, back to front.

Arse Licker	The crawler who's tongue exactly fits the groove of the manager's backside.
Arse Music	As played by the wind section. A fart, usually a long drawn-out one.
Arse Over Tip/Tit	To fall, although not necessarily head over heels, as the term suggests.
Arse Scratcher	A layabout, an idler with nothing to do all day except scratch himself.
Arse Up	To bungle or make a mess of. 'You've arsed that right up.'
Arse Wipe	a) An old and common expression for a toilet roll. b) A person who is beneath contempt. Often a 'no-good arse wipe'.
Arse Wiper	A brown noser (qv), someone who would 'wipe the gaffer's arse if he asked him'.
Arsehole	a) The anus, the hole up which people have been told to shove any number of unwanted things. b) An extremely unpleasant, untrustworthy person, commonly a 'stinking arsehole'. The worst of people may win the title 'Arsehole of All Arseholes'. c) An unpleasant, unsavoury place, the worst of which may be nominated as the 'Arsehole of the World'. d) Physical courage: 'He won't back you up, he's got no arsehole.'
Arsehole-Ache	A variation on a pain in the arse that's brought on by a pest or a vexing situation: 'I'm getting the arsehole-ache of this.' Often more colourfully said as: 'This is giving my arsehole a headache.'
Arsehole Bandit	A homosexual male seen as a villain, one you are warned against turning your back on.
Arsehole Crawler	Right up an officer's chute crawls the creeping subordinate.
Arsehole Job	A coward is someone who lacks 'arsehole' (d).
Arsehole Lucky	Double fortunate or as 'lucky as arseholes'.
Arsehole, the	Dismissal. An employee may be given 'the arsehole' or be 'arseholed off'.
Arseholed	A shortening of 'pissed as arseholes' (qv, c), meaning well drunk.
Arseholes	a) Said with venom, this is an older version of 'get stuffed'. 'Arseholes to you mate, I ain't goin' to Twickenham.' The well-known catchphrase of the cab driver. b) Nonsense or rubbish. 'Everything you say is a load of arseholes.' c) Something to be compared with. For some

		reason any adjective may precede 'as arseholes', e.g., silly as, scruffy as, miserable as, etc.
Arsenal		The genitals, especially of a well-endowed man. 'He's got some arsenal on him.'
Arse-Piss		The watery outpourings of diarrhoea.
Artful Dodger	*Lodger*	An oft-used term when it was common for householders to take in lodgers. Based on the Dickensian character from *Oliver Twist*.
Artful Fox	*Box*	A theatrical expression for a box in that establishment.
Arthritic Hand-shake Mob		Freemasons, from the finger positions needed to perform secret handshakes.
Arthur		Pronounced 'Arfur' and asked for when ordering a half pint of whatever your tipple is.
Arthur Ashe	*Cash*	A piece from the second-hand motor trade based on an American tennis player (1943–93), the Wimbledon champion of 1975.
Arthur Bliss	*Piss*	The act of urination. Also to 'take the Arthur' is to assault verbally, to 'take the proverbial piss'. Based on the knighted English composer (1891–1975).
Arthur Scargill	*Gargle (Drink)*	Beer normally, courtesy of an English trade unionist, president of the National Union of Mineworkers (NUM) from 1981–2000.
Artichoke	*Smoke*	A piece that also works as a pun, suggesting that its originator was coughing his giblets up at the time, i.e., having a hearty choke.
Artichoke Ripe	*Pipe*	A piece from a time when pipe smoking was popular, at least with those who were smoking them. Now seems to have run out of puff.
Artillery		An underworld term for weaponry.
Arvy Mariah	*Fire*	An infrequent mispronunciation of 'Ave Maria'.
Ascot Heath	*Teeth*	As Hugh Grant may have remarked of Divine Brown: 'You don't come across Ascots like hers every day.' *See* DIVINE BROWN.
Ascot Races	*Braces*	Known as 'Ascots' but probably not to the big hat brigade who gather here during 'The Season'.
Ash & Oak(s)	*Smoke(s)*	Commonly associated with telling someone to get their cigarettes out: 'Come on, flash the ash.'
Ash Tray on a Motorbike		A symbol of uselessness, what a 'doombrain' (qv) is said to be as much use as.
Aston Villa	*Pillow/Pillar*	Since both meanings are pronounced the same, an 'Aston' is equally at home as the thing you rest your weary head on or the view obstructor at a football ground.
Astroturf		A name given to an informer. Based on the all-weather playing surface, which is often known as supergrass.

At It		a) Up to no good, most commonly thieving or on the fiddle.
		b) Having sexual intercourse or a sexual relationship: 'They've been at it for years them two.'
At the Post		To be ready and waiting, as a racehorse is at the start of a race.
At the Wash		Stealing from jackets in public washrooms. An old term for a crime that's been moved upmarket to include stealing from the changing rooms of golf clubs, sports clubs, gyms, etc.
Attic		The head, one of many terms making the top of a building/body connection. An empty attic means there's not a lot going on upstairs.
Aunt/Auntie		The lavatory may be heard as 'I'm going to visit my aunt/auntie'.
Aunt Annie	*Fanny (Vagina)*	The aunt you don't want to visit if she's unwell.
Aunt Em/Emma		Morphine, from the initial M.
Aunt Fanny		An expression of disbelief: 'Yeah? And so's your Aunt Fanny.'
Aunt Hazel		Heroin, from the initial H.
Aunt Lil	*Pill*	Usually something from the chemists. Feeling unwell? Send for 'Aunt Lil'.
Aunt Lily	*Silly*	Rarely heard example, possibly after somebody's actual dopey relation.
Aunt Maria	*Fire*	An old piece that went out when old King Coal ceased to rule the fireplace.
Aunt Nell	*a) Smell*	Said as 'It don't 'alf Aunt Nell in 'ere'. Possibly after someone's redolent relative.
	b) Gel	A modern piece for hair slick.
Auntie		a) The BBC, a term coined by employees of the corporation.
		b) An elderly or middle-aged male homosexual, seen as the prissy type.
Auntie Ella	*Umbrella*	An infrequent term for a 'mush' (qv).
Auntie Ena	*Cleaner*	Refers to a charlady and appears in a rhyme:
		Have you seen my Auntie Ena
		In an office she's a cleaner
		Met a bloke from Bethnal Greena
		Since then uncle hasn't seen 'er.
Auntie Nellie	*Belly*	Often used in regard to an upset stomach, when your 'Auntie Nellie' might be playing you up.
Auntie Ruth	*Tooth*	A recently acquired gap in your dental collection will prompt enquiries as to your 'Auntie Ruth's' whereabouts.
Auntie's Ruin	*Gin*	Old alternative to Mother's Ruin.

Aunt's Sisters	*Ancestors*	A mildly amusing and relative pun.
Autumn Leaf	*Thief*	'Autumn leaves' may be thick on the ground down 'Hooky Street' (qv).
Ave Maria	*Fire*	*See* ARVY MARIAH.
Avoid Like an Infected Arsehole/Minge		Said of anything, anyone or anywhere best kept well away from. A vulgar version of the following.
Avoid Like the Plague		Said of anything, anyone or anywhere best steered clear of.
Away		A spell in prison. The habitual criminal is often 'away'.
Away to Fuck		The Scottish version of 'fuck off'.
Away/Off/Out With the Fairies		Silly, simple, daft. Where anyone considered to be an egg short of a full English breakfast is said to be. Alternatively they may be with the 'pixies'.
Awesome		Originally American but now a universally common term for anything excellent. A piece of modern teenspeak.
Awful Wedded		A spouse. See LAWFUL WEDDED.
Awkward Squad		Originally a military term for a bunch of inept recruits, it now applies to any bunch of misfits who do not respond to training or discipline.
Axe		A guitarist's term for his instrument, he himself is often called an 'axeman'.
Axle Grease		An underworld term, usually reduced to 'axle', meaning a bribe.
Ayet		Tea, in backslang mode, a 'puc of ayet' – a cup of tea.
Aylesbury Duck	*Fuck*	Only used in terms of not caring, i.e., not giving an 'Aylesbury'.
Ayrab		An Arab, he who rides a caymel.
Ayrton Senna	*Tenner (£10)*	An 'Ayrton' has become quite common in the years since the death of the Brazilian racing driver in 1994 (b. 1960).

B

B & D		Bondage and discipline. Sexual services offered by prostitutes via small ads.
Baa Lamb	*Tram*	A term that was widely used when trams were. Now they are making a comeback and we can jump on 'baa lamb' again without the RSPCA jumping on us.
Baa Lamb		A polite euphemism for bastard, often relating to a naughty child.
Bab		A kebab, as sold at the 'bab shop'.
Babbling Brook	*a) Cook*	Originally a 'babbler' was an army cook of World War One. It now applies to anyone who can wield a tin opener.
	b) Crook	Applies to any rogue or villain as a 'babbler'.
Babe		An attractive young woman, very much a term of today.
Babe Magnet		A man who attracts women and not any old 'iron'. *See* IRON HOOF *and* IRON MAGNET.
Baby Blues		Eyes, whether they are blue or not.
Baby Chute		A modern term for the vagina.
Baby Gravy		One of a great many terms for semen concerned with gravy, yoghurt, custard or cream.
Baby Maker		The penis. The worker with a lifelong productivity bonus.

Baby's Cries	*Eyes*	A rarely used example that began making a noise in the 1930s.
Baby's Pap	*Cap*	First recorded in the mid 19th century when the working man was particularly adept at turning out children and wearing flat hats, often at the same time. Hence the connection I suppose.
Baby's Pram	*Jam*	A continental breakfast, bread, butter and 'baby's'.
Baby's Public House		Where a newborn gets his drink, a breast. Also 'baby's pub' and 'baby's boozer'.
Bacardi & Coke	*Bloke*	See BACARDI BREEZER.
Bacardi Breezer	*Geezer*	A 21st-century term of youth based on a popular alcopop. Always shortened to the first element, much the same as the slightly earlier 'bacardi and coke'.
Bacca/Backy		Old terms for rolling or pipe tobacco. Well-known today in regard to 'drugfags', i.e., 'wacky backy' and 'caca bacca'. *See both.*
Bacca Box		The mouth. 'Shove this in your bacca box' translates as 'Eat this'.
Back Door		A very early term for the anus, especially one involved in letting in visitors, i.e., that of a sodomite. Older examples are 'Back Door Usher' and 'Gentleman of the Back Door'. Later came the Back Doors: Burglar, Commando, Man, Merchant and Kicker. All mean homosexual.
Back Door Job/ Work		Both relate to anal intercourse.
Back Door Man		As well as being part of the list at 'back door' (qv), it also relates, conversely, to the provider of secret sex to a married woman, an adulterer. A song with this title, written by Willie Dixon, has become a part of every blues band's set since the early 1960s.
Back Door Trots		Diarrhoea, a piece from when people had to go to the outhouse.
Back Double		A back street. More and more are subject to no-entry signs and one-way systems to deter motorists from taking short cuts, thus causing traffic jams on main roads.
Back End		The backside. 'Park your back end' – sit down.
Back Eye		The anus. Scratching an itchy one may draw the question, 'Got an eyelash twisted?'
Back Porch	*Torch*	If it's dark on your back porch, grab your 'back porch'.
Back Street Butcher		An abortionist, a piece that adequately paints its own gory picture.
Back Wheels		The testicles, which gives a new slant on getting

		your back wheels balanced. 'Get one's back wheels in' – to have sexual intercourse.
Backchat		a) A back street, the way around traffic jams is to use the 'backchats'.
		b) A reply to a telling off by someone who is supposed to take it in silence, usually a child.
Backfire		An anal emission, sometimes 'back-end backfire'.
Back-Hander		A bribe. A boxer may accept a back-hander to take a moody right-hander and fall down.
Backseat Driver		Somebody who gives unwanted instructions, not necessarily in-car advice.
Backseat Driver	*Skiver*	Someone who doesn't want to do the work but will tell you how it should be done.
Back-Wheel Skid	*Yid*	A 'back-wheeler' is sometimes used as an alternative to 'front-wheeler'. Same meat, different gravy really. *See* FRONT-WHEEL SKID.
Bacon		Money, commonly heard in the phrase 'bringing home the bacon'.
Bacon & Egg(s)	*Leg(s)*	You're up against it when you haven't got a 'bacon' to stand on.
Bacon Bonce	*Nonce*	Prison slang for a child molester. *See* NONCE.
Bacon Bonce		a) As some rashers come up thicker than others, so do people. This is one of them.
		b) A partially bald person, one whose forehead stretches to the back of his head.
Bacon Face		Somebody with a fat face. A 'chubby chops' (qv).
Bacon Lardon	*Hard On*	A recent term for an erection, probably from the suburbs.
Bacon Rind	*Blind*	Always sliced to 'bacon', usually of the short sighted, e.g., 'He's as bacon as a bat.'
Bacon Sandwich at a Bar Mitzvah		What people feel like when they are out of place or uncomfortable.
Bacon Slicer	*Shicer*	A name given to anyone who will 'carve you up'. A 'bacon' will swindle, cheat or welsh on you.
Bad		Modern youthspeak for good.
Bad Hair Day		A day when nothing goes right, even your hair won't lay down properly.
Bad News		A best avoided person, a ne'er-do-well. Also an unwelcome situation.
Baden-Powell	*Trowel*	The original scoutmaster, Robert Baden-Powell (1857–1941) has been spreading 'muck' (qv) for bricklayers for a century or so.
Baderbus		A modern term for a wheelchair. *See* BADERED.
Badered		Drunk, a sick term based on the wartime pilot

19

who lost both legs, Sir Douglas Bader (1910–82). Therefore 'legless'.

Badger
A prostitute's accomplice, who goes through a client's pockets while she keeps him occupied.

Badger Crib/ House
A low brothel where clients are routinely robbed.

Badger's/Bear's Arse
What sick people, especially those nursing a hangover, are said to look as rough as. We'll have to take it as read that the backsides of these animals are sufficiently coarse to form a simile.

Badlands
Slum or dangerous areas of a town or city. South London to an East Ender and vice-versa.

Badmouth
An American import meaning to insult, put down or generally slag off.

Bag
a) A charmless, unappealing woman who may or may not be a prostitute. Usually 'old bag'.
b) To catch. The police may 'bag' a burglar, then again they may not.
c) Sexual intercourse, maybe a connection with (d).
d) The vagina. Also the womb, a pregnant woman may have 'one in the bag'.
e) The scrotum, generally in the form of 'ballbag' or 'bollockbag'. *See both.*

Bag Filler
A woman who leads a man on but stops short of sex. *See* BAG (e).

Bag of Bones
An extremely thin person, often said these days of fashion models and anorexics.

Bag of Coke   *Poke*
Sexual intercourse. Possibly from the old illusion that the coalman was often paid in kind, as in the saying, 'Never be unfaithful with the milkman when you're in debt to the coalman'.

Bag of Flour   *Shower*
A plain old piece from the washroom. Also a rain shower: 'It's just a bag of flour, it won't last.'

Bag of Fruit   *Suit*
An old example that only fits properly when it isn't shortened. You're always cased up in your best 'bag o' fruit'.

Bag of Mystery
A sausage, also called a 'mystery bag' (qv), because only the butcher knows what's in it.

Bag of Nails
Anything mixed up or in disarray, as disorderly as the term suggests.

Bag of Sand   *Grand (£1000)*
A 'bag' is of recent coinage in the City of London.

Bag of Shit
What a scruffy person is said to look like, often with 'tied up with string' added on.

Bag of Wind
What a boasting loudmouth is often called.

Baggage
a) How a promiscuous woman is known, and has been for centuries.

		b) A man's genitals as seen by the bulge in his trousers or ballet tights.
Bagged		a) To be arrested. *See* BAG (b).
		b) Drunk, an old term for which you may still get 'bagged' (a).
Bagger		One who specialises in violently removing rings from their owner's fingers. From the French *bague* – a ring.
Bagpipe		a) A boring, monotonous speaker, one who drones on and on.
		b) The homosexual practice of having sex with a partner's armpit.
Bags		A late 19th-century term for trousers, which a century later were worn as 'baggies'.
Bail Out		To leave, often a swift getaway from a difficult situation. A term stolen from the hasty exit of pilots when their planes were going down.
Bake It		To resist the urge to defecate, to 'keep it on a low light'.
Baked Bean	*Queen*	An unflattering term for our present monarch. Also a blinding hand of poker, four 'baked beans'.
Baked Beans	*Jeans*	A term from the 1960s which mirrored the rise in popularity of both products.
Baked Hard		Said of excrement that cannot be shifted, giving rise to constipation.
Baked Potato	*Waiter*	One of several examples rhyming the restaurant lackey with 'potater'. *See* COLD, HOT *and* ROAST POTATO.
Bakers Dozen	*Cousin*	Relating to your relation, 'bakers' is an old term.
Balaclava	*Charver*	A sinister term for sexual intercourse. Charver comes from the Romany word for the taking of a woman and a balaclava has become the symbol of the rapist.
Bald as a Badger/ Billiard Ball/ Egg		Although a badger has fur, he is seen, like these other examples, as being a smoothie, a 'balloon-head'.
Bald Head	*Red*	Heard only in the snooker hall, possibly from the saying 'as bald as a billiard ball'.
Bald Headed Bandit		One of several terms linking a hairless dome with the penis. Other 'bald headed' ones are Burglar, Champion, Friar, Hermit, Intruder and Sailor.
Bald Tyre Bandit		Sounds like somebody that steals dodgy tyres but is in fact somebody who nicks people who drive on them, i.e., a traffic cop.
Ball		An Americanism for the sex act heard in many a film. 'Who's Balling Who' – the Hollywood jolly-go-round. *See* JOLLIES.

Ball & Bat	*Hat*	Although this is an ancient example, it's always been shaded by the famous 'tit for tat' (qv).
Ball & Chain		A wife, partner or regular girlfriend, symbolic of being shackled. Rhyming slangers attached it to 'Jane' (qv), a term for a girlfriend.
Ball & Chain	*Strain*	Used sarcastically when a job is being done without much effort: 'Mind you don't ball and chain yourself.'
Ballbag		The scrotum, the commonest term for the 'knacker-sack'.
Ball Buster/ Breaker		a) A heavy load. One that requires the 'balls of a donkey' to carry. Hard work in general.
		b) A dominating, nagging woman, usually a wife whose thumbprint can be found on her husband's head. Also a 'ball crusher'.
		c) An overbearing boss, a manager who will 'bust your balls' to get an order out on time.
Ball of Chalk	*Walk*	Has tirelessly stridden the road of RS for many years.
Ball of Fat	*Cat*	Descriptive of many a pampered puss.
Ball of Lead	*Head*	A piece that was first fired during World War One.
Ball Slap		Sexual intercourse, for obvious reasons.
Ballast		Food, more especially a heavy meal.
Ball-Less Wonder		A weak, cowardly person. *See* Balls (c).
Ballocks		The original spelling of 'bollocks', literally little balls.
Balloon		For safe sex 'blow' into a 'balloon', i.e., a condom. *See* Blow (k).
Balloon Car	*Saloon Bar*	Always known as a 'balloon', this old term is one of the few to effect a rhyme on both elements.
Balloons		Large breasts, the subject of the oft-repeated 'I'd like to rub 'er balloons' pun.
Balls		a) Non-kickable ones, the testicles.
		b) Nonsense. Bullshitters and liars will spout a 'load of balls'.
		c) Courage, audacity or front, something either sex can have. The brave are said to have 'balls like an elephant'.
		d) An argumentative, defiant or disbelieving retort.
Balls Up		A mistake. To make a 'balls up' is to do something wrong.
Balls, the		Descriptive of the best, the most fantastic.
Ballsache		*See* Bollockache.
Ballsed Up		The result of a mistake or something wrongly done.
Ballsitch		'Here comes old ballsitch.' A mildly abusive term for a grouch.
Ballsitch, The		An itchy scrotum.
Ballsy		Said of anyone displaying courage or determination.

Bally		A polite version of 'bloody' (qv).
Balmy Breeze	*Cheese*	Any type, colour or texture, it's all 'balmy'.
Baloney		Originally an American term for nonsense, which is now common here.
Balsam		An ancient term for money, it relieves financial conditions like 'skintitis' (qv).
Banana		a) A fool: 'I've been standing here like a banana for an hour waiting for you.' b) The penis, due to its shape and, judging by the colour, belonging to Homer Simpson. c) Homosexual, therefore 'bent', as you never see a straight banana.
Banana Boat		A vessel that's never boarded by the gullible: 'How much? What d'you think I've just come over on a banana boat?'
Banana Fritter	*Shitter*	Refers to a lavatory, the place to accomodate one suffering a bout of the banana splits (qv).
Banana Split(s)	*Shit(s)*	You either go for a 'banana' or have a touch of them.
Bananas		a) To 'go bananas' is to go berserk. To 'drive someone bananas' is to infuriate them. b) The Special Patrol Group (SPG), a branch of the police. Said to be yellow, bent and hang around in bunches.
Band of Hope	*Soap*	An appropriate piece since it is based on an old organisation that preached clean living to juveniles.
Bandit		A homosexual, a shortened form of longer terms like 'arsehole bandit', 'bum bandit', etc.
Bandit Country/ Territory		Anywhere frequented by homosexuals, be it a bar, park, area, etc. *See* BANDIT.
Bandy		Bow – couldn't stop a pig in a passage – legs.
Bang		a) An act of sexual intercourse, a coarse term often used chauvinistically by men: 'Does she bang? Like a fucking firework'. b) A drug injection, also 'bang up'. c) To hit 'I'll bang you one in a minute.' The severely bashed are 'banged up'.
Bang & Biff	*Syph(ilis)*	Two slang terms for the sex act get together for what could be the result of a bad one.
Bang/Bash/ Batter One's Bishop		To masturbate. The bishop is one of several high-ranking holy men to come in for this kind of punishment. Cardinals, Friars and even Popes get it.
Bang to Rights		To be caught with stolen property or standing over a body with the weapon in your hand and they've got you 'bang to rights', with no defence.

Bang Up		To imprison. Commonly heard of prisoners to be 'banged up'. From the sound of a cell door.
Banged Out		Of a place, to be 'packed out'. Most pubs are 'banged out' on New Year's Eve. Also to be full, as most stomachs are on Christmas Day.
Banged Up		A one-time reference to being high on drink that is now more frequently used in connection with drugs. *See* BANG (b).
Banger		a) An old car that's been round the clock and had it's share of scrapes.
		b) A term for a sausage that is practically standard English.
		c) A hypodermic needle, *see* BANG (b).
		d) A fist. Late-night travellers on the London Underground often have their 'bangers' ready throughout their journey.
Bangers & Mash	*Slash*	A 'bangers' is one of many terms for urination on stream.
Banjaxed		An Irish term for flummoxed, or to be beaten by a person or a problem.
Banjo		a) An old persons version of a guitar. Heard in the 1960s on the subject of the Beatles: 'Bloody Beedles? Can't even play them banjos.'
		b) An old navvie's term for a shovel, which later became known as an 'Irish banjo'.
		c) A large filled roll, e.g., a cheese and salad 'banjo'.
		d) To hit with a lot of force, originally an example from the army.
Bank		The vagina, especially that of a prostitute. Endorsed in terms like 'money box', 'money maker' and 'money machine'.
Banker		In gambling, a certainty or at least a good thing.
Baptise		Of a publican, to water down alcoholic drinks to make more money per bottle. Such drinks are 'baptised'.
Bar		a) A long-established term for £1. Half a bar was 10 shillings but is still used for 50p.
		b) An erection, known as 'having a bar on'.
Bar Bore		The bloke in the pub who has his regular seat, often a tankard behind the bar, and is best avoided.
Bar Fly		A regular frequenter of bars, a drunk.
Bar of Soap	*a) Dope*	Used mainly in connection with drugs, but a dimwit may also be a 'bar o' soap'.
	b) Pope	A term which seems to prove that cleanliness is next to godliness.
	c) Rope	A term from the docks that was cast off years ago.

Bar Steward		A comical euphemism for 'bastard', this has seen service in many a British comedy.
Bar Stool Preacher		That bloke down the pub who knows something about everything and offers advice on anything.
Barb		A term that is a reduction of the word barbiturate.
Barbecue Griddle	*Piddle*	Don't be surprised if, halfway through a meal, someone tells you they're going for a 'barbie'.
Barbie Doll		A typically attractive blue-eyed blonde woman built in the same mould as the toy she takes her term from. Has been around for many years but has recently evolved as a piece of RS for a moll. Since she is often seen on the arms of villains it seems to fit rather well.
Barbie Doll	*Moll*	A gangster's girlfriend.
Barclays Bank	*Wank*	One of many banks connected with the 'Wringing of the Richard'. Barclays banker – Wanker.
Bareback		To have a ride without being saddled by a contraceptive, i.e., unprotected sex.
Barf		To vomit, a piece that found it's way here from the States.
Barge & Tug	*Mug*	Old rivermen would have had a 'barge' of 'Rosie Lee' (qv).
Barges		Massive shoes as worn by men with massive feet.
Bark		A term of abuse usually directed at an old grouch. The original 'miserable old bark' may have worked at Billingsgate, as a 'bark' is fish porters' backslang for a crab.
Bark & Growl	*Trowel*	An archaic piece that has probably laid its last brick.
Barking		In full 'barking mad', it refers to total lunacy.
Barking Arsehole		One that makes constant noisy emissions.
Barking Dog		A ringing, beeping or popular television theme-playing telephone. Based on the RS 'dog and bone' (qv), and said as, 'If the dog barks while I'm out, answer it.'
Barking Dogs		Aching feet, usually said as 'my dogs are barking'. An old term which may be, but probably isn't, connected to 'dogs meat' (qv).
Barmpot		A mildly abusive expression for a fool, often heard in TV dramas set in northern England.
Barmy		Mad or eccentric. Very old but still very common, especially in the context of supporters at sporting events, most famously the barmy army who follow the England cricket team.
Barnaby Rudge	*Judge*	A Dickens of a title for a legal bigwig.
Barnacle Bills	*Pills (Testicles)*	A pill is an old slang term for a ball, which has evolved quite happily to refer to man's tender

dangly bits. Reduced to 'barnacles', from the song about a sailor of the same name.

Barnes Wallis The beknighted inventor of the bouncing bomb (1887–1979) becomes a 'splashing turd', i.e., a piece of excrement that splashes the backside as it hits the water.

Barnet Fair *Hair* Applies to a head of hair *en masse,* or lack of mass when referring to a bald man who's 'got no Barnet'. Based on an event that dates back to medieval times.

Barney A fight or a noisy argument. A common term for an everyday occurence in Albert Square, the setting of TV's *EastEnders*.

Barney Moke *Poke* A poke is a wallet and its contents, and this is a term used by those who would dip into a pocket and separate one from its owner.

Barney Rubble *Trouble* Fred Flintstone's oppo lends his name to any worrying situation. A driver with a spoonful of unleaded in his tank will be in 'Barney' if a garage doesn't loom up in the not-too-distant distance.

Baron The most dominant convict in a prison. Most commonly heard of as a 'tobacco baron', he who has control over any drugs or tobacco trafficking within his domain.

Barrel/Barrel Arse A rotund person, one with a similar shape to a barrel.

Barrel Fever What one may be suffering from the morning after a heavy drinking session. A hangover.

Barrikin An unintelligible language so therefore slang. People on the same wavelength will 'tumble' each other's 'barrikin'.

Barry McGuigan *Big 'un* Heard in a bakers shop. When asked which of the remaining three loaves he wanted, a customer replied, 'the Barry McGuigan'. Ironic since the TV boxing pundit is a former world featherweight champion and therefore more of a little 'un.

Barry White *Shite* An American soul singer lends his name to anything considered rubbish.

Barse The perineum, the bit between the 'balls' and the 'arse'.

Base Over Apex The polite version of 'arse over tip' (qv).

Bash Street Kid *Yid* A 1960s term that sees a Jew become a 'Bash Street'. Based on the anarchic gang of school children from *The Beano,* who are fast approaching pensionable ages.

Basher a) One who 'bashes'. A thug, bully or a professional punch-up merchant.

		b) A shelter made of whatever a homeless person can find to make it with.
Basic Poplavian		The cockney dialect as heard by an outsider. Poplar is in the heart of London's East End.
Basil		A piece from the 1980s for £40. A pun on the name of Basil Fawlty from TV's *Fawlty Towers*.
Basil Brush	*Thrush*	Applies to the fungal infection that can be sexually transmitted and leaves male sufferers with an itchy 'Richie'. *See* RICHARD/RICHIE. Based on a TV fox puppet.
Basil Fawlty	*Balti*	Carry-out curries courtesy of John Cleese's classic comedy creation. *See* BASIL.
Basin		An attempt at, or a portion of, something that needn't fit into a receptacle. A recipient of a racing tip may respond with 'I'll have a basinful of that'.
Basin Cut/Crop		A haircut, a short back and sides obtained by placing a basin on the head and cutting all the hair to the south of it.
Basin of Gravy	*Baby*	A leaking, bawling, sleep-reducing, time-consuming, stress-inducing, pocket-emptying bundle of happiness. That's a 'basin'.
Basket		a) A light-hearted euphemism for 'bastard'. See TISKET.
		b) A homosexual term for the male genitals that gives rise to 'basket lunch', oral sex between men.
Basket Case		A lunatic who may or may not be certified, someone who should be in a secure institution making baskets.
Bastard		a) So common it's hardly slang anymore, but a disagreeable, unpleasant person it is.
		b) A difficult, vexing or in any way a bad situation.
Bat		An unpleasant woman usually preceded by 'old'. Originally a prostitute who, like a bat, came out at night.
Bat & Ball	*a) Stall*	As trundled out on market day when barrow boys come out to play.
	b) Wall	What prisoners 'have it over' and the tormented are 'driven up'.
Bat & Bowl, to		To be bisexual, i.e., equally at home when bowling a maiden over or being on the receiving end of a full toss.
Bat & Wicket	*Ticket*	Any ticket, be it train, theatre or test match.
Bat for the Other Side		Said to be what a homosexual does.
Bath Bun	*Son/Sun*	Not often used either way.

Bats/Batso/Batty		Mad, eccentric or scatterbrained. Famously, to have 'bats in the belfry'.
Battalion		An old term for a gang of thieves and cut-throats.
Batter		A 1980s term for semen, hence to 'splatter one's batter' – to ejaculate.
Battle Axe		A spiteful woman who will cut a man down with her tongue.
Battle Bowler		The helmet of a British soldier since World War One. The bowler is the typically English hat.
Battle Cruiser	*Boozer*	A post World War Two term for a pub that's usually known as the 'battle'. Sometimes called a 'battleship and cruiser'.
Battleship(s)	*Lip(s)*	Apart from the mouth-edges, this applies to insolence. 'Let's have a little less battle' or 'button your battle' are warnings against further argument.
Batts		Shoes, Polari plate holders since the 19th century, when they were also known as 'crabshells'.
Batty		A West Indian term for buttocks, which, at the time of writing, is getting a lot of exposure in the hands of Ali G. *See* ALI G.
Batty Boy		A homosexual, *see* BATTY.
Baubles		The testicles, probably of an exhibitionist who likes to show off his trinkets.
Bayonet		The penis seen as one of many weapons. Also included in the arsenal are Dagger, Sword, Lance and Harpoon, etc.
Bazaar	*Bar*	A long-serving term for the saloon, public, spit and sawdust, etc., that has yet to hear the time bell ring. Sometimes heard as bizarre, depending on the pub I suppose.
Bazooka	*Snooker*	A term from the 1970s when the game became one of televised sport's big guns.
Bazooka		The penis, a member of the weapon store along with 'gun', 'cannon' and 'pistol'.
Bazumas/ Bazongas/ Bazookas		A trio of bosoms substitutes.
Be Lucky		A phrase of farewell mainly associated with London taxi drivers.
Beacon		A red nose, one that draws attention to itself.
Beadle		A dock policeman, a docker's term for the man who had to be wise to the ways of smuggling goods out of the gate.
Beagle		A heavy smoker. An unfunny reference to lab-tested dogs who are forced to inhale cigarette smoke.
Bean		a) Originally a guinea, later a pound, but now

common as a coin of any denomination. 'Not to have a bean' is a well-known plea of poverty.

b) The head, and also to strike someone thereon, i.e., to 'bean'.

c) A 1990s term for the clitoris, whereby cunnilingus may become a 'beanfeast'.

Beano & Dandy *Shandy*
Based on the popular kids' comics and formed when people began to take the drink-drive law more seriously.

Bear
a) An irritable person, a grouch. 'A bear with a sore head.'

b) A police officer, an American piece that reached these shores courtesy of CB radio users. Related pieces include: 'Bear Cage' – a cell; 'Bear Trap' – a radar speed trap and 'Bear in the Air' – the police officer in a helicopter.

Beard
a) A woman's pubic area. An archaic piece that's still bristling.

b) A stand-in used to perpetuate a lie. A man seen escorting a famous woman to disguise the fact that she is lesbian. Also a go-between. A beard is a typical guise of deception.

Beard Splitter
A man known to have had intercourse with a lot of women. Also a term for what he used to do it with, i.e., the penis. *See* BEARD (a).

Bearded Clam/ Oyster/Whelk
A trio of the many fish-related terms for the vagina.

Bear's Paw *Saw*
Maybe it's sharpness that connects Bruin's claws with the carpenter's right hand.

Bears-head
A miserable, short-tempered person, an extension of 'bear' (a).

Beast
a) Somebody guilty of a sex crime, especially a child molester.

b) An ugly girl or woman, from the mouth of the chauvinist.

Beastmaster
A man who marries an ugly woman. After a comic-strip and film character who consorts with animals.

Beat One's Meat
To masturbate. Any number of things are beaten in the name of solo sex, including: one's 'Burger', 'Quarter Pounder', 'Dummy', 'Puppy', etc.

Beatbox
a) A musician's term for a drum machine.

b) A large portable tape or CD player, a 'ghettoblaster' (qv).

Beattie & Babs *Crabs*
Refers to an infestation of the pubic area by crablice. Based on a music hall duo who probably deserved better.

Beaver		a) A beard, a 19th-century term that's still about. b) A bearded man, sometimes 'Beaver Jed'. c) The pubic hair of a woman, from a supposed similarity between it and beaver fur.
Beaver Cleaver		The penis, as it cuts through pubic hair. *See* BEAVER (c).
Beaver Shot		A close-up photograph of a woman's genitals seen in porn magazines and films.
Becher's Brook	*Look*	A rival to 'butcher's hook' (qv), that is probably only heard once every Grand National day.
Becker		A very brief act of sexual intercourse. Based on the name of German tennis player Boris Becker who, in 2001, hit the headlines when a woman had his baby after a 'quickie' in a broom cupboard.
Bedworthy		A less vulgar version of 'fuck', 'plunge' and 'shag', worthy in respect of a sexually attractive woman. *See all.*
Bee Stings		Very small breasts, ones that men still get a buzz out of despite their size.
Beechams		Testicles. For balls read pills, and as a jocular extension read 'Beechams', the pill-makers. It has been suggested that the word should be pronounced 'testi-kils' and that this is RS.
Beechams Pill	a) *Bill (1)*	In its modern form the 'Beechams' applies to the police. Based on the name of a laxative, which makes the term appropriate as just a glimpse of a police car in the rear-view mirror can have exactly the same effect, even when you've done nothing wrong.
	Bill (2)	A notice carried by ex-servicemen, unable to work following World War One, which stated their qualifications for begging, busking or selling bootlaces or the like on the streets of the 'land fit for heroes'. A typical 'Beechams' might say 'Wounded at Ypres' or simply 'Blind'.
	Bill (3)	Any type of bill or receipt.
	b) *Still*	A professional snapper's term for a photograph.
Beef		a) An argument or problem. 'I've got no beef with him, it's his old woman I object to.' b) Sexual intercourse. To 'beef' is an ancient forerunner of the modern to 'pork' (qv).
Beef & Mutton	*Glutton*	A cow and a sheep unite to make a pig.
Beef Brain/Head		A pair of dimwits, from a similar shop to 'Muttonhead' and 'Meathead'.
Beef Heart	*Fart*	An offering from the offal counter for back-end backfire.

Beefy		a) Big, brawny types, often a name for a bully or heavy.
		b) Anyone with a pit problem, an armpit that is, a smelly one.
Beehive	a) *Dive*	Cheating footballers take a 'beehive' in order to win a penalty and dopey refs fall for it.
	b) *Five*	Chiefly a bingo term that is sometimes heard as a 'beehiver' – a fiver (£5).
Beemal/Mal		Lamb. A piece of backslang from the meat market. A 'beemal potch' – a lamb chop.
Beemob		Bomb, a piece of backslang that was common when the Luftwaffe was doing a demolition job on London.
Beemoc		Backslang for a comb, for use when backcombing hair.
Been Round the Block		Experienced, often sexually. Alludes to a block of streets, therefore streetwise.
Beer Barrel/Gut/ Pot		The stomach, especially one stretched by beer drinking.
Beer Eater		A big fan of the juice of the hop. One who sees beer as a food.
Beer me up Scotty		A request for a beer to a bar person or whoever's round it is. Based on an oft-repeated line from TV's *Star Trek*, where it's 'beam' instead of 'beer'.
Beer Pub/Shop		Familiar terms for a pub, usually the local, 'just nipping down the beer shop'.
Beer Trap		The mouth, 'get this down your beer trap'.
Beered Up		Drunk, the result of chucking too many pints down 'Beer Street' – the throat.
Beery		Just short of being drunk. 'I may have been a bit beery, but I wasn't pissed.'
Beery Nose		A drunk. Mocking abuse aimed at the well bevvied by street urchins of yore.
Bees & Honey	*Money*	A piece from the century before last, that still has a currency.
Bees Bollocks/ Nuts		Modern vulgarisms of 'bees knees' (qv).
Bees Knees	*Business*	More of a pun than RS and refers to 'the business', an old expression for the best, the most excellent. Could also be a fitting complaint for a Brentford footballer, like a West Ham player with hammer toes, a Crystal Palace player with an eagle eye or an Arsenal man with gunner ear.
Bees Wingers	*Fingers*	Never actually heard this one so I don't know if it's about flying insects or the outsides left and right for Barnet FC.

Beeswax	*Tax*	Refers to Income Tax and is a cleverly composed play on 'bees whacks', or money (*see* BEES & HONEY) one gets whacked for.
Beetle		To hurry. 'Beetle down/along/over/up to' wherever, but get there quick.
Beetle Brain/ Head		A simpleton, terms that are symbolic of smallness so therefore someone with minimal intellect.
Beetle Crushers/ Squashers		Footwear, especially large heavy working boots, a scourge of the creeping, crawling masses.
Beetle Off		To make a departure, often a hasty one. From the image of a scurrying insect fleeing a loaded boot.
Beetles & Ants	*Pants*	Underpants are commonly dropped to 'beetles'.
Beezer		a) The nose. People have been picking their 'beezers' for a century or so. A 'boozer's beezer' – the reddened nose of a sot.
		b) An old-school term for wonderful, terrific, etc.
Beezonker	*Nose*	A cross between beezer and shonker, two terms for the hooter.
Beg Your Pardon	*Garden*	In a previous book I wrote that this was a postwar term but apparently it's older, in which case I beg your pardon.
Beggar		A polite version of 'bugger' when used in its least offensive context, i.e., 'silly beggar', but puts a different perspective on the phrase 'beggar my neighbour' (qv).
Beggar Maker		An ancient term for a publican, which in a roundabout way attached itself to a bookmaker when betting shops opened in the 1960s.
Beggar My Neighbour	*Labour*	On the labour is another version of 'on the dole', hence on the 'beggar' is to be out of work.
Beggar's Lagging		Three weeks in prison, formerly the fixed penalty for begging before it became an occupation.
Beggar Boy's Arse	*Brass (Money)*	Always short-changed to 'beggar boy's', the phrase is ancient and apt. Brass is what the poor little sod would have been after and all he would have received was a kick up the bum.
Beggar Boy's Ass	*Bass (Beer)*	It's a common sight today to see a beggar with a sleeping dog, maybe they had sleeping donkeys a hundred odd years ago when this was coined.
Beigel		On a racecard, the noughts that precede a horse's name signalling a loss. In general terms a battling loser is said to be 'as game as a beigel'. Note, this is never pronounced 'bagel'.
Beigel Basher		A Jew. A jocular pun on 'bible basher' signifying non-Christianity.

Belch		Inferior beer, an old term that is still relevant.
Belcher		An enthusiastic beer drinker, these days probably a CAMRA man.
Belfry		The head, where the insane are said to have bats living.
Bell		A telephone call, from the days before phones knew how to play selections from Beethoven.
Bell End		The head of a penis, a shape-related rather than a sound-related piece.
Bell Ringers	*Fingers*	Try ringing a bell without them.
Bell Rope		A lengthy penis, or maybe an extensively pulled one.
Belled Up		Said of a premises with a burglar alarm.
Bellman		A burglar with a specialised knowledge of alarms.
Bellows		An archaic term for the lungs that's still got some puff in it.
Belly/Toes Up		Dead. To turn 'belly up' is to die, as is to 'turn one's toes up'.
Belly Up, go		An expression for failure, if a business goes down it's said to have 'gone belly up'.
Bellyache		To complain or moan and generally give everyone else a headache.
Belly-Slop		To use the withdrawal form of contraception, i.e., to ejaculate over a partner's stomach. 'I didn't have a Johnny so I had to do a belly-slop.' A pun on the dodgy dive, the belly-flop.
Below the Belt		A comment or deed delivered underhand, sneakily or spitefully. From a low blow in boxing.
Belsen Victim		What a painfully thin person is said to resemble. After the appearance of victims of the Nazis at the Belsen concentration camp during World War Two.
Belt		a) A heavy blow. 'Someone belted me on the crust (qv) and that was the last thing I knew.'
		b) To hurry, to 'belt' along as fast as you can go.
		c) To strike, 'I'll belt you one in a minute.'
		d) A drink with a kick, 'a belt of whisky'. Too many and the term 'Belted' (drunk) comes into play.
Belt & Braces	*Races*	A term that begs you to be double careful what you place your hard-earned on.
Belt & Braces Man		An overly cautious person, someone who doesn't trust his belt to hold his trousers up so he wears braces as well, just in case.
Belt Loosener		A big meal. 'I'll have to loosen my belt for this lot.'
Belt Strainer		A big meal. One that will 'stretch the leather'.
Belt Up		To be quiet, what most people wish waffling sports commentators would do. A familiar demand for silence.

Belter		Something excellent, 'a belter of a goal'. Also heard as 'belting'.
Ben Flake	*Steak*	An example that was cooked up in the 19th century and no longer on the nosh-up list. *See* NOSH-UP
Ben Hur	*Stir*	A term for a term in prison. Coined after the success of the 1959 film of the same name.
Bend an Ear		To nag or to talk ceaselessly and boringly, often unburdening oneself of a problem by pouring it down the 'noise funnel' (qv) of some poor soul who only came out for a swift half.
Bend Down/ Over		Funnily enough this means to stand for, or allow to happen, or more commonly not to. 'I won't bend down to thugs like them.' Probably based on the passive stance of a consenting adult.
Bend the Elbow		To have a drink of alcohol, what the arm joint was made for, otherwise our mouths would be a yard above our heads.
Bended Knees	*Cheese*	Always grates down to a 'bit of bended'.
Bender		a) A very long drinking session which may involve smashing up the premises and outrageous behaviour. (In a West End pub, a man charged with being a drunken yob was heard to reply in his best thespian voice, 'Yob! How dare you? I am an actor. I insist on being called a hellraiser!')
		b) A male homosexual who may 'bend like a country lane'.
		c) An old term for the knee or elbow.
		d) Underworld jargon for a suspended prison sentence. Partial RS, Bender – Suspender.
Benghazi	*Carsey*	Refers to the lavatory and is sometimes truncated to 'the Ben'. It probably emanated from World War Two where the battle for Benghazi was the Allies' first major victory. The word 'carsey' is an example of a slang based on Italian and known as Parlyaree or Polari. Originally employed by circus and fairground people, it was picked up and popularised by mainstream theatricals and is largely used in gay circles.
Benny		a) An old term for a simpleton which enjoyed a revival when a TV character of the name and nature became a national institution after he turned up in *Crossroads* in the 1970s.
		b) Good, a piece of Polari based on the Italian *bene*. 'Benny darkmans' – goodnight.
		c) A tablet of benzedrine.
		d) A Jew, a once-typical Jewish name.

Benny Hill	*a) Drill*	A carpenter, when asked why his Black and Decker had become identified with the British comedian (1926–92), replied, 'They both bore a bit.' Obviously not a fan.
	b) Till	A modern piece for a cash register based on the man whose comic persona would have enjoyed having his buttons pushed by young women at the checkout.
Bent		a) A common piece for a homosexual, i.e., perpendicularly conflicting – not straight. b) Stolen merchandise, for sale 'on the cheap', is known as 'bent gear'. c) Dishonest or corrupt, as a bent official or policeman may be. Or rigged, as a boxing match or a horse race may be. d) Counterfeit, fake or forged goods, generally anything that deviates from the 'straight'.
Benty		The number twenty, based on the Spanish *vente* and the way it's said in Spain. The 'M benty-finko' – the M25. *See* FINKO.
Berkeley Hunt	*Cunt*	A different version of 'Berkshire Hunt' (qv) that is sometimes said as 'Sir Berkeley'.
Berkshire Hunt	*Cunt*	It is well documented that in it's shortened form of 'berk' the term has become accepted in all circles and would shock many who use it to learn of its origin. It is never employed anatomically; a 'berk' is a fool. Never said as 'Barkshire'.
Bernhard Langer	*Banger*	Based on a champion German golfer, this applies to a sausage. Not necessarily a champion German one.
Berni Flint	*Skint*	Based on a 1970s singer whose claim to fame was to appear on the talent show *Opportunity Knocks* more times than anyone else. A successful record in 1977 means he'll probably never be 'Berni'.
Bernie		The sum of one million pounds, this has been current since Motor Racing boss Bernie Ecclestone donated that amount to the Labour Party in 1997.
Berries		The testicles, where strangely enough, a boot in the 'berries' may lead to crushed 'nuts'.
Berry		An easy touch for a conman, someone ripe for the picking.
Bertie Smalls		A name given to an informer or snitch. Based on a 'supergrass' of the 1970s who informed to the police about a number of North London criminals in return for immunity from prosecution. To 'do a Bertie' – to turn Queen's Evidence.

Bertie Woofter	*Poofter*	A homosexual, and always a 'Bertie'. Based on a pun or a lisped version of the upper class twit of P G Wodehouse's imagination, Bertie Wooster.
Beryl Reid	*Lead (Dog's Leash)*	Probably greyhound track-inspired, after a British actress and comedienne (1920–96).
Berzonkers		Mad rage: 'He went berzonkers when he heard.' A hybrid of berserk and bonkers.
Bessie Braddock	*Haddock*	A fish porter's term based largely on a largely based British politician (1899–1970).
Bessie Bunter		A name given to a fat or overweight girl or woman, often in self derision: 'Look at me, I'm getting like Bessie Bunter.' The female version of 'Billy Bunter' (qv).
Best Bib & Tucker		What you are said to be dressed in when cased up in your finest clothes.
Bet Your Boots/ Bollocks/ Arsehole		A certainty, something you'd risk your prized possessions on. Often used negatively, e.g., 'Bet your bollocks, if I forget to put the lotto on my six, 'numbers will come up.' Also 'Bet your: Life', 'Neck', 'Arse', 'Eyesight', 'Shirt', 'Balls' and in Scotland your 'Chip Pan'.
Better to be Blown Up than Shown Up		Death before dishonour, in other words.
Betty Boop	*Soup*	A tasty dish, based on an early cartoon one. Served as a bowl of 'Betty'.
Betty Grable	*Table*	Named after a Hollywood actress (1916–73) noted for having a great pair of legs. Now she has two pairs.
Betty Swollocks		Unpleasantly hot testicles, a spoonerised 'sweaty bollocks'.
Bevvied		Drunk. Well bevvied – very drunk.
Bevvy		A drink, usually beer. A shortening of beverage that's been around since the 19th century.
Bevvy Shop		A pub. Originally a 'bevvy ken' (*See* KEN), it's been a 'bevvy house' as well.
Bevvy-Up		A bout of heavy drinking, the same as a 'booze-up' (qv).
Bevvypint		A pint of whatever beer takes your fancy.
Bexley Heath	*Teeth*	An area in South East London provides a rare term for the 'chomping gear' (qv).
Bible Basher/ Thumper/ Puncher		A clergyman, preacher or a generally religious person. Often someone who tries to introduce religion into the lives of those who don't want it.
Bibleback		A religious person who frowns upon the rest of us.
Bice		a) A two-year prison sentence. A two stretch.

b) £2, a 'bice of quids'. The original 'bice' was a 'bice o' deaners' – two shillings.

Bice of Tenners
£20. *Bis* is French for twice, therefore two tenners equals a 'score o' quids'.

Bicycle/Bike
A promiscuous woman, one who will stand a 'ride' (qv).

Bicycle Lamp *Tramp*
Applies to tramps and scruffbags in general and would appear to come from a time when people bothered to have lights on their bikes.

Biddy
A nosey or nagging old woman, hence 'old biddy'.

Biff
a) To punch: 'I biffed him one on the bugle.' 'Biff and stiff' – to render unconscious with a punch.
b) Sexual intercourse as a noun and verb.

Biffin
The perineum, or that bit of the body between the anus and scrotum or vagina.

Big A
A euphemism for AIDS.

Big Bass Drum *Bum*
Reduced to 'big bass' this applies to a posterior of portly proportions.

Big Ben *Ten*
The clock at Westminster strikes a reference to £10. Formerly ten shillings.

Big Blink/Sleep
Death, as in 'endless sleep'. *See* Blink.

Big Bloke *Coke*
First recorded in the 1940s in regard to cocaine.

Big Bopper *Copper*
A police officer. Based on a rock 'n' roll singer (JP Richardson, 1932–59), and from a time when the police carried, and bopped people with, truncheons.

Big Bucks
Large amounts of money, an American term that is not restricted to dollars.

Big C
a) A way of saying cancer without actually saying cancer.
b) A police caution, where that is the end of proceedings.
c) One of a long line of terms for cocaine.

Big Cheese/ Noise/Potato/ Wheel/Wig
Anybody in authority, the head person.

Big Chill
A cold-blooded term for death.

Big Dipper *Slipper*
An old piece of schoolboy jargon from the days when corporal punishment often came in the shape of a plimsoll, which would come down like a white-knuckle fairground ride on to clenched buttocks.

Big E
The elbow, but in terms of a rejection or a knockback.

Big Ears *Cheers*
Used jocularly when raising a glass. Formed on an Enid Blyton character.

Big Ears & Noddy *Body*
Based on the names of Toytown's most prominent citizens, it is said in admiration of a well-shaped

torso and dwarfed to 'Look at the Big Ears on that.' The shell-likes won't come into it.

Big Eye A stare: 'That geezer over there's been giving me the big eye all night.'

Big Figure A large person, usually a male of the type who make good bouncers.

Big Gates Prison. A time server is 'behind the big gates'.

Big Girl's Blouse A wimp, usually a spineless man. A term put into the mouths of non-cowardly women by writers of northern TV comedies.

Big H a) A user's term for heroin.
b) A posthumous term for the cause of a heart-attack victim's death.

Bighead A person full of his own importance. 'Ol big'ead'.

Big House Originally a workhouse but more recently a prison. Any large institution really.

Big I'm It A derogatory reference to a self-important person, a version of 'The Great I Am'.

Big Job Murder, an assassination, usually done for money. A hit.

Big Jobs Defecation, in a childish way.

Big Mac *Sack* Dismissal from work comes in the shape of a hamburger. May also mean bed.

Big O An orgasm, especially a female one. 'The Big O' is a term that came from America originally.

Big Time A commonly heard phrase that's used to intensify a statement. 'I love her big time' or 'I'll knock him out big time.'

Big 'Un a) £100, from a time when it was much bigger in value than it is today. Has also seen service as £10.
b) To act and talk big, known as 'giving it the big 'un'.

Big Wheels A 1980s term for an articulated lorry, as driven by a 'knight of the road' – a trucker.

Bigger State than China/ Texas To be in a state of utter chaos or confusion. The terms apply to the size of these places rather than a supposed condition. Texas is a massive US State, so to declare that you are in a 'bigger state' emphasises what a bad way you are in.

Bike What a boxer is said to be on when he back-pedals around the ring trying to catch his opponent with counter punches.

Biker A motorcycle rider, frequently heard in connection with couriers.

Bilge As spoken by those talking a load of rubbish.

Bilgewater A foul-tasting drink, especially flat beer.

Bilingual		A lying boaster, a 'know him, had her' windbag. Someone said to be fluent in two languages, English and 'bollocks' (qv, b).
Bilk		To cheat, an archaic piece that's still knocking around. A 'bilker' is one who does it.
Bill		a) One of a flock of terms for the nose, although this is way down the pecking order in usage.
		b) The police. Everyone knows this from TV but nobody is absolutely sure of its origins. Sometimes extended to 'William'.
Bill & Ben	*Pen*	Based on the names of the world's most famous flowerpot men, the term was commonly heard in betting shops.
Bill O'Gorman	*Foreman*	A 19th-century term said to be based on a real-life Irish ganger who couldn't possibly have known that he would achieve immortality.
Bill Shop		A police station, a modern version of 'cop shop' (qv).
Bill Stickers	*Knickers*	Said in the form of a name rather than the occupation of those who would be prosecuted.
Billet		To jeer or heckle, an extension of barrack, a soldier's billet.
Bill-on-a-Bike		Motorcycle police in general or singularly. 'Look out, it's Bill-on-a-bike' can apply to one or more traffic cops.
Billy Bunter	*a) Punter*	An old bookmaker's term based on the most famous fat boy in English literature.
	b) Shunter	A term from the steam railways industry for an engine that pushes rather than pulls carriages.
Billy Bunter		A name given to a fat boy or man, based on the over-stuffed creation of novelist Frank Richards (1875–1961) and played with great comic effect by British actor Gerald Campion (1921–2002) on 1950s TV.
Billy Button		A very old term for a tailor.
Billy Button	*Mutton*	The slang term for a tailor serves up this old term for sheep-meat.
Billy Cotton	*Rotten*	Based on a British bandleader (1899–1969), this is what disgruntled kids called their father if he didn't come across with a tanner (sixpence) for an ice-cream. Now he's called something much worse if he doesn't weigh in with a week's wages for a pair of trainers. Also applies to anything that has gone off, and is also what the very drunk are said to be.
Billy Goat	*Coat*	A rarely heard alternative to the female of the species. *See* NANNY GOAT.

Billy Liar	*Tyre*	Based on a film of the 1960s, this is quite fitting as a flat 'Billy' is often a moody excuse for being late.
Billy No Mates		A friendless soul, usually because he's a despicable nerk that no one likes.
Billy Smart	*Fart*	When the question 'Who let Billy Smart in here?' is asked, it's usually the one with the smug grin on their face that did it. Based on a circus proprietor (1893–1966).
Billy the Kid	*Yid*	How a Jew became a 'Billy'. Or how the infamous left-handed gun became a left-handed 'gunsel' (qv).
Billy Two Sheds		Someone who always has to go one better than everybody else. If you've got one shed, he's got two. If you've been around the world in a bath, he's done it twice.
Billy Whizz	*Quiz*	A modern piece based on a comic character relating, generally, to a pub quiz.
Billy Wright	*Tight*	A 1950s piece used by the Teddy Boy generation in relation to ill-fitting attire, when their drainpipes and winklepickers started to pinch, they were too 'Billy Wright'. Based on the enduring England football captain of the period (1924–94).
Billy-O		A name given as an example of muchness. Anyone who drinks, smokes, swears, coughs and aches like Billy-Oh is probably suffering a bad hangover.
Bimbette		A young girl, a wannabe bimbo (qv).
Bimbo		A century ago this applied to a young man but during the 1980s it achieved fame as a term for an attractive, but not overintelligent, woman. Often worn on the arms of villains and rich old men.
Bin		a) A pocket. 'Here, stick this in your bin.' Music to the ears of the skint.
		b) An asylum, a reduction of the term 'loony bin' (qv).
		c) To throw away. 'When you're finished with the paper, bin it.'
		d) A police cell and also to lock someone up in one.
Bind		A tiresome situation, a nuisance. Like when you get a puncture and you can't get the wheelnuts off because they've been tightened with a power tool. Also, what a dull person may be; to 'bind' is to bore rigid.
Binnie Hale	*Tale*	An oldish term for a con man's sob story that had a currency during this British actress's lifetime (1899–1984).

Bins		Binoculars. A term that has been extended to spectacles. Also 'Binocs' and 'Binos'.
Bint		A young woman, from the Arabic word for daughter. It was picked up and brought home by soldiers serving in North Africa during World War Two and is now widely used.
Birch Broom	*Room*	An ancient term for living quarters. Rarely visited these days.
Birch Broom in a Fit		A sweeping expression for wild, unruly hair.
Birchington Hunt	*Cunt*	A seldom-heard but old example used both anatomically and condescendingly for a prize fool or ne'er-do-well. A hunt saboteur's idea of a huntsman, in fact.
Bird		a) A very common term for a young woman, and has been since the 19th century.
		b) A con man's victim, later narrowed down to a 'pigeon'.
Bird Bandit		A man who snatches another man's 'snatch', i.e., steals his woman.
Birdbrain		A fool, of whom it may be said, 'If brains were made of birdseed, he wouldn't have enough to feed a sparrow.'
Birdcage	*Stage*	Where entertainers put themselves on dis-play. Or dat-play. Or any play really.
Birding		What predatory males are doing when they are out on the pull, or seeking female company. *See* BIRD (a). Also facetiously, 'wenching' and 'whoring'.
Birdlime	*Time*	Widely employed as 'bird', meaning a prison sentence.
Birds & Bees	*Knees*	An injured 'bird' is the mid-leg crisis dreaded by sporting folk.
Bird's Nest	a) *Pest*	Chiefly relates to a child with a God-given talent for driving adults mad.
	b) *Chest*	A human chest, especially a hairy one, therefore a male one, probably.
Biscuits & Cheese	*Knees*	An example that can't really be used in the singular but nevertheless is, so a knee is only ever a 'biscuit'.
Bit		a) A recent term for a pound coin, a shortening of 'nicker bit' (qv).
		b) The perineum. Most people don't know what this part of the anatomy is called, so when it comes to oral sex it's the 'bit' they liked licked. 'Bit-Lick' – licking the perineum. *See* BARSE.
Bit & Piece	*Niece*	Affectionately known by uncles as 'little bit', which separates her from the 'bit' that goes to a hotel with her 'uncle'.

Bit of Black/ Dark Meat/ Ebony	Black women seen as a sex objects.
Bit of Brush/ Crumpet/ Goods/Tickle/ Arse	All terms for women, used with sexual overtones.
Bit of Crackling/ Fluff/Skirt/ Stuff/Cuddle	Attractive women, every one of 'em.
Bit of Fish/ Fishpaste	The vagina, what cunnilinguists claim to have eaten.
Bit of Hanky Panky	Sexual shenanigans, what married people get up to with other people's partners.
Bit of How's Your Father	Sexual intercourse, what people at parties disappear upstairs for.
Bit of Rough	A lover, usually a male, who is a step down the social staircase, typically the lorry driver to the debutante.
Bit of Slap & Tickle	Sexual goings on which may be more slap than tickle.
Bit of Spare	A husband or wife's 'bit on the side' (qv).
Bit of the Other	Sexual intercourse. What, on many a beano, plenty of couples have gone beneath the pier for.
Bit of Tit	Said by disappointed lads who wanted everything but got only this.
Bit on the Side	An extramarital lover or relationship. What one may have or be having.
Bit Previous	Too early. Heard in a hospital canteen when somebody's will was being discussed: 'You're a bit previous aincha? He's not even dead yet.' You're also this when you jump to a conclusion.
Bitch	a) A female dog has become the major offensive term for a woman who may be a 'cat' (qv, a). Strange that.
	b) A homosexual male.
	c) Anything hard, tricky or unpleasant. A 'bitch' of a job, journey, weekend, etc.
	d) To complain, a moan-a-lot is always 'bitching' about something.
	e) An early term for a prostitute.
Bitching	Seeking sex with a prostitute. See BITCH (e).
Bitchy	A sarcastic or spiteful comment or deed.
Bite	a) To fall for, to be taken in, to swallow. The gullible and the easily wound-up are said to 'bite like a fish'.
	b) To copy or plagiarise, especially of a song lyric.

Bite the Bullet		To take what's coming to you without complaint. Before anaesthetics, men wounded on the field of battle endured the pain of surgery by having bullets placed between their teeth. Many would rather have had one between their eyes.
Bite the Dust		To die or to be beaten, a term reflecting the fate of charging Indians in many a cowboy film.
Biter		A bloodsucker, anything from a mosquito to an extortioner, taking in con men, beggars and spongers. One who 'puts the bite on'.
Bites & Scratches	*Matches*	A smoker's term for a 'box of lights'.
Bits & Bobs		One's possessions, usually of those without many. 'I've just got a few bits and bobs, that's all.'
Bitsa/Bitser/ Bitza		A cross-bred dog, one made of bitsa this and bitsa that.
Bitter/Wicked Oath		A definite oath. So help me.
Bizzies		The police, so called because they make themselves busy, i.e., they interfere.
Bizzo		Business or rather *the* business. 'I've done the bizzo' (what needed to be done). Also the best, *see* Business.
BJ		A flash way of saying that someone has performed oral sex on you. 'She gave me a BJ,' a blow job (qv).
Blab		To inform on or to give away a secret.
Blabbermouth		Somebody best kept in the dark where secrets are concerned because he can't keep his mouth shut.
Black		a) A blackmailer or extortioner, therefore to menacingly demand money is 'to put the black on'.
		b) The Black Market. Goods obtained illegally are 'bought on the black'.
		c) Dark-coloured hashish.
		d) A mistake. To 'put up a black' is to make an error.
Black & Blue	*Cue*	A snooker or pool cue. Used as a club by the sound of it.
Black & Decker	*Pecker (Penis)*	Formed on the name of a company that produces power tools, so a sexual marathon man may come to mind. Of course the name is also synonymous with doing it yourself. This is 'pecker' in it's American form and shouldn't be confused with the older British version meaning the nose. 'Keep your pecker up' conveys a totally different meaning in the States.

B

Black & Tan		A mix of black and brown beers, i.e. mild and bitter, Guinness and bitter, etc.
Black & White	a) *Night*	Descriptive of the night sky with a full moon. 'In the middle of the black' sounds just right.
	b) *Tight*	A reference to meanness and short-armed, long-pocketed folk.
Black Ace		A woman's pubic area. The shape of the ace of spades.
Black Bess	*Yes*	A definite affirmative is a big 'black Bess'. Based on an early rifle or Dick Turpin's horse.
Black Bomber		A strong, black amphetamine that was common in the 1960s.
Black Eye	*Pie*	A term that possibly arose after someone asked a barman for a 'smack in the eye' (qv).
Black Food		To those whose lunch is liquid, this is a Guinness.
Black Job		An ancient term for a funeral, for obvious reasons.
Black Man Kissed 'er	*Sister*	A piece from less enlightened times. A taunt from one child to another was 'Know your sister? A black man kissed 'er.'
Black Man's Pinch		A blood blister caused by pinching the skin.
Black Maria	*Fire*	Applies to a burn-up the fire brigade have to deal with rather than a domestic one.
Black Maria		A prison van, from when such conveyances were black. A famous term which seems to have it's origins in the US.
Black Money Box		A London taxi as seen by those aspiring to drive one.
Black Pillar Box		A Muslim woman wearing a burka, a black garment that covers the body from head to foot with a slit for the eyes, or in slang terms for posting letters.
Black Rat		a) A London Taxi. As rats abound below ground level, so cabs flourish above. A supposed mirror image. b) A uniformed police officer, no longer are they 'boys in blue'.
Black Rock Day		A very bad day when nothing goes right. After the well-known film *Bad Day at Black Rock*.
Black Rolls Royce, the		Death, symbolised by a typical hearse and used by sick people to exaggerate their condition when asked how they are feeling: 'Awful, I'm about ready for the black Rolls Royce.'
Black Stuff		a) Tarmac, made famous by Alan Bleasdale's film *The Black Stuff*, about road layers. b) Opium.

Black Velvet		A mixture of champagne and Guinness.
Black Widow		A woman who has seen off a lot of husbands.
Blackadder	*Ladder*	Formed on the name of a TV series, the fiercely ambitious will climb the 'Blackadder' of success two rungs at a time, no matter who those rungs happen to be.
Blackbird & Thrush	*Brush*	A term for a shoebrush, hence to 'blackbird one's boots' meant to clean them.
Blackhead		An illegal immigrant or asylum seeker from Eastern Europe or Arabia, typically seen as having black hair and being hard to get out.
Blackheath	*Teeth*	Heard outside a Soho cinema: 'Call that porn? I've seen dirtier films on my brother's Blackheaf.' Based on a historic part of South-East London, it's the teeth of the dentally careless.
Blackpool Rock	*Cock*	One of many terms for the male member, this one probably inspired by the George Formby song, 'With Me Little Stick of Blackpool Rock'.
Blackwall Tunnel	*Funnel*	An old term from the docks for a ship's chimney. The Blackwall Tunnel runs under the Thames between Poplar and Greenwich and is known locally as the 'pipe' or 'conduit'. At peak times it is a motorist's nightmare and so has collected many other names as well. Usually two words, the first one beginning with F.
Bladder of Fat	*Hat*	An out-of-date example that probably referred to greasy headwear that sat on greasy heads of yore.
Bladder of Lard	a) *Card*	A playing card and also a World War One bingo card, which would have been a housey-housey (qv) card on its formation.
	b) *Yard*	'The bladder' is a reference to Scotland Yard.
Bladder of Lard		A none too complementary term for a fat person.
Bladdered		Very drunk, a high intake of beer will give the bladder a hammering.
Blade		a) A man, especially a sharp, quick-witted one. b) A knife, when carried as a weapon.
Blag		a) A robbery, often with violence. A word that TV writers of police dramas would be lost without. b) A story told in order to decieve, a lie. To 'blag' is to persuade by deception, especially when trying to get into a function, club, restaurant, etc. 'It's all ticket but I managed to blag my way in.' c) To get off with a girl, to 'pull' (qv). To chat up.
Blagger		A thief, big time rather than petty.
Blanco/Blank		A white person as seen by black people.

Blank		a) A rejection or defeat, usually 'to draw a blank'.
		b) To ignore completely: 'I saw Mickey up the pub and he blanked me.'
Blanket		a) Bed, the exhausted can't wait to 'get to their blanket'.
		b) A cigarette paper, a pre-World War Two example that may still be smouldering somewhere.
		c) An overcoat, originally that of a tramp which was used in a dual capacity.
		d) An overly thick skin on custard.
Blanket Fever		A condition often called lazyitis, where the desire to stay in bed is overwhelming.
Blanket Treatment		To get beaten up by prison officers.
Blanks		As fired from the weapons of sterile men.
Blast		a) A smoke, especially the deep inhalation of 'drugfags' (qv).
		b) A good time or experience. 'It was a blast to meet you'.
		c) A party, an example that probably takes in (a) and (b).
		d) Damn. This is an old outburst of displeasure.
Blast from the Past		An old record, especially when played on the radio. Also anything or anyone that brings back a memory.
Blasted		a) Drunk, very drunk in fact. Out of one's skull, having one's senses shot to pieces either due to drink or drugs.
		b) Heavily criticised or panned, as a film, book or theatre reviewer may do.
Blaydon Races	*Braces*	Formed on the famous song of Geordieland, 'Blaydons' have long held up the trousers of bonny lads from the North East.
Bleat		a) To complain, common as 'What's he bleating about?' Also a complaint. In criminal parlance it's a convict's appeal for a reduced or repealed sentence.
		b) To inform to the police, an underworld term.
Bleeder		A mildly abusive term for a person who is less contemptible than a 'bastard'. To call someone a 'lousy bleeder' doesn't convey much venom.
Bleeding		An example that was once considered quite bad language. But not any more, it's bleedin' mild now.
Blert		A worthless, good-for-nothing ne'er-do-well. A piece often heard on TV's *The Bill*, usually referring to a young thug or a 'little blert'.

Bli/Bly	A shortening of 'blimey' (qv), usually 'oh bli'.
Blige Me	A granny's way of saying 'blimey' (qv).
Blighted	Drunk, in the same way as 'ruined', 'wrecked', 'mangled', etc.
Blighter	A version of 'bleeder' (qv) that doesn't sound at all right unless coming from the mouth of one of the upper classes.
Blimey	A reduced version of 'Gor blimey' (God blind me) that was once considered offensive. It began life as an oath and went on to become a popular expression of surprise, disappointment, etc.
Blimp	a) Anyone with an over-inflated opinion of himself, a hot-air merchant or windbag. b) A fat person, an American term that gained weight over here. c) A look, e.g., 'Let's have a blimp at that map.'
Blind	a) A cover-up, a statement or an action designed to hide the truth. b) In cards, to gamble without looking at one's hand. c) Drunk, so far gone you can hardly see. d) Night time, the all-concealing darkness of night. e) A bingo caller's term for round numbers 10, 20, 30, etc.
Blind/Blimey O'Reilly	An expression of surprise, an emphatic rendering of 'Gor blimey'.
Blind Eye	Not a thing to bother an optician with, as this relates to the anus, the sightless socket that sits between the 'blind cheeks' – the buttocks.
Blind Fart	A 'silent but deadly' emission.
Blinder	a) To perform well, i.e., 'to play a blinder'. b) An act of masturbation, from the old wives' tale that it makes you go blind. How do old wives know these things?
Blinding	Marvellous or great. Heard after a West Ham game: 'That was a blinding goal [Iain] Dowie got, pity it was in his own net.'
Blindman's Buff *Snuff*	An obsolete piece, as snuff has been replaced by cocaine in the nose-powder stakes.
Blindo	Drunk, an extension of 'blind' (c). 'I was blindo last night, dunno how I got home.'
Bling-Bling	Flash, gaudy or showy personal adornments, trappings of success for all to see, usually in the form of jewellery or a top-of-the-range car. Originally an American term that seems to be based on the name of an ostentatious panda.

Included at the insistence of exotic juggler and part-time poodle clipper Janie D, who is currently the All England ladies knob-twiddling champion.

Blink
a) A drink of anything but soft stuff, for which a 'Bit of blink' is obsolete RS.
b) A light which, when first lit, would have been a candle light.
c) A nap, from many moons ago. A bit of blink then was the bit of 'kip' (qv) of today. Hence the RS mentioned in (a)?

Blinker
A punch in the eye, from days gone by, though it's still apposite.

Blinkers
The eyes. There are none so blind as those who won't open their blinkers.

Blinking/
Blooming/
Flipping
Polite euphemisms for 'bloody' (qv).

Blinky
An unkind name given to a one-eyed person.

Blister
a) A summons ordering an appearance in court.
b) A painful punishment, often a legal one that may hurt the pocket.
c) An unpleasant person. One who is a pain to be with.

Blitz
To break into a building in order to rob it.

Blitz Out
To escape from a confinement, a prisoner's term.

Blitzed
Drunk or bombed out on drugs.

Bloater
a) An old insult to a fat person, one with a mountainous gut and cavernous bellybutton.
b) What a penis is often compared to in disbelief: 'If he's an international class winger, then my cock's a bloater.' To which someone will invariably reply, 'No, it just smells like one.'

Block
a) The head. A fool is said to be 'off his block' and a common threat of violence, especially in field of comedy is 'I'll knock your block off.'
b) A late 19th-century term for a watch, much used in conjunction with a 'tackle' (qv). The cockney, when skint, would regularly pawn his 'block and tackle' – watch and chain.
c) The part of a prison that houses the punishment cells.
d) To ban, to put a 'block' on.

Block & Tackle *Shackle*
Originally referred to fetters but got hoisted up from ankles to wrists to become handcuffs.

Block of Ice *a) Dice*
Presumably one that is running cold.

b) Shice
An old racing term that relates to not paying out on

winning bets. Many a hooky bookie 'had it over the wall' when his bag was full. *See* SHICE.

Blocked
Drunk or, more commonly these days, under the influence of drugs.

Blockhead
A stupid person, the image of someone who wears his hat on a solid block of wood.

Bloke
An example that has practically achieved standard English status as a reference to a man. It has a universal usage and in the vocabulary of girls it's a boyfriend, i.e., 'my bloke'.

Bloke-Bird
A manly woman, especially a well-muscled athlete.

Blokess
A woman who acts 'blokish' (qv). There are currently a number of celebrity 'blokesses' seeking to alter the traditional female image by making the news with behaviour designed to shock. *See* LADDETTE.

Blokish
Girls behaving badly. It's 'blokish' for them to get drunk, swear loudly, have tattoos and generally act the way men have always done. Can't piss up a wall though, can they?!

Blood Cloth
A sanitary towel but most frequently heard when spoken with a strong West Indian accent and used as a term of severe abuse or anger.

Blood Red *Head (Fellatio)*
Hence a 'blood donor' is someone who performs oral sex, i.e., she gives 'blood'.

Bloody
A multipurpose adjective used for emphasis, once considered swearing.

Bloomer
A mistake, a reduction of 'blooming error'.

Blootered
A Scottish term for being drunk.

Blotto
Extremely drunk. Heard at work on a Monday morning: 'Good weekend Tel?' 'Probably. I was blotto for most of it.'

Blow
a) A strong wind, commonly understated as a 'bit of a blow'.

b) A rest. At work, an unofficial break. To 'have a blow' may or may not involve a cigarette, but it's how the phrase probably originated. *See* (f).

c) Hashish or marijuana, a 'bit of blow'.

d) Tobacco in general, especially in prison.

e) To leave, often before the police arrive. 'Quick, let's blow.'

f) To smoke. A piece that's so old it originally meant a pipe.

g) To waste or squander; money. Also golden opportunities may be blown.

h) To lose, to blow a fortune at the card table, or to lose a game you were once winning.

i) To inhale cocaine, a snort.

j) A mild term of annoyance, 'Oh, blow' or 'blow it'. Most people I know get more annoyed than that though.

k) To ejaculate, the basis of the whaler's orgasmic cry of 'Thar she blows!' no doubt.

Blow a Fuse/ Gasket
A sudden loss of temper or burst of anger. When the heat felt under the collar gets too hot, something's got to give.

Blow Away
a) To kill, originally with a gun. What else? This being an American term.

b) To impress thoroughly. A performer on top form may 'blow away' his audience.

c) To trounce. One day Leyton Orient Football Club may 'blow away' all opposition. One day they might.

Blow Both Barrels
To ejaculate. 'I let her have both barrels.'

Blow Bubbles
To inform. 'Someone's been blowing bubbles.' From 'bubble & squeak' (qv, c).

Blow It In
To stop or to abandon a project. To take time off work or have a break.

Blow Job
Fellatio, when the full term is too much of a mouthful, 'blow' gets the job done.

Blow Me
An expression of surprise, almost a version of 'blimey'.

Blow Me Down
A mild exclamation of surprise that sounds like it's origins may have been with seamen. I know Popeye said it a lot, along with 'I'll be blowed'.

Blow Off
To break wind in juvenile terms.

Blow One's Beans
Of a man, to reach orgasm.

Blow One's Bulkheads
A colourful term for ejaculation, especially when a pregnancy ensues.

Blow One's Cork/Top
To lose one's temper, visions of being shaken like a bottle of fizz before blowing the bung out.

Blow One's Mind
To amaze or excite. Originally a user's term for the effects of hallucinogenic drugs.

Blow One's Radiator Cap
To lose one's temper after a 'welling up' of anger. To stand something for just so long before 'the cap comes off'. An image of slowly coming to the boil before overheating.

Blow One's Tubes
To ejaculate, as a submarine blows out its payload.

Blow Out
To reject, dismiss or discard. The motto of a sexual predator: 'suck 'em in and blow 'em out'.

Blow Street
The anus, down which the wind may whistle.

		Probably a pun on the original home of London's police force, Bow Street, as a 'Blow Street runner' is a breakage of wind that produces a faecal discharge, i.e., a wet fart.
Blow Street Runner		A wet fart, *see* BLOW STREET.
Blow the Gaff		To give away a secret, usually wrecking a plan or getting someone into trouble.
Blower		a) A telephone, from the days before it came with a 500-page book of instructions.
		b) When it was illegal to have televisions in betting shops, the racing service was provided courtesy of the 'blower', a public address system that was linked to the racecourses.
Blowhard		Someone who blows his own trumpet long and loudly. A 'been there, done that' boaster.
Blowsing		Glue sniffing. A term coined by 'sticky noses' (qv) in relation to their habit.
Blubber		What the obese carry to excess, hence 'blubber guts' – a fat person.
Blubber Bags		Female breasts, large ones!
Blubber Head		A fool, an expansion of 'fathead' (qv).
Blue & Grey	*Day*	An allusion to the colours of the sky.
Blue Film to a Man with No Arms		A symbol of uselessness, what a 'pranny' (qv) is said to be as much use as.
Blue Moon	*Spoon*	Applies both to the utensil which makes eating soup a simple task and to the old-fashioned (though not when it was formed) term for romancing.
Blue Peter	*Heater*	Mainly applies to the heat source of a car. Most likely after the TV programme rather than the naval flag which indicated a ship was ready to sail.
Blue Ruin		This term for cheap gut-rot gin started life as 'blue tape' which became 'blue ribbon' or 'riband' before finally emerging as 'ruin', probably as a result of drunken tongues not being able to pronounce 'ribbon' properly. Too old to be RS.
Blue Vein/Veiner		The penis erectis, due to the vein that runs along it. A number of terms for the penis come from this basis, the 'blue veined' – 'Trumpet', 'Piccolo' and 'Popgun' are among the assorted instruments and weapons involved.
Blueberry Hill	*Bill (Police)*	Based on Fats Domino's hit record of the 1950s, the 'blueberry' is a fairly recent piece.
Bluebottle		A police officer. A 'bottle' in blue. See BOTTLE & STOPPER.

Blues & Twos		The blue light and the two-toned siren of emergency vehicles.
Bluey		a) A pornographic video. A blue film.
		b) A £5 note. Also a 'blue' or 'blue un'. If you're reading this in 2050, guess what colour a fiver was fifty years ago.
		c) Lead, especially that which is stolen from a roof, often a church.
Bo Peep	*Sleep*	A well-known term based on a well-known, but useless, sheep minder.
Board & Easel	*Diesel*	An example that was first chalked up in the transport industry when you could buy a half-decent car for what it now costs to fill up a lorry with 'board'n'.
Board & Plank	*Yank*	Must be connected with the wooden actors on those dire American soaps hidden away on afternoon satellite television stations.
Boards		Playing cards, a shortening of the older 'pasteboards' (qv).
Boat		A titanic shoe or boot. 'They're not boots, they're boats' is an observation of giant footwear.
Boat & Oar	*Whore*	Not exactly a rhyme, but since the 1950s loose women have been known as 'boats'.
Boat-Hook	*Book*	How the British Library came to be full of 'boat-hooks'. A 1950s term from the docks.
Boat Person		An illegal immigrant who arrives in a country by sea.
Boat Race	*Face*	A commonly heard summing-up of a woman: 'Lovely body, dodgy boat'.
Bob		The commonest term for a shilling, can be preceded by every amount, e.g., two bob, fifteen bob, etc.
Bob & Dick	*Sick*	An uncommon alternative to 'Tom and Dick'. It seems Bob fills in when Tom's not feeling well.
Bob & Hit	*Shit*	What one can go for or step in, i.e., to defecate or the matter involved in it.
Bob & Weave	*Leave*	Time to 'bob and weave' or time we were 'bobbing and weaving'; either way it's time to go.
Bob & Weave		To keep on the move, thus avoiding authority or responsibility.
Bob Harry & Dick	*Sick*	Take a week off work with an illness and you can be on the 'Bob Harry'.
Bob Hope	*a) Dope*	The English-born American comedian (1903–2003) lends his name to drugs and an idiot. A 'right Bob Hope' is likely to 'have a button missing'.
	b) Soap	Commonly passed around in the showers, the 'Bob Hope'.

Bob Howler		A term for a moth heard in the Midlands, based on a boy called Bob Slade who howled in terror at the sight of the fluttering insect.
Bob Marley	*Charlie*	The availability of cocaine these days is reflected in the amount of terms that have sprung up for it of late. Based on a Jamaican reggae star who died in 1981, aged 36.
Bob Squash	*Wash*	An old term that applies to a public washroom. People using this facility hang up their jackets at their peril, as it is a haven for pickpockets who are 'working the Bob'.
Bobbing & Weaving	*Breathing*	A reply to the question 'How are you?' is 'Oh, you know, bobbing and weaving.' It means getting by, jogging along.
Bobbins		A term from northern England for rubbish either in the form of nonsense or anything useless. In the mill towns of Lancashire, discarded bobbins formed the basis of rubbish tips outside woollen mills.
Bobby		A policeman, after Sir Robert Peel, now most commonly heard of, though rarely seen as the 'Bobby on the beat'. The 'Bobby on a boneshaker' seems to be a thing of the past as well.
Bobby Moore	a) *Door*	A modern piece coined by football fans too young to have seen the great West Ham and England captain (1941–93).
	b) *Score*	A 'Bobby' is a recent expression for £20.
Bob's Your Uncle		Recently extended to 'Robert's your father's brother', it means that everything will turn out right.
Boche		A German, especially one in uniform and carrying a gun.
Bock		A jinx. The superstitious will declare something or somebody to be a 'bock' to them and steer well clear.
Bodes Dodgy		The omens do not look good.
Bodge		To do a job that doesn't bear inspection, a 'Wild West job', i.e., done by 'cowboys' (qv).
Bodge-Up		An unsatisfactory job, one done by someone whose screwdriver looks remarkably like a hammer, a 'bodge-up merchant' or 'bodger' for short.
Bog		a) A popular term for the lavatory; one can be in the bog or on it.
		b) To look at or peep. In a friendly game of cards a cheat may be told to 'stop bogging'.
Bog Blocker		A colourful piece for anything disgusting, something that makes you feel sick. Visions of a large, stomach churning deposit that won't be flushed.

Bog Eyed		Having eyes that show that their owner hasn't had enough sleep.
Bog Off		One of the versions of 'fuck off' that was allowed to television scriptwriters. Now that the language barrier has been lifted on TV, it is likely to be heard less and less and the F-word version more and more.
Bog Trotter		An old, defamatory reference to an Irish person which leads to some equally disparaging examples such as 'Boglander', 'Boghopper', 'Bog Rat', etc.
Bogey/Bogie		a) A piece of nasal mucous, dried, picked and ready for flicking. A 'pick 'n' flick'.
		b) Anything considered to be unlucky, a jinx.
		c) A police officer, as seen by the criminal. Like the bogey man, someone to fear. 'Bogey Wagon' – a police van or car.
Bogger		A peeping Tom. *See* Bog (b).
Boiled Beef & Carrot	*Claret*	Nothing to do with wine. Shortened to the first two elements, it refers to blood. 'There was boiled beef all over the place' could describe the aftermath of a fight, an accident or the first day of the Harrods sale.
Boiled Sweet	*Seat*	Heard in a cafe: 'You get the teas I'll find some boiled sweets.'
Boiler		A woman who refuses to believe that her sexual allure is waning and dresses lamb-fashion when she is well and truly mutton. She is almost always referred to as an 'old boiler', which in poultry terms is what a spring chicken turns into.
Boko		An old reference to the nose, especially one that's suffered some damage. 'He got stroppy so I bopped him on the boko.'
Bollitics		Political correctness seen as an absurdity. Bollocks and politics get together to produce the misbegotten bane of modern living.
Bollo		A diminutive version of 'bollocks' (c).
Bollock		To reprimand. May be from an earlier meaning, namely, to grab by the testicles while fighting.
Bollock Brain		An ancient term for a fool which now serves as a form of general abuse.
Bollock Buster		A heavy weight to carry, one likely to do testicular damage. Of a similar burden is a 'Nut Buster'.
Bollock Chops		Originally someone with a fat face, now a term of mildly mocking abuse.
Bollockache		A disagreeable situation; being stuck in traffic can be a 'right bollockache'.
Bollockbag		A variant of 'ballbag' (qv), regarding the scrotum.

Bollock-Head
A bald head, especially that of an intentionally bald man, i.e., a shaved head.

Bollocking
A severe reprimand. Much worse than a 'rollocking'. *See* ROLLOCK.

Bollocks
a) Well-known term for the testicles, where a kick is painful both physically and in a metaphorical sense; 'Redundancy came as a right kick in the bollocks.' Also to have a man under control is to 'have him by the bollocks'.

b) Nonsense, verbal rubbish. Windbags and liars are said to be 'fluent in bollocks'.

c) An emphatic refusal: 'You want me to do what? Well bollocks to that.'

d) An argumentative retort, something on the lines of 'get stuffed'.

e) An expression of disbelief: 'Bollocks, you're winding me up.'

Bollocks in Brackets
An old, imaginative description of a bow-legged man.

Bollocks-Up
A mistake, a job done wrongly: 'You've made a right bollocks-up of that.'

Bollocks, the
The absolute best. May be a castrated version of 'the dog's bollocks' (qv).

Bollocks, to have some
To be brave or daring. 'You've got some bollocks to do that.'

Bollocksed
Broken, as a car may be, or in trouble, as a motorist might be because his car is.

Bollocky
A term of mild abuse used in the third person: 'Here comes bollocky.' Sometimes 'Bollocky Bill'.

Bolt the Door   *Whore*
A time-ravaged prostitute, one you wouldn't want to be seen with. So bolt the door.

Bomb
a) A large amount of money. 'I lost a bomb on the last race.'

b) Strangely, in the theatre if a play 'goes down a bomb' it's a success, but conversely if it's a failure it's said to 'bomb'. So you buys your ticket you takes your choice.

c) A major storm at sea, where mountainous waves, hurricane force winds and a bucketful of seasickness pills are the order of the day.

d) To jump close to an unsuspecting swimmer in a way that causes maximum splash.

e) To travel at high speed, to 'bomb down the road'.

f) To cover a wall with graffiti. A piece of 1980s youthspeak that originated in America.

Bombadier	A potato, a term used by British soldiers of World War One because it sounds like *pomme de terre*, French for a spud.
Bombay Roll	The 'penis between the breasts' type of sexual activity.
Bombed	Very drunk or very high on drugs. 'I was bombed out my skull last night.'
Bomber	a) An illicit drug-pill. b) A large potent cannabis cigarette.
Bombhead	A name given to anyone whose head seems a bit too big for their body or for their hat.
Bomp On	A term from the docks, when London's Docklands were full of ships rather than tall buildings. On days when dockers turned up for work but there wasn't any for them, they had to sign on twice at the Dock Labour Board office. This was known as 'bomping on' and a workless day was a 'bomper'.
Bona	Pick any superlative, from good to excellent, and this is it in Polari form. From the Italian 'buono' – good.
Bonce	A famous term for the head based on the name given by 19th-century schoolboys to a large marble.
Bonce Ponce	Any kind of parasite that lives off whatever the head or hair can sustain it with. A flea, for example.
Bone	a) Old thief's jargon for what thieves do, i.e., steal. Hence 'boning' – out thieving. b) The skull, therefore the head. To be 'boned' is to be hit on the head.
Bone/Boner/ Bone-On	An erection or three. Also 'to bone' is to make use of 'a bone' – to have sexual intercourse.
Bone Box	a) A morbid term for a coffin, as planted in a 'boneyard' (qv). b) The mouth. People have been advised to shut their 'bone boxes' for over 200 years. c) An ambulance, an example used by good buddies on their CB radios.
Bone Off	To masturbate, one way to utilize a 'bone-on'. *See* BONE.
Bone Shaker	Any form of conveyance, originally an early bicycle, that gives its rider or passengers a bumpy ride due to inadequate springs or tyres.
Bone-Ache	Unspecified aches and pains, to 'have the bone-ache' is to ache all over.
Bonehead	a) A slow-witted person, typified in comedy as a brainless thug. b) A shaved head, the ultimate 'skinhead'.

Boner		A bad or stupid mistake, maybe something to do with a malfunction of the head. *See* BONE (b).
Bones		a) Dice, a term that's been rolling for centuries.
		b) The teeth, those that live and die in the 'bone box' (qv, b).
		c) A doctor, especially a surgeon. *See also* SAWBONES.
Boneyard		A cemetary. 'The healthiest corpse in the boneyard' – someone who dies while working out. A perfect reason why exercise should be vigorously avoided.
Bonk		a) Sexual intercourse. A term that's been common since the 1970s. To engage in a spot of 'backseat bonking' is to have sex in a car.
		b) Backslang for 'knob' meaning the penis or to have sex, this possibly accounts for (a).
Bonkers		Mad or eccentric, may be connected with being bonked on the 'brainbox' (qv) thereby rendering the recipient thus.
Bonnie & Clyde	*Snide*	Applies to designer gear what ain't. Imitation watches, perfume, clothes, etc., are 'bonnies'. Based on a pair of American gangsters of the 1930s, Bonnie Parker and Clyde Barrow, whose exploits were made into a successful film in 1967.
Bonnie Dundee	*Flea*	An elderly and once-common term. The scourge of heads, dogs and sporrans.
Bonzer		Good or great, a term that came Up Over from Down Under.
Boo & Hiss	*Piss*	The sounds of disapproval would be apt if you caught someone having one in your doorway.
Boob/Boo Boo		A mistake or a gaffe, often an embarrassing one.
Boob/Booby		A fool, originally a country bumpkin as seen by city dwellers, a clodhopper.
Boobs/Boobies		Female breasts, updates of the ancient terms 'Bubs' and 'Bubbies'. 'Booby Trap' – a brassière.
Booby Box/ House/Hatch		Very old expressions for a lunatic asylum.
Boodle		Stolen goods or money acquired by dishonest means.
Boolie		An enema. I don't know why and I hope I never have to find out.
Boom & Mizen	*Prison*	Parts of a sailing ship shouldn't conjure up visions of convicts being transported to the colonies because the term isn't very old. More likely a sailing holiday for a young offender.

Boot		A contemptuous woman, often a slur hurled at an overly officious one. Usually referred to as an 'old boot'.
Boot Trees		The feet, somewhere to hang your footwear.
Boot, the		Ejection, to be kicked out, given 'the order of the boot'. Also dismissal from a job.
Bootface		Famously a 'face like a boot', a miserable face, one that is 'as long as a boot'.
Bootlace	*Suitcase*	To prevent a calamitous trip, secure your 'boot-laces'.
Bootlicker		A well-known term for a crawler. To 'bootlick'.
Bootnose		A name given to anyone with a broken or mis-shapen nose.
Boots		Tyres. Always check the 'boots' when buying a second-hand car.
Bootsie & Snudge	*Judge*	A TV comedy from the early 1960s gave rise to his lordship being called a 'Bootsie' for a while around that time.
Booze		Alcohol or to drink it. So well-known I don't really know what it's doing here.
Boozed/Boozy		Drunk, though not necessarily falling over drunk, tipsy.
Boozer		a) A pub, a piece that's so well used that it has some RS terms of its own. b) Someone often seen propping up the bar in (a), a drunkard. a 'boozaholic'.
Booze-Up		A heavy drinking session, as opposed to a 'Booze-Down', where light refreshments are the order of the day, with maybe a glass or two of sherry.
Boracic Lint	*Skint*	Very old, very common and said as 'brassic'.
Born Again Virgin		Anyone who has not had sex for a long time.
Boron		An uninteresting idiot. If a moron knows nothing about everything then a 'boron' knows everything about nothing and will happily bore you with the details of it. A master of the unfunny quip with an endless store of knock-knock jokes. Someone to be palmed off on somebody else.
Borrow & Beg	*Egg*	An old piece that's now probably an empty shell.
Boss-Eyed		Eyes that look at each other or in opposite directions. Anywhere but straight ahead.
Boss-Eyed, all gone		When things have gone 'boss-eyed' they've gone wonky, badly awry.
Botany Bay	*a) Hay*	'Hitting the Botany' is an ancient form of getting some sleep.
	b) Run Away	To abscond is to 'do a Botany'.

Bother		Violence. A term that has accompanied youth gang fights since the 1960s and is usually spelt and pronounced 'bovver' even by non-cockneys.
Botherments		Problems, troubles or ailments. Ailments of the Father:

> *Dodgy eyes, dodgy knees,*
> *dodgy nose, chesty wheeze*
> *Dodgy ears, dodgy back,*
> *dodgy neck, joints that crack*
> *All these ailments sad to see*
> *Hope they're not heredit'ry.*

Bottle		a) To go for a drink: 'Coming for a bottle?' 'Bottling' – drinking.
		b) To hit somebody with a bottle, the cause of many a battle scar after a pub brawl.
Bottle & Glass	*Arse*	A well-known example that is only ever used in it's first element, both anatomically and in relation to courage, where the brave and bold are said to have a 'lot of bottle', and a coward may 'bottle it' or 'bottle out' of a confrontation, hence a 'bottler'. Also, in the jargon of the pickpocket, a rear trouser pocket. Anything stolen from here is taken 'off the bottle'.
Bottle & Stopper	*Copper*	Arrested at the first element for a police officer, e.g., 'So I said to these three bottles, "Ello 'ello 'ello."'
Bottle Blonde		Someone whose blonde locks are courtesy of a hair dye.
Bottle of Beer	*Ear*	Always used in full, i.e., 'A word in your bottle o' beer.' 'A word in your bottle' takes on an altogether different and unsavoury meaning. *See* BOTTLE & GLASS.
Bottle of Booze	*a) News*	Most nights at 10 o'clock it could be said, 'Nothing on? Let's watch the bottle then.'
	b) Twos (2/1 Odds)	There seems to be some contention as to whether this or 'bottle of spruce' (qv) is responsible for the common expression 'bottle' in this sense. Odds on 'spruce' I think.
Bottle of Drink	*Stink*	A nasty 'bottle' could mean that someone's 'bottle' needs corking. *See* BOTTLE & GLASS.
Bottle of Fizz	*Whizz*	To 'bottle' someone in this instance is to pick his pocket. *See* WHIZZ (b).
Bottle of Kola	*Bowler*	An old term for the traditional headwear of the city gent that is now old hat.
Bottle of Milk		An extremely white person. A term associated with new arrivals at a holiday resort, people whose bodies haven't seen the sun since their previous holiday.

Bottle of Pop	*Wop (Italian)*	May be based on the well-known Italian soft drink 'Pop Sicola'.
Bottle of Sauce	*Horse*	Refers to one that pulls a cart rather than a racehorse. OK?
Bottle of Scent	*Bent (Homosexual)*	Comes from a time when men were considered poofy if they smelt of anything other than soap or sweat.
Bottle of Scotch	*Watch*	On its formation it applied to a pocket watch. It is that old.
Bottle of Spruce	*Deuce*	Originally applied to tuppence but is now more readily associated with £2. It also applies to the playing card and odds of 2/1 are known as 'bottle'. Formed on the name of a cheap and nasty concoction known as spruce beer.
Bottle of Water	*a) Daughter*	When daddy hears he's got a little girl for a daughter this is just the stuff to wet the baby's head with, I don't think.
	b) Quarter	In the dingy world of drugs this is a quarter of an ounce.
Bottle of Wine	*Fine*	A piece laid down some years ago that refers to a punishment as poured by a magistrate.
Bottle Opener		A laxative, a piece that works perfectly when you see what 'bottle and glass' means and a 'bung' needs removing. *See* BUNG IN THE BOTTLE.
Bottle Top	*a) Cop*	This is about value, not the police. Anything that's 'not much bottle' isn't very good.
	b) Cop	In this sense cop means to catch or take hold of.
Bottled		Drunk, the result of hitting too many bottles. A 'Bottlehead' is a drunkard.
Bottled Promise		A promise given while under the influence of alcohol and as such, one likely to be broken in the light of sobriety. A piece of good advice: 'Hold to a promise that's given in ink but disregard one that is given in drink.'
Bottles of Booze	*Shoes*	In vogue since Elvis sang about his 'Blue Suede Bottles' in the 1950s.
Bottom of a Birdcage		Symbolic of dryness, what the thirsty claim to have a mouth like.
Boulder Bonce		A bald person, one whose head bears a resemblance to a giant pebble or large stone.
Bounce		a) The strength of resilient people, those that 'bounce' every time they are knocked down. Applies in a mental as well as a physical sense. b) Attributed to someone with a lot of self-confidence, often a con man or a salesman. Anyone with 'more front than Brighton'.

c) To eject from a pub, club, party, etc. Hence the need for 'bouncers'.

d) To be dismissed from a job, 'bounced out of work'.

e) To cheat or con. A gullible person may be 'bounced like a ball'.

f) As a noun or verb, sexual intercourse. Or as foreigners in TV comedies call it, 'bouncy-bouncy'.

Bounce Up   A fight. A hardened troublemaker could start a 'bounce up' at a pacifists' convention.

Bouncer   A worthless cheque. Also, more comically, an 'East European trampolinist' – a bouncing Czech.

Bouncers   Female breasts, usually of a larger variety.

Bounty Bar   A derogatory term used by black people against black people who affect white mannerisms, the inference being that, like the chocolate bar (Bounty), they are brown on the outside but white inside.

Bovver   *See* BOTHER.

Bovver Boots   Heavy, high-laced boots, usually Dr (Doc) Martens, which became synonymous with skinheads.

Bovver Boy   Another name for a hooligan, one who enjoys violence for violence's sake.

Bovver House   A pub that is well-known for trouble, where as much blood gets spilt as beer.

Bow & Arrow   *a) Barrow*   A piece from a late 20c building site, obviously a reputable one. You never see 'cowboys' (qv) with bows and arrows.

    b) Charra   When the early form of motor coach was known as a charabanc, it soon got reduced to charra only to make a further transition to a 'bow and arrer'.

    c) Sparrow   A bird much in the affections of Londoners.

Bow & Quiver   *Liver*   Refers to the human organ and that on the offal counter, but mainly it applies to feeling liverish or irritable: 'Bert's got a right bow and quiver this morning, the grumpy old git.'

Bow Locks   The part of the East End where the perennial liar and the 'Jack of Tall Tales' are said to inhabit. A pun on 'bollocks' (qv, b), which is what they talk, as in 'What a load of bow locks'.

Bowl   To walk, most commonly used to describe a strange gait, e.g., 'He's got a funny bowl on him.'

Bowl a Wide   To make a mistake, often costly, as a wide ball in cricket costs a run.

Bowler Hat   *Rat*   Applies to either the rodent or an untrustworthy person.

Bowser		An unattractive woman, from a once-common name for a dog (qv).
Bow-Wow		A dog in all its forms, from the animal to an ugly woman to shoddy or useless goods: 'I've been sold a right bow-wow with this car.'
Box		a) The anus. Mostly used by homosexuals, where rent boys are said to 'take the money and open the box'. b) A small room, especially a prison cell. c) A safe, a piece of underworld jargon: 'blow a box'. d) The vagina, an example which may or may not be related to surgeon's slang for the womb. On a TV documentary a doctor was heard to refer to a hysterectomy as 'whipping out the box'.
Box of Toys	*Noise*	Since kids + toys = a racket, this is a well-fitting term, especially for those of us who believe that no noise is good noise.
Box of Tricks	*Flicks*	The 'flicks' is old slang for the cinema and when this was coined it would have been very apt.
Boy & Girl	*Twirl*	An example of slang for slang. A 'twirl' (qv) is a key, especially a skeleton key. To a thief the tools of his trade are like his kids, his 'boys and girls'.
Boy Racer		A name given to a young man, given to driving without due care and attention to speed limits.
Boy Scout	*Shout*	Whereby 'It's your turn to get the drinks in,' becomes 'It's your boy scout.'
Boy Scouts	*Sprouts*	A greengrocer's term for Brussels sprouts, whereby 'boy scouts' are traditionally eaten with the Christmas dinner.
Boy Scout with Agorophobia		A symbol of uselessness: 'You're as much use as a . . .'
Boys in Blue	*Stew*	Nothing to do with food, to be in a 'right old boys in blue' is to be in a state of agitation.
Boysie		a) A form of address for a man, an extension of 'boy'. b) A little kiss, a peck on the cheek from Ireland.
Bozo		An Americanism for a fool or someone who acts the clown.
Bracelets		A police and underworld term for handcuffs: 'Put the bracelets on him.'
Braces & Bits	*Tits*	Known as 'braces', which is about right since breasts come in pairs.
Bracket		An unspecified part of the body up which comedians have been threatening to punch their stooges since the 1950s.
Brad Pitt	*Shit*	A modern piece based on an American film star who is flushed with success.

Bradford City	*Titty*	Reduced to 'Bradford' or 'Bradfords' if we're talking of a pair. Which we generally are.
Brads		A 19th-century term for money, though you've got more chance of seeing a snowman with a suntan than hearing it now.
Brahma		a) Anything good, great or better is said to be 'a brahma'.
		b) An attractive woman. A 19th-century term based on a Hindu god, therefore probably adapted by British soldiers serving in India.
Brahms & Liszt	*Pissed*	A famous piece based on a pair of famous composers who may or may not have been famous drunks. Johannes Brahms (1833–97), Franz Liszt (1811–86).
Brain		To knock senseless by a blow to the head.
Brain Damage		A name given to a loon, and often to an ultra-violent nutter.
Brain Failure		A condition suffered by the absent-minded or the mentally deficient.
Brainbox		A name given to anyone clever, especially a classroom swot.
Brain-Box/ Bucket/Pan		The head, even one owned by someone who shows a lack of brain power.
Brains		a) Criminal parlance, used ironically of the CID.
		b) An ironic term for the moronic. Those of whom it may be said that, 'if brains were made of dynamite, they wouldn't have enough to blow their hats off.'
Brands Hatch	*Scratch*	The motor-racing circuit takes a turn for getting rid of an itch and is also a slight injury.
Brass		Money, a northern term rarely heard down south.
Brass/Brass Hat		A senior officer in the armed forces or the police.
Brass Band(s)	*Hand(s)*	One of several music combos that make the same connection.
Brass Monkey	*Dunkie (Condom)*	So called because it offers no protection from frost, so be careful when making love in the open on a cold night.
Brass Monkeys		Cold weather. From a saying about a metallic primate with frozen testicles. Actually, on a sailing ship of yore, a brass monkey was a tray on which iron cannonballs were piled. In very cold weather the brass contracted more quickly than the iron, causing the cannonballs to fall to the deck.
Brass Nail	*Tail (Prostitute)*	A familiar piece is a 'brass'. To dress gaudily, as she may do, is to appear 'brassy'.
Brass Tack(s)	*Fact(s)*	An example of RS that has joined the ranks of standard English.

Brassed/Browned/ Cheesed Off		To be fed up in triplicate.
Brasswork		A promiscuous woman, maybe an extension of 'brassy' or the RS 'brass nail' – See both.
Brassy		A showy, ostentatious woman, one who is loud of gab and garment.
Brat		A child, usually a badly behaved one.
Brattery		A crèche, nursery or primary school. Anywhere frequented by nippers.
Brave & Bold	Cold	Does not apply to being unwell. To be 'bloody brave' is to be freezing.
Braveheart		A mocking term for a Scotsman that came into being after the 1995 film of that name, which was loosely based on the Scottish patriot William Wallace (d. 1305).
Bread & Butter	a) Gutter	A very old example when used in relation to being down and out, i.e., in the 'bread and butter'.
	b) Nutter	Getting a wide usage because everybody knows a headcase.
	c) Putter	A piece from the golf course for one of a golfer's bats.
	d) Shutter	Reflective of the inner-city high street, where shop windows are protected by 'bread and butters'.
	e) Stutter	A term not easily said by one who suffers from a speech impediment.
Bread & Cheese	Sneeze	The end result of the nose-itch.
Bread & Honey	Money	World famous as 'bread'.
Bread & Jam	a) Pram	A recent rival to 'jar of jam' (qv) in the 'baby-barrer' stakes.
	b) Tram	A term that's as old and redundant as this mode of transport.
Bread & Lard	Hard	Used sarcastically to anyone seen to be complaining unnecessarily, e.g., 'Your dishwasher's busted and you had to wash up by hand? Well how bread and lard for you.'
Bread & Scrape		A slice of bread with a thin scraping of 'bread-spread', usually butter.
Bread Knife	Wife	One of a drawerful of terms connecting her of the sharp tongue with a cutter.
Breadbasket		The stomach, as seen as a target for a punch. A piece from the boxing ring.
Breadcrumbs	Gums	Those with mouths full of 'breadcrumbs' where once were teeth, are those most likely to hold the world peanut-sucking record.
Breadspread		Any kind of fat that can be scraped on bread, from cholesterol-ridden butter to polyunsaturated other stuff.

Break One's Duck		Of a male, to lose his virginity, to get 'on the scoreboard' or 'off the mark'.
Breakneck Speed		So fast that survival would't be an option should the worst happen.
Breeze-Up/ Wind-Up		A couple of terms that relate to fear. 'Breezy' or 'windy' people are scared people.
Brek/Brekkers/ Brekky/ Breknek		Four ways of preparing the first meal of the day, i.e., breakfast.
Brenda Frickers	*Knickers*	A modern example for what are found in the drawers drawer. Known as 'Brendas' after an Irish film and TV actress.
Brew		In America it's beer, in Britain it's tea. I'm with the Yanks on this one, but only if it's British beer.
Brewer's Bung	*Tongue*	A warning to someone with a loose jaw: 'Keep that brewer's of yours still in future.'
Brewers Droop		The effect that too much beer may have on a normally upstanding and able penis, rendering it temporarily useless to a partner, who would probably rather go to sleep anyway.
Brian O'Linn	*Gin*	Victorian sots would have been partial to a drop of 'Brian' or 'Bri'. Sometimes 'Brian O'Flynn'.
Brick It		a) To steal from a shop window, smash and grab. b) To be frightened, a reduced form of 'shit a brick'.
Bricked		Castrated, usually said of pets, but is increasingly being suggested as a punishnent for sex offenders. Probably from the famous joke about the camel-keeper at the zoo who stated that his charges were castrated with a couple of house bricks. When asked if it hurt he replied, 'Only if you whack your thumbs.'
Bricks & Mortar	*Daughter*	Possibly as old as the joke: She was only a brick-layer's daughter but she never went up the wall.
Bride & Groom	*a) Broom* *b) Room*	Whereby a new 'bride' sweeps clean. Coined when a room was all working-class newlyweds could expect to move in to.
Bridger		Constipation, having a bridger means you can't go, much like traffic when a bridge goes up to let ships through, which is known as 'catching a bridger'.
Bridgets/Bridget Joneses		Large women's knickers, as worn, to much publicity, by the eponymous heroine of the 2001 film *Bridget Jones Diary*.
Brief		a) A lawyer. A term from those who need his services, based on the documented instructions he receives.

b) Down the years a 'brief' has been any kind of ticket, from a pawnbroker's one in the 19th century to a lotto ticket today. Anyone who successfully dodges a duty is said to have 'worked their brief'. *See* WORK ONES TICKET.

c) A licence, especially a driving licence. A banned driver has 'lost his brief'.

d) A membership card, particularly one held by union members.

e) A cheque. Parlance of those who specialise in passing dud ones.

f) Police jargon for a search warrant.

g) A passport, often a false one.

Brig — Prison. Originally a nautical term, but now houses criminal landlubbers.

Bright & Breezy *Easy* — Like anything else, it's 'brighton' when you know how.

Bright & Frisky *Whisky* — In short a 'brighton', it's what a few but not too many will make you.

Brighton Line *Nine* — One from the bingo hall.

Brighton Pier *a) Queer* — In early RS this applied to feeling unwell, and later to anything odd or strange. Now a 'Brighton' is solely a homosexual.

b) Disappear — A modern term meaning to run away or leave, i.e., 'time to Brighton'.

Brighton Rock *a) Cock (Penis)* — Long, hard and sucked at the seaside, see the connection?

b) Dock — The 'Brighton' is the part of the courtroom where the accused learns if he is to spend some time at one of Her Majesty's guest houses, i.e. prison.

Brig's Rest *Vest* — A rough itchy undergarment. Worn by convicts, named by convicts. But not recently.

Brill — An abbreviated form of brilliant, meaning everything's er . . . brilliant.

Bring Down — To make a happy person morose with tales of misery and woe.

Bringdown — A disappointment or a depressing situation, a pub with no beer for instance. Also applies to a tiresome person who has the knack of turning a short, interesting story into a long, boring one.

Bristles — A moustache, often one belonging to a woman.

Bristol City *Titty* — Commonly known and accepted as 'Bristols'.

British Rail *Stale* — An obvious allusion to the infamous intercity sandwich.

Brixton Briefcase — A large portable radio/tape recorder, originally owned and carried around by black youths.

Brixton Riot	*Diet*	Following the riot of April 1981, when the youth of Brixton, South London, waged war with the police, overweight people began going on 'Brixtons'.
Broad		a) A well-known Americanism for a woman, who may or may not be a prostitute.
		b) A variation of 'wide' (qv), someone usually on the edge of legality who always knows someone who knows someone who can lay his hands on . . .
Broads		a) Playing-cards, especially those in the hands of a card sharp who, incidentally, is known as a 'broadsman'. Anyone who falls for the three-card trick is a mug who 'stands the broads'.
		b) Credit cards or the like, and obviously fairly recent.
Broken Heart	*Fart*	Probably from the old rhyme scrawled on many a lavatory wall:
		Here I sit broken hearted
		Spent a penny and only farted.
Broken Wristed		A homosexual, an exaggerated form of 'limp wristed' (qv).
Bromley-by-Bow	a) *Dough*	A cab driver's term for money that is short-changed to 'Bromley'. After an area of East London.
	b) *Toe*	To 'have it on your Bromleys' is to leave or run away a bit sharpish.
Bronco Layne	*Pain*	An early 1960s term based on a popular TV western series of the period, when a pest was a 'Bronco in the arse'. American actor Ty Hardin starred as the eponymous hero of the piece.
Bronk		An erection. A penis may be 'on the bronk' or a man may 'have a bronk on'.
Bronze		Any coins that aren't silver.
Bronze Eye		The anus. To wink with the 'bronze eye' is to expose the backside to onlookers, to 'moon' (qv).
Bronze Figure	*Kipper*	An imperfect rhyme that finds itself cut up by the famous 'Jack the Ripper' (qv).
Brothel Creepers		Suede shoes with thick crepe soles, often brightly coloured. Part of the dress code of Teddy Boys in the 1950s and die-hard Teds of today.
Brother & Sister	*Blister*	As seen on the hands after a rare burst of hard graft or on the feet as a result of tight shoes or an unaccustomed burst of running.
Brother Bung	*Tongue*	Whereby 'don't ever be a crawler' becomes 'don't bung your brother up your boss's backside'. The term, which was the name of a pickle company, is based on an old slang term for a brewer, who was a 'Brother of the Bung'. Other examples in the

same vein are: Brothers of the Blade (soldier), String (fiddler), Gusset (pimp), Whip (coachman) and Brush (painter).

Brother of the Badge One who goes through the purgatory of the knowledge to earn his badge, so he can go through the hell of driving in central London and moan about mini-cab drivers. In a bygone age he was a 'brother of the whip', now he is a London taxi driver.

Brown a) Any coin that isn't silver. Heard at an old public bar card game: 'I've been waiting all night for a decent hand and when I get one all I win is a load of brown.'
b) The anus, an old term whereby sodomy is known as a 'bit of brown', or 'browning'.
c) Excrement. Also a euphemism for shit in other forms. A protester's placard during the fuel crisis in 2000 read 'Gordon's policies are a load of Brown', a reference to Chancellor Gordon Brown's insistance that the petrol tax had to remain at 84 per cent.

Brown & Mild *Wild* Refers to a loss of temper, often the result of mixing drinks like these two ales.

Brown/Bronze Wink *See* Bronze Eye.

Brown Artist A male homosexual, an example that relates to 'brown' (b). Also known as a 'brownie'.

Brown Bess *Yes* The same as 'black Bess' (qv), in that they were both early rifles.

Brown Bread *Dead* Old and the most common term for the 'popping of the clogs', an extension of which is 'Hovis' (qv, a).

Brown Bullethole A fairly recent term for the anus.

Brown Eye The anus. One of many terms connecting these two body parts.

Brown Food Bitter. A beer drinker's meal-in-a-glass.

Brown Hat *Cat* An old term that may be based on a music-hall song by Harry Champion which contains the line: 'If I can't get what I order in a pot I'll have it in me old brown hat.' Then again it may not.

Brown Hatter A male homosexual, an old term that supposedly depicts the outcome of sodomy, or 'shit stabbing', i.e., an excrement-topped penis.

Brownie A male homosexual. *See* Brown Artist.

Brown Joe *No* The equally aged opposite of 'brown Bess' (qv).

Brown Nose To crawl or suck up to, the image of kissing a superior's backside. As practised by:

Brown Noser A crawler, one with his nose up his manager's breech, hence the colour. To 'brown nose'.

Brown Paper	*Caper*	Asked of anyone doing something they shouldn't, in a place they shouldn't be doing it: 'What's your brown paper then?'
Brown Stuff		Excrement. Also, to get someone in trouble is to 'drop them in the brown stuff'.
Brown Sugar		An attractive black woman who was made famous by the Rolling Stones in 1971.
Brown Tongue		To grovel in a bigger way than the creep described at 'brown nose'. 'Brown tonguers' do this.
Brown Trouser Job		Anything that will scare the shit out of you and soil your legwear. The idea is that brown strides won't show the mess.
Brown Windsor		The anus. A derivation of the RS for arsehole – 'Windsor Castle'.
Bruce Forsythe	*Knife*	A fairly recent piece based on a well-known entertainer whose catchphrase is 'Knife to see you, to see you knife'. Or something very similar.
Brush		The pubic area, especially of a female. A vulgarism, used by men to represent a woman, is a 'bit of brush'.
Brussels Sprout	*a) Scout*	A term that's almost as old as the boy scout movement.
	b) Tout	Originally used on the racecourse concerning tipsters but now relates to the ticket tout.
Bryan Ferry	*Sherry*	Another British rock star turns to drink, this one the ex-singer with Roxy Music.
Bryant & Mays	*Stays*	Now that women no longer case themselves up in these old-fashioned corsets, the famous matchstick men no longer strike a light in RS.
Bryant and May		A light ale. Based on the well-known company of matchmakers because a match is known as a 'light'.
Bubble		a) A bogus company, one that is set up, makes money (often by conning investors) and vanishes like a burst bubble.
		b) To con or swindle, like those in (a).
		c) A name given to a bubbleheaded person, someone with a vacancy between the ears.
		d) A wet fart, a rueful look on the face of anyone who has just broken wind may indicate that they have just blown a 'bubble'.
Bubble & Blister	*Sister*	Closely related to 'Skin and Blister' (qv) but not as common.
Bubble & Squeak	*a) Beak*	If you have to appear in front of a magistrate or judge, you're 'up before the bubble'.
	b) Greek	Very familiar in the shortened form of 'bubble'. When a Greek team play at West Ham the fans will be 'forever booing bubbles'.

c) Speak		Most frequently employed in terms of informing either to the police or someone in authority, often a wife, i.e., 'to bubble up' or to 'put the bubble in'.
d) Weak		A sure sign of the flu is when you come over all 'bubble and squeak'.
e) Week		Seven days make a 'bubble'. Bubble and squeak is a dish of fried leftovers.
f) Leak		A plumber's term for a leaky pipe. Also to urinate is to 'take a bubble'.

Bubble/Bubble Up — To inform. 'Bubbled'/'Bubbled Up' – informed on. *See* BUBBLE & SQUEAK (c).

Bubble Bath — *Laugh* — The bane of the peeping Tom becomes a sign that everyone else is happy. Also used as a term of disbelief: 'You're having a bubble' translates to 'You must be joking.'

Bubble Gum — *Bum* — A lovely 'bubble', that of a shapely girl.

Bubblebrain/ Bubblehead — A mentally deficient person, someone who has 'left the doors open to let the air in'.

Bubblegum — Uncomplicated pop music of the late 1960s, typified by 'Sugar Sugar', a number-one hit by the Archies.

Bubbles — Female breasts, from the same root as 'boobs' (qv).

Buccaneer — *Queer* — Homosexuality has long gone hand in hand with sailors and the dictionary defines this early seaman as: 'A pirate, an unscrupulous adventurer.' Well boys will be boys.

Buck & Doe — *Snow* — Said with a heavy emphasis on the first element, it creates an impression of an expletive, e.g., 'Look at the buck 'n' doe out there.'

Buck — a) An American dollar, a term that has gained a usage in the UK in the expressions 'big bucks' – a lot of money and 'a fast buck' – a quick earner.
b) A young man, often a reference to a member of a gang of tearaways. It is also a term from northern England for a young criminal.
c) Sexual intercourse, well it's what rabbits are famous for.
d) An occasional euphemism for 'fuck'. There's buck all else to say about it.

Bucket & Pail — *Jail* — For a shorter sentence, say 'in bucket'.

Bucket & Spade — *Maid* — Mainly applies to a barmaid, although a spinster of the parish may be an old 'bucket'.

Bucket & Well — *Hell* — Was said in full to replace the F word in 'fucking hell', e.g., 'What the bucket and well are you on about?' Rarely heard now as nobody is shocked by bad language any more.

Bucket		a) A piece of old seaman's jargon for a ship or boat, which was either a term of affection or one of derision.
		b) An old car, often known as a 'rustbucket'. Mine have been known as far worse.
		c) To rain heavily. When it's 'bucketing down' it's 'chucking it down'.
		d) A lavatory. When you've got a 'turtle's head' poking out, the need to find a 'bucket' is great.
Bucket Afloat	*Coat*	An old term with nautical connections, a bucket being a ship. Soldiers of World War One changed it to 'bucket and float'.
Bucket of Sand	*Grand (£1000)*	A recent term from the market, the money one that is.
Bucketer		Someone who cheats a partner in crime out of their share of the loot; one who doesn't conform to the perception of honour among thieves. To 'bucket' is to cheat or deceive and is a later version of to 'well'. The 19th-century rogue would 'drop his accomplice down a well'. A 'bucket job' is a deception and in the 1960s the term related to a fraudulent company, where a criminal would fleece his more legitimate partners.
Buckle My Shoe	*a) Jew*	An old piece, but Jews are rarely heard of as 'buckles' these days.
	b) Two	Buckle my shoe the number two, a bingo call.
Bucks Hussar	*Cigar*	An example that seems to have been stubbed out.
Buckshee	*Free*	British troops serving in 19th-century Persia heard the word 'baksheesh', meaning a tip or gift, brought it back to Blighty and adapted it to a slightly different meaning. That's the history, the reality is that 'buckshee' beer is the best beer.
Buddy Holly	*a) Volley*	A footballer's term for kicking the ball in mid air, based on the legendary American musician of the 1950s who kicked the bucket in mid-air when the plane he was travelling in crashed in 1959. Buddy was 22 when he died but his songs live on.
	b) Wally	A pickled cucumber sold in fish 'n' chip shops. Also a modern reference to a fool.
Budgie		A talkative person, someone you wouldn't want to be stuck in a lift with.
Buffoon		Although not slang when used of a professional fool or a clown, it becomes a term of abuse when aimed at an everyday idiot.
Bug		a) A small electronic device secretly planted so that conversations may be listened to by, usually, professional snoopers.

b) An illness which would appear to be caused by a rotating germ carrier, hence the expression 'there's a bug going round'.

c) Something that causes defects in machinery, a gremlin.

d) To annoy greatly, e.g., 'Don't bug me, I'm not in the mood.'

Bug & Flea　*Tea*　First brewed by itching, trenchbound soldiers of World War One.

Bug Path/Run/ Walk　A parting in the hair, along which head vermin may go for a stroll.

Bug Rake/Raker　A comb, especially one carried by the 'nit nurse' (qv).

Bugger　a) Anything hard, tricky or downright impossible to do. Trying to thread a needle wearing boxing gloves can be a 'right bugger'.

b) To mess up or ruin, to bugger something up.

c) A person. Once considered an insult but now only mildly or humorously so.

Bugger All　Nothing. Having 'bugger all' in your pocket means you're holding nuppence. You're broke.

Bughouse　Any run-down building that makes you feel cootie (qv) on entering. Often true of cheap boarding houses.

Bugle　The nose, that which may be blown, hopefully on a 'bugle duster' – a handkerchief.

Bugs Bunny　*Money*　Based on the carrot-crunching cartoon rabbit in connection with 'lettuce' (qv). known as 'Bugs' or 'Bugsy'.

Bugsy　A nickname for a mad or eccentric person, one with bugs in his head.

Buick　To vomit, from the supposed sound of somebody chucking up the contents of their stomach.

Built for Comfort　Fat or at least overweight, as opposed to being built for speed. The title of a song by American bluesman Willie Dixon.

Bull　a) An ancient term for five shillings (25p).

b) A shortening of 'bullshit' (qv).

Bull & Bush　*Push*　Getting dismissed from work is known as getting 'the old Bull & Bush'. Based on a music-hall song about a pub in Hampstead, North-West London.

Bull & Cow　*Row*　An argument, often between the male and female of the species, i.e., man and wife. If hostilities persist because of the continual raking up of the past, remember this peace process: 'If yesterday's scars are allowed to fade, a new tomorrow can begin today.'

Bull/Bullshine — A military term for regimental routine seen as unnecessary.

Bull Artist/ Merchant — A 'bullshitter' (qv) by any other name is still full of it.

Bulldozer *Poser* — A vain exhibitionist, one who forces attention on himself for effect.

Bullet — a) The ace in a pack of cards.
b) Dismissal from employment, to get the bullet is to be fired.
c) A single pill or capsule of an illicit drug.

Bullets — Peas, especially hard ones or those used as ammunition for a peashooter.

Bullock's Blood — A beefy cocktail of beer and rum.

Bullock's Heart *Fart* — Seldom heard nowadays, the term that is.

Bullock's Horn *Pawn* — An archaic example that is always cut down to the first element. Many a wedding ring has been put in and got out of 'bullocks'.

Bullock's Liver *River* — An old example from the butcher's shop that dried up years ago.

Bullseye — A common term for £50, as the centre ring on a dartboard is worth 50.

Bullshit — a) A much-employed term for nonsense or a blatant lie. Someone on the receiving end may sniff the air and swear he can smell the countryside or he may just say 'That's bullshit!'
b) Empty flattery or boastful talk designed to impress.

Bullshitter — A liar or flatterer, someone who is 'full of shit'.

Bully Beef — A name given to a bully, but not to his face.

Bully Beef *a) Chief* — A convict's term for the chief officer in a prison.
b) Deaf — A term from north of the English border that is unlikely to be heard or understood south of it.

Bullywayo — A name given to a bully; a pun on the Zimbabwean city of Bulawayo, and has been since it was in Rhodesia.

Bulrush *Brush* — Refers to a paintbrush, a piece from the painting and decorating trade. These days it pays to be choosy about who you get to do your painting as the world is awash with ne'er-do-well decorators. In our multi-racial society, even Indians can be cowboys.

Bum — a) The buttocks, a term that predates most other slang and is said to be based on the sound of a fart, as the earliest references give it as 'boom'.

b) A tramp or a scrounger, anyone frequently 'on the bum'.

c) Bad, false or unfair. A 'bum deal' is no good; a 'bum rap' is a false arrest or an unfair accusation.

Bum Bandit A homosexual, the same one as described in 'arsehole bandit' (qv).

Bum Boy A homosexual, a derogatory term and has been for generations.

Bum Buddies/
Chums/Chinas A male homosexual couple. Often a jocular put-down aimed at close friends. *See* CHINA PLATE.

Bum Fodder a) An old term for lavatory paper, *see* BUMF.

b) A newspaper, from the days when it was read, torn into squares and hung on a string in the lavatory, hence 'today's news is tomorrow's bum fodder'. Also a book not worth keeping.

Bum Freezer A short jacket, one that doesn't stop the wind from blowing around the 'Khyber Pass' (qv).

Bum Licker/
Sucker Another pair of grovelling sycophants to go with the 'brown noser' and the 'arse licker'.

Bum Steer Bad or misleading advice. To be sent the wrong way is to be given a 'bum steer'.

Bum Tags Pieces of dried excrement that have attached themselves to hairs around the anus.

Bum Up To speak highly of, to praise often for publicity. TV stations 'bum up' forthcoming programmes only for them to disappoint.

Bumbershoot An umbrella, an example that's been keeping the rain off for over a century.

Bumblebee(s) *Knee(s)* In RS a 'bumblebee' in the 'flowers' takes on an eye-watering meaning. *See* FLOWERS & FROLICS. Usually though, this is bent in half at 'bumbles'.

Bumf Written information or instructions, usually compli-cated or confusing. The term is a shortened version of 'bum fodder', an old reference to toilet paper, which, presumably, is where it all ended up in the days before bums became used to the super-soft 'arse-wipe' of today.

Bumface a) A name given to someone with a cleft chin.

b) A term of derision against anyone a bit on the ugly side.

Bumfest A recent term for a large gathering of homosexual men, a gay rights march for example. Also a men-only orgy.

Bumfluff The soft facial hair of youth, a growth that's often met with sarcastic comments about letting a cat lick it off.

Bumfucker	A male homosexual, a derisive term used by those who do not share those tendencies.
Bummer	a) An unpleasant experience or a disappointment. It was originally a racecourse term for a skint-making loss, causing the loser to bum some more money, at least to get home with. It later became synonymous with hippies and the drug-taking scene of the late 1960s when it meant a bad trip.
	b) An American term for a tramp, a wandering gentleman of the road as sung about in the Dean Martin record 'Bumming Around'. On this side of the pond it's a scrounging layabout.
	c) A male homosexual, a term of abuse used by those who don't travel on the same bus.
Bummocks	A juvenile term of defiance, championed in 2001 by BBC radio presenter Sarah Kennedy.
Bump Off	To murder. Heard after a performance of *The Mousetrap*: 'Every time I thought I had the murderer sussed, they got bumped off.'
Bump Start	To get a car started by pushing it. It later became a metaphor for getting anything going by giving it a shove in the right direction.
Bumpers	a) Breasts, like the part of a car that is 'out in front'.
	b) Sports footwear, in pre-trainers days, with a thick rubber toe-cap.
Bumps	Breasts, either the shape or what most men like to bump into.
Bum's Rush	When you see a bouncer grab someone by the collar and the seat of the trousers and chuck him out, he's giving him the 'bum's rush'. Lately the term seems to be metaphorically creeping towards a 'brush off' or a 'knock-back'.
Bumswizzled	Drunk. A modern version of the very old 'swizzled', meaning the same thing. Not sure how the bum got in. *See* Swizzle.
Bunce/Bunts	Perks, bonuses, inducements to act or work. Money or goods earned on top of wages, usually by way of a fiddle. The term originated with 19th-century costermongers, the more unscrupulous of whom would use counterfeit or 'slang' weights and measures, thereby earning more for selling less. To 'bunce', is to overcharge and it's done by a 'buncer'. Possibly connected to 'Bounce' (e).
Bunch	A term employed by women when speaking of a man's genitals.

Bunch of Fives		Five clenched fingers = one fist, often waved menacingly under the chin of a potential recipient who may be asked if it is required: 'Do you want a bunch of fives?'
Bundle		a) A large sum of money, often a stake that will either win or lose you a 'bundle'.
		b) A fight, often in a school playground where the cry 'Bundle' would attract an audience.
		c) Sexual intercourse, a 'bundle beneath the bedclothes'.
		d) The bulge in tight clothing made by a man's genitals.
Bung		a) To throw, pass or hand over. 'Bung it over here' – give it to me.
		b) A bribe. A direct descendant of (a), this is a term of bribery and corruption on a large scale. Anyone in power is open to a 'bung', from politicians to sportsmen to the bloke on the gate at a venue.
Bung in the Bottle		Constipation, a clever piece that aptly unites the RS term for the anus (bottle) with that which seals its contents. *See* BOTTLE & GLASS.
Bung It In	*Gin*	A gin drinker would simply hold up his glass and tell the barman to 'bung it it'.
Bungalow		A man with large genitals but little intelligence, often a rich woman's toyboy. So called because everything's down below and there's nothing on top.
Bunghole		The anus, that of a 'barrel arse' (qv) presumably.
Bungie/Bungy		a) An old term for cheese, a bit of bread and bungie.
		b) Rubber. An old term for an eraser and also an elastic band. Now famous as 'bungee', the elasticated rope that nutters tie round their ankles before jumping off bridges.
Bun in the Oven		A well-known phrase relating to pregnancy, one of many.
Bunk		a) To abscond. To leave in a hurry is to 'do a bunk'.
		b) Rubbish, nonsense. A 'load of bunk'.
Bunkies/ Bunkipoos		Sexual intercourse, derivitives of the well-known 'bunk-up' (qv).
Bunk In		Uninvited or illegal entry. To gatecrash a party, queue jump or sneak into the pictures without paying is all 'bunking in'.
Bunk Off		To play truant or skip work for the day.
Bunk Up		To lift somebody up in order for them to reach or climb something.

Bunk-Up		Sexual intercourse, an example from the lexicon of the unromantic oaf.
Bunk-Up in a Brothel		What the totally incompetent are said to be unable to organise.
Bunny		Talk. A talkative person is said to have 'more bunny than Watership Down'. This is used as an extension of the very familiar 'rabbit'. From RS 'rabbit and pork' (qv).
Bunny Boiler		An obsessed woman who can't take rejection without taking spiteful revenge. As the character in the film *Fatal Attraction* did by boiling the pet rabbit of the married man who gave her the elbow.
Bunsen Burner	a) *Earner*	A nice little tickle that brings in some bunce , that's a 'bunsen'.
	b) *Turner*	A cricketer's term for a pitch that is beneficial to spin bowlers.
Bup/Buppie		Bread, more especially a slice of bread and butter. Sometimes refers to money.
Buppy		Originally an American term for a young well-to-do black person, a black yuppie.
Burdett-Coutts	*Boots*	An outmoded piece based on the philanthropic Baroness Angela Burdett-Coutts (1814–1906) whose acts of charity must have included putting footwear on impoverished Victorian feet.
Burglar Alarm(s)	*Arm(s)*	One of several examples rhyming on 'alarm' that are sending out warning signals to the long-dominant 'Chalk Farm'.
Burgoo		Porridge. From the Arabic, *burghul*, the term was originally used by seamen and then soldiers.
Buried		Imprisoned. Heard outside a court: 'Not a bad result really, buried for three months.'
Burke & Hare	*Chair*	Based on the infamous 19th-century Scottish murderers who donated their bodies, as well as those of their victims, to medical research.
Burlington Bertie	*Thirty*	Another piece from the bingo caller's handbook, this one is based on the famous shirtless toff from Bow. TV racing experts use it in reference to the odds of 100/30.
Burn		a) A cigarette or a smoke: 'Let's have a quick burn before we go back.'
		b) To kill, particularly by shooting.
		c) A swindle, to sell inferior goods as first class, especially drugs. Such a con man is a 'Burn Artist'.
Burn/Burn Up		A fast drive/ride in an automobile or on a motorbike.
Burn Off		To overtake another vehicle and leave it in your wake.

Burn Oil		To drive an old car. A humorous British version of 'burn rubber' (qv).
Burn Rubber		To drive. An Americanism: 'Let's burn rubber' – let's go. The effect of friction on the tyres.
Burn Up		To cause anger, to make someone so hot under the collar you can see the steam rising.
Burn(s) & Smoulder(s)	*Shoulder(s)*	Apt when you've done the mad dogs and Englishman bit and you've got shoulders that could stop traffic.
Burner		Venereal disease, to catch a 'burner'.
Burnout		The result of mental or physical exhaustion, necessitating a long rest for batteries to be recharged.
Burnt		An ancient term for contracting venereal disease. A 'burnt poker' has been an infected penis for a couple of centuries, a sort of 19th-century hot-rod.
Burnt Cinder	*Window*	Always reduced to the first element, smash and grab merchants chuck bricks through a 'burnt'.
Burnt Fingers		The result of 'playing with fire', putting yourself in a dangerous situation.
Burnt Offering		An overcooked meal, as prepared by a 'burn-toast' (qv).
Burn-Toast		A useless cook, one who seeks the help of Delia Smith to boil an egg.
Burton-on-Trent	*a) Rent*	May be no coincidence that the name of this famous brewery town should be used when very often the landlord's money was blown on its product. Also a male prostitute, a rent boy is a 'Burton'.
	b) Went	Offered by some as the origin of the expression 'gone for a burton', but I'm not convinced.
Bury		a) To beat off the opposition, to win by a wide margin, the loser being 'buried'. b) In football, to put the ball in the net, to score a goal.
Bus & Tram	*Jam*	Apt if referring to snarled-up traffic but less so if the sweet stuff is involved. In fact not at all.
Bush		a) Pubic hair of either sex. 'Beating about the bush' – female masturbation. b) Marijuana, a drug dealer's term for 'grass' (qv, a).
Bushed		Tired, worn out. An old expression of exhaustion.
Bushel & Peck	*Neck*	An old term that's got the measure of both the inside and outside of the neck. You can wear a scarf round or get a pint down your 'bushel'.
Bushel of Coke	*Bloke*	An old example that has left the coal'ole.
Bushfire(d)	*Tire(d)*	Sits alongside 'bushed' (qv), an extension that probably isn't connected.
Bushy Park	*Lark*	One of several parks, this one by Hampton Court,

to make this link. Parks being synonymous with messing about.

Business
a) Anything that needs to be done. 'Go in, do the business, and come straight out.'
b) Defecation, to do one's business is a splash in the pan.

Business Girl
Otherwise known as a streetwalker, a prostitute.

Business, the
a) Sexual intercourse, the act without any love involvement. Heard at a party: 'I dunno who she was, we nipped upstairs, did the business and came down again.'
b) The best, the absolute topmost. Often said as 'the biz'.

Busk
To improvise. If you haven't got the right tools, 'busk it' or leave it to someone who has.

Bust
To burgle. An example that first broke into slang usage in the 19th century.

Buster
a) A bet. An accumulator of four or more selections. One loser and the bet is busted.
b) A housebreaker, a burglar who first 'cracked a crib' in the 19th century.

Busting
A term of approval from the Midlands.

Bustle Punching
Frottage. The activity practised by men who derive sexual pleasure from rubbing themselves against women in crowded places.

Butch
a) A mannish woman, not necessarily but very often a lesbian.
b) Overtly masculine, a mostly homosexual term.

Butcher's Hook   *Look*
Widely used and always in the first element: 'Let's have a butchers.'

Butt
An American term for the buttocks that has become common in the UK with the popularity of America's first family, *The Simpsons*.

Butter Churn   *Turn*
A theatrical term for a theatrical act.

Butterboy
A novice, especially a taxi driver with a shiny new badge.

Buttercup
An effeminate male homosexual. *See* DAFFODIL.

Buttercup &   *Crazy*
Daisy
Used by a distraught father whose kids are driving him 'buttercup'.

Buttered Bread   *Dead*
One of many terms linking death with the staff of life. Heard in a pub:

> First Man: I see they buried Alfie Smith yesterday.
> Second Man (surprised): Is old Alfie buttered bread then?
> First Man (sarcastic): No. He's the first prize in a treasure hunt.

Buttered Bun	*One*	An alternative to 'Kelly's eye' (qv) down the bingo hall.
Buttered Scone	*One*	An alternative to the previous alternative to 'Kelly's eye' down the bingo hall.
Butterfly	*Tie*	Any form of neck tie but may relate more easily to a bow-tie.
Butthead		A stupid person, the famous cartoon partner of Beavis.
Buttie		A term from northern England for a sandwich, most famously a chip one.
Buttinski		Someone who habitually interrupts or butts in. Geddit?
Button		a) The clitoris. An old piece of advice from mother to daughter is to 'be good and keep your finger on your button'. b) The chin. In boxing, a punch that lands 'right on the button' often secures a knock-out.
Button It		A warning to 'hold your noise'. Keep your mouth shut and be quiet. Alternatively, 'put a zip on it'.
Button Your Lip		An order to be quiet, keep your trap shut. In other words: 'Put a zip on that mouth of yours.'
Buttonhole		An old term for the cavity that holds the 'button', the vagina. *See* BUTTON (a).
Buttons & Bows	*Toes*	'Shall we have it on our buttons?' translates to 'Shall we go?'
Buy		To believe or accept a story. Someone may try to sell you a dummy but you don't have to buy it.
Buy a Pup		To buy something that wasn't worth the money, to be swindled.
Buy It		To die. RAF jargon from World War Two, mostly used in the past tense of a fellow pilot who had been killed, i.e., he 'bought it'.
Buyer		In criminal and police parlance, a receiver of stolen goods.
Buzz		a) Good or pleasant. 'Thanks for the invite, it's been a buzz.' b) A thrill that may be derived from drink, drugs or life. c) A telephone call, to give someone a 'buzz'. d) A rumour, there's a 'buzz' going round. e) To pick a pocket, thieves have been 'buzzing' since the 19th century. f) To leave. 'Gotta buzz.'
Buzz Off		To leave, or an order to do so – 'Bee off with you'.
Buzzard		An old cantankerous person, that's an 'old buzzard'.
Buzzcocks		A modern euphemism for bollocks, based on a

British rock band and brought to the fore in the TV pop quiz, *Never Mind the Buzzcocks*.

Buzzer One who specialises in 'buzzing', i.e., a pickpocket.

Buzzing High on drink or drugs, or a mixture of both.

Buzzy A juvenile term for a bluebottle, the buzzing pest of summer. Also a 'buzzy-wuzzy'.

By the Cringe/ Left A couple of mild oaths. The first became well-known in the 1960s through TV's *The Likely Lads*. The second is a steal from an army parade ground.

By Pass   *Arse* A kick up the 'by pass' may be just what's needed to get a layabout moving.

Bye-Byes/Bylies Hopefully what follows a lullaby in a child's bedroom – sleep!

C

C & A		A bisexual man, one who will have a stab at 'cunts and arseholes'. Based on the well-known clothing chain which in polite circles stands for 'Coats & 'Ats'.
C & A	*Gay (Homosexual)*	Based on the high street store which, in this sense, may stand for 'cocks and arses'.
Cab Rank	*Bank*	Apt in a money goes to money sense, although most taxi drivers would deny it.
Cab Yab		Shop talk among taxi drivers.
Cabbage		a) Money, more especially the folding kind. From when pound notes, because of their colour, were known as 'greens' (qv), hence 'cabbage'. *See also* SPINACH and LETTUCE.
		b) A brain-dead person as a result of an accident or illness, a vegetable.
Cabbage Head		A simpleton, a buffoon, someone who IS as green as he's cabbage-looking.
Cabbaged		To be in the vegetative state of a drunken stupor.
Cabbie's/Cab Driver's Armpit		What a mouth that is less than fresh is said to be like.
Cabin Cruiser	*Boozer*	Something to do with pushing the boat out?
Cabman's Rests	*Breasts*	An old, obsolete piece which shows that yesterday's cabbies weren't just interested in tips.

Caboose		A prison. A well-known example from the 19th century that's still within its 'cell by' date.
Caca-Bacca		Cannabis, or 'shit' (qv, c), as loaded into a joint.
Ca-Ca/Caca/ Cack		Excrement, that which reclines in a child's potty or 'cacksack' – nappy.
Cacatorium		An ancient term for a lavatory, an old out-house.
Cackpipe		The anus. A modern equivalent of the 'Shit-Chute' (qv).
Cad		A typically upper-class rogue, an unprincipled bounder.
Cadbury Alley/ Channel		The anus. A brown stuff connection here, one that Cadbury, the well-known chocolate manufacturer, won't be happy to be involved with.
Cadbury's Snack	*Back*	Whether anatomically speaking or a reference to the back of a building, this chocolate biscuit is always reduced to 'Cadburys'.
Cady		A hat, a well-worn example that's been about for a century or more.
Cafeteria		A homosexual term for a place, usually a public toilet, to go for oral sex. In a way, a place to go and eat.
Caff		As far as I'm concerned, the only way to say cafe. Also 'kayf'.
Cage		A prison cell, where gaolbirds are kept.
Cain & Abel	*Table*	On which dinners have been served for over a century. Based on the sons of Adam and Eve.
Cakehole		An old and familiar term for the mouth, especially when telling someone to shut it.
Cakery/Cakers		A cake shop, another version of a bakery.
Calaboose		A prison, originally an American term from the Spanish *calabozo*.
Calamity Jane	*Train*	Of modern coinage, a 'calamity' seems about right considering the problems and disasters that have beset the railways in recent years. Based on the nickname of Martha Jane Canary (1852–1903), the legendary US frontierswoman best known for driving the Deadwood Stage.
Calcutta	*Butter*	A term that seems to be spreading for no other reason than that it rhymes.
Calendar		A stretch, a year in prison.
Call a Copper!		A general term of alarm akin to 'look out!' or 'ay-ay!' 'Call a copper! Granny's on the gin again.'
Callard & Bowsers	*Trousers*	Usually cut down to 'Callards' and formed on the name of the well-known confectioners.
Calvin Klein	*a) Fine*	The punishment you might receive if you were caught selling snide designer gear.

	b) Wine	Red or white, plonk or vintage, it's all 'Calvin', and is based on the American fashion designer.
Camber Sand(s)	*Hand(s)*	Another resort on the Kent coast (*See* MARGATE *and* RAMSGATE) for what is never out of your wallet when on holiday.
Camden Lock	*Shock*	A modern piece, a 'Camden' is what an electric bill is designed to do.
Camden Town	*Brown*	A brown is an old slang term for a copper coin. *See* BROWN (a).
Camel's Hump	*Dump*	To defecate is currently known as going for a 'camels'.
Camerer Cuss	*Bus*	A piece that dates back to the days of the omnibus. Based on the long-established company that specialises in antique timepieces and jewellery.
Cameroon	*Coon*	A derogatory piece that came into being after the 1990 World Cup, when the team of that country performed so well.
Camister		A vicar or priest, a 19th-century man of the cloth.
Camilla Parker-Bowles	*Rolls (Royce)*	Based on the friend of the Prince of Wales in relation to the prince of wheels, which has become a 'Camilla Parker'.
Camp		Exaggerated, posturing effeminacy, the way that 'camp' comedians get their laughs, i.e., by 'camping it up'. Homosexuals are said to be as 'camp as a row of pink tents'.
Can		a) Originally an American lavatory but now quite commonly a British one as well.
		b) A prison or a police cell. Drunks often spend a night in 'the can'.
		c) A pocket, a rare version of 'bin' (qv, a).
		d) Beer. A general term for anything that comes with a ring pull.
Can a Black Man Dance?		A reply given when a definite yes is required.
Can a Duck Swim?		A question raised when a definite yes is called for. It means 'absolutely'. Others include: Can a bird fly? Can a fish swim? Can a dog lick his own bollocks?
Can a Paddy use a Shovel?		A reply to a question where the answer is obviously yes.
Can a Scotsman/ Jock Drink?		A reply to a question that demands a definite yes.
Can a Taff/ Welshman Sing?		A question asked in response to a question that demands a positive reply.
Can It		An instruction to be quiet, often best obeyed.

Can of Coke	*Joke*	A contemporary piece of 'yoofspeak', where the cheapest jokes are usually at someone else's expense. An unbelievably bad place or situation may be a 'can o' Coke'.
Can of Oil	*Boil*	Refers to the great pus-filled swelling on the skin and is normally known as a 'canov'.
Canal Boat	*Tote*	A racecourse term concerning the totalisator.
Canary		A police informer or a confessing prisoner, someone who sings like a bird.
Canary	*Fairy (Homosexual)*	A theatrical term, probably for a chorus boy or any gay man who makes a living on the 'birdcage' (qv).
Canary Wharf	*Dwarf*	A modern and ironic piece for a small person in that the Canary Wharf Tower, in London's Docklands, was, when built, the tallest building in Britain. A 'canary', one of the seven to go UP on Snow White.
Cancer Bed		A sun bed, the tanning device as found, ironically, at a health and fitness club. From the link with the sun and skin cancer.
Cancer Stick		A cigarette. A term that was first lit in the early 1960s when the link between tobacco and cancer became an issue.
Candle Basher		A spinster of the parish, said to pleasure herself with a 'wax cock' (qv).
Candle Sconce	*Ponce*	Always shortened to a 'candle', in reference to a pimp. Also 'Candle & Sconce'.
Candle Wax	*Tax*	Heard for the first time in the 1960s after the introduction of betting tax: 'I always pay the candle in advance, it works out better if you have it off.' Likely to burn itself out now that the tax has been abolished.
Candles		Unwiped secretions seen running from the nostrils towards the mouth. A juvenile term, usually a dig at a child with silver cuffs (wiping its nose on its sleeve).
Candy		Drugs, originally heroin but later anything else that can be swallowed or sniffed.
Candyfloss	*Toss*	Those who don't care 'couldn't give a candy'.
Candyman		A drug dealer.
Cane		a) To severely criticise. Bad workmanship will get a 'right caning'. b) To inflict a heavy defeat upon. The British are used to their tennis players getting 'caned'. Also to beat someone up. c) The penis. Sits alongside 'Stick', 'Rod', 'Pole', etc. 'Bend over and get the cane,' as the actor said to the bishop. The term also slips in as reference to sexual intercourse.

		d) To steal, thieves' jargon. 'The car wasn't locked so I caned the CD player.'
Caned		Drunk or high on drugs.
Caner		An old-fashioned term for a teacher, one who never spared the rod.
Canister		The head. An old instruction to think is 'use your canister'.
Canned		a) Arrested, chucked in the 'can' (qv, b).
		b) Drunk. Possibly a connection with (a) since it was often the fate of the intoxicated. Stands up well today with the popularity of canned beers but would appear to predate them.
Cannon		*See* BAZOOKA.
Canoe(s)	*Shoe(s)*	To be kept in good repair, once they get holes in you're sunk.
Cans		Headphones, jargon from the recording studio.
Canteen Medal		A food stain on the shirt, overall or tunic. An award for the sloppy eater.
Canvas		Skin, as it covers the human framework. A tattooist may have a different explanation.
Cap		a) A shortening of capsule, one containing an illicit drug.
		b) Oral sex, probably connected to 'head' (qv) although to go 'cap & gown' (down) has been suggested, and if it is a student's term it's possible.
Cape Horn	*Corn*	The most southerly point of South America comes in for the painful condition on the most southerly point of the body.
Cape of Good Hope	*Soap*	Shortened to 'Cape of', the term has been working up a lather for about a century now.
Capeesh		Understand, based on the Italian *capisci*.
Caper		An activity, usually on the wrong side of legality: 'What's your caper?' – What are you up to?
Capital City	*Titty*	Breasts known as 'capitals' may be the talk of the town.
Captain Bligh	*Pie*	After the old salt famous for the mutiny aboard his ship *The Bounty* in 1789. Against the odds he survived to make mincemeat out of the mutineers. William Bligh (1754–1817) later became an admiral before serving as governor of New South Wales and more recently an equal partner on a plate of pie and mash.
Captain Cook	*a) Book*	Applies to any book including the one made by bookies. Inspired by the British explorer and navigator James Cook (1728–79).
	b) Look	Not too common but 'Give me a Captain Cook' means 'Let me see.'

Captain Grimes	*Times*	Refers to the newspaper and appears to be based on a character in the novel *Decline and Fall* by Evelyn Waugh. Evidently a piece from suburbia.
Captain Kettle	*Settle*	Based on a comic-book hero of a bygone generation, this term, for putting an end to an argument by violent means or otherwise, is, like the good captain, retired.
Captain Kirk	a) *Turk*	A late 1990s term following the rise in popularity of Turkey as a holiday resort.
	b) *Work*	Coined in the early 1990s, when a recession meant that people had more chance of meeting a Klingon than a job interviewer. Based on the hero of TV's *Star Trek*.
Captain Morgan	*Organ*	A theatrical piece that applies to any organ, musical or otherwise. Based on the Welsh pirate (1635–88) who ended up governor of Jamaica. Who says crime doesn't pay?
Captain Scott	*Hot*	Typical East End humour to use the name of a man who froze to death as a term relating to heat. Captain Robert Falcon Scott (b. 1868) died on an expedition to the South Pole in 1912.
Captain Sensible		A responsible, sober man. One who doesn't take risks or act the fool. A term that was in existence before the bass player with UK punk group The Damned took the name to the top of the charts in 1982 with 'Happy Talk'.
Captain's Log	*Bog (Lavatory)*	When there are rumblings in the 'poop deck', an entry into the 'captains log' is warranted.
Capture		A lesser-known version of 'Pull' (qv, a), whereby anyone out looking for a sexual conquest is 'on the capture'.
Car Surfing		The dangerous pursuit, followed by young idiots, of riding on the roof of a car.
Carbolic Naked		Stark bollock naked, almost RS but more of a pun for nudity.
Carbuncle	*Uncle*	The dictionary describes a carbuncle thus: 'An extensive skin eruption resembling a boil but much larger and having many openings.' It would seem to sum up an uncle quite nicely.
Cardboard Box	*Pox*	One of many terms for the disease you wouldn't tell your mother about. Or your wife!
Cardboard Frying Pan		A symbol of uselessness: 'You're as much use as a . . .'
Careless Talk	*Chalk*	A post-war term employed by darts players.
Carey Street, in		Based on the name of the street in London where the bankruptcy court sits. Therefore to be in Carey Street is to be bankrupt or in financial difficulty.

Carl Rosa	*Poser*	Based on a German musician (1842–89) who formed a London-based operatic society. This refers to anyone who makes out to be something he isn't, the 'Old Carl Rosa' is a pretence.
Carlo Gatti	*Batty*	Mad or eccentric, based on the name of a company that supplied ice to restaurants in London before refrigerators became the norm.
Carney		Hypocritical, not genuine, crafty. A 'carney' person will tell you one thing and something completely different to somebody else.
Carol Singer	*Ringer*	Anything or anybody that is not what they appear or claim to be is a 'carol', from a lookalike greyhound to a stolen car with moody plates.
Caroon		From the Italian *corona* – a crown, this became five shillings, now 25p.
Car-Park	*Nark*	An informer, probably because an empty car park is a likely meeting place for the police and their snouts (qv, c).
Carpet		a) Relates to the number three. *See* CARPET BAG. b) The female pubic area, whereby cunnilingus becomes 'carpet cleaning'.
Carpet Bag	*Drag*	A drag is a slang term for a three-month prison sentence, and is responsible for the term 'carpet' becoming a popular replacement for the number three. £3 is commonly called a 'carpet', as are odds of 3/1. And 33/1 is a 'double carpet'.
Carrot		A giant cannabis cigarette, the size of an average orange root vegetable.
Carrot Cruncher		A country dweller, seen by city folk as a bumpkin.
Carrot Head/Top		Someone with red or ginger hair, one who may bear the nickname 'Carrots'.
Carrying		In possession of drugs, money, a weapon or a 'bun in the oven' (qv).
Carry-Out		Drink, usually beer, bought at closing time and taken home to drink.
Carsey		A commonly heard expression for a lavatory. Also any unsavoury or disagreeable place, be it a building, town or country, may be condescendingly called a 'carsey'.
Carsey of the World		The worst place on earth, where it is is a matter of personal choice. Also the 'Carsey of all Carseys'.
Carve		To cut someone with a knife, a piece of thugspeak.
Carve/Cut Up		To drive badly by stealing another driver's road, causing them to brake or swerve.
Carve Up		To cheat or to take an unfair advantage.
Carver		A knife when used as a weapon.

Carve-Up		a) A swindle, possibly when the joint of meat you've paid for is not the one you've bought.
		b) A share-out of earnings or ill-gotten gains.
Carving Knife	*Wife*	She of the sharp tongue and cutting glances is known as the 'carving'.
Casablanca	*Wanker*	Mainly used in full but sometimes a 'cazza' as a term of abuse for a scrote (qv).
Case		a) A mad person, a loon. A suitable case for treatment.
		b) The last of anything. Your 'case' cigarette is the last one in the pack, and when you've spent your 'case' fiver, you'll be potless. From racing parlance, the last of a gambler's money kept in case he lost his fare home or in case there was a 'good thing' in the last race.
		c) An archaic piece for a brothel, probably from *casa*, Italian for house. Also called a 'caser', it's owned or run by a 'casekeeper'.
		d) To look over a place prior to robbing it, most famously in the expression 'case a joint'.
Cased Up		a) An ancient term for a house is a 'case', so when a man and woman live together they're said to be 'cased up' or living 'caso'.
		b) Dressed. To be 'cased up' in your Sunday togs.
Caser		Once referred to five shillings but has made the small change into 25p.
Casey's Court, like		Said of a place where pandemonium, chaos and uproar is in evidence, a madhouse. Based on the name of an early 20th-century juvenile show about a fictitious East End alley and the shenanigans of a gang of cockney kids who lived there. Among the stars who began their careers in the show were Charlie Chaplin and Stan Laurel.
Cash & Carry	*Marry*	This begets two offspring: 'Cash & Carried' and 'Cash & Carriage'.
Cash in One's Chips		To die, one of many colourful expressions for clog popping. *See* POP ONE's CLOGS. 'Cashed in' – dead.
Caso		Mad, certifiable or otherwise: 'Watch him, he's caso.' Also a loss of temper: 'She'll go caso when she finds out.'
Castle Rag	*Flag*	One of the oldest terms of RS in that it applies to the slang term for a fourpenny piece, a coin from the middle of the 19th century. Now it quite suitably fits that which is flown or waved.
Castor & Pollux	*Bollocks*	The names of the twins of Gemini are transferred to the twins of the ballbag.

Castor Oil(s)	*Royal(s)*	The 'castors' is a disrespectful name given to the royal family.
Cat		a) A spiteful woman, usually when she's got her claws out for another of her sex. A she-devil. Also a gay term for a catty homosexual. b) A woman who freely gives out sexual favours, originally a term for a prostitute. c) A person. A well-known piece that originated with jazz musicians and was later adapted in the rock 'n' roll era. A 'cat', like the animal, is seen to be cool. d) The vagina, a variation of 'pussy' (qv). 'Cat-bite' – VD.
Cat & Dog	*Catalogue*	Probably more of a pun than RS, but those who do their shopping at home, do it with a 'cat and dog' on their laps.
	Bog (Lavatory)	Trips to the 'cat and dog' may follow a meal at a restaurant serving questionable meat.
Cat & Kitty	*Titty*	As displayed, possibly, by a woman who puts her 'pussy' to work in a 'cathouse'.
Cat & Mouse	*House*	When this was first coined many houses had both.
Catch a Cold		To lose financially as a result of gambling or investments.
Catch Some Rays		To sunbathe, a package holiday piece of youth-speak, an extension of which is to 'catch some cosmics'.
Catch/Cop Some Zs		To get some sleep, usually in the form of a nap.
Catch Yourself On		An exclamation informing someone to get wise to the event.
Cathouse		A brothel, where 'Toms' (qv) work. *See* CAT (b).
Cats & Dogs Beer		Due to what a cloudburst is said to rain down, we get this reference to cloudy beer.
Cat's Breakfast		A mess, to make a right 'cat's breakfast' of something is to do it spectacularly badly.
Cat's Face	*Ace*	One of four in a pack of cards, perhaps the one that takes the kitty.
Cat's Lick		The brief wash of a 'soap dodger' (qv), where the tiniest amount of water is involved. Also called a 'Cat's Lick and a Promise'.
Cat's Milk	*Silk*	Relates to smoothness, hence a malt whisky may go down as smooth as 'cat's milk'. I would have thought 'cow's milk' would have been more suitable; how do you milk a cat? Gingerly I suppose.
Cat's Whiskers		The best, like the 'bee's knees' and the 'dog's bollocks'. *See both*.

Catting		Out on the pull, i.e., looking for females. Once with a view to paying. *See* CAT (b).
Cattle		Prostitutes. An ancient term which saw women as meat. *See* COW (a).
Cattle Market		Originally a brothel (*see* CATTLE), later any place where women congregate. A good place to 'pull a bird'.
Cattle Truck(ed)	*Fuck(ed)*	Commonly reduced to the first element, mainly in the context of being tired or rendered helpless. You're 'cattled' if you get two flat tyres, for instance. It's also what British tennis players habitually get at Wimbledon. The sex act is known as 'cattling'.
Catty		A kid's term for his catapult.
Caught Short		A sudden urge to defecate. Being 'caught short' is a common excuse for lateness.
Cavalier		An uncircumcised penis, or a man who owns one. Compare with 'Roundhead' (qv).
Cavy		An upper-class word of warning that comes from the Latin *cave* – beware.
Cecil		£1000 aka a 'grand', which becomes a 'g' and then a Cecil, down to Cecil Gee, the men's outfitter.
Cecil Gee(s)	*Knee(s)*	A fairly old term, based on the chain of menswear shops, where the second element is always discounted.
Cellar Flap	*Tap*	Originally applied to tap dancing but now anybody on the 'cellar' wants to borrow some money.
Centre Forward		A nine in a pack of cards. The centre forward in a football team wears the number nine shirt.
Centre Half		A five in a pack of cards. From the shirt worn by the centre half in a football team.
Centre Half	*Scarf*	A neck warmer, fittingly enough from the football terraces, since it's based on the player in the number five shirt.
Century		£100, an old term for what is now more commonly a 'ton'.
Chain & Crank	*Bank*	A piece that never really created a lot of interest.
Chain & Locket	*Pocket*	Keep your hands in your 'chains' when there are thieving 'hooks' (qv) about.
Chain Gang		Married men. A jibe used by their single drinking partners at closing time, when they can stay for 'afters' but the 'chain gang' have to go home. *See* BALL & CHAIN.
Chalfont St Giles	*Piles*	'Chalfonts' is a theatrical term for what keeps bums off seats. After the village in Bucks.
Chalk Farm	*a) Arm*	An ancient and still common piece. A gambler will 'chance his chalk'.

	b) Harm	A minder will see that his guv'nor comes to no 'chalk'. After an area in North London.
Chalky White	Light (Ale)	A 'chalky' is one of several terms for this beer.
Champagne Glass	Brass	A twice-removed example for a prostitute (see BRASS NAIL), which is suggestive of the high-class call girl who entertains visiting nobs.
Champagne Taste & Brown Ale Money		Attributed to people whose desires exceed their pockets, those who want the world but can't afford a back street in Peckham.
Chancer		Someone who risks his luck, often a con man. One who 'chances his arm'.
Chancre Mechanic		A naval term for a ship's doctor. A chancre (pronounced shanker) is an ulcer associated with VD, a once common complaint among sailors.
Chandelier	Queer (Homosexual)	That which hangs gaily from the ceiling, a chandelier that is, becomes a 'shandy'.
Channel Fleet	Street	A very old piece that seems to have sunk without trace.
Channel Port	Short	A measure of spirit, alcohol from the 'top shelf'. A 1990s term that's probably based on the cross-Channel 'booze runs', where duty-free alcohol is bought in vast quantities.
Channel Ports	Shorts	Known as 'channels' in reference to the garment that exposes the thin, pale, hairy, knobbly things that men call their legs. I have long had a suspicion that there is a competition in the rag trade to see who can come up with the worst pair of 'channels' in the world.
Char		Tea. A common old term based on the Chinese cha.
Charing Cross	Horse	In old cockney dialect, cross is pronounced 'crorse', and horses are 'charings'.
Charles Atlas		The name of the legendary Italian/American muscleman (b. Angelo Siciliano 1893–1972) is mockingly used in relation to a puny, weedy man.
Charles Dance	Chance	A meticulous planner leaves nothing to 'Charles Dance'. Based on a British actor.
Charles James Fox	Box	An ancient piece for a theatrical box that has long been known as a 'Charles James'. It's based on Britain's first foreign secretary (1749–1806).
Charley		An ancient term for a watchman, an early security guard and a once common sight on building sites and at road works.
Charlie		a) A fool, see CHARLIE HUNT. b) A snobocracy term for anything cheap and nasty, as opposed to 'Charles' which is the opposite. Class discriminatory gits!

Charlie/Charles		Cocaine, probably its most common name these days.
Charlie Brady	*Cady*	A 19th-century term for a hat that was consigned to the hatstand many years ago.
Charlie Brown	*Clown*	A professional jester or anyone who acts the fool is a 'Charlie'. From a song of the 1950s, a top-ten hit for American group The Coasters.
Charlie Chan	*Can*	Started with an advertising campaign for canned beer in the 1970s and is based on the fictional Chinese detective of book and film fame.
Charlie Clore	a) *Floor*	An elderly piece from the fight game, where to put an opponent down was to put him on the 'Charlie'.
	b) *Score* (£20)	Based on a millionaire financier (1904–79) who probably never appreciated the joy of putting on a long-since-worn pair of trousers and finding a 'Charlie' in the pocket.
Charlie Cooke	*Look*	A 1960s term based on a Scottish international footballer who rarely gave opposing fullbacks a look in.
Charlie Dicken	*Chicken*	The name of the great author is suggested here, albeit incorrectly, but RS isn't that particular. It refers to poultry, not to cowardice.
Charlie Dilke	*Milk*	An ancient example based on the long-departed politician Sir Charles Wentworth Dilke (1843–1911)
Charlie Drake	a) *Brake*	It would be interesting to *see* a fitter's reaction if a women drove into his garage and asked to have her 'Charlies' looked at.
	b) *Break*	A tea break or rest period courtesy of the comedian who first came to prominence in a double act called 'Mick and Montmorency' with Jack Edwards. Charlie's catchphrase was 'Is it tea time yet?'
Charlie Freer	*Beer*	An example from the penny-a-pint days.
Charlie Frisky	*Whisky*	Probably the long-standing oppo of 'Charlie Randy' (qv).
Charlie Howard	*Coward*	Commonly, to 'turn Charlie' is to 'bottle it' (qv). You don't need to be brave to be a coward – a piece of useless advice.
Charlie Hunt	*Cunt*	Widely used in respectable circles by people who know not what they are saying, e.g., 'You look a right Charlie in that hat.'
Charlie Mason	*Basin*	Kitchenware is not necessarily involved here. To have a 'basinful' of something is to have a go at it or get in on it, so the next time there's a tip circulating, you might want to have a 'Charlieful of it'.
Charlie Pope	*Soap*	Coined in the trenches of World War One by men who would have been caked in mud.

Charlie Prescott	*Waistcoat*	An old term for the third part of a three-piece 'whistle' (qv) which is pronounced 'wescot'.
Charlie Randy	*Brandy*	A 19th-century term based on a bloke called Randy whose first name was Charlie.
Charlie Ronce	*Ponce*	An old term for a prostitute's minder.
Charlie Smirke	*Berk*	A fool, based on an English jockey (1906–93), and an example of secondary RS (*see* BERKSHIRE HUNT). Must be used in full to differentiate it from 'Charlie Hunt' (qv) which is the same card in a different envelope.
Charlie Wiggins	*Diggings*	A theatrical term for where theatricals hang their wigs while performing away from home.
Charlies		Female breasts, a term that's been knocking about for over a century.
Charlton & Greenwich	*Spinach*	A greengrocer's term for Popeye's favourite.
Charming Wife	*Knife*	As introduced to enemy soldiers during World War One.
Charper		To search, a 19th-century piece of Polari from the Italian, *cercare*. 'Charpering omi' – a policeman.
Charra		An early motor coach, a shortening of charabanc and still going with older day-trippers.
Charver/Charva		Sexual intercourse. An old Romany term (*charvo*) that has been picked up and used by theatrical types and is now common among young males.
Charvered		Knackered, exhausted or quite literally, fucked.
Chas & Dave	*Shave*	A 1980s term based on the cockney musicians who don't seem to do a lot of 'chazzing'.
Chase/Chasing		To continue gambling, often recklessly, after a run of losing bets. To 'chase your losses'. Good rarely comes of it.
Chase One's Tail		To be very busy, to chase around like a mad thing and not seem to get anywhere. Like the cross between a fox and a foxhound who chased himself to a standstill.
Chase the Dog-End		Of men, to urinate. There's always a cigarette butt in a urinal and most men try to piss it down the drain-hole. Don't we lads? Don't we?
Chase the Dragon		To inhale the smoke of burning heroin.
Chase Yourself, go and		Go away, get lost. Either literally or as a definite rejection.
Chassis		The female body, especially a well-proportioned, shapely one.
Chatham & Dover	*Over*	Taken from the old London, Chatham and Dover railway line, this is used to emphasise finality; 'That's it, finished, all Chatham and Dover.'

Chavvy/Chavvie		A child. From the Romany word *chavo* or *chavor*, which also accounts for 'shaver' (qv), of 'young shaver' fame.
Chavvy Lavvy		A child's potty. The 'chavvy lavvy' stage follows the 'crappy nappy' one.
Chaw/Chore		To steal. Heard outside a dog track: 'I tell you the car was here. Someone's chawed it.' Also 'Nicked' in the sense of being arrested.
Chawry Goods		Stolen property, 'back of lorry drop-offs'.
Cheapo		A cheaply sold article that may be inferior or possibly just a basic model. 'I just wanted a cheapo video, nothing fancy.'
Cheat the Worms		To recover from a bad accident or serious illness, to step back from death's door.
Check One's Oil		To masturbate, it's what a 'dipstick' (qv) is for.
Cheerful Earful		Used ironically to the bearer of bad news: 'Thanks, that's just what I wanted to hear. A right cheerful earful.'
Cheerful Giver	*Liver*	Someone who happily carries a donors card for what he one day may donate, although the term predates transplant technology somewhat.
Cheese		Smegma, the guff that accumulates beneath the foreskin.
Cheese & **Crackers**	*Knackers*	The after-dinner course in relation to the testicles, or a vegetarian's lunchbox, i.e., two veg without the meat.
Cheese & Crust/ **Rice**		A couple of exclamations used by those who don't want to take the Lord's name in vain when sounding their surprise or annoyance, i.e., Jesus Christ.
Cheese Effect		A false smile, based on beamers people put on when a photographer demands we 'say cheese'.
Cheese Grater	*Waiter*	A fitting piece for the one who sprinkles the Parmesan and acts Kraftily until he gets his tip.
Cheesecutter/ **Cheeser**		A cap, originally one with a large peak, but more recently any flat headwear.
Cheeser		a) A particularly smelly breakage of wind. b) A false smile, a big 'cheesy grin'. From the word frequently said to photographers.
Cheesy		a) Anything distasteful or unpleasant, anything that may be said to 'stink'. b) Descriptive of a phoney or hypocritical person, one with the false smile seen in the 'cheese effect' (qv).
Cheesy Helmet		An unwashed, smegma-covered glans penis. *See* CHEESE *and* HELMET.
Cheesy Quaver	*Favour*	Based on a savoury snack, people have been doing 'cheesys' for each other since the early 1990s.

Cheesy-Dick		A term of abuse; when offence is meant, it's usually taken.
Chelsea Bun	*Son/Sun*	May the 'Chelsea' always shine on my 'Chelseas'. A father's 'chocolate eclair' (qv).
Chelsea Potter	*Squatter*	Known as a 'Chelsea' and probably formed on the name of the pub in Chelsea's King's Road.
Chelsea Smile		A facial scar that runs from the mouth to the ear, a modern-day duelling scar inflicted on one football supporter by a rival one.
Cheltenham Bold	*Cold*	An old term based on the home of the National Hunt Festival, where bold jumpers may fall like the temperature. Also given as 'Cheltenham Gold', after the race (the Cheltenham Gold Cup). Either way, when it's freezing, it's 'Bloody Cheltenham'.
Cherie Blair	*Fare*	A recently formed piece, due to the Labour Prime Minister's wife who hit the headlines by travelling on the railway without purchasing a ticket.
Cherry		a) A virgin of either sex, a 'lost cherry' is a loss of innocence. b) An apprentice, especially a jockey. The naive new kid at work, the butt of all the old practical jokes. c) To blush, to 'do a cherry' – to turn red.
Cherry Hog	*Dog*	A 'cherry' is a widely used piece in relation to man's best friend. It's especially common among greyhound racing enthusiasts whereby to go dog racing is to go to the 'cherries'. Cherry 'ogs are the stones of that fruit, which were used by children of the early 20th century as playthings. Tell that to today's kids and they'll be straight on the internet in search of a counsellor.
Cherry Picker	*Nicker (£1)*	A 'cherry' is spent force these days.
Cherry Red	*Head*	Tampax Fugit! As the Latin master said when he walked beneath the girl's dormitory window and a discarded sanitary towel landed on his 'cherry'.
Cherry Ripe	*a) Pipe*	A term from when pipe smoking was a common way of making people cough.
	b) Tripe	Written or spoken nonsense: 'What a load of cherry.'
Chevy Chase	*Face*	One of the earliest terms of RS, this refers to an ancient ballad about the battle of Chevy Chase, which took place near Otterburn, Northumberland in 1388.
Chew the Fat	*Chat*	A well-known piece that has transcended the realms of RS to join conventional English for a 'Mad Hatter' (qv).

Chick		A girl, a young woman at most.
Chicken		a) A cowardly person has been called 'chicken' for about 300 years. 'Chicken hearted', 'chicken livered' and 'chicken shit' are among the related insults for the not-so-brave.
		b) A boy, often a runaway, seen by homosexuals as game. Prey for a 'chickenhawk' (qv).
		c) Anyone young or inexperienced.
		d) A game of dare, where people perform feats of courage or face the risk of being called cowards.
Chicken & Rice	*Nice*	From the take-away shop comes this modern rival to the old 'apples and rice' (qv).
Chicken Feed		A small or poultry amount, especially of money. A tenner for three numbers on the lotto, for instance.
Chicken Heart	*Fart*	Used when a fetid fragrance of a faecal nature assails the nostrils: 'Who's chicken hearted?'
Chicken Perch	*Church*	Known as 'chicken', as all cockney 'parsons knows'.
Chicken Run		A daredevil game in which two cars are driven at speed towards each other, the first to brake or swerve is deemed 'chicken' (a).
Chicken Soup		A current term denoting that everything's alright or kosher. Based on a typical jewish dish that is frequently referred to as 'Jewish penicillin' because of it's restorative qualities.
Chickenhawk/ Chicken Hunter		A homosexual with a preference for young boys, or 'chickens' (qv).
Chicken's Neck	*Cheque*	An alternative to 'goose's neck', possibly for a less poultry amount.
Chickenshit		Anything considered petty, small-minded or unimportant, 'chickenshit regulations' are usually wrapped in red tape. Also *see* Chicken (a).
Chi-Ike		To barrack or taunt. Chi-iking is the bane of second-rate comedians.
Children		The tools of a housebreaker, his skeleton keys. *See* Boys & Girls.
Chill		To kill, murder or assassinate. To make a warm body cold.
Chill/Chill Out		To rest after a busy time or contest, to cool off after losing your temper and regain calm. To relax.
Chimney		An ancient term for a heavy smoker, what one puffs like.
Chimney & Soot	*Foot*	The sock filler, not the measurement, as in the complaint, 'athlete's chimney'.
Chin		To punch someone on the 'Gunga Din' (qv). 'He was ranting like a loon so I chinned him.'

China Plate	*Mate*	One of the more common terms whereby an old friend becomes an old 'china'. The 'china' is also a seaman's term for the first officer.
China Pot		The epitome of riches, e.g., 'I wouldn't do that for a china pot.' A Ming vase is seen as a great treasure.
Chinese		Anything hard to understand or figure out. Often said of the instructions to a DIY chest-of-drawers kit: 'It's all Chinese to me.'
Ching		A term for £5 that's becoming a rival to 'fiver'. From the same root as 'chinker' (qv).
Chink		a) Money; strictly speaking, a coin. But who wants to speak strictly? 'Chinks' is small change, obviously the sound of coin against coin. b) A derogatory term for a Chinese person, from a time when people didn't know it was a put-down.
Chinker		The Parlyaree version of the number five, from the Italian *cinque*.
Chinky		Anything to do with China, from a person to a Chinese restaurant and the meal served there. Sometimes 'chinky chonky'.
Chinless Wonder		A gormless, upper-class man, a typical 'lombard' (qv).
Chinny		Of a boxer, one who cannot take a punch to the chin, one easily knocked down.
Chinsplasher		An act of masturbation by way of a woman's cleavage, she receives a chinful of semen.
Chinwag		To talk, to have a bit of a natter.
Chip		a) Formerly a common term for a shilling that was used extensively by bookie's runners and those they ran to. 'Chip' each way doubles and trebles were the staple bets of small punters. Some still apply the term to a 5p piece. b) An ancient term for a child, a 'chip off the old block'. c) To barrack or give stick to. To 'chip' unmercifully may cause a victim to run up the white flag (surrender) or 'pick up his drum' (qv).
Chiphead		A technical wizard, computer buff or generally any enthusiast of the world of microchips.
Chippy		a) Easily offended, aggrieved. A short version of having a 'chip on one's shoulder'. b) A tradesman's reference to a carpenter. Also 'chips'. c) A fish and chip shop in the north of England.
Chips		a) Money. If you're 'holding some folding', you're in the 'chips'.

		b) What anything bought in Bargain Basement is said to be as cheap as. A term made popular by David Dickinson, presenter of TV's *Bargain Hunt*.
Chips & Peas	*Knees*	Whereby victims of a kneecapping have had their 'chips'.
Chirrup & Titter	*Bitter (Ale)*	An old piece that has come to the bottom of the barrel.
Chisel		To swindle. Never play cards with a 'chiseller'; he'll carve you up and cheat you blind.
Chiv/Chive		A common underworld term for a knife or a razor. Originally a Romany word, it means the weapon and also to use it, i.e., to stab or cut somebody is to 'chiv' them. Also said as 'shiv'.
Choc Ice	*Dice*	Mainly those that come with board games, probably unheard of in Monte Carlo.
Choc Ice		An American version of 'Bounty Bar' (qv).
Chocker		a) To be fed up, disgusted or 'up to here' with everything. b) To be full up or jam-packed. A reduced form of 'chock-a-block', it is most commonly applied to roads and trains during the crush hour.
Chocko		A derogatory term for a black person.
Chocky Jockey		A homosexual, he who rides the 'chocolate highway' (qv).
Chocolate		Excrement, a term that leads to several crudities concerning the anus and by extension homosexuality.
Chocolate Bandit/ Highwayman		A homosexual, seen as a 'chocolate box' (qv) thief.
Chocolate Biscuit	*Risk It*	When you've heavy work to be done, be careful. If you 'chocolate biscuit' you could end up with a dodgy 'Cadbury's snack' (qv).
Chocolate Box		The backside, see CHOCOLATE.
Chocolate Drop		A disparaging term for a black person, often heard in the 1970s TV sitcom *Love Thy Neighbour*.
Chocolate Eclair	*Prayer*	Sweet dreams may follow as a result of children saying their 'chocolates' at bedtime.
Chocolate Eye		The anus, another of many with ophthalmic connections.
Chocolate Frog	*Wog*	An Australian term for a foreigner or immigrant that is unused here, except, probably, by ex-patriot Aussies. Which kinda makes them 'chocolates' to us. *See* WOG.
Chocolate Fudge	*Judge*	How m'lud came to be known as a 'chocolate'.

Chocolate Highway	The rectum, used in connection with homosexuality. Also Chocolate: 'Freeway', 'Tunnel', 'Street', 'Lane', etc. *See* CHOCOLATE.
Chocolate Starfish/Towel Holder	The anus, a pair of modern terms pertaining to similarity of shapes.
Chocolate Tea Pot	A symbol of uselessness, what a 'wally' (qv) is said to be as much use as.
Choice	Used ironically for anything bad. The air turns blue because of 'choice' language.
Choirboy	A naive, virginal youth, a picture of innocence. 'A face like a choirboy.'
Choked	a) To be upset or disappointed. As most people are after the lotto draw. b) To be strangled or hanged, executed by the 'choker-in-chief', i.e., the hangman.
Choker	a) A disappointment, a bad result. Like losing your dentures and finding a pound of Brazil nuts. b) A scarf or cravat, formerly a neckerchief, when such a thing was a prized possession. c) The hangman's noose, later an underworld term for anything used to strangle someone.
Choker/Chokey	Prison. Said to be from the Hindustani word *chauki*, meaning a shed. Couldn't it be from the place where people are hanged or 'choked'?
Chomby/Chomb	Derogatory terms for a black person.
Chomp	To eat or bite, to make use of your 'chompers' (qv).
Chompers	The teeth, the tools of dinner demolition.
Chomping Gear	The teeth, a well-known term for the 'biters'.
Choochy Face	A term of endearment from the 1960s, usually said to someone while pinching their cheek.
Chop	a) To give up doing something. To pack up smoking is to 'chop' the habit. b) The price of failure, most glaringly paid by football managers. Their heads, permanently on the block, may roll after a string of bad results. Odds are laid about who will get 'the chop', i.e., dismissed, next.
Chop/Chopping Sticks *Six*	A brace of terms from the bingo hall, although a 'chop' is sometimes used as £6.
Chopper	a) A customised motorbike, so called because it has been 'chopped' about to suit its rider. Sometimes called a 'chop'. b) The penis. A common term especially popular with comedians who specialised in the double entendre. Many a sketch included a fireman being told to get his chopper out.

		c) A helicopter, mainly used in a military sense.
Choppers		Teeth, especially detachable ones, i.e., 'false choppers'.
Chops		a) The cheeks, jowls, jaw, lips and mouth. A slap round the 'chops' may follow an improper suggestion.
		b) Fingerprints. An old term that apparently comes from London's Chinatown.
Chow		An old term for food, most commonly heard in American war or prison films.
Chozzer		A police officer, maybe a mispronunciation of 'cozzer' (qv).
Christmas Card	*Guard*	Takes in all types, from a fire guard to a railway worker to the soldier that minds the queen.
Christmas Cheer	*Beer*	A drunk may truthfully state, 'The last time I was sober was eight Christmases ago.'
Christmas Crackered	*Knackered*	To be exhausted, broken or in trouble is to be 'Christmassed'.
Christmas Crackers	*Knackers*	The pulling of which is guaranteed to make the eyes water. *See* KNACKERS.
Christmas Dinner	*Winner*	An old newspaper vendor's cry 'All the Christmas dinners', in regard to the racing results.
Christmas Eve	*Believe*	Would you 'Christmas Eve' it? 'Adam and Eve' have a rival.
Christmas Log	*Dog*	Chuck one on the fire and you'll have the RSPCA at the door. Worse, Rolf Harris!
Christmas Shop	*Strop* (Masturbate)	Doing your Christmas shopping in the privacy of your own home doesn't necessarily mean you have the Argos catalogue in your hands.
Christmas Tree(s)	*Knee(s)*	The seasonal indoor toilet your dog pines for in cold weather represents those that have been known to tremble behind the bikeshed. Not necessarily in cold weather.
Christopher Lee	*Pee/Wee*	The British actor, famed for his roles in horror films, gets back in character as a 'vampire's kiss' (qv).
Chrome Dome		A bald head or a name given to the owner of such a 'napper' (qv, a).
Chubb/Chubb Up		To lock or lock up, a key term in prison. From the name of a lockmaking company.
Chubby Chaser		A man whose sexual preference is for obese women, or men if that way inclined. Sometimes referred to as a 'Chubby Checker', a humorous play on the name of an American singer.
Chubby Chops		A fat-faced person, a non-malicious jibe. A 'balloon face'.
Chuck Up		a) To vomit, especially after a drink. The trouble

with living near a pub is people tend to 'chuck up' in your front garden. Sometimes reversed to 'upchuck'.
b) To smell. What people who neglect their personal hygiene tend to do.

Chuckaway Charlie
An ironic name for a man who is known to be careful with his money.

Chucking-Out Time
Closing time down the pub.

Chuff
a) A euphemism for 'fuck', used up north, e.g., 'chuffing 'eck'. Looks like it could be a piece of dyslexic backslang.
b) The backside. 'Raise your chuff' – get off your arse. Sometimes said as 'chufta'.
c) To break wind, a more polite version of 'fart'.

Chuff Adder
A male homosexual. A piece of word play involving 'chuff' (b), 'puff' (qv) and the venomous snake, the puff adder.

Chuffed
A common term for being pleased, well satisfied, 'dead chuffed'.

Chummy
A nameless third person, about whom a police officer is speaking. Usually a suspect.

Chump
a) The head, most commonly heard in the phrase 'off his chump' – mad.
b) A buffoon, an idiot. Somebody easily fooled.

Chunder
To vomit. A well-known piece that was brought up from Australia.

Chunk of Beef *Chief*
Anyone in charge has long been known as a 'chunka'.

Chunk of Wood *Good*
A 19th-century term that was used mainly in a negative sense, i.e., anything bad was 'no chunk of wood'.

Chunnel
A popular term for the Channel Tunnel, the pipe that joins us to Europe.

Churcher
An extinct term for a threepenny piece, a once acceptable amount to put in a collection plate.

Churchyard Cough
A jocular piece that has long been used against people heard 'coughing themselves into a coffin'.

Chute
The rectum, a reduced form of 'shit-chute' (qv).

Chutist
A homosexual, a man who shoots up a 'chute'.

Chutzpah
A Yiddish term for audacious cheek, more sauce than HP.

Cigarette Holder(s) *Shoulder(s)*
Heard at a football match on a freezing day:
> Her: Got a hanky? My nose keeps running.
> Him: No. Use your sleeve.
> Her: No. This is my new coat.
> Him: Well I've been using your cigarette.

Cilla Black *Back*
More people cry off work with dodgy 'Cillas' than

anything else. Based on the TV personality and singer whose voice makes some people wish they had dodgy ears.

Cinderella	a) *Smeller (Nose)*	People who get on your nerves may get right up your 'Cinder'.
	b) *Yellow*	Mainly used in connection with pool or snooker balls, although it may be the nickname of a coward.
Circle		An ancient term for the vagina, used by Shakespeare in *Romeo and Juliet* and many other writers since. 'A round of applause' – a convoluted term for VD ('circle and clap').
Circus		A sex show, more Chopperfields than Chipperfields. *See* CHOPPER (b).
Cisco Kid	*Yid*	An old term based on a Western film hero. A cowboy from Mexico as opposed to Stamford Hill.
City Banker	*Wanker*	An obnoxious person, courtesy of the office wallah and close rival to 'merchant banker' (qv).
City Tote	*Coat*	When summer heads for sunnier climes for the winter, put your 'city tote' on. Formed on the name of a bookmaking firm.
Civilian		Underworld jargon for someone who is neither a criminal nor a police officer.
Clackers		False teeth, ill-fitting ones, by the sound of it.
Claim		a) To grab hold of someone in a fight, a term used by bouncers. 'I claimed the geezer giving it the big 'un and slung him out. It died down a bit after that.' b) To arrest. Underworld speak for an occupational hazard, i.e., being 'claimed'.
Claimo		A fortuitous accident, one where no-one is hurt but an insurance claim will pay dividends. It also applies to a 'moody' (qv, b).
Claire Rayners	*Trainers*	A contemporary term for modern footwear designed for physical activity, based on an agony aunt who clearly wasn't.
Clam		An ancient term for the mouth and by extension a person who can keep his mouth as tight as a clam. Someone to be trusted with a secret, a 'tightlip'.
Clam Up		To say nothing, often during interrogation, but sometimes through shyness. The complaint of a would-be wooer: 'I know what I want to say to her, but when I see her I just clam up.'
Clanger		A mistake, a glaring blunder. 'Clangers' make a racket when they are dropped.
Clap		The oldest term still in use for venereal disease, once specifically gonorrhoea, but now includes other diseases. To be infected is to be 'clapped up'.

Clap Trap		The vagina of a prostitute or a promiscuous woman. And by extension the woman herself. *See* Clap.
Clapped Out		Run down, worn out and generally NFG (qv). Generally used in connection with an old car. Or not so old if it's an ex-minicab.
Clappers		An old military term for the testicles, possibly related to 'bell rope' (qv).
Clapster		A promiscuous man, one often caught in a 'clap trap' (qv), and so a regular at the clinic. *See* Clap.
Claret		Blood. An example that has flowed from the boxing ring into general usage. Especially common with young thugs and football hooligans. Criminals aren't averse to spilling it either.
Claret & Blues	*Shoes*	A modern piece based on the colours of West Ham United FC and worn as 'clarets'.
Clark Gable	*Table*	How, every meal time, women get to lay the actor known as the 'King of Hollywood' (1901–60).
Clark Kent	*Bent*	Can mean homosexual, but mainly means corrupt. How the alter-ego of the ultimate goodie, Superman, becomes dodgy.
Clay Pigeons		Pedestrians, seen as targets by motorcycle couriers in London, where people tend to step on to crossings and cross busy roads with little regard for what may be bearing down on them.
Clean		a) Free of anything incriminating when searched by the police or customs. b) No longer addicted to drugs. c) To give someone a severe telling off, to 'ruck the life out of'.
Cleaned Out		Made penniless by bad bets or dodgy deals.
Clear as Mud		Unclear, as a complicated explanation or instruction may be.
Clement Freuds	*Haemorrhoids*	Based on the lugubrious TV personality who, as a Liberal MP, has also occupied a seat in the House of Commons. Painfully known as the 'Clements'.
Clemmed/ Clammed		Starved. A term mainly heard in the north of England, especially by the residents of TV's *Coronation Street* when Betty's hotpot is off the menu.
Clever Dick	*Brick*	As laid by a 'clever dickie'.
Clever Mike	*Bike*	An old term, possibly named after an early stunt cyclist. Or maybe one who had the sense to have lights on his bike, not like today's idiots who don't realise they're invisible at night.
Click		a) A robbery, a successful piece of thieving is a 'good click'.

b) To obtain some money. Heard in a 'spit and sawdust': 'He must've clicked, he was skint this morning.'

c) To succeed in the pursuit of sex. Heard at a party: 'There must be something wrong with me. Even Micky Moonface has clicked.'

Clicketty Clickers *Knickers* Ladies underwear, in brief, 'clicketties'.

Clink
a) One of the commonest terms for a prison, even though the original Clink, in Southwark, was burnt down in the Gordon Riots of 1780.

b) Metal money, stuff that clinks when it's knocked together.

Clinker
A piece of excrement stuck to a hair that is attached to the anal area.

Clip
a) To swindle or cheat someone out of their money. The con of a prostitute – clipping – whereby she will take a customer's money, tell him to wait somewhere and scarper.

b) To kill, originally by shooting. A piece from gangsters about gangsters: 'We only clip each other.'

Clip Joint
A club or bar in which customers are enticed into buying exhorbitantly priced drinks for hostesses, giving them the impression that they are paying for the girl's favours, which they rarely are. *See* CLIP (A).

Clipdick
Circumcision provides the reason for this derogatory term for a Jewish man.

Clit/Clitty
Familiar abbreviations for the clitoris.

Clithopper
A promiscuous lesbian, to be found in prison or on the ladies tennis circuit, apparently.

Clitwobble
Said to be what a woman gets when she is sexually attracted to someone.

Clobber
a) An old term for clothes, which became popular in the 1960s when the young, for too long clones of their parents, became fashion conscious. Carnaby Street became world famous for its 'clobber shops'.

b) Personal possessions and belongings. A rent dodger will pack up his 'clobber' and have it on his toes before the landlord arrives.

c) Famously to strike but also to punish without violence in the sense of rough justice. Harsh treatment at the hands of a magistrate may be met with the complaint 'I've been clobbered.'

Clock
a) An old term for the face. A 'busted clock', that of someone who has had a close look at someone else's fists.

b) A gullible person, one easily 'wound up'. *See* WIND UP.

c) The heart, an extension of 'ticker' (qv).

d) To hit. A common threat is 'I'll clock you one in a minute.'

e) To look at. Obvious 'wigheads' (qv) are often the subject of a sniggered 'Clock the gagga.'

f) To recognise, as in 'I clocked who she was as soon as I saw her.'

g) To alter the mileage on a vehicle to make it more saleable. Such a motor has been 'clocked'.

Clod/Clodhopper
Clodpole — A stupid person, an oaf. Originally an ignoramus or three from the country.

Clodhopper *Copper* — Applies to a copper coin. An old penny was universally known as a 'clod'. Also a police officer, who may be known as 'Plod the Clod'.

Clodhoppers — Big feet or alternatively large footwear. Either way, visible means of support.

Clog — a) Virility, a young man in his prime is 'full of his clog'.

b) To kick, especially in sport. A team that relies on aggression rather than skill is said to be full of 'cloggers'.

Clog/Cloggy — Because of their traditional footwear, these relate to the Dutch.

Clone — a) A homosexual who dresses in typically gay attire, the macho moustachiod look. The 'Clone-Zone' – their world.

b) A fashion follower rather than an individualistic dresser. Also an imitator, the world is full of Barbie 'clones'.

Clot — A fool, an example from countless British comedies.

Clothes Peg *a) Egg* — Formed when bad eggs were common, so a clothes peg would have been a handy piece of nose-wear.

b) Leg — As a footballer was being carried off on a stretcher, his opponent protested his innocence to the referee: 'But ref, it was a fifty-fifty ball.' 'Yes,' replied the official, 'Now he's got a fifty-fifty clothes peg. Name?'

Clothesliner — A petty thief, typically, but not necessarily, one who steals from clotheslines.

Cloud Seven *Heaven* — To be on 'cloud seven' is a very common expression for happiness.

Clout — a) The vagina. An overheard conversation: 'He was doing OK with this bird, till his wife came in and caught him with his hand up her clout.'

b) To hit. A 'clout round the ear' has long been an effective deterrent to unruly kids.

Cloven Hoof	*Poof (Homosexual)*	A devilish rival to the very common 'iron hoof' (qv).
Clown		A term of abuse directed at a fool or an idiot. Someone not suffered gladly.
Cloy		To steal, especially from pockets. A 'cloy' or 'cloyer' is the thief or pickpocket.
Clubs Are Trumps		A witty old example which reverses the adage that 'the pen is mightier than the sword'. The pun on the weapon and the playing-card indicates that violence will win out over argument.
Cludgie		A lavatory, a northerner's 'carsey' (qv).
Clum		An awkward, ham-fisted person. A shortening of clumsy.
Clutchfist		Anyone with a vice like grip on their money. 'Clutch-fisted' – tight.
Coachman on the Box	*Pox*	A piece from pre-penicillin days for VD, and known as the 'coachmans'.
Coal Heaver	*Stever/Stiver*	An obsolete example for an old slang term for a penny.
Coal(s) & Coke	*Broke*	Refers to being potless (qv), or put another way, devoid of the receptacle required to urinate in.
Coal Sack		An English version of a blocked turning or cul-de-sac.
Coalboxed		Ruined, a plan that has been totally wrecked, as in 'that's coalboxed that idea'.
Coalman's Sack	*Black*	Applies to being dirty. A parent's rebuke to a grubby child: 'Look at you, you're coalman's. Go and have a scrub.'
Coat		To tell off, a severe 'coating' is a right 'rollocking'. Also applies to a physical beating or 'shellacking'. *See* SHELLACK.
Coat & Badge	*Cadge*	Formed on the name of the Doggett's Coat and Badge, which is the oldest annual sporting event in Britain. Contested by rowers, the course is the four- and-a-half miles stretch of the Thames between London Bridge and Cadogan Pier, Chelsea. People on the scrounge are often said to be 'on the Doggett's'.
Coat Hanger	*a) Banger*	Mainly an old car but sometimes a sausage.
	b) Clanger	It's a mistake to drop a 'coat hanger'.
Cob		A bad mood. Anyone with a 'cob on' is best left alone.
Cob of Coal	*Dole*	One of the older examples for unemployment benefit.

Cobber		A mate in Australia or an oppo in Oz.
Cobbler's Awls	*Balls*	'Cobblers' is probably the most common term of RS for the testicles. It's also an argumentative retort, i.e., 'Cobblers! You don't know what you're talking about.'
Cobbler's Stalls	*Balls*	A corruption of 'cobbler's awls' (qv).
Cock		a) Ultra-familiar and long-standing term for the penis and therefore to have sexual intercourse.
		b) The top man or champion. The 'Cock of the North' is the title given to the top northern flat jockey at the end of the season.
		c) A showoff, the 'Cock of the Walk' is a man who is full of his own importance, as is a 'Cockalorum'.
Cock/Cocker		A non-offensive term of address for a man, usually a stranger. What a stallholder or cab driver may call a customer.
Cock a Deaf 'Un		To pretend not to hear or to take no notice of. To turn a blind eye. Eh?
Cock Alley/ Lane/Pit		The vagina, some of the terms relating to the point of male intrusion.
Cock & Hen	*a) Pen*	The oldest of the terms for a scribbler, which in it's day would have been a scratcher, i.e., a nib and inkwell job.
	b) Ten	A common reference to £10.
Cock Linnet	*Minute*	The time people are kept waiting. It may be more or less, but 'I'll be with you in a cock linnet' means 'hang on a while'.
Cock Rock		Heavy rock music, typified by the macho strutting of rock-band vocalists.
Cock Sparrow	*a) Arrow*	An old public bar term for a dart, a game of 'cock sparrers'.
	b) Barrow	A market trader's term for what he wheels to his field of business.
Cock Sparrow		A friend, usually in the greeting 'Wotcha me old cock sparrer.'
Cock Teaser		A flirting woman, or one who goes in for foreplay but stops short of allowing a climactic situation. Sometimes shortened to a 'CT', as in the song by the British blues band, Blues and Trouble.
Cockaleekie	*Cheeky*	A warning to an insolent child: 'Don't be cockaleekie or I'll smack your legs.'
Cocked Hat	*Rat*	Applies to a human rodent, a person not to be trusted or an informer.
Cockerel & Hen	*Ten*	Always reduced to a 'cockle', which is lazy pronunciation of the first element, this originally

applied to ten shillings but has been revalued to become a well-used expression for £10. A 'cockle' is also a ten-year stretch in prison, and ten years of marriage.

Cockroach	*Coach*	A motor vehicle, the 'beano bus'.
Cocksucker		A derogatory term for anyone who deserves such abuse. Often used of a sycophant in much the same way as 'arse licker'.
Cock-Up		A mistake, a polite form of 'fuck-up'. SNACU is the repeatable version of SNAFU (qv).
Cocky		Swaggering, arrogant or impudent. We all know someone who fits the description.
Cocoa		a) A derogatory term for a black person, from a time when derogatory terms were the norm.
		b) Semen, whereby to ejaculate is to 'come your cocoa'.
Cocoa		c) *See* COFFEE & COCOA.
Coconut		a) The head, usually shortened to 'use your coco'.
		b) Another example of an abusive term used by black people against others of their race who are seen to embrace a white culture. *See* BOUNTY BAR *and* CHOC-ICE.
Coconuts		Large breasts, from the resemblence and the fact that they both produce milk.
Cod		Fake or false, a parody. Cod French is a phony French accent. Cod hair is a wig.
Cods		A well-known term for the testicles. A 'kick in the cods' is a setback.
Cod's Roe	*Dough (Money)*	The long-standing moan of a losing punter is that he has 'done his cod's'.
Cod's Roe(ing)	*Snow(ing)*	When it's cold enough for 'cod's', suck a Fisherman's Friend.
Codswallop		Nonsense or rubbish. Many a TV programme has invited the comment 'What a load of codswallop'.
Coffee & Cocoa	*Say So/ Think So*	Common but unusual in that it's always reduced to the second element as a term of disbelief, e.g., 'D'you think he'd be selling the car that cheap if it was a good 'un? I should cocoa.'
Coffee & Tea	*Sea*	Nice to get away for a while and dip your feet in the 'coffee', even if it's only to Blackpool, where the sea resembles it.
Coffee Stalls	*Balls*	Reduced to the 'coffees' in relation to the testicles; so men, beware of coffee grinders!
Coffin Dodger		An old person, especially one who has recovered from an illness. Used condescendingly of an obnoxious old git.

Coffin Nail		A pre World War Two term for a cigarette, which confirms that people knew the dangers of smoking long before government health warnings.
Coke		a) The common name for cocaine.
		b) Phlegm. People have been coughing up lumps of 'coke' ever since Jimmy Bean did in the song 'What a Mouth', a music-hall hit for Harry Champion and, in 1960, for Tommy Steele.
Cokies/Cocos		Old-fashioned baggy trousers, the type of legwear that Coco the Clown and others of his ilk might wear.
Cold Fish		A cold, unemotional person, one who coddn't care less about anybody or anything.
Cold Potato	*Waiter*	If your spuds are 'taters' (qv), tell the 'cold potater' to get you some hot ones.
Coldstream Guards	*Cards*	Playing-cards, based on the ace regiment who have long been minding kings and queens.
Collar		a) Hard work. An overheard job description: 'It's collar but the money ain't bad.' The image of a carthorse in it's collar.
		b) Police jargon for an arrest, a shortened version of 'having your collar felt'. The arrest of a long sought-after felon is a 'good collar'. Also used as a verb.
		c) The head on a glass of beer, especially a Guinness when it's known as a 'dog collar' (qv).
		d) To take or grab as in 'Collar that table and I'll get the drinks in.'
Collar & Cuff	*Puff*	A homosexual male, an old but rarely heard example.
Collar & Tie	a) *Lie*	People were telling 'collars' long before the now-common 'porkies'. *See* PORK PIE.
	b) *Spy*	Usually refers to the workplace snitch, who runs bosswards with tales of everyday shirking folk.
Collared		Arrested. Also in the sense of being detained. An overheard excuse: 'Sorry I'm late, old Frank collared me up the market and I couldn't get away.'
Colleen Bawn	*Horn (Erection)*	At a stroke, this is reduced to a 'colly', and is based on the name of the heroine of the 19th-century opera, *The Lily of Killarney*.
College		Prison seen as a university of crime, therefore specifically Borstal or any other young offenders' prison.
Colney Hatch	*Match*	Based on the name of the mental institution in North London in regard to what it's inmates shouldn't play with.
Colonel Blimp	*Shrimp*	Seafood, courtesy of cartoonist David Low's bumptious creation.

Colonel Gadaffi	*Taffy*	Courtesy of the Libyan leader, the Welsh have all become 'colonels'.
Colonel Prescott	*Waistcoat*	Based on an officer and gentleman sportsman, whose game, mayhap, was snooker.
Colonic		A nonalcoholic drink for drivers, a mixture of cola and tonic.
Comb & Brush	*Lush*	A drink of an alcoholic nature and therefore also a drinker of an alcoholic nature.
Come		To have an orgasm, to come to a climax. Also (sometimes spelt 'cum') a reference to semen.
Come a Clover	*Tumble(d) Over*	A World War One term that was probably apt when the bullets were flying; it's what too many young men did. It's also an accident waiting to happen, e.g., 'Tie your laces up or you'll come a clover.'
Come a Cropper		To fall, trip up or suffer some misfortune, both physically and metaphorically.
Come a Tumble	*Rumble (Find Out)*	A worker who regularly ventures into the black economy may be told: 'If your boss comes a tumble he'll march you straight down the nick.' A term that signifies a downfall.
Come Across		To allow sex. An oft-repeated question among young men when speaking of a girl is 'Does she come across?'
Come & Go	*Snow*	Vulgarists enjoy reducing this to the first element, e.g., 'There's no racing at Sandown 'cos there's come on the course.' In extended form 'coming and going' is snowing.
Come On		To start menstruating, by far the commonest expression for what may be a 'blessing' or a 'curse'.
Come One's Guts		To confess, to give information to the police.
Come Out		A shortened version of 'come out of the closet', meaning to admit to being a homosexual. To be 'outed' is to be dragged out by someone else.
Comeback		A repercussion. A successful crime or deception depends on there being no 'comebacks'. Also a retaliation or a witty retort.
Come-On		A lure or enticement, usually of a sexual nature. An unspoken invitation.
Comic Cuts	*Nuts (Testicles)*	Cut at 'comics' for where it's no laughing matter to get a kick. Based on an early comic book. Australians use the term for 'guts', the stomach.
Comic Cuts		An appellation given to a joker, usually by the butt of one of his jokes.
Comic Singer(s)	*Fingers*	As rare today as a comic song in the charts.

Comical Farce	*Glass*	Probably coined after an ancestor of mine was seen putting putty around a window.
Commo		A communist, a militant socialist, an old-style trade unionist.
Con		a) An abbreviated form of confidence trick, a swindle, carried out by a 'con man' or 'con artist'. b) A convict, an insider's term for someone inside.
Con-Charge		Motorists will see this as an apt abbreviation of the Congestion Charge, the fee they must pay for the dubious privilege of driving through central London and other British cities from 2002–3. For 'con' read 'rip-off'.
Con & Col	*Dole*	What these diminutives of the name 'Colin' have to do with signing on I don't know.
Conan Doyle	*Boil*	Based on the author, Sir Arthur Conan Doyle (1859–1930), the large septic beast that appears on the skin is always known as a 'Conan'. Also to boil, whereby a kettle may be on the 'Conan'.
Concertinas		Trousers that are too long for the wearer, from the many folds around the ankles.
Concrete Lifebelt		A symbol of uselessness; what a fool may be considered to be as useful as.
Conger Eel	*Squeal*	The slippery fish comes in for a slippery person, as this is what an informer does.
Conk		a) The nose, especially one a bit on the large side, or one belonging to a boozer. 'Claret conk' - a wine drinker. Previously applied to the head. b) To hit, to punch on the nose or to knock someone out by 'conking' them on the head.
Conk Out		a) Mechanical breakdown, most commonly said of a car that warrants a call to an emergency service: 'I don't know what's wrong with it, it's conked out.' Sound familiar? b) To die or to a lesser extent, to lose consciousness.
Conkers		The testicles. A euphemism for 'bollocks' as an argumentative response.
Conko/Conky		A nickname given to someone with a big nose.
Connaught Ranger	*Stranger*	Based on an old Irish regiment, a 'Connaught' is an underworld term for an unknown 'face', one that could belong to an undercover police officer.
Connection		a) A drugs' supplier. b) The relationship between a criminal and a friend in high places whose price provides protection.
Constant Screecher	*Teacher*	Relevant more to 'caners' of yesteryear than today's teachers who are more likely to be screeched at.

Constipated Said of a road that is blocked, jammed up or closed due to an accident.

Constipation *Station* A probable allusion to motionless trains and hold-ups on the line.

Conyo The Anglicised version of the Spanish *cono*, meaning cunt. A term brought back in the 1960s by young Brits who dossed away the summer months in Spain, especially at the resort of Lloret-de-Mar.

Cooey A pigeon. From the noise it makes.

Cooked Drunk. The excessively so may be 'done to a T' or 'ruined'. 'Half-cooked' – tipsy.

Cooking a) Working well, as in 'now we're cooking'. 'Now we're cooking with gas' is a recent phrase for working very well.
b) Beer, especially bitter. A 1970s term that was heard on a TV sitcom and caught on for a while.

Cool a) Calm, to keep your cool is to stay in control.
b) Good. A fashionable term among the young who probably don't realise that their grandads may have used it.
c) Look. An old example of backslang used by lookouts at illegal gambling games: 'Cool, Delo Lib' – Look, Old Bill.

Cool Brittania Britain under Tony Blair's New Labour government. A term much in vogue at the time of writing, and one that has long described British summers. Once in power, Mr Blair sought to present a younger, trendier image than British politics was used to.

Cool Hand Luke *Fluke* Based on a well-known film of the 1960s in regard to a lucky accident, especially in a pool or snooker match. Known as a 'cool hand'.

Cooler A prison cell, especially one for solitary confinement.

Coolie A derogatory term for a Chinese or Asian person, especially an obsequious one.

Coon An offensive term for a black person. 'Coon Town' – a black area of a town or city.

Coon's Age An American expression for a long time that's based on the longevity of the raccoon. Now heard in the UK as a result of western films.

Coot A fool, usually an elderly one as the term is generally preceded by 'old', e.g., 'soppy old coot'.

Cootie A head or body louse, any kind of infestation that makes your skin crawl. The feeling you get when in a dirty place or next to someone in need of a bath, 'Standing next to him's making me feel cootie.'

Cop	a) Value, the worth of something. Anything no good is said to be 'not much cop'. b) An arrest, famously 'It's a fair cop,' the supposed reaction of a criminal caught red-handed. c) To catch something that is thrown or something that's going round, e.g., to 'cop for a dose of the flu'. d) To take a bribe, to be 'on the cop'. e) To obtain or acquire, especially some drugs.
Cop/Copper	A police officer, one who puts the pinch on. *See* Cop (b).
Cop a Plea	To admit to a lesser offence in the hope of getting off a more serious one.
Cop It/Out	To get a reprimand, often a smacked bum. Used in a threat: 'Behave or you'll cop out.'
Cop Shop	A police station.
Cop-Out	A cowardly evasion of a situation, to take the easy way out.
Copper	A derogatory term for an informer, especially a criminal who may 'turn copper'.
Copper Nob/ Coppertop	A brace of old terms for a ginger-haired person.
Copper's Nark	A police informer, from the Romany word *nak*, meaning nose, which ties in with 'snout' and 'snitch'. *See both.*
Cork	An imaginary requirement for women with a dire need to urinate when there isn't a 'bucket' (qv, d) about.
Cork It/Up	A couple of ways to tell someone to shut up. The image of damming the mouth.
Corked	Constipated, on the same lines as having a 'bung in the bottle' (qv).
Corker	Anything good, a term on the lines of 'belter' and 'cracker'. An attractive woman is a 'corker'.
Corkscrew	a) Bent. Applies to anybody or anything seen as not straight, therefore any form of corruption is said to be 'as bent as a corkscrew'. Also refers to a homosexual. A 'Hairpin' or a 'Dog's Hind Leg' can be equally as bent. b) A laxative, what's needed when you feel as though you've 'sat on a cork'. *See* CORKED.
Corn	Money, the working man has had to earn his 'corn' for centuries.
Corn Flake *Fake*	Anything that isn't what it seems, including funny money, snide jewellery and a 150-year-old mahogany hi-fi cabinet.

Corn on the Cob	*Job*	A piece from the suburbs for what's needed to earn one's corn.
Corned Beef	a) *Chief*	The chief officer in a prison, the 'head screw'.
	b) *Thief*	Applies to a petty criminal or one who could break into a tin of corned beef without a key.
Corned Beef City		A large council housing estate, where all the houses are said to look the same, as tins of corned beef do. In East London it's a jibe against Dagenham, which once had the largest council estate in Europe.
Corned Beef Legs		Red blotchy legs, a result of standing in front of a fire. From a similarity in appearance.
Cornish Pastie	*Tasty*	Used in relation to a member of the female sex as a rule and cut to her being 'a bit Cornish'.
Corns & Bunions	*Onions*	A term from the greengrocers that also implies great skill, wisdom or knowledge: 'He knew his corns when it came to painting alright.' A summation of Michelangelo.
Corporal		£2. *See* STRIPE (b).
Corporal Klinger	*Ringer*	An example heard briefly when the TV series *M.A.S.H.* was at its height, concerning unregistered players in amateur football matches. The memorable soldier from the series put in many an appearance at Hackney Marshes. *See* RINGER.
Corpse		To kill, to turn someone into a dead body. On stage it's when a performer forgets his lines, or 'dies'.
Cory		A well-established piece for the penis. From the Romany word, *kori*, meaning a thorn, hence a 'prick'.
Cosmic		A modern term for anything marvellous, or out-of-this-world. Often used ironically for anything mundane, or of this world.
Costard		An archaic term for the head, a 'costard' being a large apple in normal language.
Cottage		A place, usually a public lavatory, where homosexuals get up to their tricks. Or down to them.
Cottaging		Of homosexuals, hanging around public lavatories for casual sex.
Cotton Wool	*Pull*	The hunt for sexual quarry is known as being on the 'cotton'.
Couch Case		A mad person, a suitable case for a lie-down in a psychiatrist's office.
Couch Potato		Originally an American term for anyone content to idle away their time by lying on their sofas and watching TV all day while their brain vegetates like a potato. *See also* SOFA LOAFER.
Couch Slouch		A lazy person, someone with a morbid fear of the TV remote breaking down.

Cough		To confess to a crime, often after forceful questioning: 'Blow some more smoke in his face, he'll cough.'
Cough & Choke	*Smoke*	As a noun or a verb this couldn't be more apposite.
Cough & Drag	*Fag*	A fitting term for a cigarette, no-smoking policies send workers outside for a 'cough and drag'.
Cough & Sneeze	*Cheese*	The 'cough' course doesn't sound a very appetising way to end a meal.
Cough & Splutter	*Butter*	If this comes from the same grocer as 'cough and sneeze' (qv), shop somewhere else.
Cough Drops		Mental faculties. If an old woman is 'all there with her cough drops', her brain is still in good working order, even if her body is wearing out.
Council Gritter	*Shitter (Anus)*	Based on the vehicle that unloads it's brown contents on icy roads.
Council Houses	*Trousers*	Whereby leg-holders become 'councils'.
Counting House		The face. A pun on countenance, first uttered a century ago.
Country Cousin	*Dozen*	An old term largely heard on the racecourse. Also number twelve in the game of bingo.
Couple of Bob	a) *Gob (Phlegm)*	If you see a 'couple of bob' on the pavement, best leave it where it is. A 'bob' was a shilling.
	b) *Job*	If a 'couple of bob's' worth doing, it's worth paying someone a couple of bob to do it properly.
	c) *Swab*	A piece from the pub in connection with the dart team, it's the damp rag needed to wipe the scoreboard.
Coupon		A Scottish expression for the face, on which a punch is known as 'filling in a coupon'.
Cousin Ella	*Umbrella*	Probably the only cousin you've got who's in any way useful.
Cousin Sis	*Piss*	An old reference to boozing, i.e., to go on the 'cousin Sis'.
Couter		An ancient term for £1 that no longer appears to be in circulation.
Cove		An archaic term for a man. A 16th-century 'geezer' that still gets a mention, especially when he's a 'strange cove'.
Covent Garden	*Pardon*	Can be begged and granted. Originally applied to a farthing, a long-extinct coin.
Covered Wagon	*Dragon*	An ugly or disagreeable woman. Said of a man whose address book is full of ugly women: 'He's pulled more covered wagons than a carthorse.'
Cow		a) A woman in several guises. She's the obnoxious 'rotten cow', the downtrodden 'poor cow' and as a wildcat she's a 'cow when she gets going'. Originally though, she was a prostitute.

		b) A hard or tricky job, 'a cow of a job'.
Cow & Calf	a) *Half*	See Cow's Calf.
	b) *Laugh*	Heard in a night club:
		1st Man: You cowing at me?
		2nd Man: Yes
		1st Man: Why?
		2nd Man: You're the comedian.
Cow & Gate	*Late*	When a woman is 'cow and gate' for her period, it is usually a sign that she'll soon be buying baby food, which makes the name of this pap-producing company a suitable term.
Cow Juice		Milk. An ancient piece that is being employed in a TV advertisement at the time of writing.
Cowboy		a) A rogue tradesman such as a 'cowboy' builder or repair man, who will do a quick bodge job before riding off into the sunset with your money.
		b) An orthodox Jew, most famously in London, a Stamford Hill cowboy. This is due to there being a large population of them in this part of the capital and the wide-brimmed hats worn by the men.
Cowboy Outfit		A firm or gang of incompetent workers, the foreman of which is the 'trail boss' (qv).
Cowdenbeath	*Teeth*	A Scottish term for what fills a 'Queen of the South' (qv).
Cows & Kisses	*Missus (Wife)*	In mid 19th-century parlance a cow was a common reference to a woman, though not considered as offensive as it is now, so this very old term makes sense when you under-stand that it means 'women and kisses'. Unless there was some secret perversion that went undocumented.
Cow's Calf	*Half*	A revamped version of 'cow and calf', in that 50p or a half a quid and a six-month prison sentence or half a stretch is universally known as a 'cow's'.
Cow's Cunt		A term of abuse for someone infinitely more obnoxious than a 'cow's son' (qv).
Cow's Lick	*Nick*	An insider's reference to prison.
Cow's Licker	*Nicker (£1)*	The bovine tongue is always used in full so as not to confuse it with a 'cow's calf' (qv).
Cow's Son		Said as one word 'cowson', a well-used cockney term of abuse. 'Gertchoo cowson' – to quote cockney musicians Chas and Dave.
Cozzer		A police officer, a cross between a copper and a rozzer.
Crab		a) A disagreeable or irritable person, usually referred to as an 'old crab'.

b) A persistent borrower of money, someone to avoid or run the risk of getting 'nipped' (qv).

c) Of a vehicle, to career sideways in an accident or a skid. The frantic words of a coach driver heard over his radio: 'She's crabbin' Ted.'

Crabs
Pubic lice. Crab-like nasties that set up home in the nether regions and cause embarrassing itching.

Crack
a) An archaic term for the vagina, thus a general term for a woman, especially a prostitute.

b) An addictive form of cocaine.

c) The split between the buttocks, and also in gay parlance the 'buttock-hole', the anus.

d) A good time, a mainly Irish expression. The Cheltenham Festival attracts thousands of Irish racegoers who, win or lose, enjoy the 'crack'.

e) First class, excellent. A term much employed by the Irish.

> Her: What do you think of my vagina, Jim?
> Him: It's a fair crack, love, so it is.

f) To break into, as a safecracker may do and a 'cracksman' is a burglar. To 'crack' a tenner is to break into a ten pound note. Also to break open a bottle is to 'crack' it.

Cracker/
Cracking/
Crackerjack
A trio of superlatives.

Crackerjacks/
Crackheads
People who are addicted to crack cocaine.

Crackers
Mad, eccentric. A word to describe someone who may be a sandwich short of a packed lunch.

Crack-House
A place connected with crack cocaine, where it may be made, sold or used.

Crackle
An underworld term for money, specifically bank-notes. From the sound of a crisp new forgery.

Crackling
An attractive woman or women in general seen to be 'a bit tasty'. A nice bit of 'crackling'.

Crackpot
a) A mad or eccentric person, a 'nut-nut'. The term derives from 'crack-pate'.

b) A mad or eccentric idea or theory. Like the one that tells us that men who wear tight underpants can't father chickens.

Cracks
An old word for nuts, the shelled variety that need cracking.

Cradle Snatcher
A person, normally a woman, who has an amorous attachment to someone much younger. Men are more likely to be known as lucky bastards.

Crank-Up	A drug user's term for plunging a needle into themselves, to crank an addict into life.
Crap	a) To defecate and the end result of a 'sit-down job' (qv). Also to be beaten up is to have the crap kicked out of you.
	b) Nonsense or rubbish in the 'bullshit' way of things, e.g., 'That's crap and you know it!'
Craphouse	A lavatory or what may pass for one in that it's in a dirty, filthy state.
Crapology	Silly talk. The stuff and nonsense spouted by a 'crapologist', a specialist in bullshit.
Crapper	a) A lavatory, the inventor of the flushing toilet being Mr Thomas Crapper, God bless him.
	b) The anus, same pastry but different filling to the 'shitter' (qv).
Crappo	Cheap, worthless tat. Goods as sold in your average pound shop.
Crappy	Rubbishy, cheap: 'What, you don't think a £2 garlic press is a crappy wedding present?'
Crap-Rack/ Krap-Rack	A backslang version of a car park.
Crashing	First rate, excellent. A sort of cross between 'cracking' and 'smashing'.
Crate	An old aeroplane. A term that was later extended to any old vehicle, including an old-fashioned bicycle.
Cratehead	A fool or simpleton, the image of a big square bonce with nothing in it.
Craterface	An unkind name given to a person with a pock-marked face.
Crawlarse	A vulgarism of crawler, a toady who may be known as a 'crawlarse bastard'.
Cream	a) To beat comprehensively in a sporting contest. The loser has been 'creamed'.
	b) To give someone a severe beating, to 'whip them to cream'. Also to kill.
	c) Semen or vaginal secretions. He may 'come his cream' while she may 'cream her knickers'. To become overexcited, whether sexually or not, has drawn the expression, 'cream his jeans/pants'. One particularly excitable TV and radio football commentator seems to be on the point of doing so every time England score.
	d) To steal from an employer, especially in an occupation where cash is involved. Known as 'creaming', or skimming the cream off the top.

Cream Crackered	Knackered	Exhausted, 'creamed', as they say.
Cream Crackers	Knackers	A low blow is a punch in the 'creams', which is liable to drop you to your 'biscuits and cheese' (qv).
Cream Puff	Huff	People in a bad mood often leave in a 'cream puff'.
Cream Puff		a) A wimp or weakling, someone easily blown away. b) An effeminate male homosexual.
Cred		An abbreviation of credibility, most commonly 'street cred', to be wise to the ways of life and be respected for it.
Creep		An unpleasant person who may or may not be a sycophant, but most definitely is a scumbag.
Creeper		a) A thief, especially a burglar who specialises in robbing hotels or brothels. b) A soft-soled shoe of the 1950s, the blue suede type of the Teddy Boy. c) A drug, especially a joint, which doesn't have an immediate effect. It creeps up on you.
Creepers		Body lice, bedbugs, fleas, etc., anything that makes your flesh creep when they creep over your flesh.
Creeps		A feeling of repugnance or fear, the unease felt in the presence of a 'creepy' person or in a spooky place. 'This place would give a ghost the creeps.'
Creepshow		Horrible or grotesque, a modern term to describe a situation or person that fits the bill. 'His wife's a right creepshow.'
Creepy		Descriptive of a weird person or an old run-down place.
Cremated		Badly beaten by an opponent who was too hot for you, or ruined by a bad business deal or stock-market collapse. Also the effect of an overhot oven on a piece of meat.
Crevice		How 19th-century slangists described the narrow opening or fissure that is the vagina. An example still in use by their descendants.
Crew		A gang, especially of football supporters who band together for violence with rival 'crews'.
Cribbage Peg	Leg	One of several terms linking leg with peg, making them close partners in rhyme.
Crimbo		A fairly recent term for Christmas, the season of Slade on the radio and Morecambe and Wise on the telly.
Crimea	Beer	Formed by soldiers of a bygone century, the Light (ale) Brigade, perhaps.
Crinkle		Banknotes, therefore money: 'If I can get hold of some crinkle I'll meet you later.' A single note is a 'crinkler'.
Crinkly		An old person as seen by a young 'un.

Cripple & Crutch *Touch*
To touch someone is an old phrase for borrowing money from them, so anyone who 'cripples' his mum for a few quid is not necessarily a bad person.

Croak
a) To die, an unsympathetic example from around the time Nelson was croaked by a Frog.
b) To kill, an underworld term. 'Just put the frighteners on, we don't want to croak him.'

Croaker
a) A professional murderer, a hit-man. *See* CROAK (b).
b) Someone about to knock on death's door, a terminally ill person. *See* CROAK (a)
c) A doctor, especially one who deals with drug addicts, prisoners or, more recently, old-age pensioners.

Crock of Shit
What the totally luckless would find at the end of a rainbow, as opposed to a crock of gold.

Crocodile *Smile*
An urge to get someone smiling: 'Come on show us your teeth, give us a crocodile.'

Crocodile Dundee *Flea*
Had a slight usage when the film of this name was popular, in reference to a dog's boarders, as in: 'The dog won't bite you but his crocodiles might.'

Crocus
A quack doctor, one whose diagnoses and cures are likely to 'croak us'. *See* CROAK (b).

Cronk
A run-down car, an 'old cronk' is a likely MOT failure.

Crosby Stills & Nash *Slash*
Urination 1970s style, courtesy of a successful rock group made up of Americans David Crosby and Stephen Stills and Englishman Graham Nash.

Crouton *Root On*
A modern term for an erection, an example of slang for slang. *See* ROOT.

Crow
a) A disagreeable woman, usually an 'old crow'.
b) A lookout, one who tips the wink for a three-card trick team. To crow is to make a noise, so therefore it is also to inform.

Crowded Space *(Suit) Case*
A term used by thieves who make a living by stealing luggage from airports, stations or other crowded spaces.

Crown
To administer a severe blow to someone's head. To fall and crack your head is a 'crowner'.

Crown & Anchor *Wanker*
One of many terms for a useless or obnoxious git. Strange how people considered thus are also deemed to be 'not worth a wank'.

Crown Jewels *Tools*
Appropriate since a tradesman's tools are precious to him and don't come cheap. Also a frequent reference to a man's baby-making equipment, especially the main member.

Crucial
A West Indian term of approval from the 1970s that was adopted by young whites in the 1980s.

Crud	Any kind of dirt, grease or grime, a euphemism for 'shit'. Also the dried evidence of a wet dream, be it on pyjamas, pants or bedclothes.
Cruddy	Descriptive of anything, or anybody, dirty or disgusting.
Cruise	To walk or drive around looking for casual sex.
Crumb	A body louse. A comment to people scratching themselves: 'What you got, crumbs?' A term that attached itself to a human equivalent. A louse is a rotten, contemptible person. A 'lousy bastard' is a 'crumb'.
Crumble	Old age. Nurses on a geriatric ward are on 'crumble duty'. At a wedding, while their parents were dancing to Hank Mizell's 'Jungle Rock', their juniors changed the words to 'Crumble Rock'.
Crumble Rumble	A fight or altercation between elderly people. The mooted fight between aging boxers George Foreman and Larry Holmes in 1998 was so called. Though probably not to their faces.
Crumbly	An old person through the eyes of youth, to whom old age is seen as a period of body parts wearing out, seizing up, dropping off and falling out.
Crummy	No good, worthless. A 'crummy job' is a dead-end one.
Crumpet	a) The vagina and thus a woman or women in general, as seen through the lustful eyes of men. More than one beauty with brains has been tagged 'the thinking man's crumpet'.
	b) A fool, a less obscene version of 'cunt' (qv, c).
Crusher	An old term for a policeman, that takes a swipe at the legendary size of his feet. *See* Beetle Crusher.
Crust	What's earned to give one a living. To 'get a crust' is to get a wage.
Crust of Bread *Head*	Applies physically rather than mentally. You may scratch your 'crust' while using your 'loaf'. *See* Loaf of Bread.
Crusty	A particularly filthy person. Often deliberately so, in order to cause offence.
Crutch	a) The genital area of either sex, another version of crotch. I remember in the 1950s a woman who would roam the streets of Poplar with her hand up her skirt; this poor deranged character bore the nickname Dolly Crutch.
	b) Something, usually a split matchstick, used to hold the last remnants of a drug fag.
Crutch Cheese	The secretion that collects in an unwashed vagina. The female version of 'knob cheese' (qv).

Cry Beef		To shout an alarm at a crime scene; the call of 'stop thief' at the sight of a pickpocket doing his worst, for instance.
Cry Hughie/ Ralph/Ruth		To vomit. Three popular references to throwing up, based on the noises made when retching.
Crystal Palace		A euphemism for the exclamation 'Christ Almighty!'
Crystals		A drug user's expression for amphetamines or cocaine.
Cube		a) An ultra-unfashionable person, the epitome of uncool, a super square.
		b) The hallucinogenic drug LSD, so called because it was frequently taken on a sugar cube. Users are known as 'cubeheads'.
Cuckoo		Mentally inadequate, an old term for craziness.
Cuckoo's Nest		A mental institution, famously the one in the film that *One Flew Over. See* CUCKOO.
Cucumber	*Number*	Mainly used in connection with a telephone number, e.g., 'Give me your cucumber and I'll call you back.'
Cuddle & Kiss	*a) Miss*	An old, obvious term for a girlfriend, coined when a kiss and cuddle was all a boy could expect until about the 95th date.
	b) Piss	Quite common when slashed to the first element, e.g., 'Watch my beer while I go for a cuddle.' Liberty takers, however, are given to taking the 'cuddle and kiss'.
Cuddled & Kissed	*Pissed*	The frequently 'cuddled' may wind up addled or puddled.
Cue Ball		A black person's term for a white one. From the colour of that ball in the game of pool.
Cuff Link	*Drink*	Originally an Aussie term that probably arrived here in a can of Fosters.
Cumulot		To ejaculate, a pun on King Arthur's gaff.
Cunning Stunt	*Cunt*	A spoonerism based on the old joke: What's the difference between a circus and a strip club? One has cunning stunts. A humorous euphemism for an idiot.
Cunny		The vagina, a euphemism for 'cunt'. This dates back to the 18th century, when a brothel was a 'cunny warren' and frequenters paid for services with 'cunny money'.
Cunt		a) The vagina, a taboo and once-unprintable term that put *Lady Chatterley's Lover* in the book charts and the law court in 1960.
		b) A woman or women in general. A 'cunt-house' is a pub or club known for its high female patronage; it therefore attracts a large number of predatory males.

c) A fool, someone who does something completely wrong or stupid, whose actions may be described as 'cuntish'.

d) An obnoxious, despicable person. Such a widely used term of abuse that there must be a world full of horrible bastards about.

Cunt of All Cunts		The most detestable or the most stupid person imaginable.
Cunt Teaser		The male equivalent of a 'cock teaser' (qv).
Cunted		Very drunk, a shortening of 'drunk as a cunt'.
Cunthead		A total idiot, a complete fool, a one hundred per cent wally. Someone who makes a 'dickhead' look bright.
Cunt-Itch		a) Female randiness, what a woman has long been said to get when she wants sex.
		b) Vaginal thrush, a crude and somewhat selfish term used by men whose partners are in the throes of an attack, e.g., 'No sex for me for a while, she's got the cunt-itch.'
Cuntocks		A term of abuse among friends, sometimes shortened to 'ocks'.
Cunt's Blood		A term of abuse based on the monthly outpouring of a woman.
Cunt-Shop		An old term for where sex is bought and sold, a brothel.
Cuntstable		A play on constable which is often tauntingly directed at police officers.
Cunt-Struck		A man obsessed by sex, possibly one of the 'Dirty Mac Brigade' (qv).
Cup of Tea	a) *Pee/Wee*	If you hear someone in the pub say he's going for a 'cup of tea', he isn't.
	b) *See*	Used mainly as a term of farewell: 'I'll cuppa tea you later.'
Cupid Stunt		Stupid cunt. A spoonerism introduced by British comedian Kenny Everett (1944–95) in his TV show of the 1970s. Fools and idiots have gone by this name ever since.
Currant Bread	*Dead*	Should be used in full, as referring to the passed-on, as 'currant' sounds wrong somehow.
Currant Bun	a) *Nun*	A recent term for the woman of habit.
	b) *Run*	More specifically 'on the run', or 'on the currant'.
	c) *Son*	A father's pride and joy is his 'currant'.
	d) *Sun*	Most widely used version of the term, which is also commonly used for the *Sun* newspaper.
Currant Cakes	*Shakes*	Refers to the DTs, (drinker's trembles or delirium tremens).

Currant Cakie	*Shaky*	Descriptive of how you feel the day after a heavy night's drinking, or any circumstance that makes you feel wobbly.
Currants & Plums	*Gums*	An invitation to a toothless person to smile is: 'Come on, flash your currants.'
Curry & Rice	*Price*	An example from the racecourse that may relate to the price of a hot favourite.
Curry Muncher/ Wallah		Originally an Indian, but these are now terms for any Asian capable of cooking up a curry.
Curse		The menstrual period, the bane of everyone's life.
Curtains		The end of something. If you're caught on the fiddle, it could be 'curtains' for your career. Based on the 'final curtain', the end of a theatrical performance.
Cushti/Kushti		The toppo (qv) cockney word of approval, and was, long before John Sullivan put it to regular use in the TV series *Only Fools and Horses*.
Cushti Manti		If 'cushti' means good, then 'cushti manti' is very good, excellent.
Cushti Rye		Good or top man, from the Romany words *khushto* – good, and *rei* – gentleman.
Custard		Semen. To 'come your custard' is to ejaculate and 'instant custard' is premature ejaculation.
Custard & Jelly	*Telly*	A common excuse for having some 'afters' up the pub is: 'Well there's nothing on the custard.' In the newspaper industry, the *Daily Telegraph* (the tele) is also known as the 'custard'.
Custard Cream	*Dream*	'Bo Peep' perchance to 'custard', as Shakespeare might have written had he come from Stratford, E15. *See* Bo Peep.
Cut		a) Very drunk, as opposed to being 'half cut' – tipsy. b) To tamper with an illicit drug for profit, to adulterate it.
Cut a Chuckle		To laugh, to have a little giggle.
Cut a Rug		To dance, usually to a rock 'n' roll song.
Cut & Carried	*Married*	An unusual variant of 'cash and carried'. *See* Cash & Carry.
Cut(s) & Scratch(es)	*Match(es)*	An old reference to 'strikes' that's still alight.
Cut of One's Jib		Character, the way one acts: 'I like the cut of your jib.'
Cut Some Cheese		To fart and let out a particularly nasty niff, like the smell of pungent Stilton. *See* Cheeser.
Cut Some Slack		To give a bit of leeway to someone in order to take the pressure off, to 'loosen the rope a bit'.
Cut Yourself a Big Slice of Cake		To talk highly of yourself, self-appreciation on a grand scale.

Cut-Downs/ Cut-Aways		Shorts made by cutting the legs off a pair of jeans.
Cutesy		Cringe-makingly cute or sickeningly sweet, especially a child performer.
Cut-Purse		An early pickpocket whose title derives from their deftness in cutting the string of a money bag attached to the belt of their victim.
Cutter		A knife, usually a weapon but not necessarily.
Cutty Sark	*Nark*	The old tea clipper sets sail again as a police informer.
Cyclops		The backside of a persistent farter, a one-eyed monster with foul breath, like the one of Greek mythology.
Cyril Lord	*Bald*	Suitable since this is based on the name of a carpet and rug manufacturer (1911–84), and a 'rug' is a slang term for a wig.
Czecha Ball/ Bald Head		Anyone with his head shaved. A term coined before it became fashionable with certain people. A shaved head used to be seen as a punishment or an identity remover, as in Nazi concentration camps, and films of Czech prisoners gave rise to this term.

D

D for Dunce	*Bunce*	Reduced to 'deefer' in reference to money earned that the taxman will never know about. Hopefully.
DA		A hairstyle, popular in the 1950s with Teddy Boys. Heavily greased hair is slicked back at the sides so that the back resembles a 'duck's arse' or DA.
DTs		Delirium tremens, known as the shakes. It's the trembles after an overindulgence of alcohol.
Dab		Backslang for bad, whereby a publican who sells 'dab reeb' is deemed a 'dabeno', a bad one.
Dab On		To sign on at the unemployment office in order to get benefit.
Dabs		An old underworld term for fingerprints which lends itself to rebutting a denial, e.g., 'Come on, own up. Your dabs are all over it.'
Dacha		The Polari version of the number ten, based on the Italian *dieci*.
Dachshund		The correct name of a 'sausage dog' has lately become a term for a large piece of excrement. The producer of such a turd may proclaim: 'I'm not sure, but I think I've just given birth to a dachshund.' Normally pronounced 'dash'ound'.
Dad & Mum	*Rum*	Often ordered as a tot of 'daddy'.

Daddler		A small coin, originally a silver threepenny piece and now a silver fivepenny piece.
Daddy		a) The best or most superior, i.e., 'the daddy of them all'. Also to emphasise an illness: 'I've got the daddy of all colds.'
		b) The dominant prisoner in borstal, as witnessed in the film *Scum*.
		c) An older male homosexual or a masculine lesbian.
Dad's Army		The mocking name given, in World War Two, to the Home Guard, which was made up of men too old for active service. Since the TV series, however, the term has been dragged back to life to refer to any group made up of men of more mature years than those using the term.
Dad's Army	*Barmy*	Based on the well-known TV sitcom in reference to anyone who may be seen as being a penny short of a shilling.
Daffadown Dilly	*Silly*	An old term based on an even older slang term – 'Daffydown Dilly' – meaning a dandy.
Daffodil		One of several flowers representing an innocent and naive youth, most commonly a young homosexual. Others include: 'buttercup', 'daisy', 'iris', 'lily', 'pansy' and 'tulip'.
Daffy		a) An unspecified, but large, amount. Many a batsman has scored a 'daffy' of runs for his county, but for England they manage a 'daffy' of ducks.
		b) Mad, eccentric or daft. Common but still regarded as slang.
Daft & Barmy	*Army*	A soldier may say that he was daft to join and barmy to stay in. Then again he may not.
Dagenham Girl Piper	*(Windscreen) Wiper*	A dopey statement heard in a spares shop: 'There's nothing wrong with me Dagenham Girls when it's not raining.'
Dagger		*See* BAYONET.
Dago		An offensive term for an Italian or Hispanic person.
Daily Bread	*Head*	An old term for the head of a family, when father put the food on the table and his would be done.
Daily (Tote) Double	*Trouble*	An old term based on a defunct bet. The Daily Tote Double was the dividend paid on the winners of the third and fifth races of a meeting. Those in bother are in a bit of 'daily' or 'daily tote'.
Daily Express	*Dress*	Refers to the garment and the act of putting it on. A piece from the Tory rag trade?
Daily Mail	*a) Ale*	A regular drinker likes his daily pint of 'Daily'.
	b) Bail	An example from the underworld for the accused's temporary release money.

	c) Nail	A term from the carpentry trade for what the hammer was made to whack.
	d) Tail	This takes in many guises. It's the backside whereby busy people may work their 'Dailys' off; it's a prostitute (see BRASS NAIL); the waggable part of an animal; and it's to follow, when a PC may be on a suspect's 'Daily'.
	e) Tale	A deception, especially when told by a con man.
Dairy Box	Pox	Venereal disease. Reduced to the 'dairy', an unpopular complaint based on a popular box of chocolates.
Dairylea		Smegma, penile cheese-spread. Based on a well-known, non-penile cheese-spread.
Daisy		See DAFFODIL.
Daisy Beat	Cheat	To 'daisy' someone is to swindle them, a term from the 19th century.
Daisy Beaters		The feet, a 19th-century term for the flower tramplers.
Daisy Bell	Hell	Expressions of anger, disappointment or frustration are 'blooming', 'bloody' or 'fucking Daisy'. Formed on the name of a famous music-hall song.
Daisy Chain		Group sex. Three or more people indulging in a linked act.
Daisy Cutter		In cricket, to bowl in such a way that the ball stays close to the ground.
Daisy Dormer	(Bed) Warmer	An obsolete term for an obsolete piece of equipment based on a long-dead music-hall star.
Daisy Root	Boot	An old but still wearing-well term for a 'trotter-case' (gv). Also, a more recent term for a car-boot, hence a 'daisy' sale.
Damage		The cost of something, as in 'What's the damage?'
Damager		Almost RS for a manager, one who may damage your job prospects.
Damn & Blast	Last	Heard on a racecourse: 'Damn and blast, my horse came in damn and blast.'
Damon Hill	Pill	The link between Britain's former world motor-racing champion and pills has to be speed, therefore amphetamines.
Damp		a) A drink, similar to a 'wet' (qv, a). Same beer, different bottle.
		b) A feeble or inept person, only slightly drier than a wet one.
		c) The vagina and thus a general term for a woman in sexual terms: 'a bit of damp'.
		d) Of a woman, to be sexually aroused, having a knicker-creaming attraction to someone.

Dan Dares	*Flares*	The comic-book hero from the future sees action as legwear of the past.
Dan Leno	*Beano*	A drunken day-trip to the seaside, taken by a bunch of boozers in a charra. Formed on the name of the first superstar of British comedy (1860–1904)
Dance		a) An archaic term for a flight of stairs, even older is the term 'dancers'.
		b) To steal from the upper floors of a building. A direct step down from (a).
		c) To hang, from the leg movements of the victim. A term that spawns several others, including; 'dance upon nothing', 'dance on air' and 'airdance'.
Dancer Cases		Shoes, boots, slippers, etc. Any kind of footwear that encases your 'dancers' – feet.
Dangle/Dangler		The penis, a couple of terms about which it's often asked, 'How's it hanging?'
Dangleberries/ Dingleberries		Pieces of excrement stuck to anal hair that make your eyes water when you tug them out. Or so I'm told.
Danglers		a) The testicles, an example that's been hanging around for well over a century.
		b) A less than sexy term for suspenders.
Danny La Rue	*a) Blue*	Based on the well-known entertainer, this applies to anything blue, including a snooker ball, a dirty joke or a pornographic video – a 'Danny' film.
	b) Clue	A condescending remark to an idiot: 'You ain't got a Danny.'
Dapper Dan		A name given to a well dressed man: 'He's a right old dapper Dan.'
Darbies		An archaic term for fetters or shackles, which later came to mean handcuffs. Based on the old phrase 'Father Darby's Bands', a restrictive agreement between a money lender and a borrower.
Darby & Joan	*a) Alone*	A loner spends most of his time on his 'Darby'.
	b) Moan	Based on an elderly married couple from an 18th-century ballad, this would appear to be a pertinent example since old age and moaning seem to go hand in hand.
	c) Phone	An old term that probably hasn't been used for a mobile.
Darby/Derby Kelly	*Belly*	A very old and very well-known piece that is generally reduced to 'Darby' or 'Darby Kell'.
Darby Bands	*Hands*	Derived from an ancient phrase, 'Father Darby's bands'. This was a binding agreement between a money lender and a debtor, which was heavily stacked in the lender's favour.

Darkers		Sunglasses, for obvious reasons.
Darkie		A derogatory name for a black person.
Darkmans		An archaic term for the night-time, as opposed to 'lightmans' (qv).
Darks		The night. Owls, bats and newspaper packers come out in the middle of the 'darks'.
Darky Cox	*Box*	Seating area in a theatre, as described by your theatrical type.
Darling Buds of May	*Gay (Homosexual)*	Had an instant currency in 1991 when a hugely popular TV series was made of H E Bates' novel about the Larkin family. Almost overnight gay men became 'darling buds'.
Darling Daughter	*Water*	What to swallow a 'mother's little helper' (qv) with?
Darling Wife	*Knife*	A World War One term for the old woman. One can only wonder how many letters left the Front addressed a 'darling wife' and was delivered to a widow.
Darren Gough	*Cough*	The Yorkshire and England fast bowler will be as one with ill health for ever more, courtesy of RS.
Date		An idiot or fool, the well-known 'soppy date'.
Date & Plum	*Bum*	An old term that's always pruned to the first element:

> *Wife: The dog's been full of mischief today.*
> *Husband: Yeah? Well his date'll be full of my boot if he keeps on.*

David		Semen. A modern pun on the name of England's goalkeeper, David Seamen, who is known to fans as 'Spunky'.
David/Davy		An old type of oath. If somebody gave their 'Davy/David', they were swearing on their honour, giving their 'affadavit'.
David Beckham	*Peckham*	How the present England football captain takes a slang-for-slang route towards becoming a necktie. See PECKHAM RYE.
David Bowie	*Blowy (Windy)*	A massive understatement heard after the hurricane that struck southern England in 1987: 'A bit David Bowie last night wasn't it!' It was like calling the Pope a bit religious. Formed on the name of a British rock singer.
David Gower	*Shower*	The former England cricket captain lends his name to BO-bashing in the bathroom. It would be fitting if it got extended to a sudden cloudburst; after all, it wouldn't be the first time he came out of the sky to interrupt a cricket match. On a tour of Australia he and fellow player John Morris hired a plane and buzzed their team mates as they played a match.

Davy Crockett	*Pocket*	Formed on the name of the early American frontiersman and senator (1786–1836), the term dates from the 1950s when a popular Disney film of the man's exploits had fathers all over Britain, dipping into their 'Davys' to buy their sons a Davy Crockett hat.
Davy Jones's Locker		Where those lost at sea are said to end up. Davy Jones – the evil spirit of the sea.
Davy Jones's Locker	*Knocker*	Many a rentman, tallyman or any unwanted caller has had to 'take it out of Davy Jones till pay day'. Also a name given to any notorious non-payer; a 'Davy Jones' never pays his debts.
Davy Large	*Barge*	An old riverman's term based on an old riverman. Mr Large was a well-known dockworker who became a union official.
Day & Night	*Light*	Applies to most forms of the word. It's what wasteful offices leave on day and night, what someone without matches will ask for, and, best of all, a light ale.
Day's a Dawning	*Morning*	An obvious piece and said as 'See you in the Daysa.'
Dazzler		The sun, an occasionally heard example for the occasionally seen star.
Dead & Alive		A miserable, sour-faced person. Someone who is anything but the life and soul of the party.
Dead & Alive Hole		A gloomy, miserable place; a pub, for example, with no atmosphere.
Dead Body		A lifeless individual, somebody who is content to stay in while his friends go out, often a spent force, as in: 'He used to like a glass of beer but he's turned into a dead body.'
Dead Duck		A useless person or thing, a total failure. Anything said to be 'dead in the water'.
Dead Eye		Another old term giving the eye a look-in in connection with the anus.
Dead Eye Dick		A homosexual male, one who practises anal intercourse. *See* DEAD EYE.
Dead from the Neck Up		What somebody terminally stupid is said to be, 'braindead'.
Dead Loss	*Boss*	An often relevant piece used by workers about the one who couldn't run the proverbial drinking session in a beer factory.
Dead Meat		A corpse or someone on the verge of dying. Also used as a threat, e.g., 'Do that once more and you're dead meat.'
Dead Rabbit		A penis, unable to rise to the occasion either due to impotency or drink. Or maybe one that's 'tipped

it's load', as owned by someone who wanted to do it twice before he did it once.

Dead Soldier/ Man/Recruit	An empty bottle. After a party the room may be strewn with them.
Dead Weight	A member of a team or workforce who is no longer needed, someone being 'carried' by his colleagues and, so, is facing the axe.
Deadbeat	A person who doesn't amount to much, one who is permanently broke and always on the cadge. A workshy layabout.
Deadhead	A fool, another version of 'numbskull' (qv).
Deaf & Dumb *a) Bum*	Applies to both the buttocks and the anus, therefore you may compliment a woman on her shapely 'deaf and dumb' and she may tell you to poke your compliment up the same term.
b) Plum	A term from the fruit and veg market.
Dealer	Someone who sells or deals illicit drugs.
Deaner	An old shilling that survived decimalisation and is now 5p. An example of Polari, from the Italian for money, *dinero*. Potless people still 'haven't got a deaner'.
Dearie Me *Three*	Old hands at bingo will know this.
Death Warmed Up	What the very ill or tired are said to look like.
Deck	a) To knock down, to put someone on the floor with a punch. b) A small portion or packet of an illicit drug.
Deck Cargo	A waterman's term for female breasts, especially jumper-bulging ones.
Deck It	To make a car go flat out, to 'floor' the accelerator.
Decko/Dekko	A famous term for a look, to have a 'decko'. From the Urdu, *dekho* – look.
Decorators	*See* HAVE THE DECORATORS/PAINTERS IN.
Deeach	The head, as spoken in backslang. 'Deelab deeach' – bald head.
Deedle	A dim person, a dunce. From the old jibe 'Duncey duncey deedle, can't threadle a needle'.
Deelab	Bald. A backslang headful of nothing. 'Deelabby tun' – baldy nut.
Deenah/ Deenach	A hand, backslang for help me is 'give us a deenach'.
Deep Sea Diver *Fiver (£5)*	An example that's been floating around as a 'deep sea' since the 1970s.
Deep Sea Fisherman	A confidence man, often a card sharp, operating on ocean liners.
Deep Shit	What you are said to be in when in serious trouble.

Deep Six		A grave, to 'deep six' someone is to bury them. Six feet under – dead and buried.
Deep Throat		Fellatio, when the penis is taken deep enough into the mouth so as to tickle the tonsils. From the famous porn film starring Linda Lovelace (1952–2002), the term later became a covert name for an informant from the US Watergate scandal.
Deeracks/Dracks		Playing cards, an old example of backslang, 'an emag of deeracks' – a game of cards.
Deeray		A backslang yard, made up of three 'teef'.
Deerib/Drib		A young woman of backslang, a 'bird', to 'lup a deerib' – to pull a bird.
Deerut		Excrement, a backslang turd. Evict a deerut – to defecate.
Deetees/DT's		The common name of delirium tremens.
Def		Originally a black American youth term for anything excellent, it landed on these shores in the 1980s.
Defrosted		A loss of cool, what a person gets when he's angry. Stay frosty – keep cool.
Delhi Belly		Diarrhoea, as suffered by visitors to India of the long past and visitors to Indian restaurants of the present.
Delo		Old. An example of backslang common in markets. 'Delo' goods are past their best.
Delo Lib		The police, or 'old Bill' in backslang.
Delo Nam		Old man, often the backslang version of a husband.
Delo Namow		Old woman, often the wife, in backslang. Pronounced 'delo namma'.
Deloes		Old people, a 'delo elpoc', backslang's Darby and Joan, an old couple.
Delog		Gold, the precious medal of the backslang olympics.
Demolish		Crack cocaine, a 1980s term based on the effect on the life of an addict.
Denis		A term once used for the police, that is a play on the name of the former footballer Denis Law.
Denis Law	*Saw*	A carpenter's term formed on the name of a former Scottish international footballer known for his sharpness in front of goal.
Dennis Wise	*Rise*	A modern term among young working men seeking a pay rise. Based on an England international footballer of the 1990s.
Depth Charge		A pint of beer with a smaller glass of spirit dropped in it and drunk in one go.
Derby Brights	*Lights*	Illuminations, probably theatrical ones.
Derby Kelly	*Belly*	See DARBY KELLY.
Deri		A derelict building used by tramps.

Derry & Toms	*Bombs*	Formed during the blitz when 'Derrys' were flattening the East End of London. Sadly ironic that the first element should be the name of a place that saw so many bombs towards the end of the 20th century. Derry and Toms was a department store that closed in 1973 after 111 years trading in London's Kensington High Street.
Derry-Down-Derry	*Sherry*	An aged theatrical piece, known as 'DDD', 'Three Ds' or 'Derry-Down', it's based on a character in a verse, believed to be the creation of Edward Lear.
Desdy		A persistent whinger, a pun on Desdemona or 'desde-moaner'.
Deshy		An East End term for an immigrant from Bangladesh, many of whom reside in the East London borough of Tower Hamlets.
Des O'Connor	*Goner*	Anyone or anything that falls victim to the Grim Reaper is said to be a 'dezzo'. In racing terms it can be a fallen horse. Sadly, sometimes it's both. Based on a London-born entertainer.
Desmond		A student's term for a lower second university degree, a 2/2, based on the name of the South African clergyman and anti-apartheid campaigner Desmond Tutu.
Desmond Hackett	*Jacket*	Based on a British newspaper sports columnist and always cut to a 'Desmond'.
Desperate Dan	*Tan*	The desired colour of a sun worshipper or sun-bed enthusiast, courtesy of the tough guy of a children's comic who gets his tan with a blow torch.
Dethroned		A homosexual male who has been thrown out of a public lavatory in which he has been seeking a sexual conquest.
Deuce		Originally a term for tuppence in old money but now a common expression for £2. A 'deuce' is also a two-year prison sentence.
Deuce & Ace	*Face*	In the words of a man who won't back down: 'Better to have your face punched in than to lose it.'
Dewdrop		A drop of nasal fluid hanging from the nose, often seen in cold weather.
Dewey/Dooey/Duey		The number two, Polarily speaking. From the Italian *due*.
Dex/Dexie/Dexo/Dexy		Dexedrine, an amphetamine popular in the 1960s with British youth.
Dhobying		The washing of clothes, a term from India that was probably brought back by soldiers.
Dial		The face, a miserable dial is one that could stop a clock.

D

Diamond		a) The cockney seal of approval, a 'diamond geezer' is a 'good 'un'. b) A Jewish prostitute, a play on the name of the diamond, the Koh-i-Noor – Cohen 'ore.
Diana Dors	*Drawers*	Jokingly dropped to 'Dianas' when mentioning women's unmentionables. Named after a British actress (1931–84).
Dibble		A policeman, a name nicked from the officer in the TV cartoon series *Top Cat*.
Dibs		A 19th-century term for money that gets little interest today.
Dicey		Risky, an RAF term for anything dangerous.
Dick		a) A universally known term for the penis that has been extended to mean the sex act. b) A fool, from the same dangling root as 'plonker' and 'prick' (*see both*). c) A policeman, more specifically a detective. A term most commonly connected with a private investigator, i.e., a 'private dick'. d) A child, a backslang version of kid, but you'd never hear a man talking of his little 'dick'.
Dick Dunn	*Sun*	A 19th-century term for the 'dazzler' based on a bookmaker, well-known in his day.
Dick Emery	*Memory*	A man with a bad 'Dick' needn't have a social problem, just as a man charged with having a short one doesn't necessarily have to feel ashamed. Based on a British comedian (1917–83).
Dick 'n' 'Arry	*Dictionary*	An old schoolboy's term that necessitates inclusion. Often known as a 'Dicky', it's what you are holding.
Dick Turpin	a) *Gherkin*	An imperfect rhyme for a pickle, the tag to the 'what's green and robs stagecoaches?' joke.
	b) *Thirteen*	A piece of RS that doesn't quite come off, but old-time bingo callers used it. Based on the English highwayman (1705–39).
Dick van Dyke	*Bike*	A piece of East End slang based on the American actor, who is generally accepted as having the worst cockney accent in history after his performance in the 1964 film *Mary Poppins*.
Dickhead		An idiot, a complete 'dick for brains', as mentioned in the acronym lombard (qv).
Dickory Dock	a) *Clock*	'Dickorys' have been telling the time for over a century.
	b) *Cock* *(Penis)*	Rumour has it that the nursery rhyme was written about a gentleman called Woodcock, who apparently had a hickory 'dickory dock'. Sadly this cannot be confirmed.

Dicky

a) The penis, a somehow less vulgar version of 'dick'. Often extended to 'Dicky Dido'.

b) Descriptive of anything faulty, or in danger of failure. Famously a 'dicky ticker' – a weak heart.

c) Unwell, out of sorts, sickly. People tend to have a day off when they feel a bit 'dicky'. Like the unfortunate soul in 'Bimteazle':

> *When bimteazle comes you'll get ants in your*
> *   gums,*
> *Your kneecaps will wither and shrink;*
> *Your ears will perspire, your toes will catch fire,*
> *Your elbows will drop in the sink.*

> *There's the case of a man called Sebastian Flann*
> *Who was spanking a crow one night*
> *When his tonsils exploded, his nostrils eroded,*
> *His teeth began spinning with fright.*

> *'It looks like bimteazle', said Doctor McFeezil,*
> *There's only one thing we can do –*
> *For the only known cure is to fall in a sewer*
> *Whilst beating yourself with a shoe.*

> *With an old brogue in hand they did as they*
> *   planned*
> *And took the poor chap to a drain.*
> *His thumbnails were fest'ring, the world seemed*
> *   against him*
> *For now it had started to rain.*

> *As they lifted the grate he plunged to his fate*
> *As he frantically battered his hide,*
> *But the waters around him rose quickly and*
> *   drowned him;*
> *The coroner said 'Sewercide'.*

Dicky Bird	*Word*	Applies to the spoken rather than the written word, the silent never say a 'dicky bird'.
Dicky Bow		A bow-tie, to be worn with a 'dicky dirt' (qv).
Dicky Diddle	*Piddle*	A rarely used stand-in for the famous 'Jimmy Riddle', which smacks of too many shakes.
Dicky Dirt	*Shirt*	An old but long-enduring example; fashions may change but 'Dickys' go on forever.
Dicky Up		To get dressed up in your best clobber, including your best shirt. See DICKY DIRT.

D

Did/Diddy/ Diddicoi		A gypsy or an itinerant tinker, from the Romany word *didakei*, meaning a half-bred gypsy.
Diddies		An archaic term for breasts, not necessarily small ones.
Diddle		a) A 19th-century term for the penis that also became a word for sexual intercourse. b) To molest sexually, especially a child. A 'diddler' – someone who would do such a thing. c) To cheat or swindle, a practice carried out by a 'diddler'. d) To masturbate, or to sexually stimulate by hand or finger.
Diddley Diddley Band		An Irish folk group, one that uses the violin to the fore and gets people jigging with their traditional music. 'Diddle' is an 18th-century term for the sound of a violin.
Diddlo		A modernish term for anyone mad, strange or not quite right.
Diddy		Small. A term popularised by comedian Ken Dodd with his little pals, the diddy men.
Diddy Ride		To splash a woman's chin, i.e., to masturbate between her breasts. *See* DIDDIES.
Didn't Ought	*Port*	What good girls supposedly said when asked if they wanted another drink. Didn't stop them having one though.
Didn't Oughta	*Water*	A very old example which could find a new currency as a warning against swimming in the seas around Britain.
Die		To fail, especially of a comedian who doesn't get a laugh.
Diesel Boots/ Shoes		Cheap, workaday footwear of the 'diesel do for work' variety.
Diesel Fitter	*Bitter (Ale)*	Always halved to a pint of 'diesel'.
Diesel-Dyke		A particularly masculine-looking lesbian.
Dieu et Mon Dright		A World War One version of 'fuck you Jack, I'm alright', that was used dismissively towards anyone behaving selfishly. *Dieu et mon droit* – God and my right – the English royal motto.
Dig		a) To appreciate, like or understand, a famous example from the jazz world. b) To punch, as in 'I knew he'd see it my way after a couple of digs in the ribs.'
Dig in the Grave	*Shave*	An old expression for the scraping of the face that is always shaved to a 'dig'.
Dig Out		To criticise or abuse somebody who may, after a barrage, tell his critic to 'dig someone else out for a change'.

Dig My Grave	*Shave*	A humorous rival to the older 'dig in the grave': 'Won't be long, I've got to dig me grave.'
Digitate		Of a woman, to masturbate. Extensive use of the finger.
Digs/Diggings		Temporary accomodation or lodgings, a term that is especially prevalent in the theatre.
Dilberry/ Dingleberry		Another pair of terms for what's described in 'clinker' (qv).
Dilbert		A fool. A relation of 'wally' (qv), since they are both from the same pickle jar. A dill pickle, for which dilbert is an extension, and a wally amount to the same kind of gherkin.
Dildo		A fool in the same vein as a 'prick', although based on an artificial one.
Dill		A fool, see DILBERT.
Dilly		The penis, usually a child's one, probably from a dill pickle.
Dimmo		A fool, a 'twenty-watt bulb', i.e., someone who is not too bright.
Dimp		A cigarette butt, one with a few drags left in it, a tramp's delight.
Dimwit		The same mug as described in 'dimmo' (qv).
Dinah		a) Nitroglycerine, an underworld term based on 'dynamite'. b) A male homosexual, either from the female name or a play on the word catamite.
Ding		To hit, specifically to punch in a one-sided row, or half a 'ding dong' (qv).
Ding Dong		A noisy argument or fight, presumably when people knock seven bells out of each other. *See* DING *and* DONG.
Ding Dong	*Sing Song*	When this was coined it referred to a bunch of people gathered round a piano, giving it a lot of vocal. It later evolved into a general party or 'knees-up'.
Ding Dong Bell	*Hell*	Most commonly heard in the phrase 'fucking ding dong', an expression of surprise.
Ding Dongs		An old term for bell-bottomed trousers.
Dingaling		Originally an American term for a loon, which with the aid of TV caught on in Britain.
Ding-a-Ling		The penis, a piece that achieved notoriety over here when the BBC banned Chuck Berry's record 'My Ding-a-Ling', which went to number one anyway.
Dingley Dell	*Bell*	Used in connection with telephone calls, i.e., 'Gimme a dingley tomorrow.' The phone was a futuristic fantasy when Charles Dickens 'composed' the place for *The Pickwick Papers*.

Dink		a) To hit, the difference between this and 'ding' (qv), is you can 'dink' someone with a weapon. b) A small person, a dinky one. c) A buffoon, a prize idiot.
Dinkle		A parent's reference to a small boy's penis, like 'dilly', 'willy' and 'winkle'.
Dinks		A young professional couple, from the acronym 'Dual Income No Kids'.
Dinnyhazer		A knockout punch, a speciality of a bruiser named Dinny Hayes.
Dip		Sexual intercourse, often a quickie. As in 'dip your wick'. *See* HAMPTON WICK.
Dip & Dive	*Drive*	Sounds more relevant to flying than driving.
Dip/Dipper		A pickpocket, old underworld terms for an occupation that still thrives on the underground.
Dip Your Bread In!		Have a go, take a chance. Once a catchphrase of British comedian Jim Bowen.
Dipping		The picking of pockets, or 'dipping Davy's'. *See* DAVY CROCKETT.
Dippy		Descriptive of an eccentric, slightly mad person.
Dipstick	*Prick (Penis)*	An appropriate term when used anatomically but is mostly heard in connection with a fool.
Dirt		a) Excrement, human or more commonly 'dog dirt'. b) Money, a 19th-century term for the filthy lucre.
Dirt in One's Eye		To have an itchy anus, the scratching of which will evoke the question, 'Bit of dirt in your eye?'
Dirt Road/Track		A couple of references to the anus, up which sodomites may travel.
Dirtbag		a) A promiscuous woman, originally an American term, now commonly heard in Britain. b) An obnoxious, repugnant person. Another type of 'scumbag' (qv).
Dirtbox		The anus. A course vulgarism used when telling someone where to shove an unwanted article.
Dirty		a) Untrustworthy, sneaky. A back-stabber or a cheat is a 'dirty bastard'. b) A woman who will do anything sexual, a 'dirty bird'. c) An underworld term for anything to steer clear of, something that doesn't seem right.
Dirty & Rude	*Nude*	What all nakedness was in pre-permissive times, and still is to people of a certain generation.
Dirty Daughter	*Water*	What grubby young ladies need to be dipped in.
Dirty Den	*Pen*	A term that came and went with the popular character from television's *EastEnders*.
Dirty Dick		A name given to someone who is in need of a

scrub, sometimes extended to 'Dirty Dick of the Boneyard'.

Dirty Dick	*Nick*	The 'dirty' is a rare term for a police station. The original 'Dirty Dick' was one Nathaniel Bentley, an 18th-century dandy, whose fiancée died on the eve of their wedding. He spent the rest of his life in squalor, and when he died in 1809 his house was a complete tip, although he was filthy rich. A pub, Dirty Dick's, was built on the property in 1870 in London's Bishopsgate and still survives.
Dirty Faces	*Laces*	A 1940s example that may arise from the dishevelled state of the old street sellers of boot and shoelaces. Many were wounded ex-servicemen who could find no other employment during the peace.
Dirty Leper	*Pepper*	Not really what you want to hear at dinner, 'Pass the dirty leper.'
Dirty Mac Brigade		Men who frequent sex shops and private cinemas, typically dressed in overcoats to cover up their erections.
Dirty Money		a) A bonus paid to labourers when a job that is dirtier than usual needs doing. b) Money made from dealing drugs.
Dirty Old Jew	*Two*	A bingo caller's term from the pre-PC days when the game was called 'housey-housey' (qv).
Dirty Rotter	*Squatter*	A recent term for an unauthorised resident, usually shortened to a 'dirty'.
Dirty Tyke	*Bike*	The dictionary gives three definitions of 'tyke', so this is about a dirty dog, a dirty child or a dirty Yorkshireman.
Dirtybones		A name given to a soap-shy person who may be so ground in with grime that 'even his bones are dirty'.
Dirtywack		Someone who clean avoids washing either himself or his clothes, a soap-dodger.
Dis/Diss		To put someone down, to treat with disrespect. 'Dissing' may be a cause of trouble.
Dish		a) A sexually attractive person of either sex, a 'tasty dish'. b) A homosexual term for the buttocks.
Dish of the Day	*Gay (Homosexual)*	An appropriate example given the gay connection with 'dish' (qv, b).
Dismal Desmond		A miserable, permanently down-in-the-mouth person, one with a face like a slapped bum.
Disobey the Pope		To waste babies, i.e., to masturbate.
Div/Divvy		A thick person, one slow to catch on, a mug.
Div		To swindle. 'Div the vicar' – to steal from the Church collection plate.

Dive		a) In football terms to feign a foul by falling over in the hope of getting a free kick or penalty; in boxing to pretend to be knocked out, i.e., to 'take a dive'.
		b) To perform cunnilingus, to 'go down'.
Dive/Diver		Old terms for a pickpocket, newer is 'skydiver'. *See* SKYROCKET.
Divebombing		A tramp's term for picking up cigarette ends.
Divine Brown, go	*Go Down (Fellatio)*	So apt it's like divine providence for the slangman. Ms Brown is the prostitute caught by Los Angeles police officers with her face down British actor Hugh Grant's trousers in 1995.
Diving		Picking, or going down, people's pockets.
Diving Suit		An appropriate term for a condom, protection against the terrors of the deep should there be any.
Divot		A toupee, from the resemblence to a piece of turf, apart from the colour.
Divvy Up		To divide and share out what may or may not be ill-gotten gains.
Dixie Lid	*Kid (Child)*	A term from the army where a 'dixie' is an iron cooking pot, used to make military custard, soup, porridge, etc. It can also be used to boil eggs *en masse* for the dipping in of soldiers.
DIY		A jew, yid in backslang.
DIY Job		An act of masturbation, as performed, with or without tools, by the handy.
Do		a) A party, famously 'a bit of a do'.
		b) Excrement, also said as 'dos', as in 'doggie dos'. Also 'do-do'.
		c) To kill, commonly in the mock threat, 'I'll do you if you keep on.' Also 'do for' and 'do in'.
		d) To inflict a severe beating, also 'do over'.
		e) To imitate, as in the TV programme 'Who Do You Do', a showcase for impressionists.
		f) To sue, to 'do' someone for every penny.
		g) To swindle. Any tourist who buys Tower Bridge has been 'done'. Also 'do up'.
		h) To undergo, to 'do' time.
		i) To prosecute, to be 'done' for a crime.
		j) To rob, to 'do' a jeweller's.
		k) To take drugs.
		l) To have sexual intercourse with.
Do a Disappearing		To vanish, to leave the vicinity, especially when being sought by the police, an enemy or a debt collector. A clipped version of 'do a disappearing act' that can act as a warning for someone to go

away: 'If you know what's good for you, you'll do a disappearing.'

| **Do a Runner** | | *See* RUNNER. |

Do As You Like *Bike* — From a time when cyclists kept to the road, knew what a red light meant and could get nicked for riding without lights. Now they do as they like.

Do Flies Like Dogshit? — A question raised in answer to a question that demands a positively yes reply.

Do For — a) To severely beat up, to murder, a reduction of 'do time for'.

b) To eat everybody's share of food, e.g., 'You gannet, you've "done for" the whole cake.'

Do It Yourself Sex — Masturbation, the pleasure of those who delight in their own handiwork.

Do Me a Favour *Neighbour* — An imperfect rhyme but may be a perfectly fitting example if liberty-takers live next door. For many, the ideal 'do me' is one who's not there when he's not wanted.

Do Me Good *Wood* — What people started their fires with, when coal fires were the norm. Possibly the best thing that ever started a fire was a 'tarry block', a wooden brick that once made up the top layer of a road which was then covered with tar. During the war and into the 1950s, when roads were relaid *en masse*, millions of the things found their way into people's coal-cupboards. Course you couldn't burn them without a fireguard, too many stones in them. These, when heated, had a tendency to hurl themselves out of the flames like miniature comets.

Do Me Good(s) *Wood(s)* — Applies to Woodbine, the much-loved cigarettes of World War One soldiers. The term flies in the face of health warnings and was used defiantly by smokers when cigarettes were first linked to cancer.

Do My Dags *Fags (Cigarettes)* — An old and extinguished term based on the name of a children's game of yore, which meant 'follow my lead' or 'do as I do'. Known as 'do mes', and apt as kids would follow their parents into a cigarette packet.

Do One — Go away! A retort that sits somewhere between 'get lost' and 'fuck off' and is a cut-down version of something like 'do a runner!' or 'do a disappearing!' (qv).

Do One's Bollocks/Crust/Nut/Pieces — Some examples of 'going into one', a raging fury that is.

Do One's Brain In/Head In		To drive insane. A common excuse for being down the pub: 'Her nagging is doing my head in.'
Do Paddys like Guinness?		A reply to a question that requires an answer in the positive.
Do Some Metalwork		To make a hasty exit, to 'make a bolt for the door', especially to 'do a runner' from a restaurant without paying the bill.
Dock Asthma		An underworld term for the feigned gasps of surprise made by the accused when evidence is produced against them in court.
Docker		A cigarette, half smoked and put out for finishing later.
Docker's Hook	*Look*	Oldish, but never grabbed the attention away from 'butcher's hook' (qv).
Doctor & Nurse	*Purse*	A mugger will snatch a 'doctor' and leg it.
Doctor Cotton	*Rotten*	One of many terms making a cotton/rotten connection.
Doctor Crippen	*Dripping*	The infamous wife murderer (1862–1910) gives his name to the infamous toast topping, which is to healthy eating what the man was to marriage guidance.
Doctor Dolittle		A name given to a man with a passion for unattractive women, because, like the good doctor who gave his name to a 1967 film, he talks to the animals. *See* ANIMAL (b).
Doctor Feelgood		A name given to a doctor who freely prescribes drugs to his patients.
Doctor Jekyll	*Freckle (Anus)*	Freckle is an Australian term that found it's way to Britain in the 1980s. Mr Hyde's alter ego became attached to it soon after.
Doctor Legg	*Egg*	Used in a caff by a building worker to the amusement of his pals; when ordering a fry-up, he ordered two 'Doctor Leggs'. Based on the GP in TV's *EastEnders*.
Doctor Who	*Two*	Based on the long-running TV series, this term from the bingo hall has recently been put into service as £2.
Doctor's Orders		The number 9, famous at the bingo hall.
Do-Dad		A name given to something you can't remember the name of.
Doddle		A simple task, a pushover. So common it's no longer slang really.
Dodgements		Another version of 'dodgy' (qv) in all its forms.
Dodgework		A lazy, bone-idle layabout. Someone not given to hard work, an accusation often hurled at those who walk the corridors of power in local government and MEPs, whose only function in life is seemingly to go to functions.

Dodgy		a) Stolen or illegal goods, spivs specialised in 'dodgy merchandise'.
		b) Dubious, not to be trusted. If something looks too cheap or too good to be true, it's probably 'dodgy'.
		c) Anything bad, a situation, meal, shirt, wig, etc. All can be described as 'dodgy'.
		d) Tricky, as a 'dodgy' manoeuvre may be.
Dog		a) An unattractive person, lately more likely to be a woman.
		b) Anything useless or faulty, a second-hand car may turn out to be a 'dog'.
		c) A sausage, from an early belief that they were made with dog meat.
		d) A euphemism for God which is, apparently, too old to be backslang, although many assume it to be. 'Dog's honour' is a false oath.
		e) A wig, a mocking term for a 'golden syrup' (qv).
		f) A share that performs badly on the stock exchange.
		g) To follow, to 'dog around'.
Dog & Bone	*Phone*	A term that first saw service with the old-fashioned Bakelite jobs. Now, given the popularity of the mobile, millions of people can be seen walking their 'dogs' every day.
Dog & Boned	*Stoned*	Known as 'doggo' in connection with being out of one's jolly old nut on drink or drugs.
Dog & Cat	*Mat*	An apposite term since either of these pets will make the mat in front of the fire its own.
Dog & Duck	*Ruck (Fight)*	Probably formed on the name of a rough-house of a pub, rather than a fight twixt feather and fur. My old Scobie-dog would have run a mile if a duck had started on him.
Dog & Pup	*Cup*	Originally an Australian term for either a sporting trophy or what your average sheep shearer wouldn't be seen dead drinking from.
Dog/Doggie Breath		Bad breath and also a term of abuse. A bonus when the abused has a breath problem.
Dog Collar		An oversized head on a pint of Guinness, reminiscent of the black and white of a cleric's garb. 'If I'd wanted a vicar I'd have gone to church' – a complaint from an unsatisfied customer.
Dog End		A common expression for a cigarette butt.
Dog Eye		A look-out for a three-card-trick team. 'Dog eyed – sharp eyed.
Dog Trick		A dirty deed, an act of treachery: 'What a low-down dog trick that was.'

Doggett's Coat & Badge		*See* COAT & BADGE.
Doggie Fashion/ Dogfuck		Sexual intercourse whereby the man – well you know the rest.
Dog's Bollocks		a) The best, the greatest thing out, is called thus.
		b) A term of abuse, usually preceded with 'Oi'.
Dog's Dick		The yardstick by which cleanliness is measured, i.e., 'as clean as a dog's dick'. From the care and attention a dog gives to licking his genitals.
Dog's Meat	*Feet*	Commonly said of aching feet: 'My dogs are barking like mad.'
Dog's Tooth	*Truth*	Apart from the obvious 'you wouldn't know the dog's tooth if it bit you on the arse,' this is used as an oath, something akin to 'God's truth'. But be careful, a liar may swear he's telling the 'dog's tooth' like he may swear on 'dog's honour' instead of God's.
Dog's Wife		A disagreeable or spiteful woman, in short, a bitch.
Doings		A word used to replace the name of something that you can't lay your memory on.
Doink		A fool, idiot or generally thick person.
Doll		An amphetamine or barbiturate pill, from the mid-1960s book and film *The Valley of the Dolls*.
Doll/Dolly		A term that over the years has gone from a prostitute to an attractive young woman.
Dollar		In old money this was five shillings. It has survived decimalitis to a point, in betting offices people speak of having 'dollar' yankees rather than 25p ones.
Dollop		A piece of excrement, especially a lump of 'pavement poop'.
Dolly		a) An example of Polari meaning nice, attractive, etc. In gayspeak, a 'dolly boy' is a good-looking young man.
		b) A traffic cone. Miles of 'dollies' on a motorway means men working ahead, or more likely a man leaning on a shovel being watched by another smoking a fag.
Dolly Bag		An old term from the docks for a stocking that dockers secreted inside their trousers in order to smuggle out tea, sugar, etc.
Dolly Bird		An attractive girl, a piece from the 1960s that's as dated as an old calendar.
Dolly Cotton	*Rotten*	What a situation or food may turn and also what too much booze will make you. *See* ROTTEN.
Dolly Dimple		A name given to an obese person, be they male or female.

Dolly Mixtures	*Pictures*	Sweets are synonymous with going to the cinema. They usually come in rustly wrappers which are synonymous with me LEAVING the cinema.
Dolly Shop		An unlicenced pawnbrokers, where the proprietor is likely to act as a receiver of stolen goods.
Dolly Varden	*Garden*	Formed on the name of a character from Dickens' *Barnaby Rudge*. Apart from your own small part of the world, it applies to 'the' garden, i.e., Covent Garden – the fruit and vegetable market.
Dome		The head, especially a bald one; a 'shiny dome'.
Don		A 19th-century term for a Spaniard, famously heard in Sir Henry Newbolt's poem 'Drakes Drum'.
Don Revie	*Bevvy (Drink)*	A term coined by boozers of the 1970s after the then-manager of the England football team (1927–89), previously successful with Leeds United.
Dona/Donah		A woman, Polari fashion. From the Italian *donna* – woman.
Donald Duck	*a) Fuck*	The number-one bird in Disneyland lends his name to the sex act and if it doesn't bother him, then he 'don't give a Donald'.
	b) Luck	Those said to have been born under a bad sign, don't get the best of 'Donald'.
Donald Peers	*Ears*	A nagging wife will give you GBH of the 'Donalds', and it's down to a British vocalist (1910–73).
Donald Trump	*Dump*	Defecation in the name of the millionaire property developer from the USA, whose name is already a 'wind-break'. *See* TRUMP.
Done For		Broken or ruined, as a car engine may be. Or doomed, as the car's passengers may be if it breaks down in the middle of a desert.
Done Like a Kipper		To be fitted up, stitched up and generally well beaten, conned or wound-up, in which case the flattened victim is 'kippered'.
Doner Kebab	*Stab*	A recent term that's as likely to be heard in the past tense. 'I hear someone was donered here last night.'
Dong		a) To hit, the other half of 'ding dong' (qv). *See also* DING. b) The penis, one with a large 'bell end' (qv)?
Donkey		a) An awkward, slow person, especially a sportsman. b) A manual labourer, one who does the donkey work.
Donkey's Years		A very long time. An old term that is connected to the length of a donkey's ears. It is, therefore, either a pun or 'donkey's ear' is a lost piece of rhyming slang for a year.

Donnybrook		A brawl, from the Donnybrook Fair, held near Dublin, where rucks are the norm.
Don't Be Rude	*Food*	An old term, often bitten off at 'don't be': 'You'll feel better with some don't be inside you.'
Don't Make a Fuss	*Bus*	An ancient term that's as apt today as it ever was. To make a fuss about the foul-mouthed, loutish behaviour of your fellow passengers is likely to get you a mouthful of abuse or worse. Especially from the schoolchildren.
Doob		A term from the 1960s for an amphetamine pill.
Doobry		A word used in place of the one on the tip of your tongue, sometimes extended to 'Doobry Firkin'.
Doodah		a) A word used instead of the one that has slipped your mind. b) A word used instead of one that may be considered taboo. An itchy penis may be termed an itchy 'doodah'.
Doofer		a) An impromptu word for something, the name of which escapes you, sometimes extended to 'oofer doofer'. b) A half-smoked cigarette, put out and placed behind the ear. One that will 'doofer later'.
Doog		Good. The backslang seal of approval. A 'doogeno' – a good one.
Doolally		Out of your bonce mad, crazy. Based on the Deolali military sanitorium in Bombay, where mentally ill soldiers were sent to recuperate. The madness suffered by these soldiers acquired the name 'Doolali Tap', a condition still attached to anybody of an eccentric nature.
Doombrain		A stupid person, a dullard. If brains were made of flour, a 'doombrain' wouldn't have enough to sustain a weevil.
Doon		An incompetent or a novice. Until he's learned to do a job skillfully he'll remain a 'doon'.
Door To Door	*Four*	A housey-housey or bingo term.
Doorknob	a) *Bob* b) *Job*	A pre-decimalisation term for a shilling (5p). When you reach a certain age the only 'doorknob' open to many is driving a mini-cab, the last refuge of the unemployed and the unemployable.
Doorstep		a) A thick slice of bread or a jaw-stretching sandwich. b) Of a journalist, to hang around the house of a newsworthy person in the hope of a story.
Doorstep Baby		An illegitimate or unwanted child. From the place where desperate mothers may place a newborn in the hope of a better upbringing.

Doozy		Very good, bordering on the excellent. A 'doozy' of a book.
Dope		a) A stupid person, an idiot. One who thinks that Margate is a liaison between an American president and his mother. b) Information, especially about something that can be gambled on. c) A drug. People under the influence are said to be 'doped up to the eyeballs'.
Dopehead		A common term for a drug addict.
Dopey		A name given to a dullard, a 'dopey git' may be a card short of a full deck.
Doppelganger	*Banger (Sausage)*	A term, coined by a television scriptwriter, which is double unlikely to be heard off TV.
Do-Re-Mi		Money, an extension of 'dough' (qv).
Doris Day	*a) Gay (Homosexual)* *b) Way*	An American singer and filmstar of the 1950s and 1960s is the reason a gay man is called 'Doris'. To be 'on your Doris' means you're in transit or you're being moved on by the police.
Dork		A fool, an Americanism that has jumped the Atlantic via Hollywood. Over there it is also an expression for the penis.
Dorothy Squires	*Tyres*	A term from the 1950s based on a British singer (1915–98), that is always reduced to the lady's Christian name, e.g., a set of 'Dorothys'.
Dose		a) A venereal infection, famously a 'dose of the clap'. b) A prison sentence, a 'dose of porridge'.
Dosed Up		Infected with VD, knocked off your bike, so to speak, i.e., no riding for a while.
Dosh		Money, a common and much in vogue term with the 'loadsamoney' type.
Doss		Sod. A horrible git in backslang is a 'nettor doss' – a rotten sod.
Doss		a) To sleep, especially rough, or in lodgings, to 'doss down'. Also a place to sleep; the homeless have to find a new 'doss' every night. b) A simple task, akin to a 'doddle' (qv). Something you can do with your eyes closed. c) The number two, from the Spanish *dos*, well-known to Spain's British dossers circa 1970. *See* DOSSER (b).
Doss Money		The money required for a night's lodging. Hard to believe that in the early part of the 20th century people paid a penny to drape themselves over a rope, strung up in some stinking basement, to get a

night's kip. Hence a heavy sleeper is said to be able to sleep on a clothesline.

Dossbag A modern reference to a sleeping bag, the dosser's friend.

Dosser a) A tramp, vagrant or generally someone who sleeps rough. Also a temporary boarder.

b) Someone who gets by without working, a layabout, one content to 'doss around'.

Dosshouse A hostel or shelter for the homeless. Also the home of a scruffbag, on the lines of a 'shit-hole'.

Dossy Simple, mentally inadequate. A special-school case.

Dot To punch, commonly to dot someone's eye, to give them a shiner.

Dot & Carried *Married* To 'dot and carry one' is to walk with a limp. This old term therefore brings into play the time-honoured view of marriage being a handicap. Also used are 'dot and carry' and 'dot and carriage'.

Dot & Carry One How someone with an old-fashioned wooden leg was said to have walked. The peg would have made a dot in the dirt while the good leg was carried. Therefore to limp. Also 'dot and go one'.

Dot & Dash a) *Cash* A seldom-heard piece but when it is, it's 'dot'.

b) *Tash* A moustache. An old term from the army, possibly the Signal Corps?

Dot Com Bollocks Hi-tech jargon, state-of-the-art gobbledegook, like instructions on how to use a computer and the new language needed to understand it. Also a cynic's view of the Internet.

Dot Cotton *Rotten* Based on a character from TV's *EastEnders*, this is a piece that was waiting to happen.

Dot on the Card A certainty, a piece that originates from the racecourse but now refers to anything that's more than likely to happen. *See* DOTS & CAREFULS.

Dothead An Indian woman, because of the mark on her forehead called a *bindi*, which shows she is married.

Dots & Carefuls A racecourse term from the 1940s that relates to 'having your card marked'. A dot was drawn next to the selection and a dash next to the danger, the one to be careful of.

Double A word used to replace extremely or very, as in 'double unfortunate' or 'double fair', etc.

Double Arsed A description of someone with a fat bum, anyone who's all behind.

Double Banker/ Header A sporting contest where the points value to the winner is worth twice as much because their opponent is their closest rival, i.e., points gained by the victor and lost by the vanquished.

Double Beanshoot — Not a large portion of vegetables in a Chinese, but to ejaculate twice without withdrawing. *See* BLOW ONE'S BEANS. Also known as a 'double shot'.

Double Bubble — Twice the normal rate of pay, double time.

Double Carpet —
a) In racing terms, the long odds of 33/1. *See* CARPET BAG.

b) A six-month prison sentence, a 'carpet' being three months. *See* CARPET BAG.

c) If a 'carpet' is £3 then this is obviously £6.

Double Dutch — What any unintelligible language, jargon, gobbledygook or DIY instructions are said to be.

Double Eyed — A condition ascribed to the untrustworthy, when a 'double-eyed bastard' can't find his knife, it can usually be found between someone else's shoulder blades. The blinkers (qv) of a two-faced person.

Double Fin — £10, or two fivers. *See* FIN.

Double Flusher — A gigantic piece of excrement that laughs off the first onslaught of water.

Double Guts — What an overweight person is deemed to have, therefore a name given to a fat person.

Double Handful — £10, derives from a fiver being a 'handful' (qv).

Double Top — £40, a term from a darts match; 'double top' is double 20.

Double Whammy — A couple of blows delivered in quick succession. A 'whammy' will have you reeling but the 'double' one is the knock-out blow. Not necessarily a physical thing; a verbal assault and a pair of dirty tricks may also cause somebody to fall for a 'double whammy'.

Double Yolker   *Joker* — Usually asked of somebody taking the 'wet stuff', an unfunny comedian who is 'having a laugh' or on a 'wind-up': 'What are you, some kinda double yolker?'

Doublet & Hose   *Nose* — Since actors are the only people likely to wear this attire, this was probably conk-ockted in the theatre.

Douchebag — A no-good, despicable person. One whose children have a lot to live down to.

Dough — Originally a US term for money, but so well-known in Britain, it's almost part of the language.

Doughboy —
a) A punch, usually a knock-down blow, to be 'flattened by a doughboy'.

b) An American soldier, commonly heard when they were stationed in Britain during World War Two.

Doughnut		a) A modern term for a fool, a 'thickhead'. One who is a cake short of a tea-party.
		b) A truck driver's term for a roundabout, as both are round in appearance.
		c) A tyre. The very height of unsweet is a flat 'doughnut' on the M25 on a rainy night.
Doughy		Stupid, thick. In 'knead' of some common sense.
Douglas Hurd	a) *Third*	A piece of student slang for a third-class honours degree from the 1980s.
	b) *Turd*	A piece of excrement. Based on a former conservative MP, whereby a 'sit-down job' on the toilet is known as 'dumping a Douglas'. Also the one reclining on the pavement awaiting somebody's boot.
Dover Boat	*Coat*	One to keep you warm on the cross-channel ferry, possibly with deep pockets to hide the duty-frees.
Dover Harbour	*Barber*	Men used to go to the 'Dover' for a fourpenny all off; now they go to a hairdresser for the same haircut and can get charged a fortune.
Down Among the Dead Men		Drunk, the dead men being empty bottles. *See* DEAD SOLDIER.
Down the Carsey/Drain/ Pan/Plug(hole)		A cotchel of terms that all relate to a loss, a waste or a chance that has gone begging. Every lotto draw is another nicker 'down the carsey'. Lost dreams may also disappear down the Chute, Gurglar (qv), River, Sewer, Sink, Swanee, Toilet and Tubes.
Down the Drain(s)	*Brain(s)*	Possibly a barbed comment on a wasted education, there are none so thick as those who don't want to learn.
Down the River		Where the betrayed claim they have been sold. Often a striker's complaint against his union.
Down the River/ Road		In prison. Where anyone spending time at Her Majesty's is said to be.
Down to Larkin		Free, the reply you want to hear when you ask how much.
Downer		A depressing person, a moaner. Someone you could happily pawn and lose the ticket for. Also a variation of 'bummer' (qv) in respect of a depressing situation.
Downers		Tranquillising drugs, barbiturates.
Downhill		The second half of a prison sentence.
Downhills		*See* UPHILLS.
Downstairs		a) Hell, an ancient euphemism symbolising a descent.
		b) The general genital or anal areas, used shyly by those with a 'bit of trouble downstairs'.

Doxy		A prostitute, a term that's been on the game for hundreds of years.
D'Oyly Carte	*Fart*	Generally dropped as a 'D'Oyly', after operatic impressario Richard D'Oyly Carte (1844–1901).
Dozen Sailors, drunk as a		Well and truly oiled, twelve times as drunk as one drunken sailor.
Dozy		Stupid, a term of abuse hurled at a none-too-bright individual.
Drack/Dracula		An ugly person, usually a male put-down of a woman, one you wouldn't want a love bite from.

Drag
a) Three months in prison, a term more common in its RS version, 'carpet bag' (qv).
b) A vehicle, a term that has seen some modernisation since it's formation. It originally referred to anything that was drawn or 'dragged' by horses.
c) A draw on a cigarette, sometimes the cigarette itself, especially if marijuana's involved.
d) A street or road, famously the 'main drag'.
e) Women's clothes when worn by men, originally a theatrical piece for the long dresses that 'dragged' along the ground. Also artistes who got 'dragged up' became known as 'drag acts'. The term later got attached to men's clothes as worn by women.
f) Anything, anywhere or anybody considered depressing or boring. Also a disappointment can be a 'right drag'.
g) A person who holds someone else back or keeps them down, a millstone.

Drag Dyke/King	A masculine lesbian given to wearing men's clothes.
Drag Queen	An effeminate male homosexual who wears women's clothes.
Dragging	Originally this was stealing from horse-drawn carts but later got tagged on to stealing from motor vehicles. *See* DRAG (b).

Dragon
a) An ugly woman, originally a term for an ageing prostitute. A man with a predisposition towards the unprepossessing is said to have 'done more dragons than St George'.
b) A domineering, fearsome woman. One whose husband's head bears her thumbprint.

Dragon Breath	A slur upon someone with halitosis or, at least, one who hasn't brushed away last night's curry.
Dragonchops	An unattractive woman, an extension of 'dragon' (qv, a).
Drain/Drain Off	A couple of ancient terms for urinating, the

drinking man has been going for a 'drain off' for over a century.

Drain the Dragon/ Lizard/Snake
Fairly modern terms from the youth of the nation for urinating.

Drain the Radiator/Tank
To urinate, examples from military drivers of World War Two.

Drape
The long, wide-shouldered jacket that was favoured by Teddy Boys of the 1950s. 'Drapes' is an older, originally American, term for clothes.

Dratsab
The backslang rendering of bastard, often preceded by 'kaycuffing'. *See* KAYCUFF.

Draw
a) A winning bet, money 'drawn' from a bookmaker.
b) Tobacco or cigarettes, commonly 'Got any draw?'
c) A descendant of (b) relating to any kind of smokeable drug.

Draw Some Mud
A wet fart, i.e., to break wind and bring out a little bit of anal content.

Dread
A Rastafarian, someone with dreadlocks.

Dream/Dreams
Drugs, originally opium or morphine and later cocaine.

Dreck
From the German for excrement we get a term for anything considered to be rubbish or 'crappy', i.e., 'what a load of dreck' or 'drecky'.

Dreg/Dregs
A no-good horrible person, a wrong 'un, someone from the 'dregs of society', who may be a 'dreg' or the 'dregs' and may acquire the name 'Dregsy'.

Dribbler
An unkind name given to an incontinent man. An excuse for the constant smell of urine that follows him is: 'He can't help it poor sod, he's a dribbler.'

Dribs & Drabs   *Crabs*
Refers to crab lice, an infestation of the pubic area. A scratching Aussie has 'dibs and dabs'.

Drill
An ancient term for sexual intercourse, also the part that does the 'drilling' – the penis.

Drill for Marmite
To have anal sex, Marmite being brown. But 'Marmite' is also RS for shite so maybe that's the connection.

Drink
A small financial inducement or a tip, originally the price of a pint but now a bit more substantial. Tell someone 'there's a drink in it', and they are liable to 'see you alright' or 'look the other way'. The bigger the 'drink' the bigger the 'turn' (qv).

Drink, the
An old term for the sea, and to London's dock workers of yesteryear, the Thames. Probably other rivers to other dockers.

Drinker		A pub or club, especially one that doesn't stick to lawful opening hours.
Drip		A slow, dithering or ineffective person whose Christian name is often preceded with 'drippy'.
Drip/Dripper		Of a man, to have gonorrhoea, from the discharge from his penis.
Drip Dry	Cry	Apt when reduced to the first element, e.g., 'Come on, don't drip, tell me what's wrong.'
Drip, the		To purchase anything 'on the drip' is to buy it on hire purchase; no mass outpouring of money here, just the gradual 'dripping' of the payments.
Dripping		Descriptive of a weak, ineffectual person. Someone completely 'wet' (qv).
Dripping & Toast	Host	Whereby a publican becomes 'mine dripping'.
Drongo		A fool or simpleton, an Australian term of abuse that has been adopted by young Brits.
Drop		a) A delivery of stolen or illegal goods, and also the place where it is made. b) Refers to bribery in noun and verb form. A 'drop' may relate to a 'drink' (qv) and to 'drop' someone a few bob will get the job done. c) To 'drop' an opponent is to knock him down, a piece from in and out of the ring. On the battlefield it's to kill. d) To swallow an illicit drug, famously to 'drop some acid'. e) To pass forged banknotes or cheques.
Drop a Bollock/ Brick/Clanger/ Right 'un		Things that escape our grasp when we make a mistake.
Drop Anchor in Bum Bay		To have anal intercourse; sounds like an old sailor's term.
Drop of Nonsense		Strong drink, something that will separate you from your senses and have you talking drivel.
Drop Off the Perch/Twig		To die. What a bird, lying on it's back with it's feet in the air, has done.
Drop One		To break wind, commonly, 'Who's dropped one?'
Drop One's Guts		To break wind in a spectacularly noxious fashion, causing much nostril pinching.
Dropdead		Extremely impressive, famously 'dropdead gorgeous'.
Dropper		A criminal who passes counterfeit money.
Dropsy		A bribe or the money used for one. When a deal stinks, it might be a 'dropsy' you can smell.
Drugfag		A joint, a term used by people who don't smoke them.
Druggy/Drughead		A couple of terms for a drug user.

Drum		a) A road or street, an old term from the Romany *drom*.
		b) A dwelling, be it a house, flat or room. If it's lived in, it's someone's 'drum'.
Drum & Bass	*Face*	A modern term based on a noise that masquerades as music.
Drum & Fife	a) *Knife*	An old term from the army that's know as a 'drum and' (pronounced 'drummond').
	b) *Wife*	A term that dates from a time when wife beating was sadly more common than it is today, so it's easy to imagine a bullying husband jokingly referring to his wife as 'the drum'.
Drummer		a) A burglar, a low-life who will 'turn a drum over'. See DRUM (b).
		b) A vagrant, a tramp who travels the road. See DRUM (a).
Drumming		Posing as a travelling salesman in order to ascertain which houses are empty in order to rob them.
Drummond & Roce		A knife and fork, from the unison of two terms of RS, 'drum and fife (Drummond) and 'roast pork' (Roce).
Drumsticks		The legs, people have been walking round on their 'drumsticks' since the 19th century and trousers have been known as 'drumstick cases' for about the same length of time.
Duane Eddys	*Readies*	Cash money, courtesy of an American guitarist who had hits over four decades.
Dub		An ancient underworld term for a key that was most commonly heard in prison, where the 'dubsman' (warder) 'dubs up' (locks the prisoners in the cells).
Dubbed Up		An old term from prison for being locked in a cell.
Dubber		A thief, a specialist when it comes to picking locks.
Dublin Trick	*Brick*	Well-known on yesterday's building sites but has probably been laid to rest.
Duchess of Fife	*Wife*	A well-known piece, long believed to be responsible for the term 'dutch', as in the music hall song 'My Old Dutch', but it ain't necessarily so, to quote another old song title.
Duchess of Teck	*Cheque*	Known as a 'duchess' she went arm in arm with her old man (see DUKE OF TECK). The term got cashed in long ago.
Duchess of York	*Pork*	A piece from the late 1980s for pig-meat.
Duck & Dive	a) *Skive*	To avoid work by keeping your head down, i.e., 'ducking and diving' out of sight of your guv'nor.
	b) *Survive*	Ask somebody with no obvious income how he's

getting on, and invariably he'll reply, 'Oh you know, ducking and diving.'

Duck, drunk as a The happily bevvied may declare themselves to be as 'drunk as a duck' and don't give a fuck.

Duck's Arse A name given to a mean, stingy person, one said to be 'as tight as a duck's arse', and that's watertight.

Duck's Arse *Grass* Sometimes shortened to a 'DA', this is a slang for slang term for an informer. *See* GRASSHOPPER

Ducky A term of address to a homosexual male. Call a straight man 'ducky' and he'll take offence.

Dudley Moore *Sore* The comedian and jazz pianist (1935–2002), born on the fringe of London's East End, lends his name to any unpleasant condition involving skin eruptions. Most commonly a 'Dudley' is a cold sore.

Duff a) Anything worthless, useless, broken or counterfeit. A snide Rolex can be all four.
b) The backside, the original 'kick up the duff' came from a northern boot.

Duff Up To beat up, to give someone a thorough bashing.

Duffer A fool, a term of abuse most commonly hurled at old people, indicating senility.

Duke It Out To fight with fists, well that's how it starts. *See* DUKES.

Duke of Argyll *File* An underworld term for the prisoner's favourite cake ingredient.

Duke of Argylls *Piles* Sounds like the Scottish nobleman has a painful hereditary seat.

Duke of Fife *Knife* A term that's been on the table for over a century.

Duke of Kent a) *Bent* Applies to anything misshapen, such as a car bumper after an accident or Quasimodo. Anything or anyone crooked, like goods for sale down the pub, coppers, sportsmen, etc. And famously, it refers to a homosexual.

  b) *Rent* From the days when home ownership was not for the working man, and the landlord used to knock for his 'Duke of Kent'. Whether he got it or not is another thing.

Duke of Teck *Cheque* Beware 'rubber dukes', they bounce. An old term that may be responsible for a 'duke' being a term for a restaurant bill.

Duke of York a) *Chalk* Has been scribbling on the blackboard of RS since the late 19th century and is still to be heard at darts matches.

  b) *Cork* The bung that seals a bottle, a vintage term.

  c) *Fork* When joined by the 'Duke of Fife' (qv), you're in noble company at dinnertime. Also applies to the

		fingers, for which 'forks' is an old term, and by extension the hands. *See* Dukes *and* Forks.
d)	*Pork*	A piece that is still cooking after scratching around for quite a while.
e)	*Talk*	Less common than 'Rabbit & Pork' (qv), but wasn't always so, this being the older of the two.
f)	*Walk*	An example that was strolling off cockney tongues in the 19th century.

Dukes — The hands, or more specifically fists, famously 'put up your dukes' – an invitation to fight. In singular form it's a hand of cards. It is a long-held belief that the term is a piece of convoluted RS – 'Duke of Yorks' – forks (fingers) = hands = fists.

Dull & Dowdy *Cloudy* — An obvious piece in relation to the weather but can also be applied to unclear beer.

Dumb — Stupid or ignorant, famously to 'act dumb' – pretend you don't understand, feign ignorance.

Dumb-Bell/ Cluck/Head/ Ox — An assortment of abusive names chucked at an assortment of fools, idiots and thickos.

Dumbo/Dummo/ Dum Dum — Shafts of abuse directed towards the stupid.

Dummy — a) A fool, a condescending term for a pillock.
b) Fake, misleading or untrue. If you're told you've bought a genuine top-of-the-range item when in fact it's a genuine load of rubbish, you've been sold a 'dummy'.
c) The penis, a man's most suckable feature.
d) An ancient term for a wallet, as sought by a 'dummy hunter' – a pickpocket of yore.

Dummy Up — To keep quiet and say nothing, especially when not helping the police with their inquiries. A dummy is a mute person.

Dump — To defecate, an Americanism for a 'sit-down job', now well established in British lavatories as people commonly 'go for a dump'.

Dump/Dumpage — Excrement. 'Today's dinner is tomorrow's dump,' the tenet of someone who is not exactly a gourmet.

Dump On — To abuse or take liberties with someone, literally to 'shit on' them.

Dumper — a) A lavatory, the place where 'dumpage' is 'dumped'.
b) The anus, that which 'dumps' the 'dumpage'.
c) Someone who gets sexual gratification from excrement, a crap-happy chappie.

Dumper Truck *Fuck* — The unconcerned just couldn't give a 'dumper'.

Dumpling		A fool, a rival of the 'pudding' (qv) in the kitchen of idiocy.
Dumplings		Breasts, a piece that's well-known through it's long-standing ability to raise a titter in the hands of British comedians.
Dumps/Dumpsies		Money returned to a losing card player in a friendly game. It may or may not have to be repaid.
Dunkie		An old term for a condom, when worn it's 'dunked'.
Dunking		Sexual intercourse, whereby a man 'dips his wick' in a 'furry cup'.
Dunkirk	*Work*	The scene of a lot of hard work in 1940 and used as 'See you later, I'm off to Dunkirk.'
Dunlop Tyre	*Liar*	Tread carefully round the bald-faced teller of untruths known as a 'Dunlop'.
Dunop		£1 as spent in backslang. 'Net dunop' – a tenner.
Dust		a) Cement, a term from the building site for what has yet to be mixed with sand.
		b) Powdered drugs. Also the cut-down name given to 'angel dust'.
		c) The supposedly dried-up semen of an elderly man. An unkind jibe: 'You must come dust at your age.' Also, 'My nan and grandad don't do it any more, well it's too much trouble hoovering her out afterwards.'
		d) To kill, an old term for what someone may be turned to. An older meaning is to beat up, and 'dusted' can mean either dead or done-over.
		e) To leave in a hurry, what you won't see someone's heels or arsehole for.
Dustbin		A name given to a person or a possibly a pet who will eat absolutely anything at anytime.
Dustbin Lid	*Kid*	The 'dustbins' is an old and familiar term for the nippers. Had William Bonney come from the East End, he no doubt would have been known as Billy the Dustbin.
Dusters		The testicles. Not sure why, maybe something to do with the famous Chinese gentleman, Wun Hung Lo, who, it's said, left a trail in the dust as he walked.
Dustin Hoffmans	*Rothmans*	An American actor comes in as a brand of cigarettes, tobacconists report young men asking for 'twenty Dustins'.
Dustpan & Brush	*Thrush*	To have a touch of 'dustpan' is to have a fungal infection of the genitals, forcing female sufferers into furtive bouts of snatch-scratching.
Dust-Up		A fight, an old term for a bout of fistiknuckles.

Dusty		a) An old person, an example on the same lines as a 'crumbly' (qv).
		b) A cruel nickname given to an elderly man, said to 'blow out dust' when he ejaculates. After, of course, he has 'blown the dust off his toolkit'. See DUST (c).
Dutch		a) A wife. Generally accepted to be a reduction of 'Duchess of Fife' (qv), maybe aye maybe no. Maybe it's just a reduction of duchess.
		b) A name given to a lesbian, the inference being that Holland is the land of the dyke. (See DYKE.)
Dutch Beer		Any dull, insipid, headless beer. Like Holland, it's flat.
Dutch Peg(s)	*Leg(s)*	So I said to this bloke with no 'dutches' at the bus-stop, 'How you getting on?'
Dutch Plate	*Mate*	Fairly old but far less common than 'china plate' (qv).
Dwell Up		To stop, hold on or wait. Often an instruction to someone running off at the mouth.
Dycue		£1. A backslang quid (di-q).
Dyke		a) The best-known term for a lesbian. Nobody is sure what the origin of this is, although a strong contender is that it is based on the story of the little Dutch boy who stuck his finger in a dyke to prevent a flood. The connection being that a finger is the longest part of the anatomy to be inserted into a lesbian.
		b) A lavatory, the actual pan. You're never in the 'dyke', but on it.
Dykey		Having the appearance or the leanings of a lesbian.
Dynamite	*Fight*	Generally reduced to a 'dyna', whether the Marquis of Queensbury is involved or not. (See QUEENSBURY RULES.)
Dynamite		a) A potent drug, especially heroin.
		b) A sensational, potentially explosive piece of news, especially when famous or powerful people are involved.
		c) An expression of delight that follows good news.
		d) A very efficient person, often a sportsman: 'There's a new player on the darts team, he's dynamite.'

E

E		The nickname for the drug Ecstasy.
Each Way		Bisexual, someone who bends both ways. A bisexual couple are an 'each way double'.
Ear Basher/ Bender'		A talkative person or a nag, one who hands out an 'ear bashing' or 'bends an ear'.
Ear Sex		Dirty talk over the telephone.
Earache		Constant nagging, an excuse for going for a pint: 'She don't leave off giving me earache.'
Earls Court	*Salt*	Based on that part of West London which is famous for it's Exhibition Centre and Australians in bedsits, the latter giving rise to the area being known as 'Kangaroo Valley' and the 'Bedsit Jungle'. The 'Earls Court' is passed at the table.
Early Bird	*Word*	A fairly old piece, 'an early in your ear'ole' is usually a bit of good advice.
Early Door	*Whore*	An ancient piece for she who is willing to get her 'early doors' (qv) off.
Early Doors	*Drawers*	An old, jocular term for women's underwear. It is based on an old music-hall custom of paying a few coppers extra to get in early, thus beating the crush when the hoi polloi filed in.
Early Hour(s)	*Flower(s)*	A piece from the flower market, and aptly based on the time vendors have to arrive to pick up the best bloomers.

Early Morn	*Horn* *(Erection)*	An apposite piece as men often wake up in this state. A visit to the lavatory usually takes it down a peg.
Earner		A lucrative job or situation, almost always cash-in-hand and often illegal. Famously 'a nice little earner'.
Ear'ole		a) A fool, someone with a vacancy between the 'sound funnels'.
		b) To listen into a conversation, to 'ear'ole in'.
Ear'oles		A name given to someone who listens into a conversation: 'Speak up, ear'oles over there can't hear.'
Eartha Kitt(s)	*a) Shit(s)*	Based on an American singer, this is either to defecate or to have diarrhoea, i.e., 'a touch of the Earthas'.
	b) Tit(s)	Largely secondary to (a) but a mention in a *Sunday Times* article in 2001 warrants an appearance.
Earwig		To eavesdrop on a conversation: 'Careful, I think someone's earwigging.'
Earwig	*Twig*	In this case it's to understand or to catch on.
Earwigging		A reprimand, a severe telling off.
East & South	*Mouth*	Was in use before the 'tater trap' underwent a directional change to the well-known 'north and south' (qv).
East & West	*a) Chest/ Breast*	Anatomically applied to a male or female, either can have a sore 'east and west'.
	b) Vest	Underwear, what's needed to enhance the slob effect of a 'sofa loafer' (qv).
East India Docks	*a) Pox*	Based on one of the old docks of East London where foreign seamen arrived, caught the 'East Indias' and left, taking their disease to another port.
	b) Socks	An old example that has probably disappeared under the same bulldozer as the docks.
Easter Bunny	*Money*	The ball-churning dream machine, which has made 'If I win the lotto' a national catchphrase, provides us with a multimillion-to-one chance of having enough 'Easter' to never have to waste it on necessities again. A wish called squander, so to speak.
Easter Egg	*Leg*	The seasonal confection, usually in the shops on Boxing Day, is one of several terms to make the egg/leg connection.
Easy/Easy Meat		A gullible person, someone easily duped or wound up.
Easy Rider	*Cider*	A piece from the 1970s, based on the 1969 film of the name, that is ordered as a pint of 'easy'.
Easy Rider		A cool, laid-back type of person, one with a high annoyance threshold.

Eat		To perform cunnilingus. Other terms on the menu include 'eat pussy', 'eat fish' and 'eat fur pie'.
Eat Crow/Dirt/ Shit		To suffer humiliation by swallowing an insult without reply, to back down.
Eau De Cologne	a) *Phone*	A term from the racecourse known as an 'odour' or 'odie'.
	b) *Polone (Woman)*	A theatrical piece for a young theatrical piece. *See* Polone.
Eclipse		A particularly thick person, what he is said to be as bright as. Someone who is 'as dim as a ten-watt light bulb', and then some.
Ecnep		Pence in backslang. 'Owt ecnep' – two pence.
Ecnop		A ponce, in backslang form.
Eco Freak		A put-down directed at anyone concerned with the environment; one who will glue, nail or tie himself to a meadow to stop the road builders.
Eco Warrior		A fanatical environmentalist, one prone to screwing himself to a tree to prevent it from being felled.
Ecstasy		The common name of the drug methylene dioxymethamphetamine (MDMA).
Edgar Allan Poe	*Dough (Money)*	A racecourse term, based on the American writer (1809–49) whose stories have made a wealth of 'Edgar Allan' for filmmakers since the birth of motion pictures.
Edgar Britt(s)	*Shit(s)*	A piece from the 1950s, based on a flat jockey of the period, that applies to the runs as well as the normal dumping of yesterday's dinner.
Edinburgh Fringe	*Minge*	A recent term for the vagina, probably coined by a participant of the Edinburgh Festival.
Edmundo Ros	*Boss*	Based on a Latin American bandleader, seldom off the box in the 1950s and '60s. 'Edmundo' shares a podium with 'Joe Loss' (qv) in the gaffer stakes.
Edna May	*Way*	A way of telling someone to push off is 'Gawn, on your Edna.' Based on a music-hall star.
Edward Heath	a) *Beef*	Jointly known as 'Edward' and 'Ted Heath' (qv).
	b) *Teeth*	Formed on the name of a former conservative prime minister, a renowned 'gnasher flasher' when he laughed. Known as 'Edwards' and sometimes 'Ted Heath' (qv).
	c) *Thief*	An extension of 'Ted Heath' (qv).
Edwin Drood	*Food*	One of several of Dickens' characters to make the list, this from the novel he was writing when he died. Probably a theatrical term coined by a starving actor in need of some 'Edwin'.
Eecaf/Eesaf		Faces in the mirror, or backslang versions of the face.

Eefil		Backslang for life. A prison sentence for the evil, which, handily, it sounds like.
Eefink/Eefin		Backslang versions of a knife. When in food-cutting mode it's partnered by a 'kayrof'.
Eefoc		Coffee, brewed in backslang. A proper 'puc of eefoc' in a proper 'eefoc puc'.
Eejit		What an idiot sounds like in Ireland.
Eek		The face, a piece from the gay and theatrical lexicons, a shortened version of 'eecaf' (qv).
Eekibe		A bicycle. A backslang bike.
Eelim		A backslang mile, consisting of 1760 'deerays'.
Eels & Liquor	*Nicker (£1)*	The liquor involved here is not alcohol but the gravy that accompanies stewed eels and sold only in eel-and-pie restaurants. A pound is an 'eels'.
Eemag		A game, backslang fashion, or THE game if prostitutes are involved.
Eemoc		To ejaculate. To 'come' in backslang.
Eemoc Nye		Come in, a backslang welcome. The unwelcome may be told to 'kaycuff fo' (qv).
Eemosh		Backslang for home: 'Come on, let's go eemosh.'
Eenin		The number nine in backslang.
Eenob		A backslang bone. This has also seen service as the penis.
Eerif		A fire, a backslang version of what keeps the house warm.
Eeseech		Cheese, a bit of backslang 'bungie' (qv). Eeseech and noino crisps anyone?
Eeson/Eesong		The nose, backslang style.
Eevach a Kool		Have a look, a backslang glance.
Eevif		Backslang's number five. 'Evif dunops' – five pounds.
Eff/Effing		A euphemism for fuck/fucking in various guises. 'eff all', 'eff off', 'effing hell', etc.
Eff & Blind		To use bad language, usually in temper.
Egabac		A cabbage, as spoken by a backslang-spouting market porter.
Eganaro		An orange, a piece of backslang from the fruit market. 'Eganaro eesooj' – orange juice.
Egg & Spoon	*Coon*	A derogatory term for a black person.
Egghead		a) A name given to a bald-headed person, usually one with a natural head of skin rather than a shaved one. b) A fool, an example that flies in the face of standard English, where an egghead is a brainbox.
Eggs & Ham	*Exam*	A recent piece that's more of a pun from recent students.

Eggy		Annoyed, irritated or uptight, the result of being 'egged' – wound up.
Egon Ronay	*Pony*	An example of secondary slang. A 'pony' is a well-known term for defecation (*see* PONY & TRAP), so to go for an 'Egon' is to go to the lavatory. Based on the famed gastronome who knows all the best places to fill up with 'scran' (qv), and now, it seems, where to get rid of it.
Egyptian Hall	*Ball (Dance)*	Based on an exhibition hall which stood in Piccadilly from 1812 until it was demolished in 1905.
Egyptian PT		Sleep. An example that mocks the legendary laziness ascribed to Arabs by serving British soldiers in the area during World War Two.
Eiffel Tower	*Shower*	A peeping Tom's delight, an eyeful in the 'Eiffel'.
Eight Ball		A black person, the colour of the eight ball in the game of pool.
Eighteen Carat		First class, anything from the top drawer. Also, a complete idiot is an 'eighteen carat cunt'.
Eighteen Carat	*Claret*	Although this could apply to a fine wine, it's main application is to do with blood.
Eighteen Pence	*Sense*	Said of anyone acting pillockishly: 'He never did have any eighteen pence.'
Einstein's Homework		A humorous reference to sportswear made by Nike, whose logo is a tick.
Eisenhower	*Shower*	World War Two term after the US general and later president Dwight D Eisenhower (1890–1969) Sometimes reduced to an 'Eisen', it applies to ablution.
Elbat		A table, the backslang partner of a 'riach' (qv).
Elbow		a) Dismissal, to 'give anyone the elbow' or 'elbow them' is to get rid of them. b) Part of a pickpocket gang, the one who distracts the victim with a nudge of the elbow.
Elbow Bender		A regular drinker, a drunk. God's gift to publicans.
Elderberry		An ageing homosexual, a jocular reference to older fruit. *See* FRUIT.
Elephant & Castle	*a) Arsehole*	The things people have told their fellow human beings to shove up their 'elephants' is enough to make even Jumbo's eyes water. Based on an area of South-East London.
	b) Parcel	A term from the Post Office about that which should be dropped if marked 'fragile'.
Elephant's Trunk	*Drunk*	To get kaylied is famously 'to cop an elephant'.
Elizabeth Regina	*Vagina*	A humorous piece from the theatre, possibly Her Majesty's.
Elky Clark	*Mark*	Applies to a starting point or meeting place: 'Be on the Elky at nine.' Based on a Scottish boxer

(1898–1956), a British and European flyweight champion of the 1920s.

Ella   Ale, a backslang glass of beer. A 'teenip of Ella' – a pint of ale.

Ellen Terry   *Jerry*   An archaic piece formed on the name of a Shakespearean actress (1847–1928), who probably deserves better than to be remembered as a chamber pot.

Eloesra   The anus, a backslang 'arse'ole'. Say 'Ello Ezra' to a contemptible person and he won't have a clue as to what you're calling him.

Eloppa/Elpa   An apple, a piece of backslang from the fruit market. Something to keep the 'rotcod' (qv) away.

Elpanip   A pineapple, a chunk of backslang from the fruit market. The fruit of the good Samaritan in Japan. Help a nip – geddit?

Elrig   A girl, the backslang partner of a 'yob' (qv).

Elsie Tanner   *Spanner*   A 1960s term for a nut turner formed on the name of a popular character from TV's *Coronation Street*.

Eltob   A backslang bottle. An 'eltob of kaylim' – a bottle of milk.

Elton John   *Con*   The knighted musician goes on record as any kind of 'stitch-up', 'tuck-up' or 'take-on', always as an 'Elton'.

Embalmed   Dead drunk.

Emlup   A plum, a piece of backslang fruit.

Emma Freuds   *Haemorrhoids*   Known as 'Emmas' and more of a pun than RS really. It's probably something this TV and radio presenter has had to put up with all her life. I blame the parents.

Emmerdale Farm   *Arm*   Based on the name of a long-running TV soap-opera and, like the programme, RS loses the 'farm': 'Alright, if you're twisting my Emmerdale I'll have a double.'

Emperor, as drunk as an   Extremely drunk, ten times more so than a lord.

Emra   The arm, a piece of backslang anatomy.

Emulsion   Semen. To 'give a coat of emulsion to' – to have sexual intercourse – but, ironically, not when the 'painters are in' (qv).

End   a) The penis, famously 'to get your end away' – to have intercourse.

b) A piece from the rock 'n' roll era meaning the greatest, 'the end' is the absolute best. Also 'endsville' and the 'living end'.

c) A share in the proceeds of a robbery: 'What's my end come to?'

Endless Sleep		Death, made famous in the 1958 hit record by Marty Wilde.
Enemy		A humorous term for a wife used by men who are about to leave the safety of a bar: 'Time to face the enemy I suppose.'
Enforcer		A sledgehammer, underworld jargon for what you don't have to be hit with to know it hurts. In the police it's something to bash doors in with.
Engelbert Humperdinck	*Drink*	A mouthful from the 1960s that's reduced to an 'Engelbert' or a 'Humperdinck', never both. Formed on the name of a chart-topper of the period, who only found fame and fortune after changing his name from Gerry Dorsey to that of a 19th-century German composer.
Engineer's Spanner	*Tanner*	Time's up on this old term for sixpence in old money.
Engineers & Stokers	*Brokers*	An old term for those who come and snatch back goods for which payment has not been kept up.
England's Last Hope		Mockingly said of a weakling. Also someone suffering the fragility of a hangover, someone as unheroic as you can get.
English Channel	*Panel*	This is a reference to an old state sickness benefit regulation. People drawing sick pay for thirteen consecutive weeks had to appear before a panel of doctors who would decide whether payment could be continued or not.
Eno		The number one in backslang.
Enoch Powell	a) *Towel*	Heard round a Spanish swimming pool: 'This is ridiculous, every bloody sunbed's got an Enoch on it.'
	b) *Trowel*	The tool of the bricklayer's trade, based on the controversial British MP (1912–98).
Enzedder		A World War One term for a New Zealander.
Epsom Races	a) *Braces*	A 19th-century term that will be used for as long as men need to hold their trousers up.
	b) *Faces*	An ancient term for an ancient in-crowd, it would seem.
Equaliser		A gun, a term that's been in force in America since the gangster era of the 1920s.
Erase		To murder, literally to rub out. A professional killer is an 'eraser'.
Erb/Erbert		A 1960s term for a young, unsophisticated working-class male, one of 'a bunch of Erberts' – a gang of youths. Before that, 'Erbs' were fools and scruffbags, and the world was awash with dopey-looking, scruffy and spotty Erberts.
Eric		In the popular TV series *Auf Wiedersehn Pet*, set in

		Germany, the Germans were known as 'Erics' and the name stuck off screen for a while.
Eric/Eric Shaun		A couple of stand-up puns that relate to an erection.
Erk		Someone to be looked down on, used by those who do the looking. In military terms it's the lowest rank and to the upper classes it's everybody else.
Ernie Marsh	*Grass*	No drugs or narks involved here, just an old term for nature's carpet. Don't know who old Ernie was, maybe a parks' gardener.
Eros & Cupid	*Stupid*	A recent term from the suburbs, whereby the Greek and Roman love archers get together to produce a 'wally' (qv) or a nonsensical situation.
Errol Flynn	a) *Bin*	A waste bin, hence to dispose of something is to 'Errol it'.
	b) *Chin*	To take it on the 'Errol' is to accept what's coming to you, to take it like a man. Based on the Australian filmstar with a big reputation (1909–59).
Errol Flynns	*Bins*	A racecourse term that originally applied to binoculars but made the transition to spectacles.
Erth/Earth		The number three in backslang. 'Erth-pu' – the gambling game, 'three-up'.
Esclop		Police in backslang, pronounced 'slop'.
Eskimo Nell	*Bell*	Even though telephones no longer ring, people are still inclined to give each other an 'Eskimo'.
Eskollobs		The testicles, or 'bollocks' in backslang.
Eslabs		The testicles, the backslang version of 'balls'. 'Go squeeze yer eslabs' – get stuffed.
Eslag		A glass. A backslang pint-holder, an 'eslag of rettaw' – a glass of water.
Esra/Ezra		A backslang backside or 'arse'.
Esroch		A horse in the backslang stakes. Not necessarily one that runs backwards.
Evening Breeze	*Cheese*	Sometimes carries the prefix 'sweet', which may be a bit ironic when the wind brings forth cheesy aromas.
Evening News	*Bruise*	Often refers to a love bite, which is usually news from the previous evening. Based on a defunct London newspaper.
Everton Toffee	*Coffee*	People have been percolating pots of 'Everton' for well over a hundred years.
Evil		In the contrary world of today's youth, 'evil' is marvellous.
Evlewt/Evlenewt		Backslang versions of the number twelve.
Excess Baggage		Of a person, to be surplus to requirements, someone no longer needed. A passenger.
Exchange & Mart	*Tart*	Based on the weekly publication for those wishing

to buy or sell anything, this aptly refers to a woman who sells herself and often buys trouble.

Exchange Spit
To kiss, not exactly the stuff of Mills and Boon. Neither is to 'Eat Face' – another kiss.

Excremental
Anything considered rubbishy or no good, in other words 'crappy' or 'shitty'.

Execution Day
Washing day, the day the washing is hanged out.

Exes
Expenses. 'Exes' are still fiddled after a century or more.

Exhibition
A live sex show where full sex is enacted.

Exis
The backslang version of the number six. 'Flach a neezod' – half a dozen.

Exop
Venereal disease, a dose of backslang pox.

Extra
Excellent: 'Stand on me, the Guinness in this place is extra.'

Extract the Michael/Urine
To mock or take a liberty. Extended versions of 'take the Micky' and 'take the piss'. From RS 'Micky Bliss' (qv).

Eye
A time-honoured euphemism for the anus. *See* DIRT IN ONE'S EYE.

Eye in the Sky
A police surveillance helicopter, or a local radio airplane that reports on the traffic.

Eye of a Needle Job
A bout of diarrhoea, from the saying that a sufferer could 'shit through the eye of a needle without splashing the sides'. Also suspicious-looking food or drink, anything that looks likely to cause frequent visits to the lavatory: 'This fish smells like an eye of the needle job to me.'

Eye Opener
a) An old name for a sodomite's penis. *See* EYE.

b) A livener, a 19th-century term for the first drink of the day, which later got hijacked by drug users for their first fix of the day.

c) A laxative, something that will bring on an urge to purge following a bout of 'shut eye' (qv).

Eyeball
a) To stare at, often threateningly. Many a fight has started with the words 'Who are you eye-balling?'

b) A meeting. Parties seeking to meet require an 'eyeball'.

Eyeballs
A name given to a person with prying eyes: 'Oi Eyeballs! What're you staring at?'

Eyeballs in the Sky   *Spy*
A humorous term for someone with a watching brief, a security person who keeps an eye on a CCTV screen. A piece that would work if it wasn't RS and is based on an annual feature of the *Daily Mirror* strip cartoon, the Perishers.

Eye-Hole
The opening in the tip of the penis. Heard in the urology department of a hospital: 'And they've got a camera on the end of a tube which they shove down your eye-hole.'

Eyelash   *Slash (Urinate)*
A threat heard in a nightclub: 'I'm going for an eyelash, don't be here when I come back.'

Eyes
a) Spectacles, especially those of the very short-sighted, without which they can't see.
b) A guide dog, the eyes of the blind.

Eyes a Winking,
Simplicity itself: 'The Aussie bowlers are going through our batsmen like eyes a winking.'

Eyes Front   *Cunt*
Said at the approach of a despicable nerk: 'Look out, eyes front.'

Eyes of Blue   *True*
Often said as 'two eyes of blue' – too true, signifying complete agreement.

Eyetie/Iti
An Italian, as in the drunken Italian on an airplane – a high tiddly eyetie.

Eyewash
A deception or a lie, 'a load of eyewash' is said or done for the sake of appearances.

F

FA	*See* FANNY ADAMS.
Face	a) A unknown person, especially in police and criminal circles, e.g., 'Who's the face?' Or down the pub you may be informed: 'Your mate was in earlier with a couple of faces.' Conversely, it is also police jargon for a known criminal.
	b) A top person, a leader. A piece from the 1960s mod culture.
	c) Oral sex, giving 'face' is another take on giving 'head' (qv).
Face Furniture	Glasses, a term associated with television's Dame Edna Everage, the possessor of some spectacular spectacles.
Face-Ache	A term given to an ugly or miserable-looking person. Someone with a 'face like a smacked arse'.
Factory	a) An ancient term for a police station that has seen service in TV's *The Bill*.
	b) Anywhere drugs are manufactured.
Factotum	The vagina of a woman who puts it about. A punning euphemism for 'fuck totum' or has sex with everybody. The latin *totus* – all.
Fag	A cigarette, an example that is probably used more than the actual word.

Fag/Faggot		An American term for a homosexual that is well-known in Britain through films.
Fag Packet	a) Jacket	Entry into the best places is forbidden without a fag on.
	b) Racket	Applies in all senses of the word, all of which can be used at Wimbledon. Firstly it's the tennis bat, secondly it's the exhorbitant prices they charge for the traditional strawberries, and thirdly it's the noise people should make about having to pay them.
Fag-Ash Lil		A name given to a woman who smokes heavily.
Faggot		An unpleasant, miserable woman. An 'old faggot' is often a constantly carping neighbour.
Faggot Tunnel		The mouth, where to stuff pieces of chopped offal. Often said as: 'Get this down your faggot.'
Fag-Hag		Originally a US term for a woman who associates with male homosexuals.
Fag-Hole		The mouth, an alternative to 'cakehole' (qv) from a time when smokers weren't considered antisocial.
Fains/Fainites		A kids' call for a truce or break in proceedings during a game. Also heard as 'fainies', 'faints', 'fainlites', etc., depending on where it's hollered. Ineffective when little heads are being flushed in toilet bowls.
Fainting Fits	Tits	Sounds like a pair to make men swoon.
Fair Cop		The supposed comment made by 'honest' villains to an arresting officer after being caught red-handed.
Fair Enough	Puff (Homosexual)	Said as 'fairy nuff', but not often.
Fairy		a) A male homosexual. Originally an American term, it has minced around the globe and achieved worldwide recognition. b) A 19th-century term for a drunken woman, which in the early 20th century became attached to a tinselled tart – a garishly dressed prostitute.
Fairy Snuff		A punning version of 'fair enough'.
Fairy Story	Tory	Always employed in the first element, giving access to many humorous possibilities. 'Vote Fairy', for instance.
Fairy Story/Tale		An unbelievable lie or excuse, one that may be decried as: 'If I want fairy tales I'll watch Jackanory.'
Fall Guy		A scapegoat, somebody used by others to 'take the fall'.
False Alarm	Arm	Always used in full, as asking a woman to hold something in her 'falsies' is likely to lead to violence.

Family Jewels		A man's genitals seen as his most treasured possessions.
Family Tree	*Lavatory*	An old example that's used as: 'I'm just going to water the family tree.'
Fan		The vagina, a 19th-century term later made famous by comedian Max Miller in his song about the fan-dancer who 'fell down and damaged her fan'.
Fancy Dan		A flashy person, often a sportsman, who looks the part but doesn't always deliver the goods.
Fancy Man		a) An adulterer, the illicit lover of an attached woman. b) A pimp, a 19th-century piece that's still knocking around.
Fancy Piece		A mistress, a 'bit on the side'. Originally a gaudily dressed prostitute.
Fancy Woman		A mistress, the feminine equal of 'fancy man' (a).
Fangoggling		Looking at naked women, either openly as in strip clubs or secretly, Peeping-Tom style.
Fanlight		The vagina, or 'fanny', a 1960s term based on the song 'Fanlight Fanny', a hit for British singer Clinton Ford.
Fanny		a) A common term for the vagina and has been for well over a century. b) To deceive. A con man will try to 'fanny' you by giving you a load of old 'fanny' – nonsense.
Fanny/Faff About		To be indecisive or fussy: 'Will you stop fannying about and make your mind up?' Both 'fanny' and 'faff' are probably euphemisms for 'fuck'.
Fanny Adams		A well-known term for 'fuck-all' or FA, to use the girl's initials, meaning nothing. Famous also as 'Sweet Fanny Adams ' or 'Sweet FA', as in the rebuke to the nosey 'It's got sweet FA to do with you.' Formed on the name of an eight-year-old murder victim of 1867.
Fanny Blair	*Hair*	An ancient piece that may incorporate the pubic variety.
Fanny Craddock	*Haddock*	Applies to the fish on a dish as served up by one of the first TV cooks (1909–94).
Fanny Flange		The clitoris, a crudism from the 1990s.
Fanny Hill	*Pill*	Based on the promiscuous heroine of John Cleland's book *Memoirs of a Woman of Pleasure*, this chiefly applies, rightly enough, to the contraceptive pill.
Fanny Itch		Thrush, or vulvovaginitis as it is scratched in Latin.
Fanny Rag		A sanitary towel. A term brought back by World War Two soldiers from wherever they encountered a bloody resistance.

Far & Near	*Beer*	As ordered at the 'near and far' (qv).
Far Out		An exclamation of delight at anything considered marvellous or out of this world. It also describes anyone or anything weird and wonderful: 'The 'joint' was so far out I was flicking the ash on Pluto.' *See* JOINT (a).
Faraway Place	*Case*	Generally a suitcase and probably coined by a holidaymaker who, on his return to London, found that his luggage was *en route* to Melbourne or Mexico, or some other faraway place.
Farmer Giles	*Piles*	'Farmers' is by far the commonest of many references to the anal horrors.
Farmer's Daughter	*Quarter*	A drug user's term for a quarter of an ounce of their chosen poison.
Fart		a) An anal emission of wind, not really slang but it's coarseness demands inclusion. b) An example of worthlessness, i.e., 'not worth a fart'. c) A derogatory term for a fool, famously a boring old fart.
Fart About/ Around		To lark about or play the fool, usually to the annoyance of somebody.
Fart in a Colander		A short stay. To be 'in and out like a fart in a colander' is indicative of the briefest of visits.
Fart Sack		A sleeping bag, your own personal 'pong-pouch'.
Fart-Arse About/ Around		To mess around or shillyshally: 'Stop fart-arseing about and pass the ball' – a football spectator.
Farting against Thunder		Unlikely to be heard or noticed, so therefore wasting one's time. What anyone complaining to a government body or cowboy builder is said to be doing.
Fartleberries		Little bits of dung stuck to bum-hairs. 'Clinkers' (qv).
Fashion Victim		A slave to the latest fads and trends, no matter how ridiculous he may look. One who often draws the comment: 'You wearing that for a bet?'
Fast		Amphetamine, another version of 'speed' (qv).
Fat & Wide	*Bride*	As she may appear on a seaside postcard, or may allude to the belle of a shotgun wedding.
Fat Farm		Where people with a lot of weight and a lot of money go to lose some pounds, a health farm.
Fat Guts	*Nuts*	Refers to the edible kind, especially peanuts when eaten at the bar and smacks of an overindulgence.
Fatboy Slim	*Gym*	An aptish piece, for where the overweight go to get fit, based on the working name of British DJ Norman Cook.

Fathead		A fool; the fatter the head, the thinner the brain.
Father O'Flynn	*Gin*	An old term based on an even older song, downed as a 'drop o' Father'.
Father Ted	*Dead*	A recent piece based on a TV sitcom. The eponymous hero was played by actor Dermott Morgan who sadly died in 1998 aged 45. Such was the irreverent humour of the show that I doubt he'd have minded his inclusion here.
Fattening Frogs for Snakes		Working hard for the benefit of someone else, the title of a song by American bluesman, Sonny Boy Williamson.
Faulty		Descriptive of a hopeless, stupid or uncoordinated person, one who was 'made wrong' and should have been sent back at birth.
Faw		A term from northern England for a gypsy, based on a band of Scottish gypsies named Faa.
Fawney		A centuries-old term for a ring that's still around.
Feargal Sharkey	*Darkie*	How a white Irish singer becomes a black person.
Feather & Flip	*Kip*	Pertaining to sleep and by extension, bed, this has been part of the tramp's lexicon since a few coppers bought a night's feather.
Feather Plucker	*Fucker*	Only used in a jocular vein. If someone is seriously meant to be called a 'fucker', words would not be minced.
Feather(s)		An ancient example for pubic hair that more recently lent itself to that area in general.
Features		The face, a term that is used as a form of address in the same way as the more common 'moosh' (qv), but when prefixed with anything abusive – prick, shit, cunt, etc. – it's a good insult.
Feck		A euphemism for 'fuck' used by TV scriptwriters especially common in the sitcom *Father Ted*.
Feeb		a) Beef, a piece of backslang that was commonly served up at London's Smithfield market. b) A simpleton, or someone who passes for one with a feeble-minded comment or deed.
Feed the Fishes		a) To drown, a 19th-century seaman's term. b) To be seasick, to add to the ocean's mass with vomit.
Feed the Flies		'I'm just taking the dog to feed the flies.' It's what Rover does when it squats to do it's business. Unless you pick the mess up, of course.
Feed the Pussy		What a woman does when she has sexual intercourse.
Feed the Worms		To die and be planted in the ground to become 'wormfood' (qv).

Feel Fine	*Nine*	A rare example for £9, but be careful who you ask for a 'feel'.
Feel Like Shit		To feel unwell, especially if nursing a hangover.
Feet & Yards	*Cards*	Refers to playing cards, whereby 'feet' are cut, shuffled and turned into hands.
Femme/Fem		A feminine lesbian as opposed to a masculine or 'butch' one. From the French word for woman, it also applies to an effeminate male homosexual.
Fence		A receiver of stolen goods, the proprietor of a 'fence shop' who was known as a 'fencing master' in the 18th century. Also in verb form, to 'fence' is to buy and sell bent gear.
Ferret		a) The penis, an old term for what, like the animal, has a natural liking for holes. Also a reference to the sex act. To 'Exercise the Ferret'.
		b) A German guard in World War Two prisoner-of-war camps, one who made regular searches for signs of escape.
		c) To cheat or con, an ancient term that lives on in the shape of an untrustworthy person or someone who looks like he can't be trusted, as in 'ferret faced'.
Feygele		A male homosexual, the yiddish version.
Fiddle		A swindle or fraud, a dishonest way of making money. So common that it's hardly slang any more. Also a verb, as in to 'fiddle the books'. The one up to no good is a 'fiddler'.
Fiddle/Fiddling Stick		The penis, apt examples for what men like to have fiddled with.
Fiddle Face		Anyone with a long miserable face, reminiscent of a violin.
Fiddle-De-Dee	*Pee/Wee*	Always slashed to a 'fiddley', may have something to do with button flys.
Fiddlers Three	*Pee/Wee*	Old King Cole's string combo are reduced to playing in the toilet.
Field of Wheat	*Street*	Nice sarcasm here. A dirty, littered, traffic-choked street will be pointed out as a nice 'field o' wheat'. Also anything favourable may be 'right up your . . .'
Fife & Drum	*Bum*	The buttocks. Naughty kids often got a smack on the 'fife' before it became possible to sue the smacker for assault.
Fifteen Two	*Jew*	An example borrowed from the game of cribbage for the 'Red Sea pedestrian' (qv).
Fifty Winks		Death, the long sleep. An extension of forty winks – a nap.
Fighting Fifth	*Syph(ilis)*	An old soldier's term for what was originally an old sailor's disease.

Figure of Eight	*Plate*	A twice-removed example for oral sex. *See* PLATE OF HAM.
Filbert		The head, an old term for the 'nut' based on a nut, the fruit of the hazel.
File		A long-established example for a pickpocket, also to pick a pocket.
Fill In		To beat up, to give someone a good hiding.
Fillet of Cod	*Sod*	Reduced to the first element as a form of mild admonishment: 'Come 'ere you little fillet.'
Fillet of Plaice	*Face*	Heard in a department store, a man to a woman, discussing Christmas presents: 'Why don't you get your mother some wrinkle cream, she's got a fillet like a chewed toffee these days.'
Fillet of Veal	*Steel (Prison)*	Steel is an archaic slang term for the 'big house' and this is an ancient term.
Filleted		Total disappointment, to have the stuffing knocked out of you. Another version of 'gutted' (qv).
Filth		A common term for the police that started in the underworld and rose to mainstream slang to be used by anyone who falls foul of the law in the slightest of ways. A motorist who gets a tug for not wearing a seat belt in a traffic jam is likely to say that he's been pulled by the 'filth'.
Filthy		Money, a shortening of 'filthy lucre', not likely to be used by the empty of pocket.
Filthy Beast	*Priest*	Formed in recent times in the light of many reports of sexual abuse of children by Catholic clergymen.
Fin		An ancient term for an arm and, a bit later, a hand. A one-armed man is known as 'finny'.
Fin/Finn/Finuf		Old terms for £5 based on the backslang version of the yiddish *funf* – 5.
Find		To steal. The mock innocence of a thief, as in 'I found it in some bloke's pocket.'
Fine & Dandy	*Brandy*	How a medicinal tot is supposed to make you feel.
Finest		A mocking term regarding the police force: 'Here they come, England's finest.'
Finger		To inform on someone, to point a finger at. Also an informant, one with a 'diabolical digit'.
Finger & Thumb	*a) Chum*	A man with no 'fingers' has no-one to count on.
	b) Drum	A tramp's term for the road (see DRUM, a). 'Fingers' also lay down the beat in a band.
	c) Mum	Only ever used in the third party. You might talk about your 'finger' but you wouldn't call her it.
	d) Rum	An old but still current term among rum drinkers.
Finger/Finger Fuck		Sexual stimulation of the vagina with a digit.

Finger Pie		Manual stimulation of the vagina. When a girl doesn't consent to full sex, sometimes a chap has to be content with a bit of 'finger pie'. The Beatles added 'fish' to the term in the song 'Penny Lane'.
Fingers		A nickname given to a pickpocket.
Fink		A contemptible person in every way. A back-stabbing snide who cannot be trusted.
Finko		The number five, from the Spanish *cinko*, and the way it's pronounced in Spain, i.e., thinko.
Finsbury Park	*Arc (Light)*	An example from the technical side of the film business.
Fire Alarms	*Arms*	A military term for firearms and a civilian anatomical term.
Fired Up		a) Very drunk or 'well alight'. b) Very angry, and ready for a row.
Fireman's Hose	*Nose*	Always reduced to the first element, e.g., 'Don't pick your fireman's, you'll go bandy.'
Fireproof		Safe from blame or trouble. Said of anyone who continually 'gets away with murder'.
Firk		A centuries-old euphemism for 'fuck'.
Firm		A crime organisation or gang, famously the one run by the Kray twins. Also, the hooligan element of West Ham supporters are called 'the Inter City Firm'.
Firming		A severe beating administered by a gang, or 'firm' (qv).
First Aid	*Blade*	Refers to a knife as wielded by a thug and inspired by what his handiwork will bring about. Also applies less menacingly to a razor blade.
First Aid Kit(s)	*Tit(s)*	'First aids' are nature's comforters.
First Lot		An old serviceman's reference to World War One: 'I done my bit in the first lot, I was too old for the second.'
First of May	*Say*	An old term regarding speaking up for oneself, having your 'first of May'.
Fish		a) The vagina, an example that has sparked a net-full of related terms, including: 'Fish Market', 'Fish Shop' and 'Fish Tank'. *See* BEARDED CLAM. b) A drinker, what a drunkard is said to drink like. c) A victim of a con man, someone 'Reeled In' (caught) by a 'fisherman' (qv).
Fish & Chip	*Tip*	A 'fish' is a gratuity or a piece of information, in regard especially to a horse or greyhound.
Fish & Chips	*Lips*	In many cases, when shortened to 'fishes', this is a descriptive example.
Fish & Shrimp	*Pimp*	An American piece that only made it here on a small scale.

Fish & Tank	*Bank*	An underworld term for a likely target.
Fish Breakfast/ Dinner/Supper		Cunnilingus, depending on what time of day you eat. *See* FISH (a).
Fish Fingers		Fingers after vaginal stimulation, used by lads when discussing the extent of a sexual encounter: 'She wouldn't go all the way, all I got were fish fingers.'
Fish Porter's Armpit		What anything suspect or highly suspicious is said to smell, reek or stink like. Fishy (qv) in the extreme, like cockney caviar (prawn's eyes masquerading as sturgeon's roe). The term is likely to be tossed about in the wake of political sleaze or following a 'fixed' result.
Fisherman		A con man, one always on the look-out to catch a 'fish' (qv, c).
Fishermans		A touch of the 'fishermans', denotes jealousy or envy, to be as 'jealous as a fisherman'. The idea is that the fisherman's friend keeps getting sucked. Fisherman's Friends are a type of warming confectionary.
Fisherman's Daughter	*Water*	Shortened to 'fishermans', this is an old accompaniment to scotch.
Fishing		Indulging in sexual intercourse. *See* FISH (a) *and* ROD (b).
Fishy		Highly suspicious, how anyone or anything that doesn't seem pukka may smell.
Fist Fuck/Fisting		The sexual practise of thrusting the whole of the hand up a partner's vagina or anus.
Fist Magnet		A person with the kind of face others want to punch, and often do. Not someone to go drinking with.
Fistiknuckles		A fight, a version of 'Fisticuffs', the loser of which may end up 'Shitting teeth'.
Fit		A term of approval, especially of a good-looking person.
Fit Up/Fix Up		Evidence made up to incriminate an innocent person, an example often hurled at the police. Also a verb, to 'fit up' is to plant such evidence.
Five Acre Farm(s)	*Arm(s)*	An archaic piece that has long since been ploughed over.
Five Bellies		A name given to an obese person, one with several beer-guts.
Five Finger Shuffle		One of several terms for masturbation that bring the fingers into play. Others include 'five finger job', 'five finger solo', 'five finger exercise' and 'five on to one'.

Five Furlong Job		Anybody unable to last very long at anything. Most commonly applied to someone who bails out of a party or drinking session through premature drunkenness. Five furlongs is the minimum distance for a horse race.
Five Pinter		An ugly girl, one who may not look so bad after five pints of beer.
Five Star Nap	*Jap*	A World War Two term based on the (old) *Star* newspaper's top racing tip of the day.
Five to Four	*Sure*	Based on odds that are short enough to represent a reasonably sure thing, this is usually said in disbelief or astonishment at a statement, i.e., 'Are you five to four?'
Five to Two	*Jew*	A racecourse term, where jews have long been an integral part of the scene, whether as bookmakers or punters. 5/2 are odds of 2½/1.
Five to Twos	*Shoes*	An old, worn-out example.
Fiver		A so-common-it's-not-really-slang-anymore piece for £5. Also a 'five spot', which is more usually a £5 note.
Fix		a) An injection of a narcotic, a term that lent itself to milder forms of addiction, e.g., a weekly 'fix of the TV series *Coronation Street*. b) Refers to bribery and corruption. In a sporting contest, when the 'fix' goes in, the crooked win.
Fixed Bayonet		The penis erectus, one that's ready for battle.
Fizzer, on a		To be in trouble and likely to face a disciplinary hearing. Army slang for 'on a charge'.
Fizzhouse		A beer enthusiast's term for a pub that doesn't sell real ale.
Flag Unfurled	*World*	Originally applied to a 'man of the world', but now aptly applies to our planet in general.
Flake/Flako		A mentally unbalanced person, a 'nutter' (qv). Someone 'not the full two weeks', i.e., a day short of a fortnight.
Flake of Corn	*Horn* *(Erection)*	Waking up with a 'flake' on could signify breakfast in bed.
Flako		Drunk enough to flake out.
Flaky		Mentally unbalanced, crazy. An American term, given to the world by President Reagan in his assessment of the Libyan leader, Colonel Gaddafi in 1986.
Flam		A 19th-century term for a lie. Probably a reduction of 'flim-flam', an earlier term for a tall story. In the U.S. a 'flim-flam' is a con trick.
Flaming		An acceptable version of 'fucking', 'Flaming Nora' is a famous northern lady, whoever she is.

Flanagan & Allen *Gallon* Used solely in connection with the measurement petrol used to be sold in. Now we have to know that there are four and a half litres to the 'Flanagan' before we can work out how much we are being ripped off by. Bud Flanagan (1896–1968) and Chesney Allen (1894–1982) were a British comedy double act, part of the Crazy Gang.

Flange Trouble A humorous term for a nonspecified problem that gives a man 'waterworks' trouble. Weak flow, dripping or slow starting may prompt the remark 'I need a new flange.'

Flanker A trick or a con, famously to 'work a flanker' is to 'pull a stroke'.

Flannel Nonsense or rubbish, well-known as 'a load of old flannel'. Also to 'flannel' someone is to flatter them in order to obtain some kind of result.

Flap a) A length of hair that some men comb from one side of the head to the other in a vain attempt to cover up the bald truth, when in fact they are fooling nobody but themselves. Also known as a 'comb-over'.
b) To talk too much, an example seen in the terms to 'Flap One's: 'Chops', 'Gums', 'Jaw', 'Mouth' and 'Tongue'.

Flaphead A name given to a man who arranges his hair to cover his baldness. *See* FLAP (a).

Flapper An old term for an arm, to twist someone's 'flapper' is to force them into something. Ironically, it's also the empty coat sleeve of a one-armed person.

Flapping Track An unlicensed greyhound track, known as a 'flap', where known dogs run under assumed names for the purpose of betting.

Flaps The labia, the folds of skin that enclose the opening of the vagina.

Flaps/Flappers The ears, a nickname for anyone with conspicuously large lugs is 'Flapper'.

Flarge A shortening of camouflage, solely a reference to a piece of hair combed in such a way as to disguise it's owner's bald patch. *See* FLAP (a).

Flash a) Ostentatious and showy in dress as well as nature. A 'Flash Boy' or 'Flash 'Arry' is an extrovert Jack the Lad, who could probably fix it for Jimmy Savile.
b) The immediate effect of a drug injection.
c) To indecently expose oneself, the act of that sad exhibitionist, the 'flasher'.

Flash of Light *Sight* Anyone who dresses loudly, gaudily or over-the-top is a 'right flash o' light'.

Flasher		*See* FLASH (c).
Flat		a) A reduction of 'flat broke' – completely without funds.
		b) A 1970s term for a credit card and a 1990s term for a phone card.
		c) A placid, unflappable person who, like the dwelling, is always on one level.
Flatbacker		An old term for a prostitute, one who lies back and thinks about money.
Flatch/Flach		A half in backslang. 'Flatch a voss' – 50p or half a 'sov'. 'Flatch a teenip' – half a pint. Therefore a 'flatch' is a half pint of beer or 50p. In old money a 'flatch an enwork' was half a crown. *See* TOSHEROON.
Flatfoot		Originally a foot soldier, but famously got transferred to the constabulary – a policeman.
Flats		Playing cards, an old hand as a slang term.
Flavour of the Month		The current fashion or trend, expected to be a 'flash in the pan'. Taken from an American ice-cream slogan.
Flaybottomist		An 18th-century term for a teacher, just here to show how times have changed.
Flea & Louse	*House*	Descriptive of the seedy, run-down hovel that was all too common in the East End of London when the term was coined.
Flea Bag	*Nag*	Nothing to do with a woman who 'keeps on keeping on', but with a scruffy old horse.
Fleabag		a) An itchy old soldier's term for a sleeping bag or a bed.
		b) A dirty, 'truggy' (qv) person. One who makes you feel cooty just to look at him.
		c) An old dog, often a term of affection: 'Come here, you old fleabag.'
Flea Bite		A small, irritating person, an aggravating little nuisance.
Flea Raker		A well-known term for a comb, school kids once used it for the one brandished by the 'nit nurse'.
Fleapit		a) An old term for an old-fashioned cinema, one with the name of Troxy, Regal, Pavilion, etc.
		b) A long-since-cleaned dwelling, with wall-to-wall littering.
Fleas & Lice	*Ice*	Applies to ice as used to chill drinks. Interesting to see a barmaid's reaction when you ask if she's got any 'fleas'.
Flea's Footpath		An old term for a parting of the hair. A bald head is a 'Flea's Skating Rink'.

Fleece	Female pubic hair and by extension a woman – a 'piece of fleece'.
Flexible	Bisexual, able to bend both ways.
Flexible Friend	A credit card, an example taken from a TV advertisement for *Access*.
Flick	An early term for a film which is still very much in use, as in 'skinflick' (qv). It's derived from 'flicker', which is what films were seen to do because of gremlins in early projectors.
Flicker	A bogie, one of the pick and flick variety or one that's been rolled dry, often seen being ejected from a car window because it's owner cannot wipe it without letting go of the steering wheel.
Flicking/Flipping	A pair of lightweight versions of the word 'fucking', much loved by kids and scriptwriters. 'Flippin' kids' – Tony Hancock's catchphrase on radio's *Educating Archie*.
Flicks	The 'flicks' is a well-established reference to the pictures, the cinema.
Flicks 'n' Chips	An old example of a night out, especially a date, which consisted of the cinema followed by fish 'n' chips. Coined in the days when both were relatively cheap.
Flid	An unsympathetic cockney reference to a thalidomide victim. Thlid – flid.
Flim	An ancient piece for £5 or a five-year prison-sentence, both of which are still current. Possibly a reduced version of 'flimsy' (qv).
Flimp	To steal, often in a small way, e.g. 'Who's flimped my beer?' 'Flimping' was originally the crime of stealing from the person, 'mugging' from a previous era.
Flimsy/Flymsy	An 18th-century term for a banknote, especially a fiver, based on the thinness of paper at the time. Later, it also became a reference to a counterfeit note, so 19th-century race meetings and fairs would be the stamping ground of the 'flimsy kiddy', an early passer of 'funny money'.
Flip	To become enraged, to 'lose it'. Many a fight has occurred because someone 'just flipped'; also 'flip out'. Both are shortened versions of the 'flipping' of the 'lid', 'top', 'turret', 'wig', etc.
Flipper	The limb that helps creatures to swim is an old expression for a hand, but strangely not when people swim, when it becomes a dirty great rubber foot. 'Gimme your flipper' – shake hands.

Floater		a) A 19th-century term for a drowned corpse, especially one that had been robbed and dumped in a river or sea. Still in use as a suicide or accident victim. b) An old student's expression for a mistake. c) A piece of excrement that refuses to be flushed away. The end product of a light meal?
Floaters		a) Spots before the eyes, also known as 'eyeflies' and 'dancing dollies'. b) Unwanted foreign bodies in a glass of beer, usually a sign that the pipes need flushing.
Flob		To spit. A spectator's retort after an Arsenal player spat in the face of a Hammeroid (qv): 'If he'd flobbed in my face I'd have killed him.'
Flog		a) To masturbate. Among the plethora of terms beginning with 'flog', which all reach the same climax, are: flog one's 'dong', 'donkey', 'Horace' and 'meat'; also flog the 'bishop', 'drunken sailor', 'infidel', 'pirate', etc. b) To sell, usually 'on the cheap' and often because of hardship: 'I've had to flog the car since I got laid off.'
Floored		Legless, falling down drunk.
Floozie		A promiscuous woman. From the lips of a cheated wife, she's a trollop, a whore.
Flop		A temporary place to sleep, be it lodgings or a friend's floor. Also to sleep: 'You can flop at my place till you find somewhere.'
Flophouse		A cheap lodging house or a shelter for the homeless.
Florence & Dougal	*Bugle (Nose)*	A 1970s term based on a couple of characters from TV's *Magic Roundabout*, whereby a bunged-up 'Florence' needs blowing. *See* Bugle.
Florin(s)		The pre-decimal two shilling coin now represents defecation or diarrhoea, in a piece of twice removed slang. A florin (or 'flo') was a two-bob bit and in RS a 'two-bob bit' is a shit.
Flounder & Dab	*Cab*	Originally applied to a horse-drawn taxi but survived mechanisation so that people still hail a 'flounder'.
Flour Grader		A pasty-faced person, one whose face looks to be covered in flour. Based on the cartoon character from the *Homepride* flour commercials.
Flour Mixer	*Shixa/Shicksa*	An example from Jewish cockneys regarding a girl who is not of their own religion.
Flower Pot	a) *Cot* b) *Hot*	Where all little seedlings get their heads down. Used almost exclusively in terms of a scolding, to

'cop a flower pot' is to 'cop it hot', i.e., to be severely reprimanded.

Flowers & Frolics *Bollocks* An Irish term for the testicles and also rubbish talk, whereby 'You're talking a load of bollocks' becomes 'You're talking a bunch of flowers.'

Flowery Dell *Cell* An old term for where the prisoner does his time, generally reduced to a 'flowery'.

Flue The vagina, the female duct.

Fluff A 19th-century term for female pubic hair, which later became a reference to women in general. Well-known as a 'bit of fluff'.

Flunkey & *Paki* A derogatory term for a Pakistani, usually reduced
Lackey to a 'flunkey'.

Flush A lavatory, especially a public one.

Flusher A toilet attendant, someone who minds a 'flush' (qv).

Fly a) A police officer, a derivation of 'bluebottle' (qv): 'Let's scarper, this place'll be swarming with flies in a minute.'

b) To be knowledgeable, aware and sharp-witted. Con men, spivs and the like are 'fly-boys'.

Fly by Night Descriptive of an untrustworthy person, originally a 'here today, gone tomorrow' con man.

Fly by Night *Tight (Drunk)* A century-old description of someone who has had a skinful.

Fly by Nights *Tights* A term that flew in when stockings went out as primary legwear.

Fly Food Dog's mess. Heard in a park: 'The state of this place, it's like a bluebottle's Wimpy bar.'

Fly My Kite *Light* Ancient and lost to the wind. 'Got a fly me?' was a request for a match.

Fly Tipper *Nipper (Child)* A term to be used in the first element, whereby 'How's the flies?' puts kids on the same plane of peskiness as the insect.

Flyblow A good for nothing, despicable person. Someone devoid of any social nicety. A whoreson based on a maggot.

Flyer a) Anyone who commits suicide by jumping off a tall building.

b) A racing term for a quick start: 'The four dog got a flyer and was never headed.'

Flying a) To be high on alcohol or drugs.

b) To be on a winning streak or a good run of form. What in-form jockeys or football teams are said to be.

Flying Duck *Fuck* Used only in terms of not caring, i.e., when you don't give a 'flying duck'.

F

Flying Trapeze	*Cheese*	For a hundred years or so, people have been savouring the winning combination of a nice glass of 'rise' and a knifeful of 'flying'. *See* RISE & SHINE.
Fly-Pitching		Selling goods at an unauthorised place, usually from a makeshift stall or a suitcase. The vendor is a 'fly-pitcher'.
Fly-Posting		Putting up posters or advertisements on unauthorised walls or on boarded-up shopfronts as is the wont of the ubiquitous and, as yet unprosecuted, Bill Stickers.
Fly-Tipping		Dumping rubbish at unauthorised places and making eyesores out of fields and parks, etc.
Fog and Mist	*Pissed*	To be well 'fog & mist' aptly describes being blind drunk.
Foghorn		Someone who talks loudly, one who booms and doesn't care who hears. As opposed to a 'Shoehorn' – someone who mumbles 'into his boots'.
Folding/Folding Stuff		Paper money. The perpetually skint are seldom 'holding any folding'.
Food & Drink	*Stink*	Most commonly used when the stench of somebody's dinner has passed through their intestines and escaped noisily from their back-ends.
Foop		A homosexual, a backslang version of 'poof'.
Football Kits	*Tits*	As this is always reduced to 'footballs', it just has to apply to big ones that are fun to play with.
Foreign Language	*Sandwich*	A 1990s term that may be apt if it's mortadella in ciabatta.
Fork		a) An early term for a pickpocket and also to pick a pocket. *See* FORKS. b) A euphemism for 'fuck', fairly common as 'fork off'.
Fork & Knife	a) *Life*	Generally used as: 'not on your' or 'never in your' 'fork and knife'.
	b) *Wife*	An old piece that has never really taken hold.
Forks		An old expression for the fingers and by extension the hands. Fork to fork combat, therefore, is not a fight over the dinner table.
Form		a) Previous criminal convictions. Based on racecourse jargon and used by the police when reading a prisoner's record like a racecard, i.e., reviewing past performances. b) Luck, as spoken by someone resigned or used to losing: 'With my form I'd fall in a rose bush and come up smelling of shit.' Also an exclamation akin to 'just my luck': 'Form innit! I get's all the way up north for the semi-final and some bastard nicks my money and my ticket.'

Term	Slang	Definition
Forrest Gump	*Dump*	To go for a 'Forrest' is the 1990s way of defecating. Based on an Oscar-winning film. *See* DUMP. Can also apply to an unsavoury place or a dive.
Forsyte Saga	*Lager*	A 1970s term for the popular beer based on a popular TV serial, a dramatisation of John Galsworthy's novel. A down-in-the-mouth person may be asked: 'What's up? You look like you've lost a whisky and found a Forsyte.'
Fortnum & Mason	*Basin*	The Piccadilly store lends it's name to a recepticle and more mockingly to a type of haircut, whereby a 'Fortnum' is placed over the head and any protruding hair is lopped off.
Forty Four	*Whore*	An old reference to a prostitute, a successful one if this is her chest size.
Forty Snoozewinks		A brief nap, a recent extension of the old 'forty winks'.
Foul-Arse		A name given to anyone given to dropping loud, smelly farts. One with a 'barking arsehole' (qv).
Four by Two	*Jew*	Once said, unkindly, to be the average size of a jewish nose, in inches presumably. Actually a four-by-two was a piece of rag issued to soldiers to clean their rifles.
Four Poster	*Toaster*	The traditional bed of a honeymoon suite comes in as the traditionally popular wedding gift.
Four Wheel Skid	*Yid*	A 'four wheeler' is a less common version of a 'front wheeler'. *See* FRONT WHEEL SKID.
Fourpenny All Off		As can be seen by the price, this is an old term for a close haircut. Still used by the elderly.
Fourpenny Bit	*Hit*	An ancient term based on an archaic coin, which is still heard as a 'fourpenny one'.
Fourpenny One		A smack, whack, clump or thump, they're all 'fourpenny ones'. *See* FOURPENNY BIT.
Fourth of July	*Tie*	An example brought over here by Yanks and mainly ignored by the British.
Fox		An attractive, sexually alluring woman. Commonly described a 'foxy'.
Fox & Badger	*Tadger (Penis)*	A piece of RS from the 1990s for a 19th-century term for the 'rogering stick'.
Fox & Hound	*Round*	Applies to a round of drinks, hence the expression 'Whose fox and hound is it?'
Foxtrot Oscar		Fuck off. From the initial letters as used in the phonetic alphabet.
Fractured		Having no money, a different version of 'broke' (qv).
Frame		a) The human body. Heard in a 1960s disco: 'Nice frame, shame she's got a moustache.' b) To invent or plant evidence in order to obtain a

conviction or transfer blame. The victim of this 'frame-up' has been 'framed'.

c) Police jargon for what a suspect is said to be in: 'We've got a witness who puts you right in the frame.'

Frame-Up		*See* FRAME (b).
France & Spain	*Rain*	Normally reduced to 'frarney'; what the year 2000 will be long famed for in Britain.
Francis Drakes	*Brakes*	Inspired by the English admiral and navigator (1540–96) who in 1588 put the brakes on the Spanish Armada, thus ensuring that no Briton would ever have to eat paella.
Frank Bough	*Off*	Refers to food, especially milk that's on the turn, whereby rank scoff becomes 'Frank Bough'. Also used in relation to leaving, e.g., 'Time I was . . .'
Frank Skinner	*Dinner*	A modern example from the young generation based on a British comedian.
Frank Zappa	*Crapper (Lavatory)*	The founder member of the Mothers of Invention rock band (1940–93) comes in as the seat of necessity.
Frankie Durr	*Stir (Prison)*	A 1960s term based on a classic winning British jockey of the period (1925–2000). *See* STIR.
Frankie Fraser	*Razor*	Fittingly based on the name of a well-known villain turned film and television celebrity, who was noted for his use of the barber's tool as a weapon.
Frankie Howerd	*Coward*	A British comedian (1917–92) lends his name to the type of person he often portrayed on stage, screen and television.
Frankie Laine	*Chain*	Formed at the height of this American singer's popularity, it refers to the old-fashioned toilet flusher. Even though it's all but disappeared from the modern bathroom, people still pull the 'Frankie'.
Frankie Vaughan	*Prawn*	The popular shellfish takes on the name of a popular British entertainer (1928–99).
Frazer Nash	*Slash (Urinate)*	Formed on the name of the car makers of the 1920s and '30s, who in recent years have made electric rickshaws. The term has been running a long time, much like a modern Chinese cabbie will be if he ever gets stuck in gear.
Freak		a) One whose sexual preferences deviate from the norm, e.g., a masochist is a 'pain freak'.

b) A 1960s term for a hippy, one which the flower-power-shower themselves were happy to use.

c) A suffix denoting someone's personal obsession, e.g., 'health freak', 'fitness freak', etc.

Freak-Out		a) To lose control, to behave wildly, originally as a result of a bad experience with LSD. Anyone who suffers a loss of temper or becomes mentally unhinged is said to have 'freaked'. b) A wild gathering of young people engaged in drug-induced dancing. The rave of the 1960s.
Freckle		The anus, an Australian reference to the 'brown spot'. 'Freckle Puncher' – a male homosexual.
Fred Astaire	*Hair*	This differs from the ultra-familiar 'Barnet Fair' (qv) in that it applies to individual hairs. You wouldn't find a 'Barnet' in your dinner, but a 'Fred'. Based on an American entertainer (1899–1987)
Fred Astaires	*Stairs*	An old term for what the man famously danced up and down on in films.
Fred Karno's Army		An incompetent or useless bunch of people, a term formed during World War One in regard to a squad of new recruits and based on a chaotic British comedian (b. Fred Westcott, 1866–1941).
Fred Perry	*Jerry (Chamberpot)*	A bit out of order that the finest male tennis player we've ever had in Britain (1909–95), should have ended up under the bed.
Free the Slaves		To achieve orgasm by masturbation. Too often in the same shirt may fray the sleeves.
Freebasing		Purifying cocaine by heating it with ether and then smoking the residue or inhaling the fumes.
Freeloader		A sponger, originally an American one but now an international traveller.
Freemans		Anything gained for nothing, most commonly a drink. Sometimes known as 'Harry Freeman's'.
Freighted Up		Financially secure, well provided for. Often as a result of prudently invested gains of an ill-gotten nature.
French		Oral sex. A 19th-century term based on the belief held at the time that 'those vile Frogs' were responsible for all sexual deviancy, pornography and venereal diseases.
French Disease/ Gout/Measles/ Pox		Some of the many terms for venereal disease based on the assumption that 'them over there' invented it. Others include: 'French – 'Crown', 'Cannibal' and 'the Frenchman'. All particularly relevant to syphilis.
French Kiss	*Piss*	One of several terms rhyming kiss with urination.
French Loaf	*Rofe*	A slang for slang example from the racecourse. 'Rofe' being 'four' in backslang.
French President		A taxi-driver's term for having the meter running. It's a pun on President François Mitterrand, whose surname sounds like 'meter on'.

French Screwdriver		A hammer, from a supposed belief that the French are unable to use tools that require a modicum of thought.
Frenchie		A condom, a cut-down version of a 'French letter'.
Fresh		A mocking description of someone who smells decidedly unfresh.
Fresh Fish		A newcomer, especially a new recruit or prisoner. Seen as newly caught.
Fresh Fish/Meat		A condescending term for a young prostitute who is new to the game.
Friar Tuck	a) *Fuck*	Can be used in most senses of the word. Those who don't care 'couldn't give a Friar', the bemused may wonder 'what the Friar Tuck is going on', but most commonly it is used in connection with the sex act. Prostitutes plying their trade around the old East End of London would proposition potential clients with 'D'you wanna Friar Tuck?' to which the stock answer was 'I'd sooner fry a sausage.' 'Thank the monk' – 'thank fuck'.
	b) *Luck*	A passenger in a taxi was bemoaning his 'Friar Tuck', and was advised by the driver to cheer up as things could be worse. 'How?' asked the fare. 'You could look like Robin Cook,' (qv) came the reply.
Fridge Freezer	*Geezer*	A modern piece of youthspeak heard spoken of a Chelsea supporter – 'a fridge from the Bridge' – Stamford Bridge, the home of Chelsea FC.
Fried		Very drunk, whereby those who drink like a fish may end up 'as fried as a lump of cod'. Also to be 'drugged up to the eyeballs'.
Fried Bread	*Dead*	One of several terms linking the staff of life with death.
Fried Egg	*Leg*	One of many terms linking eggs with legs, this one originally came from Australia.
Frig		a) To masturbate, an archaic term which is well-known from the activities of the sailors in the rugby song 'The Good Ship Venus', who took to 'frigging in the rigging'.
		b) A common euphemism for 'fuck' in all it's forms, i.e., 'frig off', 'frigging hell' and also the sex act.
Frightener		A heavy, someone sent to scare a witness, juror, debtor, etc., with threats of violence.
Frighteners		Threats of violence as delivered by a 'frightener' (qv). Famously 'to put the frighteners on'.
Fritz/Fritzies		One or more Germans, a term widely used during World War One by British soldiers.

Frock & Frill	*Chill*	A very old reference to a cold.
Frog & Feather	*Leather*	A pickpocket's term for a wallet, known as a 'frog'. A case of one form of pond life being the jargon of another.
Frog & Toad	*Road*	One of the most well-known pieces of RS, normally shortened to the 'frog'.
Frog/Froggy		These much-used terms for a French person have been in constant use since they became an enemy of Britain at the end of the 18th century. Frogland – France.
Frog in the Throat	*Boat*	A World War One term that was coughed up and spat into obscurity soon after.
Frog Spawn	*Horn (Erection)*	A 'frog on' for short. Or not so short as the case may be.
From Here to Blooms		A long distance. Racing parlance for the distance a horse has won by. Blooms was a well-known Jewish restaurant in Whitechapel, East London, so the phrase was probably coined by on-course Jewish bookmakers who, wherever they happened to be, would have been far from Blooms, since the East End has never had a racecourse. The restaurant is now situated in Golder's Green, North London.
From Soup to Afters		From start to finish. The working-class version of 'from soup to the cheese board'.
From Soup to Cheese Board		From start to finish, a piece with its roots on the racecourse to describe a horse that led all the way. Older is the American 'from soup to nuts'.
From Trap to Line		From beginning to end, an example with its roots at the greyhound track, i.e., from the starting trap to the finish line: 'From trap to line it's 52 miles from the pick-up to the drop', as said by a London courier.
Front		a) Audacity, nerve or effrontery. A daring person may have more front than Dolly Parton. b) The face behind a usually dishonest business but not the owner. Someone with no criminal record 'fronting' for someone who has. c) To confront. Bullies may back down or bash-up, but you won't know unless you 'front' them.
Front Door/ Entrance/ Parlour/Room		Some terms for the vagina which liken a woman's body to a house. Some that don't are: 'Front Arse', 'Front Bum' and 'Front Crack'.
Front-Wheel Skid	*Yid*	Whereby a child of Israel is known as a 'front wheeler'.
Frosty		A name given to a cocaine dealer. The drug has long been known as 'snow', hence a dealer is a

'snowman'. After the seasonal song 'Frosty the Snowman'.

Fruit

A male homosexual. Not sure if this was a gaffe or not, but in his radio show, Michael Parkinson was talking to Sir Ian McKellen about the actor's impending talks on gay rights at the prime minister's residence in Downing Street. Parkinson ended the interview with 'I hope your talks prove fruitful.'

Fruit & Nut *Cut*

Applies to an injury. By sending your head into battle you may 'fruit' someone with your nut.

Fruit Bat/Fly

A couple of terms for women (ugsome one's in the case of 'bat') who prefer the company of gay men, rather than straight ones'.

Fruitcake

a) A male homosexual, an extension of 'fruit' (qv).
b) A mad, eccentric person. What loons are famously 'as nutty as'.

Fry

To electrocute. An American term associated with the electric chair. In Britain it's a domestic thing, or a reason to keep away from railway tracks. An electric fly-trap is a 'fly-frier'.

Frying Pan *a) Fan*

Refers to an admirer. A performer may be told: 'I've been a frying pan of yours for years.'

b) Hand

An old reference to the maulers, and it matters not about the 'd', it's never sounded anyway.

c) Man

Usually the 'old frying', meaning a husband or father.

Fubar

Originally an American military term for an operation gone wrong or a situation out of control. Now any kind of wreck, including people ruined by drink or drugs who can be 'Fucked Up Beyond All Recognition' – FUBAR.

Fuck

a) Sexual intercourse, a term that's been representing the old in and out, as noun and verb, since Shakespeare's time. Although he never used the word in his writing, certain passages and puns in his plays show that he knew it. The use of the French version (*foutre*) in *Henry IV* part 2, for instance.
b) A fool, in terms such as 'dumb' or 'stupid' – fuck.
c) The slightest amount, when you 'couldn't give a fuck'.
d) To render helpless, e.g., to cut off the hands of a habitual nose-picker will fuck him completely.
e) A replacement word for hell when a strong refusal is given, as in 'Like fuck I will!'. Also, anything done in a devil-may-care manner is done 'just for the fuck of it'.

Fuck About/ Around	To play the fool: 'Don't fuck about, this is serious.' To tamper or experiment with: 'Don't fuck around with things you don't understand.' To waste someone's time: 'Don't fuck me about. Do you want it or not?'
Fuck All	Absolutely nothing: 'It's got fuck all to do with you.'
Fuck Me/Fuck me Gently/ Rigid	Exclamations of amazement or trepidation.
Fuck My Old Boots/Daisies	An exclamation of surprise that began in the army but is well-known in civvy street. *See* DAISY ROOTS.
Fuck Off	a) To leave, and also a vehement indication that you want someone to get lost.
	b) An expression of disbelief: 'Fuck off, you're having me on.'
Fuck One's Fist	To masturbate, to 'give your hand one'.
Fuck Up a Wet Dream	What a completely useless, incompetent man is said to be able to do.
Fuck Up	a) To make a mistake, often with serious repercussions: 'Fuck this up and you're finished.'
	b) To ruin, break or mess up. Also what drink and drug addiction can do to a person.
Fuck With	To mess with, to get on the wrong side of, someone: 'Don't fuck with me!'
Fuck You	A term of dismissal akin to 'get stuffed'.
Fuck You Charlie	An old term of dismissal or disinterest that is euphemistically reversed to 'chuck you farley'.
Fuck You Jack, I'm Alright	A well-known term of selfishness that originated in the navy.
Fuckable/ Fuckworthy	Highly fanciable, someone you wouldn't kick out of bed. You should be so lucky!
Fucked	a) Totally exhausted, worn out: 'You'll have to carry on without me, I'm fucked.'
	b) Anything that's broken down and no longer usable.
	c) Drunk or high on drugs.
	d) Beaten, floored or rendered helpless. Ironically, like a woman with an impotent partner.
Fucked Up	a) Ruined, broken or messed up, be it a plan, an object, an exam, or anything being worked on. Also people who are dependent, or 'fucked up' on drugs or alcohol.
	b) Traumatised, psychologically unsound. Shell-shocked soldiers for instance.
Fuckface	A term of abuse that is not necessarily abusive.
Fuckhead/ Fuckwit	A pair of morons, a couple of brainless dolts.

Fucking		a) The commonest intensifier that needs no description, a child of three could tell you.
		b) A severe telling off, on a level with a 'bollocking' but worse than a 'rucking'.
Fucking Ada/ Arseholes/Hell		Exclamations of disappointment, annoyance or surprise.
Fuckpig		A low, contemptible person, the British version of the American 'pigfucker', which may be an insult to the pig.
Fuckpot		A contemptible, obnoxious person. 'Horrible fuckpots' shouldn't be trusted.
Fuck-Truck		A vehicle used in the pursuit of sex, another model of 'passion wagon' (qv).
Fuck-Up		a) A blunder or a failure; military history is littered with them.
		b) An incapable, incompetent bungler; military history is littered with them as well.
Fudge		Excrement, mostly used in an unsavoury connection with homosexuality in terms such as 'Fudge Nudger', 'Fudge Packer' and 'Fudge Puncher'. 'Fudge Tunnel' – the anus.
Full/Full As		Drunk. Among the many trailers to 'Full as' are: 'an egg', 'a tick' and 'a fat bloke's vest'.
Full Monty		The whole lot, the complete set. Everything. The title of a successful film about a group of male strippers for whom the 'full Monty' is a complete strip.
Full Moon	*Loon*	An appropriate term for anyone given to acting crazily. The connection between the moon and lunacy is plain to see.
Full of Shit		What a liar, braggart or teller of tall stories is said to be. Also, euphemistically 'full of it'.
Fully Rigged		Dressed up for an occasion. A bridegroom in his top hat and tails is said to be in 'full rig'.
Fun & Frolics	*Bollocks*	Originally an Irish term for where it's no fun to take a knock.
Funbags/ Funsacks		Breasts, the perennial source of untold amusement to most men.
Fungus		Whiskers, therefore 'Fungus Face' or 'Fungus Features' – a bearded man.
Funnel		The anus; the escape route for yesterday's dinner.
Funny		Anyone who is weird or creepy is said to be a bit 'funny', as is somebody who is slightly touched, whose brain is slightly out of whack.
Funny Bones		A naturally funny person, a born comedian. Someone who will make you 'laugh like a leper', i.e. laugh your head off.

Funny Cods		A name conferred on someone given to witty or sarcastic remarks: 'Alright funny cods, that's enough, a joke's a joke.'
Funny Face(s)	*Lace(s)*	A juvenile term that applies to shoe or boot laces: 'Mind you don't trip over your funny face.'
Funny Fag		A joint, that which gets nonsmokers sniffing the air and wondering what that strange smell is.
Funny Farm		A mental institution, a later version of a 'loony bin' (qv).
Funny Feeling	*Ceiling*	Fitting when you've had a few and the 'lid' won't stop spinning.
Funny Money		a) Money from the 'Bank of Toytown'; counterfeit bank notes or dodgy £1 coins.
		b) The British view of foreign currency, now particularly the euro.
Fur		The female pubic hair and, by extension, a woman. Heard in a club: 'Not a lot of fur about.'
Furburger/Fur Pie		The vagina, as 'eaten' by a cunnilinguist.
Furpiece		The vagina and, by extension, a woman: 'Seen the new furpiece Dave's dragging around?'
Furry Cup		The vagina, what cunnilinguists are said to drink from.
Furry Muff		Currently a jocular rendition of 'fair enough'.
Fusilier	*Beer*	An ancient term that is still on parade but mainly with old soldiers.
Fusiliers	*Ears*	An old soldiers' term for the spectacle hangers.
Fuzz		a) The police, an American term that was taken up in the 1960s by hippies and discarded soon after. Now outdated.
		b) Female pubic hair or wispy male facial hair.

G

Gabby Hayes

A name given to a talkative, or gabby, person: 'Him with all the gab.' Based on an American actor (1885–1969), a star of countless western films.

Gable/Gable End

The head, the highest part of a wall for the similar part of the body.

Gaff

a) A well-known term with a convoluted history. From the Romany *gav*, meaning a market town. It began life in the early 19th-century as a fair, and by the end of that century had transferred to any place of entertainment, chiefly a cheap theatre or music hall, famously a 'penny gaff'. By the time of World War One it had come to refer to any kind of place (soldiers used it for their trenches) and by the 1930s it became what we know it as today: a house, flat or any kind of dwelling. Buckingham Palace is the queen's 'gaff'.
b) A trick or device that aids a deception or a swindle, especially among cardsharps. Exposing such chicanery is known as 'blowing the gaff', a term well-known now for divulging information.
c) A cigarette, a backslang fag.

Gaffer

A boss, someone in authority. A term often fired at a publican.

Gaga		Senile through old age and by extension being mentally skew-whiff at any age.
Gage/Gauge		Marijuana, hashish or cannabis, as smoked in Britain since the 1960s but earlier in the US.
Gagga		A wig, especially an obvious one.
Gagging		Thirsty. Hot days tend to get people gagging for a pint, cold days a cup of tea.
Gagging for It		Eager for sex, a term used by men about women, e.g., 'She was gagging for it, so she got it.'
Gali/Gauley		A Bengali, a piece from London's East End, which has a large population of Bengali immigrants.
Galoot		A clumsy, awkward person who has been stepping on toes since the 19th century.
Gam/Gamaroosh		Oral sex, usually the act of fellatio. From the French *gamahucher* – the performance of oral sex.
Gam Cases		Originally stockings but now tights, leggings or trousers. Anything that you keep your legs in.
Gamble & Procter	*Doctor*	Loosely based on the pharmaceutical company, Proctor & Gamble, which is loosely connected with healthcare.
Game		Available for sex, therefore a prostitute. 'On the game' – working as a prostitute.
Game as a Beigel		See BEIGEL.
Game Bird		A promiscuous woman, one who only goes with friends and strangers.
Game of Nap	*a) Cap*	Based on a card game and refers to the old style of cap rather than the baseball variety, which seems to be taking over the world.
	b) Crap	Refers to the act of defecation: 'Sorry I'm late, I had to go back for a game o' nap.'
Gammon		An 18th-century term for a deception or a pretence. To 'gammon' someone is to humbug them or give them a load of moody (qv).
Gammon Rasher	*Smasher*	Anything marvellous or smashing. Be careful when using it in connection with a woman as she may think you're calling her a pig.
Gammy		Lame, crippled or injured, famously a 'gammy leg'.
Gams		A long-standing term for the legs, originally skinny, spindly ones.
Gander		A well-known example for a look or glance.
Gandhi's Revenge		Diarrhoea that follows an Indian meal.
Gang Bang		Group sex consisting of a bunch of men and one woman.
Ganja		Marijuana, a term synonymous with Rastafarianism.

Gannet		A glutton, after the sea-bird with a see-food diet, i.e., it eats whatever it sees.
Gap		The mouth. Since the 19th century tactless people have had to mind their 'gaps'.
Gap between a Bedouin's Toes		What the mouth of someone who has had too much to drink may be said to be like on waking.
Garden Gate	a) *Eight*	As well as a bingo term, a 'garden' is a common term for £8.
	b) *Magistrate*	Old, but lawbreakers still go up before the 'garden'.
	c) *Mate*	This rare alternative to 'china plate' (qv) was more commonly heard as a reference to the first officer in the merchant navy.
Garden Gates	*Rates*	An old term that was common until first, the poll tax and then, the council tax became the local government charges.
Garden Gnome	*Comb*	There are many connections in slang between a head of hair and a garden. Hair is 'grass', scissors are 'shears' and a comb is a 'rake' as well as a 'garden'.
Garden Hop	*Shop (Inform On)*	An early 20th-century term from the underworld relating to betrayal.
Garden Hose	*Nose*	Appropriate if the said shonker is long or dripping.
Garden Path	*Bath*	Common to be in the 'garden' when the doorbell rings.
Garden Plant	*Aunt*	Generally used in the third person, when speaking of a 'garden and carbuncle' (qv).
Garden Shed	*Red*	The red ball in the game of pool: 'I'm garden sheds, you're cinderellas.'
Gareth Hunt	*Cunt*	Another branch of the Hunt family tree gets to make a rhyme for a fool or a 'wrong 'un', this one a British actor.
Gargle		A drink, especially an alcoholic one as sold at a 'gargle house' – a pub.
Gargled		Drunk, the result of chucking too much 'gargle' down your 'gargler' (throat).
Garibaldi Biscuit	*Risk It*	On noticing his lorry was well overloaded, a driver was heard to remark: 'It's only got to go a couple of miles so I'll garibaldi it.'
Garret		The head, another example of the top room representing the 'top end'. See ATTIC, LOFT, etc.
Garretty		Crazy or mad, especially a loss of temper: 'The old man took one look at the room and went garretty.' Also, 'off one's garret' (qv).
Gary Ablett	*Tablet*	A 1990s term from the world of the young drug-taker. Based on a footballer who made his name kicking a 'pill' about for Liverpool FC. See PILL.

Gary Glitter	a) *Bitter*	Beer, have this one on an ex-pop singer.
	b) *Shitter*	Appears quite fitting since he makes a living from rock 'n' roll. *See* Rock 'n' Roll (b) and you'll see what I mean.
Gary Lineker	*Vinegar*	People were actually sprinkling 'Gary' on their chips before the former England footballer's 'salt and Lineker' crisps adverts appeared on TV in the late 1990s.
Gas		a) Anything good, pleasurable or enjoyable. Also a person who is fun to be with, like Jumpin' Jack Flash apparently.
		b) Idle, uninteresting chatter. The specialist subject of a 'gasser'.
Gas Guzzler		A car that drinks a lot of petrol. A low-miles-per-gallon job.
Gas Meter Thief		A small-time criminal, one with low aspirations.
Gasbag		A talkative person, a term aimed at many a DJ.
Gash		a) The vagina, and by extension women in general seen as sex objects, often a prostitute.
		b) Rubbish, trash or anything worn out or useless, e.g., an empty pen is 'gash'.
		c) Spare or available. May be a further extension of (a), in that spare or unattached women may be available.
Gasp & Grunt	*Cunt*	An uncommon variant on 'grumble and grunt' (qv).
Gasper		A cigarette from pre-government health-warning days.
Gassing		Pretending to be from a gas company in order to gain entry into an old person's flat with the intention of robbing them.
Gat		A gun, originally an American term, a shortening of Gatling.
Gate		An old term for the mouth, famously 'Shut your gate!' – hold your noise!
Gate Arrest		The re-arrest of a prisoner, for an outstanding offence, as he leaves prison at the end of a sentence.
Gate Fever		Nervousness felt by prisoners as their sentence comes to it's close. They are said to be 'gatey'.
Gate of Life		An archaic and perennially apt term for the vagina.
Gates of Rome	*Home*	Be it ever so humble, there's no place like your 'gates o' Rome'.
Gatter		Beer, a 19th-century pint.
Gavas/Gavvers		An underworld term for the police, sometimes said as 'gabbers'.
Gavel & Wig	*Twig*	To 'twig' is to scratch an itchy anus, and is crudely based on the savoury snack, a twiglet. The

inference being that it resembles a faecal-stained finger after a 'good old scratch' or 'gavel'.

Gay & Frisky   *Whisky*   An old term for a long-serving member of the 'top shelf' fraternity.

Gay & Hearty   *Party*   An old-fashioned term from when gay meant happy. The term aptly describes a 'knees-up' (qv).

Gay Gordon   *Traffic Warden*   Based on the name of the dance you may want to do on the grave of the one who gave you that ticket.

Gaylord   A homosexual male, an extension of gay.

Gazongas   Breasts, large ones.

GBH of the Ear'ole   Perpetual or persistent nagging: 'I'd better go or she'll give me GBH of the ear'ole for a week.'

Gear   a) A drug user's term for whatever they happen to be after: 'Got any gear?'
b) Descriptive of anything good, a term popularised by the Beatles in the 1960s. Now well dated and used almost mockingly, like 'fab'.

Gearbox   The female genitals, as penetrated by a 'gearstick' (qv).

Gearstick   The penis, an oft-used in-car double entendre especially when teaching a girlfriend to drive, when 'put your hand on me gearstick' jokes are all the rage. Possibly RS for dick/prick.

Gee   The person planted in the audience of a street-seller who 'gees-up' the crowd by rushing to be the first to 'buy' whatever's on offer.

Gee Up   a) A wind-up or a practical joke. To 'gee someone up' is to get them going. Often a 'gee up' will go too far, in which case the victim may become 'geed up' – angry.
b) To encourage, to get the best out of. A captain's job is to 'gee up' his team, i.e., get them going, which is the traditional way of getting a horse or donkey moving.

Geese   A Portuguese person, originally a World War One soldier. Also people from Portugal in general: 'Friendly people, your Geese.'

Geezer   Presently, probably the commonest term for a man. It certainly is in London where it's sometimes reduced to 'geez'.

Geezerbird   A masculine lesbian or a well-muscled female athlete.

Gel   A leg in backslang. A 'gel of kayrop' – a leg of pork.

Gelt   The yiddish word for money has been in circulation since the 17th century and still has plenty of spending power. Sometimes said as 'gelter'.

Gen		a) A long-dead term for a shilling that was often used in conjunction with backslang, 'net gens' – ten shillings.
		b) Information, to 'gen up' on is to find out all you can about a subject.
Gender Bender		A transsexual or transvestite, one who bends the rules of convention.
General Booth	*Tooth*	Based on the name of William Booth (1829–1912), the founder of the Salvation Army. How well off he was in the choppers department I know not.
General Election	*Erection*	A polite allusion to a standing member.
General Smuts	*Nuts* *(Testicles)*	Reduced to 'generals', probably to signify their importance. Based on the name and rank of a Boer War general and later prime minister of South Africa, Jan Smuts (1870–1950).
Genial		Anything good, a 1990s term that takes in everything from nice to excellent.
Geoff Hurst	a) *First*	England's World Cup hero of 1966 becomes a first-class honours degree at university.
	b) *Thirst*	Those gagging for a drink may claim to have a raging 'Geoff Hurst'. The ex-footballer was knighted in 1998.
Geoffrey Chaucer	*Saucer*	What the unrefined drink from when their tea is too hot, never heard of a 'flying Geoffrey'. After the English writer and poet (1342–1400).
George & Ringo	*Bingo*	Heard occasionally in the heyday of the Beatles, after musicians George Harrison (1943–2001) and Ringo Starr.
George & Zippy	*Nippy*	Based on a pair of TV puppets from the 1970s, this relates to cold weather and is not descriptive of Japan.
George Bernard Shaw	*Door*	Putting the wood in the hole is always reduced to closing the 'George Bernard'. Based on the Irish writer (1856–1950)
George Blake	*Snake*	Refers to a slippery, untrustworthy person, and since it's based on a British traitor would appear to be perfectly fitting.
George Melly	*Belly*	The jazz-singing art critic comes in as a paunch.
George Michael	*Cycle*	A piece from the young people's lexicon of the 1990s based on a British singer/songwriter.
George Raft	a) *Draft*	An example from the used car trade for a banker's draft. Based on an American film actor (1895–1980).
	b) *Draught*	A waft of cold air: 'There's a right George in here.' Also refers to draught beer.
	c) *Graft*	A reference to hard work, but given this actor's well-documented underworld connections, it could also apply to corruption.

George Robey	*Toby*	Based on the English comedian who was billed as the 'prime minister of mirth' (1869–1954), this originally applied to a road, for which 'toby' is an old slang term. Now more readily connected with this brand of beer.
George the Third	*Turd*	Applies to that reeking piece of gunge on the pavement that you didn't see, otherwise you would not have stepped in it. Based on the king of Britain and Ireland (1738–1820), who reigned from 1760 until his death.
Georgie Best	*a) Guest*	Refers to an invitee but is mainly used in sense of 'be my guest': 'D'you mind if I sit here?' 'Be my Georgie.'
	b) Pest	Based on the legendary Irish footballer and drinker, this applies to the drunken pest who won't leave you alone when your one desire is to be left alone.
Germ		A small, loud and irritating person, a candidate for a squirt of Harpic.
Germaine Greer	*Beer*	One of many terms that have emanated from the 'middle classes' in recent years. Based on an Australian feminist, journalist, TV panellist and probably several other 'ists'.
German Band	*Hand*	An early 20th-century term that is always reduced to 'Germans', and inspired by the fact that such musicians were a common feature in London's parks at that time. 'German job' – masturbation.
German Flutes	*Boots*	A 19th-century term from the woodwind section that's been given the breeze, i.e., blown out.
Geronimo		To ejaculate. The American war-cry gets a second coming as a yell of orgasm. From the Apache Indian chief (1829–1909).
Gerry		An old person, a shortening of geriatric. A particularly common term among nurses.
Gerry Cottle	*Bottle*	A container but mostly a reference to courage. Based on the name of a circus owner, which seems apt enough considering the 'Gerry' needed to stick one's head in a lion's mouth. *See* BOTTLE & GLASS.
Gert & Daisy	*Lazy*	Based on the comic stage personas of Elsie and Doris Waters, this is used as a direct attack on the layabout: 'You'd know what sloth meant if you weren't too Gert and Daisy to look it up.'
Gertcha/ Gertchoo		An old cockney expression of contempt or dismissal, along the lines of 'gerd-ah-dovit you', which is usually followed by a relevant expletive, famously 'gertchoo cowson'.

Gertie Gitana	*Banana*	An old term based on the British music-hall turn (1888–1957) who gave the song 'Nellie Dean' to the drunk's repertoire.
Geseech		The face, a 19th-century term for a less than pretty dial, one that needs a lie-in when it comes to beauty sleep.
Get		A bastard, largely used in the North, where it may come out as a fool, as in, 'You stupid get.'
Get/Gets		An underworld expression for an escape from prison.
Get a Creep On		To go faster, to speed up a bit: 'Come on, let's get a creep on, we're well late.'
Get a Jerk/Jig/ Shift/Wiggle/ Wriggle On		Some of the many terms demanding a bit of speed, variants of 'get a move on'.
Get At		To bribe, threaten or nobble in order to secure the right result, most commonly sportsmen, jurors and racehorses are 'got at'.
Get Fucked		A defiant retort of the strongest order.
Get Horizontal		To get into a position to have sex, i.e., to lie down.
Get in the Game		To become aware of a situation, often an instruction to someone who doesn't see, or is slow to fall in with, a joke: 'Come on, get in the game.'
Get It On		a) To have a sexual relationship: 'I see Tom's left his wife. He's been getting it on with some bird in his office.'
		b) To have a fight, a boxer's challenge to a rival: 'Let's get it on.'
Get It Up		To get an erection, to arouse John Thomas from his slumbers.
Get Knotted		A defiant retort of the mildest order. *Compare* GET FUCKED.
Get Shot Of		To throw away, to get rid of. In criminal terms to dispose of any incriminating evidence.
Get Stuffed		A defiant retort that falls somewhere between 'get fucked' and 'get knotted' in severity.
Get the Glory		To become religious, especially a prisoner who sees the light during a sentence, either for real or as a scam.
Get to Fuck		A stated desire for somebody to go somewhere else.
Gherkin		A fool or an idiot, same vegetable but different vinegar to a 'wally' (qv).
Ghettoblaster		A large portable radio/cassette player capable of blasting out music at a high rate of decibels.
Ghost		a) An extremely pale person, one who looks like 'death warmed up'. Also a derogatory term for a white person, used by black people.

b) To move silently and without disturbing the surroundings. Also to secretly follow someone.

c) A Muslim woman dressed in a white burka. The popular image of a ghost being a form covered in a white sheet.

Gianfranco Zola *Cola* Pepsi, Coke or whatever passes for cola in a pub takes the name of an Italian footballer, a star player at Chelsea, *c.* 2000.

Gianluca Vialli *Charlie (Cocaine)* A late 1990s example based on an Italian footballer who played for, and later managed, Chelsea. As a player he spent his career getting up the noses of opposing defenders.

Giblets In standard English this is the innards of a bird; in slang, however, people have them too: 'How can you say you enjoy smoking when you spend half the day coughing your giblets up?'

Gig Lamps A 19th-century term for spectacles. A gig was a light, two-wheeled carriage which, necessarily, had a lamp on either side. Wearers of glasses have long been known as 'giggers'.

Giggle & Titter *Bitter (Ale)* Commonly known as 'giggle' and apt as it gets people merry.

Giggle Juice/ Water Alcoholic drinks that get you 'merry & bright' (qv).

Giggle Stick A cannabis cigarette, often used by non-users at the smell of a 'joint' (qv): 'Someone's smoking a giggle stick.'

Gilbey's Gin *Chin* A boxer's downfall is a glass 'Gilbey's'. *See* GLASS JAW.

Gillie Potter *Trotter (Foot)* A British comedian from the early 20th century (1887–1975) lends his name to a term for a foot that steps back about 400 years. A 'Gillie' is also a pig's trotter sold as food.

Gimp Originally applied to anyone with a defective leg but got transferred to the mentally askew – 'lamebrains' – and also the clumsy, awkward type.

Gimpy An unkind name given to a cripple or 'clum' (qv).

Gin & Fuck-It A woman whose sexual favours can be bought for the price of a drink.

Gin Gan An Indian, specifically a Bengali or 'Gali'. A pun on the song 'Gin Gan Goolie' – 'Gin Gan Gali'.

Gin Gans The testicles, the 'Gin Gan Goolies'.

Gin Lane An ancient term for the throat. Cheap rotgut gin was the favourite gargle of the poor, as it led them away from reality for the duration of it's effectiveness.

Ginchy		Attractive, stylish or smart, an example from the early 1960s. The title of a hit record for British guitarist, Bert Weedon.
Ginger Ale	*Gaol*	A piece originally from the US, therefore an American ginger ale.
Ginger Beer	*a) Queer*	Widely used in the cut-down form of 'ginger'. Hence a 'ginger's' – a pub frequented by gays.
	b) Engineer	A term from the navy for the bloke who makes the boats go.
Ginger Pop	*Cop*	Generally arrested at the first element in reference to a police officer.
Gink		Originally an American term for an idiot but used here for a man, a fellow. Famously, Colonel Blink the Short-Sighted Gink – from the *Beezer* comic.
Ginormous		Massive, a well-known mix of enormous and gigantic, often used as an overexaggeration. A ginormous spot on the nose may seem bigger than it actually is.
Ginty		An Irish person, a shortening of the typical Irish name McGinty.
Giorgio Armani	*Sarnie (Sandwich)*	A piece that was in vogue in the 1990s and based on the name of an Italian fashion designer who strives to be in vogue all the time.
Giraffe	*Laugh*	A current retort to anyone 'extracting the urine' is: 'You're having a giraffe aintcha.'
Girl & Boy	*a) Saveloy*	An early piece for an early take-away.
	b) Toy	A fitting piece when the girl and boy are under 7 years. Over that and toys give way to mobile phones, computers and designer wear.
Girl/Girlie		Terms of derision aimed at weak or sissyish men: 'It's only a little spider you big girl.'
Girlieboy		An effeminate, young male homosexual, a derisive term used by boyish boys.
Girls & Boys	*Noise*	An appropriate term if ever there was one.
Gismo		A name given to something one doesn't know the name of, often a highly technical part of a machine.
Git		A venomless version of 'bastard' in that a kiddie-pest can be a 'right little git'. Although a 'rotten git' can be a nasty piece of work. The southern version of 'get' (qv).
Give & Get	*Bet*	The origin of this speaks for itself. You give the bookie your money and if you're lucky you get your winnings. A more common scenario is you give him your money and he gets to keep it.
Give & Take	*Cake*	A piece that's been served up with the afternoon 'Rosie Lee' (qv) since the 19th century.

Give a Damn/ Fuck/Monkey's/ Shit/Toss		To care about, though most commonly used in the negative, as in 'I couldn't give a . . .'
Give a Dog a Bone		To have sex with an ugly woman, even if you're an ugly man. *See* BONE *and* DOG.
Give a Sample		To urinate, a piece that's currently making a splash on TV. To 'take a sample' is to hold up to ridicule, or to 'take the piss'.
Give Five		To slap hands with someone to congratulate or seal a deal. A 'high five' is the hands-in-the-air slap, much in evidence in cricket matches.
Give it Some Boot/Clog/Welly		To accelerate, to 'put the pedal to the metal' by sticking your booted foot down. The use of welly has taken off in a different direction in that it is used as a term denoting force or strength. A foreman may tell a flagging labourer to 'Give it some wellie with that shovel.'
Give it Some Stick		To get stuck into something, to apply some force or pressure.
Give it the Big 'Un		To verbally intimidate or to act in a boastful or belligerent manner. Also to 'give it large' or 'large it'.
Give One		To have sex with. Originally a piece of male chauvinism that has been hijacked by the feminists, whereby 'I'd give her one' is now heard as 'I'd give him one' as well.
Give One's Hand One		To masturbate, to 'have it away with one's fingers'.
Give the Air/ Breeze		To get rid of, to dismiss, to wave or blow away. Often used when turning off the TV, to 'give it the air'.
Gladys Knight	*Shite*	To go for a 'Gladys' is to defecate and it is based on an American soul singer whose backing group were called the Pips, which aptly enough is a slang term for a series of farts that signify an imminent need for a 'sit-down job' (qv).
Glam Rock		A music genre of the early to mid 1970s featuring flashily dressed and made-up groups and singers, typically Gary Glitter, David Bowie, Sweet, etc.
Glarney		A marble, a term from the early 20th century, when marbles were common playthings.
Glasgow/ Gorbals Kiss		A head butt, a piece from the Scottish mean streets, or is it part of a Scot's mating ritual?
Glasgow Boat	*Coat*	To be worn when the wind blows round the Clydebank shipyards.
Glasgow Ranger	*Stranger*	Generally shortened to 'Glasgow', especially

when used by look-outs watching for police while a 'spieler' (qv) goes through his patter, whether he is selling from a suitcase or inviting people to find the lady in the three-card trick.

Glass
a) An underworld term for diamonds, whereby you can have genuine or fake glass and cut or uncut glass.

b) To hit someone in the face with a broken glass, the commonest injury in a pub fight. The victim is said to have been 'glassed'.

Glass Case *Face*
Heard at the end of a 'Grab a Granny' (qv) night: 'I didn't realise how old she was till the lights came on. Her glass was like a piece of second-hand chewing gum.'

Glass Eye at a Keyhole
A symbol of uselessness, what a 'plonker' (qv) is said to be as much use as.

Glass Jaw/Glass Chin
A supposed condition suffered by boxers who can't take a heavy punch on the chin.

Glass of Beer *Ear*
Good advice often comes as a result of a word in your 'glass of beer'.

Glass of Lunch
A lunch that consists of an alcoholic drink, usually beer, instead of food.

Glass of Plonk *Conk (Nose)*
Usually applies to a large red one, the result of an overbending of the elbow.

Glasshouse
A military prison. The name, given by inmates of the glass-roofed prison at Aldershot barracks, caught on and was given to all similar institutions.

Gleamer
What anything considered excellent, brilliant or dazzling is said to be. A sparkling or star performance is a 'gleamer'.

Glenn Hoddle *Doddle*
A simple task, courtesy of the former England footballer who went on to manage the national side. As a player, sportswriters never seemed to tire of the headline 'A Doddle for Hoddle'.

Glenn Miller
An underworld term for disappearing without a trace, i.e., to 'do a Glenn Miller'. A reference to the American bandleader (b. 1904) who was a passenger in an airplane that was lost over the English Channel in 1944.

Glenn Roeder *Soda*
Heard in an East End pub since this ex-footballer's appointment as West Ham manager in 2001: 'Put a splash of Glenn Roeder in that scotch.'

Glim/Glimmer
A torch, as carried by a member of the underworld while up to no good. A 17th-century housebreaker first carried a lantern known as a 'glim', which also served as a term for fire, and later a match.

Glimmer		To hold on to the urge to defecate is to have one on a 'glimmer', i.e., cooking on a low heat.
Glitterati		Fashionable celebrities from the world of show business and the arts, regular targets of the paparazzi.
Glitz		The presented face of show business, the glamour, showiness and bright lights.
Glop		a) A thick, sticky liquid, a piece that readily transfers to semen and ejaculation. A 'wet dream' (qv) will result in sheets full of 'glop' and a masturbator will 'strop till he glops'. *See* STROP.
		b) Inedible or unappetising food: 'I can't eat this glop.'
		c) To swallow greedily, to guzzle a glass of beer. To 'glop' it down.
Gloria Gaynors	*Trainers*	Footwear, based on an American singer whose records were aimed, aptly enough, at people's feet. If you're looking for any 'sole singer' jokes, make 'em up yourself.
Glorious Sinner	*Dinner*	A mid 19th-century term that seems to have purported that only the decadent got to eat.
Glory Be	*Tea*	An occasionally brewed alternative to 'Rosie Lee', which has often been spouted in connection with an evening meal: 'Wash your hands, your glory be's on the table.'
Gluebag		A mentally unstable person, a 'headcase': 'You never know how he'll react, he's a total gluebag.'
Glue Pot	*Twat (Vagina)*	Touching which results in a sticky finger.
Glug		To drink alcohol: 'I always glug a drop of scotch at bedtime, it helps me sleep.'
Gnashers		A well-known term for the teeth, those that are gnashed. 'Gnasher Snatcher' – a dentist.
Gnat Bites		Small breasts, a piece of male chauvinist mockery. Like 'bee stings' (qv).
Gnat's Piss		A weak, insipid drink, especially tea, which is often winced at as 'gnats'. Also applies to cheap or low-alcohol beer or lager.
Go a Bundle On		To like very much, to strongly fancy. Or not, as in: 'Mine's nice but I don't go a bundle on yours.'
Go all the Way		To have sexual intercourse, an adolescent piece used in describing a conquest: 'I didn't think she'd go all the way on the first date, but she did.'
Go Ape		To go berserk, to 'do a King Kong'.
Go Down		To perform oral sex, either fellatio or cunnilingus.
Go Figure		An exclamation of puzzlement akin to: 'You work it out. I can't.'

Go Into	To borrow from: 'I'll go into the old woman for a few quid.'
Go into One	To lose one's temper, to go into a rage: 'All I did was slag off his haircut and he went into one.'
Go Scratch/Go Scratch Yourself	A refusal, a definite knockback akin to 'get lost'.
Go Squeeze Your Balls!	Get lost! Go away and do yourself some damage! Sometimes reduced to 'squeeze 'em'.
Go the Limit	To have sexual intercourse, a term used by young men when talking of their latest 'pull': 'I got a sticky finger but she wouldn't go the limit.'
Go Through	To have sexual intercourse. Famously the Max Miller joke: 'My wife weighs twenty stone. What I go through.'
Go through the Card	A sexual encounter in which various positions and practices are carried out.
Go to Hell in a Handcart	To come to a bad end. A favourite saying of journalist Richard Littlejohn, who is convinced that this is the fate awaiting mankind. *To Hell in a Handcart* – the title of his 2001 novel.
Go Upstairs	To drink spirits in a pub. Beer is poured at bar level but the shorts are higher up.
Go Walkabout in the Bush Down Under	Of a woman, to masturbate. To wander through the undergrowth.
Go-Ahead	Forward-thinking or progressive, especially of a person, e.g., a 'go-ahead' manager.
Goalie/ Goalkeeper	The ace in a pack of cards, the keeper wears the number one shirt.
Goat	a) A miserable old man: 'Stop moaning you old goat.'
	b) A bad man or one who does you a bad turn. The driver who cuts you up may be a 'goat' of a driver; a jobsworth barman who won't serve you a minute past closing time gets a similar tag.
Gob	a) A 17th-century term for the mouth that's still about. 'Gobby' people still have too much to say.
	b) A punch in the mouth: 'D'you want a gobbing?'
	c) To spit. Part of the punk culture of the late 1970s was 'gobbing', when groups and their audiences would engage in 'gob fights', i.e., spit at each other.
Gob Iron	A mouth organ or harmonica, a musician's term.
Gob Job	Fellatio, another version of a 'blow job' (qv).
Gobble	The word for noisy eating is a 19th-century term for fellatio, as popular today as it ever was.

Gobbler		Someone who actively enjoys performing fellatio.
Gobbler's Gulch		A place where homosexuals meet for sex. *See* GOBBLE.
Gobshite		A term of abuse for a contemptible or despicable person, largely used in the north of England and in Ireland.
Gobsmacked		Astonished, left speechless with a gasted flabber. A well-known and oft-used term.
Gobstopper	*Chopper (Penis)*	Often used in connection with oral sex: 'Suck it and see if it changes colour.' Based on a sweet that does when you do.
God Almighty	*Nightie*	Probably one of those sexy, not-to-be-slept-in jobs that get men drooling and taking the Lord's name in vain.
God Damn	*Jam*	Has been spread on 'holy ghost' (qv) since the Lord only knows.
God Forbid	a) *Kid*	Coined in the days when the method of birth control was often the prayer 'God forbid we have any more God forbids.' On the whole it wasn't a successful method.
	b) *Lid (Hat)*	A seldom-worn piece, although it has been heard in connection with a crash helmet (a skid-lid), the inference being 'God forbid I should ever need it'.
	c) *Quid*	Heard at a market butcher's stall at closing time: 'God forbid I should rob myself but who'll give me a couple of God forbid for this piece of beef?'
	d) *Yid*	An obvious piece since this expression is as much a part of Jewish tradition as matzos, salt beef and the Ten Commandments. From the silent prayer of the Jewish taxi driver: 'God forbid the bulb in my For Hire sign should go.' To the assurance of the baker: 'God forbid I should ever sell you a stale beigel.'
God in Heaven	*Seven*	A piece from the bingo hall.
God Love Her	*Mother*	A piece that's used in the third person, when talking about your 'Gawd luvver'.
God Save the Queens	*Greens*	A jocular reference to green vegetables and used in full when trying to get the kids to eat them.
God Squad		Any religious group, especially one trying to preach the gospel by knocking on street doors or setting out their stalls in crowded places, like shopping precincts, markets, etc.
Goddess Diana	*Tanner*	If this old coin was still with us it would no doubt have been renamed a 'Princess Diana'.
Goer		a) Anything mechanically sound, something that works: 'The car may be old but she's a goer.'

b) A promiscuous woman, one who 'goes like a rabbit'.

Gofer — An errand boy or a lackey, someone sent to 'go for' this or 'go for' that.

Goggle — To stare, an ancient piece of voyeurism.

Goggle Box — A 1950s term for a television. Early TVs resembled great boxes and were goggled at in wonder.

Goggles — Originally a term for the eyes, which later got transferred to glasses. Also a nickname for a spectacle wearer.

Going-Over — A beating, anyone who has been on the wrong end of an assault has had a 'going-over'.

Gold Ring — *King* — At the moment this applies to a playing card, but if his mother ever moves over, there's a ready-made piece of RS for Charles III.

Gold Watch — *Scotch* — A very common term for whisky that is never said in short.

Golden Hind — *Blind* — Said sympathetically: 'Bad eyes? She's almost Golden Hind, poor cow.' Inspired by the name of the vessel in which Francis Drake plundered the Spanish treasure ships while sailing around the world in 1579–80.

Golden Oldie — Originally a radio presenter's term for an old record that's still worth listening to. It later got transferred to anything good for it's age, including people.

Golden Shower — A urine shower, part of a prostitute's list of services.

Golden Syrup — An obvious wig, from the merging of the rhyming slang 'syrup of fig' – wig, known as a 'syrup', and 'golden' in the guise of outstanding. A giant mockery.

Goldie Hawn — *Prawn* — A 1990s update of the older 'Frankie Vaughan' (qv), based on an American film actress.

Goldilocks — *Pox* — One of many references to VD, this is the type caught through sharing a bed with a bear or three. Also to be fed up with something: 'I've got the right Goldilocks of this.'

Golliwog — *Dog* — Applies to all mutts but mainly to greyhounds, whereby to go dog racing is to go to the 'gollies'.

Golliwog(gy) — *Fog(gy)* — When you can't see your hand in front of your face, you've either got your eyes closed or it's 'bloody golly'.

Gollopagoose — A greedy person, a glutton. Someone who could swallow (gollop) an item of poultry.

Golly/Gollier — A lump of phlegm coughed up and spat where anyone can tread in it. In Australia it means to spit.

Golly/Golliwog — Offensive terms from the 1950s for a black person.

Gom		A gormless, soppy-looking person. The bloke on holiday that the time-share sharks home in on.
Gone		a) Drunk or drugged out of one's skull. Also to be enthralled or taken over by music.
		b) Mad, crazy. Off one's head.
Gone for a Burton		Originally an RAF term from World War Two for dead, especially a shot-down pilot. It later got expanded to anything missing or broken. Since there are so many plausible explanations for the term, the true meaning remains uncertain.
Gone Native		Police jargon, said of an officer who has turned criminal.
Gone to Bed	*Dead*	Sadly stated: 'Old Steve's gone to bed and he ain't getting up.'
Gone West		Passed, failed or dead: 'That's another idea gone west.'
Gonef/Ganef/ Gonnof/Gunnef		A thief, no matter how it's said or spelt (it's actually from the hebrew *gannath* – thief), it's someone who has 'gonnof' with someone else's property.
Goner		A dead person or one who is doomed or terminally ill.
Gonga/ Gongapooch		The anus, a pair of old terms used to tell people where to shove the unwanted. Gongapooch is a Hindu word for bum.
Gonies		The testicles, a corruption of gonads. An American merging of both is 'gonicles'.
Gonk		a) A fool, a slow-witted dolt. Based on a troll-like doll of the 1960s which resembled a slow-witted foolish dolt.
		b) A prostitute's client, from the same source as (a).
Gonzo		An embellished version of 'gone' (qv, a, b): 'Sorry if I made a pest of myself last night. I was gonzo' – an apologetic drunk.
Gonzo the Great	*State*	To be in a bad way, a state of panic, agitation or drunkenness is to be in a right old 'Gonzo'. A 1990s term based on the name of a character from TV's *The Muppet Show*.
Good & Bad	*Dad*	An old term for the old man.
Good News		Sexual intercourse, used especially as the result of a conquest or a successful 'pull': ' We slipped out of the party and I gave her the good news in the car.'
Good Ship Venus	*Penis*	Based on the title of a well-known rugby song, it's a ship to go down on.
Good Time Charlie/Jane		A man (Charlie) or woman (Jane) with loose morals.

Good 'Un		Someone who can be trusted, as opposed to a 'wrong 'un' (qv), who can't.
Goodie & Baddie	*Paddy*	Reduced to a 'goodie' in reference to an Irish person, even if they are a baddie.
Goodnight Kiss	*Piss*	Another of many terms rhyming kiss and piss, although not one of the better-known ones.
Goods, the		Incriminating evidence or information, the job of an undercover cop is to 'get the goods' on a suspect.
Goof		a) A fool, a senseless or dull-witted oaf. Goof-proof – foolproof.
		b) To make a mistake or a complete mess of something. To 'goof up'.
Goofy		a) Stupid, thick or dopey, like the Disney dog.
		b) Having large protruding teeth, famously a 'goofy grin'.
Googy		An egg, an ancient piece of backslang said as a stuttered g-ge.
Gooliboos		The testicles, an extension of 'goolies' (qv).
Goolies		The testicles, from the hindu word *goli* meaning a ball or pill. Commonly to have someone by the 'goolies' is to have them under your control. Also to 'goolie' is to strike below the belt.
Goon		a) An idiot, the thick-headed dolt of the 1930s, who became synonymous with loonism in the 1950s radio series *The Goon Show*.
		b) A henchman or hired muscle, someone not paid to think.
		c) A prisoners-of-war term from World War Two for a German guard.
Gooner		A supporter of Arsenal Football Club, a play on the team's nickname, the Gunners.
Goose		To poke or pinch someone's backside, to touch them up.
Goose & Duck	*Fuck*	A couple of birds come in for sexual intercourse but it's the first one that gets all the attention, as it's always known as a 'goose' or to 'goose'.
Gooseberry Bush		Female pubic hair, where babies are said to be found under.
Gooseberry Pudden	*Woman*	Used as the 'old gooseberry' meaning the wife. Not a great rhyme but who cares?
Gooseberry Tart	*a) Fart*	Similar gut droppage to 'apple tart' (qv). Same pastry, different filling.
	b) Heart	One of several fruit puddings making this connection.
Goose's Neck	*Cheque*	Always reduced to the first element, a duff cheque is a 'rubber gooses' – it bounces.
Gordon & Gotch	*Watch*	Always stopped at a 'Gordon', this is based on a

small firm from East London which dealt in books and magazines before getting into computers and moving to a city address.

Gordon Bennett   A familiar euphemism for 'gor blimey'. Same initials, same sentiment.

Gorilla   a) A hard, violent man, often a hired thug or an enforcer.

b) A 1970s term for £1000, the worth of two 'monkeys' (qv).

Gorillas in the   *Pissed*   A 1990s term for inebriation based on the 1988 film
Mist   of this title. You're well 'gorillas' when you see pink elephants in the Red Lion.

Gorm   For a 'gorm' *see* GOM.

Gospel Oak   *Joke*   Formed on the name of an area of North-West London and about as common these days as a 'gospel' on TV's *EastEnders*.

Got Out of Pawn   *Born*   Oldish and used jokingly in connection with refuting gullibility: 'What d'you think, I've just been got out of pawn?'

Goy   A Jewish word for a non-Jewish person.

Grab a Granny   For a young man to 'pull' an older woman. 'Grab a Granny Night' – an over-40s night at a pub or club.

Grabbers   A 19th-century term for the hands that's forever apt.

Graeme Hick   *Dick/Prick*   The penis, courtesy of the England cricketer, born in Rhodesia.

Graft   Hard work, a labourer's lot. 'No-one ever got rich grafting for a living' – a layabout's excuse.

Grafter   Someone who works hard. Also anyone with their fingers in a lot of pies, who goes to great lengths to earn a few quid.

Graham Gooch   *Hooch*   An England cricket captain comes in as a brand of alcoholic drink much loved by the young, drink-from-the-bottle brigade. A term from 1990s youth.

Grand   A universally well-known term for £1000.

Grand Coolie   *Ham*   Probably unheard for forty years but when this title
Dam   formed a top-ten hit for Lonnie Donegan in 1958 the 'Grand Coolie' sandwich was popular in some quarters. The Grand Coulee Dam crosses the Columbia river in Washington state.

Grandfather   *Cock (Penis)*   If a cleaner offers to polish your grandfather clock,
Clock   let her!

Granite   *Shoulder(s)*   'Put Your Loaf on My Granite' – a song from the RS
Boulder(s)   charts. *See* LOAF OF BREAD.

Grannie Grunt   *Cunt*   No anatomical usage here. A 'grannie' is someone who is annoyingly sensible or old womanish, the

Sunday driver with the three-mile queue of traffic behind him, for instance.

Grannie's Wrinkle *Winkle*
The seafood, part of the traditional cockney Sunday tea is known as a 'grannies'.

Granny
a) A person, could be a young man, who behaves like an old woman in that they are fussy, prissy or granny-like.
b) The unspecified thing that people who take a fearful beating have removed by their assailants. 'I saw this poor Arsenal supporter getting the granny kicked out of him by some Spurs fans.'

Granny Lane
The inside lane of a motorway, the one favoured by slow, granny-like drivers.

Grapefruits
Breasts, a piece from the fruit basket, along with 'apples' and 'melons'. *See both.*

Grapes
A well-used euphemism for haemorrhoids, those that give a sufferer the pip.

Grapevine *Line*
The major employment here is a clothesline. Never actually heard of a drowning person being thrown a 'grape'. May also be a rival of 'Patsy Cline' (qv).

Grass
a) A well-known, long-smouldering term for marijuana.
b) The hair, thus to 'cut the grass' is to get a haircut.
c) An informer, a well-known shortening of 'grasshopper' (qv). To 'grass up' – to inform on.

Grass in the Park *Nark*
An informer, an extension of 'grasshopper' (qv), in that the police are called the 'narks' (qv).

Grasshopper *Copper*
So familiar in the shortened version 'grass' that it has passed into everyday language for an informant. Still applies, as originally intended, to a police officer, but very much secondarily.

Grave Digger *Nigger*
'Grave diggers' is an old expression for spades, the card suit. A 'spade' is also a black person.

Gravel & Grit *Shit*
Always reduced to the first element, whereby the constipated are in dire need of a 'gravel'.

Graveyard
An old term for the mouth, teeth being known as 'tombstones' (qv).

Graveyard Shift
Night work, especially of shift workers. Sometimes they're on days and sometimes on the 'graveyard'.

Gravy
a) Semen, to 'pour one's gravy' is to ejaculate.
b) Symbolic of the best or an extra bonus. The 'gravy on the pudden' is akin to the 'icing on the cake'. Also in the saying 'the navy gets the gravy but the army gets the beans'.

Grease
a) Money, especially in the context of a bribe, famously to grease someone's palm.

b) Butter, margarine or one of those buttery-type spreads.

c) A lubricant. A homosexual's aid to better buggery.

Grease Burger   An inferior hamburger, especially one sold from a van or a stall.

Grease Monkey   A mechanic, especially a motor fitter.

Greaser   a) Originally a Teddy Boy, a reference to the mittfuls of Brylcream he slicked his hair down with.

b) A Rocker, a derogatory term used by Mods during the 1960s. 'Greasers' were motorcycle enthusiasts, given to wearing dirty jeans and leather jackets, an affront to their sartorial rivals.

Greasy Spoon   A transport caff or eating house of the type that give health inspectors nightmares.

Great Unwashed   A well-known expression for the common people, the hoi polloi, the rabble.

Grebo   From the 1980s, a scruffy, loutish rock-music fan.

Greek   Anal intercourse and a man who indulges in it, based on a supposed Greek inclination.

Green Crystal Job   A 1970s term that is still in effect regarding drinking and driving. Early breathalysers had yellow crystals that turned green in the event of a positive test, therefore anyone over the limit may say: 'One for the road? No thanks. I'm probably a green crystal job already.'

Green Gilbert   A thick, green lump of phlegm, usually seen reclining on the pavement. Also called a 'greenie'.

Greenacre   An accident. A piece that was common in London's docks industry, when it had one. Formed on the name of an accident-prone docker.

Greener/Greenie   A naive person, a novice in the ways of life. Someone said to be 'as green as a frog's bollocks'. Green has been the colour of an innocent since the 17th century, when the countryside was known as the 'green', as was a country dweller who, to the townie, was seen as a gullible clod and ripe for the taking. Green man – the country.

Greengage   *Stage*   A theatrical expression for the boards that are trodden.

Greengages   *Wages*   A 19th-century term for a weekly pay packet, often shortened to 'greens'.

Greens   a) Sexual fulfilment: 'Where are you getting your greens from since you split with your wife?'

b) Paper money. *See* CABBAGE *and* SPINACH.

Greens & Brussels	*Muscles*	Apt since we are told from an early age that green vegetables make us big and strong.
Gregory Peck	*a) Cheque*	A term that's common with the criminal fraternity and people who would rather be paid in cash. To 'sausage a Gregory' – to cash a cheque. *See* SAUSAGE & MASH.
	b) Neck	Based on an American actor (1916–2003), this has acquired a wide usage in Christian name form: 'Go and have a wash, and don't forget your Gregory.'
Gregory Pecks	*Kecks (Trousers)*	Scousers have been wearing kecks for generations, now they wear 'Gregorys'.
Greville Starkey	*Darkie*	This British ex-jockey is a forerunner to 'Feargal Sharkey' (qv) as a reference to a black person.
Grey Mare	*Fare*	An example from the days of the horseless carriage that still applies to bus, train and even plane fares.
Grief		Trouble or pain. A pest or tight shoes might give you grief.
Griff		Information. 'What's the griff?' – What's the word?
Grimsby Docks	*Socks*	Given Grimsby's connection with the fishing industry, this has to apply to footwear that cover kipper feet or socks that reek of dead haddock.
Grind		A common term for an act of sexual intercourse. Also to 'grind' – to have sex.
Grinder		A sportsman who wears down an opponent by hard work and relentless pressure. The nickname of Canadian snooker player Cliff Thorburn, world champion in 1980.
Grinders		The teeth, for reasons that are bitingly obvious.
Gristle Grabber		A two-faced, back-stabbing person. You can't trust a 'gristle grabbing bastard'.
Grizz		A grey beard, especially on a man.
Groan & Grunt	*Cunt*	A seldom used alternative to 'grumble and grunt' (qv).
Grocer's Shop	*Wop*	A 'grocers' is a 1970s term for an Italian. *See* WOP.
Grogan		A thick head of hair, a typical Irish name for a typically Irish trait. In America 'grogans' are bushy sideburns.
Groin/Groyne		A ring containing a stone, especially a diamond.
Groove		a) A scar, especially a facial one.
		b) Anything enjoyable or pleasurable. Originally a jazz fan's term, whereby to be 'in the groove' meant to be in tune with a piece of music, like a needle in the groove of a record. The term was taken over in the 1960s by the hippy generation and expanded so that anything that gives pleasure is a 'groove'. Also to 'groove' is to enjoy oneself, to have a good time.

Groovy
A 1960s term, well loved among the fashionable set, for anything considered great, wonderful, excellent, etc. Never caught on at street level and I don't think I ever met anyone who said it, except as a mockery of those who did. It's now used derisively of 1960s fashion.

Grope
A clumsy, often unwanted, fondle for sexual pleasure. A 'groper' can be a sex pest.

Grosvenor Squares   *Flares*
Often used condescendingly by young people when they see anybody wearing this wide-bottomed leg-wear, whether it be on a die-hard hippy or their parents' wedding photos (although fashionable as we go to press). Always 'Grosvenors'.

Grot
a) Rubbish, tat. Anything useless or substandard.
b) Dirt, muck or squalor. A slovenly person may live in a 'grot-hole'.

Grotbag
A dirty, squalid, altogether unsavoury person.

Grotty
Descriptive of anyone, anything or anywhere dirty, squalid or unpleasant.

Groucho Marx   *Sparks*
A building-site workers' reference to an electrician. Always a 'Groucho', after the American comedian (1890–1977).

Groupie
A girl who hangs around, and offers herself sexually to, rock musicians.

Growl & Grunt   *Cunt*
A rarely used alternative to 'grumble and grunt' (qv).

Gruesome & Gory   *Cory (Penis)*
Always a 'gruesome', and inspired by the old 'touch it again it's gruesome more' joke.

Grumble & Grunt   *Cunt*
In the reduced form of 'grumble', this applies to women as sex objects. Men go out to pull a bit of 'grumble'.

Grumble & Mutter   *Flutter (Bet)*
Inspired by what a losing punter does all the way home from the track or betting shop.

Grunge
Dirt, grime or anything distasteful, an American version of 'grot' (qv, b).

Grunt
To break wind: 'Why don't you go to the carsey? You've been grunting like a pig all day,' – said by a long-suffering victim of a 'foul-arse' (qv).

Grunter
a) An ancient term for a pig that got transferred to a policeman in the 19th century. *See* PIG.
b) A piece of 1980s kidspeak for a miserable adult, an old moaner.

Guardianista
A term from millennium year coined by columnist and broadcaster Richard Littlejohn. It refers to left-wing officials in local government and education who typically read the *Guardian* newspaper and try to inflict their will on the rest of us.

Guff		a) Empty talk, lies or nonsense: 'Don't give me that old guff.' b) Any messy, sticky or greasy substance, often semen. 'I'm not having your guff seeping out of me all day' – a refusal of early morning sex. c) To break wind, and if a 'bubble' (qv, d) is involved, then 'guff' (b) may be also.
Guillemot	*Twat*	The sea bird swoops in as an expression for a fool, generally in the guise of a 'gilly'.
Guinea Pig	*Wig*	A mocking piece heard at the sight of a ghastly gagga (qv) that resembles a small furry animal: 'Cop the geezer with the guinea pig on his head.'
Guiver/Gyver		A well-dressed, swaggering young working-class man, thus 'to have all the old gyver' is to be full of confidence.
Gumby		A fool or a moronic dunce. From a character in TV's *Monty Python's Flying Circus*.
Gummy/Gums		A toothless person, either term is often used as a nickname.
Gump		A fool or simpleton, typically the character immortalised by comedian Sir Norman Wisdom.
Gumshoe		A private detective or a plain clothes police officer. Originally an American term, where a gumshoe is a galosh, the idea being that detectives wear soft shoes while uniformed officers wear boots.
Gun		a) An old term for a man's personal weapon, i.e., his penis. b) To hit the accelerator pedal with force, to 'gun the motor'. c) A smoker's pipe: 'Oh no! Grandad's loading his gun again. Someone hide the matches.'
Gunfire		Anal 'gunfire', that is, an outbreak of wind, loud reports fired from the anus: 'Did I hear gunfire?'
Gunga Din	*Chin*	Based on a character of Rudyard Kipling's creation, the 'Gunga' has a wide circulation.
Gunge/Gunk		A messy, greasy or sticky substance. 'Gunge' being the British version of the American 'gunk'. 'Gungy' and 'gunky' are the common adjectives.
Gunner Sugdens		Long, baggy, old-fashioned shorts. The type worn by this character in the TV sitcom *It Ain't Half Hot Mum* played by diminutive singer/comedian Don Estelle.
Gunpowder Plot	*Hot*	Possibly from standing too close to the bonfire on November 5. Happy memories of a 1950s nipper-hood: 'Pleased to Remember'

We went and took our grannie's table, struggled with it down the stairs,
Put it on a homemade barrer with a pair of broken chairs.
Two boys dragged an ancient sideboard, a nipper helped them with a drawer
And having prised it off its hinges, triumphant vandals lugged a door.
All was taken to a bombsite, piled into a pointed heap;
A guy was put into position, like a guard but sound asleep.
Reams of paper stuffed inside it, someone's dad set it alight –
Soon the flames were soaring upward, burning fiercely, burning bright.
Sparklers sparkling, bangers banging, happy faces glowing red;
Blazing timber roaring loudly, rockets whizzing overhead.
In the morning all was different, glowing embers marked the spot
Where the greatest ever bonfire celebrated the Gunpowder Plot.

Gunsel — A Yiddish term for a gunman, a hired thug.

Gupta — An Indian or Pakistani, a piece that came into existence in the 1980s with the TV series *Only When I Laugh*, which featured an Indian character called Gupta.

Gurgler — A lavatory, for obvious reasons. A 1950s term so hardly in its first flush of youth.

Gutrot — A low-quality alcoholic drink – bad beer, cheap wine or dodgy spirit.

Guts/Guts Gotcha — A glutton or at least someone with a hearty appetite. A 'greedy guts'.

Gutted — To be deeply disappointed, highly devastated or just plain sorry. 'Gutter' – a huge disappointment.

Guv/Guv'nor — General terms of address to people in authority, well-known in television police dramas. Also an address to strangers: 'Where to, guv?' – just about every cab driver who ever drew breath.

Guy — To run away, to escape. Also to 'guy off'.

Guy Fawke *Walk* — A 19th-century term and one that is most commonly connected with an easy victory, especially of a horse or greyhound: 'The favourite Guyed it.' Based on Guy Fawkes, the gunpowder plotter (1570–1606).

Guzunder — An old term for a chamber pot, that which 'goes under' the bed. Or did in the days of the outdoor lavatory.

Guzunter *Punter* — An old example for the bookie's bread and butter. The term is a variation of 'guzunder' (qv). Fitting then, that bookmakers like nothing more than a losing punter, or one that goes under.

Guzzle — a) To drink, especially vast quantities of beer. To drink beer quickly is to 'gas guzzle'.
b) Beer, a surfeit of which will get you 'guzzled' – drunk. 'Guzzle-guts' – a regular beer drinker, often a drunkard, or a glutton, a permanently hungry 'scoff-the-lot'.

Gyp		a) To cheat, swindle or refuse to honour a debt. Also a 'rip off': 'Three quid for a choc-ice? What a gyp.' b) Pain or discomfort, common for an injury to give you 'gyp'.
Gyppo		A familiar version of gypsy, taking in travellers and tinkers.
Gypsy's Kiss	*Piss*	Old and very common for men to leave their beers to go for a 'gypsys'.
Gypsy's Warning	*Morning*	Always halved to the first element: 'See you in the gypsys.'

H

H		Heroin, a term common to addicts, dealers and the drug squad.
Hack It		To handle a situation, to manage: 'We had to let old Wag go, he couldn't hack it any more.'
Hack Off		To annoy, irk or generally give someone the 'right raving hump'.
Hackney Marsh(es)	*Glass(es)*	An old term for a drinking vessel, but newer in the form of spectacles or binoculars.
Hackney Wick	*Prick (Penis)*	Given Hackney's location in East London, it's a puzzle as to why this is of secondary usage to the widely used 'Hampton Wick' (qv).
Haddock & Bloater	*Motor*	An example from the time before King Car ruled.
Haddock & Cod	*Sod*	Always reduced to the first of this finny duo and used as a mild expletive. A cheeky child may be called a 'saucy little haddock'.
Haemorrhoid Hitman		A male homosexual, a reference to anal intercourse. *See also* PILEDRIVER.
Haggis		A Scottish person, sometimes jock-ularly named 'Angus 'Aggis'.
Haggisland		Scotland, as described by a Sassenach. Also the 'Land of the Rising Haggis', which conjours up thoughts of people throwing up after eating one.

Hail & Rain	*Train*	An ancient piece that has all but run out of track.
Haircut		A short prison sentence, time served between haircuts.
Haircut & Shave	*Grave*	Heard in the moan of a harrassed father whose wayward son was bent on sending him to an early haircut. Also to paraphrase the saying: 'There'll be two dates on your haircut but all that matters is the little dash between them.'
Hairpin		A homosexual who, like a hairpin, is 'bent'.
Hair-Up		A fight between women, where the hair-pull is a common hold. The female version of a men's 'tear-up' (qv).
Hairy		a) Dangerous, precarious or frightening, probably from 'hair-raising'.
		b) Anything old or out of date. Something so old, it's got whiskers on.
Hairy Doughnut		A 1990s term for the vagina, one of a million. Some too crude even for me.
Hairy Fairy		A particularly hirsute male homosexual.
Hairy-Arsed		Rough, tough and aggressive. Said of someone nursing a bruised face: 'Serves him right, he got lairy with some hairy-arsed lorry driver and came unstuck.'
Hale & Hearty	*Party*	Apt in that it conjours up pictures of healthy enjoyment. But not on the morning after.
Hale & Pace	*Face*	Based on a British comedy double-act, whereby a miserable person may have a 'Hale and Pace like a squeezed orange'.
Half		A half of a pound, i.e., 50p. Originally ten shillings.
Half a Crown	*Brown*	Heard in the snooker hall regarding this coloured ball. A not-too-apt example, as a half a crown was a silver coin worth 12½p in today's currency.
Half a Dollar	*Collar*	Said in reduction as 'arfer', often in connection with a dog's collar, although probably not at Crufts. A dollar was 25p-worth of pre-decimal currency.
Half a Gross	*Dose (VD)*	How a dose of the clap becomes an 'arfa'.
Half a Nicker	*Vicar*	Shortened to 'arfer', it may seem an irreverent reference to his Reverence. Half a nicker is 50p.
Half a Stretch		An underworld term for six months in prison. *See* STRETCH.
Half a Surprise		A black eye. Taken from the song: 'Two lovely black eyes. Oh what a surprise.' Thus one shiner.
Half & Halfer		A bisexual, half one way and half the other.
Half Inch	*Pinch*	Very familiar in relation to stealing and to a lesser

extent to being arrested. An example that is never shortened.

Half Iron
A bisexual, fifty per cent of the RS 'iron hoof'.

Half of Marge *Sarge*
An underworld reference to one who leaves a nasty taste in the mouth, a police sergeant.

Half Ounce *a) Bounce (Beat Up)*
I hope you never find out how many 'half ounces' there are in a pounding.

b) Bounce (Cheat)
Anyone thick enough to try to find the lady in the three-card trick deserves to be 'half ounced'.

Half Ounce of Baccy *Paki*
A variant of 'ounce of baccy' (qv), and reduced to 'half ounce' in relation to a Pakistani child.

Half Ouncer *Bouncer*
A doorman, a professional 'chucker outer'.

Half Past Two *Jew*
One of many terms culminating in 'two' for the chosen one.

Half Pint
A child or a grown-up who didn't grow very high.

Half-Soaked
Foolish, daft. How a halfwit may be described up North.

Half Stamp *Tramp*
An early 20th-century term, possibly based on a slow walk. A stamp being a slang term for a walk.

Half-Mast
A semi-erect penis, usually that of a drunken man who can't quite fly the flag.

Halfway House
The halfway point between a flaccid and erect penis, a semi-erection. Also known as a lazy lob.

Ham
A ham-ateurish actor, one given to overacting.

Ham & Beef *Chief*
A 19th-century prisoner's reference to a chief warder.

Ham & Egg(s) *Leg(s)*
Usually employed in relation to the shapely female variety: 'Nice hams. What's her face like?'

Ham Shank *a) Wank*
A 1990s term for 'rubbing up the right way'. Also anything valueless isn't worth a 'ham shank' and a worthless or despicable person is a 'ham shanker'.

b) Yank
A World War Two term for an American that's still common. During the 2001 foot-and-mouth crisis, the tourist trade suffered as a result of a shortage of 'ham shanks' visiting our shores.

Hambone *Phone*
Occasionally used but is, by and large, gobbled up by 'dog'. See DOG & BONE.

Hammer & Discus *Whiskers*
Facial hair, probably as grown by East European athletes of yore who swept the board at chucking-heavy-objects-great-distances events. The men weren't bad either.

Hammer & Nail *Tail*
Normally reduced to the first element, it means to follow. Show me someone driving at 30mph and I'll show you a driver being 'hammered' by the police. A dog may also wag it's 'hammer'.

Hammer & Saw *Law*
Normally used in connection with a police officer: 'Look out here comes the hammer.'

Hammer & Tack	*Back*	Once common on building sites when a foreman wanted the navvies to put their hammers into it.
Hammer		a) To thrash thoroughly or to criticise severely. Poor workmanship is rightly hammered. b) A bodyguard or hired muscle, someone with a knockout punch. c) An ancient term for the penis that is still banging away, especially as an expression for the sex act: 'She's like a nail, she wants constant hammering.' d) To work hard and long on a laborious task. To 'hammer' away. e) The accelerator pedal: 'Sorry officer I didn't realise I had the hammer down.' f) An inclination, one's own thing: 'I think I'll go to the pictures, that's more my hammer.' – Tony Hancock (The Poetry Society).
Hammered		Drunk. When you wake up feeling like someone is trying to smash your skull from the inside, you know you've been hammered.
Hammeroids		West Ham United supporters, so called because they consider themselves to be a pain in the arse of rival fans.
Hampden Roar	*Score (£20)*	A 1980s term based on the noise that Scottish football fans make at Hampden Park.
Hampstead Heath	*Teeth*	Very old and still widely used in the reduced form of 'Hampsteads' or 'Hamps'.
Hampton Court	*Salt*	It's not only women in porn movies who pass the 'Hampton'. *See* HAMPTON WICK.
Hampton Wick	*Prick (Penis)*	A well-known term and one that is unusual in that it can be reduced to both elements. The male member is commonly termed 'Hampton'; indeed Hugh Jampton has been a character in many a comedy sketch. The second part is equally familiar; coitus is known as 'dipping one's wick' and few people realise what 'you get on my wick' actually means.
Han Solo		Masturbation, handling your own sex life. A pun on the character in the film *Star Wars*.
Hancocks		Half an hour. A 1950s term that may still have a currency with fans of British comedian Tony Hancock (1924–68), whose radio show, *Hancock's Half Hour*, drew millions of listeners: 'I'll be with you in an 'ancocks.'
Hand & Fist	*Pissed*	A piece that's never shortened. if you had too much to drink, trust me, you was 'hand and fist'.
Hand Job		Masturbation, often a service offered by a prostitute.

Hand Shandy		Masturbation, often the first sex received from a girlfriend: 'I finally got a hand shandy off her.'
Handbags at Twenty Paces		A fight where neither protagonist really wants to hurt the other, a something of nothing, a heat of the moment flare-up. Especially common on the football field, where feuds come, go and are forgotten at the final whistle.
Handful		a) Due to having five digits, that number of anything is a 'handful', e.g., it's five people, five runners in a race, a winning distance of five lengths and odds of 5/1.
		b) A five stretch, i.e., a five-year prison sentence.
		c) £5. *See* DOUBLE HANDFUL.
Handful of Sprats		Vaginal stimulation, a term from the 1950s that connects the vagina with the smell of fish. Before the sexual revolution in the 1960s a young man thought he was doing OK if he got this far: 'I got a bit of tit and a handful of sprats.'
Handicap	*Clap (VD)*	A pertinent example, whereby having a 'handicap' makes you a non-runner in the sex stakes.
Handicap Chase	*Face*	Usually employed at the sight of a custard-curdling geseech (qv): 'Look at the handicap on him.'
Handle		a) An ancient term for the nose, also known as the 'handle of the face' and the 'face handle'.
		b) A name, nickname or alias; whatever you're known by is your 'handle'.
Handley Page	*Stage*	An old theatrical piece for the theatrical boards, based on Sir Frederick Handley Page (1885–1962), the pioneering British aircraft designer.
Hands & Feet	*Meat*	A vegetarian's nightmare, often reduced to 'hands'.
Handshake		A tip or a bribe. Much can be achieved by a decent 'handshake'. 'Did you shake the waiter's hand?' – Did you give the waiter a tip?
Handsome		A well-known cockney term of approval for anything considered excellent or delicious. If a bigger superlative is required, the term is doubled to ''andsome 'andsome'.
Handwriting		The size and appearance of someone in relation to someone else: 'He was about your handwriting.'
Handy		Anything good, useful or admirable. Anyone 'handy' with their fists takes in all three.
Handyman		An impotent man or one who suffers from premature ejaculation. He has to bring his partner to orgasm by hand.
Hang a Louie		Make a left turn, an initial connection.
Hang a Ralph		Make a right turn, from the initials of right and Ralph.

Hang One On		To punch: 'I'll hang one on you if you don't hold your noise.'
Hangar Lane	*Pain*	This is pain in the sense of a nuisance or annoyance and is a diminuitive of 'pain in the neck' or 'arse'. The term is appropriate because Hangar Lane is a notorious road junction in West London, where traffic jams are the norm.
Hangings		A World War Two term for a man's genitalia, probably best-known to British soldiers who spoonerised a well-known wartime song into 'We're Gonna Wash Out Our Hangings on the Seigfried Line'. A defiant 'Bollocks!' to Hitler.
Hangnail	*Snail*	Not so much the mollusc but a slow, dawdling person, especially the pain behind the wheel of a car with dead flies on the REAR window.
Hang-Up		An emotional problem or an obsession: 'He's got more hang-ups than an art gallery.'
Hank Marvin	*Starving*	The name of this British guitarist was possibly first uttered in an RS sense by a dieter who was a shadow of his former self.
Hanky Panky		Trickery or deceit, especially sexual goings-on behind a partner's back: 'He's up to the old hanky panky.' Based on an old slang term for a magician's handkerchief, a cover for his tricks.
Hannibal Lecter	*(Ticket) Inspector*	The scourge of the fare dodger, based on the character who is on a different train to everyone else as far as 'fare' is concerned, the cannibalistic antihero in the film *Silence of the Lambs*.
Hans Christian Anderson		A police officer who makes up evidence to get a conviction. Based on the Danish writer of fairy stories (1805–75), this can apply to anyone given to telling tall tales.
Hansel & Gretel	*Kettle*	In old cockney sculleries the 'Hansel' was always on the go. Based on the fairy-tale siblings.
Hansom Cabs	*Crabs*	Crab-lice, known as 'hansoms', which these parasitic critters that infest the pubic area are anything but.
Ha'penny		The vagina, an old-fashioned piece of motherly advice to her daughter: 'Keep your hand on your ha'penny.'
Ha'penny Dip	*a) Kip (Sleep)*	Based on an old East End custom whereby shopkeepers would lay on a halfpenny bran-tub or lucky dip. Used in connection with a short sleep: 'I'll have half hour's ha'penny in the armchair before we set off.'
	b) Ship	A piece that was common among London's dock

		workers, when dock workers were common in London.
Ha'penny Stamp	*Tramp*	Short-changed to the first element, symbolic of a down-and-out's financial situation.
Ha'porth		A very small, insignificant amount, a shortening of 'halfpenny worth'. An idiot is someone said to be without a 'ha'porth' of sense, otherwise known as a 'daft ha'porth'.
Happy Bollocks		A piece used ironically of an eternally miserable, ill-tempered man, usually without his knowing.
Happy Dust/ Powder		A powdered drug, especially cocaine.
Happy Fag/Stick		A marijuana cigarette.
Happy Hour(s)	*Flower(s)*	If you come home late and the dinner's ruined because you been in the pub for the happy hour, a bunch of 'happy hours' won't cover it. Sometimes extended to 'happy half hour(s)'.
Happy Juice		Any alcoholic drink that gets people merry.
Happy Pill		A drug in tablet form, especially a tranquilliser.
Happy-Pratt		A piece used ironically of a perpetually miserable, disagreeable woman, generally behind her back. She may alternatively acquire the name 'happy crutch'.
Harbour		A 19th-century term for the vagina, often the busy one of a working girl.
Harbour Light	*Right*	Applies to correctness. If everything is alright, it's termed 'all harbour light' or 'all harbour'.
Hard/Hard Arse		a) A miserly, tight-fisted person: 'Hard? He wouldn't give his shit to the crows.' b) A tough, ruthless and uncaring person.
Hard Baked		Said to be the condition of unborn excrement when one is constipated.
Hard Case/Nut		A tough, uncompromising person.
Hard Cheese/ Cheddar		Bad luck. An expression aimed at someone bemoaning their bad fortune.
Hard-Faced		Brazen, shameless or unfeeling. 'A hard-faced bitch.'
Hard Hit	*Shit*	To go for a 'hard hit' is to defecate.
Hard Labour	*Neighbour*	Could be apt if getting on with 'them next door' is hard work.
Hard Stuff		Strong alcohol, especially Irish whiskey. famously 'a drop of the hard stuff'.
Hard-On		A well-known and long-established term for an erection, which in recent years has also come to refer to a desire for – to have a 'hard-on' for.
Hare & Hound	*Round*	An exact variation of 'Fox & Hound (qv). Both

terms are more likely to be based on the names of pubs rather than any so-called country sport.

Haricot Bean	*Queen*	A theatrical term for an overt homosexual.
Harold Lloyd	*Celluloid*	An old underworld term for an aid to house-breaking. Based on an early American film comedian (1893–1971).
Harold Macmillan	*Villain*	Reduced to an ''Arold', whereby the ex-British prime minister (1894–1986) becomes a baddie.
Harold Pinter	a) *Printer*	A recent piece concerning a peripheral part of a personal computer system.
	b) *Splinter*	A piece that first caused pain in a timber yard in the 1960s. Always cut to an ''Arold, after a British playwright and dramatist, now Sir 'Arold.
Harold Wilson	*Stillson*	A British prime minister (1916–95) takes his seat in the house of common slang as a plumber's term for what is also known as a monkey-wrench. Became Baron Wilson of Rievaulx.
Harp		A harmonica, especially one as played by a blues musician.
Harpic		A name given to anybody a bit mentally misaligned. After the brand of lavatory cleaner that will, according to the advert, 'clean round the bend'.
Harpoon		A user's term for a hypodermic syringe.
Harpoon	*Spoon*	An old term that was often fired in the docks when the mobile canteen came round.
Harris Tweed	*Weed*	A term for the skinny, little, ineffectual type, often the butt of a bully. He'd do well to remember that when the bullied stand up, the bully stands down. Sometimes.
Harry/Henry		Heroin, from the initial.
Harry Bluff	*Snuff*	Used to be quite common, but then so did snuff.
Harry Dash	*Flash*	Lairy people may acquire this nickname.
Harry Grout	*Snout* (Cigarette)	Based on a character from the TV sitcom *Porridge*. Set in a prison where the genial Harry Grout was the tobacco baron. Not to be confused with 'Harry Wragg' (qv).
Harry Huggins	*Muggins*	Normally said in self-admonishment for letting somebody get away with something. A foreman may prevent a worker from taking a liberty because: 'If you get caught, who'll cop a bollocking? Harry Huggins here.'
Harry Lauder	a) *Border*	A theatrical term for a stage hanging, and also what soldiers of the Border regiment called themselves.
	b) *Order*	What should be obeyed, and also a publican's alternative to those three terrible words 'time gentlemen please', which is 'Last Harry Lauders'.

	c) Warder	An ancient underworld term for a prison officer based on a Scottish entertainer (1870–1950), who was knighted in 1919 for his contribution to the war effort.
Harry Lime	Time	Based on a well-known film character of the 1940s, this applies to the time of day. A stock reply from the 1950s to someone who constantly asked the 'Harry Lime' was 'Half past, kiss me arse and tuppence back on the bottle'.
Harry Monk	Spunk (Semen)	Always comes down to 'Harry'.
Harry Nash	Cash	An old, localised docker's term appropriately based on a former wages' clerk in the industry.
Harry Potter	Squatter	The young wizard of JK Rowling's imagination comes in as an example of a 2002 trespasser. Heard in a pub: 'Talk about fat, he's scared to take his strides off in case he gets Harry Potters in 'em.'
Harry Randall	a) Candle	Coined by soldiers of World War One, who needed 'Harrys' to light up their trenches.
	b) Handle	A 19th-century term based on a British music-hall comedian (1860–1932), and heard when a drunken hotel guest rang reception and complained that he couldn't get out of his room. 'Just open the door and come out,' advised the receptionist. 'I can't,' replied the guest. 'There's only two doors, one leads to the bathroom and the other's got a Do Not Disturb sign on the Harry Randall.'
Harry Ronce	Ponce	Along with 'Charlie', 'Johnny' and 'Joe', the Ronce family seem to have turned living off immoral earnings into a family business. See all.
Harry Tagg(s)	Bag(s)	Originally a theatrical term for luggage, it later transferred to trousers, for which 'bags' is an old slang term, and took on the form of 'Harolds'.
Harry Tate	a) Eight	A bingo caller's term and also an old reference to £8.
	b) Late	Based on the British comedian (1872–1940) who has become a monument to bad time-keeping.
	c) Mate	A wartime term from the merchant navy, regarding the first officer.
	d) Plate	It can be the best china or a tin one, if you eat off it, it's a 'Harry Tate'.
	e) State	To be in a 'right old Harry Tate' is to be in a state of nervousness or excitement.
Harry Tate(s)	Weight(s)	The fat may be carrying too much 'Harry' but this was mainly a term regarding a popular brand of cigarettes, Player's Weights.
Harry Tom & Dick	Sick	When you feel a wee cough coming on, it's time for a week off on the 'Harry'.

Harry Wragg	*Fag (Cigarette)*	The name of this English jockey (1902–85) will live on for as long as people smoke.
Harvest Moon	*Coon*	An abusive term for a black person.
Harvey/Harvey Smith		To 'do a Harvey Smith' is to make the time-honoured British two-finger salute – a V sign. Based on the name of a British horseman who, at the 1971 Hickstead show-jumping trials, made such a gesture, allegedly, at one of the judges.
Harvey Nichol	*Pickle*	The Knightsbridge store lends it's name to being in a predicament. Those in a 'preserve' (qv) are in a 'bit of a Harvey'.
Harvey Nichol(s)	*Pickle(s)*	All forms of preserves are 'Harveys'.
Has Beens	*Greens*	Originally a convict's term for green vegetables that, presumably, have been boiled to a pulp.
Has Judith Chalmers Got a Passport?		A retort used in reply to a question where the answer is an obvious 'yes'. The lady has spent most of her TV career travelling the globe in the holiday programme *Wish You Were Here . . . ?*
Has Pinnochio Got Wooden Bollocks?		A reply to a question that warrants an obviously positive answer.
Hash		A user's term for hashish.
Hat & Coat	*Boat*	An old term from the docks, often regarding a refrigerated cargo ship, the unloading of which required the docker to wear his hat and coat.
Hat & Feather	*Weather*	Generally used in full when complaining about 'this poxy hat and feather' but sometimes in humorous weather vein as 'Hatton', as in: 1st man: 'What's the hatton like?' 2nd man: 'Raining, you'd better put your hatton.'
Hat & Scarf	*Bath*	Can't really see the relevance of this. Who wears a scarf in the bath?
Hat Holder/Peg/ Rack		The head in triplicate, all from a time when headwear wasn't restricted to baseball caps.
Hatch		A drinker's term for the throat, the liquid goes 'down the hatch'.
Hatchings, Matchings & Dispatchings		Christenings, weddings and funerals, the only times most of us go to church.
Hattie Jacques	*Shakes*	A British comedy actress (1924–80) gets on the RS cast list as a term for drunken trembles.
Have a Down On		To dislike intently, often without just cause.
Have a Liver		To be peevish or grumpy: 'Keep away from the boss today, he's got a right liver.'
Have a Pop At		To insult, rile or generally have a go at someone:

'He was having a pop at me so I decked him.' Also 'have a dig at' and 'have a chop at'.

Have It Away
a) To have sexual intercourse, usually illicitly: 'They've been having it away for ages.'
b) To escape, run away or simply to leave: 'Come on it's late, let's have it away.'
c) To steal something, most often from a shop.

Have It In
Crudely put, to have sexual intercourse.

Have It Off
a) To have sexual intercourse, usually with someone else's partner.
b) To fight. 'If he keeps digging me out we're gonna have to have it off.' See DIG OUT.
c) To secure a result. Four winners in an accumulator and you've 'had it off'. Also, criminally speaking, to carry out a job successfully.

Have It on One's Toes
To escape, run away or 'leave a bit sharpish'.

Have It on the Thumb
To hitch a lift: 'I ran out of juice in the middle of nowhere, so I had to have it on the thumb.'

Have It through the Slips
To make a getaway without being caught, like a cricket ball avoiding a slip fielder.

Have Over
To swindle, cheat or short-change someone. 'Either that barman can't count or he's had me over.'

Have the Arsehole With
To be fed up or bored with: 'The film started off OK but I got the arsehole with it after a while.'

Have the Decorators/ Painters In
To have a period. The tradesmen who come around every month and, ironically, put the block on 'whitewashing the interior' (qv).

Have the Ike
To be fed up: 'I've got the ike of this programme; what else is on?'

Hawaii
£50, a 1990s term taken from the '70s TV series *Hawaii Five-0*.

Hay Bag
A promiscuous woman, one to 'hit the hay' with.

Haystack   *Back*
Applies anatomically – there are many dodgy 'haystacks' about – and also to the rear of a building, the tradesman's entrance is usually 'round the haystack'.

Head
a) Oral sex, both fellatio and cunnilingus. At the same time it's a 'double header'.
b) A drug user's term for a like-minded person.

Head Rake
A comb, that which rakes the 'grass' (qv).

Head-Banger
a) A fan of heavy-metal music, one who nods and shakes his head in time with the sounds.
b) A dangerously violent, evil-tempered person. A 'nutter' (qv).

Headcase		A mentally off-line or eccentric person, one given to doing crazy things, a 'loon' (qv). Also someone who indulges in mindless violence, a thug. Often referred to as a 'header'.
Headlights		Breasts, from the shape of the headlights on early automobiles.
Headshrinker		Originally an American term (what else?) for a psychiatrist, now equally well-known in Britain in the reduced form of a 'shrink'.
Heap		An old, unreliable, rust-bucket of a car. In full, a 'heap of shit'. Also a 'pile/pile of shit'.
Heap of Coke	*Bloke*	'A heap, big heap.' As Geronimo may have described his largest brave had he come from Bow or possibly, 'Arrow.
Hearth Rug	a) *Bug*	An ancient piece that may make a comeback, as the vermin has, in insanitary hotels.
	b) *Mug*	An old reference to a fool or simpleton, someone regularly stepped on.
Hearts of Oak	*Broke*	Refers to being financially challenged: 'I can't come out, I'm flat busted hearts.'
Heat		a) Trouble, aggravation or pressure. Funny that, when the 'heat' gets too much for some people, they go on holiday to somewhere hot.
		b) A large police presence in an area following a crime. Also, by extension, the police are known as 'the heat'.
Heaven & Hell	a) *Shell*	A wartime term from the army regarding a projectile.
	b) *Smell*	Rotten smells don't half 'heaven'.
Heavenly Bliss	*Kiss*	Old, made in America, and apt, especially when not confined to a mouth-to-mouth arrangement.
Heavens Above	*Love*	A happy example when applied to a new romance, people are not quite earth-bound when in 'heavens'.
Heavy Bevvy		a) Strong beer, a term generally aimed at real ale. Or in a 'fizzhouse' (qv), the strongest beer available – a pint of 'heavy'.
		b) A long drinking session ending in inevitable inebriation.
Heavy Gear/Shit		Strong varieties of marijuana.
Heavy Mob		A team of strong-arm men that crosses the divide of law and disorder, stretching from a gang of villains to officers of the Flying Squad.
Hebe/Hebie		A Jew, a shortening of Hebrew.
Hedge & Ditch	*Pitch*	A playing area, the spot where a stallholder may set up shop or a bookmaker's 'joint' (qv).
Hedgehog	*Wog*	An example from the xenophobe, who maintains that all 'hedgehogs' start at Calais.

Heebie Jeebies		A state of nervous anxiety or irrational fear. Also withdrawal symptoms after coming off heroin addiction and the shakes that may accompany a hangover.
Heeshie		An effeminate male homosexual or transvestite, an update of the 19th-century 'he-she'.
Heist		A robbery, an American piece that has stolen it's way into the British vocabulary.
Hell/Hellfire/ Hell's Fire		Terms of anger, annoyance or disappointment. Often preceded by 'fucking' as an intensifier.
Hell on a Bad day		A miserable, depressing, generally terrible place to be. Like a working man's club on a karaoke night or the A & E department of a British hospital.
Hell's Bells/ Teeth		A couple of exclamations of surprise or disappointment. 'Hell's bells! Is that the time?'
Hell's Waiting Room		A diabolical, nightmarish place. An ancient term for a field hospital, prison, asylum, etc.
Helmet		A common term for the head of the penis.
Helter Skelter	*Shelter*	Originally an air-raid shelter, now thankfully obsolete except in the reminiscences of people who survived the Blitz. Still applies to a bus shelter though.
Hen		A woman, an old term that is responsible for the 'hen party', the 'hen night' and the 'henpecked' husband. A common address to a woman in Scotland.
Henley Regatta	*Natter*	An old source of friction between man and wife is when he's waiting for his dinner and she's having a 'Henley' with her next door.
Henrietta	*Letter*	A girl who gets addressed as a boy when shortened to a 'Henry'.
Henry		An eighth of an ounce of cocaine or cannabis. A dealer and user's term based on Henry VIII.
Henry Fonda	*Honda*	Based on an American film star (1905–82) and limited to would-be taxi drivers doing the knowledge. It refers to a Honda 90 motorcycle, the most common 'knolly bike'.
Henry Halls	*Balls (Testicles)*	'Henrys' is a 1950s term based on a British bandleader (1898–1989).
Henry Meville	*Devil*	From a line in an 1887 ballad called 'Tottie' and used as 'What the Henry Meville's going on?'
Henry Moore	*Door*	Based on the English sculptor (1898–1986), this is a piece of student slang, so a 'Henry' is likely to be the door of an art college.
Henry Nash	*Cash*	An elderly piece that doesn't appear to have been saved.
Henry the Third	*Turd*	The long-reigning English monarch (1207–72) rivals

fellow kings George III and Richard III in the excrement stakes. If ever the present Prince of Wales becomes Charles III, well, I hope he knows what's in store for him. Henry reigned from 1216 until his death.

Her Indoors

One's wife. The catchphrase of Arthur Daley in the 1980s TV series, *Minder*, caught on in a big way and is still very common.

Herb

Marijuana, a West Indian term, imported by Rastafarians and adopted by anyone who likes a puff.

Herbie Hides — *Strides*

A 1990s, young 'Erberts' term for trousers based on a British heavyweight boxer, once a holder of a version of the world title. *See* STRIDES.

Here & There — *Chair*

Never shortened: 'Pull up a here and there and have a bite to eat.'

Herman Fink — *Ink*

A term that was first drawn up in the theatre before the ballpoint took over.

Herring & Kipper — *Stripper*

Always reduced to the first element, and since strip shows have moved from clubs to pubs, suggestions to go to one have been rebuffed with: 'No, I don't wanna see some old herring taking her clothes off, let's go for a quiet pint.'

Herring Bone — *Phone*

A 1990s term, the 'herring' is mostly used in connection with the ubiquitous mobile job.

Hey Jude — *Food*

Based on the title of a Beatles song from 1968, which makes a food faddist, gourmet, celebrity chef or any other kind of foodie a 'Hey Judy'.

Hi Diddle Diddle — *a) Fiddle*

Refers to gaining by dishonest means, which may take the form of petty larceny in the workplace or a much larger tax fraud. A working man's maxim: 'If you see a fiddle, get on it. No-one ever got rich working for a living.'

b) Fiddle (Violin)

As played by a 'hi diddle diddler.'

c) Middle

Often a reference to the bull's-eye on a dartboard, the nearest dart to the 'hi diddle' throws first.

d) Piddle

From the nursery rhyme in which the little dog 'hi diddled' himself o' laughing to see such fun.

Hi Jimmy Knacker — *Tobacco*

Refers to pipe or rolling tobacco and is based on the name of a street game of the dim and distant past. *See also* OI JIMMY KNACKER.

Hibber-De-Hoy

An early 20th-century version of 'hobbledehoy' (qv), but meaning a young hooligan. Sometimes said as 'yibber-de-hoy', which gets condensed to 'yib'.

Hickory Dickory Dock — *Clock*

An extended version of 'dickory dock' (qv) and known as a 'hickory dickory'.

Hide & Seek — *a) Boutique*

A term from the 1960s, the decade when young

		people ceased to be fashion clones of their parents, and 'clobber' shops called boutiques sprung up everywhere.
	b) Cheek	Refers to impudence or sauce. Liberty-takers tend to have a load of it. Sometimes used anatomically, usually when a peck on the 'hide and seek' is concerned.
High		To be well under the influence of drugs. 'Sky-high' – 'stoned out of one's skull'.
High as a Kite	Tight	A reference to being drunk, a common term that's been hanging around since the early 20th century.
High Noon	Spoon	A 1950s term formed on the name of the classic Western film.
High Roller		Someone who doesn't waste money on necessities. An extravagent spender and gambler.
High Stepper		A fashion-conscious person, one who keeps apace with current trends.
High Stepper	Pepper	A seasoned campaigner on the table of RS.
Highland Fling	a) King	At the moment this is a playing card, when we get another male monarch, who knows?
	b) Sing	A post-war term found on a Billy Cotton record called 'The Marrow Song', with vocals by Alan Breeze, the band's resident 'Highland Flinger.'
Hill & Dale	Tale	As spun by a con artist or a beggar in order to separate a 'mark' (qv) from his money.
Hillman Hunter	Punter	Based on an old make of car, this, unsurprisingly, was coined by used car dealers in reference to a customer. It now applies to a customer of any trade.
Himbo		The boyfriend of an older woman, the male version of a 'bimbo' (qv).
Hip/Hep		a) An old-fashioned term for being fashionable and in touch with current trends in clothes, music, and so on.
		b) Aware. To be 'hip/hep' to a situation is to be 'in the know'.
History		A threat or prediction of impending doom: 'If orders don't pick up soon, this firm's history.'
Hit & Miss	a) Kiss	By which, 'kiss me' masochistically becomes 'hit me'.
	b) Piss	Can be used in regard of urine or booze. While 'on' the 'hit and miss' people regularly go 'for' one.
Hit & Run	a) Done	Mainly applies to being swindled. If you've been 'taken', you've been 'hit and run'.
	b) Sun	Fittingly suggestive of the fleeting appearances put in by the sun during a typical British summer, as described in the following: The Sun. British Tour '98

Burning hot it sets with the coming of night
Inferior beings depend on its might
Great fiery mass that circles the sky
Controls man's existence, he has no reply
Infinite power yet strangely forbidden
In summertime to the people of Britain.

Hit
a) An underworld term for a murder or an assassination.
b) A drag on a 'drugfag', an injection of heroin, a noseful of cocaine. A single dose of a drug.
c) A robbery, especially of a shop, bank or post office.
d) To adulterate or dilute drugs before selling them.
e) To borrow money off someone or to hustle them for some: 'He gave me a sob story then hit me for a score.'
f) A visit to an Internet website.

Hit the Post
To be unlucky. Two winners and a second, beaten a short head in a win treble and you've 'hit the post'.

Hiver
An AIDS sufferer – HIVer.

Hobbledehoy
Mistakenly given by some as RS for boy, including myself in *Cockney Rabbit*. Since it is a 16th-century term for a youth, it's far too old.

Hob-Nailed Boot
What anybody lacking tact or diplomacy is said to be 'as subtle as'.

Hobson's Choice   *Voice*
A common term that originated in the theatre, possibly when a singer was being castigated for having a 'dodgy Hobsons'.

Hod of Mortar   *Porter*
An archaic expression for a type of beer now only served at beer festivals.

Hog
a) A motorbike, a term coined by Hell's Angels of the 1950s and still used by their counterparts.
b) An extinct term for a shilling, which was similarly known as a 'grunter' and a 'pig'.

Hoggins/'Oggins
Sexual gratification. To paraphrase Spike Milligan: The only way to stop a British soldier from wanting his 'oggins is to shoot his bollocks off.

Hogsnorton
A gluttonous person, a pig. Based on a fictional place of a 1930s radio show.

Hoick
To noisily bring up phlegm and spit it out. To 'hoick it up'.

Hoist
To burgle. An 18th-century term for the two-man caper of climbing through an upstairs window, whereby one, who was known as the hoist, would allow himself to be stood upon by the other to

effect a high-rise entry. It later became a reference to picking pockets.

Hoister
A thief, especially a shoplifter. 'Hoisters' usually have something cheap to sell.

Hokey Cokey *Karaoke*
A 1990s term for the pub entertainment much loved by the lager and 'I Will Survive' brigade. The more discerning will do the hokey-cokey, turn around and go somewhere else.

Hokey-Pokey
A 19th-century term that is forever associated with Italian ice-cream vendors regarding their product. 'Hokey-pokey' was their cry as they pushed their handcarts through the streets, a far cry from today's 'hokey-pokey man' with his van and his annoying 'Teddy Bear's Picnic' chimes.

Hold Your Noise
An insistence on somebody's keeping their mouth shut, usually said in anger.

Holding/
Holding Folding
To be in possession of money. Or if you're 'not holding', you're skint.

Hole
a) The anus, the orifice with seemingly more terms of slang than there are light-years to Uranus.
b) The vagina, and by extension women in general as sex objects: a 'piece of hole'. When men have had sex they claim to have 'had their hole'.
c) The mouth: 'Shut your hole up!'

Hole in One's
Own Shoe
To be your own worst enemy, the cause of your own misery.

Hole in the *Pound*
Ground
A 'hole' is an elderly and now uncommon reference to £1.

Hole in the Wall
A piece that has become a well-known term for a cashpoint machine.

Holed Below the
Water Line
Unable to achieve an erection. A medical problem or temporary impotence brought about by too much alcohol. Either way, like a ship that strikes a rock below water level, you're sunk.

Holler
a) To give information to the police.
b) To run, especially on an errand: 'Just gonna holler over the shop for a paper.'

Holler & Shout *Kraut*
Appropriate since Germans tend to get a bit loud, especially around hotel swimming pools. Until someone mentions the war, that is.

Holler Boys *Collar*
Holler
Originally applied to a detachable shirt collar of a bygone age, when it was known as a 'holler boys'. Based on a line from a poem denigrating Guy Fawkes.

Holy Friar *Liar*
Never shortened and only used in a light-hearted manner. If someone has defamed you, you wouldn't call him a 'holy friar', you'd call him a liar.

Holy Ghost	a) Host	Usually the landlord down the local.
	b) Post	A racing term for the starting post: 'The runners are at the holy'. Sometimes also the winning post.
	c) Post	A theatrical term for what the postman brings, from the days before junk mail.
	d) Toast	Generally served as a slice of buttered 'holy'.
Holy Joe		Originally a naval term for a clergyman but now applied to any religious man: 'He's turned into a right holy Joe since he got religion.'
Holy Land		A 19th-century term for a part of a town or city populated by Jews, originally Whitechapel, in London's East End.
Holy Nail	Bail	One of those that secured Christ to the cross comes in as money required to secure the temporary release of a prisoner.
Holy Smoke	Coke	Originally applied to the fuel but now refers to the the drink, Coca Cola.
Holy Water		Water, with a goodly measure of whisky in it.
Holy Water	Daughter	The apple of her father's eye is his little 'holy water'.
Holyfield's Ear	Year	Based on the 1997 world heavyweight title fight between Evander Holyfield and Mike Tyson, in which the latter seemingly tried to ascertain whether a boxer's ear actually tasted like a cauliflower by biting a great chunk out of his opponent's 'listener'. For this act of cannibalism Iron Mike received a lifetime ban from the sport but was granted leave to re-apply for his licence twelve months later. A year, therefore, quickly became known as an 'olyfields. Although, it must be said, not for long.
Home on the Range	Strange	Anything out of the ordinary or unusual may be described as 'very home on the range', like seeing George Best drinking from a cup for example. Based on an old cowboy song.
Homework		An attractive woman, a nice piece of 'homework'.
Honcho		A manager, leader or man in charge. The 'head honcho' is the boss of bosses. Originally an American forces' term based on the Japanese han'cho – group leader.
Honeypot		The vagina, as possessed by the sexually alluring, who attract men like bees round a 'honeypot'. Incorrectly described in *Cockney Rabbit* as RS for twat, the term is older than rhyming slang.
Hong Kong	a) Pong	Not sure if this is apt as I've never been there. But pong is Chinese for smell, isn't it?
	b) Wrong	When a plan has gone boss-eyed, it's gone 'Hong Kong' or sometimes 'Hongkers'.

Honk	a) To smell, or more pungently, to stink to high heaven.
	b) To vomit, especially of a drunk when his head is down the toilet, 'honking' up the supper that he didn't want in the first place.
Honked/ Honkers/ Honking	Varying descriptions of being drunk, suburbia style. Middle-class terms that probably started in the officers' mess.
Honking Down	Pouring with rain, akin to 'pissing down'.
Honky	A derogatory term for a white person used by non-whites.
Hooey	Rubbish, nonsense. A term with it's roots in excretia, so 'what a load of hooey' is probably 'what a load of shit'.
Hoof	a) An archaic term for the foot, especially a big one: 'Look at the bleedin' great hooves he's got.'
	b) To kick. Unskilled footballers tend to 'hoof' the ball upfield. 'Hoof It' – kick it.
	c) To walk: 'We've missed the last bus, we'll have to hoof it.'
Hoof It	To abscond or escape. Runaways 'have it on the hoof'.
Hoofer	A professional dancer, a well-known term for those who 'hoof' (dance) for a living.
Hooha	A commotion, a hullaballoo.
Hook	a) A thief, especially a pickpocket; one who uses his fingers to good (or bad) effect. *See* HOOKS.
	b) To steal, especially to pick a pocket.
	c) A catch, snag or stumbling block. If it seems too good to be true, it probably is. There's sure to be a 'hook' somewhere.
Hook It	To run away, to abscond. Same boots, different laces to 'hop it' (qv).
Hook Up	To meet. What people planning a rendezvous agree to do: 'Let's hook up and discuss it.'
Hooker	A well-known term for a prostitute, although it was well-known in America before it was here.
Hooks	The fingers and by extension hands. People have been getting their 'hooks' into things for centuries.
Hooky	a) An old reference to a Jew, from a supposed hook-nosed appearance.
	b) Stolen goods, in other words 'bent gear'.
	c) Truancy. To 'play hooky', probably from the same root as 'hook it' (qv) or the older 'hook off' – to run away. Sometimes spelt 'hookey'.
Hooky Street	The imaginary thoroughfare immortalised in the

theme song from TV's *Only Fools and Horses*. Inhabited by rogues, it's where stolen goods can be bought and dodgy deals slapped hands-on.

Hoolivan A police van with protected windows for use at riot scenes.

Hoop/Hoople A ring, but mainly in the sense of the anus: 'Soon as I get the chance I'll be away from here quicker than a whippet with mustard round his hoop.'

Hooray Henry A snobbish young man from a well-to-do family who indulges in drunken loutish behaviour. An upper class 'yobbo' (qv).

Hoosegow An American expression for a prison, sometimes heard in Britain.

Hooter The nose, an example that is as familiar now as when it was first blown in the 1950s.

Hoover a) A sports or a top model car; one that draws the girls, or picks up bits of 'fluff'. A reworking of the 1940s term 'vacuum cleaner'.

b) To eat or drink like a mongrel, i.e., quickly and noisily. The image of food being sucked off the plate by a vacuum cleaner.

Hop Originally a 19th-century term for opium, which later came to mean any illicit drug.

Hop it To run away or abscond. Also an exclamation akin to 'Get lost! Go away!'

Hop It & Scram *Ham* A localised piece that is sliced and eaten as 'hop it'.

Hop the Wag To play truant from school, a 19th-century term for an unofficial day off.

Hophead A beer drinker or a drug addict. *See* HOP *and* HOPS.

Hopping Hut *Slut* A 1950s term which may have it's roots in reality. It was common for wives and kids to go hop picking while the old man stayed behind in London to work. And with all those lusty rustics about, well, it didn't take long for a girl to get a bad name: 'Never mind what my old woman says, do you think I'd have a hopping hut for a mistress?' – A man to his upset girlfriend.

Hopping Pot *Lot* A widely used term that is generally contracted to the first element: 'That's your hopping' means that's your lot, there's no more.

Hoppy a) An unsympathetic name given to a lame or one-legged person.

b) A name given to a beer drinker or a drug addict. *See* HOPHEAD.

Hops Beer. From the drink's main ingredient we get a

		wife's complaint that her old man is 'more fond of his hops than his oats'.
Hopscotch	*Watch*	With a leap in time, this children's game continues the kiddie connection with what used to be known in the underworld as a 'Toy' (qv).
Horace		The penis, thus to 'flog one's Horace' is to masturbate.
Horizontal Dancing		Sexual intercourse. Think of any dance from barn-dancing to the waltz, precede it with 'horizontal', e.g., the 'horizontal rumba', and someone, somewhere has probably done it.
Horizontals		Sexual intercourse, sometimes known as the 'old horizontals'.
Horlicks		A popular euphemism for 'bollocks' (qv). 'What a load of Horlicks' is an expression for rubbish, and to make a right 'Horlicks' of something is to make a mess of it.
Horn		The commonest and longest-standing term for an erection. To 'have the horn for' is to lust after.
Horn of Plenty	*Twenty*	One of a cornucopia of terms from the bingo hall.
Horny		Sexually aroused, lustful, a term no longer restricted to men; randy women can also be 'horny'.
Hors d'Oeuvres	*Nerves*	A rarely served suburban version of the cockney 'West Ham Reserves' (qv).
Horse & Carriage	*Garage*	An example from a time when we bought petrol in gallons and air was free.
Horse & Cart	*a) Fart*	Normally employed in the past tense, or when the horse has bolted, so to speak: 'Who's horse and carted?'
	b) Heart	A 19th-century term for the 'pump' (qv). Also used ironically to anybody who performs a heartless act: 'You're all horse and cart, d'you know that?'
	c) Start	A new beginning is a new 'horse and cart'. Also a mocking remark to a motorist having ignition problems: 'Won't horse and cart? Get a horse and cart.'
Horse & Trap	*a) Clap (VD)*	A dose of the 'horse' is usually a reference to gonorrhoea.
	b) Crap	To go for a 'horse' is to defecate, and it's also what's produced. But not as regular as 'Pony & Trap' (qv).
Horse & Trough	*Cough*	Specifically a smoker's cough, when he's 'horsing his offal up'.
Horse Piddle	*Hospital*	A hospital, a pun as much as anything else.
Horses & Carts	*Darts*	Always curtailed to a game of 'horses'. On its own a dart becomes a horse.

Horse's Collar		A larger than average vagina, especially one belonging to a promiscuous woman that's said to be stretched by overuse.
Horse's Hoof	*Poof (Homosexual)*	A 'horses' is a less used variation of the well-known 'iron hoof' (qv).
Horsey Set		Upper-class country folk, those who ride to hounds.
Hot		a) What stolen goods are said to be, as is the thief who took them is when the police are after him.
		b) To be sexually aroused is to be 'hot for it' and to 'have the hots for' is to fancy someone rotten.
Hot & Cold	*Gold*	Known on Hooky Street (qv) in the melted-down form of 'hot', often in regard to jewellery that's the 'other way', i.e., bent.
Hot Beef	*Thief*	A term which, in the 19th-century, was supposedly a cry of alarm, a rhyme on 'stop thief!' Can't imagine a robbed person messing around with RS while chasing a thief, so maybe it was used mockingly by amused onlookers.
Hot Cross Bun	a) *Gun*	An underworld term of secrecy, the fear factor would prevent anyone staring down the barrel from yelling 'Look out! He's got a hot cross bun.'
	b) *Nun*	If a 'hot cross' was toting a 'hot cross bun (a)', would she be a member of the Armourlite Order?
	c) *Run*	To be on the 'hot cross' is to be on the run from the police. Or the wife.
	d) *Son/Sun*	Unusual but not unheard in either of these settings.
Hot Dinner	*Winner*	A term from the racing world that suggests a good meal follows a good result.
Hot Potato	*Waiter*	A 'hot pertater' sounds like an efficient table jockey, or one in a curry house.
Hot Toddy	*Body*	Refers to the body beautiful and is inspired by the name of a hot alcoholic drink that's nice to go to bed with. The connection is obvious.
Hotel		A police station, a PC's term for his place of work.
Hotting		Stealing cars for fun, which has become known as joy-riding even though it causes misery for the victim.
Houdini		To 'do a Houdini' is to escape, an underworld term based on the legendary escapologist, Harry Houdini (1873–1926).
Hound		A young male hooligan. An overheard conversation: 'The old Bill's pulled me for not wearing a seat belt and over the road a couple of hounds are kicking hell out of a bus shelter.'
Hounslow Heath	*Teeth*	An archaic example that has had the bite put on it by 'Hampstead Heath'.

House of Fraser	*Razor*	Originally a Scottish term known as a 'hoosie', it has since travelled south where it is generally called a 'howser' and relates mostly to a razor as used as a weapon, although it can also refer to a shaver. Based on the retailing chain.
House of Lords	*Cords*	A 1970s term for casual corduroy trousers.
House of Wax	*Jacks (£5)*	An example of secondary slang. *See* JACKS ALIVE. In Ireland it refers to a lavatory. *See* JAKES.
House to Let	*Bet*	Oldish but never really got moving.
Housemaid's Knee	*a) Key*	Generally mislaid and searched for as a 'housemaids'.
	b) Sea	A note for posterity: This week the Ecuadorian oil tanker, *Jessica*, ran aground and is, even now, polluting the 'housemaids' surrounding the Galapagos Islands.
Housewives' Choice	*Voice*	Based on a long-running radio request programme of yesteryear, this often applies to the shrill, raucous voice of a shrieking woman, especially a mother castigating an unruly child.
Housey-Housey	*Lousy*	To feel unwell, run-down or to itch. Based on a slang term for the game of lotto or bingo.
Hovis		a) Dead, an extension of the RS 'brown bread', based on the well-known brand of that product.
		b) The head of a black person, especially when used in a fight. Mike Tyson is well-known for 'slinging in the Hovis'. Based on the RS 'loaf of bread' – head. Hovis is a brown loaf.
How D' You Do	*a) Shoe*	A 19th-century term for a 'trotter case', but you've got more chance of opening a Weetabix wrapper without tearing it, than hearing it these days.
	b) Stew	This is a stew in the sense of a state of difficulty or mental agitation, when you're in a right old 'how d'you do' you're in trouble. Applies secondarily to the dish.
Howard's Way	*Gay (Homosexual)*	A 1980s term, based on a popular TV series of the time, that was generally curtailed at 'Howards'.
How's Your Father		a) A well-known euphemism for 'fuck' in a couple of senses. People, having indulged in a quick bout of intercourse, have had a quick 'how's your father' and it's what folk may smoke, drink, swear or stink like.
		b) A bad state of affairs: 'Well here's a nice how's your father.'
		c) A term used to refer to something, the name of which has either been withdrawn from your

memory bank or you never knew it in the first place: 'Where's the how's your father that fits on to the wossname?'

How's Your Father

a) *Lather*
Nothing to do with soap, but to get into a state about something, to work yourself up into a 'how's your father'.

b) *Palaver*
Anything complicated or bothersome is a 'right old how's your father'.

Huckle
An effeminate homosexual, originally an American one. Heard in a recent British TV comedy.

Huckleberry Finn *Gin*
Originally an Australian term but 'Huckleberry' or 'Huck' has found it's way into British glasses. Based on the eponymous hero of a Mark Twain novel.

Huff
A solvent used for inhaling. To sniff glue is to 'huff' it and a 'huffer' is another term for a 'sticky nose' (qv).

Huggins Not Muggins, the name's
A reply given to anyone requesting you do something stupid, like lend cash to a known knocker.

Hugh Jampton
A name given to a man with a large penis. A pun on Huge Hampton. *See* HAMPTON WICK.

Hugh Jooter
A punning name given to a man with a large nose. *See* HOOTER.

Hughie
a) To vomit, the name similar to the one that echos round the lavatory bowl on disgorgement.

b) A green piece of phlegm, a play on the name of the entertainer and TV quizmaster Hughie Greene (1920–97).

Hughies
Greens. From the same root as 'Hughie (b)', it has applied to any green vegetable since the 1960s.

Hugs & Kisses *Missus*
Hardly complimentary to refer to the wife as 'the 'ugs', but it's meant to be.

Humdinger
Anything or anybody spectacularly good or remarkable. A well-known import from the USA.

Hump
a) To 'have the hump' is a well-known phrase for being fed-up, depressed or angry: 'You're giving me the right 'ump' – You're getting on my nerves.

b) To have sexual intercourse: 'If I ain't in bed and humping by midnight, I'm going home.'

Humped-Up
Annoyed, angry or irritated. To generally have the 'hump' (qv, a).

Humpty Dumpty
a) Broken or ruined. When a plan goes 'Humpty-Dumpty', it has gone wrong, and like the eggy thing in the nursery rhyme, it's gone to pieces.

b) Names given to anyone who lives in a permanent state of depression or is constantly angry. A miserable moaner who could give an Asprin a headache.

Humungous   A juvenile term for anything huge, massive, etc.

Hunchfront   A very large-breasted woman, the type the more average-sized woman refers to as deformed.

Hundred to Eight   *Plate*   It's a funny fact of life that you may have a plate for years and all the time you've got it, that's all it is, an old 'hundred to eight'. But as soon as it gets smashed it acquires antique status. Hundred to eight are bookmaker's odds of 12½/1.

Hundred to Thirty   *Dirty*   Bookmaker's odds get a quote in reference to grubbiness: 'I can't wear this shirt, it's hundred to thirty.'

Hung   To be well endowed of the genitals, as in 'hung like a horse/donkey/elephant/bull, etc. The less well endowed are said to be hung like various types of rodent – mouse, field mouse, etc.

Hung Up On   Obsessed or infatuated with someone or something. People get 'hung up on' other people, their work, hobbies, music, etc. Someone somewhere is probably hung up on Accrington Stanley FC.

Hungry Horace   A name stolen from a children's comic and given to a permanently hungry person, often a young larder- and fridge-raider.

Hunt Not Cunt, the name's   A reply given to anyone asking you to do something stupid, like tell a well-known psychopath his breath smells.

Huntley & Palmer   *Farmer*   A 1990s term from the suburbs that gets trimmed to a 'Huntley', which may appear apt if gentleman farmers, horses and hounds are involved.

Huntley & Palmers   *Farmers (Piles)*   Based on a well-known biscuit company, this is secondary slang for haemorrhoids and is known as 'Huntleys'. *See* FARMER GILES.

Hurricane Deck   *Neck*   The upper deck of a ship comes in for an upper part of the body.

Hurricane Lamp   *Tramp*   The second element gets blown away here, leaving vagrants, methers, dossers, gentlemen of the road, etc., as 'hurricanes'.

Hurry-Up Wagon/Van   Terms from down the ages for police vans, which have included the horse drawn 'hurry-buggy', the 'black Maria' and the modern 'Transit Tug-Truck'.

Husband & Wife   *Knife*   A fairly old example which sees the 'husband' doing the carving.

Hush Puppie   *Yuppie*   A derogatory term for the high-earning, high-profile type, many of whom 'colonised' London's Docklands in the 1980s.

Hustle		a) To take money under false pretences, to swindle. A 'hustler' is someone who will do whatever it takes to make a few quid. b) To engage in prostitution. A 'hustler' is one of many terms for a streetwalker.
Hustle Your Bustle		Hurry up, get your skates on and let's get moving.
Hustler		Someone who deliberately plays badly at snooker, pool, darts, etc., in order to get an attractive wager on himself in a later game.
Hyde Park	a) *Mark* b) *Nark* *(Informer)*	A theatrical term for an actor's mark. Based on London's biggest park, where ears can be whispered into without being overheard.
Hydraulics	*Bollocks*	The testicles. The dictionary describes 'hydraulics' as 'the science of the conveyance of liquids through pipes, etc., especially as a motive power.' Apt then that a carefully aimed boot would have a serious effect on this. Also 'What a load of hydraulics!' – a colourful way to express disbelief.
Hymie		A derogatory term for a Jew, a shortening of the Jewish name Hyman.
Hype		Intensive and excessive publicity. A term that has become common in connection with the entertainment world, where many an act has been 'hyped up' out of all proportion, only to be found wanting where talent was concerned.
Hype/Hypo		Junkie's terms for a hypodermic syringe.

I

I Am Back	*Crack (Cocaine)*	A 1980s piece that may reflect the addictive power of crack, i.e., 'I am back for more.'
I Desire	*Fire*	A 19th-century term for the traditional house-warmer that was known as an 'Idey'.
I Know You Now		A schoolboy retort on being told his best friend has a girlfriend.
I Suppose	*Nose*	An example that's been running since the 19th century.
Ian Rush	*Brush*	A piece formed in the 1980s on the name of a Welsh international footballer of the period which is most commonly used in connection with a paintbrush.
Ice		a) An underworld term for diamonds, well-known through it's use in many a crime movie.
		b) Protection money, especially payments to the police for closing an eye to after hours drinking and illegal gambling. Such 'bungs' (qv) keep the heat off.
		c) To kill, a piece that originated in the American underworld before journeying to Britain via Hollywood.
		d) To snub or ignore somebody, to give them the cold shoulder.
Ice Cream Freezer	*Geezer*	Usually melted down to the first two elements: 'My sister's new ice-cream's a right poser.'

Ice Maiden A cold, aloof or frigid woman, one guaranteed to cool a man's ardour.

Icebox A prisoner's term for the solitary confinement cell. The cooler.

Ice-Cream a) Someone who talks tough but melts away when it comes to the crunch. Not a good man to have on your side. A mug.

b) A derogatory term for a white person, a piece of 1970s black youthspeak.

Ice-Cream Habit Occasional drug use, that of someone who indulges because they want to, not because they need to.

Ice-Creamer An Italian, based on the common occupation of 19th-century Italian immigrants, i.e., making and selling ice-cream. For many, the first Italian they ever knew was the 'hokey-pokey man' (qv).

Iceman a) A professional killer, a hit-man. See ICE (c).

b) An underworld term for a specialist jewel thief. See ICE (a).

c) A cold, unemotional man, also the unflappable, nerves of steel type.

Iddy A jew, almost a backslang version of 'yid'. Often extended to 'Iddy Boy'.

Ideal Home *Comb* A ironic term from the 1950s in that, in an ideal home, it wouldn't keep getting mislaid.

Idiot Board A theatrical term for a cue-card, the visual prompt for performers who haven't learnt their lines.

Idiot Box A television, a term from the 1950s used con-descendingly by the intelligentsia of the period, the implication being that those with inferior brains watch TV.

Idiot Dancing A 1960s term for frenzied, often drug-induced, gyrating to rock music, which involves much head and arm shaking but not a lot of foot movement.

Iffy a) Questionable, suspect or dangerous. Anything that's risky or not quite right. It's the weather when it looks as though it might rain, food that doesn't smell fresh, or hopping across Niagara Falls on a tightrope while juggling three bottles of gelignite.

b) A dishonest or untrustworthy person, also stolen or snide goods.

If You Can't Fight Wear a Big Hat A piece of useless advice which reasons, uselessly, that if a mug makes himself look taller by wearing a large titfer he won't get picked on. It doesn't work, and bullies just take the piss out of the hat and beat the wearer up anyway, as a hundred years' worth of victims will testify. Yes, it's an old piece of useless advice.

Ikey/Ikey Mo
Derogatory terms for a Jew, based on the typically Jewish names Isaac and Moses.

Ilie Nastase — *Carsey (Lavatory)*
Based on a Romanian tennis player whose on-court outbursts seemed designed to take the piss out of his opponents and scare the shit out of umpires.

I'll Be There — *Chair*
An early piece from the public bar, known by it's first two elements: 'Who's in the I'll be?'

I'm Afloat — *a) Boat*
An obvious term that was used by 19th-century dock workers and shortened to an 'ima'.

b) Coat
As old as (a) and generally refers to an overcoat.

I'm So Frisky — *Whisky*
Usually nipped to 'a drop of I'm so'.

I'm Willing — *Shilling*
A piece that was probably obsolete before the coin.

Imshee/Imshi
An Arabic expression meaning 'go away', which was imported into Britain by soldiers serving in the Middle East during World War One.

In & Out — *a) Snout*
Refers to a snout in it's guise as a nose and also a cigarette or tobacco.

b) Spout
Applies to something that's been ruined or rendered useless and is always preceded by 'Up the'. A pregnant woman is 'up the in and out'.

c) Sprout
A greengrocer's term for a Brussels sprout.

d) Stout
Beer. The stuff that's also known as 'black food'.

e) Tout
Originally applied to a person who made a living by selling tips to racecourse punters. It now also applies to a seller of exorbitantly priced tickets.

In a Deuce
In a pair, especially two people: 'There was a dozen blokes looking for trouble and we was in a deuce, so we legged it.'

In & Out
Sexual intercourse, to indulge in 'the old in and out'. Often just 'In-Out'.

In & Out Like a Fart in a Colander
A fleeting visit, a very short stay.

In & Out Man
An opportunist thief, one who goes about his business courtesy of an open door or window.

In Bed/Cahoots With
Allied to or in partnership with somebody, especially in illegal activities.

In Between — *Queen (Homosexual)*
Originally an Australian term for a 'girlieboy' (qv).

In Collar
In work, employed: 'I've been "In Collar" since I got slung off the dole.'

In Dock
To be out of action and laid up. A broken car in a

		garage or a sick person in hospital are 'in dock'. From dry dock, where ships go for repairs.
In Like Flynn		To be on to a good thing or in a favourable position, especially where a member of the opposite (or same if so inclined) sex is concerned. Based on the supposed sexual proficiency of actor Errol Flynn (1909–59).
In Lumber		In trouble, if you're in deep trouble, you're in 'dead lumber'.
In Queer Street		In financial difficulties. Where anybody skint and with bills to pay is said to be.
In Shit Street		In trouble or great difficulty. Any street that isn't paved with gold is said to be paved with shit. So tread carefully.
In Swell Street		The direct opposite of being 'in Queer Street' (qv). Where the well-off live.
In the Chair		As occupied by the person whose turn it is to buy a round of drinks: 'Who's in the chair?' – who's round is it?
In the Closet		Where hides a homosexual yet to 'come out' and declare his/her sexuality.
In the Club/ Pudding Club		Ultra-familiar expressions for being pregnant. *See* PUDDING.
In the Mood	*Food*	A hungry person is in the mood for some 'in the mood'.
In the Nude	*Food*	A jocular play on 'in the mood' (qv) which may suggest a different type of 'nosh' (qv).
In the Raw		Naked, to have one's nude on. Also a schoolboy expression for when he gets a handful of breast beneath it's owner's bra.
In the Shit		In trouble, those in 'deep shit' are in a disaster area.
In the Trap		Ready and waiting to go, as a horse or greyhound is at the start of a race: 'I'm in the trap, as soon as the cab arrives I'll be leaving.'
Indian Charm(s)	*Arm(s)*	An Eastern rival to 'lucky charm' (qv).
Inkspot		A black person, a 1950s term that may or may not be based on the black American vocal group of the period, the Inkspots.
Inkwell		A 19th-century term for the vagina, symbolic of being dipped.
Inky Blue	*Flu*	A 1970s term for the illness that can be counter-acted by having an 'inky' jab.
Inky Smudge	*Judge*	The man of law who will officially blot your copybook aptly becomes an 'inky'.
Ins & Outs of a Cat's Arsehole		What nosey people and intrusive questionnaires are said to want to know.
Insects & Ants	*Pants*	Refers to underpants. In brief, 'insects'.

Inside Left		The ten in a pack of cards. When football teams had inside lefts, ten was their shirt number.
Inside of a Long Distance Runner's Sock		What a mouth is said to be like when it is less than fresh.
Inside of a Wicket Keeper's Glove		What a mouth is said to be like when in need of refreshment.
Inside of an Arab's Underpants		When you've got an awful taste in your mouth and reeking breath, this is what you may say your mouth is like.
Inside Right		The eight in a pack of cards. Footballers playing in this position wore the number eight shirt.
Inside Right	*Tight*	An old-fashioned position on the football field relates to one whose hands are too big for his pockets.
Inspector of Manholes		A male homosexual, an early 20th-century term that needs no delving into.
Instant Custard		To ejaculate within seconds of penetration, premature ejaculation. *See* CUSTARD. An 'instant custard job' – intercourse when both partners are mutually 'gagging for it'.
Intelligence Department		The head, where nature's computer is housed.
Intercoursed		Exhausted, a play on being fucked or shagged out.
Interior Decorating		Sexual intercourse, when the inside walls get a coat of 'emulsion' (qv).
Irene Handl	*Candle*	An example that's been in existence since the early 1970s, when industrial action taken by miners in 1972 forced the closure of power stations and plunged the country into darkness. The name of this British actress (1902–87) was heard when rooms needed light.
Iris		*See* DAFFODIL.
Irish Jig	*a) Cig*	How a 'coffin nail' (qv) became an 'Irish'.
	b) Wig	An 'Irish' is an obvious and much derided vanity shield.
Irish Rose	*Nose*	An old piece that seems to have been picked for the last time.
Irish Screwdriver		A hammer, from a supposed perception that the Irish are incapable of using a tool that doesn't require brute strength.
Irish Stew	*a) Blue*	Refers to all things blue, including melancholia.
	b) True	Said in agreement: 'Too Irish stew.' Or for emphasis: 'Too bloody Irish.'
Irish Way		Anal sex between a man and woman, a supposed Catholic form of contraception.

Iron		a) Money, one of several terms linking a metal to coinage.
		b) A crowbar, especially when in the hands of a housebreaker.
		c) A gun, originally an American piece. 'Iron-mongery' – firearms.
		d) An underworld term for a knuckleduster.
Iron Duke	*Fluke*	A term from the billiard hall that relates to a lucky shot. The Iron Duke was a nickname of the Duke of Wellington (1769–1852).
Iron Girder	*Murder*	Not necessarily the 'top-job' (qv), but more relative to a spoilt child who is allowed to get away with 'iron girder', or a liberty taker: 'There'll be iron girders if the gaffer tumbles to what you're up to.'
Iron Hoof	*Poof (Homosexual)*	An extremely common piece that is always minced to the first element: 'Actors? They're all a bunch of irons.' Not a good nickname for West Ham United though, who are known as 'the Irons'.
Iron Hoop	*Soup*	An ancient term based on a plaything of a bygone era that has now been rolled into oblivion.
Iron Horse	a) *Course*	A racecourse, based on an early nickname for a train.
	b) *Toss*	Cockney dialect makes this 'torse' and it is a reference to tossing a coin to settle an argument: 'Alright, I'll iron you for it. Heads I drink, tails you drive.'
Iron Magnet		A heterosexual male who attracts attention from homosexuals, a gay icon. *See* IRON HOOF.
Iron Mike	*Bike*	Boxer Mike Tyson inspires a term that wouldn't have been out of place years ago when cycles were heavyweight beasts of iron.
Iron Tank	*Bank*	One that would appear to be hard to 'knock over'.
Irons		Eating utensils, i.e., a knife, fork and spoon: 'to lay the irons out' – to set the table.
Is the Pope a Catholic?		A question asked in reply to a question that requires a positive answer.
Isaacs		A name given to a fat person based on the name of the well-known London shellfish vendor Tubby Isaacs.
Isabella	*Umbrella*	A piece that's been keeping the rain off cockney heads every summer for over a century.
Isadora		A long scarf. The dancer, Isadora Duncan (1878–1927) was killed when her scarf got caught in a car wheel while her neck was still in it.
Isle of Man	*Pan*	An example that's never shortened: 'Bung the bangers in the Isle o' Man and I'll butter the "Nat King Coles"' (qv).

Isle of Wight	a) *Alright*	When everything's 'cushti' (qv) it's 'all Isle o'Wight'.
	b) *Light*	What to switch on when it gets dark and a cigarette's no good without one.
	c) *Right*	Applies in terms of direction: 'Chuck an Isle o'Wight at the next corner.' And also correctness, if you're not wrong you must be IoW.
	d) *Tight*	What mean, miserly people are said to be and when your clothes get 'Isle o'Wight', it's time to lose weight.
Itch & Scratch	*Match*	Long been the cheapest way to light a fag.
Ithnom		A month in backslang. 'Exis Ithnoms' – a six-month prison sentence.
Ivy		A thick or gormless woman, a female 'Wally' (qv) whereby a dopey couple may be celebrated around Christmas time as 'the Wally and the Ivy'.
Ivories		a) The teeth. From the 18th century, a time when gnashers probably more closely resembled ebonies, and the mouth was an 'ivory box'. The term still has some bite in it as drinkers still 'rinse their ivories'.
		b) Dice, as thrown since the 19th century.
		c) Piano keys and thus the instrument itself. Good pianists 'tickle the ivories', average ones hammer them.
		d) Billiard balls, early ones were made from ivory.
Ivory Pearl	*Girl*	Not necessarily a white one.
Ivory Thief/ Snatcher		A dentist, terms from the time when dentists took your teeth out rather than filled them. Also 'Gnasher-Snatcher'.
Ixnay		No or none, the pig Latin version of 'nix' (qv), a well-known term of refusal.

J

J Arthur Rank	a) Bank	In this sense the term is probably obsolete, it's demise due to the popularity of (b).
	b) Wank	Employed extensively in the shortened form of 'J Arthur'. Based on the British film producer and entrepreneur who became Lord Rank (1882–1972).
J Carroll Naish	Slash (Urinate)	Stopped in mid-flow at 'J Carroll', this is based on the name of the American actor (1900–73) who played Charlie Chan in a long-running TV series.
Jabby		A shortened, East Londoner's term for an immigrant from the Punjab, a Punjabi.
Jack		a) A police officer or a detective, originally a term from the north of England but now nationwide.
		b) The penis, especially an erect one: 'I just have to look at her and I get a jack on.'
		c) To ejaculate, probably an abbreviation but may be an extension of (b). 'Primojack' – premature ejaculation.
		d) A centuries-old term for a lavatory.
Jack & Danny	Fanny	A well-known term for the vagina: 'I must've been drunk, I kissed her Jack & Danny.'
Jack & Jill	a) Bill	Applies to any horrible piece of paper with a charge on it, be it gas, phone or restaurant, etc. It's also a receipt.
	b) Hill	Since this is what the pair in the nursery rhyme

		climbed, it would seem to be an appropriate and obvious example.
	c) *Pill*	A piece in everyday use among drug users and probably the sick.
	d) *Till*	A piece that has become common in regard to a cash register.
Jack & Jill		A male and female partnership in the police, either detectives or PCs on patrol together.
Jack & Joan	*Alone*	More correctly on one's own. Either a misheard version of 'Jack Jones' (qv), or the famous Mr Jones could be a century-old corruption of this. It's certainly a better rhyme, but either way it makes no difference. If you're keeping yourself company, you're on your 'Jack'.
Jack & Vera	*(Daily) Mirror*	A slightly imperfect rhyme but one that's used in the newspaper distribution industry, and if it's good enough for them. . . . Based on Mr and Mrs Duckworth from TV's *Coronation Street*.
Jack/Jack Shit		Nothing or a very small amount: 'You don't know jack about anything.'
Jack/Jack Tar		A sailor, a term that has been well-known since Brittania first ruled the waves.
Jack Benny	*Penny*	Based on an American comedian (1894–1974) who was famed for his penny-pinching meanness.
Jack Dee	*Pee/Wee*	In vogue at the turn of the millennium and since it is based on one of today's better comedians I foresee him being a star of stage, screen and urinal for years to come.
Jack Doyle	*Boil*	The painful skin eruption based on a colourful Irish boxer of the 1930s (1913–78) whose gimmick was to sing in the ring. Had he danced as well, would it have been the lancer?
Jack Flash	a) *Crash/ Smash*	Refers to a road accident and is possibly an allusion to a speeding motorist.
	b) *Hash*	A drug user's term for hashish, based on the well-known jumping man of the Rolling Stones hit.
Jack Frost	*Lost*	The famous iceman provides a chilly reference to an ignorance of whereabouts: 'If this isn't the B229 we're Jack Frost.'
Jack Horner	*Corner*	Applies to what may be stood in, turned or cut, and is sometimes called 'Little Jack Horner' after the boy in the nursery rhyme.
Jack in a Box		An ancient term for what an expectant mother is carrying, an unborn child.
Jack It In/Up		a) To stop doing something, to abandon a project, to leave one's job, etc.

		b) To die. A dead person is said to have 'Jacked It'. When you spend time with 'Jack Jones' you're on your own, or 'on your Jack'.
Jack Jones	*Alone*	
Jack Ketch	*Stretch*	A term from prison, courtesy of the man who curtailed many a stay by stretching the miscreant's neck or putting an axe through it. Ketch (d. 1686) was an English executioner whose name became identified with the job of hangman.
Jack Malone	*Alone*	An alternative to 'Jack Jones' (qv), but since it also comes down to being 'on your Jack', it's no alternative at all.
Jack of Dibs		A generous man, one who is free with his money, *see* DIBS: 'Have you seen the Jack of Dibs? He'll lend you his arsehole and shit through his ribs.'
Jack of Legs		A tall, long-legged, gangling man or boy. Otherwise known as 'Lanky' or 'Longshanks'.
Jack of No Trades		A useless individual in relation to work, especially when it comes to home maintenence, DIY and anything mechanical. A reversal of a 'Jack of all trades'.
Jack of Spades	*Shades*	Sunglasses, worn as 'Jacks'.
Jack of Tall Tales		A liar, one whose stories border on fantasy.
Jack Off		To masturbate, originally one off an American wrist.
Jack Randall	*Candle*	The name of a 19th-century prize fighter burns on with this archaic term.
Jack Sprat	a) *Brat*	A precocious or unpleasant child is a 'right little Jack Sprat'.
	b) *Fat*	Cut the 'Jack Sprat' off the bacon in a greasy spoon sandwich and there's not much left between the slices. Ironically based on a nursery rhyme character who wouldn't touch the stuff.
Jack Straw		An insubstantial man, one commanding no respect. Literally a man of straw, after the leader of the peasant's revolt of 1381 and not the Foreign Secretary of 2002.
Jack Surpass	*Glass*	An archaic term for a glass of alcohol, based on. . . I don't know who or what it's based on.
Jack Tar	*Bar*	Not necessarily a harbour or riverside bar, even if it is based on the slang term for a sailor.
Jack the Lad		A boastful, swaggering, self-assured young man, who assumes himself to be 'top Johnny' (qv).
Jack the Lad	*Bad*	Descriptive of something that is no longer fresh: 'This milk's Jack the Lad.'
Jack the Ripper	a) *Kipper*	A well-known piece based on the infamous Whitechapel murderer of 1888.
	b) *Slipper*	A term that was used by schoolboys when the

		slipper was a mode of corporal punishment that made sitting a painful experience.
	c) Stripper	A piece that hails from the 1970s, when it became common for pubs to put on striptease shows.
Jack Up		To inject an illicit drug. 'Jacked up' – under the influence of drugs.
Jack-a-Dandy	*Brandy*	Based on an alternative name for will o' the wisp, itself the common name for *ignis fatuus*. This is the phosphorescent light that can be seen hovering over swampy ground at night, so the term may be inspired by the blue flame of ignited brandy.
Jackanory	*Story*	Refers, obviously, to that which is told to a child but is mainly used in the sense of a lie; a teller of tall tales tells 'Jackanorys' and behind his back the term is often his nickname. It is also used in the underworld for an informer because it's what he tells the police.
Jackdaw	*Jaw*	Employed anatomically but more readily associated with a scolding. To 'cop a jackdaw' is to be told off.
Jackdaw & Rook	*Book*	An old term with it's roots in the theatre, where the book was a script.
Jacket & Vest	*West*	The 'jacket' is an old reference to the West End of London.
Jackie Dash	*Slash (Urinate)*	Formed in London's docks on the name of a union official who found fame as a writer and artist. A council building in the recently rebuilt Docklands bears his name, at the back of which drunks stop late at night for a 'Jackie'.
Jackie Trent	*Bent*	Applies to anything that isn't straight but mainly in the sense of corruption; a crooked lawyer, a rigged result or stolen goods, for example. They're all 'Jackie Trent'. Based on a hit singer of the 1960s.
Jack-in-the-Box	*Pox (VD)*	Originally a reference to syphillis, 'Jack' later came to mean any of the antisocial diseases.
Jacks Alive	*Five*	A very common term for £5 is a 'Jacks'. A 'pair of Jacks' is a tenner.
Jacksie/Jaxie		The anus, a well-known and much used example: 'You'll get my toe up your jacksie in a minute.' A threat, not a promise of deviant sex.
Jackson Pollocks	*Bollocks*	The testicles and also rubbish. Based on an American abstract artist (Paul Jackson Pollock 1912–56), about whose work it has probably been said 'What a load of Jacksons.'
Jacobs Crackers	*Knackers*	The testicles, that fragile part of the anatomy based on a brand of fragile biscuit. Known as the 'Jacobs' and sometimes given as 'Jacobs Cream Crackers'.

Jacques Cousteau, do a		To dive, a term from the football terraces regarding a player who tries to con the referee by falling to the ground in order to gain a penalty or free kick. Also called a 'Jacques Cousteau job'. Based on a French diver, a maker of underwater documentaries (1910–97).
Jaffa		A sterile man, based on a Jaffa seedless orange.
Jag		A 17th-century term for a bout of drinking, therefore an archaic booze-up. In the 1950s the term took on another meaning when it was used in the same way for drug taking and, later, glue sniffing.
Jagged		Drunk or high on drugs or solvents.
Jagger's Lips	*Chips*	The singing Stone's salient features often provide late night sustenance after a couple or ten pints of 'Mick Jagger' (qv).
Jail-bait		A sexually alluring girl who is under the age of consent, relations with whom can land a man in court.
Jake/Jakey		Methylated spirit, or meths to one who drinks it.
Jakes		A centuries-old term for a lavatory, one that is still engaged but mostly in the navy. In Ireland it is said as 'Jacks'.
Jam		a) A well-known term for luck: 'You've got some jam, you.' 'Jammy' – lucky.
		b) Blood discharged during the menstrual cycle.
Jam Duff	*Puff (Homosexual)*	A sweet for a sweetie.
Jam Jar	*Car*	A well-known piece that's been in existence since the birth of the car, although originally it applied to a tram car.
Jam Pie	*Eye*	A 1990s version of the well-established 'mince pies'. Time will tell if it stays on the table.
Jam Rag		An old and well-known term for a sanitary towel and, more recently, a tampon.
Jam Roll	*a) Dole*	Refers to unemployment and is used as being on the 'jam roll'.
	b) Parole	An underworld term for the conditional discharge from prison.
Jam Sandwich/ Butty		A modern term for a police patrol car, from it's appearance of white with a red stripe along it's sides.
Jam Tart	*a) Fart*	Based on a sweet but the result of a 'jam tart' is anything but.
	b) Heart	Has been used anatomically but the main usage is towards the suit in a pack of cards.
	c) Sweetheart	Originally applied to a girlfriend but somewhere

along the line the jam got eaten and 'tart' became a byword for women in general, and on the tongue of a jealous wife, an immoral one.

Jamaica Rum	*Thumb*	The 'Jamaica', what henpecked husbands are under and hitchhikers 'have it on'.
James		Student talk for a first-class honours degree, a 'James the First'.
James Gang		A name given to a firm of 'cowboy' (qv) builders based on the legendary American outlaw, Jesse James (1847–82), and his band of rogues.
James Hunt	*Front*	Applies to confidence, whereby an audacious person may be said to have 'more James Hunt than Brighton'. Based on a British racing driver (1947–93), who was World Champion in 1976.
James Riddle	*Piddle*	The formal version of 'Jimmy Riddle' (qv) is quite a common outpouring.
Jammy Dodger	*Roger*	A 1990s piece for sexual intercourse based on a popular biscuit, which is apt when you think about dunking it.
Jampon		A humorous take on a tampon, *see* JAM (b).
Jampot		A rival to 'honeypot' (qv) in the vagina stakes.
Jane		A woman, especially a girlfriend: 'We won't see Will tonight, he's out with his new Jane.'
Jane Russell	*Mussel*	The name of an American film actress is taken for the seafood that's popular in the pub of a Sunday lunchtime.
Jane Shore	a) *Floor*	A 19th-century term that no longer sees a footstep.
	b) *Whore*	A term that has long been in use as a 'Jane'. It was coined by 19th-century sailors who no doubt made humorous associations with 'shore' leave. Based on the 16th-century mistress of King Edward IV.
Janet Street Porter	*Quarter*	A 1980s term used by drug users for a quarter of an ounce of an illegal substance. Based on a TV personality and journalist.
Jankers		A military term for punishment, commonly heard in Civvy Street by way of British cinema.
Japanese Flag		What the anus, during a long bout of diarrhoea, is said to resemble. You've seen the flag so this needs no delving into. And would you want to?
Jap's Eye		A 1990s term for the penile opening, due to the slit shape of what's more commonly known as the 'eye-hole' (qv).
Jar		a) A well-known term for a pint of beer. b) A piece of fake jewellery, especially a diamond. 'Jar up' – to sell someone snide sparkle.
Jar of Jam	a) *Pram*	Put this down to the fact that whenever a clean

J

baby is put in a 'jar of jam', somehow it always manages to get sticky.

b) Tram An elderly example that became extinct in London when trams did, but now that they are running again in South London, a comeback may be in the offing.

Jarred/Jarred Up Drunk, the result of a jar too many. *See* JAR.

Jasper Carrot *Parrot* That which sits IN a birdcage and talks humorously as represented by a Brummie comedian who sits ON a 'birdcage' (qv) and talks humorously.

Jaw a) To talk incessantly, a gabby neighbour can keep you 'jawing' for ages.
b) To tell off, to scold: 'You'd better tidy your room or your mum'll jaw.'

Jawdropper Anything shocking, be it a film, story or revelation, something that leaves you 'jawdropped'.

Jazz Band(s) *Hand(s)* 'Jazzes' are a modern version of the traditional 'Germans'. *See* GERMAN BANDS.

Jazz-House A lively pub, one with loud music. A 1960s term used derogatorily by people who prefer a quiet pint.

Jean-Claude *Ham* Too long a term to be called anything but 'Jean-
Van Damme Claude'. Based on the Belgian action-movie hero in regard to what's sold on the cold meat counter. If it has anything to do with bad acting, it didn't come from me, right?

Jekyll & Hyde *Snide* Very pertinent in the sense of being two-faced. Also applies to fake or counterfeit goods, a copied painting, a moody Rolex, a dodgy banknote, etc. They're all Jekylls. Based on the novel *Dr Jekyll and Mr Hyde* by Robert Louis Stevenson.

Jekyll & Hydes *Strides* How trousers or jeans became known as 'Jekylls'.

Jellied Eel(s) *Wheel(s)* Applies not only to an actual wheel but to transport in general: 'Have you got jellied eels?' – have you got a car?

Jelly a) An ancient term for semen, to 'jack one's jelly'. *See* JACK (c).
b) An underworld term for gelignite, several fictional safecrackers have been called 'Jelly'.

Jelly Bean Drugs. Any form of pill or capsule.

Jellybone *Telephone* A localised term used by some courier controllers.

Jem Mace *Face* An archaic piece based on the legendary 19th-century boxer from Norfolk (1831–1910). Known as 'The Swaffham Gypsy', he became the world heavyweight champion in 1870.

Jenny Hill *Pill* A drug taken for medicinal purposes, based on a music-hall entertainer (1851–96).

Jenny Lee	a) *Flea*	A term that was once as widespread as the blood-sucking parasite.
	b) *Key*	These days this is 'Jenny' at her commonest.
	c) *Tea*	A 19th-century term that has been supplanted by the famous 'Rosie Lee'.
Jenny Lind/Lindy	*Wind/Windy*	Can apply to the weather or to internal gases that work their way out one way or another. The lady was a Victorian singer known as the 'Swedish Nightingale' (1820–87).
Jenny Linder	*Window*	A 19th-century term for the casualty of a 'smash and grab' raid.
Jenny Riddle	*Piddle*	The little-known sister of the famous 'Jimmy Riddle' (qv).
Jenny Wren	*Ben (Truman)*	Downed to a pint of 'Jenny' in reference to this brand of beer.
Jere		a) Excrement, an ancient term based on the Romany *jeer*.
		b) The backside, an early showman's term that was adapted by pickpockets, for whom stealing 'off the jere' meant 'dipping' into a back pocket.
		c) A male homosexual, a piece that is either an extension of (b), whereby a 'jere boy' is a variation of 'bum boy' (qv) or RS for queer boy.
Jeremiah	*Fire*	Applies to a domestic fire which once was exclusively fuelled by coal. It was common to 'put another piece of merry on the jerry'. *See* MERRY OLD SOUL.
Jeremy Beadle	*Needle*	To give someone the 'Jeremy' is to anger or annoy them and is aptly based on TV's arch practical joker, whose show, *Beadle's About*, seemed to be about trying to give some poor unsuspecting soul a heart attack.
Jericho	*Po*	Named after an ancient city that was the scene of a biblical demolition job. Gideon, the leader of the Israelites, in order to save money, brilliantly hired some musicians (whose hourly rate was cheaper than the navvies of the day) to blow their trumpets and bring down the walls. Thus revealing many a hapless Canaanite sitting with fingers in ears on their decorous chamberpots midway through fear-induced defecation. When they were cleaned these pots became prized spoils of war and were known as 'jerries'. This story was told to me by a direct descendant of Gideon who had many such family heirlooms. Due to circumstances, however, he was being forced to sell them from the back of

a van on some waste ground off the Mile End Road. 'Not for ten pounds, not for eight, not even six. But to you, and I'm robbing myself . . .'

Jerk A well-known, originally American, term for a fool or a contemptible person.

Jerk/Jerk Off American terms regarding masturbation which, although heard in Britain, will never replace 'wank' or 'toss'. *See both.* 'Jerk the gherkin' – to masturbate.

Jerk-Off An obnoxious or useless person, the American version of 'wanker' (qv).

Jerry a) A Word War One term for a German, which saw service again when the second lot broke out.
b) A 19th-century term for a chamberpot, now most likely to be heard on TV's *Antiques Roadshow*.

Jerry Diddle *Fiddle* How shady goings-on were described a hundred years ago. In America it's a violin.

Jerry Lee *Pee/Wee* There may be a whole lotta shakin' goin' on when you're bursting for a 'Jerry Lee'. Based on the American rock 'n' roll singer and pianist Jerry Lee Lewis.

Jerry Quarry *Lorry* A 1960s example based on a tough American heavyweight boxer of the period (1945–99), who fought for the world title and lost only to the top fighters of his time.

Jerry Riddle *Piddle* A 19th-century piece which may have something to do with chamberpots.

Jerry-cum-Mumble *a) Rumble* If anyone is 'Jerry' to what you've been up to, you've been found out or rumbled.
b) Tumble An archaic example that originally referred to a fall. It later became widely used as 'jerry', meaning to understand: 'I was jerry to what he meant' – I tumbled (understood) what he meant. *See* TUMBLE (b).

Jessie An effeminite homosexual male, a term that later saw service as any cowardly or sissyish man.

Jesus Boots A 1950s term for sandals, footwear much favoured by beatniks and, apparently, Jesus.

Jesus Freak A fervent or born-again Christian, one given to preaching to those not wanting to be preached at.

Jew A miserly person, one tight with his money. From a long-held belief that a Jew never possessed a coin or banknote he didn't love or could bear to part with.

Jew/Jew Down To get the better of someone financially by fair means or foul, from the supposed skill of a Jew in the art of haggling.

Jewish Lightning		Arson. The burning down of an unprofitable business premises for the insurance.
Jewish Penicillin		Chicken soup, so called because of the Jewish belief in it as a cure-all.
Jewish Tank		A London taxi. Jewish mothers dream of their sons becoming doctors, lawyers, scientists, etc. Many have to settle for taxi drivers.
Jig		A lie, a ruse or a swindle. The 'jig is up' when it's exposed.
Jig It/Up		Of a horse or greyhound, to win easily. To 'dance in'.
Jig-a-Jig/Jiggy-Jig		Sexual intercourse; an expression, it seems, that every nationality in the world understands.
Jig-Saw Puzzle	*Muzzle*	Heard in the late 1990s when a law was passed forbidding owners of certain breeds of dog from walking their pets without first fitting the animal with a 'jig-saw'.
Jigger		A derogatory term for a black person.
Jiggle & Jog	*Frog*	Refers to a French person. A condescending view of the Arsenal football club of 2001 by a Spurs fan: 'They've got more jiggles than the resistance had in the war.'
Jill		A policewoman, the female version of 'Jack' (qv, a).
Jill Off		Female masturbation, an equal rights version of 'jack off' (qv).
Jim		A man who gets sexual pleasure from watching prostitutes ply their trade or from browsing in sex shops. One of the 'dirty mac brigade' (qv).
Jim & Jack	*Back*	Anatomically speaking, people have been suffering 'Jim and Jack' pain since the 1960s.
Jim/Jimmy Skinner	*Dinner*	After a 'heavy bevvy' a man went home and demanded his 'Jim Skinner'. His wife threw a pork chop at him, causing him to stagger back, trip over the dog and smack his head heavily against the door frame. 'Thanks love,' he smiled, 'but I won't bother with the vegetables.'
Jim /Jimmy Mason	*Basin*	To have a portion of something is to have a basinful or a 'Jimmyful'.
Jim Brown	*Town*	A 19th-century term for the West End of London.
Jim/Jimmy Prescott	*Waistcoat*	A piece that's been in the back of the wardrobe gathering moth-holes for many years.
Jim-Jams		a) Nervousness, apprehension. An attack of the 'jim-jams' may precede an important event. b) Originally the shaky uneasiness following a drinking session, but now also tremors brought on by drug taking.
Jimmy Boyle	*Foil*	A drug user's term for kitchen foil, as used for

'chasing the dragon' (qv) and smoking heroin. Based on the name of a British writer.

Jimmy Britts	*Shits*	The 'Jimmys' is a bout of diarrhoea, based on an American boxer (1879–1940) who in 1902 claimed the world lightweight title.
Jimmy Floyd Hasselbank	*Wank*	A 21st-century term for an act of masturbation that is known simply as a 'Jimmy Floyd'. Based on a Dutch international footballer who joined Chelsea in 2000.
Jimmy Grant	*Immigrant*	On its 19th-century formation this meant an emigrant, someone leaving for the colonies. In Australia, however, the term was reversed to a new arrival.
Jimmy Hill	*Pill*	Based on an ex-footballer and current TV pundit, this refers to a prescribed or an illicit drug.
Jimmy Hix	*Fix*	A drugs-related piece for a shot in the arm.
Jimmy Logie	*Bogie*	Relates to a piece of nasal residue and is based on an Arsenal and Scotland footballer of the 1950s.
Jimmy Nail	*a) Sale*	When prices are down there must be a 'Jimmy' on.
	b) Stale	A Geordie actor and singer comes in as a rival to 'British Rail' (qv), but if we're talking sandwiches, he'll never be as apt.
Jimmy O'Goblin	*Sovereign*	Not her maj but £1. Seldom used but 'sov' is very popular.
Jimmy Riddle	*Piddle*	By far the most familiar member of the 'Riddle' clan, whereby people on the point of bladder-burst are 'breaking their necks for a Jimmy'.
Jimmy Rollocks	*Bollocks*	As with 'Johnny' and 'Tommy' (*see both*) this represents the testicles, and is what a certain alternative comedian, struggling in an East End pub, was said to be as funny as a boil on.
Jimmy White	*Kite (Cheque)*	A 1980s term based on the London-born snooker player who has seen his fair share of big money 'kites'. Normally passed as a 'Jimmy'.
Jimmy Wilde	*Mild (Ale)*	Based on the former world flyweight boxing champion from Wales and formed around the time of World War One, when both man and beer were in their heydays. The diminutive Wilde (1892–1969) is rated as one of Britain's greatest-ever fighters.
Jimmy Young	*a) Bung*	A backhander or bribe is usually shortened to the Christian name: 'I gave the gateman a Jimmy so we'll be alright.'
	b) Tongue	Aptly based on the name of a hit singer of the 1950s and later a beknighted radio personality who obviously does a lot of talking: 'Stop flapping your Jimmy' – keep quiet.
Jingle Bell	*Girl*	A 1980s term that demands the cockney pronunciation of girl as 'gel'. 'Saveloys and jingles' – boys and 'gels'.

Joan of Arc	a) *Lark*	Not really used in connection with playing about but said after a narrow escape or in a difficult situation: 'Sod that for a Joan of Arc.' Had the Maid of Orleans (1412–31) been the Maid of West Ham she would no doubt have said it herself when they lit the fire.
	b) *Park*	Even in the best-kept 'Joan of Arc' there's a piece of dogshit. A cockney cynicism.
	c) *Shark*	This time, the fiery French heroine comes in as a predatory fish and an unscrupulous person.
Joan Rivers	*Shivers*	Refers to fear-induced trembling, the creeps: 'He gives me the Joans.' Based on an American comedienne who, for a while in the 1980s, was popular in Britain.
Joanna	*Piano*	A very well-known piece from a time when the working man loved nothing more than a pint and a sing-song round the 'old Joanna'.
Job		a) To punch. People who get 'jobbed' tend not to get up in a hurry.
		b) To put the blame on someone, to 'frame' (qv). Famously to 'do a job on'. Also to cheat. A 'job jockey' won't try to win a race.
Job & Finish		To work unscheduled hours, to leave as soon as the job is finished. An incentive to work hard and fast.
Jobbed		Finished. 'Another job jobbed' – another chore done.
Jobbie/Jobby		To defecate and also what's ejected. A piece from north of the border, whereby a Scot may step in a 'wee jobbie'.
Jobsworth		A minor official, one who zealously upholds company regulations because 'it's more than my job's worth' not to. But shouldn't it be 'less than his job's worth?'
Jock		a) The typical name for a Scot. Although based on a man's name it can be either sex. The 'Jockos' – the Scottish football team, as named by the English.
		b) An old term for a jockey, more recently a DJ.
		c) An 18th-century term for the genitals, hence a jockstrap.
Jockey's Whip	*Kip*	To catch a little bit of 'jockeys' is to grab a 'bit of blink' – get some sleep.
Jockey's Whip(s)	*Chip(s)*	May accompany a steak or represent a stake.
Jockstrap		A Scotsman. 'Jock' with a strap tagged on.
Jodrell Bank	*Wank*	An extensively used example for the 'polishing of one's telescope', always as a 'Jodrell'. Based on the giant observatory in Cheshire, England.
Joe Baksi	*Taxi*	A piece from the 1940s based on an American boxer of the period (1922–77) who found fame by

coming to England to beat the British heavyweight champion, Bruce Woodcock.

Joe Blake	a) Cake	A 19th-century piece that is no longer sliced due to the regular use of (c).
	b) Stake	Once heard at gambling arenas for money that is gambled.
	c) Steak	A term that is not in the least bit rare.
Joe Blakes	Shakes	A reference to the DTs, or the trembles of the well 'mangled' (qv).
Joe Brown	Town	A 19th-century piece that was probably coined by itinerant entertainers, circus folk or the like.
Joe Buck	Fuck	Sexual intercourse from the 1970s by way of the stud character in the Oscar-winning film of 1969, *Midnight Cowboy*.
Joe Cole	Dole	21st-century parlance for unemployment benefit used by young out-of-workers. Based on a current England footballer, whose talent ensures he will never have to 'dab on' (qv).
Joe Daki	Paki	A recent example that has become common in the East End of London, but then so has the Pakistani immigrant.
Joe Erk	Berk	A twice-removed example (*See* BERKSHIRE HUNT), which has to be used in full to distinguish it from Joe Hunt, which is the same but different.
Joe Goss	Boss	An old piece for the foreman or guv'nor, based on an English bare-knuckle fighter who was top man in the heavyweight division from 1876 until 1880.
Joe Gurr	Stir (Prison)	A piece that's been serving time since the 1930s.
Joe Hook	a) Book	A 1930s example but it now seems a case of 'Joe Hook has left the library'.
	b) Crook	A perpetual lawbreaker for the best part of a century which derives from the slang word for a thief – a 'hook', a dealer in 'hooky (stolen) goods'.
Joe Hunt	Cunt	Generally reduced to a 'Joey' when used in connection with a fool or a mug, but when an obnoxious littleworth is involved, 'Joe Hunt' doesn't get shortened.
Joe Loss	Toss	Based on the name of a British bandleader (1909–90), this is used either in the sense of not caring, i.e., not giving a 'Joe Loss', or to the only thing the England cricket team is ever likely to win against Australia, the 'Joe Loss'.
Joe Macbride	Ride	Sexual intercourse, late 20th-century style.
Joe Ronce	Ponce	Another of the family Ronce (*see* CHARLIE, HARRY and JOHNNY RONCE) who have been protecting prostitutes since the 1920s.

Joe Rook	a) Book	Specifically the one made by an on-course bookmaker, a piece that has been in existence since bookies needed a permit rather than a license to fleece punters.
	b) Crook	A thief, possibly based on a misheard version of 'Joe Hook'.
Joe Rookie	Bookie	Time was, anyone could set themselves up as a bookmaker at a racecourse or dog track, many of whom would operate outside the bounds of legitimacy. Which would explain the association with 'Joe Rook' (qv, b).
Joe Rourke	Fork (Hand)	Specifically the hand of a 'dip', Mr Rourke is therefore a pickpocket. The term has also been used as a rhyme on 'crook'.
Joe Royle	Boil	A 1980s term for a pus-filled nasty, based on an England international footballer.
Joe Savage	Cabbage	A 19th-century term that has most likely been boiled into obscurity.
Joe Shmoe		A simpleton or a mug: 'What, my round again. Who am I Joe Shmoe?'
Joe Skinner	Dinner	One of three J Skinners that have been dished up since Victorian times. See JIM and JOHNNY.
Joe Soap	Dope	Refers to a fool or a mug, the one in the crowd most likely to step in something. Another 'Harry Huggins' (qv). As a term of mild abuse it's reduced to 'soaper'.
Joe Strummer	Bummer	A 90s example regarding an unpleasant or unlucky experience, a 'sickener'. Based on a rock musician who gained fame as singer/guitarist with the punk group 'The Clash' in the 1970s. He died in 2002, aged 50.
Joe Tank	Bank	A World War Two piece that is now seldom, if ever, used.
Joey		a) An old term for a clown based on the famed English clown Joseph Grimaldi (1779–1837). Outside the circus tent any fool can be a 'Joey'.
		b) A parcel or package smuggled into a prison by a visitor.
		c) An extinct term for the long-departed coin, the threepenny bit.
Joey the Plum		A fool or a dupe. The one who usually gets the blame.
Jogue		An old, underworld term for a shilling (5p). Sometimes known as 'jug'.
John		a) An American term for a toilet, now well-known in Britain through television.
		b) A prostitute's customer, the jargon of the girls themselves.

John Bull	a) *Full*	Anything from a stadium to a stomach can be 'John Bull'. But the main reference is to being full of alcohol, i.e., drunk.
	b) *Pull*	Mainly used in reference to being stopped by the police, but also to 'go out on the John Bull' is to go in search a sexual encounter.
John Cleese	*Cheese*	A piece of middle-class slang based on the English comedy actor and writer. Refers to any kind of cheese, be it Cheddar, Stilton or Norwegian Blue. Or is that a parrot?
John Dillon	*Shilling*	Based on the name of a racehorse, the term beat the coin in the obscurity stakes.
John Hop	*Cop (Police Officer)*	They say that you are approaching old age when the 'Jonnops' begin to look youthful. When the judges start looking younger, you're there. Sometimes a 'John Hopper' – copper.
John Major	*Pager*	A 1990s piece for the bleeping radio device based on a British prime minister of the period.
John O'Groat	*Coat*	It makes no difference that the 's' is missing, for years people have been wearing their 'John O' Groats'. Oh there it is.
John O'Groats	*Oats*	Refers to sexual satisfaction. When a man has had his 'Johnoes', he's 'had his end away'.
John Peel	*Eel*	Applies to a jellied or stewed eel, culinary traditions of working-class London. Based on the old traditional song 'd'ye ken', and not the old traditional disc jockey.
John Prescott	*Waistcoat*	The New Labour politician, better known as 'Two Jags', becomes the latest member of the Prescott boys to represent the third part of a suit. *See* CHARLIE, COLONEL *and* JIM PRESCOTT.
John Selwyn Gummer	*Bummer*	'What a John Selwyn!' As this Tory MPs daughter might have said when, in 1990, she was famously forced by her father, the agricultural minister, to eat a hamburger in public to prove the safety of British beef. A bummer is an unpleasant, disappointing or distressing occurrence.
John Thomas		A 19th-century term for the penis, which gained notoriety and a wide usage after the publication of *Lady Chatterley's Lover* by DH Lawrence in 1959. Often shortened to 'John', 'Johnny' or 'J T'.
John Wayne	*Train*	A 1950s term that seems to have run out of track since this American film star (1907–79) stopped shooting Indians from one.
John-John		A derogatory term of address for an Asian man, often heard spoken by Alf Garnett during his

visits to the corner shop in TV's *Till Death Us Do Part*.

Johnnie Ray   *Day*

A 1950s term based on a popular American singer of the period (1927–90). It was used by young national servicemen when lamenting the fact that it had been 'one of those Johnnie Rays'.

Johnny

a) A condescending term for anybody whose name is unknown, e.g., the window cleaning Johnny, Johnny Law (a policeman), Johnny Newbloke (a newcomer), etc.

b) An all-purpose prefix for any race or nationality: Johnny Frog (Frenchman), Johnny Dago, Johnny Turk, etc.

c) A Jack in a pack of cards: 'The first Johnny deals.'

Johnny/Johnny Bag

A condom. The name being an enlargement of John (*See* JOHN THOMAS), this then is literally a bag for the penis. Well-known when cased-up in rubber. *See* RUBBER JOHNNY.

Johnny Cash   *a) Hash*

A drug user's expression for hashish.

    b) Slash (Urinate)

To irrigate the desert, courtesy of an American country-and-western singer (1932–2003) and occasional actor in westerns.

Johnny Cotton   *Rotten*

If it's rank, putrid or generally not fit for human consumption, it's 'Johnny Cotton'.

Johnny Foreigner

A generic term for anybody who isn't British, he who must shoulder the blame for all the world's ills: 'I blame Johnny Foreigner.'

Johnny Giles   *Piles*

A 1970s version of 'Farmer Giles' (qv), based on an Irish international footballer of the period.

Johnny Horner   *Corner*

An old term that was sometimes used to signify the nonspecific whereabouts of someone: 'He's gone round the Johnny' often meant 'he's up the pub'.

Johnny Rann   *Scran (Food)*

A largely unheard version of 'Tommy O'Rann' (qv).

Johnny Reggae

A young West Indian male, a piece that has been in use since the 1971 hit record of this name by UK group, the Piglets.

Johnny Rollocks   *Bollocks (Testicles)*

One of a trio of Rollocks, the others being 'Jimmy' and 'Tommy'. *See both.*

Johnny Ronce   *Ponce*

The last of the Ronce boys in the prostitute-minding game. *See* CHARLIE, HARRY and JOE RONCE.

Johnny Rutter   *Butter*

First spread in the 19th century, rarely, if ever, heard now.

Johnny Skinner   *Dinner*

When this was coined it would have been cooked in a scullery.

Johnny Vaughan   *Porn*

One of the first terms of the 21st century, as a British comedian turns blue.

Johnny Walker	*Talker*	Refers to 'trappy' people, sometimes an informer, but mainly to people who talk incessantly and drive you mad. Based on a brand of whisky, the connection with loose tongues is obvious.
Johnnydom		A condom, a humorous extension of 'Johnny' (qv).
Johnny-on-the-Dot		A fastidious time-keeper, someone who, if he says he'll see you at two, will be there on the dot.
Johnson		A prostitute's enforcer, a pimp, especially if black. A term from the early 20th century based on the name of the first black world heavyweight boxing champion Jack Johnson (1878–1946).
Joint		a) The most widely known term for a marijuana or hashish cigarette, which originally applied to a pipeful of opium.
		b) A bar, originally a disreputable one. A nightclub where cheap women cost a fortune.
		c) A gambling club and by extension an on-course bookmaker's pitch, a 1930s piece that got attached to early betting shops.
		d) Any establishment or dwelling place, much like a 'gaff' or 'drum'. *See both.*
Joint of Beef	*Chief*	A reference to the boss man: 'Who's the joint o' beef round here?'
Joker		A man, especially an incompetent or strange-looking one: 'Who's this joker?'
Jollies		Gratifications, sexual or otherwise. To 'get your jollies' is to indulge in whatever makes you happy.
Jollop		Medicine, especially a laxative that will hopefully bring forth a 'dollop' (qv).
Jolly		In a betting event the 'jolly' is the favourite.
Jolly/Jolly Nob		An 18th-century term for the head, still heard occasionally as a whack or knock on the 'jolly'.
Jolly Along		To keep someone happy by telling them what they want to hear whether it's true or not.
Jolly Bean		An illicit pill or tablet, a 1960s term for benzedrine or amphetamine. A play on jelly bean.
Jolly Joker	*Poker*	Strangely not the card game but the implement for poking a fire, which somewhat dates the term to the days of coal fires.
Jolly Popper		An occasional rather than habitual drug user.
Jolly Roger	*Lodger*	From a time when people commonly supplemented their wages by letting out the spare room and taking in a 'jolly'. Based on the pirate flag, which suggests care should be taken when letting strangers into the house.

Jolly-Up
A drinking session or a party, where a good time is had by all. Sometimes called a 'jollyo'.

Jolson Story   *Cory (Penis)*
Based on the name of a 1946 film on the life of singer Al Jolson (1886–1950), the term appeared later as a 'Jolson', relating to what you wouldn't show your mammy.

Jonathan Ross   *Toss*
An updated version of the earlier 'Stirling Moss'. For 'I couldn't give a Stirling' read 'I couldn't give a Jonathan'. Based on a British TV personality and journalist.

Josser
A fool or a simpleton, a 19th-century term for anyone with his 'hat on crooked'.

Joy of My Life   *Wife*
Often said with tongue firmly in cheek.

Joy Pop
To inject drugs on an irregular basis, as a 'Joy Popper' does because he wants to rather than needs to.

Joy Stick   *Prick (Penis)*
Probably a description that results in a fortuitous piece of RS. However, it does rhyme and it has been used in this guise.

Joynson-Hicks   *Six*
A theatrical piece from the 1920s that is based on Sir William Joynson-Hicks (1865–1932), a Tory home secretary of the period. The number's long been up on this one.

Jozzer
The penis, a late 20th-century piece that may be an abbreviated 'John Thomas' (qv).

Jubbies
A late 20th-century term for late 20th-century breasts.

Judge Dredd   *Head*
A newspaper strip cartoon inspired a film and this late 1990s example.

Judi Dench   *Stench*
A 1990s term based on the British actress whose awards successes would confirm that this has nothing to do with her performances. Her dameship just happens to rhyme with a bad smell.

Judy
A well-known term for a woman in the north of England, which has become attached to a prostitute.

Judy & Punch   *Lunch*
A 1990s piece, probably from the middle classes because working-class people 'don't do Judy'. The midday meal break is dinner time.

Jug
a) Prison, a common term that derives from an old Scottish word 'joug', meaning a pillory. A serving convict is 'in jug', having been 'jugged' or 'jugged up' – imprisoned.

b) A pint of beer. Men commonly go for a few 'jugs' and fall over when they're 'jugged up' or 'jugged'. A drunkard is a 'jughead'.

Jug & Pail   *Jail*
The well-known term 'jug' (qv), meaning prison,

was in place long before this. 'Jug & Pail' is an early 20th-century piece that may have reflected cell furnishings.

Jug/Jughead		A fool, somebody who, if brains were made of dripping wouldn't have enough to fry a chip.
Juggins		Somebody readily put-upon, the fool who is easily parted from his money. A dupe.
Jughead		Somebody with a large head, especially when equipped with 'jug handles' – big ears.
Jugs		Breasts, as in 'milk jugs'.
Juice		a) Alcohol, originally an American term but now the British also go out on the 'Juice'. An over-indulgence will get you 'Juiced' or 'Juiced Up' and a drunkard is a 'Juicer' or 'Juicehead'. Anywhere that sells alcohol is also a 'Juicer'.
		b) Fuel, be it petrol or diesel for engines or paraffin for heaters and lamps.
		c) Electricity, where to switch on is to turn on the 'juice'. To suffer electrocution is to be 'Juiced'.
Juicy Pits		Sweaty, shirt-drenching armpits, common at summer weddings.
Julian Clary	a) Fairy	A 1990s term for a homosexual, which almost wrote itself based, as it is, on a gay British comedian.
	b) Lairy (Flash)	In regard to being gaudily dressed this is as appropriate as (a), given that his stage attire is blindingly loud (does that make sense?). Also applies to anyone 'giving it the big 'un'.
Julian Dicks	Six	A former West Ham footballer switches sports by becoming a big hit in cricket.
Julius Caesar	a) Cheeser	A cheeser is an early diminutive of 'cheese cutter' – a flat cap, which explains why the Roman emperor sits atop cockney heads.
	b) Freezer	Interesting that the term for what can make ice-cream should be based on someone from Italy. Mayhap he was the original 'hokey pokey man'.
	c) Geezer	A late 20th-century piece whereby 'Who's that man?' becomes 'Who's that Julius?'
Jumbo's Trunk	Drunk	An infrequently used piece to describe someone who stayed too long at the watering hole.
Jump		An old and well-known term for sexual intercourse. Heard in a London bar: 'If we don't get a jump in this place there's something wrong with us.'
Jumper		A thief who specialises in stealing from offices, a reduced version of 'stair jumper'.
Jumping Jack	Black	Refers to a black person and sometimes the snooker ball.

Jump-Up		To steal from the back of a lorry; cheap goods are usually the result of someone being 'at the jump-up'. A specialist thief in this field is a 'jump-up merchant'.
Jungle Bunny		A derogatory term for a black person which has been in use since the 1950s.
Jungle Jim/ **Jimming**	*Swim/* *Swimming*	A piece that lived and died in the 1950s when the TV series of this name came and went. It's star, Johnny Weismuller, was a former screen Tarzan and an Olympic swimming champion to boot, so the term was apt at the time.
Jungle Juice		Strong alcohol of the cheap and nasty kind. Originally the home-brewed concoctions of World War Two soldiers serving 'up the jungle'.
Jungle Music		A common example used disparagingly by the elderly, who describe any music with a beat as this.
Jungly		A disdainful term to describe an unsophisticated, uncouth or bad-mannered person.
Junk		Addictive drugs, especially heroin, on which 'junkies' get hooked.
Junk Food		Food with low nutritional value, typically hamburgers, hotdogs, and chips, etc.

SCHNITZELBURGER BLUES

I've travelled here, I've travelled there, I've journeyed hither and thither
I've scaled the highest mountain and crossed the widest river
From east to west, from north to south, been there and back again
I've sailed the seven seas and every single mile in vain
I've roasted in the desert sun, the arctic nights were murder
Yet nowhere could I find the legendary schnitzelburger.

I've had schnitzel soup in Guadeloupe
In Mexico schnitzel con carne
And schnitzel and Guinness, stir fried in gin is
A favourite in Killarney.
I once stopped off in Dusseldorf
And sampled schnitzel strudel
Whilst in Bangkok they make the stock
For schnitzel stew from poodles.
I've had schnitzel à l'orange en France
Curried schnitzels in Bengal
And I had a stab at schnitzel kebab –
In downtown Istanbul.
Gerschnitzelfish is a wondrous dish

In kosher Tel Aviv
The schnitzel and pasta in Venice just has ta
Be tasted to be believed.
In Peking the schnitzel chow min
Is the tastiest of dishes
And the schnitzel quiche on Bondi beach
Was flamin' well delicious
Once in York I charged my fork
With schnitzel in the hole
And a schnitzel inside when it's Kentucky fried
Is a gastronomic goal.
I've had schnitzel pie in Peckham Rye
Schnitzels barbecued in Crete
And a schnitzel sandwich in anyone's language
Is a tasty teatime treat.
I've had schnitzels raw on a Japanese floor
In New York schnitzelfurters
But where on Earth does anyone serve
That elusive schnitzelburger?

Junk Mail		Unwanted advertising sent by post, the garbage that goes straight from letter box to dustbin, turning the postman into a waste delivery agent.
Junkie/Junkhead		A couple of the many terms for a drug addict, 'junkie' being the commonest.
Junkie Jim		A name given to a drug addict: 'Look out, here comes Junkie Jim.'
Just as I Feared	*Beard*	A piece that's always trimmed to a 'just as'.

K

K		Modern speak for £1000 based on the kilo, which contains that many grams.
K/Key		A dealer's term for a kilo of any drug.
K B/Kaybee		The initials of a 'knock back' indicate a rejection: 'I've had enough KBs for one night, I'm gonna concentrate on getting pissed.' The dejected moan of a would-be ladies' man.
Kaker		Anything nasty or unpleasant, from the yiddish word for excrement.
Kamikaze		An expression used in cold weather, when there's a nip in the air.
Kangaroo	a) *Jew*	A well-known term that's often used for on-course Jewish bookmakers, especially, it would appear, in the jumping season.
	b) *Screw*	Prisoners slang for a prison officer, usually in the reduced form of 'kanga'. It also applies secondarily to wages: 'He's never short of a few bob so he must be on a good kangaroo.'
Kaput		Broken down, usually beyond repair, from the German word for knackered.
Kate Adie	*Lady*	Based on a TV news reporter, who not only appears as one of her sex but mainly in the guise of a ladies toilet, the 'Kate Adies'.

Kate & Sidney	*Steak & Kidney*	A piece from caff society of years gone by for a steak and kidney pie or pudding. I seem to remember it from school dinner days as 'snake and pygmy'.
Kate Carney	*Army*	A very well-known piece that is based on a music-hall artiste (1869–1950). Coined by World War One soldiers and used by squaddies as the 'Kate' ever since.
Kate Moss	*Toss*	A 1990s term based on a British fashion model. This is an update of the earlier 'Joe Loss' (qv), in that now the uncaring couldn't give a 'Kate' and a dispute may be settled by the 'Kate Moss' of a coin.
Katharine Docks	*Socks*	Based on the dock near the Tower of London which closed in 1968, which is possibly when this term was last used.
Kaycab		The back in kaycabslang.
Kaycollobs		Bollocks, backslang testicles. Sometimes said lazily as 'kaylobs'.
Kaycuff		The backslang version of 'fuck', sexual intercourse not necessarily from the rear. 'Kaycuff fo' – fuck off. 'Kaycuffing dratsab' – fucking bastard.
Kayken		The neck. In backslang a pest looks like a 'nyap in the kayken' – a pain in the neck.
Kaykirp/Kirp		The penis, a 'prick' in backslang.
Kaylied		Drunk, a well-known term for raising a glass too many. Possibly connected to kali, a type of sherbet from which a drink could be made. *See* Sherbet.
Kaylim		Milk, a drop of backslang 'cow juice'.
Kaylobs		*See* Kaycollobs.
Kaynab		Underworld backslang for a bank. 'Kaynab boj' – bank job.
Kaynaw		Masturbation, a backslang 'wank', whereby a 'pull and push' becomes a 'push and pull'. Said as a 'kayner' or 'caner'.
Kaynits		A smell. A backslang stink. Food that has gone off is 'kaynitso' (pronounced 'kenitso').
Kaynups		Semen. Backslang spunk.
Kaynurd/ Kennurd		Drunk, a backslang result of going out on the 'Sip' (qv).
Kayrof		A fork, the backslang oppo of an 'eefink' (qv).
Kayrop		Pork, an example of backslang from the meat market. A 'gel o' kayrop' – a leg of pork.
Kayrow		Work. 'Kayrow is the curse of the drinking classes,' as Oscar Wilde might have said had he been familiar with backslang.

Kecks		A well-known term in the north of England for trousers that travelled south during the 1960s. *See* KICKS/KICKSIES.
Keek/Keech		Scottish excrement, a term well-known to fans of the TV series *Rab. C Nesbitt.*
Keep Dog-Eye		To keep a look out, or a watch on. A piece of underworld jargon.
Keep One's End Up		To do one's share of the work, to pay one's way, especially in the pub.
Keep One's Hair/ Wig On		To stay in control of one's emotions; to stay calm. The inference being that if you keep a cool head you've no need to 'tear your hair out' as angry, hot-headed folk are said to do. 'Keep your Hair On!' – calm down! Other versions include keeping one's 'Shirt' and 'Whiskers' on. Another evolvement is 'Keep Your Teeth In' as enraged denture wearers have a tendency to become detached from their man-made 'mouthbones' during arguments.
Keep the Population Down		To masturbate, to waste 'baby gravy' (qv).
Keith Moon	*Loon*	A 1960s example based on a rock drummer (1947–78) whose outrageous exploits led him to being known as 'Moon the loon'. This is a piece that wrote itself.
Kelly's Eye		The number one at the bingo hall. Based on someone called Kelly who had a famous 'mince'.
Ken		An archaic term for a house, which is involved in many examples of slang. 'Bawdy Ken' – brothel, 'fencing Ken' – a place to take stolen goods, 'Boozing Ken – pub, etc., 'Ken Buster' – burglar.
Ken Dodd	*Wad*	Refers to a large roll of banknotes produced from a pocket or from under the stairs of a house in Knotty Ash. Based on a British comedian who fell foul of the taxman.
Ken Dodds	*Cods (Testicles)*	'Kick 'im in the Ken Dodds' is an instruction to fight dirty. And hard grafters work their 'Kens' off.
Kenneth Branagh	*Scanner*	A modern term for a modern piece of equipment, part of a home PC system. Based on a British actor, director and dramatist of the classical theatre.
Kennington Lane	*Pain*	Based on a road in South London near the Oval cricket ground, whereby a batsman facing a demon fast bowler without his protective cup could end up reeling in 'Kennington'.
Kensington		Artificial blood and guts in the film industry, a theatrical pun on Kensington Gore, a road in West London.

Kentish Town	*Brown*	A nearby rival to 'Camden Town' in relation to copper coinage, originally pre-decimal pennies.
Kermit		A French person, a 1980s term based on the name of the muppet frog. *See* FROG.
Kermit the Frog	*a) Bog (Lavatory)*	Based on a character from TV's *The Muppet Show*, people have been hopping to the 'Kermit' since the 1980s.
	b) Snog	A passionate 'Kermit' will often give rise to a 'frog spawn' (qv), which may result in sprogs born.
Kerry Packered	*Knackered*	When you're worn out and tired you're 'Kerried'.
Kerry Packers	*Knackers*	The testicles, known as 'Kerrys' thanks to the Australian entrepreneur.
Kettle & Hob	*a) Bob*	One of an elite band of male Christian names to have a piece of RS. Always shortened to 'kettle', but not often these days. The term once applied to a shilling. Sometimes 'kettle on the hob'.
	b) Fob	One of the many possible explanations as to why a watch is known as a 'kettle' (a fob watch). *See* KETTLE. Since there are so many theories this has to be treated as only a possibility; use it if you like but don't bank on it being valid.
Kettle		A watch. Whoever it was who first referred to a watch as a 'kettle' could not have dreamt of the arguments he was to trigger a century later. Some believe it to be a piece of rhyming slang: 'kettle and hob' – fob. I have no confidence in this. A fob is a chain (in full a fob chain) attached to a watch. It is also a pocket in a waistcoat where a watch sits. So why refer to a timepiece by it's accessory? Another RS theory is that a 'kettle' is an old slang term for a bottle, therefore a 'kettle of scotch' – a watch. Another theorist states that a watched kettle never boils, but that's a watched pot, isn't it? A slang expert tells us that early watches were cumbersome and resembled teapots, so why a 'kettle' and not a 'teapot'? If an answer is necessary, then maybe the best one is that, to satisfy a mass market, the cheapest and easiest metal to make the casing from was found in rag-and-bone yards in the shape of scrap kettles. Who knows for sure? Maybe Kettle was the name of some Victorian Del Trotter who sold them on the cheap. Most probably a watch is called a 'kettle' for the same reason a ring is called a 'groin' and £1 a 'nicker', it just is! Just as it has been a 'turnip', a 'thimble', a 'toy' and a 'soup'.

Kevin		A young working-class male, seen as boorish and unsophisticated by his upper-class counterparts and whose behaviour is seen as 'Kevinish'. From a supposedly working-class name.
Kew		A sennight. A week in backslang. 'Nevis yads in a kew' – seven days in a week.
Key		An archaic term for the penis, which still does a turn in a 'keyhole' or 'lock'. *See both.*
Keyhole		a) The vagina, that which accepts a 'key' (qv). When a man is being unfaithful he is said to be 'putting his key in the wrong keyhole'.
		b) To rob a building by picking the lock, an underworld term for an activity that belongs there.
Keyholing		A 1950s term for busking outside the front door of a building.
Keystone Cop	*Chop*	When the curtain came down on the crazy comedy crew of the silent screen, they endured in butcher's shops in lamb and pork form.
Khyber Pass	*a) Arse*	A very familiar piece that has almost gained respectability, a kick up the 'Khyber' has spurred mobility since the 19th century.
	b) Glass	An example that has been in existence since the days of the Raj but with the popularity of (a), drinking from a 'Khyber' takes on an unsavoury, if not deviant, sense.
Kibosh		An eighteen-month prison sentence, a piece from the 1940s when the term was also recognised as 18 pence (1 shilling and sixpence).
Kick		a) A defunct term for sixpence in old money. 'One and a kick' was the same as a 'kibosh' (qv).
		b) To give up a habit, whether it be booze, fags drugs or to pack up being a nun.
Kick & Prance	*Dance*	A function and what you do when you get there. 'Lilley and kick' – a dinner and dance. *See* LILLEY & SKINNER.
Kick in the Bollocks		a) A shock, a body blow: 'This redundancy has come as a complete kick in the bollocks.'
		b) Lacking finesse, tact or diplomacy: 'As subtle as a kick in the bollocks'.
Kick It		To die, a reduced form of 'kick the bucket': 'He seems lost since his old lady kicked it.'
Kick One		a) A defiant retort akin to 'drop dead!' or 'kick a bucket!'
		b) To die, to put the boot into the proverbial bucket.
Kick, the		Dismissal from a job, another way of getting 'the boot'.

Kick-Bollock & Bite		A name given to anyone who lacks finesse, someone for whom reasoned argument is superfluous to requirements.
Kickers		A 19th-century term for the feet, which later got passed on to boots and shoes.
Kicks/Kicksies		A couple of ancient terms for trousers, now more commonly worn as 'kecks' (qv).
Kid Creole	*Dole*	A 1980s term for unemployment benefit based on a pop group of the period, Kid Creole and the Coconuts.
Kiddie, the		The man for the job. How a 'Jack of all trades' will describe himself: 'You want your place decorated? Then look no farther, I'm the kiddie.'
Kidney Punch	*Lunch*	Always truncated to 'a bit of kidney', often in relation to a pie and a pint.
Kidology		The art of lying, of laying a ruse as a trap for someone to fall into in order to take advantage. A successful con is 'all kidology'.
Kidstake	*Fake*	To be at the 'kidstakes' is to be on the wind-up, i.e., to try to con or kid someone with a phoney story.
Kike		A derogogatory, originally American term for a Jew. Illiterate Jewish immigrants coming to New York, unable to sign their names, would draw a circle as their mark. The yiddish word for circle is a *kikel*.
Kilburn Priory	*Diary*	Based on a long-gone medieval convent in Kilburn, North-West London, this mainly relates to the diary of a police officer.
Kilkenny	*Penny*	A piece from our previous coinage which may still be part of someone's small change.
Kilkenny Cats	*Bats (Mad)*	A reference to anyone who is mentally out of whack, based on a fabled story of animal cruelty, whereby some soldiers in 18th-century Ireland tied a pair of cats together by the tail and threw them into a ring to fight. At the approach of an officer a trooper sliced through their tails with his sword, explaining that they had eaten each other up to their tails.
Kiltie		A Scotsman, originally a World War One soldier as termed by other British tommies.
Kin'ell		A piece made famous by cockney comedian Jimmy Jones who, in his stage act, replaces 'fucking hell' with this.
King Canute(s)	*Boot(s)*	A seldom-used variation of the perennial 'daisy roots', based on the king of England (d. 1035).
King Death	*Breath*	An old expression for halitosis is 'dodgy king death'.

King Dick	a) Brick	An example from an old building site.
	b) Thick (Stupid)	'Is he King Dick or what?' a question asked of a king-size dickhead.
King Dickie	Brickie	Bricklayers have probably revelled in this term for years.
King Farouk	Book	A post-World War Two term for a 'reader' based on the last king of Egypt (1920–65).
King Lear	a) Ear	A well-known piece based on Shakespeare's play. Heard in a shopping mall: 'Did you see that? A baby about three months old with it's King Lear pierced. Ridiculous!'
	b) Queer	How a king becomes a queen. An elderly theatrical piece, the term, that is.
Kingdom Come	a) Bum	In the days when corporal punishment raised cane in the classroom, teachers were known as 'flaybottomists' which means they would have flogged many a little 'kingdom' to kingdom come.
	b) Rum	'A kingdom! A kingdom! My horse for a kingdom!' As Richard III might have said had he been a cockney alcoholic.
Kings & Queens	Beans	Mainly refers to baked beans whereby 'kings on holy ghost' is a common pairing. See HOLY GHOST.
King's Head	Shed	Although for many men their shed is a place of retreat, for others it's a place where the tools live and so symbolises jobs that need doing. For these men it's a term of wishful thinking: 'If you want me I'll be down the King's Head.'
King's Proctor	Doctor	An uncommon, if not obsolete, piece. The 'quack' or the 'sawbones' will usually suffice.
Kinifee		A knife, a dopey pronunciation of the word.
Kink		A sexual deviant, or a pursuit he likes to deviate to. A 'kinky' person favours kinky behaviour.
Kip		a) A place to get a night's sleep, a dosshouse, hostel, shop doorway or box in Cardboard City. A well-known term for a bed.
		b) To sleep, usually in the form of a nap. People commonly grab a few hours 'kip'. Sometimes extended to 'kippingtons'.
Kipper		a) Another fish-related term pertaining to the vagina. Also a 'kipper box'.
		b) A wide tie, a symbol in the 1950s of a 'spiv'.
		c) Someone who cannot be trusted or relied upon; a coward. A World War Two term used in the forces about anyone who, like a kipper, was seen as two-faced and with no guts.
		d) See DONE LIKE A KIPPER.

Kipper & Bloater	a) *Motor*	Cars, vans, coaches, fish-lorries, etc. They're all 'kippers'.
	b) *Photo*	Refers to all types of photograph, from holiday snaps to the one that separates the first and second in a horse or dog race.
Kipper & Plaice	*Face*	Always reduced to the first element, often about a 'moosh' of no great beauty.
Kipper/Kiphouse		A place to get some sleep, usually a dosshouse.
Kipper Season		The slack period of a trade, like winter for seaside hoteliers. So called because they can afford smoked salmon when the money is rolling in but they have to make do with kippers when it's not.
Kiss & Kuddle	*Muddle*	Never shortened, to be in a right old 'kiss and cuddle' is to be in a state of confusion.
Kiss Me Hardy	*Bacardi*	The reputed last words of Lord Nelson (1758–1805) taken in jocular vein. Whether it is reduced to 'kiss me' or not depends on the sex of the bar person.
Kiss Me Quick	*Prick*	More likely to be associated with a fool than the male member. Based on the fact that on a beano there is always one person who dons a 'kiss me quick' hat and acts like a complete pillock. Such a person is a 'kiss me'.
Kiss of Life	*Wife*	As used by the man whose liver has been saved by marriage, no doubt.
Kiss-Arse		A crawler, another version of an 'arse licker' (qv).
Kisser		The mouth, a 19th-century piece of boxing slang that still takes the punches.
Kissum		Backslang music. 'Kissum lah' – music hall.
Kitchen Range	*Change*	Always curtailed at 'kitchen' in relation to what is never checked by men buying drinks.
Kitchen Sink	a) *Chink*	A Chinese person, an uncommon alternative to the well-used 'tiddleywink' (qv).
	b) *Stink*	An example that is often di-stink-ly appropriate.
Kite		a) An archaic term for the stomach. 'Blow out your kite' – eat.
		b) A well-known term for a cheque that began life as a mid 19th-century term for paper, probably because it blew away in the wind, and by the end of the century it had become a letter. In the early 20th century the crime of stealing cheques from letters had become known as the 'kite lark' and the term got transferred to the cheque itself, where it has languished ever since.
		c) An alcoholic or junkie, someone who is permanently 'as high as a kite'.

d) An aeroplane, a piece of RAF slang that became well-known through old war films.

Kite Flyer/ Dropper/Man
Criminals who specialise in cheque-related crimes.

Kiting
The crime of passing dud or stolen cheques, the speciality of a 'kiter'.

Kit-Kat   *Pratt*
A 1990s term for a fool, one who takes the biscuit. Heard on a street corner as a long-legged beauty in a mini-skirt passed two stalk-eyed young men:
> 1st Man: *'Phwoahh look at that! It shouldn't be allowed.'*
> 2nd Man: *'Shouldn't be allowed you kit-kat? It should be compulsory.'*

Kit-Kat Shuffle
To masturbate, especially of a woman. Based on the the popular chocolate wafer that comes in a bar of four fingers.

Kleenex
A stupid person, a dimwit. After the tissue that is said to be double-thick.

Klutz
A fool, a clumsy blockhead. Originally an American term based on a yiddish word for a lump.

Knackered
a) Worn-out or exhausted, a common term that derives from 'knacker' – a broken-down horse, one fit only for the knacker's yard.

Knackered
b) Broken, ruined beyond repair. Cars that have 'breathed their last' are totally 'knackered'.

Knackers
A well-known term for the testicles that has it's roots in a stable. Originally to knacker was to geld, to cut off a horse's 'knackers'. Also used as a defiant retort.

Knee Bender
A religious person, one who takes a low position to talk to the 'Man Upstairs'.

Knee Trembler
Sexual intercourse in a standing position, usually a 'quickie' up against a wall and often paid for. Brooklyn Beckham wasn't the first baby to be named after the place of his conception; I went to school with a boy called Bikeshed, who WAS the result of a 'K T'.

Knees-Up
An old-fashioned party, one with much leg-cocking, song-singing and bevvy-boozing. One where Mother Brown will, at some point, make an appearance.

Knicker Loosener
An alcoholic drink given to a girl in the hope of an interesting end to the evening.

Knickers
A defiant retort, a polite version of 'bollocks' much used on TV. Possibly a toned-down corruption of 'knackers' (qv).

Knife & Fork   *Pork*
A fairly common term for pig meat which is usually said in full at the butchers: 'Got a nice bit of knife and fork for you here Mrs.'

Knob		A well-known term for the penis and also what it's used for, i.e., to have sexual intercourse is to 'knob'.
Knob Cheese		Smegma, 'Dairylea of the penis'.
Knob Custard		Semen, see CUSTARD.
Knob Polisher/ Shiner		Terms of abuse akin to 'wanker'.
Knobbly Knee(s)	*Key(s)*	Asking if anyone has seen your 'knobbly knees' usually prompts a saucy response.
Knobhead		A stupid person, another version of the more common 'dickhead' (qv).
Knob-Itch		Thrush, the penile irritation of the sexually transmitted condition.
Knobrot		An old term for syphillis, now used for any form of venereal disease, usually by some insensitive clod who hasn't got it.
Knob-Throb		A desire for or to lust after someone, to 'fancy someone rotten' is to have a 'right knob-throb' for them. Indicative of an erection.
Knock/Knock Bet		A certainty, or at least a very good thing. Now mainly heard in the sense of gambling, a strong favourite in a race for example, but originally it referred to a promiscuous woman.
Knock		a) To welsh, to fail to repay a debt. An overheard conversation about a bookmaker: 'He's knocked people from Ascot to York.' 'Knocker' – one who fails to honour a debt. Unscrupulous bookmakers are said to inhabit 'Knocker's Row'.
		b) To criticise, famously 'Don't knock it till you try it.' A critic is a 'knocker'.
		c) An ancient term for sexual intercourse, often with a prostitute, thus 'a quick knock'.
		d) To impress, as in the music-hall song 'I Knocked 'Em in the Old Kent Road'.
Knock 'Em Bandy/Cold/ Dead/Stiff		To evoke a favourable impression: 'You'll knock 'em bandy in that get-up.'
Knock Off		a) To steal. Stolen goods and getaway cars are 'knocked off'.
		b) To have sexual intercourse: 'He's been knocking off his boss's wife for years.'
		c) To finish work. You're on overtime if you work past 'knocking-off time'.
Knock it on the Head		To stop doing something, to pack in. Time to stop work? Knock it on the head then.
Knock on the Door	*Four*	Another example of bingo callers' slang, a 'knock' is rarely used for £4.

Knock Out		To sell goods, usually stolen or smuggled, on the cheap: 'Smuggler Terry's knocking out fags if you want some.'
Knock Over		To rob, very often an armed robbery. If the post office has been 'knocked over', it must be pension day.
Knock Up		To make pregnant, a common term that was conceived in America.
Knockback		A rejection or refusal, a long-unemployed man was heard to moan that when it came to job applications he'd had more knockbacks than Quasimodo at a disco.
Knocker		a) The pubic area of a woman, possibly from the shape of a door-knocker.
		b) A non-payer of a debt. *See* KNOCK (a).
		c) A critic. *See* KNOCK (b).
Knocker & Knob	*Job*	May be accessories to the door of opportunity, which during times of recession was slammed in millions of faces.
Knockers		A well-known term for breasts, especially large ones as owned by the girl who may acquire the nickname, Norma Snockers.
Knocking On		Getting old. Want to annoy someone? Tell 'em they're knocking on a bit.
Knocking Shop		A common term for a brothel. Also, any place in which a lot of sexual activity takes place may draw the comment: 'It's like a knocking shop.'
Knollers		The testicles. Almost a cross between 'knackers' and 'bollocks'. *See both.*
Knolly Bike		Any low-cc motorcycle that would-be taxi drivers learn the streets, or do the knowledge, on.
Knothead		A stupid person. Heard in a cafe:
		1st Man: 'The only Cyril I know is Willie Ryan's father.'
		2nd Man: 'What's his name?'
		1st Man: (sarky) 'Cyril Smith you knothead.'
Knotty Ash	*Cash*	A 1980s term inspired by the clash between comedian Ken Dodd and the Inland Revenue. The inference being that the chief diddy-man's home in Knotty Ash contained cash-money that was beyond the taxman's ken.
Know One's Onions		To be aware, often used saucily about a woman: 'She knows her onions.'
Knuckle		a) A fight, when two protagonists exchange fists you're likely to hear the cry 'Knuckle!'
		b) To hit, to impose one's fists on someone.

Knuckle Sandwich		A well-known expression for a 'bunch of fives', a punch.
Knuckle Shuffle		Masturbation, a piece that rubs along with 'hand shandy' (qv).
Koh-i-Noor	*Whore*	A Jewish prostitute, which is more of a pun on Cohen whore than RS. Based on the famous diamond that is kept in the Tower of London.
Kojak		A bald tyre, based on a bald TV detective of the 1970s: 'You're driving round on a set of Kojaks and you wonder why the old bill gives you a tug.'
Kool Toul		A look out, one who keeps his eyes peeled in backslang. Also a warning.
Kosher		A well-known term that tells you that everything is as it should be. Kosher goods are legitimate or genuine and kosher people can be trusted. From the Hebrew *kasher* – proper.
Kotchel		An unspecified number, usually a lot. A tout may have a 'kotchel' of tickets to sell. The term originally applied to a bundle of banknotes, but TV series like *Minder* opened it up to a bundle of anything.
Kraut		Now the commonest reference to a German. A reduction of sauerkraut, it originated in America and has almost kicked 'Jerry' out of Britain. 'Krautland' – Germany.
Kremlin		New Scotland Yard, the London police headquarters, a piece from the people who work there.
Kung Fu Fighter	*Lighter*	Known as a 'kung fu' by the young generation of smokers of the 1990s.
Kunta Kinte		A black person, a piece that came into existence in the 1970s. Based on the name of the hero in the novel *Roots* by Alex Haley, which was made into a very popular TV serial.
Kurva		A prostitute, from the Yiddish *kurveh*, a piece that's been on the street since the 19th century.
Kushti		*See* CUSHTI.
Kuwaiti Tanker	*Wanker*	A term of abuse that seemingly ran aground after the Gulf War of 1991.
Kvetch		To moan, whinge or complain. Another piece of yiddish from America that's well-known here.
Kyf/Kyfer/Kifer		A woman or women seen as sex objects, something akin to 'crumpet' (qv). Predatory men go in search of some 'kyfer'. The term has also been used in regard to sexual intercourse, sometimes as 'kifering'.
Kylie Minogue	*Rogue*	A piece of 21st-century youthspeak. Due to the popularity of this Australian songstress, ne'er-do-wells are now known as 'Kylies'.

L

L K Clark	*Mark*	*See* ELKY CLARK.
Labour, the		An old name for the labour exchange, the predecessor to the Jobcentre, and therefore a term for unemployment. If you were on the dole you were 'on the labour'.
Lace Curtain		A gay term for a long foreskin.
Lace Curtain	*Burton (Beer)*	Originally applied solely to this brand of beer but was later extended so that any type of beer became known as 'lace'.
Laddette		A young woman who behaves like a young man, in a loud, uncouth, beer-swilling way. A female lager lout.
Laddish		Behaviour seen as typical of the young working class male. Drunken, brawling, uncouth, loud, chavinistic, macho. Perm any five from six, throw in a football fan, give him the sexual appetite of a jackrabbit and you've got a 'lad'.
La-Di-Da		Stuck-up, snobbish, snooty, etc. 'She's gone all la-di-da since she became a model.'
La-Di-Da	*a) Car*	Coined when only the upper classes owned their own 'lardys'.
	b) Cigar	Generally condensed to a 'lardy' and shows the inequality of yesteryear, when the la-di-das smoked cigars and the hoi polloi made do with Woodbines.

	c) *Star*	A theatrical term for a headline performer and also used for the *Star* newspaper.
Ladies & Gents	*Sense*	Usually said in relation to an idiot, like the one-armed man who broke his wrist trying to change the time on his watch: 'He ain't got the ladies he was born with.'
Lady From Bristol	*Pistol*	'"Stand and deliver!" yelled the highwayman as he cocked his 'lady'. As Dick Turpin's cockney biographer would have written.
Lady Godiva	*Fiver*	A well-known but rarely used term for £5 based on the English noblewoman (d. 1080) who allegedly rode naked through Coventry market in protest at the taxes imposed by her husband, the Earl of Chester.
Ladyboy/ Ladyman		A couple of 1990s terms for a homosexual male, especially an effeminate one.
Lag		a) A prisoner, especially a long-serving one or a recidivist. 'Lagged' – sentenced or imprisoned. In the 17th century 'lag' was a term for water, and in the sense of a convict it began life as a reference to transportation, when ne'er-do-wells were sent overseas.
		b) To urinate and what is produced. An exact replica of 'piss', with the same source as (a).
Lag/Lagging		A prison sentence, especially one of three years and over. As served by a 'lagger'.
Lager & Lime	*Time*	A noughties term that, in terms of lateness, comes down to 'Look at the lager.'
Lager Lout		Put simply, a young man who acts like a lout when he's 'lagered up' – drunk on lager.
Lagered Up		Drunk, a modern youth version of 'beered up'.
Lagged		Drunk, a piece that follows the wavy line of 'pissed'. *See* LAG (b).
Lahdi/Lardy		Last. A name given to someone who hangs back when rounds of drinks are being bought, one who thinks that the last round will be the cheapest because people will have had enough.
Lairy		Flash in dress and manner, lippy.
Lakes of Killarney	a) *Barmy*	Generally used in the reduced form, whereby the daft are 'lakes' or 'lakie'.
	b) *Carney*	Refers to a two-faced, person: 'What a right lakie scrote him next door. Says one thing to me and something completely different to someone else.'
Lal Brough	*Snuff*	Commonly known as 'lally' when snuff was commonly sniffed.

La-La		Under the influence of drink or drugs, a state also known as being in 'La-La Land'.
Lallies		a) The legs, an example from the theatre, well-known through radio shows of the 1960s.
		b) Breasts, an old term that was used coyly by women regarding their own. Hence 'lally holder' – a brassière.
Lam		To run away or to escape, commonly heard as 'on the lam' – on the run.
Lambeth Walk	*Chalk*	An example heard in snooker halls and pubs with pool tables.
Lame Duck	*Fuck*	A reference to sexual intercourse. Heard at a bus-stop:

> *Posh Woman: 'You are the ugliest, dirtiest, scruffiest, smelliest man I've ever had the misfortune to meet.'*
>
> *Tramp: 'No chance of a lame duck then?'*

Lamebrain		An idiot, someone who is mentally off-course. A 'cripplehead'.
Lamp		a) To look at, an example that first saw service as an eye.
		b) To hit someone, to punch their lights out. Originally a punch in the eye mayhap. *See* (a).
Lancashire Lass(es)	*Glass(es)*	A very old term from the north of England that refers to spectacles and drinking glasses.
Lance		The penis, a long weapon, and therefore also to 'lance' a woman is to have sex with her.
Land of Hope	*Soap*	An old piece that seems to have been thrown away with the bath-water.
Land One		To connect with a punch. 'I landed him one, then he landed me with six.'
Landowner		Anyone, originally a World War One soldier, who is dead and buried.
Lard		Human fat, as in 'tub of lard' a well-known expression for a fat person. In America 'lard arse' fits the bill.
Lardy		A derogatory name given to a fat person.
Larro		Oral sex, a backslang blow-job most commonly used in homosexual circles.
Larrup		To beat up, to thrash. To administer a severe larrupping.
Lash		To urinate, a piece that falls somewhere between a 'lag' and a 'slash'.
Last Card in the Pack	*a) Back*	Anatomically speaking, people have been putting their 'last cards' out since the 19th century.
	b) Sack	To draw the 'last card' is to be dismissed from

		employment, perhaps through too many days off with a dodgy 'last card'. *See* (a).
	c) Snack	An old theatrical term for a bite to eat, perhaps a roll to sink the teeth in.
Last Shake of the Bag		A name given to the youngest child in a family, a piece that relates to the last hurrah of the father's 'ballbag' (qv).
Last Turkey in the Shop		A colourful description of the male genitals when flaccid, the image of a hanging turkey neck.
Latcheco/ Lachiko		A person who sees value in anything he finds, someone who will pick up an elastic band because it 'may come in handy' or if he finds enough he'll be able to sell them. A scavenger.
Laugh & Joke	*Smoke*	Refers to a smoke of any kind, be it cigarette, cigar, pipe or a 'funny fag'.
Laugh & Titter	*Bitter*	Beer. The drink that cheers and gets you merry. Can make you fight like Tom and Jerry (qv).
Laughing Gear		The mouth, famously 'get your laughing gear round that' when given food or drink.
Laurel & Hardy	*Bacardi*	Named after the most famous comedy duo of all time, Stan Laurel (1890–1965) and Oliver Hardy (1892–1957), and generally shortened to the first name, in which case Mr Laurel often acquires new partners, most commonly 'holy smoke' (qv), i.e., 'Laurel & Holy'.
Lava		Semen. To 'blow' or 'let go one's lava' is to ejaculate.
Lavender		A male homosexual; lavender water is seen as a typically feminine scent.
Lawful Wedded		A spouse, a piece that, as often as not, is changed to 'awful wedded'.
Lawn		The hair, thus to 'get the lawn mowed' is to get a haircut. In gay terms it's pubic hair, and a 'mowed lawn' is a shaved pubic region.
Lay		a) An unromantic term for a sexual partner, often used of a promiscuous woman who may be termed an easy 'lay'. b) To have sexual intercourse, originally an American piece and still more likely to be heard over there.
Lay Me in the Gutter	*Butter*	Spread as 'lay me', but not for a very long time.
Lay One On		To punch someone, the laying on of fists.
Lay Out		To knock someone out in a fight.
Lay-Off		To hedge a bet, a bookmaker's term.
Lazyitis		The imaginary medical condition of the bone-idle.
Lazzy		Elastic, an old schoolboy's term for a piece of

'stretch' for the making of a catapult. Now applies to an ordinary elastic band.

Lead in One's Pencil
Virility, a symbol of male potency.

Leaf
a) Marijuana. A 1960s term whereby a smoker may 'blow some leaf'.

b) An old term for £1 that still has a small currency even though it stems from a time when a pound was a green note.

Leak
To urinate, usually in the form of 'having' or 'taking a leak'. The incontinent may 'spring' one.

Leaky Bladder *Ladder*
A particularly high one is more likely to put a strain on the bowel rather than the bladder, especially in the acrophobic.

Lean & Fat *Hat*
A 19th-century term that's been swallowed up by the well-worn 'titfer'. *See* TIT FOR TAT.

Lean & Linger *Finger*
A term that suggests loitering may have something to do with idle hands. But then it may not.

Lean & Lurch *Church*
An ancient term for some of our most ancient buildings.

Leap
To indulge in sexual intercourse. Honeymooners tend to leap all over each other for the duration.

Leather
a) An old underworld term for a wallet or purse. Also a pickpocket, a 'Leather Merchant'.

b) To beat someone as a punishment, to hit with a leather belt or shoe: 'If ever I got lippy, the old man would give me a good leathering.' 'Put the leather in' – to kick someone.

Lee Marvin *Starving*
Based on an American film actor (1924–87) who is best remembered for his tough-guy roles and for being 'Born Under a Wanderin' Star'. Now his name will forever more be connected with a rumbling belly.

Lee Van Cleef *Beef*
A piece heard in a carvery in the shortened form of 'Lee Van'. Certainly seems to know his way round a dinner plate, this old spaghetti western star (1925–89).

Left & Right *Fight*
Apt in that it is indicative of punches thrown or boots put in.

Left Back
The three in a pack of cards. Footballers in this position wear the number three shirt.

Left Footer/ Hander
A Catholic, a Protestant term for those who 'kick with their left hands'.

Left Half
The six in a pack of cards. From the football shirt number that once related to the left half.

Left-Handed Batsman
A homosexual, one who 'bats for the other side'.

Left Hander
A homosexual, a 1960s term for someone that, according to a homophobe, isn't right.

Left in the Lurch *Church*
A 19th-century piece that is formed on the words of a music-hall song about someone being jilted at the altar.

Leg Before Wicket
a) *Ricket*
A mistake, when you've made a right l.b.w. you've cocked-up big time.

b) *Ticket*
Nearly always reduced to the initials, it refers to the obvious and also in a sense of a task well done, i.e., 'That's the l.b.w.' Anyone slightly off his noodle is said to be 'not all the l.b.w.'.

Leg It
a) To run away or escape. Absconders have been 'legging it' for well over a century.
b) To have sexual intercourse, a 1980s reduction of getting one's leg over.

Leg of Beef *Thief*
An uncommon variant of the common 'Tea Leaf' (qv), which seems to be based on the nursery rhyme denouncing Taffy the Welshman.

Leg of Mutton *Button*
Often truncated to the first element for comic effect: 'Mum, a leg's come off. Can you sew it back on for me?'

Leg of Pork *Chalk*
An example, heard in a pub, which seems to have hopped from the dartboard to the pool table.

Leg Openers
Drinks given to a woman in the hope that she will shed her inhibitions and her underwear.

Leggner
A one-year prison sentence, a 'stretch' (qv). A shortening of 'stretch one's legs'.

Legholders
Trousers, jeans, leggings, etc. Anything you can pack your legs in.

Legless
Falling over and bashing your head on the pavement drunk. 'As legless as a tree' – so drunk you can't move.

Legover
Sexual intercourse, from the well-known 'get one's leg over'. 'Legover Land' – a red light district.

Legs
The number eleven, a well-known piece that's left the confines of the bingo hall. Sometimes £11.

Leicester Square *Chair*
Always restricted to the first element: 'Pull up a Leicester and take the weight off your plates.'

Leisure Hours *Flowers*
Since the 19th century, bunches of 'leisures' have been peace offerings.

Lemon
a) A fool or a dupe: 'I've been standing here like a lemon for an hour waiting for you.'
b) Anything worthless or useless. If you've been sold a 'lemon' you've wasted your money.

Lemon & Dash a) *Flash*
A lairy person may be a bit too 'lemon' for most people's liking.

	b) *Slash*	Urination can be known as going for a 'lemon'.
	c) *Wash*	An ancient piece that began life as a term of ablution before becoming a public lavatory. It then got taken over by the criminal classes, whereby pickpockets 'working the lemon' were lousy scrotes who made a living by stealing from coats hung up in public washrooms.
Lemon & Lime	*Time*	Best get a move on when you're running out of 'lemon'.
Lemon Curd	a) *Bird*	The feathered type is secondary to a woman, obviously one who's a bit tasty.
	b) *Turd*	The sweet in the street that gets under your feet.
Lemon Drop	*Cop*	'Watch it! Lemons.' – A warning cry from a look-out at the sight of the police.
Lemon Flavour	*Favour*	A friend indeed may do a friend in need a 'lemon'. Also a phrase of disbelief: 'You're gonna take up exercise? Do me a lemon, you're too out of condition to get fit.'
Lemon Squash	*Wash*	Always 'lemon' your 'Germans' before 'Lilley' (look 'em up for yourself). Also interchangeable with 'lemon & dash' (b), thirteen and a bakers really.
Lemon Squeezer	*Geezer*	Always reduced to the first element. A naive heterosexual's view of a gay bar: 'I don't like this gaff, it's full of lemons.'
Lemon Squeezy	*Easy*	A hard-pressed manager of a small boy's football team was heard to tell his losing side: 'You're making it lemon squeezy for them, they're cutting through us like eyes a winking.'
Lemon Tea	*Pee/Wee*	A colourfully apt example.
Lemonade	*Spade*	Applies to a black person and the suit in a deck of cards. *See* SPADE.
Len Hutton	*Button*	Formed on the name of a former England cricket captain (1916–90) but now seems to be at the end of it's innings.
Length		a) A six-month prison sentence, half a stretch.
		b) The penis, most commonly heard in the phrase 'slip her a length'.
Lenny the Lion	*Iron* *(Homosexual)*	An example of twice removed RS. 'Iron hoof' (qv) has become so widely used that it has picked up a term of it's own. Based on the name of a ventriloquist's dummy from the 1950s.
Leo Sayer	*All Dayer*	A 1990s term for an all-day drinking session based on a British singer/songwriter. When the hits dried up, the man who became the butt of endless piss-taking emerged as an extended piss-up.

Les/Lesbo/ Lezzie/Lezzo		Some of the many terms for a lesbian that come with mix 'n' match spelling.
Leslie Ash	a) *Gash*	Men-behaving-badly speak for the vagina.
	b) *Slash*	Urination can be known as going for a 'Leslie'. Based on a British actress, a co-star in the popular TV sitcom *Men Behaving Badly*.
Letch		A shortening of lecherous, often a derogatory term for a man who lusts after younger women.
Lettuce		Banknotes, a term that started when they were green. *See also* GREENS *and* CABBAGE.
Lever Arch Files	*Piles*	'Lever Arches' is one of the later additions to the RS list of terms for haemorrhoids.
Levy & Frank	*Wank*	The pulling of the pudden has long been known as a 'Levy'. Formed on the name of an old London company of restauranteurs.
Lick-Arse/ Lick-Boots		A couple of terms for a crawler, a guv'nor's man or woman. 'Careful what you say in front of the lick-arse over there.'
Licknep		A pencil, a backslang 'scribbler'. Nep – a pen. One puts licknep to repap (paper) to write a rettle (letter).
Lid		a) A ceiling, an example from the decorating trade. 'Tosh the lid' – paint the ceiling. b) A hat, a piece that's still wearing well after more than a century. Now also a crash helmet. c) A measure of marijuana, enough to fill the lid of a tobacco tin, approximately an ounce. d) A wig, something else that covers the dome apart from (b).
Life & Death	*Breath*	Apt in that without breath there is no life, but this is used mainly in the case of someone with bad breath. Anyone who suffers with 'dodgy life' is liable to acquire the nickname Ally Tosis.
Life & Soul		A jolly person, the one most likely to be at the front of the conga line, the life-and-soul-of-the-party type.
Life Peer	*Queer*	A homosexual, based on the stereotyped sexuality of the nobility as seen by the common man.
Liffey Water	*Porter*	A 19th-century term for this type of beer. It also applied to any type of black beer, most famously Guinness, which is brewed near the river Liffey in Dublin.
Lift		a) To steal, an archaic piece that's still with us, commonly in shoplifting. Also to pick pockets. b) To arrest, maybe a play on 'nick'. *See* (a).
Lig		To freeload, sponge or generally ponce on someone

else's generosity. A theatrical term from the 1960s when a gatecrasher or uninvited guest became a 'ligger'.

Ligger		Someone who likes to be seen in the company of the rich and famous, a hanger-on. Related to 'lig' (qv), which may be an acronym of Least Important Guest.
Light & Bitter	*Shitter (Anus)*	Based on a popular pairing of beers, of which a bad one will get the 'L & B' working overtime.
Light & Dark	*Park*	Coined in the days when a family day out often constituted a day in the park, arriving in the morning and leaving when they were turned out by the parkie around dusk.
Light Ender		A member of the upper class, one not seen to do very much for a living. Someone perceived as 'having it easy': 'These bloody light enders, can't they understand, that life is as precious to me as to man?' – any fox who was ever hunted.
Light Fingers		A thief, especially a shoplifter or a pickpocket. One gifted in light-fingered enterprises.
Light of Love	*Guv*	An example of convict irony from the 1940s regarding a prison governor.
Light of My Life	*Wife*	Often said sarcastically of a battle-axe.
Lighthouse		The reddened nose of a drinker, especially when large and able to warn shipping of danger.
Lightmans		A 19th-century term for daytime, as opposed to 'darkmans' (qv).
Lightning		An ironic name given to anyone slow.
Lights		a) Senses, hence to 'punch someone's lights out' is to knock them senseless. b) Matches, a once-common term for the early lighter. A 'box of lights'.
Like a Well-Oiled Brake Shoe		Said of a chaotic situation, one that doesn't run smoothly or is totally out of control. The direct opposite of a well-oiled machine. Get oil on your brake shoes and you won't stop till you crash.
Like Japan		Cold. Or put another way, nippy.
Like Shit from China		A fantastic, unbelievable story. Like shit from China, it's far-fetched.
Like Southend Pier		Said of anything obvious or conspicuous because, like the pier at Southend, 'it sticks out a mile'.
Lilac		An effeminate homosexual, a variation of 'lavender' (qv).
Lilley & Skinner	*a) Beginner*	Applies to someone new to a job or a novice, who is known as a 'Lilley'.
	b) Dinner	Based on a company of shoemakers, men have

long been forced to cut short a visit to the pub for fear of their 'Lilley' ending up in the dustbin or the dog, which is often the same thing.

Lillian Gish — *Fish* — Formed on the name of an American actress (1896–1993), it applies only to a fish on a platter. Pity that a woman whose film career lasted from 1912 to 1987 should be remembered as a lump of fried cod. Still, it's a kind of immortality, I suppose.

Lillian Gished — *Pissed* — A Scottish term for being drunk, given the Scots version of pissed is pished.

Lils — Breasts, especially large ones, which become 'massive lils'.

Lily — An effeminate male, a sissy. Another flower in the field book of homosexuals.

Lily Savage — *Cabbage* — A 1990s term based on the tarty alter-ego of British comedian Paul O'Grady gets on the menu. Aptly, the character knows how fond men are of their greens.

Limehouse Cut — *Gut* — Based on an East London waterway in reference to a paunch; a boozer's belly can be a massive 'Limehouse'.

Limp Wristed — Weak, effeminate or sissyish. Outside the gay community, homosexuals are known as 'Limp Wrists' or 'Limp Wristers'.

Lincoln's Inn — a) *Fin* — A 'Lincolns' is an old reference to a hand, for which 'fin' is an even older piece of slang.

b) *Finn* — A finn is an old racing term for £5. From finnuf, backslang for *funf*, the Yiddish for five.

c) *Gin* — A 19th-century piece that's been pushed aside by the likes of 'Vera Lynn' (qv). Based on one of London's inns of court.

Line — A portion of cocaine, heroin or other drug, scraped into a line to be sniffed.

Linen Draper — *Paper* — Specifically a newspaper and always folded to a 'linen'.

Lionel — The penis, a convoluted piece that derives from rhyming slang. 'Hampton Wick' – prick, gets shortened to 'Hampton' and therefore gets connected with the jazz musician Lionel Hampton. To 'larrup one's Lionel' is to masturbate.

Lionel Bart — *Fart* — An East London-born songwriter (1930–99) gets on the RS stage as 'arse music' (qv).

Lionel Blair — *Chair* — A 1970s piece from the world of showbiz, formed on the name of a British dancer, making him an ideal partner for 'Betty Grable' (qv).

Lionel Blairs	*Flares*	A 1970s term for flared trousers, known condescendingly as 'Lionels'.
Lion's Lair	*Chair*	An old term that was probably an allusion to the old man's chair, the one that nobody else may sit in.
Lion's Roar	*Snore*	An apt example, especially in relation to the Sunday afternoon drunk who falls asleep in a chair and snores his way through the film on the telly.
Lion's Share	*Chair*	A corruption of 'lion's lair' (qv).
Lip		Back-chat, insolence or cheek as delivered by a child or a subordinate.
Lip Service		Fellatio, a piece of prostitute's jargon, a pun on the phrase 'to pay lip service to'.
Lippy		Descriptive of a cheeky person or one with too much to say for himself: 'You have to watch that lippy bastard, he says things in jest but loud enough for the guv'nor to hear.'
Listeners		The ears, a word in the wrong 'listener' usually means someone's being 'bubbled up' (qv).
Listing to Starboard		Rolling drunk, an old nautical piece probably coined after a surfeit of rum.
Lit		A pallet, a 1980s term used by lorry drivers whose bit of 'bunce' was selling pallets to a 'lit firm'.
Lit Up		Drunk another version of 'alight' (qv).
Little & Large	*Marge*	A reference to margarine, which is older than the British comedy duo that carry this handle.
Little Bo Peep	*Sleep*	Based on the dozy shepherdess and said as getting some 'Little Bo'.
Little Boy Blue	*Screw*	An early 20th-century term for a prison officer based on a horn-blowing kid in a nursery rhyme.
Little Boy's/ Girl's Room		A couple of well-known euphemisms for a lavatory.
Little Brown Jug	*Plug*	This old song title lends itself to an electric plug or the one in the sink. More vulgarly though, to a tampon.
Little Ike		A child, probably a cockney reduction of 'little tyke': 'Come 'ere you saucy little ike.'
Little Miss Muffet	*Stuff It*	An indication of what can be done with something that is not wanted: 'You can take your advice and Little Miss Muffet.'
Little Nell	*Bell*	Based on a character from Dickens' *Old Curiosity Shop* and mainly applies to a doorbell.
Little Peter	*Meter*	An old term for a gas or electric meter that has to be fed with money and was often a target for burglars. The term fits perfectly, a meter being a small 'money box' and a 'Peter' being a big one, i.e., a safe. *See* PETER.

Little Red Riding Hoods	*Goods*	An underworld term, where stolen goods are known as 'Little Red Ridings'.
Little Titch(y)	*Itch(y)*	Based on a diminutive music-hall comedian and often employed when gnats and mosquitos are doing their worst. Titch was born Harry Relph in 1868 at the time of an infamous court case about the claim of a stranger to be the heir to the Titchborne family fortune. Nicknamed Titch, the name stayed with Relph until his death in 1928 and it is due to him that short people will always be called titch.
Little-Legs		A name given to a short person, like the one the scientist crossed with a supermodel and got a little of what he fancied.
Littleworth		An insignificant person or a low, nasty one. Someone who is even disliked by his dog. Ode to a Littleworth: *Oh Slippery McBride you are such a snide that I wish I were a splinter. I'd crawl in through the hole in your shoe and torture you all winter.*
Live Eel	*Field*	An archaic piece of cockney that was coined before London became the urban sprawl it now is.
Lively		a) A predominantly cockney word meaning quickly or sharpish. When in danger of getting caught you need to get away 'a bit lively'. Also an alternative to hurry up: 'Lively, the taxi's here.' b) A sarcastic nickname given to a person who has only one speed about everything he does – slow. A one-paced individual who may also be known as a 'sloth'.
Livener		An alcoholic drink, especially the first one of the day, one to wake you up.
Liver-Lips		Large lips and also an unkind nickname for someone with such 'mouth edges'.
Liverpool's at Home		The menstrual cycle, a reason given by men for not having sex, based on Liverpool FC being known as the Reds. *See* REDS.
Liza Minnelli	*Telly*	A 1980s term based on an American actress and singer and used as: 'Anything on the Liza?'
Lloyds List	*Pissed*	A City of London example for being drunk, based on the trade and shipping paper.
Load		Semen, most commonly heard in connection with being shot, i.e., 'shoot one's load'.
Load of Hay	*Day*	A 19th-century piece that appears to have had it's 'load of hay'.
Loaded		a) Very drunk or 'drugged up to the eyeballs'.

b) Seriously rich. Heard in a bar:
1st Man: 'He's loaded now, goes out with film stars, but I can remember a time when the only birds he could get were prozzies.'
2nd Man: 'Yeah, a real bags-to-bitches story.'

Loaf

An elderly person who exudes a musty smell, not unlike stale bread, due to wearing the same clothes for too long.

Loaf of Bread   *a) Dead*

A well-known term that is seldom, if ever, used in this context.

b) Head

Most commonly used in relation to the internal workings of the noggin, hence the ultra-familiar directive to think: 'Use your loaf.'

Lob-On

An aroused penis: 'I was reading this book on the train and I started getting a lob-on. Very embarrassing.' 'Lazy lob' – a semi-erection.

Lobster & Crab   *Cab*

Possibly coined by the taxi driver who parked up outside an overcrowded temple, hoping to pick up some crushed Asians.

Lock

An ancient term for the vagina, that which takes into it a 'key' (qv).

Lock-In

An after-hours drinking session, when the pub doors are locked with the punters inside.

Loco

Crazy, insane. A well-known description of any-one mentally out of line.

Loco Weed

Marijuana, a term stolen from the name of a plant that grows in the American West and sends cattle crazy when they eat it.

Locus

To drug someone prior to robbing them. A 'locus' was originally a mixture of beer and snuff, later beer and cigar ash did the trick. More up-market thieves use chloroform or any other knock-out drops. To 'locus someone away' was to Shanghai them, i.e., to drug them and force them into becoming a seaman.

Locust

An unfussy eater, someone who will tuck into absolutely anything and eat you out of house and home.

Lodger

A flea or head louse, what anyone seen scratching themself may be jokingly asked if they've got.

Loft

The head, in a similar way to 'attic' (qv).

Loghead

A thick, stupid person. A 'blockhead' in his natural state.

Loid

An abbreviation of celluloid, a thin piece of plastic such as a credit card used for opening locked doors. A housebreaker's term that's known to the police.

Lollipop		A 19th-century term for the penis, crudely used in connection with oral sex.
Lollipop	a) Cop	An infrequent reference to the police: 'Let's go before the lollies get here.'
	b) Drop	This is drop in the form of a gratuity, therefore to give someone a 'lolly' is to tip them.
	c) Shop	To 'lolly' someone is to inform against them, the betrayed may claim to have been 'lollied up'. Occasionally used for a shop, kids on an errand are sent up the 'lollipop'.
Lolly		A well-known term for money which may derive from the Romany word *loli* meaning red, which is an old slang term for copper coins. It may also come from rhyming slang where 'lollipop' – drop, is a gratuity.
Lombard		A rich but stupid or obnoxious person, a monied moron. From the acronym Loads Of Money But A Right Dickhead.
London Fog	Dog	Probably an extinct species now, nobody ever uses anything but 'cherry' in regard to a pooch. *See* CHERRY HOG.
London Taxi	Jacksie (Anus)	Possibly coined when a cab driver derided a tip and got a boot up his 'London taxi'.
Londonderry	Sherry	A 19th-century piece that's rarely, if ever, called for today.
Lone Ranger	a) Danger	Never used in a sense of peril but as a term of exasperation: 'Any Lone Ranger of you ever getting a drink?'
	b) Stranger	An underworld term often directed at someone suspected of being a plainclothes police officer, which is apt because the Lone Ranger was a well-known TV western series about a masked, therefore unknown, lawman.
Lonely Art		Masturbation. This pun on 'lonely heart' aptly sums up a solitary sex life.
Long & Linger	Finger	Originally an American piece that may mean a finger or to inform on, to point the finger at.
Long & Short	Port	The drink that may be long with a mixer or short on it's own. And that's the long and short of it.
Long Acre	Baker	An old example that is based on a historic London street, one which has been associated with Pepys, Cromwell, Dickens, Chippendale, various lords and ladies and John Logie Baird. But no famous 'Masters of the Rolls', i.e., bakers.
Long Firm		A fraud. A dishonest business where goods are bought on credit and sold off quickly. The 'firm'

		then disappears, leaving the vendors with an unpaid bill.
Long John		Silver coins, based, obviously, on the fictional pirate and used as: 'Got any Long John for the car park?'
Long Streak of Misery		A miserable-looking person, the glum, prophet-of-doom type who seems happy to be depressed.
Long Streak of Piss		A very tall, thin person. Often used as a friendly insult.
Long 'Un		A common expression for £1000, once well-known as £100.
Long-Pockets		A name given to a tight-fisted person, someone with 'short arms and long pockets'.
Lonsdale Belt	*Gelt (Money)*	An underworld term for money based on the trophy British boxers receive for winning a British title. Always used as 'Lonsdale', after the sporting Earl (1857–1944) who founded the prize.
Loo-Be-Loo	*Flu*	A piece heard in the 1950s as 'Looby', based on Andy Pandy's girlfriend on children's television.
Loon		A crazy person, an abbreviated lunatic. Someone given to wild or eccentric behaviour. Also used in verb form, where to loon or loon about is to act madly.
Loonbucket		A mad, eccentric person. An extension of 'loon' (qv), but I don't know where the bucket came from.
Loony/Loony Tune		An insane person, one who is 'safer in than out'. A 'care in the community' case.
Loony Bin		A well-known term for the cuckoo's nest that one flew over.
Loop the Loop	*Soup*	An old term for the first course, from asparagas to zucchini it's all 'loop de loop'.
Loopy		Mad, both in the sense of craziness and anger: 'If I'm late again tonight the wife'll go loopy.'
Loose Jawed		Descriptive of a gossip, someone who can't be trusted with a secret.
Loose Screw		What the mentally insecure are said to have. Alternatively they may 'have a screw loose'.
Loot		A common reference to money, a term that started life meaning booty or plundered goods.
Lootworthy		Anything that may be financially worth investing in, something likely to pay dividends.
Lop-Cock		A circumcised penis, one with lopped-off foreskin.
Lord & Master	*Plaster*	An example from an office first aid box which doubles as a path in the labyrinth of terms that eventually lead to the backside. See PLASTER OF PARIS. Extended to 'Lord & Mastered' it becomes an expression for being drunk, i.e., 'plastered'.
Lord & Mastered	*Plastered*	Drunk. See LORD & MASTER.

Lord/Lady Muck		Titles given to phoney snobs, people seen to be putting on airs and giving it the 'high nose'.
Lord Lovat	*Shove It*	Based on the aristocratic brigadier of the commandos during World War Two and pronounced 'Lord love it', this is used as a suggestion as to what can be done with the unwanted or unwelcome.
Lord Lovel	*Shovel*	A navvy's term from the 19th century that was probably used ironically as the only nobleman who ever dug a hole.
Lord Mayor	*Swear*	A very common reference to bad language that may be extended to 'Lord Mayoring'.
Lord of the Manor	*Tanner*	Until this coin's demise this was one of the oldest terms of RS.
Lord of the Pies		A fat person, may be the bloke who ate all the pies at every football ground in Britain. A pun on William Golding's novel *Lord of the Flies*.
Lord of the Rings		The title of Tolkein's trilogy gets punned in reference to a promiscuous male homosexual. *See* RING (a).
Lord Sutch	a) *Clutch*	A motor mechanic's example based on Screaming Lord Sutch, a rock singer turned Monster Raving Loony Party political candidate (1940–99). He never got to be an MP but is immortalised in RS, which is much more prestigious.
	b) *Crotch/ Crutch*	Ill-fitting trousers may be too tight round the 'Lord Sutch'.
Lord Wigg	*Pig*	Apart from the animal, this applies to a glutton or a discourteous person: 'Excuse my Lord Wigg, he's a friend.' Based on British politician George Wigg (1900–83).
Lord(s) & Peer(s)	*Ear(s)*	Whereby a clip round the 'Lord' amounts to corporal punishment.
Loretta Young	*Tongue*	Based on an American film star of yesteryear (1913–2000) who tongue wrestled the leading men of her day. 'Hold your Loretta' – keep quiet.
Lorna Doone	*Spoon*	Only in RS can the beautiful heroine of a romantic novel end up in a bowl of spotted dick and custard.
Lorry Driver's Crutch		What an unfresh mouth is said to be like.
Lose It		To go mad. To lose control either temporarily in a fit of rage or permanently, as in a mental breakdown.
Lost & Found	*Pound*	An old reference to £1. Heard at a street market: Trader: 'Who'll give me a little lost and found for this lovely Elizabethan ashtray?' Woman: 'Elizabethan?' Trader: 'Well, Elizabeth the second.'

Lot		a) An old underworld term for a car, something akin to a 'heap' (qv). b) Semen, commonly to 'come one's lot' is to ejaculate.
Lou Reed	*Speed*	A late 20th-century term for amphetamines based on the American singer-songwriter who walked on the wild side in 1973 and enjoyed a perfect day in 1997.
Loud & Clear	*Dear*	Anything overpriced is 'too loud', and that's how we should complain.
Louse House		A cheap and nasty hotel or lodging house, one where you'll share a bed with other 'lodgers' (qv).
Lousy		Mean, tight-fisted. A 'lousy' git wouldn't feed his spit to a goldfish.
Lousy Lou	*Flu*	I have no idea who the Lou in question is but he or she must be knocking on a bit as this is a pretty old example.
Louthouse		A rough pub, one frequented by the local hounds.
Love & Hate	*Weight*	Refers to the constant battle between the human being and the scales, whereby we love to eat but hate to get fat.
Love & Kisses	*Missus*	Everyman's reference to his wife. Right up till the end of the honeymoon.
Love & Marriage	*Carriage*	A probable allusion to the horse-drawn conveyance used at a traditional wedding.
Love Bubbles/ Bumps/Lumps		Some of the many terms for breasts that inhabit the great brassière of slang.
Love-in-a-Punt		Weak beer, so called because it's 'fucking near water'. Also any spirit that's been watered down.
Love-Juice		Semen, hence to 'squirt one's love-juice' – to ejaculate.
Lover's Tiff	*Syph*	Despite the rhyme, this is not restricted solely to syphilis but to venereal diseases in general. Although there would be more than a tiff if one partner infected the other.
Low Light Job		A bowel movement waiting to happen. 'I've got one on a low light, I'll have to find a carsey soon.'
Low-Down Bum		A short person. A midget or dwarf, like the one in the Sad Story: <blockquote>A midget ran off to the circus, billed as 'Jiblet the Baritone Clown' But now he's a sad falsetto. The lavat'ry seat fell down.</blockquote>
Lowlife		Anybody considered socially unacceptable, a criminal or objectionable person.

Lubbly Jubbly		The advertising slogan for the 1950s orange drink Jubbly, has become a well-known term of approval. Other dictionaries give it as 'Lovely Jubbly' but those of us who remember the drink know better.
Lubricate One's Larynx		To have a drink, especially a beer. Another way of 'getting the dust out your throat'.
Lubricated		Drunk, a variation of getting well oiled.
Lucky Charm	*Arm*	Based on that which is supposed to give evil the elbow and keep you from 'arm.
Lucky Dip	*Whip (Round)*	Lucky the 'dip' who picks the pocket of the one holding the 'lucky dip', i.e., a collection of money.
Lucky Dip(s)	*Chip(s)*	May be based on the traditional way of eating a bag of chips and the luck involved in not picking a manky one.
Lucky Legs		Very thin legs, said insultingly to be 'lucky they don't break'.
Lucozade	*Spade*	A derogatory reference to a black person, often shortened to 'luke'.
Lucy Lastic		A name given to a promiscuous woman, one whose knickers are on and off so often that the elastic is stretched.
Lucy Locket	*Pocket*	Refers to where one's hands are happy to linger, often to the annoyance of a foreman, from whom 'Take your bleeding hands out of your Lucys and do some work,' is a common rucking.
Lug/Lughole		The ear, terms that have been commonplace for generations. 'Luggers' – a 19th-century term for earrings. 'Pin back your lug 'oles' – listen.
Luger Lout	*Kraut*	A World War Two German as described by a wag watching the *Great Escape* for the umpteenth time.
Luggage		The male genitals. Depending on how he's fixed, a man may be carrying excess baggage or be travelling light.
Lulu		a) In the game of bingo, a mistaken claim. b) Anything outstanding or remarkable. A 'lulu' of a shiner – a lovely black eye.
Lumber		To indulge in heavy petting. Serious, passionate snogging.
Lumbered		Burdened with, weighed down. 'Landed in the cart' – to quote a line from Lonnie Donegan's hit record of 1961, 'Lumbered'.
Lumberjack	*Back*	Anatomically speaking, this is a clever reworking of the word lumbar, especially when crying off work with an iffy 'lumber'.

Lumme		An exclamation of surprise or interest, from (Lord) love me.
Lummox		A large, lumbering, clumsy person. Commonly known as 'you big awkward git'. A corruption of 'dumb ox'.
Lump		a) A well-built or obese person, either way a 'big lump', which often describes a bouncer. b) A motor fitter's name for a car or lorry engine.
Lump of Coke	*Bloke*	Large gentlemen are often referred to as 'big lumps'. Coke is coal with it's gases removed.
Lump of Ice	*Advice*	Often needed when you're in hot water.
Lump of Lead	*Head*	A 19th-century term that aptly describes a weighty bonce after a heavy night.
Lump of School	*Fool*	An ancient term that may sound familiar when shortened, as in: 'You stupid great lump.'
Lumpadump		A piece of excrement, most commonly a dog's: 'Mind the lumpadump.' *See* Dump.
Lumping		Large, heavy and ungainly, a lumping great oaf is a habitual 'clum' (qv).
Lumps		a) Breasts, in military parlance a woman is a 'lumpy jumper'. b) Punishment, when you do wrong you have to 'take your lumps'.
Lumpy Gravy	*Navy*	The Royal Navy as termed by members of the other services.
Lunchbox		The male genitals, a term from the 1980s which seems to have started on the athletics track, with the advent of tight lycra shorts.
Lungs		Breasts, particularly large ones. Heard in a swimming pool: 'She won't sink with a pair of lungs like that to keep her afloat.'
Lunk/Lunkhead		A dull-witted fool, an idiot who, if brains were made of tobacco, wouldn't have enough to roll a dog-end.
Lurghi		An unspecified ailment, every symptom known to man can be labelled the 'dreaded lurghi'.
Lush		a) A well-known expression for a drunkard that started life as an 18th-century term for an alcoholic drink. b) A sexually attractive woman, often on the buxom side and known as a 'lush bird'.
Lush Roller		A mugger or pickpocket who preys upon drunks. In other words, a scumbag.
Lushed/Lushed Up		Drunk, suffering from a surfeit of 'lush' (qv, a). 'Lushy' – an alcoholic.
Lusher		A prostitute who makes a living by targeting drunks.

Luvvie

A member of the acting profession, from the typically effusive greeting between actors.

Lycra-lout

A Noughties term for a cyclist, a lycra-clad 'peddler' who seems to be colour-blind when it comes to traffic lights.

M

Mac Gimp	*Pimp*	A prostitute's bully, known as a 'mac' or a 'magimp'.
Macaroni	*Pony*	a) A long-established term for £25: 'I had a maca each way the winner so the drinks are on me.' b) A piece of twice-removed RS that refers to excrement and defecation. The reduced form of 'pony & trap' has become a byword for 'crap', so people may go for a 'maca' or step in a lump of it.
Macaroon	*Coon*	An offensive reference to a black person.
Mace		A swindle or con. Also in verb form, to 'mace' someone is to have them over, thus 'working the mace' is to obtain goods on credit with no intention of paying. The victim has been 'maced'.
Macer/Maceman		A couple of references to a swindler, con artist, knocker, etc.
Mackerel & Sprat	*Pratt*	As usual the 'sprat' gets swallowed up and a fool becomes a 'right mackerel'.
Mad Beer		Strong ale; brain-befuddling or violence-inducing beer.
Mad Hatter	*Natter*	A term that can't be shortened: 'I stopped for a Mad Hatter with him next door and couldn't get away.' Based on the character from *Alice's Adventures in Wonderland*.

Mad Mick	Pick (Axe)	An example that's been commonly heard on building sites for many years.
Madame De Luce	Spruce (Deceive)	Extensively employed in the first element, a con artist will try to 'madame' you and a liar will give you a 'load of old madame'.
Madame Tussaud	Bald	Aptly used when describing someone with less hair than a waxwork model. A piece of useless advice – worrying about losing your hair will make you go Madame Tussaud.
Madza/Medza/ Midza		A half, an old piece of Polari, from the Italian *mezzo* – half. 'Madza reckin' – 50p. *See* RECKIN.
Mae West	Breast/Chest	Based on an American film actress (1892–1980) who is remembered as much for her one-liners as for her films.
Maggie May	Gay (Homosexual)	A late 20th-century piece based on the eponymous heroine of a couple of popular songs. Applies mainly to gay men who are known as 'Maggies'.
Maggie Thatcher	Scratcher	A 1990s term for a scratch card, the game that promises the winner instant capitalist status. Aptly based on former Prime Minister Margaret Thatcher.
Maggot		a) A despicable, horrible person. A rotten sod who may be a 'maggot in the apple of life'. b) The body of a fat, white man, often spotted on beaches in early summer.
Maggot in an Orchard/ a Fruitbowl		What the unwanted are about as welcome as.
Magic Mushroom		A hallucinogenic mushroom of the genus *psilocybe* containing the alkaloid psilocybin.
Magistrates Court	Short	A drinker's reference to a measure of spirit, a 'drop of magistrates', which is appropriate since it's where a lot of people end up as a result of too many.
Magoo		A newborn baby, from an assertion that all babies look like the cartoon character Mr Magoo.
Magsman		Originally a first-class con man, now demoted to a term for a petty thief.
Mahatma Gandhi	a) Brandy	Generally reduced to the first element, which to the cockney comes out as 'me'atma'.
	b) Shandy	A bit confusing really seeing that it is also used for brandy, but since the Indian nationalist (1869–1948) was a teetotaller this seems the most apt.
Maiden's Water		Weak beer, now associated with fizzy bitter or lager.
Maidstone Jailer	Tailor	An ancient piece that seems to have fallen off the peg along with the made-to-measure suit.

Main Squeeze		A girlfriend, boyfriend, wife or husband. Your favourite cuddle.
Mainline		A main vein into which drug addicts inject narcotics, also a verb for that activity. 'Mainliner' – a junkie.
Major Loder	*Soda*	A piece from the racing fraternity, based on a once-famous owner, that refers to the natural partner of whisky.
Major Stevens	*Evens*	The only time that odds can be evens is in the betting game.
Make		a) To have sexual intercourse. Sexaholics will make it anywhere and anyway they can. b) To steal. A 'good make' is a successful robbery. c) To recognise or identify, a piece from the police slangbook.
Make a Move		To leave, to go: 'Let's make a move.' Sometimes extended to 'make a movie'.
Make One		a) To 'make a party', i.e., to accompany: 'If you fancy a pint tonight I'll make one with you.' b) To make an escape from prison. On the outside it's to leave or 'make a move'.
Make Tracks		To run away or escape, but commonly to leave: 'Come on, time we were making tracks.'
Make Yourself Busy		To get involved in business that doesn't concern you, to poke your nose where it isn't wanted: 'What're you making yourself busy for? It's got nothing to do with you.'
Makings		A convict's term for the recipe for a cigarette, i.e., tobacco and papers. Outside prison it's in similar use with drug users.
Malarky		Nonsense, rubbish or stupidity: 'You don't expect me to believe this malarky do you?'
Malcolm Scott	*Hot*	A term from the theatre based on a long-forgotten female impersonator, known in his day as a dame comedian.
Malky		To strike with considerable force. A Scottish term often heard on the TV sitcom *Rab C. Nesbitt*.
Malteser		A 1980s name given to a black man with a shaved head. A similarity in appearance to the sweet.
Man & Wife	*Knife*	A cutter from the early part of the 20th century.
Man Alive	*Five*	A piece of bingo-caller's jargon that sometimes sees service as £5.
Man in the Moon	*Loon*	Refers to a mad person or an eccentric. 'Man in the Moon Alert' – beware, nutter at large.
Man o' War	*Bore*	Apt when applied to the old soldier who trots out tales of heroism in the western desert, etc., *ad infinitum*.

Man on the Moon	*Spoon*	A piece that must have begun to cause a stir after Neil Armstrong's giant leap for mankind in 1969.
Man the Lifeboats		To make a quick escape when danger threatens: 'Man the lifeboats quick, it's the old bill.'
Man Trap	*Crap*	To defecate but mainly that piece of excrement that lies in wait on the pavement for an unsuspecting foot to be drawn into it.
Manchester City	*Titty*	'Manchesters' is a rare alternative to the oft-mentioned 'Bristols'. *See* Bristol City.
Manfred Mann	*Van*	A piece from a 1960s haulage company based on a successful British rock group of the period, which took it's name from their South African keyboards player.
Mange		What anything that has gone mouldy or bad may be said to have: 'This apple's got the mange.' An extension of the parasitic skin disease in animals, which means that anyone with a skin complaint may also be said to have 'the mange'.
Mangle & Wring(er)	*Sing(er)*	Normally used of a singer of no great vocal talent, like the person who regularly takes the stage at the local and 'mangles' Frank Sinatra's 'My Way'.
Mangle & Wringer	*Finger*	An underworld term based on a device that can be used as a finger flattener.
Mangled		Drunk. 'Well mangled' – as loaded as a lorry-load of lords.
Manhole		The vagina, especially one owned by a promiscuous woman.
Manhole Cover	*Brother*	A piece that's mainly used in the third person and stunted to 'manhole'.
Manj/Manjarie		Theatrical slang for food, based on the Italian *mangiare* – to eat.
Manor		One's own district or territory, the area covered by a police station.
Mantovani	*Fanny (Vagina)*	Based on Annunzio Mantovani (1905–80), whose orchestra had several hits during the 1950s, this applies to women as sex objects. Boys go out to pull a 'bit of Manto'.
Manyana		Tomorrow. From the Spanish *manana*. 'Always manyana' – the moan of the partner of a procrastinator.
Map		A 19th-century term for the face, especially one with typical features of it's origin, e.g., a typically Jewish-looking person may have a 'face like the map of Israel'.
Maracas	*Knackers*	A fairly common term for the testicles, most often employed as a mock threat: 'You'll get a kick in the maracas if you ain't careful.'

Marble		The head, from the shape of the plaything and used as: 'Use your marble' – think!
Marble Arch	*Starch*	An old term for an old product based on an old construction in London.
Marble Halls	*Balls (Testicles)*	An old expression that comes down to 'marbles', probably based on the famous Marble Hall – the entrance hall at the Arsenal football stadium at Highbury.
Marbles		a) The testicles, either because of their shape or from rhyming slang 'marble halls'. b) Sense, mental capability: 'My old man's 92 and he's still got all his marbles.' c) Money, often as a gambling stake: 'Let's see the colour of your marbles.'
Marbles & Conkers	*Bonkers (Mad)*	Based on two games of childhood this is always reduced to the first word, which is fitting enough in that adults who continue to play such games and enter championships are considered by the rest of us to be 'marbles'.
Mare		a) A woman. A feisty one may be a 'mare when she's roused' and a downtrodden one, a 'poor little mare'. b) A rare but old term for a queen in a pack of cards.
Margaret Rose	*Nose*	The 'Margaret', a once familiar name for the shonker.
Margate Sand(s)	*Hand(s)*	Always reduced to the first element: 'Get yout thieving Margates off!' – don't touch!
Maria Monk	*Spunk*	A 19th-century example that mostly concerns semen but may also refer to courage or spirit. Based on the eponymous heroine of a pornographic novel of 1836.
Maricon		A homosexual, from the Spanish and therefore heard and brought back from the Costas.
Marie Corelli	*Telly*	An example from the very early days of television which is based on the pseudonym of romantic novelist Marie Mackay (1855–1924).
Marigold		One of many floral names given to an effeminate male homosexual.
Mario Lanza	*Cancer*	An Australian import for the Big C based on an American opera singer (1921–59) who became a star of Hollywood musicals.
Mark		a) A meeting place or a starting point: 'Be on the mark at seven sharp.' From the mark that athletes have to get on before getting set to go. b) A victim of a con trick or a practical joke. Also somebody 'marked down' as a potential target to a pickpocket or mugger.

Mark Someone's Card		To put somebody right, to warn them. A well-known development of the racecourse custom of a tipster marking your racecard.
Marlo		Bad, a 1970s piece that's based on the Spanish 'malo' – bad. The 'Marlo Mince' – the evil eye. *See* MINCE PIE.
Marmalise		To thrash thoroughly, to beat to a pulp, a jokey word popularised by comedian Ken Dodd.
Marmite	*Shite*	Rubbish, nonsense, shoddy gear or, to give it a name, crap, becomes a 'load of Marmite'. Based on the spread, which may seem visually apt.
Marmite Driller		A homosexual male, based on rhyming slang 'Marmite' – shite, an allusion to anal intercourse. 'Marmite motorway' – the anus.
Maroon		A fool, someone who is a cross between a moron and a buffoon it would seem.
Marquis of Lorne	*Horn (Erection)*	A 19th-century piece that has probably reached it's climax. Based on John Campbell (1845–1914), later Duke of Argyll and governor-general of Canada.
Marquis of Granby		A name for a bald-headed man based on a once common pub sign showing the marquis (John Manners, 1721–70) in all his hairless splendour.
Marrer		A mate in the north-east of England, a Geordie's pal.
Marrers		The knees. *See* MARROWBONES.
Marrowbones		An ancient term for the knees, best known from a line in the music-hall song 'I'm Henry the Eighth I Am' – 'I dropped down on me marrowbones and sang God Save the King'.
Mars & Venus	*Penis*	Used jokingly as a 'Mars bar' especially in relation to oral sex: 'If you're hungry I've got a nice Mars bar for you to get your teeth round.'
Mars Bar	*Scar*	A 1970s piece of yob yab that's normally used to describe a facial scar caused by a blade.
Martin Luther King	*String*	Used in the newspaper distribution business as 'Martin Luther'. Based on the American civil rights campaigner (1929–68).
Martin-Le-Grand	*Hand*	*See* ST MARTINS-LE-GRAND.
Marty Wilde	*Mild (Ale)*	Had a slight currency in the 1950s when this British singer was making hit records and the beer was still popular.
Mary		A drug user's term for morphine.
Mary Ann	*a) Fan* *b) Fan (Vagina)* *c) Hand*	Originally a hand-held but later an electric cooler. 'Fan' is an old slang term for a woman's 'hot-spot'. An old term that was often employed as a fist.

Mary Ann		An effeminate homosexual. Also an unmanly non-gay man, often one dominated by his wife.
Mary Blane	a) *Rain*	Drought conditions have probably set in on this 19th-century piece.
	b) *Train*	A 19th-century underworld term that seems to have come off the rails.
Mary Ellens	*Melons (Breasts)*	A 1980s term for the larger-sized bra filler.
Mary Green	*Queen*	In short the 'Mary' only applies to the playing card.
Mary Hinge		A hirsute vagina Spooner-style. A hairy minge.
Mary Jane/ Mary Jew Anna/ Mary Warner/ Mary Warnera		Some of the many terms punning on marijuana. Others include: 'Mary and Johnny', 'Mary Anne', 'Mari' and 'Mary Weaver'.
Mary Rose	*Nose*	Often associated with a super snozz, one whose owner is said to be able to smell his own breath. Seems to be based on Henry VIII's flagship, which was famously raised from the Solent in 1982 after 437 years on the seabed.
Marylou	*Glue*	A woman not to be sniffed at even if you're stuck with her on a blind date.
Mashed Potato	*Waiter*	Another spud gets on the menu along with 'baked', 'roast', 'hot' and 'cold' for the man who'll bring them to you.
Masher		A fashionable young person from the 19th century, a Victorian Mod. A swell.
Massive		A piece of black youthspeak for a gang, usually preceded by it's location, the Penge massive, for example.
Master Bater		A bachelor, one whose girlfriends are few and far between and therefore thought to be an excessive masturbator.
Match of the Day	*Gay*	The BBC's long-running football programme gets on the ball as a term for homosexuality.
Matheson Lang	*Slang*	A 1920s term that belongs here, based on a Canadian actor (1879–1948), a London matinee idol and silent-film star.
Maud & Ruth	*Truth*	An example from the pens of TV scriptwriters of the 1970s.
Mauler/Maulie		Old expressions for a hand, originally, probably, that of a brawler as it also represents a fist.
Max Factor	*Actor*	Not necessarily he who treads the boards in make-up, but a person who feigns injury, illness or innocence to gain an advantage, an Argentinian footballer is a classic example. Based on the well-known cosmetics company.

Max Miller	*Pillow*	Based on the great English comedian who, according to his act, 'pillowed' every barmaid in Brighton. Known as the 'cheeky chappie', Miller (1895–1963) is reckoned to be the guv'nor of stand-up comedy.
Max Walls	*Balls (Testicles)*	Often shortened to 'Maxies' after a Londoner considered by many to be a genius of comedy. Towards the end of his career, however, Wall (1908–90) proved to be a fine serious actor.
Maxwell House	*Mouse*	A 1960s term for a verminous house-guest based on a popular brand of coffee.
Mazawattee	*Potty*	Formed on the name of an old brand of tea in relation to anyone who is 'two ounces short of a pound' – crazy: 'Don't listen to him, he's mazawattee.' Also given as a reference to a child's waste collector or 'sprog-bog'.
Mazuma		Money, a Yiddish term from the days of our previous coinage.
Mazzard		An archaic term for the head, which has also seen service as the face. So take it as anything above neck height. A mazzard is a wild cherry.
McGarret		£50. An extension of 'Hawaii' (qv). The chief character in *Hawaii Five-0* was Steve McGarret.
McGinty		See GINTY.
McTavish		See TAVISH.
Me & You	a) *Menu*	A piece long thought to be RS but would appear to be more of a play on words.
	b) *Screw*	An example that relates to sexual intercourse but not in group sex apparently.
	c) *Two*	A term from a holiday bingo game.
Meat		a) A woman seen as a sex object, therefore commonly a prostitute, where 'fresh meat' is a girl new to the game and 'tough meat' is one that's hardened to it. 'meat shop/house' – a brothel. 'Meat salesman' – a pimp.
		b) The penis, well-known in the 'meat and two veg' trinity. 'Meatbeater', 'meat handler' – a pair of habitual masturbaters. 'Meat injection' – sexual intercourse, 'meat gravy' – semen.
Meat & Two Veg	*Reg*	The diminutive of Reginald is 'meat'.
Meat Eater		A prostitute, male or female, who will perform fellatio.
Meat Pie	*Fly*	Apart from an unsavoury reference to the flying pest, this also applies to what should be adjusted before leaving – a trouser fly.
Meat Rack		A place such as a bar, station, park, etc., where homosexuals go to meet sexual partners.

Meat Wagon		The commonest term for a police van since it was a 'black Maria'.
Meathooks		Curls, based on a 19th-century fashion whereby young costers (costermongers) would wear a curl on their temples. This was known as a 'meathook'.
Meaty		A well-rounded, sexually attractive woman.
Mechanic		a) An expert card-sharp, an ace cheat.
		b) An underworld term for a hit-man, a professional killer.
Mechanical Digger	*Nigger*	A derogatory term for a black person which in less enlightened times was reduced to the first element.
Medicine Man		A condescending term for a quack doctor, especially a useless GP who may also be a 'witch doctor'.
Medza		A half, an example of Polari based on the Italian *mezzo*. In old money 'Medza caroon' was a half-a-crown (12½p).
Meet		A rendezvous, often one where criminality is involved, although anyone can 'make a meet'.
Meg Ryan	*Iron*	A piece of secondary RS for a homosexual – see IRON HOOF. Based on an American film actress.
Mega		A popular piece of late 20th-century youthspeak for anything huge, highly successful, great, etc. 'With the right publicity we could be talking mega wonga' – words a compiler of a slang dictionary would love to hear from his publisher. *See* WONGA.
Melody Lingers	*Fingers*	A term that's been around for quite a while in the reduced form of 'melodies'.
Melonhead		A police constable, from the way his helmet shapes up to half a melon.
Melons		Breasts, large ones. Heard on a TV quiz show: *Quizmaster (to female contestant): 'And you are?'* *Girl: 'Melanie.'* *QM: 'Yes, I can see that but what's your name?'*
Melvyn Bragg	*a) Fag*	A cigarette, a piece that first got fired-up in the late 1990s.
	b) Shag	Based on a popular TV presenter and author whose novel *A Time to Dance* was, in 1992, made into a television serial. The production contained many sex scenes and the act of lovemaking immediately became known as a 'Melvyn'.
	c) Slag	A contemptible person, a 1990s rival to the well-known 'toe rag' (qv).
Men of Harlech	*Garlic*	Some 'men of Harlech' hanging around a room will apparently keep vampires away. Once they start singing they'll keep everyone away.

Mensch		A Yiddish term for a strong, dependable man. Someone to be trusted.
Merchant Banker	*Wanker*	A 1980s term of abuse coined by East Enders in regard to the yuppie types who moved into the newly developed part of the area at that time.
Merlin the Magician	*Pigeon*	Only known as 'Merlin' because of the number of syllables involved. Not to be confused with an actual bird called a merlin.
Merry & Bright	a) *Light*	Fittingly applies to illumination. It was once a big thing for cockneys to go to Southend in Essex to see the 'merrys'.
	b) *Tight*	Although 'merry' is a familiar colloquialism for being drunk, this has been used for extra emphasis when a drink has gone straight to a head: 'I'm feeling a bit merry and bright.'
Merry Go Round	*Pound*	A 'merry' is an old reference to a £1.
Merry Old Soul	a) *Coal*	When coal fires were all the rage it was common for people to put some 'merry' on them.
	b) *Hole*	From the nursery rhyme about 'Old King Cole', this applies to any orifice, including the anus.
Meryl Streep	*Sleep*	An American film actress comes in as an alternative to the ancient 'Bo Peep'. Someone without a conscience may tell you that thay have no trouble 'Meryling', that they can do it with their eyes closed.
Meshuggener/ Meshugger		Mad, crazy, insane, etc. Well-known Jewish terms for a mental case.
Metal		Money, a term that alludes to gold, i.e., precious metal, and so doesn't apply simply to coinage.
Metallics		Coins, an old example that is still adding weight to men's pockets.
Mether/Metho/ Methy		An alcoholic, one given to drinking meths. Terms that are often used in relation to tramps and down-and-outs.
Mettle		An archaic term for semen. To 'fetch mettle' is to masturbate and a 'fetch-mettle' is a dated term for a prostitute.
Mexican Wave	*Shave*	A 1990s term based on that stand-up-and-wave thing that spectators do at sporting events.
Miami Vice	*Ice*	Based on a US television series from the 1980s, this was heard in a West End club when a customer wanted some 'Miami' in his scotch.
Michael		a) A drugged drink. *See* MICKEY FINN. b) A makeshift or temporary lavatory as used on a building site, where this was heard. A pun on the name of the British politician Michael Portillo, or Portaloo.

Michael Caine	*Pain*	Based on the knighted, South London-born actor, this is how a friend in need can become a 'Michael in the Khyber Pass' (qv). With apologies to Sir Maurice for comments made in *Cockney Rabbit* which may have caused offence when none was intended.
Michael Hunt	*Cunt*	The formal name of Mike, the bloke in the schoolboy prank who gets a girl to innocently ask someone if they've seen Mike Hunt.
Michael Miles	*Piles*	One of a daffy of terms for the dirtbox disorder, this is based on a popular TV quizmaster (1919–71) of the 1950s and 1960s.
Michael Schumacher	*Tobacco*	A 1990s term based on a German racing driver who has long been associated with Marlboro cigarettes, in a business largely sponsored by tobacco companies.
Michael Winner	*Dinner*	Like many of the 1990s terms, this, after a British film director and food critic, was first served up in suburbia.
Mick		A well-known term for an Irishman and by extension anything Irish. 'Mick Beer' – Guinness, Murphy's, Beamish, etc. 'Mick Firm' – a building firm where most of the navvies are Irishmen.
Mick/Micky Bliss	*Piss*	Seldom used in relation to urination but in terms of 'taking the piss', meaning to deride or insult. Taking the 'Micky' is supremely common in this guise and is used by people who don't realise that they are using RS. Sometimes extended to 'Extracting the Michael'.
Mick Jagger	*Lager*	A term used by the Scots, but then you'd have to be a jock to make the rhyme.
Mick O'Dwyer	*Fire*	A 19th-century domestic fire based on an unknown Irishman.
Mickey Finn/ Mickey		A potent knock-out drop slipped into a drink and passed to an unsuspecting victim. Based on the name of the Chicago saloon-bar owner from the late 19th century who perfected the technique.
Mickey Mouse		Anything considered a joke, i.e., inferior or second rate. Something not to to be taken seriously.
Mickey Mouse	*a) House*	The giant rodent of Disneyland has become the commonest of terms for the two-up two-down.
	b) Scouse	A piece that was originally used mockingly by London football supporters against their Merseyside rivals. The derision stems from the non RS meaning of the term, which is second rate or inferior. Mickey Mouser – scouser.

Mickey Rooney	*Loony*	An American film actor gets a role as somebody who is mentally off course.
Mickey Rourke	*Pork*	A 1990s example from the meat market based on an American film actor.
Mickie Most	*Toast*	A 1970s term for hot bread based on a British record producer (1938–2003), seen regularly at the time on the TV talent show *New Faces*.
Micky Blisser	*Pisser (Penis)*	To pull someones 'Micky' is the same as taking the 'Micky'. Same boots different laces really.
Micky Duff	a) *Puff*	A piece that relates to drugs for the smoking of: 'I'm partial to a bit of Micky.'
	b) *Rough (Unwell)*	Based on an English boxing trainer and promoter, this is generally used about the appearance of somebody after a night's carousing: 'You alright? You look a bit Micky Duff.'
Microchip	*Nip (Japanese)*	Shortened to a 'micro', this is a relevant example as the Japanese have long been at the forefront of microchip technology. It is also indicative of the widespread perception of the size of the average son of Nippon.
Microdot		A drug user's term from the 1960s for a small dose of LSD.
Middle Leg		A 19th-century term for the penis. Lucky the man whose 'middle leg' ends at a foot.
Middle Stump		The penis. Men with a venereal disease are said to have had their 'middle stump' knocked out.
Midland Bank	*Wank*	A fairly well-known piece for DIY sex. 'Midland Banker' – wanker.
Mighty Mouth		A big-mouth, someone not to be trusted with a secret. A 'blabbermouth'.
Mighty Quinn		A 1960s term for LSD made famous by British group Manfred Mann in the eponymous hit single of 1968.
Mike/Michael Bliss	*Piss*	Exactly the same as Mick/Micky Bliss (qv).
Mike Dickin	*Chicken*	A radio presenter gets on the menu for poultry, usually when cooked. A 1990s term and one which the man will probably hate.
Mike Malone	*Phone*	Sounds like this is based on a tough Irishman, but he can't get the better of the 'dog'. *See* Dog & Bone.
Mile End	*Friend*	After an area of East London, where a Mile End in need is a pest.
Milk		a) An ancient term for semen. You're on the point of orgasm when your 'milk' is about to boil over. To 'milk' is to masturbate and a 'milker'/'milkman' is someone who does it to excess.

		b) To siphon petrol from a car when your own has run out: 'There's no garages round here, we'll have to do some milking.'
Milk Jug	*Mug*	An old piece relating to someone easily duped, one who 'stands the broads'.
Milker		An old term for the vagina, so called because it 'milks' a penis. *See* MILK (a).
Milkman's Horse	*Cross (Angry)*	Old cockney pronunciation of 'crorse' make the rhyme on this dated, and the term is probably obsolete.
Milky		Descriptive of a cowardly, weak person. A term also associated with an effeminate or unmanly man.
Milky Bar		An extremely pale person, especially a new arrival on the beach of a hot resort. Based on the name of a bar of white chocolate.
Milky Way	*Gay (Homosexual)*	Based on the sweetie that can be eaten between meals. Seems apt enough.
Millennium Dome	*Comb*	A 1990s piece that was coined while the multi-million pound building in Greenwich was being constructed.
Miller's Daughter	*Water*	An example that made it's first cup of tea in the 19th century.
Milligna		A typing error, a piece Spike Milligan composed when describing himself as Spike Milligna, the well-known typing error. Included in deference to the great man (1918–2002).
Million		a) A great person, someone worth knowing, another version of 'diamond' (qv). A shortening of 'a million dollars', anyone described as a 'million' is a good 'un. b) Something considered to be at such long odds against that there is no chance of it occurring, a million-to-one chance: 'Pass your test? You're a million if you drive like that.'
Millions On		An absolute sure thing, something that is such a certainty that it's odds are millions to one on it happening: 'The day I forget to do the lotto, it's millions on my numbers coming up.'
Millwall Reserves	*Nerves*	South London rivals of the more common 'West Ham Reserves' (qv).
Millwally		A Millwall FC supporter, as seen by fans of rival teams. A hybrid of Millwall and 'Wally' (qv, b).
Milton Keynes	*a) Beans*	Any beans can be 'Miltons', but usually it's the ones that sit comfortably on 'holy ghost' (qv, d).
	b) Queens	Refers to homosexual men and is often a reference to an establishment that caters for them, a 'Miltons' bar for instance.

Mimi

A selfish person, one who puts himself first, who is all 'me me'.

Min/Minnie

The vagina, well-used terms that are probably derived from 'minge' (qv).

Mince Pie   *Eye*

A very well-known piece, common for the eyes to be referred to as 'minces' or 'mincers'.

Mincer

A male homosexual, from the affected manner of an effeminate man.

Mind Bending/ Blowing

Fantastic, amazing, staggering. Terms that have risen above their original contexts as the effects of an hallucinogenic drug to describe anything that may astound: 'That anyone can earn so much for kicking a football about is mind blowing.'

Mind Games

A battle of wills between people trying to out-think each other. Psychological warfare.

Minder

A bodyguard, originally one who watches the back of a criminal. After the success of a TV series of the name, anyone who sought protection, from entertainers to sports stars, had their 'minders'.

Mindfuck

Thoughts of a sexual encounter, to fantasise about someone. To mess with someone's mind; to baffle.

Mind's Eye

The anus, a mocking reference to someone considered to have his brains in his backside.

Minesweeping

A 1960s term for stealing drinks off tables of discos while their owners are dancing. Many have got drunk in this manner and many have caught gum disease.

Ming

a) The police, a London underworld term that sees the Met as the baddies. Based on the name of the evil enemy of Dan Dare. 'Ming on the wing' – the police are coming.

b) To smell bad, to stink. Food that's gone off is 'minging'. Also, by extension, anything that's considered rubbish. 'Minger' is the new 'stinker' and may describe a bad performance.

Minge

a) The vagina, a piece that's been in use since the 19th century and has roots in Romany. The word is also used as a substitute for 'cunt' (qv), in all it's forms.

b) Applies to women in general.

Mini Moke   *Smoke*

A 1990s term that relates to a cigarette, one that may or may not contain drugs. Based on a small car.

Mini Mouse

A name given to a woman with shapeless, thin legs and wearing a mini-skirt. A pun on Disney's Minnie Mouse, who has such 'standers' (qv).

Mint Sauce

Used by punsters of anyone who is on the run, anyone who has 'gone mint sauce' is 'on the lam'. *See* LAM.

Minted		Financially secure. Worth more than a few bob – a mint, in fact.
Misbehave	*Shave*	When a man goes into the bathroom saying he's going to 'misbehave', you now know what he's going to do. Or do you? 'Ain't misbehaving, gonna grow a beard for you.' – The song Fats Waller might have written had he been born in New Cross, London, and not New York.
Miss a Penalty		To make a glaring mistake, the type that makes you put your head in your hands and look to the heavens.
Miss Fitch	*Bitch*	An elderly reference to a spiteful woman.
Miss Piggy	*Ciggy*	Whereby the siren of the Muppet Show becomes smoky bacon.
Missing Slate		What the mad or eccentric are said to have.
Missionary		The only white person in a group of blacks, an allusion to the godly souls who travelled to Africa to inflict religion on people who were probably happy enough without it.
Mither		To complain, whinge or make a fuss, a term from the north of England that's well-known elsewhere through its use on TV's *Coronation Street*.
Mitt		A hand, often one screwed into a fist: 'Put your mitts up.'
Mix & Muddle	*Cuddle*	One of life's little ags is when you're lying in bed on a cold night having a nice 'mix & muddle' and you have to get up for a 'cuddle & kiss' (qv).
Mix/Mixer		A troublemaker, one who deliberately 'whisks his tongue' to cause a stir.
Mizzle		To leave or escape. A hasty exit: 'I don't like the atmosphere in here, let's mizzle.'
Mizzog		A miserable person: 'What's up with you, you mizzog? You've had a face longer than a stretch limo all day.'
Mo		A name given to an informer. A pun on mowing the 'grass' (qv). *See* GRASS (c).
Moaning Minnie		A name given to a persistent moaner, a World War One term based on the noise made by German Mortar shells. From the German 'Minenwerfer' – mortar thrower.
Mob		To nag, an old term from rural England.
Mobile		A tea break, an old term from the docks relating to a mobile canteen, a van that arrived at break times carrying tea and food, or 'splosh' and 'nosh'. *See both.*
Mobile Dungheap		A dirty, scruffy, smelly person. Sometimes a 'moving dungheap' or 'reeking pile of shit on the move', to name but two 'truggoes'. *See* TRUG.

Mobo/Moby/ Mobe		Recent terms heard on TV regarding a mobile phone.
Moby Dick	*a) Nick*	Refers to a prison or police station. Convicts get banged-up in, and drunks sleep one off in, the 'Moby'. Based on the novel by Herman Melville.
	b) Prick (Penis)	Doesn't necessarily have to be like the whale of the novel, i.e., a great white one. A 'Moby' is also a fool, much the same as a 'plonker' (qv).
	c) Sick	Time away from work through illness is known as being on the 'Moby'. It may sound like a venereal disease but it isn't.
Mockers		A curse. To put the mockers on someone is to bring them bad luck. 'Mockers and bockers' – a double dose of malediction.
Mockingbird	*Word*	An old piece from the theatre that's been killed off by 'dicky bird' (qv).
Mockney		Someone from the middle classes who tries to sound like a cockney. Film and TV have produced some spectacular 'mockneys' down the years.
Mocktail		A nonalcoholic cocktail.
Mods & Rockers	*Knockers (Breasts)*	Based on a couple of youth cultures of the 1960s, it applies to those of the fuller variety, the type which have caused men to wax lyrical down the ages. 'Look at the mods on that!' is a phrase that springs to mind.
Mog/Moggie		Well-known terms for a cat. Also a cheap fur coat: 'Is that genuine mog?'
Mogadored	*Floored*	Refers to being baffled or beaten by a problem. The assembly instructions to anything bought at a DIY store 'mogadors' most people. Mogador is a place in Morocco so the term may have been coined in the Forces.
Moke		A 19th-century term for a donkey, the much-cherished beast of burden of the costers (costermongers) of the period.
Molly Maguired	*Tired*	Possibly Irish in origin as the widow Maguire was the leader of anti-landlord activists in 1840s Ireland. Her name was taken some thirty years later by a group of militant miners in Pennsylvania, about whom a film was made in 1970. It may be then that the term is based on the film title. Oh well, at least you've had a history lesson.
Molly Malone	*Phone*	The seafood seller from the fair city of Dublin has for years been seen off by the 'dog'. *See* DOG & BONE.
Molly O'Morgan	*Organ*	Originally a barrel-organ but later any organ, not necessarily a musical one, became a 'Molly'.

Momma		An unattached female follower of a gang of Hell's Angels.
Momser		A contemptible or obnoxious person. A term much used by Jews, but then it is Yiddish for bastard.
Mona Lisa	a) *Freezer*	Where else but in RS can a great work of art be mentioned in the same breath as a fish finger?
	b) *Pizza*	One Italian dish for another.
Mona Lott		A name given to a perpetual whinger. An obvious pun.
Money Box/ Maker		The vagina, especially the professional one of a prostitute.
Money in the Bank		A certainty, a must-win situation.
Monica Rose	*Nose*	A 1960s term for the 'snozz' based on a cockney TV personality and comedienne of the period.
Moniker		A 19th-century term for a name that is still used when a 'squiggle' (qv) is required: 'Put your moniker on this.' Therefore a 'moniker' is also a signature. The origin of the term is not known.
Monk		A 19th-century of abuse that is not necessarily malicious. Probably short for monkey.
Monkey		a) A Japanese person since World War Two, possibly because the soldiers of Nippon specialised in jungle warfare.
		b) A well-known term for £500, but no-one seems to know why.
		c) A menial, a general dogsbody: 'You be quiet! I'm talking to Tarzan, not his monkey.'
		d) Drug addiction, 'carrying a monkey' or more commonly to have a 'monkey' on one's back.
		e) Descriptive of anyone devious or tricky, someone not entirely trustworthy: 'Watch him, he's a right monkey bastard.' In snooker and pool a 'monkey shot' is a fluke.
		f) Anything suspicious, not right, bad or seemingly dodgy. Monkey seafood will give you the runs.
Monkey's		What people couldn't give when they don't care. A damn. Sometimes they couldn't give a 'monkey's fuck', a 'monkey's toss' or a 'monkey's bollocks'.
Monkey's Cousin	*Dozen*	An example from a game of bingo.
Monkey's Tail	*Nail*	A piece from the carpentry trade of long ago.
Monolithic		In a state of intoxication courtesy of drugs; in a word, 'stoned'.
Monopoly Money		A vast, unobtainable sum: 'I don't mind paying a reasonable amount but they're talking mono-poly money.'

Montezumas	*Bloomers*	An old term for the type of underwear that would have been consigned to history had it not been for the seaside postcard. Based on the 15th-century Aztec ruler.
Montgomery Clift	*Lift*	Applies to an elevator and also a ride: 'Give me five minutes and I'll give you a Montgomery.' Based on an American actor (1920–66).
Moo		A disagreeable woman, another version of 'cow' (qv). Also as the famous 'silly moo' – a stupid woman.
Mooch		To beg, cadge or scrounge. A 'beer bandit' will come into the pub, 'mooch' a pint or two and leave. 'Moocher' – a sponger or beggar.
Moody & Sankey	*Hanky-Panky*	Applies to a deception, something that isn't quite what it seems is referred to as 'Moody'. The week off work with a Moody backache isn't for real, and a con man will give you a 'load of old Moody'. Dwight Moody and Ira Sankey were a pair of American revivalists who toured Britain in 1875, so people have been making up 'Moody' excuses for well over a century.
Moody		A bogus insurance claim following a 'moody' accident or robbery. *See* MOODY & SANKEY.
Moody Shrewdie		A successful dodge or short cut that is not strictly within the law or rules. A clever ruse or pretence that achieves an objective.
Mooey		a) The face, an extension of its original meaning, the mouth. b) A 19th-century term for the vagina that still gets a mention.
Moolah		A well-known term for money, which applied to dollars and cents before pounds and pence.
Moon		a) A month, used in terms of a long time: 'I haven't seen Lenny for many a moon.' Also refers to a month's prison sentence. b) The face, especially a round one. c) To expose one's buttocks to the world, typically through a car or coach window.
Mooner		A mad person, someone affected by the full moon. In America it's a psychopathic criminal.
Moonhead		A name given to a bald-headed man: 'He took his hat off and I thought the moon had come out.'
Moonlight Flits	*Tits*	Obviously the type men would do a bunk for.
Moonrock		A drug user's term for crack cocaine laced with heroin.
Moonshine		Nonsense, rubbish. A term that's akin to 'bullshit' (qv) but predates it by a couple of centuries.

Moose		A 1990s term for an ugly woman. A 'Loose Moose' – an ugly woman who is also promiscuous.
Moosh/Mush		a) A well-known term for the face which comes from boxing circles where it specifically meant the mouth. It first met a fist in the 19th century.
		b) A stranger, in the same way as 'face' (a): 'Who's the moosh in the corner?' Also a term of address to a man: 'Wotcha moosh.' *Moosh* is the Romany word for man.
Moozo		A late 20th-century term for a Muslim heard often in the days immediately following September 11, 2001.
Mop & Bucket	*Fuck It*	If you're ever in the company of nuns and you hit your thumb with a hammer, this is the thing to holler.
Mopho/Mofo		An abbreviated mobile phone: 'I've tried his mopho, it's switched off.'
More or Less	*Dress*	Applies to the garment and is probably based on the shifting necklines and hemlines of fashion.
Morecambe & Wise	*Rise*	A pay rise courtesy of the comedy double-act who have become as much a part of Christmas viewing as the queen. The term is reduced to a 'Morecambe', ask your boss for one. Eric Morecambe (1926–84) and Ernie Wise (1925–99).
Moriarty	*Party*	Often reduced to a 'Morry' and is based on the arch enemy of Sherlock Holmes and Neddy Seagoon.
Mork & Mindy	a) *Windy*	From a 1970s American TV sitcom comes this 1990s term for a blow.
	b) *Indy*	The newspaper, *The Independent*. A term from that industry.
Morning Glory		a) A racehorse that looks a world beater on the early morning gallops but doesn't show the same class on the racecourse.
		b) Sex before breakfast. A touch of the old 'in and out' before the old up and out.
Morning Glory	*Cory (Penis)*	Would appear to refer to one that stands tall and erect on waking.
Morph		The drug user's term for morphine.
Morris Minor	*Shiner (Black Eye)*	Based on a once popular make of car, the minor battle scar is usually reduced to the first element.
Mortar & Trowel	*Towel*	A 19th-century piece not often heard outside a building site washroom.
Moshing		Wild and aggressive dancing. A 1980s term, when rock fans took 'idiot dancing' (qv) to a level of violence. It often involved going on to the stage and diving into the crowd.
Moss		A 19th-century term for female pubic hair. 'Mossy Cottage' – the vagina.

Most, the		A 1950s import from America regarding the best, the greatest, etc. Now well dated.
Mot		A woman in the 18th century, but later a widely used term for a prostitute. 'Mot house' – a brothel. A later version of 'mort'.
Mother & Daughter	a) *Water*	In the first element an archaic term for the wet element, i.e., a glass of 'mother'.
	b) *Quarter (Post)*	An old riverman's term for a riverside post to which boats are tied.
Mother Brown	*Town*	The star of an East End knees-up is sometimes used in connection with London's West End.
Mother Goose	*Juice*	The old bird who puts in an appearance in the pantomime season comes in as a term for motor fuel, be it petrol or diesel.
Mother Hubbard		A complete lie, a 'fairy story' (qv): 'Don't give me that old Mother Hubbard.'
Mother Hubbard	*Cupboard*	A fairly obvious piece from the world of nursery rhymes concerning a provisionless woman and her hungry dog.
Mother Kelly	a) *Jelly*	Applies to the sweet and to the eels accompaniment. It's also what your legs turn to when gripped by abject fear.
	b) *Telly*	That which now has more channels than good programmes to fill them. Based on the lady with the famous doorstep.
Mother Machree	*Tea*	A not-too-often brewed cuppa based on a 19th-century Irish ballad.
Mother of Mine	*Nine*	A popular song title gives the bingo caller another example. Sometimes £9.
Mother of Pearl	*Girl*	Often preceded by 'the old' or 'my old' and meaning a wife. A lot of older cockneys refer to their other halves as 'mother' or 'mum'.
Motherfucker		A no-good, despicable person. A well-known Americanism for the lowest of the low. Often reduced to 'mother', where it is also used in the same way as 'bastard' when speaking of a third party: 'Why is it that the ugliest mothers seem to get the best-looking women?'
Mother-in-Law	*Saw*	A carpenter's term for the main tool of his trade.
Mother's Little Helper		A piece from the 1960s regarding the tranquilliser valium. Otherwise known as 'housewives' choice', the term first saw the light of day as the title of a Rolling Stones song in 1966.
Mother's Milk		A 1960s term for Guinness, which has seen service down the years as gin and brandy.
Mother's Pride	*Bride*	An apposite term for the radiant star of the

wedding. Especially if she resembles a loaf of bread.

Mother's Ruin   *Gin*   An early and very familiar example that is symbolic of what was traditionally a woman's drink. Not a great rhyme but apt in a lot of cases, especially back then.

Motion Lotion   Petrol or diesel, whatever keeps your motor running.

Motor Boat   *Throat*   A rival to the old 'nanny goat' (qv) that may be used threateningly: 'If I get my hands round his motor I'll give it full throttle.'

Motormouth   A fast-talking person, often someone who speaks before thinking and gets somebody else into trouble: 'Trust motormouth to drop me in it.'

Mott   The pubic area of a woman, particularly when it has an abundance of hair.

Motting   The pursuit of women for sex, 'on the pull' (qv). *See* MOTT.

Motzer   A Jew, a piece that derives from 'matzo', a wafer of unleavened bread for Passover.

Mouldies   Copper coins, originally those of our no-longer-current currency.

Mouldy   a) Tight-fisted: 'Put your hands in your pocket you mouldy git and get us a drink.'
b) Old fashioned or out of date, commonly heard as 'mouldy oldie' – an old record.

Moulin Rouge   *Stooge*   A theatrical term for a comedian's foil, based on a famous theatre in Paris and pronounced the London way, 'moolin'.

Mountain Bike   *Dyke (Lesbian)*   A 1990s variation on the older 'Raleigh bike' (qv).

Mountain Passes   *Glasses*   Scenic routes for spectacular viewing.

Mountains of Mourne   *Horn (Erection)*   Probably inspired by appearances above the sheets due to stirrings beneath. Based on the title of an Irish song.

Mouse in the Pantry   An underworld term for a thief among thieves, somebody who helps himself to more of the cheese than he's entitled to. Someone with a fiddle.

Mouse Trap   *Nap*   Refers to forty winks. Or in Nelson's case, twenty.

Mouth Almighty   A loud mouth, often a person who may be so described:

> *The person with the loudest voice*
> *Often speaks the littlest sense*
> *Which proves the theory which maintains*
> *The bigger the mouth, the smaller the brain.*

Mouth Breather		A stupid, moronic person, especially the thuggish type. A term that suggests someone of a primitive species, a Neanderthal (qv).
Mouth Off		To shout, holler or generally make a lot of noise: 'Your uncle was down the pub last night, mouthing off as usual.' Also to boast or brag.
Mouthful		A torrent of verbal abuse, a telling off. 'I got a right mouthful off the old man last night.'
Mouthwash	*Nosh (Fellatio)*	A piece that goes down well when it comes to aptness.
Mouthy		Cocky, lippy: 'Don't get mouthy with me or I'll maim you.'
Mouthy Codlins		A name given to someone with a lot to say for him/herself. Someone with 'mouth enough for three heads'.
Moxie		Originally an American term for courage or daring. The brave are said to have 'plenty of moxie'.
Mozart & Liszt	*Pissed*	A piece that was composed in the theatre and performed on TV and radio before gaining a wider usage. Based on the composers Wolfgang Amadeus Mozart (1756–91) and Franz Liszt (1811–86).
Mozzie		A mosquito. The blood-sucking horror that necessitates 'mozzie nets'.
Mozzle		Luck. An old piece of yiddish often heard in the downhearted lament of a loser: 'It don't pay to be good, it seems the bigger bastard you are the more mozzle you get.' Mozzley – lucky.
Mozzle & Brocha	*Knocker*	Originally used in association with door-to-door salesmen whose job it is to go 'on the knocker'. The term now lends itself to borrowing; a neighbour may be 'on the mozzle' for a cup of sugar. From Yiddish 'mazel' – good luck, and 'brocha' – good health.
Mr Hyde	*Snide*	A variant of 'Jeckll and Hyde' (qv) but this one relates to a person rather than an object: 'Don't trust him, he's a right Mr Hyde.'
Mr Magoo	*a) Clue*	Aptly based on a myopic cartoon character who never knows what's going on, it relates to the ignorant, naive or plain stupid, those who 'ain't got a Mr Magoo'.
	b) Poo (Defecate)	A piece from suburbia. Cockneys don't go for a 'Mr Magoo', they go for a 'game of nap' (qv).
Mrs Chant	*Aunt*	Bears no relation to the relative but to the toilet, for which 'aunt' is a polite euphemism. This appears to have been one in the eye for Mrs Ormiston Chant (1848–1923), a moral crusader of her day. A

19th-century term, when people with one in the 'waiting room' would need to 'visit Mrs Chant'.

Mrs Doyle   *Boil*   A 1990s formation based on the much blemished housekeeper in the TV sitcom *Father Ted*.

Mrs Duckett   a) *Bucket*   A piece that was common in the fishmonger trade and has been employed on building sites.

b) *Fuck It*   Seldom used as an expletive unless a mishap befalls one while in the company of the kids or the vicar, but said with the right volume and intonation it does give a certain satisfaction.

Mrs Mopp   A cleaner, a 1940s piece based on a charlady character in the legendary radio series *ITMA*.

Mrs Mopp   *Shop*   The place to do the 'Mrs Mopping'. Based on a character from the wartime radio show *ITMA*.

Mrs More   *Floor*   One can walk on, sit on and, when drunk, fall on the Mrs More. From the music-hall song 'Don't Have Any More Mrs More'.

Mub   The bum. A piece of backslang for the backside. 'Mubber' – a 'foop' (qv).

Muck   a) Semen. An overheard conversation: 'It was the first time in ages, I come so much muck I'll be soiling her gussets for weeks.'
b) A builder's term for a mixture of sand and cement. 'Muck up!' – a bricklayer's cry for the 'hoddy' to bring more mortar.

Mucker   A good mate. Originally a soldier's term for a friendship forged in battle, when men 'mucked in' together.

Mucking Fuddle   A fairly common spoonerised state of confusion.

Mud in Your Eye   *Tie*   A 'mud' is an old example that has been consigned to the wardrobe of oblivion.

Muddy Trench   *French*   Possibly a World War One double rhyme on 'bloody French', which is how the English have been known to view 'them over the Channel'.

Mudguts   A term of abuse that is hurled at someone with an odorous wind problem.

Muff   The pubic region of a woman, a piece that has been warming men's fingers since the 17th century.

Muff Diving   A well-known term for cunnilingus, or to 'go down' on a woman as practised by a 'muff diver'.

Muffin   The vagina, a mid 20th-century term from the same bakers as 'crumpet' (qv), which similarly doubles as a term for a woman as a sex object.

Muffin Baker   *Quaker*   A 19th-century piece that applies to constipation. A quaker is a name given to a piece of 'hard baked' excrement that causes a blockage, thus causing the sufferer to tremble and quake in their straining attempt at forcing it out.

Muffin the Mule *Fool* A fairly old term for the sawney type who's 'painting the ceiling in his best hat'. Based, not on a depraved perversion, but on the name of a 1950s TV puppet.

Mug a) The face, although not generally a pretty one. An 'ugly mug' is more common than a 'lovely mug'. This 18th-century term has also represented the mouth.

b) A fool, somebody easily tricked, meat for a con-man's pie. 'Mug-in-a-book' – someone who puts up the money for a bookmaker to set up a stall, for which he is promised the proceeds minus a percentage. The proceeds are much lower and the bookie's percentage much higher than he is told. This was a common occurence at dog tracks before bookmaking became regulated.

c) Anyone inept at a given pursuit, be it sporting or occupational, is often deemed a 'mug at the game'.

Mug Book A book containing pictures of known criminals kept at police stations.

Mug Punter God's gift to bookmakers, a person who bets stupidly.

Mug Shot A well-known term from TV for a police photograph.

Mug Up To learn or revise a subject prior to an examination.

Muggins A fool, a term that is often used in self pity: 'Muggins here'll cop the blame for that.'

Muggo A tea break, an old term from the docks that meant that the 'mobile' (qv) had arrived.

Muldoon Since the 1960s, a name given to anyone prone to spots. Based on Spotty Muldoon, a character invented by comedian Peter Cook in his guise as E L Wisty.

Muller a) To beat severely, to thrash, much in the same way as 'hammer'. A victim of a beating or a sporting opponent can be 'mullered'. Also to pan; if this book gets 'mullered' by the critics, I've had it. Not sure where it comes from, perhaps from the name of a device for grinding drugs or possibly the name of the German footballer Gerd Muller, who broke the hearts of the English by scoring the goals that knocked us out of the 1970 World Cup. If you heard the term before 1970, forget that second theory.

b) To eat or drink greedily: 'He came in, mullered his dinner and went straight out again.'

Mulligan Stew   *Two*   Based on services slang for Irish stew, this has been put forward as an explanation as to why a 'mulligan' is the name given to a second attempt at a mis-hit shot in a game of golf.

Mulligatawny   *Horny*   A hot tasty dish would seem pretty appropriate for sexual arousal, when he has a 'knob-throb' for her and she has a 'clitwobble' for him. *See both.*

Multi-Faced   An extremely untrustworthy person, at least twice the snake a 'two-faced' person is.

Mum & Dad   *Mad*   As well as a reference to someone with his 'boots on the wrong feet', this applies to a loss of temper, apt as parents are prone to it: 'His old woman'll go mum and dad when she sees the state he's in.'

Mumble &   *Butter*   People have been spreading 'mumble' on their
Mutter   'Uncle Fred' for nigh on a hundred years.

Mummysuck   A sissy, someone dominated by his mother. A 'mummy's boy'.

Mump   To beg or scrounge. Heard at a bus stop: 'You can't move on the Tube now for foreign mumpers.'

Mumper   A beggar or scrounger. *See* Mump.

Mump Hole/   A place, such as a cafe, hospital canteen, coffee
House   stall, etc., used by police officers on patrol as a 'nip-in' (qv), where free food and drink is obtained in return for services rendered, like extra protection or a blind eye to minor misdemeanors.

Mums & Dads   *Pads*   Those that protect the little legs of cricketers.

Munchies   An American term for food snacks that has arrived on these shores via TV.

Munchkin   A small child, in which case the term is used lovingly, or a short adult, whereby it's an insult. From the name of the little people in the film *The Wizard of Oz*.

Muppet(s)   a) An underworld term for officious people in uniforms, like young PCs, traffic wardens, store security guards, etc. Also a lay magistrate. From a 1970s TV puppet show.
b) An idiot or anybody seen as being a 'bit of a joke', someone who can't be taken seriously: 'Manager he may be, he's still a muppet.' Also a cruel reference to an ugly or mentally retarded person.

Mur   A backslang drop of rum. 'Murder' – red rum.

Murphy   A spud, potatoes perceived as the staple diet of the Irish. Also known as an 'Irish apple'.

Murray Mint	*Skint*	The too-good-to-hurry mint does a too-broke-to-worry stint. Why worry about what you haven't got?
Muscle		A strong-arm man, either as an enforcer or a bodyguard.
Mush		See MOOSH.
Mush/Mushroom		Old terms for an umbrella. A 'mush' was common parlance of on-course bookmakers for an important part of their equipment. Before the marker pen, prices were chalked up. Not easy when it's raining.
Mushroom		A worker who is deemed unimportant, one who is 'kept in the dark and shat on'.
Mushy Brained		Senile. A term used about anyone whose brain has supposedly 'turned to mush'. 'Mushy brains' is an abusive name for an idiot.
Mustard		Skilful, 'hot stuff'. What George Best was at football and Malcolm P Barnoldswick was at 'fangoggling' (qv). Until he got caught. Also a sexually accomplished woman: 'Hot? She's mustard.'
Mustard & Cress	*Dress*	Always a 'mustard', perhaps in relation to a hot little number.
Mustard Pickle	*Cripple*	An imperfect rhyme, but a 'mustard' is the 1990s equivalent of the widely used 'raspberry ripple'.
Mustard Pot	a) *Hot*	The contrary nature of the British is never more apparent than when talking about the weather; it's too 'taters' in the winter and too 'mustard' in the summer (sometimes).
	b) *Twat (Vagina)*	As owned by an alluring lady that gets the 'saveloys' (qv) voicing their desires: 'I wouldn't mind dipping my sausage in her mustard pot.'
Mustard Pots		Brown boots, a piece that comes from a time when black boots were the norm. People wearing brown footwear were mockingly asked if they had dipped their feet in a mustard pot.
Mutt		An unattractive person, an alternative to 'dog' (qv): 'I've been with so many mutts I've had to get vaccinated against the mange.'
Mutt & Jeff	*Deaf*	A very well-known piece that is commonly used as 'mutton'. Based on a couple of American cartoon characters from the 1930s that regularly featured in British newspapers.
Mutt's Nuts		The best, a poetic version of the 'dog's bollocks' (qv).
Mutton Pie	*Eye*	A 19th-century term that is well in the shadow of 'mince pie', but a person with an eye defect or a squint is often called 'mutton-eye'.
Mutton-Eye		A name given to somebody with a squint.

My Word	*Turd*	Just the right exclamation when you slip on one, crack your head on the pavement and get dog's mess all over your best suit. I should think so!
Myrna Loy	*Saveloy*	Not a great rhyme but widely used as a 'Myrna' in the double act with pease pudding. Based on an American actress (1905–93).
Mystery Bag		A sausage; only the butcher knows what's in it.
Mystic Meg(s)	*Leg(s)*	A piece that's been kicking about since the spaced-out crystal gazer first materialised on TV's National Lottery show.

N

NFG		Useless, lousy, rubbish. Generally No Fucking Good.
Nab		To arrest or catch someone in the act of wrongdoing. A well-known term from the 19th century when a policeman was known as a 'nabber'.
Nadgers		The testicles, a post-war version of 'knackers' (qv).
Naff		a) A popular euphemism for 'fuck', much used in TV scripts as in 'naff all', 'naff off' , 'naffing hell', etc. b) Descriptive of anything trashy like a clockwork Nativity scene. Out of date like a 1960s film set in 'swinging London' where everyone goes about saying 'groovy'. Or glaringly bad like the cabaret at a two-star boarding house in Felixstowe.
Nag Pie		Marriage. What bachelors never have to eat.
Nail		a) A cigarette, especially a drugfag. Another nail in the coffin. *See* COFFIN NAIL. b) An arrest, 19th–century term that sees criminals getting 'nailed', possibly by the 'hammer'. *See* HAMMER & SAW.
Nail in One's Own Shoe		To be your own worst enemy, to be the cause of your own grief.
Nailed On		A racing term for a horse or dog that appears to be a certainty.
Nails & Tacks	*Fax*	A 1990s term for what no office is complete without, a 'nails' machine.

Nam/Nammow		Man/woman, a backslang couple, where she is pronounced 'nammer'.
Namslop		A policeman, a backslang lawman. 'Nammerslop' – a policewoman. *See* SLOP.
Nana		A 1940s term for an idiot that was often used in British comedy films in the post-Word War Two period: 'I feel a right nana dressed like this.'
Nance/Nancy Boy		Well-known terms for an effeminate man or a homosexual. Both are commonly associated with professional male dancers, chorus boys and the like.
Nancy Lee	a) *Flea*	A 19th-century piece that was common when poverty caused fleas to be common.
	b) *Tea*	Older but less famous version of 'Rosie Lee' (qv).
Nanny Goat	a) *Boat*	A World War Two term that's rarely, if ever, used these days.
	b) *Coat*	'Nannies' are frequently worn on building sites in the guise of donkey jackets.
	c) *Throat*	The first sign of a cold or flu is a sore 'nanny'.
	d) *Tote*	Possibly the widest usage of the term is in racing circles for the totalisator: 'The favourite paid evens a place on the nanny.'
Nanny Goat Shitting on Tin, like a		A colourful expression that's used to describe the voice of a terrible singer.
Nanny Goating	*Courting*	Not a great rhyme but a very old term for an old-fashioned word.
Nanti/Nants		Nothing, none or devoid of, a piece of Polari based on the Italian *niente* – nothing. 'Nanti dinari' – no money.
Nanti Maginty/ Nanti Genighty		Extended versions of 'nothing', said for emphasis. 'Genighty' is a backslang version of 'thing', and 'maginty' may be likewise but is probably a mispronunciation of 'naginty'.
Nantucket	*Bucket*	Had a limited employment on a building site of the 1970s.
Nap & Double	*Trouble*	A 1930s piece that seems to have its roots in the turf, possibly from the financial trouble caused by losing bets.
Napoo		A piece from the trenches of World War One meaning finished, gone, no more. From the French 'Il n'y en a plus' – there is no more of it.
Napper		a) An 18th-century term for the head that is still in use. Centre forwards have long demanded the ball be crossed to their 'nappers'. b) A 1990s drug user's term for a sleeping pill.
Napper Wrapper		A 1980s, East Ender's term for a turban as worn by a Sikh. *See* NAPPER.

Nark		a) An informer, anyone who points a finger at another to a figure of authority. Most commonly associated with a police informer, sneeringly known as a 'copper's nark'. The term comes from the Romany *nak* meaning nose, which ties in with similar terms 'snitch' and 'snout' for anyone who pokes his nose in.
		b) To stop, an old cockney term used as 'nark it' – pack it in.
Nark/Narks		A police officer and the service he works for: 'He was a complete loon before he joined the narks then he went all the other way.'
Narked		Annoyed or irritated, how you feel when around someone who 'gets up your nose'. *See* NARK (a).
Narking Dues		Punishment meted out because of information given against one. What such prisoners are said to be serving.
Narky		Irritable, ratty. 'She's a narky mare when the painters are in.' *See* PAINTERS.
Naseem Hamed	*Spamhead (Bald)*	Based on a world featherweight boxing champion from Sheffield, this applies to the prematurely bald rather than a shaved head. *See* SPAMHEAD.
Nat King Cole	a) *Dole*	A piece from the late 1950s that was an update of 'Old King Cole' (qv). Thus 'on the Nat'.
	b) *Mole*	Although gardeners may be plagued with 'Nats', this generally applies to a mole on the skin.
	c) *(Bread) Roll*	Based on an American singer/pianist, this makes for a very common lunch, a pint and a 'Nat King Cole'.
Nathaniel	*Hell*	An old term that is pronounced 'Nathan-iell'.
National Debt	*Bet*	A reference to gambling which would be more appropriate if it were 'personal debt'. But it ain't!
National Front	*Cunt*	A 1980s term for an obnoxious person based on the right-wing political movement.
National Hunt	*Front*	People with a lot of cheek, boldness or face are said to have 'more National Hunt than Cheltenham.'
Native		An old term for a black person, coined before mass immigration when black people were most commonly seen in films set in Africa.
Naughties		A sexual act with someone you shouldn't be doing it with, an extra-marital relationship may start with a bit of 'naughties'. Also known as 'naughty-naughties'.
Naughton & Gold	*Cold*	A rare alternative to 'taters' (qv) as far as temperature is concerned, this mainly applies to the illness, whereby sufferers may have a 'Naughton'. Based on Charlie Naughton (1887–1976) and Jimmy Gold (1886–1967), a British comedy team who formed part of the Crazy Gang.

Naughty		An understatement from the underworld regarding someone or something very bad. A murderous thug may be described as a 'bit naughty'.
Naughty Bits		The genitals, a piece first heard on the TV show *Monty Python's Flying Circus* and which caught on.
Nause		To mess-up, ruin or throw a spaniel in the works: 'You naused that up, it should be a spanner.'
Nautical Miles	*Piles*	Normally shrunk to 'nauticals', this is another reference to the condition that non-sufferers find amusing.
Navasota	*Motor*	A piece from London's long-vanished docks industry, based on the name of a ship that used to sail between the capital and Argentina carrying refrigerated beef.
Navigator	*Potato*	An archaic term for the 'earth apple' that was once employed in the cry of itinerant baked potato vendors as 'Navigator Scot', which served as 'potatoes hot'.
Nazi Spy	*Pie*	A wartime expression for, predominantly, a meat pie.
Neanderthal		A thug. Typically a shaven-headed, tattooed yob, seen nutting police truncheons whenever the England football team play abroad.
Near & Far	*Bar*	From the days when pubs had a saloon and a public bar; when it's your round it's your turn up the 'near and far'.
Near Enough	*Puff (Homosexual)*	An example from pre-politically correct times, when the close approach from behind of someone so inclined would draw the remark: 'That's near enough.' Sometimes said as 'nigh enough'.
Nebbish/Nebich		A Yiddish expression for a total loser, a nobody. The 'never had nothing, never will' type.
Neck		Audacity, impudence or nerve. Often heard as 'Brass Neck'. Also 'Neck It Out' – to keep one's nerve.
Neck Breaker		A full bladder, as possessed by those who are 'breaking their necks for a piss'.
Neckich		A chicken, a piece of backslang poultry. 'Neckich and piches' – chicken and chips.
Neck-Oil		Alcohol, usually beer. Ties in with the 16th-century verb to 'neck' meaning to swallow alcohol and the oft-used expression 'Get this down your neck.' – drink this.
Ned Kelly	*a) Belly*	Based on the name of an Australian outlaw (1855–80), this import, which generally applies to a beer-gut, is a rival of the long-established 'Derby Kelly' (qv).
	b) Telly	A 1970s term that's rarely switched on in Britain.
Ned Skinner	*Dinner*	A 19th-century term that's no longer served up.

Neddy		An underworld term for a cosh, a bonce-basher since the 19th century.
Needle		To annoy, irritate or generally give someone a hard time. To 'get the needle' is to become annoyed.
Needle & Cotton	*Rotten*	Applies to anything that is less than pleasant, from a maggot-ridden apple to a nasty person. It may also refer to the person's insides and the gases they give off after eating the apple.
Needle & Pin	*a) Gin*	An old piece that's usually crashed down to a 'drop of needle'.
	b) Thin	An example that would appear to be supremely apt, an overenthusiastic weight-watcher may end up painfully 'needle'.
Needle & Thread	*Bread*	Often used in conjunction with 'stammer and stutter' (qv) to form a convoluted example. A slice of 'needle and stammer' would be impossible for the uninitiated to fathom out.
Needle Match		A contest where there is genuine bad feeling between the rivals. A boxing match is often hyped up as such to increase the revenue.
Needles & Pins	*Twins*	Like the well-dressed dwarf who sat on a tack, this is short, sharp and to the point. Pins and needles are identical, except around the eyes.
Neergs		Greens, a piece of backslang from the green-grocery trade.
Neetenin		The number nineteen in backslang.
Neetevif		The number fifteen in backslang.
Neetexis		The number sixteen in backslang.
Neetheg		The number eighteen in backslang.
Neetnevis		The number seventeen in backslang.
Neetrith		The number thirteen in backslang.
Neetrofe		The number fourteen in backslang.
Nell Gwyn	*Gin*	The mistress of Charles II lends her name to the spirit of the East End, often in the guise of 'a drop of Nellie'. An actress, born in 1650, she bore the king two sons before dying in 1687.
Nellie		A weak, ineffectual person, often heard disparagingly in northern comedies as 'big soft Nellie' or 'great hairy Nellie'.
Nellie Bly	*Fly*	Applies to the flying pest of summer and also to that which is left undone on a flasher's trousers. Based on an American reporter (1864–1922) who, in 1890, circled the world in a record 72 days.
Nellie Dean	*a) Green*	A 1950s reference to a green snooker ball. The next colour up to the 'Cinderella' (qv).
	b) Queen	A reference to a homosexual male, especially an

		older one, hence 'an old Nellie'. Based on the title of a music-hall song that was in the repertoire of every drunk who ever walked home late at night.
Nellie Deans	*Greens*	A greengrocer's term for green vegetables which is usually boiled down to 'Nellies'.
Nellie Duff	*Puff (Breath)*	Through breath we get life, hence the well-known phrase 'not on your Nellie' – not on your life.
Nelson Eddy(s)	*Ready/ Readies*	Can be used impatiently while waiting for someone: 'Ain't you Nelson Eddy yet?' But it is mainly used in connection with cash money: 'If you've got the Nelsons you can take it away with you.' Formed on the name of an American musical actor (1901–67).
Nelson Mandela	*Stella (Artois)*	The former South African president and political prisoner lends his name to a brand of lager, giving a whole new meaning to the phrase 'Free Nelson Mandela'.
Nelson Riddle	a) *Fiddle*	Based on the name of an American musician and composer (1921–85) but has nothing to do with violins. People who make a living on the very edge of legality are said to have a few 'Nelsons' going.
	b) *Piddle*	The act of urination and what's passed as the result of it. The term is generally used in full.
Nerd		Originally an American term for a dull, studious person, the non-drinking, non-smoking, never-get up-to-no-good type. Someone with a particular interest, e.g., a computer nerd, a comic nerd, someone said to be in need of a life. 'Nerdy' – descriptive of that type of person.
Nerk		A piece that started off as a non-offensive term for a fool but later became a stronger term of abuse: 'Drop dead you despicable nerk.'
Nervo & Knox	a) *Box*	Mainly applies to the 'goggle box', the television, and is generally turned down to a 'Nervo'. Based on the comedy pairing of Jimmy Nervo (1890–1975) and Teddy Knox (1896–1974) who were part of the Crazy Gang.
	b) *Pox (VD)*	Usually truncated to the name of the first partner, which is a result for the one who actually makes the rhyme. He might have wanted a clap in his professional life but he wouldn't want to be remembered as a dose of one.
	c) *Socks*	A 'pair of Nervos' is a theatrical term from the 1940s.
Nervous Wreck	*Cheque*	What many a pools winner has reportedly been while waiting for the man from Littlewood's to come and confirm their win.

Net		The number ten in backslang. 'Net dunops' – ten pounds.
Netter		£10, a backslang tenner. *See* NET.
Nettie		A lavatory, a piece that's common in the north-east of England.
Nevele/Nevel		The number eleven in backslang.
Never Again	*Ben (Truman)*	A term for a brand of beer that is based on what every hungover person says every time they wake up with a dead-head.
Never Fear	*Beer*	A very old piece, perhaps based on the bravado that may come from a few bevvypints.
Neversweat		A name given to a lazy person, a loafer or someone with an easy, effortless, sweat-free job.
Nevis/Neves		The number seven in backslang. Nevis canaries – seven dwarfs. *See* CANARY WHARF.
New Delhi	*Belly*	An appropriate example for the rumbling one after particularly powerful curry.
Newgate Gaol	*Tale*	An archaic term for a hard-luck story based on London's notorious but long-demolished prison.
Newgate's Knocker		A term that is symbolic of dirtiness or darkness: 'Wash your neck, it's as black as Newgate's Knocker.'
Newington Butts	*Guts*	Based on a road name in South London, this applies to both the stomach and to courage. You may have a disease of the 'Newingtons' and also the 'Newingtons' to battle against it.
News of the World		A gossip, someone unable to keep a secret. A blabbermouth: 'Keep shtum, here comes the News of the World.'
Newted		Drunk. Not sure how these amphibians got the reputation for being boozers, but most drinkers end up 'pissed as a newt' from time to time.
Newton & Ridley	*Tiddly (Drunk)*	A 1990s piece that is comically based on the fictitious beer sold in the Rover's Return in TV's *Coronation Street*.
Newton Heath	*Teeth*	An old northern term based on the original name of Manchester United football club.
Nezzod		Twelve, a backslang dozen. 'Nezzod googies' – a dozen eggs.
Niagara Falls	*a) Balls*	A term of dual usage in that it relates to the testicles and the nonsense people spout when they talk 'a load of Niagaras'.
	b) Stalls	A theatrical reference to that part of an auditorium.
Nibble		Bar snacks, traditionally peanuts, crisps, seafood, etc. placed on public house bars on a Sunday lunchtime for customers to nibble with their pints. 'Nibble and Guzzle' – food and drink. Later

		extended to 'Nibbles' regarding party snacks as used by British chef Jamie Oliver in a TV advert.
Nice Enough	*Puff (Homosexual)*	Widely known as 'one of those nice boys' or 'he seems nice enough'.
Nice One, Cyril	*Squirrel*	Based on a catchphrase of the early 1970s which was started by Tottenham Hotspur supporters and directed at their fullback Cyril Knowles (1944–91). It was taken up and used in an advertising campaign for a brand of bread and soon it seemed as though everyone was saying it. It even became the title of a song that reached the charts in 1973. Squirrels have become a common sight in parks and gardens in and around London, which is why the tree-rat has become known as a 'nice one'.
Nicely Done		Pleasantly drunk, a piece that sees the time between sobriety and inebriation as cooking time. From 'stone cold' – sober, through 'half cooked' – tipsy, to 'ruined' – paralytic.
Nick		a) A police station, well-known on the manor as the 'local nick'.
		b) A prison, a well-known piece that's been doing time since the 19th century.
		c) Any offence that carries a penalty, a term that's often associated with motoring offences, a 'Kojak' (qv) tyre, for example, is a 'nick'.
		d) To steal. Thieves have been 'on the nick' for centuries.
		e) To arrest. Thieves have been nicked for going 'on the nick' for as long as (d).
Nick Cotton	*Rotten*	A piece that had to happen, 'nasty Nick' is the meanest, rottenest character to ever tread the streets of Walford in the TV soap *EastEnders*.
Nick-Bent		To be homosexual for the duration of a prison sentence. *See* NICK *and* BENT.
Nickel & Dime	*Time*	An American piece that found it's way over here and could become part of the procrastinator's motto – 'There's no time like the future.'
Nicker		A well-known piece for £1 that doesn't get pluralised – £30 is thirty nicker.
Nicker Bits	*Shits*	The pound coin was introduced in 1983 and immediately christened a 'nicker-bit'; this term for diarrhoea appeared shortly afterwards.
Nicky Butts	*Nuts*	A late 1990s example whereby a bar snack is known as a bag of 'Nickys'. Based on a Manchester United and England footballer, it has also obtained a testicular meaning.

Nifty		a) A 1970s term for £50. A tenner on a five-to-one chance earns you a 'nifty fifty'. b) Swift: 'As soon as I saw her old man I legged it a bit nifty.'
Nig		Gin. A backslang 'drop of nonsense' (qv).
Nigel		A name that is thought to epitomise, and so is given to, any upper-class male: 'You don't want to go in there, it's running alive with Nigels.'
Nigel Benn	*Pen*	Still in the early rounds of its fight with the long-reigning 'Bill and Ben' (qv), which is well ahead on ballpoints. Based on a former super-middleweight boxing champion from Ilford. Time will tell if he can deliver a knockout blow to the flowerpot men.
Nigerian Lager		A 1970s term for Guinness, due to it's blackness.
Night & Day	*a) Grey*	A reference to the ageing process as seen in the colour of a mature head of hair.
	b) Play	A 19th-century reference to a theatrical performance.
Night Boat to Cairo	*Giro*	A term that relates to a cheque from the DSS, mainly concerning dole or sickness benefit. A piece that was coined by young unemployed people of the 1980s and is based on a song by the British band, Madness, from 1980.
Nig-Nog	*Wog*	An abusive term mainly used against black people, although it originally referred to all foreigners irrespective of colour.
Niki Lauder	*Powder*	The name of the Austrian Formula One racing driver was never one to be sniffed at in his heyday. Sadly though, it is now, since he does the rounds on the drugs circuit as any powdered narcotic.
Nimby		Someone who is all for new roads or buildings as long as they are on someone else's doorstep and 'Not In My Back Yard'.
Nine Penn'orth		An old underworld term for a nine-month prison sentence.
Nine-Bob Note		From the expression 'bent as a nine-bob note', meaning crooked or corrupt. Anything, in fact, that isn't straight, including sexuality; therefore a 'nine-bob note' is also a homosexual.
Nip		a) A Japanese person, a term that now rivals the long-established Jap. b) To tap someone for some money: 'I went into the Oak to get a sub off the guv'nor, and Jack walked in and nipped ME for a fiver.' See CRAB (b).
Nip-In		A cafe, pub or other place of refreshment where people regularly nip in for a quick drink or a bite. A coffee stall may be a 'nip-in' for cab drivers.

Nipper		a) Originally a small child, for which the term is no longer considered slang, it now applies to a small adult: 'What d'you let her talk to you like that for? She's only a nipper.' b) A persistent borrower, someone who tends to forget about repayment. *See* NIP *and* CRAB.
Nipperhood		Childhood, the happy days when you were a nipper.
Nips		A 1970s abbreviation of nipples, female ones obviously. 'Nip-tease' – a woman wearing a top but no bra.
Nish/Nisht/ Nishta		A Yiddish term meaning nothing, or free: 'It was a teriffic do, all you could eat and drink and all for nish.'
Nit		A fool, a much-used term in early radio and TV comedy shows.
Nit/Nitto		Underworld warnings to keep quiet. The clump of a policeman's boot is often heard after a whispered 'Nitto!'
Nit/Nitto/Nitso		No, nothing or none. Variations of 'nix'. To be holding 'nitso' is to be broke.
Nit Nurse		The nurse who inspects the heads of primary school children for parasitic intruders.
Nits & Lice(s)	*Price(s)*	An example from the racecourse coined by the odds-layers of around a century ago.
Nitty-Gritty		A common American import relating to the specific details of something.
Nix		No, nothing or none, a 19th-century term that comes from the German *nichts* – nothing. From the jargon of the underworld, whereby: 'I don't know nix' is an example of NOT helping police with their inquiries.
Nix/Nixes		Strong instructions to stop doing something or to keep quiet, the same as 'nit/nitto' (qv).
Nixies		Freebies, anything that isn't charged for. Complimentary tickets for example.
No FT		An underworld term meaning 'no comment' which is used in reply to police questioning. It comes from the advertising slogan of the *Financial Times* – 'No FT. No Comment'.
Noah's Ark	*a) Dark*	A piece that's been around since they brightened up the 'Noah's Ark' with gas-lamps.
	b) Lark	Fun, often used to placate the butt of a wind-up: 'No offence. Just having a Noahs with you.'
	c) Nark (Informer)	Possibly the term in it's commonest form, a 'Noahs' is not a popular person. It also spoonerises very cleverly, 'oah's (whore's) nark, representing extreme despicability.

| | d) Park | An old example that is still in use. People walk, play and allow their dogs to foul the footpaths in the 'Noah's Ark'. |

Nob
a) An archaic term for the head and also a whack on it. Thieves would 'nob' a victim before robbing them.

b) A member of the upper classes, one of those said to live on 'Nob Hill'.

Nobber
The number nine based on the Italian *nove* – nine.

Nobbins
Money thrown into a boxing ring by the crowd in recognition of a good contest. From the old term 'nob' – to collect money

Nobble
a) To cheat, especially at cards. Cheating at Patience is an example of pointless 'nobbling'.

b) To interfere with a racehorse or greyhound to prevent it from winning.

c) To use devious or underhand methods to ruin the chances of a rival or business competitor; many a result has been secured by 'nobbling' the opposition.

d) To bribe, threaten or intimidate members of a jury in order to get a favourable sentence.

Nobbler/Nobby
The end piece of a loaf, the crust. A curse: 'May you lose all your teeth and always get the nobby.'

Nobby
a) Smart, elegant or well turned-out as the 'nobs' (b) would have been when the term was coined.

b) Clever, brainy, good with one's 'nob' (a), as a 19th-century clerk would have been, which is why people with the surname Clark often draw the nickname 'Nobby'.

Nobby Halls *Balls (Testicles)*
Based on the eponymous, unitesticular hero of a comic song. A huge disappointment is a kick in the 'Nobbys'.

Nobby Stiles *Piles*
Named after a hard tackling member of England's victorious World Cup team of 1966, who was a constant pain in the arse of his opponents. 'Nobbys' for short.

Nod
In boxing, to get the referee's decision is to get 'the nod'.

Nodad
A diabolical item of clothing, said by cockney comedian Jim Davidson to derive from the phrase 'No dad I don't wanna wear it.'

Noddle
The head, a term that's survived since the 16th century. 'Use your noddle' – a long-standing order to think.

Noddy
A feeble-minded fool, a 17th-century term that lives on in the police force, where the name is given to

new, young PCs by their older colleagues, who are similarly known as 'plods' (qv). Both terms are names of residents of Toytown, as written about by Enid Blyton.

Noddy Bike — A moped, originally one used by the police.

Noddy Holder(s) — *Shoulder(s)* — A piece from the 1970s based on the singer with the hit band Slade. Now an actor and TV personality, perhaps he should revamp Paul Anka's 1959 hit 'Put Your Noddle on My Noddy'. Then again, perhaps not. *See* NODDLE.

Noggin — A 19th-century term for the head that is still in use.

Noggin/Nog — A fool, idiot or simpleton. An old term for the class dunce.

Noghead — Somebody mentally on the wrong course, a fool.

No-Goodnik — A good-for-nothing, unreliable, despicable person. A piece from the 1930s that still hits the spot.

Noino/Noyno — An onion, an example of Covent Garden backslang.

Noise — Drug user's slang for heroin.

Noise Funnels — The ears, nature's sound inlets.

Nommus — The backslang version of someone. Used by 19th-century criminals as a warning cry: 'Nommus eemocking' – someone's coming.

Non Compos — Senselessly drunk, out of one's skull. A 19th-century term from the Latin *non compos mentis* – of unsound mind.

Nonce — A child molester, a paedophile. An underworld term that has gained a wide usage. From the word non-sense. The activity makes no sense to the normal person. A 'kiddie diddler' is also called a 'peedo'.

Non-Skid — *Yid* — A 1940s term for a Jew that seems to have slid out of sight.

Noodge — A pathetic person, a loser. A pest that people tend to avoid.

Noodle — The head. People have been using their noodles to think with since the 18th century.

Nook & Cranny — *Fanny (Vagina)* — The dictionary gives 'nook' as a secluded place and a 'cranny' as a crack. Apt or what?

Nookie — Sexual intercourse, a term that was commonly heard in the 1970s, probably because it doesn't sound offensive. Dr Nookie was a character in a *Carry On* film and Nookie Bear is the popular dummy of British ventriloquist Roger De Courcy.

Nooner — A lunchtime drink: 'I'll see you in Ted's Bar for a nooner.'

Nora Batty — *Tatty* — A 1990s term for anything that's in a bad condition, often used in connection with the bodywork of a car. Based on a character from TV sitcom *Last of the Summer Wine*.

Norm

A gay term for a heterosexual male that's generally used derogatively. 'Norman Normal' – a name given to a conventional man.

Norma Snockers

A name given to a girl with large breasts, a pun on enormous knockers.

Normandy Beach   *Speech*

The D-Day destination often sees action at wedding receptions, when the best man goes over the top with a 'Normandy' designed to embarrass the groom.

Normous Nutt

A name given to anyone whose head seems too large for his body, also a 'big-head'. 'Anything you want to know, ask Normous Nutt, he knows everything' – a pun on 'enormous nut'.

North & South   *Mouth*

A very famous piece that was immortalised in the music-hall song 'What a Mouth', which was a hit record for London-born singer Tommy Steele in 1960. Unlike most terms this is never shortened; it's always used as: 'Just cos you've got hairs round your north and south there's no need to talk like a cunt.'

North Pole   *Hole (Anus)*

An old example that has lost out to 'South Pole' (qv), which has the edge in directional relevance.

Northants   *Pants*

Probably based on the county cricket club rather than the county itself. The fearful may soil their 'Northants'.

Norvie

A northener, according to those in the south. Whether or not they refer to the southerner as a 'Suvvie' I don't know.

Nose

a) An 18th-century term for an informer, the original 'nark' (qv).

b) A spy, someone paid to 'nose round' and report back; the time and motion man in a company, for instance.

c) A nosey person, especially an eavesdropper: 'Watch out we've got a right nose behind us.'

d) A 19th-century term for a detective, private or otherwise.

Nose & Chin   *a) Gin*

A 19th-century term for that which turns the nose red and makes the chin wag.

b) Win

Not uncommon for a gambler to have a bet 'on the nose', that is, to win rather than each way. The term originally applied to a penny, which in the 19th century was known as a 'win'.

Nose Candy

Cocaine, a term well-known among users.

Nose Itch of Summer

Hay fever, a term that was heard in the 1970s TV series *Catweasel*.

Nosebleed Position
Of a football team, to be in an unusually high position in a league table: 'We've never been this high before, the manager keeps getting nosebleeds.' From the fact that they can be brought on by altitude.

Nose-Ointment
An overly inquisitive, nosey person: 'You're a right old nose-ointment! When will you learn to mind your own business?'

Noser My Knacker   *Tobacco*
Reduced to 'noser' or 'nosey', the term literally means 'smell my testicles'. This was an old cockney reply to an admonishment, much the same as 'balls' or 'bollocks' is today, and is said to have originated in the 19th century as a smoker's retaliation to complaints by non-smokers.

Nose-Shit
Nasal residue, bogeys. Rollers, eaters or flickers, they all count as nose-shit.

Nosh
a) A well-known term for food, originally a snack but later a meal of any proportion. The term is a Yiddish word and appears in 'posh nosh' – cordon bleu cookery and 'noshery' – a place to eat.

b) Oral sex, usually fellatio but women can be 'noshed' as well since the term also means to eat. 'Sixty-niners' go in for mutual 'noshing' and prostitutes may earn 'nosh-dosh'.

Nosher
a) A person with a large appetite, someone with a love of food.

b) Someone with a talent for performing fellatio, one who gives a great 'nosh'.

c) A term of address to a man: 'How's it going, Nosher?'

Nosh-Up
A meal, especially one at a function. A wedding breakfast for instance or a barbecue. 'Nosh-up list' – a menu.

Nostril Intruder
A pest, someone who 'gets up your nose'.

Not All There
Mentally deficient, as shown in a multitude of terms like 'a brick short of a load', 'not a full pint' 'a penny short of a shilling', etc.

Not Many Benny
An ironic expression meaning definitely yes: 'Do I want another drink? Not many Benny.'

Not On
Unacceptable behaviour or an intolerable situation: 'This is not on!'

Not Right
Mad, eccentric, mentally wrong: 'If he's right you can cattle me.' *See* CATTLE TRUCK.

Note
An old term for £1, even if pound notes have turned into pound coins. A £15 item is still said to cost fifteen notes.

Noughties
A term given to the years 2000–2009.

Novices Chase	*Face*	A racegoer's term for someone who isn't exactly pretty: 'Nice body, shame about the novices.'
Now and/or Never	*Clever*	An example from the 19th century which may have been used ironically at a display of stupidity: 'Oh, that was now and never!' Which goes to show that you don't have to be clever to be a dunce.
Nuclear Sub	*Pub*	A modern term for a modern pub, both used by modern youth.
Nudger		The penis, a mid 20th-century piece, although a 17th-century term for a man to have sex is 'nudge'.
Nudnik		A Yiddish term for a dull, boring person. Someone you don't want to sit next to on a long-haul flight, the sort who knows how many different sized staples there are.
Nuke		a) To thoroughly beat, to trounce, either in an act of violence or figuratively in a sporting victory. b) To cook or warm-up food in a microwave oven, a godsend for the single man is the 'ready to nuke' meal. 'Nuke' is the reduced form of nuclear, as if you needed telling.
Nuker		An 1980s term for a microwave oven.
Number Ones		A juvenile reference to urination, used by adults in polite circles.
Number Twos		Defecation, a childish reference sometimes known simply as 'numbers'.
Numb-Nut		A fool, another form of 'thick-head' (qv).
Numbskull		A fool, a 'deadhead'. Someone deemed to be a couple of inches short of a yard.
Numpty		A fool, or more to the point 'a right fucking idiot', the one seen at 'cunt' (c).
Nun's Fanny/ Minge		A symbol of dryness: 'You won't roll a fag with that tobacco, it's as dry as a nun's fanny.' Also, what the thirsty may claim to have a mouth like.
Nun's Habit	*Rabbit*	A piece of secondary RS, 'rabbit' (see RABBIT & PORK) has become so common that it has acquired it's own term, just to make things interesting.
Nuppence		No money. To have 'nuppence' in your pocket is to be skint, to have no pence.
Nuremberg Trials	*Piles*	Bottom nasties known as 'Nurembergs'. Where top Nazis known as war criminals faced their accusers in 1945–46.
Nursery Rhyme	*Crime*	An example from the 1990s which is a reflection of the fact that child crime is on the increase.
Nursery Rhymes	*Times*	Refers to the top people's newspaper, which may cause 'Angry of Tunbridge Wells' to dash off a letter to the editor.

Nut		a) A well-known all-purpose term for the head. To 'use your nut' can either be to think or to butt someone, and to be 'out of your nut' is to be drunk or stoned. b) A mad person, either certifiably insane or one who does crazy things. Like the mad investor who dabbled in shocks and stares. c) The glans penis, an old rival to 'acorn' (qv). d) To butt someone, to 'sling the nut in'.
Nut Buster		*See* BOLLOCK BUSTER.
Nut Crusher		A domineering woman, one who has an emasculating effect on a man.
Nut House		A psychiatric hospital, where 'nut doctors' and 'nut nurses' go about their business.
Nutcase		A well-used term in regard to a mad person, anyone 'a bit mental'.
Nutcrackers	*Knackers*	Seems to be an extension of 'nuts' where the testicles are concerned, but it's a term to bring tears to the eyes of the hardest of men.
Nutmeg(s)	*Legs*	A piece of footballer's jargon, whereby to play the ball through an opponent's legs is to 'nutmeg' him.
Nutney		A juvenile term for defecation and its end product.
Nut-Nut		Anyone who is mentally below par, often an unkind nickname for such a person, probably without their knowledge of it.
Nut-Rock		a) A bald person, one whose head resembles a boulder. b) A crazy, mad person, often the name by which such a person is known.
Nuts		a) A very well-known term for the testicles, where a kick is known as a 'nutcruncher' or a 'nutser'. A freezing swimming pool was once described as being 'nut-shrivelling cold'. b) Breasts, a term that is often cracked by the chauvinist. c) Insane, crazy, eccentric. A piece so well-known that it hardly qualifies as slang anymore. 'Nuts about' – in love with.
Nuts, the		The best, a variation of 'the bollocks' (qv).
Nut-sack		The scrotum, a different rendering of 'ball bag' (qv). Also known as a 'Sack of Nuts'.
Nutshell		A crash helmet, something to protect the 'filbert' (qv).
Nutter		A crazy, often violently mad person. Also a person with a dangerous occupation or hobby, like a jump jockey, an ice-speedway rider or someone who indulges in mafioso baiting.

Nutty Crazy, commonly heard as 'nutty as a fruit cake'.

Nyap/Niap A pain, a piece of backslang that's used mainly in connection with a nuisance, whereby a 'pain in the arse' becomes a 'nyap in the esra'.

Nympho A promiscuous woman, one with an insatiable appetite for sex. 'Nymph' – a 17th-century term for a prostitute.

O		A coy euphemism for oral sex.
Oak		A joke without the j. It has been given as a piece of one word RS, but is probably a deliberate mis-pronunciation, said for an 'oak'.
Oak & Ash	*Cash*	A term that emanates from the theatre, where a couple of trees take to the boards as a couple of quid.
Oars & Rowlocks	*Bollocks*	Used anatomically but mainly when the smell of 'bullshit' is in the air: 'What a load of oars and rowlocks you do talk.'
Oats		Sexual gratification, said as 'getting one's oats'.
Oats & Barley	*Charlie*	A 19th-century term that in its time has referred to all things 'Charlie-ish'. It's one of the few Christian names to be endowed with a piece of RS, and a night-watchman has long been called a 'Charley'. It's been an example of slang for slang on a couple of occasions, as a fool (*see* CHARLIE HUNT) and a ponce (*see* CHARLIE RONCE). Most recently 'Oats' has been a reference to cocaine.
Oats & Chaff	*Path*	An archaic reference to a footpath that's probably been paved over.
Obadiah	*Fire*	Known as an 'Obey', this refers to a domestic fire.
Obbo		A police term for keeping someone under observation. In the military it's known as 'obs'.

Occabot		Tobacco, the roll-up ingredient in backslang.
Ocean Liner	*Shiner (Black Eye)*	A fairly old piece that appears to have sunk without trace.
Ocean Pearl	*Girl*	A 19th-century term for a girlfriend that doesn't seem to have made it to the 21st.
Ocean Wave	*Shave*	One of several terms for the destubble-ising of the 'boat' (qv).
Odd		A 19th-century term for a homosexual male, an alternative word for 'queer'.
Oddball/Oddbod		A weird, strange or eccentric person, one who follows his own path. A loner.
Odd-Lot		A police car. 'Odd' being a short version of squad and 'lot' (qv).
Odds & Sods		Bits and pieces, miscellaneous odds and ends, a piece that found fame in the 1970s as the name of an album by British rock band, The Who.
Odds Against		Not likely to happen, something you shouldn't bank on, practically an impossibility. Like picking your nose with gloves on. 'She might turn up but it's big odds against.'
Odds On		The opposite of 'odds against' (qv), a certainty: 'I've never won a ha'penny on the pools but if I stop doing it, it's odds on my numbers'll come up.'
Oedipus Rex	*Sex*	Doesn't sound particularly wholesome since it's based on an ancient Greek who killed his father and married his mother.
Off One's Bonce/Block/ Chump/Nut/ Top		Among the many terms that apply to madness, all relate to 'off one's head'.
Off One's Rocker/Trolley		Terms of insanity that, unlike 'off one's bonce', etc., do not bring the head into play.
Offer Out		To challenge to a fight, to figuratively call for someone to 'step outside'.
Office		a) To warn, to tip off when danger threatens. An underworld term from the 19th century whereby the warned is 'given the office'. b) An age-old euphemism for a lavatory, originally an ironic term for backyard restroom.
Office Wallah		A man who works in an office, a disdainful reference used by manual workers, who consider that 'desk jockeys' and 'pen-pushers' have an easy time of it.
Office Worker	*Shirker*	An example used by manual workers and labourers, who find the phrase 'hard day at the office' amusing and scornfully remark: 'Call that

		bloody work?' Therefore anyone seen to be not pulling his weight is labelled an 'office worker'.
Oggins		*See* HOGGINS.
Oh My Dear	*Beer*	A pint of 'oh' is an old bar order which is as rare now as a mild and bitter.
Oh My Gawd	*Bald*	A long-lost aquaintance whose hair loss is apparent may be greeted with: 'Oh my Gawd, he's gone oh my Gawd.' Extreme baldness is sometimes stressed as 'Oh my good Gawd'.
Oi Jimmy Knacker	*Tobacco*	Pipe or rolling tobacco was commonly known as 'oi Jimmy' or just 'oi'. *See* HI JIMMY KNACKER.
Oik		A working-class person with no social graces, a term used condescendingly by his 'superiors'.
Oil		Alcohol. 'On the oil' – on the booze.
Oil Lamp	*Tramp*	Doesn't necessarily apply to 'hobo scruffians', any ragged-arsed, couldn't-care-less-how-they-look scruffbucket can be labelled an 'oil lamp'.
Oil Leak	*Sikh*	A 1990s term for he who wears a 'napper wrapper' (qv).
Oil Slick	*Spick (Spaniard)*	Formed in the early days of the package holiday to the Costas, when young Spanish males typically used masses of hair cream, and with copious amounts of Latin smarm, greased their way into the beds of female tourists.
Oil Tanker	*Wanker*	An abusive term directed at the obnoxious and the useless, like the pilot of one of these oversized vessels who, through rank bad navigation, hits something or runs aground causing collosal damage to the environment.
Oiled		Drunk. 'Well oiled' – falling over backwards drunk.
Oily Rag	*Fag*	An old example that is still smouldering as an 'oily'.
Oink		To eat greedily, or like a pig: 'Who's oinked all the biscuits?'
Oinker		a) A police officer, an extension of 'pig' (qv). b) A greedy person, a pig. Someone whose snout doesn't leave the trough till it's empty.
Okey Doke	*a) Coke*	In the 1980s this innocently applied to Coca Cola, but in the next decade, when cocaine became easily available, the term descended into the world of drugs as 'okey'.
	b) Poke	Condensed to 'okey', this refers to a wallet or more specifically to what it contains. A low-life term of the pickpocket.
Old and Bitter		Originally related to the mother-in-law, but later to any terminally miserable pensioner. Based on an out-of-date mix of beers.

Old Bag	*Hag*	In it's original form this applied to an old or infected prostitute. It has since become a supremely common term for any disagreeable woman.
Old Bill		a) A well-used term for the police, said to be based on the name of a cartoon character used by the police in a recruitment drive in 1917.
		b) A common term for the penis. An overheard reminiscence: 'There used to be an old perv in Poplar known as Joe the Wanker, he'd walk about with his hand in his pocket jerking his 'old Bill' in front of kids.' Funny thing is, people laughed at him. Today they'd stone him.
Old Boots		What tough meat is said to be like.
Old Buck		Backchat, cheek or lairy talk: 'Any more of your old buck and you'll get a slap.'
Old Chap/Fellow		The penis, as in: 'So I said to this bloke with a watch on his old chap. Got the time cock?'
Old Coot/Git/ Goat		Well-known examples for a miserable, cantankerous old man.
Old Fogey	*Bogey*	Refers to nasal residue or 'nose shit' and is based on an old term for an invalid soldier. Lusting after a 'page three' girl, a *Sun* reader was heard to remark: 'I'd eat her ol' fogeys I would.'
Old Harry		What stale or tough food is said to be as hard as.
Old Heave Ho		What the unwanted are given. Anyone dismissed from their job, dropped from a team, thrown out of a building or dumped by a lover are given the 'old heave ho'. From the nautical image of being thrown overboard.
Old Iron & Brass	a) *Grass*	Applies to the green green stuff of Tom Jones' home. Overly officious parkies delight in keeping people off the 'old iron'.
	b) *Pass*	An old military term for what's required to leave barracks.
Old Jamaica Rum	*Sun*	Always decreased to the first two elements, this old naval term has probably sunk below the horizon.
Old King Cole	*Dole*	The nursery rhyme monarch has long been associated with unemployment benefit, but the only merry old souls in the dole queue are the ones employed in the black economy.
Old Kit Bag	*Fag*	Based on a popular World War One song, when catching a smoking-related disease was deemed preferable to stopping an enemy-related bullet.
Old Money		Non-metric measures. Anything sold or quoted in metres, litres, euros and centigrade is symbolically queried as 'What's that in old money?'

Old Nag	*Fag*	A long since stubbed-out piece that was first ignited by World War One Tommies who presumably smoked till they were hoarse.
Old Oak	*Smoke*	Refers to London, long known as the Smoke.
Old Rag	*Flag*	A piece that was flying long before it became 'offensive' to run the Union Jack and the Cross of St George up the 'old rag-pole'.
Old Sweat		A veteran in any field, but originally an old soldier. One who has put years of sweat into his trade.
Old Whip	*Ship*	An early seaman's term for his own ship, that is, the one he is currently serving on.
Oliver Cromwell	*Tumble (Understand)*	Comes from a time when cockney dialect would have produced a rhyme. Just as Bromley and Romford were pronounced Brumley and Rumford, so Cromwell would have been Crumwell or Crummell, a suitable match for 'tumble'. 'Now do you, Oliver?' Like the man (1599–1658), the term is long dead.
Oliver Reed	a) *Speed*	A young drug user's term from the 1980s relating to amphetamines. Known as 'Olly' and based on a well-known British actor and boozer (1938–99), this originally applied to another drug. *See* (b).
	b) *Weed*	Tobacco. Known as the 'dreaded Ollie' it applies to all forms of 'smoke' including the illicit kind.
Oliver Twist	a) *Fist*	An ancient example that is always shortened to the Christian name of Dickens' orphan: 'You'll feel my Oliver if you ain't careful.'
	b) *Pissed*	Descriptive of folk who have presented their glasses and asked for more.
	c) *Wrist*	Rarely used in any other sense than masturbation, whereby 'one off the wrist' becomes 'one off the Oliver'.
Ollie Beak	*Sikh*	Just what the connection is between someone of this religion and a television glove puppet of the 1960s, I don't know. But someone had a hand in it. Ollie was a cheeky owl with a Scouse accent, a regular on children's programmes.
Ollocks		A lazily said version of 'bollocks'.
Ology		A science degree. A humorous piece based on a TV ad for BT in which a boy tells his Jewish grandmother that he has failed all his exams except sociology. To which she replies that having an 'ology' makes him a scientist.
Omar Sharif	*Grief*	This is grief in its slang form of trouble or problems: 'I hope I'm not gonna get any Omar over this.' Based on an Egyptian-born film star and renowned bridge player.

Omee/Omi		A man. From the Italian *uomo*, this piece of Polari is well employed in the repertoire of camp comedians.
Omee Polone/ Polony		A male homosexual, a combination of both sexes of Polari. *See both.*
On		Menstruation: 'You can't. I'm on.' – A monthly knock-back.
On & Off	*Cough*	Obviously not based on the consumptive pest who always seems to sit behind me in the cinema and goes on and ON, coughing his offal up.
On a Pension		An underworld term that applies to a bent police officer, one who takes a regular 'bung'.
On a Promise		Due to receive something to your benefit, a bribe, a 'bung', a tip-off, etc. In this sense it's mainly an underworld term, but in the sense of an impending sexual union or if a racing tip is in the pipeline, it's anybody's.
On a Solomons		On to a good money-making scheme or racket, on the road to riches via Solomon's Mine.
On Blob		Undergoing menstruation, a term used by men following a monthly knock-back: 'I couldn't, she's on blob.'
On Doog		No Good, a backslang reject.
On One		Out thieving, on a job.
On One's Ace		On one's own, the ace card being a one-spot.
On Spec		At a risk, to buy something 'on spec' is to take a chance on it by not getting it checked out. Short for 'on speculation'.
On the Blink		Faulty, not working properly. A piece from the early days of electricity.
On the Cards		What anything that's likely to happen is said to be.
On the Ear'ole		A well-known piece that relates to borrowing or scrounging. Beggars and cadgers are said to be this.
On the Elbow		To scrounge or cadge, probably from the nudge in the ribs with an elbow and the whispered: 'Lend us a . . .'
On the Floor	*Poor*	A very common piece that has transcended the ranks of RS because of it's total suitability. To be on the floor is as low as you can get.
On the Fly		In a rush, having no time: 'Tell me later, I'm on the fly at the moment.'
On the Game		Working as a prostitute, a common term for the oldest profession.
On the Hurry-Up		On the quick, at full speed. How people on 'job and finish' (qv) work.
On the Job		An old and well-known euphemism for having sexual intercourse.

On the Knock

a) The underworld occupation of touring homes in order to persuade or intimidate people into selling their valuables at knock-down prices.

b) How goods bought on credit or on instalments are said to have been acquired. Probably due to the weekly knock on the door from the tallyman.

On the Knocker

a) An old expression for working as a door-to-door salesman.

b) To borrow or cadge, from the image of knocking on a neighbour's door when you fancy an omelette but need some eggs.

On the Mud

An almost empty beer glass, one in need of replenishment: 'Whose round is it? I'm on the mud here.'

On the Nest

Of a man, to be engaged in sexual intercourse: 'Sorry I'm late, I've been on the nest all night.'

On the Other Bus

Said to be the preferred transport of a homosexual.

On the Other Side of the Road

Where a homosexual is said to drive.

On the Thumb

Hitch-hiking, thumbing a lift: 'I missed the last train so I had to have it on the thumb'.

On the Turkey

Underworld slang for being on the run or 'on the trot'. From the 1963 hit record 'Let's Turkey Trot' by American singer Little Eva.

On the Wagon

Teetotal, no longer drinking alcohol. In full 'on the water-wagon'.

On the Way Out

Dying, often said mockingly to people who don't look well: 'You look like you're on the way out.'

On the Wonk

Crooked. Anything 'wonky' (qv) can be said to be 'on the wonk'.

On Tick

On duty, present. From the old custom of ticking the school register to signify a pupil was in.

On Your Bike!

An expression of rejection or refusal akin to 'get lost', 'go scratch', 'take a hike', etc.

On Your Cycle!

Get lost! Lose yourself! Go somewhere else!

Once a Week   *a) Beak (Magistrate)*

An example that was probably coined by an habitual ne'er-do-well.

b) Cheek

An allusion to non-edible sauce as poured on by a liberty-taker in the form of a 'oncer'.

Once Every Pancake Day

Something that rarely happens: 'You visit me once every Pancake Day.' – The exaggeration of an elderly parent. The same as 'once in a blue moon'.

Oncer

£1, originally a pound note but a 'nicker bit' is a 'oncer' these days.

One & Eight   *Plate*

Takes in all kinds of plate including crockery, a

forger's plate and what's passed around in church. Sometimes, but rarely, used as twice-removed slang for feet: 'My one and eights are killing me.' *See* PLATES OF MEAT.

One & Half   *Scarf*   Either a headscarf or a choker can be a 'one-an-arf'.

One & T'other   *a) Brother*   A bit confusing really because this is also used for . . .

    b) Mother   In either case it is always employed in full and in the third person, usually as 'one another'.

One and Eleven- pence Three Farden   A phrase from the days of our old money which was used comically instead of 'I beg your pardon'. 'Farden' was the common pronunciation of a farthing. (Ask your grandad!)

One Eyed Trouser Snake   The commonest of a number of one-eyed beings representing the penis. Others include 'Admiral', 'Guardsman', 'Monster', 'Python', 'Worm', etc.

One for His Nob   *Bob*   A once common reference to a shilling (5p). The term represents something extra and so still survives in the guise of a tip. 'Give the driver one for his nob.'

One for the Tarmac   A last drink, an extension of 'one for the road'.

One Handed Clock   A symbol of uselessness: 'You're as much use as a . . .'

One in the Departure Lounge   Impending defecation, what people have when they're 'squeezing their cheeks together'. Also 'One in the Waiting Room.'

One Off the Wrist   An act of masturbation, an old term, one that has stood the test of time and motion.

One Up the Wheel   Urination, an old lorry driver's term based on where he relieved himself.

One Way Pockets   Said to be the pockets of a skinflint, money only goes one way. In!

One(s) & Two(s)   *Shoe(s)*   One gets one's 'ones' from one's personal 'ones' maker. As Princess Anne might say if she were the Pearly Princess Royal.

One-Er   A racecourse term for £100, pronounced 'wunner'.

Oneymans   Money (said as unnymans). A variation of the pig-latin 'oneymay'. 'Nanty oneymans' – broke.

Onion   a) One of many terms from the fruit and veg stall that make a connection with the head. 'Off one's onion' – mad.

b) A fool, an idiot, an old rival to 'wally' (qv). Same jar, different pickle.

Ons   In football, an old word for a throw-in: 'Our ons ref!'

Oof/Ooftish   Money. 'Ooftish' is the Yiddish version of the

German *auf Tische* – on the table. The term then, originally applied to money used for gambling, so 'oof' was probably a 19th-century kitty. 'Oofy' – well-off, 'oofless' – skint.

Oofter

A homosexual, a 'poofter' (qv) with the P taken out of him.

Ooh La La *Bra*

A coy piece from a less permissive era, probably from the stage.

Oojamaflip

A dopey word used for something, the name of which has escaped your memory box.

Oono

The number one based on the Spanish 'Uno'. The polari version is Oona (*See* Una).

Open a Mouth

To start an argument: 'I may as well have another pint, she'll open a mouth now whatever time I get in.'

Open the Door *Four*

An example from an old bingo game.

Oppo

A good friend, a partner. Originally a military shortening of one's opposite number.

Opportunity Knocks *Fox*

A piece that's been in existence since the wily one became the urban dweller it now is. Always an 'opportunity' – why use one syllable when you can use five? Well that's slang. Probably based on the name of a TV talent show.

Orange

A term penned by an amateur poet for a word that a rhyme can't be found for, since nothing in the English language rhymes with 'orange': 'I come up with a good line and find it ends with an orange.'

Orange Pip *Nip*

A Japanese person is known as an 'orange', which colour-wise would appear to be inapt.

Orange Squash *Dosh (Money)*

An example from the 1990s that is mainly used by those with empty pockets: 'I can't get out tonight, I ain't got the orange.'

Orchestra Stalls *Balls (Testicles)*

Whereby the scrotal area is commonly known as the 'orchestras'.

Organ

A well-known term for the penis. 'Play an organ solo' – to masturbate.

Organ Grinder *Minder*

A reference to a bodyguard that brings tears to the eyes.

Orinoko *a) Cocoa*

The popular bedtime drink has long been known as a cup of 'ori'.

b) Poker

An old piece for the fireside implement that was always cocknified to 'orinoker'.

Ornaments

A man's genitalia. If a woman offers to arrange, dust, or in any way interfere with your ornaments – let her.

Orphan Annie   *Fanny (Vagina)*   Based on a cartoon character whose adventures were staged on Broadway and filmed in Hollywood, this has been heard in a cautionary warning against anything that should be given a wide berth. Roadworks on the M25 for example or a pub where the guv'nor drinks lager should be avoided like an infected 'orphan'.

Oscar Asche   *Cash*   Always curtailed to 'Oscar', this is a time-honoured piece formed on the name of a long-forgotten actor (1871–1936).

Oscar Wilde   *Mild (Ale)*   Not often heard now that this beer is all but obsolete in London. Based on the Irish writer and outstanding wit (1854–1900) who courted controversy by courting Lord Alfred Douglas.

Oswald   A drug dealer's term for an ounce, an extension of oz, the symbol of that weight.

Otcho   The number eight based on the Spanish *ocho* – eight.

Other End   The West End of London as described by East Enders. When they've got a few bob they go 'up the other end' or, if they live in Albert Square, 'up West'.

Other Way   Bent, either of goods or people. Things that have 'fallen off the back of a lorry' or sold on the black market are 'the other way'. Also a well-known term for a homosexual.

Otis Redding   *Wedding*   An example from the 1960s, based on an American soul singer (1941–67), usually in regard to someone else's nuptials: 'I won't be able to play cards this week, I've got an Otis to go to.'

Otter   The number eight, a piece of Polari based on the Italian word *otto* – eight.

Ouch-House   A rough pub or club, one where fights and, therefore, cries of pain are common. A pun on out-house, another shit-hole.

Ounce of Baccy   *Paki*   With the prevalence of the Asian tobacconist this term just had to happen. Often reduced to an 'ouncer'.

Out   Living openly as a homosexual after coming 'out of the closet'. Also to expose somebody as a homosexual against their will: 'Pay the price or get outed' – a blackmailer's demand.

Out of It   Drunk or intoxicated, out of one's head due to drink or drugs.

Out of One's Bonce/Box/ Mind/Nut/ Skull   All of these 'out of one's head' related terms apply both to being mad and to being high on drink or drugs. On a non-cephalic note 'Out of One's Tree' strikes the same chord.

Out of One's Pram		Experiencing a loss of temper or agitation: 'Alright, don't get out of your pram' – calm down.
Out of Order		Unacceptable, as objectionable behaviour or an intolerable situation may be. Anything way beyond the pale is 'bang out of order'.
Out of the Game		So drunk as to be unable to swallow another drop or to fall asleep through drunkenness: 'I should have paced myself, I was out of the game by ten o'clock.'
Outers		No longer wanted, barred: 'Tone down the language pal or you're outers,' – a publican to a drunk.
Outside Right/ Right Winger		The seven in a pack of cards. Footballers in this position wear the number seven shirt.
Ovary Tickler		The penis, a pun on 'ivory tickler' (qv) – a pianist, which is a common pun for a penis.
Over the Stile	*Trial*	An ancient example that's employed as being 'sent' or having to 'stand over the stile'.
Overall		A working man. The direct opposite of a 'suit' (qv).
Overcoat		A condom. An early 1920s example that came back into fashion in the wake of AIDS.
Overcoat Maker	*Undertaker*	An obvious allusion to a 'wooden overcoat' – a coffin.
Over-Ripe Fruit		An old homosexual male, one considered to be past his best. *See* FRUIT.
Owen Nares	*Chair(s)*	A 1930s example that originated in the theatre and is based on an actor (1888–1943) from the early days of cinema. Although his name was Nares, one chair was an 'Owen'.
Own Goal		a) A piece of unsympathetic police jargon for a suicide.
		b) A mistake that affects no-one but yourself: 'I scored an own goal today. I put diesel in the car instead of unleaded.'
Owt		The number two in backslang. 'Owt kews' – two weeks.
Oxford Bag(s)	*Fag(s)*	You're getting old if you can remember when twenty 'Oxfords' cost an 'Oxford' (*see* OXFORD SCHOLAR). Based on wide baggy trousers, once the height of fashion.
Oxford Scholar	*a) Collar*	An early 20th-century term, a time when collars were detachable. 'Oxfords' have come in all shapes and sizes since.
	b) Dollar	A dollar was 5 shillings in sterling and is still used by some die-hards for 25p. The term therefore still has a small currency. Always shortened to an 'Oxford' or an 'Ox'.

Oxo Cube	*Tube*	The London underground system has long been known as the 'Oxo'.
Oyster		a) A tight-lipped person, one whose mouth, like an oyster, remains closed.
		b) A great, glutinous glob of phlegm seen lying on the pavement. A piece that's been exuding germs and disease since the 19th century.
Oyzens		Trousers. Cockneys have been wrapping their legs in their 'oyzens' for generations.

P

PFQ	Extremely rapid. Pretty Fucking Quick in fact. The Anglo Saxon version of PDQ.
PO	A polite way to tell someone where to get off: 'Tell him to PO' – tell him to piss off.
Pack	A cap, backslang headwear. Doesn't apply to a baseball 'pack', even if it is worn backwards.
Packet	a) The male genitals, a gay term that's usually a reference to the bulge in a man's trousers. b) Trouble, wrongdoers expect to 'cop a packet' if they are caught or found out. In the army, if a soldier 'cops a packet' he receives a wound, often a fatal one. c) Excrement, especially when a baby has 'done a packet' in it's 'shitsack' – nappy.
Paddington Bear *Pear*	A 1970s rival to 'Teddy Bear' as a market trader's cry. Based on the Peruvian bear created by writer Michael Bond. Paddington became a TV 'star' in 1976.
Paddlers	a) The feet, a term from the time when they were the only part of an Englishman's anatomy that saw the sea. b) Children's footwear for the beach, protection from sharp stones and crabs.

Paddy		a) An Irish person of worldwide renown.
		b) An old underworld term for a padlock.
Paddy & Mick	a) Pick (Axe)	As wielded by those archetypal partners in grime on a building site.
	b) Thick (Obtuse)	Based on the two typical Irishmen who, for years, have kept a host of comedians in business. Apt in a non-PC way.
Paddy O'Rourke	Talk	Not sure who this Irishman is, maybe typically the one whose lip-prints are all over the Blarney Stone. One who could talk a nun out of her knickers.
Paddy Rammer	Hammer	An old piece that has probably whacked in its last nail.
Paddy Wagon		A police van, originally an American term from the late 19th century, which is probably a reflection of the number of Irish policemen patrolling the beat there at the time. Now common here.
Padlock	Cock (Penis)	A 1970s term that was trapped in the phrase: 'She could pick my padlock anytime.'
Pain		Anything or anybody troublesome or problematical, a reduction of a 'pain' in various parts of the anatomy, such as: 'arm', 'arse', 'bum', 'butt', 'crutch', 'neck' and for men only, 'balls', 'bollocks' and 'nuts'.
Pain in One's Own Arse/ Neck		One's own worst enemy. Said of someone who is often the cause of his own misery.
Pain in the Neck	Cheque	An example that may have been coined by the recipient of a bouncer.
Painful Experience		A pest, often a drunken one: 'He's a right painful experience when he's had a few.'
Painted Peeper		A 19th-century black eye, common back then when differences were settled 'outside on the cobbles'. Another term for a shiner is a 'peeper in mourning'.
Painters		See HAVE THE DECORATORS/PAINTERS IN.
Pair of Nickers		A common and fairly obvious term for £2. See NICKER.
Paki		a) A nationwide term for a Pakistani and, loosely, any immigrant from the Indian subcontinent.
		b) Originally a Scottish term for a shop run by Asians: 'I'm nipping to the Paki for some fags.'
Paki Black		Dark-coloured hashish from the Indian subcontinent.
Palatic		Drunk, 'pissed as a dozen newts'. A term that's seemingly used by those too far gone to be able to say paralytic.
Paleface		A white person, a derogatory term used by black people that was taken from the red Indians of early Hollywood westerns.

Pall Mall	*Gal*	A 19th-century term that's no longer heard as cockney dialect has changed. Gals are now gels.
Palm Oil		Money used for a bribe, to 'grease someone's palm'.
Pampass Grass	*Arse*	A piece seen in a newspaper article after the England football team's 1986 World Cup defeat by Argentina, when Diego Maradona punched the ball into the English net, an action he later described as the 'Hand of God'. It was suggested that he should take his holy hand and thrust it up his 'pampass grass'.
Pancake		A flat-chested girl, a common piece that needs no explanation.
Pangy/Pangy Bar		Old Romany terms for £5, once common at racecourses.
Panoramas	*Pyjamas*	A piece that's mainly employed when getting children ready for bed. Based on the long-running TV current affairs programme.
Pansy		A well-known old term for an homosexual male.
Pansy Corps		Homosexual men, a pun on the German armoured division, the Panzer Corps.
Pantomime Cow	*Row*	A light-hearted variation of 'bull and cow' (qv), which refers to the type of argument where nothing gets thrown but insults and threats, much to the amusement of onlookers.
Pants		a) The 2001 vogue word of defiance which is an update of the older 'knickers'. The slogan for a recent charity drive was 'Say Pants to Poverty'. b) Nonsense, rubbish or generally bad – the most dire.
Pants & Vest	*Best*	An old beer drinker's reference to best bitter that's rarely called for these days.
Papa Oscar		Piss Off. From the initials used in the phonetic alphabet.
Paper Bag	*Nag*	To verbally larrup someone. Many a last pint has been refused because 'I couldn't stand her papering me all night.'
Paper Bag Job		An ugly person, one considered too gruesome to have sex with unless they had a paper bag over their head.
Paper Doll	*Moll*	A term from the 1960s that refers to a prostitute or a girl who is used to decorate the arm of a villain.
Paper Fireguard		A symbol of uselessness, what a 'doon' (qv) is said to be as much use as.
Paper Hat	*Pratt (Fool)*	A typical 'paper hat' is someone who thinks a judo expert is an Israeli financial consultant.

Paper Johnny		A symbol of uselessness, what a 'dickhead' is said to be as much use as. *See* JOHNNY/ JOHNNY BAG.
Para/Parro		Shortened versions of paranoid: 'He's well para since someone accused him of being a nonce.'
Paraffin	*Gin*	A term used humorously to confuse new bar staff.
Paraffin Lamp	*Tramp*	Always reduced to the first element, often as an insult to those with truggy inclinations, i.e., 'soap dodgers' and 'dirtywacks'. *See both.*
Paralytic/ Paraletic/Para		Excessively inebriated, 'as drunk as a houseful of lords'. Also 'paralysed', the paralysis of booze.
Paranada		A freebie, usually a drink or a meal. From the Spanish *por nada* – for nothing.
Parcel Bouncer		A postman. Apparently packages marked 'Fragile' bounce the highest.
Park Spoiler		A 1990s term for a traveller, tinker or gypsy. From their habit of turning parks and other green spaces into rubbish tips.
Parker-Bowles	*Rolls (Royce)*	As Lady Penelope might have said had International Rescue operated out of the Isle of Dogs instead of a Pacific one: 'Park the Parker, Parker.' An alternative to 'Camilla Parker-Bowles' (qv).
Parky		Cold, chilly. Worrying conditions for brass monkeys (qv).
Parlamaree	*Gee*	An underworld term for the member of a team of street traders who 'gees-up' the crowd by rushing to buy whatever's on offer.
Parleyvoo		The French language: 'Speak the ol' parleyvoo do you?' from the French *parlez vous*. 'Do you speak . . . ?'
Parlyaree/Polari		A mode of slang based on the Italian language which originated in the theatre and is now well established in the gay lexicon. From the Italian *parlare* – to talk. *See* BENGHAZI.
Parney/Pawnee		Water. From the Hindi word *pani* and brought home by soldiers of Queen Victoria. It applies to any body of water, a pond, lake, etc., but mainly to rain. 'It looks like parney again.'
Partick Thistle	*Whistle*	The Scottish football team comes in for what the referee blows and what the crowd do to get him to blow it at the end of ninety minutes when their team is leading by the odd goal.
Passion Killers		Unsexy women's underwear, bloomers, drawers or anything with a reinforced gusset.
Passion Wagon		A vehicle used for the enticement and seduction of women. A piece that came into existence with soldiers of World War Two.

Paste		To beat, thrash or administer a thorough bashing or 'pasting'.
Pasteboards		A 19th-century term for playing cards that's still in the shuffle.
Pat & Mick	*Prick (Penis)*	A 19th-century term that's hardly ever mouthed these days.
Pat & Mike	*Bike*	Those two Irish lads in tandem again in a term from the 19th century.
Pat Cash	*Slash (Urination)*	A 1990s term based on an Australian tennis player, the 1987 Wimbledon champion.
Pat Malone	*Alone*	Originally the Australian alternative to the better known 'Jack Jones', but in the same way. If you are 'on your Pat', you only have yourself for company.
Pat Mann not Batman, the name's		A reply to someone who wants you to do something risky or daring: 'You want me to do what? Sorry, the name's Pat Mann not Batman.'
Patch		A bald spot on a man's head. A man with such a pate should wear a hat when the weather is 'patch blistering hot'.
Patrick Swayze	*Crazy*	A piece from the 1990s that sees the mad, eccentric or the ultra-violent become 'Patrick'. Based on an American film star of the period.
Patsy		A victim of a deception, a fall guy. An American version of a 'mug' (qv).
Patsy Cline	*Line*	Although based on an American country-and-western singer, this has nothing to do with dancing. The line in question is of white powder, Cocaine. Patsy died in an air crash in 1963 aged 30.
Patty Hearst	*First*	Student slang for a first-class honours degree based on an American heiress and bankrobber. Kidnapped in 1974, she later joined her captors in the urban guerrilla game.
Paul Anka	*Wanker*	A 1960s term based on a Canadian singer/song-writer, which is generally used when discussing an obnoxious or useless person: 'He's a Paul Anka, treats his old woman like a punchbag.'
Paul McKenna	*Tenner*	£10, courtesy of a well-known TV hypnotist.
Paul Weller	*Stella (Artois)*	A 1990s term for a popular lager, based on a British singer/songwriter, once a member of the band, The Jam.
Pavarotti		A 1990s term for a 'tenner' (£10) based on the world's most famous tenor, Luciano Pavarotti.
Pavement Pizza		A gutful of vomit puked up on a pavement, the appearance of a mass of ingredients.
Paw		A hand, a 300-year-old example that's still

commonly heard in the warning: 'Keep your paws off.' To 'paw' – to handle somebody roughly, especially in a sexual context where it's to grope.

Paw Cases   Gloves, a 19th-century term for mitt warmers.

Paydirt   To 'hit paydirt' is to meet with success, to make a profit. Originally an American term that is commonly heard in old films about gold prospectors.

Pazzer   A parent, a term used by 1990s teenagers.

Peabrain   A mentally challenged dolt, an ignoramus seemingly with a brain the size of a small green vegetable, who has to take special care when blowing his nose, in case he ejects the grey matter.

Peace & Quiet   *Diet*   Some endure the battle of the bulge and fight the flab in order to shed some suet just to get some peace and quiet from a loved one.

Peanut Butter   *Nutter*   A modern term which sees a loon labelled as a 'peanut'.

Pearl Harbour   Cold weather, when there's a nasty Nip (qv, a) in the air.

Pearlies/Pearly Whites   A couple of 19th-century terms for teeth that may have been used ironically since most choppers at the time would have been various shades of off-white.

Pearly Gate   *Plate*   A dinner plate, as represented by Heaven's door.

Pearly King   *Ring (Anus)*   'Ring' or 'ringpiece' are old terms for this part of the anatomy, hence the choice expression: 'Poke it up your pearly!' 'Pearly burner' – a hot curry.

Pearshaped   Messed up. When a situation is no longer ordered or organised, it's said to have 'all gone pearshaped'. When a perfect circle becomes misshapen.

Peas in the Pot   *Hot*   This is hot in all it's forms. The weather may be 'too bloody peas', it may describe a person's skill or expertise and it is also an old reference to an alluring or lustful woman. To 'have the peas' for someone is to 'have the hots' for them, even if it doesn't sound very sexy.

Pease Pudding Hot   *Snot (Nasal Mucus)*   Based on a nursery rhyme, this is always reduced to the first two elements: 'I need a clean hanky, this one's full of pease pudding.'

Pea-Shooter   *Hooter (Nose)*   Not to be confused with 'pee-shooter', which is a different extremity altogether. The term is used by some as a reference to a car horn.

Pebble Mill   *Pill*   Based on a long-running TV programme, this refers to pills that are popped rather than taken as directed. A case of 'pebbles' getting you stoned.

Pebbles   The testicles. It must be assumed that Fred and

Wilma Flintstone weren't aware of this when they gave their daughter this name.

Peck — A centuries-old term for food. 'Peck and tipple' – food and drink. 'Peckish' – hungry.

Peck & Perch — Board and lodging or bed and breakfast. *See* PECK and PERCH.

Pecker — a) The nose, an extension of 'beak' (qv). This is the British definition, the American version takes a more southerly route. *See* (b).
b) The penis, the American rendition that gives a whole new meaning to the phrase 'keep your pecker up'.

Peckham Rye — *Tie* — A well-known piece that's always condensed to a 'Peckham' in reference to what supposedly creates a good impression when worn. Based on an area of South-East London.

Pedigree Chum — *Come* — A term for the unromantic clod in that it applies to semen and orgasm. Based on a brand of dog food.

Pedlar's Pack — *Sack* — A 1970s term for dismissal from a job: 'I've been threatened with the pedlars.'

Peeler — A policeman, an archaic piece based on Sir Robert Peel (1788–1850), the founder of the modern police force. *See* BOBBY.

Pee-Shooter — The penis, that which discharges pee.

Peg It/Peg Out — To die. A couple of old terms inspired by the game of cribbage, where to peg out is to finish.

Peggy Sue — *Clue* — A 1970s term for those lacking street credibilty, those who 'ain't got a Peggy Sue'.

Peg-Legger — *Beggar* — A cruelly apt piece that came into being after World War One, when limbless soldiers, unable to find work, were reduced to begging.

Pelf — Money, a piece that's been around for centuries. 'Pelfry' – loot acquired by burglary.

Pen & Ink — *Stink* — An old and very common expression for a bad smell. Also to complain is to kick up a 'pen and ink'.

Pen & Inker — *Stinker* — A dated term for a scoundrel or a particularly tough problem.

Pen Pusher — An office worker, a term used sneeringly by manual workers.

Penalty Kick — A certainty, or very close to one. Overheard at Romford Stadium: 'I think this four dog's a penalty kick.' It actually 'hit the post' (qv) and finished second.

Pencil — The penis, generally the one of a little boy. Big boys, however, like theirs to have lead in. 'Pencil and tassle' – the genitals of a boy.

Penciller		An old term for a bookmaker's clerk, a pre-betting shop one.
Penholder(s)	*Shoulder(s)*	An example from the 1960s that was first heard in the theatre.
Penn'orth of Bread	*Head*	A stale reference to the 'turret' from a time when bread could be bought for a penny.
Penn'orth of Chalk	*Walk*	Always shortened to the first element, often when sending someone out of earshot: 'Take a penn'orth, I wanna talk to your mother, private like.'
Penny Banger	*Clanger (Mistake)*	An appropriate piece from the days when fireworks were cheap. Drop a 'penny banger' and it may blow up in your face.
Penny Black	*Back*	Based on Britain's first postage stamp and employed only in an anatomical sense, this fits a work dodger's excuse. He'll phone in with a 'bad penny' then stick it to his bed.
Penny Bun	a) *One*	Only really used in connection with gambling, whereby odds of a 'cockle' to a 'penny bun' is 10/1. *See* COCKEREL & HEN.
	b) *Son/Sun*	One of several examples from a baker's shop making the same connections.
Penny for the Guy	*Pie*	Seems a much more reasonable request down the chip-shop than a 'smack in the eye' (qv).
Penny Locket	*Pocket*	The thirsty may be as dry as a snooker player's 'penny locket'.
Penny Stamp	*Tramp*	An old term for one whose worth slightly more than the 'ha'penny stamp' (qv).
Penny-a-Mile	*Smile*	Always used in a reduced form: 'Come on, cheer up, give us a penny.'
Penny-a-Pound	*Ground*	Terra firma has always been known as the 'penny'. To knock someone down is to 'penny' him.
Penny-Come-Quick	*Trick*	Originally a fitting term for a con trick, which for a good 'artist' was a quickly earned 'penny'. It later came to represent any trick, before disappearing.
Peppermint Flavour	*Favour*	A 1960s term that is often said in disbelief, whereby 'you must be joking' becomes 'do me a pep'ment'.
Peppermint Rocks	*Socks*	'Peppermints' (pronounced pep'ments) is a rarely used alternative to 'almonds'. *See* ALMOND ROCKS.
Perch		A bed, generally a temporary one. A 19th-century term among the poor who often sought a 'perch for the night'. *See* PECK & PERCH.
Percher		A gullible person; one easily conned.
Percy		The penis, famously pointed at the porcelain during urination.

Percy Thrower	a) *Blower (Phone)*	Even with today's technology telephones are still known as blowers, so you're still liable to be on the 'Percy' for ages, pressing numbered options.
	b) *Mower*	A totally suitable piece based on the original TV gardening expert (1913–88). If it cuts the grass, it's a 'Percy'.
Perisher		A badly behaved or annoying person, a semi-abusive term that falls somewhere between 'rotter' and 'bleeder' (qv).
Perry Como	*Homo*	An old term for the old-fashioned term for a homosexual male. Based on the name of an American singer (1912–2001) for no other reason than its rhyming factor.
Peruvian Pisshole		What a foul-smelling place is said to stink like. Also 'Peruvian dosshouse'.
Peruvian Poof		A man, not necessarily a homosexual, who is acting in an unmanly or cowardly way. Someone who won't have 'afters' (qv) because the 'wife'll kill me' for example, may be so derided: 'Come on, you Peruvian Poof, stay and have a drink.' Not sure why 'Peruvian', probably alliteration.
Perv/Pervy		Sexual perverts in all their many forms.
Pete Murray	*Curry*	A 'ringstinger', courtesy of a British radio and TV personality, is sometimes dished-up as an alternative to the more common 'Ruby Murray' (qv). *See* RING BURNER.
Pete Tong	*Wrong*	Applies to a worsening situation, one that's all going 'Pete Tong'. Based on a British DJ.
Peter		a) An enduring underworld term for a safe. The origin of the term is unknown, maybe from the disciple who was a symbol of strength, or perhaps the old phrase to rob Peter to pay Paul. Whatever, thieves have been robbing 'Peters' for at least two centuries. b) A 19th-century term for a prison cell, another form of strongbox. *See* (a).
Peter Cook	*Book*	A 1960s term for a 'reader' that never really caught on. Based on a British comedian and writer (1937–95).
Peter O'Toole	*Stool*	Mainly applies to a bar stool which is fitting enough given this Irish actor's bar-fly reputation. Incidentally, how come, when famous actors get out of their skulls on drink and wreak havok on pubs and hotel bars, they're called hellraisers, while the rest of us are drunken yobbos?
Peter Pan	*Van*	A 1980s piece from the light haulage industry

seems to have taken off in the courier trade. Like the boy of J M Barrie's creation, 'Peters' are now flying all over the country.

Peterman   A thief specialising in cracking safes, who may also be a 'Peter Blower'.

Peters & Lee   *a) Pee/Wee*   Lennie Peters (1939–92) and Di Lee were a hit-making duo of the 1970s and the term came and went with their records, a slash in the pan you might say. Some may still go for a 'Peters' in deference to Lennie, a great East-End singer.

     b) Tea   Too many cups of which will lead to an overwhelming desire to (a).

Petrol Tank   *Wank*   Based on the vulgarly sung first line of the song 'Granada': 'I once had a wank in an old petrol tank in Granada.' Applies to an act of masturbation and what the useless or obnoxious aren't worth. 'Petrol tanker' – an obnoxious or useless person, a 'wanker' (qv).

Petticoat Lane   *Pain*   Based on London's famous Sunday market at Aldgate, this applies either to physical pain or to a nuisance, whereby a pain in the neck becomes a 'petticoat in the Gregory Peck' (qv).

Petty not Getty,
  the name's   A reply to someone asking an exorbitant amount of money for something: 'How much? Sorry, the name's Petty, not Getty.' An allusion to the Getty family, one of the richest in the world.

Pewter   a) An old term for money, especially silver coins. Put some 'pewter' outside on New Year's Eve and you'll never be skint in the coming year – an old superstition.

b) A 1990s reduction of the word computer. Coined in the 1990s and used by, well, me for one.

Peyton Place   *Face*   A 1960s term based on a long-running American TV soap of the time, which made famous 'Peytons' of it's stars.

PG Tips   *Lips*   'Pee gees' refers to the larger lips, as worn by the chimpanzees in the famous TV adverts for this brand of tea (which incidentally is known as Monkey Brand).

Pheasant Plucker   *Fucker*   Not too sure if this famous spoonerism is admissable as RS. Used in the same context as 'He's a nice bastard' – meaning the opposite. A 'pheasant plucker' therefore is not a pleasant f . . . . .

Phil McBee   *Flea*   A term from before World War One that doesn't seem to have survived Two.

Phil the Fluter	Shooter (Gun)	Known as a 'Phil' and named after the song about an Irish musician who had a celebrated ball.
Philharmonic	Tonic (Water)	The perfect accompaniment for 'Vera Lynn' (qv).
Photo Finish	Guinness	The world-famous stout is sometimes downed to a 'photer'.
Phyllis Dixie	Pixie (Homosexual)	Pixie is a 19th-century variation of fairy and this 1940s term is based on a wartime dancer (1914–64) who was billed as the 'Queen of Striptease'.
Physical Jerk	Berk (Fool)	An example of secondary slang (see BERKSHIRE HUNT) that sees an idiot as a 'physical'.
Phyzog/Phyz		The face in terms of it's looks. You can have an ugly 'phyzog' but not a dirty one. A shortened form of physiognomy.
Piccadilly	a) Chilly	Cold weather brings about much grumbling about how 'Piccadilly' it is.
	b) Silly	Normally gets reduced to the first two syllables: 'Don't be so bloody picca.'
Piccalilli	Willie (Penis)	A case of the pickle representing the schnickel (qv).
Piccolo & Flute	Suit	A rare alternative to the well-worn 'whistle and flute' (qv).
Piccolo(s) & Flute(s)	Boot(s)	A seldom-heard example. 'Daisy roots' is the guv'nor in this branch of the footwear department.
Pich		A chip, the backslang partner of 'shif' (qv). 'Piches' – chips.
Pick & Choose	Booze	A piece that seems to sum up the multitude of different drinks there are to pick and choose from.
Pick up One's Drum		To storm off in a huff, an example based on the comedy antics seen in the eccentric British band Sid Milward and the Nitwits, regularly on TV in the 1950s and '60s. Whenever the drummer was told off, he would pick up his instrument and storm off stage.
Pick up Sticks	Six	Another piece from the bingo hall.
Pick Us a Winner		A phrase used when someone is caught descaling a nostril with his finger.
Pickle		The penis, a piece that's based on a pickled cucumber, which, apart from the colour, is aptish. 'Tickle the pickle' – to masturbate.
Pickle & Pork	Talk	The garrulous 'can't half pickle'.
Pickled		The worse for drink, an ancient term for being drunk or 'as pickled as an onion'.
Pickled Onion	Bunion	In normal circumstances pickled onions sit nicely on plates of meat. Not at this table! See PLATES OF MEAT.
Pickled Pork	a) Chalk	A 19th-century term for the much-used scribbling stick.

	b) Talk	An unheard example which seems to be based on drunken pigs.
Picture in the Attic		A term that's used derogatorily against a young person who behaves like an old one: 'He's definitely a picture in the attic that Terry, it's not normal for a bloke of his age to have a cob-on all the time.' Based on Oscar Wilde's novel *A Portrait of Dorian Gray* in which Gray's portrait ages but he doesn't.
Piddle		To urinate and the discharged liquid. So common as to hardly be slang any more.
Piddled		Drunk, a piece that's considered less vulgar than 'pissed'. 'Piddly' – slightly drunk.
Pie & Liquor	*Vicar*	The man of the cloth becomes a man of the scoff that's sold in pie and mash shops. The liquor in question is the gravy sold in these establishments.
Pie & Mash	*a) Cash*	In the cab and courier games a 'pie and mash' job is a fare or job not on account. Based on a traditional London dish.
	b) Flash	An ostentatious, trappy, big-headed know-all may be described as being: 'Too pie and mash for my liking.'
	c) Slash (Urination)	Very common for those on the point of 'blowing a washer' to disappear behind whatever cover is available for a 'pie and mash'.
Pie & One	*a) Son*	Based on the same fare as at 'pie and mash', i.e., a pie and one portion of mash.
	b) Sun	How hopes of having a decent summer become 'pie' in the sky.
Pie Can		A fool, a dope. An example frequently heard in TV programmes set in the north.
Piece		a) Originally American but now a universal term for a gun.
		b) A women seen as a sex object: 'That new secretary's a fair piece.' Also a 'piece of skirt'.
Piece of Piss		Anything considered to be easy, a doddle. The RAF version of a 'piece of cake'.
Piece of Shit		A contemptible person, a rat. Sometimes extended to a 'reeking piece of shit'.
Pieces of Eight	*Weight*	The aim of the dieter is to 'do some pieces'.
Pie-Eyed		Very drunk, unable to see straight.
Pig		a) A slow racehorse or greyhound. A dejected complaint of a losing punter is that his selection had 'run like a pig'.
		b) A vehicle that keeps breaking down. An East End company ran a fleet of old lorries which their drivers

christened 'Thunderpigs', a jocular inversion of the wonder machines in TV's *Thunderbirds*.

c) A police officer, a piece that's been around since the early 19th century but found universal fame during the middle of the 20th. 'Swine gums' – said to be a copper's favourite sweet.

d) A job that may be difficult or tricky to do, or just plain horrible.

e) An ugly fat woman. 'Did you see that pig Joey had in his car last night? Talk about squeals on wheels.' She may also be called a 'porker'.

f) A greedy person, a glutton. Someone who will eat anything on the basis that 'it'll all get turned to shit anyway'.

g) A sexist male as seen by women, a mysogynist. An 'MCP' – male chauvinist pig.

Pig & Roast	*Toast*	A term coined by soldiers of World War Two, a piece that's heavy on irony due to the lack of cordon bleu dishes served up on the front line.
Pig in the Middle	*Piddle*	Either used in full or condensed to a 'pig', but never a 'piggy'. An announcement of 'I'm going for a quick piggy' means something completely different. *See* PIGGY BANK.
Pig It		To behave in a rude or disgusting manner or to live carelessly in squalor. Can't help thinking that pigs get a lot of bad press.
Pig Latin		The type of slang that everyone knows, but not by name. 'Agfay' – fag, 'oday' – dough (money) are a couple of examples. Know the one?
Pig Out		To eat to excess or to overindulge in anything. To be greedy.
Pig Wagon		A later version of 'pigmobile' (qv).
Pigging		A euphemism for 'fucking', commonly heard on TV when an intensifier is needed.
Piggy Bank	*Wank*	An act of masturbation that's usually rubbed down to the first element: 'She wouldn't drop her Dianas so I had to settle for a piggy.' *See* DIANA DORS.
Piglet		A rude, obnoxious child, a term you can use without sounding offensive. But you know what you mean!
Pigmobile		A 1960s term for a police vehicle coined, apparently, by hippies when police drugs raids were frequent events. *See* PIG (c).
Pig's Ear	*Beer*	By far the commonest term for 'brown food', the original pub-grub.
Pig's Fry	*Tie*	A seldom-used alternative to the common 'Peckham Rye' (qv).

Pig's Trotter	*Squatter*	A 1970s term for a someone who dips their snout in someone else's trough.
Pigsty		An obvious term for a police station from the 1960s. *See* Pig (c).
Pigswill		Verbal garbage, rubbish: 'I've heard some pigswill in my time, but that. . .'
Piker/Pikey		A traveller such as a gypsy or tinker, an old term with it's origins in turnpike, a road with a tollgate.
Pile-Driver		A male homosexual, a connection with sodomy and haemorrhoids.
Pilgarlic		A bald-headed man, originally one whose hair has fallen out due to VD. From the image of a peeled clove of garlic.
Pill		a) A ball, originally a cannon-ball or a pellet, but later anything ball-shaped, from a marble to a football.
		b) A 19th-century term for a bore, or somebody who is 'hard to take'.
Pillar & Post	*Ghost*	Whereby the Holy Trinity become the 'soap, currant and holy pillar and post'. *See* Soap & Lather *and* Currant Bun.
Pill-Head		An amphetamine or barbiturate addict.
Pillock/Pill		A general term of abuse against anyone considered an idiot, often a petty official or a neighbour who complains about you parking outside his door.
Pillocks/Pills		Euphemisms for 'ballocks' and 'balls' relating to the testicles and what some people talk. In slang, pill and ball are the same thing and, as a hillock is a small hill, 'pillocks' and 'ballocks' are small balls, hence the contents of the 'ballbag'.
Pillow		To bed someone, to have sexual intercourse: 'He's only been here a fortnight and he's already pillowed half the typing pool.'
Pillow Biter		A male homosexual, one on the receiving end of anal sex. The 'Official Receiver'.
Pimple		A hill, an old lorry driver's piece: 'The drop should be just over the next pimple.' 'Over the pimple' – past it.
Pimple & Blotch	*Scotch (Whisky)*	Commonly condensed to a 'drop of pimple'.
Pimple & Wart	*Port*	A piece that's used in full to avoid confusion with 'pimple and blotch' (qv). The term also once applied to a quart, a measurement of a quarter of a gallon.
Pin & Needle	*Beetle*	An old term for the insect that has long been cockneyfied to a beedle, as in:- Insecticide.

> *Studley Needle saw a beedle*
> *Crawling up the wall*

He knocked it off with a dirty cloth
And made the ugly bug bawl.

Pinball Wizard
A police term for someone who claims to have seen and heard nothing. Based on the deaf, dumb and blind kid in Pete Townsend's rock opera *Tommy*, who was a dab hand at pinball.

Pinch
a) To steal, so well-known that it hardly seems like slang any more, but slang it is! 'Pincher' – a thief.
b) To arrest, underworld jargon for an occupational hazard. 'Pincher' – a police officer.

Pineapple
A World War One term for a hand grenade based on it's appearance.

Pineapple Chunk   *a) Bunk*
A naval term from World War One, seamen used to sleep on 'pineapples'. It was later picked up by prisoners of war whose main aim in life was to escape or 'do a pineapple'.

b) Drunk
A 1990s piece from suburbia, yet to oust the old cockney 'elephant'. *See* ELEPHANT'S TRUNK.

c) Junk
Heard at a recent car boot sale: 'You'll be lucky to find something valuable amongst all this old pineapple.'

d) Spunk
(Semen)
A Scottish term for what's ejaculated north of the border.

Pineapple Yourself
Go away, get lost or fuck off. From the colourful expression of dismissal: 'Go and fuck yourself with the rough end of a pineapple.'

Pinhead
An idiot, someone thought to be mini-brained. Also a small-minded, petty person.

Pink
a) Homosexual, the term that preceded 'gay'.
b) A supporter of left-wing politics but not a communist. A 'pink under the sink' is less extreme than a 'red under the bed'.

Pink Lint   *Skint*
An infrequent interloper into the popularity of 'boracic lint' (qv) as an expression for having nuppence in your pocket.

Pinkie
A white person, a derogatory term first used by black Americans.

Pinky & Perky   *Turkey*
What is traditionally eaten on festive occasions, courtesy of a brace of TV puppets who happen to be pigs. A slice of 'pinky' is therefore not a slice of pork.

Pinned Up
a) Tense, on edge, thus frightened. A piece from the trenches of World War One.
b) A drug user's term for being under the influence of a drug that reduces the pupils of the eyes to pinpricks.

Pins		The legs, very common for the old and frail to be 'dodgy on their pins'.
Pip		To break wind but not very loudly, a fart that falls between a 'rip snorter' and a 'silent horror'.
Pipe		a) To look at or watch, an old underworld term: 'Pipe the geezer in the corner. Old Bill or what?'
b) A tunnel, commonly the tunnels Blackwall and Rotherhithe, the 'pipes' connecting East and South-East London.
c) A drug user's term for a vein.
d) The penis, the outlet of a man's waterworks.
e) To cry, a piece that's been around since the 18th century. 'Pipy' – weepy.
f) To talk. Hence 'pipe up' and 'pipe down'.
Pipe & Drum	*Bum*	The anus and therefore the basis of the choice expression 'poke it up your pipe', an indication of where the unwanted may be dispatched to.
Pipe Your Eye	*Cry*	It is debatable as to whether this is genuine RS or not but it has been given as an example for so long that it warrants inclusion as such.
Piper		a) A smoker of crack cocaine, from the use of a pipe to smoke it.
b) A look-out or someone who keeps an eye on things, especially the work-place spy. *See* Pipe (a).
Pipes		The human breathing system, the lungs and the airways that lead to them.
Piss		a) To urinate and the liquid that's produced, a piece that's so much a part of everyday speech that it really shouldn't still qualify as slang. Politely reduced to 'pee'. 'The luckiest bastard who ever pissed in a pot.' – The summation of a fortunate person.
b) Alcohol, people commonly go 'on the piss'.
c) Weak beer or lager, stuff that's mainly water: 'Was this brewed or passed?'
Piss/Piss Away		To waste or squander: 'If he's pissed his wages up the wall I'll kill him.'
Piss About/ Around		To play the fool, to mess around. Also to waste time, either your own or more annoyingly, someone else's. Sometimes said as 'piss-ball about/around'.
Piss Artist		A regular drinker, a drunk. A well-known drunkard is often just known as an 'artist'.
Piss Flaps		A crude term for the labia, even cruder is 'cunt lips'.
Piss Home/In		To win a race easily: 'This favourite pissed home last time out.'

Piss in the Swimming Pool	To spoil something, to ruin a good thing. To wreck it completely is to 'piss in the swimming pool off top board'. A same-but-different version of muddying the water.
Piss It	To succeed with ease: 'Drive like that on your test and you'll piss it.'
Piss Off	a) To annoy, anger or to generally give someone the hump: 'You're really pissing me off, d'you know that?'
	b) To leave, to go away or an order for someone to do so.
Piss Oneself o' Laughing	To laugh uproariously, to cachinate oneself into a state of incontinence.
Piss Proud	Descriptive of the penis when basking in the glory of an erection due to it's owner's awaking to the need of a piddle.
Pissed	a) Drunk. Pissed as a 'Fart', 'Newt', 'Pudden' – very drunk.
	b) Out of true, not square or straight. Askew. A term that's often heard on building sites, describing a badly built wall, a twisted door frame, etc.
Pissed/Pissed Off	Originally American terms for being angry or very annoyed.
Pissed Off	Fed-up, bored: 'I need to find another job, I'm well pissed off with this one.'
Pisser	a) A lavatory, especially a pub urinal. 'It must be Roger's round, he's in the pisser again.'
	b) The penis, a term most commonly employed by the butt of a wind-up: 'You're pulling my pisser' – you're taking the piss.
Pisshead	A drunkard, someone who finds it hard to eat on an empty stomach.
Pisshole	A dirty, scruffy or unsavoury place, a piece that takes in anywhere from a room to a town to a country: 'From what I saw of Istanbul it's a pisshole.'
Pisshole/ Pisshouse	A lavatory, well-known terms that usually relate to a urinal.
Pissing Down	Raining heavily, a term that's commonly heard during the English summer.
Piss-Poor	a) Bad, useless or inferior. The moan of a football supporter: 'Last week we were world beaters but today we were piss-poor.'
	b) Poverty stricken: 'Everybody talks about the good old days, but the truth is we were piss-poor.'
Pisspot	An archaic example for a chamberpot, po or potty.

Pisspot	*Sot (Drunkard)*	An enduring term for a boozer.
Piss-Take		A mockery, a wind-up or a liberty. A pile of bricks masquerading as an exhibit of modern art, for example.
Piss-Tanked		A cigarette made soggy by wet lips, a piece from pre-filter days.
Piss-Up		A drinking session, a common description of a drunken party.
Piss-Up in a Brewery		What the totally inept are said to be unable to organise.
Pissy/Pissy-Arse		A drunken person, not necessarily a regular drunkard. 'You pissy-arsed git, what time did you get in last night?'
Pistol		The penis, another term which sees the member as a weapon, especially when cocked and ready to fire.
Pit		a) A well-known term for a bed, especially a single man's one.
		b) A reduced form of armpit, people with BO are said to have a 'pit problem'.
Pit Juice		Sweat generated from the armpit, which may be combatted with 'pit spray' – deodorant.
Pit Spray		*See* Pit Juice.
Pitch & Fill	*Bill*	Originally applied to men with this Christian name, later referred to a poster or hand-bill.
Pitch & Toss	*Boss*	A reference to him or her in charge, based on an old gambling game.
Pitkin		A gullible fool, a dupe. A 1950s term based on the oft-used surname of the character portrayed on film by Norman Wisdom: 'What a Pitkin'.
Pits		The absolute worst. A horrible person, place or situation can be described as 'the pits'. Based on the 'stink-holes' that are untreated armpits.
Pixie		A homosexual man, a variation of 'fairy' (qv).
Pixilated		Drunk. 'Out of one's brains', or 'silly drunk'.
Pizza Hut	*Slut*	Based on the chain of pizza restaurants, this is how a promiscuous woman became a 'pizza'.
Plain & Gravy	*Navy*	The 'plain' is an old reference to the Royal Navy based on that culinary delight, the dumpling and gravy.
Plain & Jam	*Tram*	A term that is sitting on a back-burner waiting for this form of transport to make a comeback.
Planet of the Apes	*Grapes*	Cut down to 'planets' since the 1960s, when a film and TV series of this title hit the screens.
Plank/Plank-Head		A stupid person, a dim-wit, someone as 'thick as a plank'.

Plant		a) An undercover police officer or spy, a 19th-century piece that still gets a lot of use especially in TV crime programmes. Also somebody 'planted' in a crowd surrounding a street vendor, the first to buy the 'bargain of the week'. b) To secrete incriminating evidence in the possessions or the property of a suspect in order to get a conviction.
Planting		A funeral, an old term for the sad occasion when the deceased is 'planted' – placed in the ground. To 'plant' – to bury.
Plaster		To shell or bombard heavily, an old military term.
Plaster of Paris	*Aris*	A thrice-removed piece that leads, eventually, to the backside. 'Aris' is the shortened form of 'Aristotle' which in turn is slang for 'bottle', which is a reduction of 'bottle and glass'. We have now arrived at the 'arse'.
Plastered		Drunk, originally a military term so may be based on 'plaster' (qv) in the sense of 'bombed' (qv).
Plastic		a) A false, phoney or insincere person, someone who isn't genuine. A 'plastic smile' isn't for real. b) Any type of credit or bank card. Cash is flash but plastic's practic.
Plastic Toasting Fork		A symbol of uselessness, what a 'doughnut' (qv) is said to be as much use as.
Plate of Beef	*Chief*	A convict's term for a chief warder.
Plate of Ham	*a) Gam (Fellatio)*	Always reduced to the first element, it is supremely common, whereby 'to plate' becomes a verb. Gam is an abbreviation of 'gameroosh' which is a corruption of an old French word for the performance of oral sex, *gamahucher*. Many a filthy comment was raised in the early days of betting shops when it was announced over the blower that a race was delayed due to a horse being plated. 'It's a good job jockeys are little, it saves 'em getting their knees dirty' is one I seem to remember.
	b) Tram	When trams went out of sight in London, this went out of mind.
Plate of Meat	*Street*	The original meaning before getting pluralised to dance to a new tune. *See* PLATES OF MEAT.
Plate(s) & Dish(es)	*Wish(es)*	As written on greetings cards and inscribed by authors of books on slang: 'Best plates and dishes'. Originated in the theatre, probably as part of a pantomime script.
Plate-Rack	*Hack*	A 19th-century term for this type of horse. Not sure if it has ever applied to a journalist.

Plates & Dishes	*Missus*	The 'plates' is an old reference to the wife.
Plates of Meat	*Feet*	The fame of this term is legendary and the leg-ends are always known as 'plates': 'My plates are so hot I could do the ironing with 'em.' 'Plate holders' – footwear.
Platters of Meat	*Feet*	A rarely used variant of 'plates of meat', except maybe in matters of the patter of tiny 'platters'.
Play Silly Buggers		To act the fool, mess around or generally act pillockishly.
Play Solitaire/ Solo		To masturbate, a couple of terms that symbolise single-handed sex.
Play the Hop		To take an unofficial day off school, to play truant.
Play the White Man		A still common term from pre-PC days meaning to play fair, keep to the rules, be honourable.
Pleasure & Pain	*Rain*	Apt since the umbrella-maker's pleasure is the holidaymaker's pain.
Pleat		A facial scar, normally a vertical one.
Plink-Plonk	*Vin Blanc*	A term coined on the battlefields of World War One. Plonk was soldiers jargon for mud, which was likened to the cheap wines available, a result of which, 'plonk' has become a common hand-me-down for any dodgy wine. Red or white.
Plod		A 1970s term for a policeman based on PC Plod, the lawman of Enid Blyton's Toytown. Later, as 'the Plod' it became a reference to the police force in general. 'Plod the Clod' – a uniformed officer. *See* CLODHOPPER. 'Ploddess' – a policewoman.
Plonk		a) Cheap, indifferent wine. A term coined by World War One soldiers who likened dodgy wine to (b). *See* PLINK-PLONK. b) Mud, so called by the men who knew a bit about the stuff: World War One soldiers.
Plonker		a) A well-known 1960s term for the penis when it was commonly used in connection with winding someone up, i.e., to 'pull someone's plonker'. b) A stupid person, a piece that is derived from (a) in the same way as the older 'prick' (qv).
Plop		To defecate, from the sound of a rectal ejective hitting the water. 'Plopsy' – the resultant splash-maker.
Plot-Up		To park a vehicle, a piece of taxi driver's jargon: 'I was plotted-up at the airport for two hours and all I got was a local.'
Plough		To have sexual intercourse, an ancient term with a seed-sowing connection. Shakespeare used it in the play *Anthony and Cleopatra*.
Plough the Deep	*Go to Sleep*	An archaic piece that hit rocky ground years ago.

Plug		a) A tampon, a 1990s term that's crudely used by men who selfishly consider themselves to be the victims of their partner's indisposition. b) To shoot someone, an old example from the Hollywood western. c) To have sexual intercourse, an 18th-century term that's still in use. 'Plug' – the penis.
Plugged In		Aware of the current trends and fashions, a variation of 'switched on'.
Plugged-Up		To be in the throes of a period, an unsympathetic piece of malespeak: 'No 'oggins for me today, she's plugged-up.'
Plum		A fool, a 'prune' (qv) by any other name would be as stupid.
Plum Duff	*Puff* *(Homosexual)*	A 1970s term for an unmanly man, hence to act 'plummy' is to behave effeminately.
Plumbing		The human urinary system, one's 'waterworks': 'He's got to go to the hospital about his plumbing, I think he needs a new washer.'
Plumpette		A fat girl or young woman, especially one seen putting some consideral strain on a swimsuit.
Plums		The testicles. A common term for a disappointment is a 'kick in the plums'.
Plunge		Of a man, to have sex with a woman, the image of an inward thrust.
Plunger		The penis, an old term for the part that makes an entry, or plunges in.
Plungeworthy		An attractive, desirable woman. One who scores high on a man's 'plungeometer'. *See* PLUNGE.
Plymouth Argyll	*File*	An underworld term for the tool, based on an English football team.
Plymouth Argylls	*Piles*	A double painful condition. People with 'Plymouths' have 'grapes' the size of footballs.
Plymouth Cloak	*Oak*	An old term for an archaic piece of slang for a cosh or cudgel.
Pock		A police officer, a backslang cop. The 'pocks' – the police.
Poch		A backslang chop, either pork or lamb. A piece from the meat market. Poch and piches – chop and chips.
Pocket Billiards		The old British game of playing with the genitals through a trouser pocket; the Yanks play 'pocket pool' or 'pocket pinball'.
Pocket Rocketeer		A man who habitually plays with his genitals through his pocket.
Podger		Originally a cosh but now applies to the penis and therefore sex.

Poet		An early 20th-century term for a man with long hair, a piece that's still used by people of the Pre-60s short-back-and-sides generation for whom long hair once represented the arty-farty type.
Pogo Stick	*Prick (Penis)*	A piece from the 1970s that also represents a fool or an obnoxious person: 'What a pogo.'
Poison		An unpleasant person, one best left alone. A snide.
Poison Dart	*Fart*	A smell of poison gas may demand the question: 'Who's fired a poison dart?'
Poison Dwarf		A nasty little person, one best not argued with first thing in the morning, or when it's too early to start on shorts.
Poke		a) A 19th-century term for a wallet and by extension what it contains, i.e., money. A piece generally used by pickpockets. b) Sexual intercourse, an example that's endured for well over a century.
Poke-Hole		The vagina, that which gets poked. *See* POKE (b).
Poker		The penis, that which does the poking. *See* POKE (b).
Pokey		A well-known American term for a prison or a cell.
Polari		*See* PARLYAREE.
Pole		The penis, and by extension what it is used for. To 'pole' is to indulge in intercourse.
Pole-Hole		The vagina, that which gets 'poled'. *See* POLE.
Polish & Gloss	*Toss (Masturbate)*	A piece that generally comes down to 'polish': 'She said she never goes the whole way on a first date, so she gave me a quick polish.'
Polisher		A sycophant, a crawler. A truncated version of 'apple polisher' (qv).
Political Asylum		A clever term for the House of Commons, where gather England's elected nuts.
Poll		a) Someone who talks a lot, a convict's term based on that talkative bird, Polly Parrot. b) The head. An ancient word which, although not really slang, is used by old East Enders as if it were. People with nits would scratch an itchy poll.
Poll Topper		A wig, that which tops the 'poll' (qv).
Polly Flinder	*a) Window*	An old term used by glaziers and window cleaners. Based on a little girl in a nursery rhyme, who obviously felt the cold.
	b) Cinder	With the demise of the coal fire, this is mainly used humorously to describe overcooked food, which may be burnt to a 'Polly Flinder'.

Polly Parrot	*Carrot*	A piece from the fruit and veg market that could be off-putting for a vegetarian.
Polly Wolly Doodles	*Noodles*	The popular fast food. If you want to see bafflement try asking for crispy 'polly wollys' at the Chinese take-away. Based on a traditional song.
Polo Mint	*Skint*	The mint with the less fattening centre comes in as a protest of the potless: 'I'm polo till payday.'
Polone/Polony		A girl or a young woman. An example of Polari based on the Italian *pollone* – a chick.
Poltroon		In the 1950s, this 16th-century word for a coward became, thanks to British comedian Tony Hancock, a term for a fool. His popularity ensured that idiots all over the country became 'poltroons'.
Pom/Pommie		An English person according to an Australian. Based on 'pomegranate', an Aussie-type rhyme for immigrant.
Pompey Whore	*Four*	A streetwalker from Portsmouth gets the bingo-caller treatment.
Ponce		a) A man who lives off a prostitute's earnings, a pimp. b) A sponger, someone who would have to pack up smoking if you did. To 'ponce' – to cadge. c) A derogatory expression aimed at a disliked person, often a stranger, like the driver who cuts you up, or the wheel clamper who . . . well just the wheel clamper. d) An overtly effeminate male homosexual, a showy individual.
Ponce About		a) To live an aimless, irresponsible life. To get what you can, when you can, from whom you can. b) To act in a flashy, effeminate manner.
Ponce About/ Around		To play the fool, to mess about, to waste time. Another version of 'arse', 'fuck' and 'piss about'. *See all three.*
Ponced Up		Formally or overly dressed: 'I feel a right pranny ponced up in this monkey suit.' Also 'Poncified'.
Poncy		Of an homosexual, to behave in an affected or theatrical way.
Pongo		a) An early 1960s term for a black person that was used by the upper classes as they looked down their noses at the rest of the world. b) An ancient naval term for a soldier, possibly connected to (c). c) A name given to a smelly individual, usually behind his back. One who emits a nasty pong. d) A name given in the early 1970s to someone with a big nose. After a character in a TV advert

who used his enlarged proboscius to sniff out pink paraffin.

Ponies
Racehorses, hence to 'play the ponies' is to gamble on them, to follow racing.

Ponte
The Polari term for £1, based on the Italian *pondo* – a weight.

Pontoon
From the card game, a 21-month prison sentence. In pre-decimal currency it related to twenty guineas which was twenty pounds and twenty shillings, thus £21, an amount still relevant to the term.

Pony
A long-standing and well-known term for £25, many use no other expression for the amount.

Pony & Trap   *Crap*
A very well-known term, both in reference to defecation and its product. Also used in connection with rubbish or bad merchandise in that anything considered to be 'crappy' can be described as 'pony'.

Poo
An abbreviated term for shampoo which has attached itself to champagne.

Poo/Poo Poo
Juvenile terms for defecation and the mess it produces. From 'poo' – a stink. 'Pooey – smelly.

Pooch
a) A familiar expression for a dog, originally an American one. There is a story of a Dagenham man who, for a joke, entered his scruffy old mongrel in a dog show under the name of 'Poochy Woofkins of Day-jen-ham'. They were both ejected.
b) An unattractive woman, a variation of 'dog': 'He pulls so many pooches, he's more likely to catch hardpad than a dose.'

Poodle
A slow, leisurely stroll or drive: 'It's a nice day, let's have a slow poodle round the park.'

Poof
Probably the best known term for a homosexual that exists, giving rise to extended terms like 'Poofhouse' and 'Poofter'.

Poofed Up
Gaily or extravagantly dressed, a term not necessarily levelled against a homosexual but someone deemed to be dressed like one.

Poofhouse
A pub frequented by homosexuals.

Poofism
Homosexuality: 'He's heavily into poofism' – he's a practicing homosexual.

Poofist
Anyone prejudiced against homosexuals, a homophobe.

Poofy
Having the traits of a homosexual, effeminate.

Poomp
A juvenile term for a fart, often the 'silent but violent' variety.

Poona
A 19th-century reference to £1, originally a sovereign.

Poony		A fool or a dope. It is pronounced to rhyme with the way a northerner says 'funny'. Possibly related to 'poonce', a 19th-century term for the vagina, i.e., 'pratt' (qv). *See also* PUNAANY.
Poop		To defecate and the result of a lavatorial visit. 'Poop scoop' – a piece of equipment for picking up dog's mess.
Pooper		The anus. When your 'pooper's making little buttons', you're excited.
Poor Relation	*Station*	Formed, presumably, when rich relations had cars but is hardly relevant these days, when every family has a means of transport and even the rich find rail travel expensive.
Poove		A homosexual, a 1960s variation of 'poof' (qv).
Pop		a) An unspecified distance, a 'short pop' isn't very far but a 'fair old pop' is. b) An orgasm, famously to 'pop one's cork'. c) To pawn, a piece that's been about since the 19th century. 'In pop' – in pawn. 'Pop-shop' – pawnshop. d) To take a drug, either orally or by injection. e) To hit someone, specifically to punch them. f) To insult, scold or generally have a go at someone: 'You having a pop at me?'
Pop a Window		To break a window as part of a 'smash and grab' raid, an underworld term.
Pop Goes the Weasel	*Diesel*	A bit of a mouthful so always reduced to 'pop'. An example from the haulage trade.
Pop One's Clogs		To die, a familiar term that may have something to do with pawning a dead person's footwear. *See* POP (c).
Popcorn	*a) Horn (Erection)* *b) Porn*	Generally reduced to a 'poppy' and apt, as both may be found in a Soho cinema. Commonly associated with dirty books, blue films and sex on the Internet.
Pope of Rome	*Home*	An ancient term for where the heart is, there's no place like 'pope-a'.
Popeye the Sailor	*Tailor*	The old spinach-munching cartoon salt (qv, c) comes in as a 'needle wallah'.
Popper		A small vial of amyl nitrite which is broken and inhaled by drug users.
Pop-Pop		A moped, from the sound it makes, as opposed to the roar of a motorbike.
Poppy		A well-known old cockney term for money which is probably related to 'pop' (c), i.e., money obtained by pawning something.

Poppycock		A 19th-century term for nonsense or rubbish which is still common. It literally means soft shit, from the Dutch word for just that – *pappekak*.
Pork		Of a man, to have sexual intercourse, an American import from the 1970s.
Pork & Beans	*Portuguese*	A development of soldiers of World War One, which is probably more of a pun than RS.
Pork Chop	*Cop (Police Officer)*	An example that goes hand in cuff with the common slang term for 'plod' and co, 'pigs'.
Pork Chop at a Jewish Wedding		What people feel like when they are out of place or uncomfortable.
Pork Pie	*Lie*	Enjoys nationwide usage thanks to TV exposure, often in the form of 'porky pie'. 'Porkies' – lies.
Porker		a) A police officer, a 1970s variation of 'pig' (qv, c). b) A fat person, an old derivation of 'pig' (qv, f).
Porky		Fat. A name often cruelly given to a fat person. Someone said to be 'a fine figure of a pig'.
Porky Pig	*Big*	Used in terms of size and as a mild rebuke against someone who has done you no favours but thinks he has: 'You've put me down for a fiver's worth of raffle tickets have you? Well that was Porky Pig of you. You're very generous with my money.' Based on a cartoon character.
Porridge		a) Imprisonment, from what was the staple prison breakfast. The term became well-known in the 1970s, when a TV sitcom bearing the name became staple viewing. b) The brain, from the similarity in appearance between the grey matters of the cranium and the breakfast bowl. c) Semen, as pumped out by the 'Porridge Gun' – the penis.
Port & Brandy	*Randy*	An appropriate piece since this concoction may be used by the saloon-bar lothario as a knicker loosener for his girlfriend.
Poser		Someone who wants to be noticed, a show-off. Someone who poses for effect. Not a genuine person.
Posh		A shop. A backslang 'seller'.
Posh Sydney		A name given to an upper-class boy by a lower-class one. 'Posh Sydneys' attend Eton and Harrow. Based on a character from early American comedy films.
Posh & Becks	*Sex*	A piece from millennium year based on the celebrity couple whose everyday antics kept them in the newspapers on a daily basis. Victoria Adams, a singer known as Posh Spice, and her husband, England footballer David Beckham (Becks), who famously had sex in Brooklyn, New York.

Postage Stamp	*Ramp*	The ramp is a common expression for the bar of a pub, therefore: 'Get up the postage' means 'It's your round.'
Postman's Knock	*Clock*	Probably formed on the basis that you could set your 'postmans' by the postman's knock.
Pot		a) A lavatory. An old term that gives us 'on the pot' – on the toilet.
		b) A familiar term for marijuana, even to those who never smoke it. Someone who does is known as a 'pot-head'.
Pot & Pan	*Man*	Generally a term for a husband or father known as the 'old pot and pan'.
Pot House		A lunatic asylum, an infrequent version of 'mad house'.
Pot of Glue	a) *Jew*	Now known more familiarly as 'potters'.
	b) *Queue*	A fitting term, it's not uncommon to get stuck in one at the post office on pension day.
Pot of Honey	*Money*	A 19th-century term whereby the penniless are 'potless'.
Pot of Jelly	*Belly*	An old term of derision for a fat gut, which should be dished up in full, as a reference to a 'pot' speaks for itself.
Potash & Perlmutter	*Butter*	A play of this name was produced in London in 1914 and the term duly followed. You now have more chance of getting sunstroke down a pothole than of ever hearing it again.
Potato Mashers	*Gnashers (Teeth)*	An example that would work equally as well in a non-RS context. Teeth are perfectly adapted for mashing spuds.
Potato Peeler	*Sheila (Woman)*	An old piece from down-under which has a currency among ex-pat Aussies in London, where women are more likely to be known as 'Janes', 'Jills' or 'Renes'.
Potato Pilling	*Shilling*	How this old amount of money became known as a 'tater'.
Potato Trap		A 19th-century term for the mouth that has probably only ever been said as 'tater trap'.
Potatoes in the Mould	*Cold*	Very well-known and never said as anything but 'taters'. Refers to the temperature, not the illness.
Pot-House		A mad person, a loon. A 'candidate for the van'.
Potless		Flat broke, without the proverbial pot to piss in.
Pots & Dishes	*Wishes*	A theatrical piece, probably from a pantomime.
Potted		a) Under the influence of marijuana. *See* Pot (b).
		b) A term for being drunk that comes from a time when a tankard was called a pot.
Potty		Crazy, mad or eccentric, a well-known and oft-used example. Sometimes shortened to 'pots'.

Poultice		An obnoxious, unpleasant person. A general term of abuse that usually follows an adjective, e.g., 'fat poultice'.
Pound Note	*Coat*	An elderly piece which was based on the banknote that is consigned to the memory bank.
Pound Noteish		Pompous, snobbish, stuck-up. An old term based on the perceived wealth of the well-off.
Pound of Butter	*Nutter*	Applies to any loon, from the wildly dangerous to the mildly strange, the eccentric who lives in a world of his own because he doesn't care for the only alternative.
Pound of Lead	*Head*	An old example that was generally reduced to the first element. A pounding 'pound' may describe a hangover.
Pound One's Flounder/Meat/ Pork/Pudden		Some examples of male masturbation.
Pounds & Pence	*Sense*	A piece that's generally used to have a go at those lacking any common sense: *1st Man: 'Ain't you got any pounds and pence?'* *2nd Man: 'Sorry, my mind is somewhere else today.'* *1st Man: 'Well as long as YOU know where it is.'*
Powder One's Nose		To sniff a powdered drug, commonly cocaine. A user's term. 'Powder' – any drug in powder form.
Powder Puff		a) A 1920s term for an effeminate male homosexual, based on a typically feminine thing that brings 'puff' (qv, b) into play. b) A weak or gentle non-gay man, a 'softie'. One easily pushed around and, so, often the butt of a bully. Also a henpecked husband.
Powdered Chalk	*Walk*	A less exercised version of the well-worn 'ball of chalk' (qv).
Power & Glory	*Cory (Penis)*	How men feel about their standing member.
Pox		A venereal disease, originally syphilis. A misspelling of 'pocks' from the pock-marks on the skin of a sufferer. 'Pox doctor' – a specialist at the special clinic who may also be a 'poxdoc'.
Pox of, the		To be fed-up with, a common expression of unhappiness: 'I've got the right pox of this traffic.'
Poxy		Descriptive of anything of inferior quality, worthless, useless or unpleasant.
Pozzy		Jam, as consumed in the trenches by soldiers of World War One.
Pranny		a) A 19th-century term for the vagina which seems to be a hybrid of 'pratt' and 'fanny'.

Prat/Pratt

b) A fool, a dope. An example that's used as a mild rebuke or insult, much like 'pratt'.

a) A 16th-century term for the backside that seems to have emigrated to America, where it's much more likely to be heard than here. 'Pratfall' – a humiliating failure, literally to fall on one's arse.

b) The vagina, common in this sense since the 19th century, when it seems to have replaced (a).

c) A fool, a dope. A piece that has become strangely acceptable, considering it is a variant of 'cunt' (qv, b).

Prat About/ Around

To act the fool, to mess about. *See* PONCE ABOUT (a).

Pratty

A term of abuse directed at a man behaving in an unmanly, girly manner. If you see a bloke in a linen shop sorting through the doilies, some may say it's a 'pratty' thing to do. He is therefore being 'pratty'.

Prawn

A jokey reference to a fool or an idiot: 'I feel a right prawn in this get-up.'

Prawn Crackers *Knackers (Testicles)*

Currently in use and always in the first element. A low blow is a punch up the 'prawns'. Based on a number on a Chinese menu.

Prescott

A punch, specifically a left hander. Based on the New Labour politician, John Prescott, who, in 2001, famously aimed such a blow at a protester who threw an egg at him.

Preserve, in a

In trouble or a difficult situation, an extension of 'in a pickle'.

Press & Scratch *Match*

Cigarettes are rarely lit by 'presses' any more, they've been shot down by the disposable 'spitfire' (qv).

Pretty Lips

A derogatory name given, since the 1930s, to a person with full, prominent lips: 'Here comes Pretty Lips.'

Previous

a) A criminal record, a reduction of previous convictions used by police and criminals.

b) The cockney version of early or premature: 'We're well previous, we might as well go for a pint.' Also, strangers who talk to you like they've known you for years are said to be a 'bit previous' – a bit forward.

Prick

a) The penis, this ultra-common example has been in use since the 16th century.

b) A fool, an idiot or an obnoxious person, something akin to 'plonker' (qv).

Prick Tease/ Teaser

A woman who leads a man into believing that she is sexually available but stops short of intercourse, leaving the man all dressed up with nowhere to go. So to speak. Such a woman is also known as a 'PT'.

Prick-Lick

Exactly what it sounds like, fellatio. 'Nodding dog' – an ugly woman who performs a 'prick-lick' on the back seat of a car.

Pride & Joy *Boy*

Mainly a reference to a newborn son and used for as long as he's the apple of his parents eyes.

Prile/Prial

Of playing cards, three of a kind. 'Prile of priles' – three threes. From 'pair royal' because three pairs can be obtained from three cards.

Prince Albert

In body piercing, a ring attached to the penis. Legend has it that the German husband of Queen Victoria (1819–61) considered the genital bulge in his tight trousers to be offensive so he had a ring inserted into his manhood to which he attached a weight that pulled down on the offending member, thus reducing the size of his embarrassment. The truth may be that old Germans liked decorative helmets.

Princess Di *Pie*

Current among the younger generation, this took a respectful dip after the death of the Princess of Wales (1961–97), but seems to have returned to a chip shop near you. Just goes to show, you can't keep a good woman down. You can't keep a bad 'Princess Di' down either.

Private Ryan *Iron*

A piece of secondary slang for a homosexual (*see* IRON HOOF) based on the award-winning war film of 1998, *Saving Private Ryan*. Here referred to as 'Raving Private Ryan'.

Privet

The remaining hair that grows round the back of a bald man's head.

Pro

A 'pro'-fessional working girl, i.e., a prostitute. Also a 'prozzy'.

Prod/Proddy

Terms used by Northern Ireland Catholics in regard to protestants.

Prong

A 1940s term for the penis and consequently sexual intercourse: 'I pronged her in the NAAFI and still had a hard-on when I jumped on the lorry taking us to the docks.' – A soldier leaving for war.

Provide a Specimen

To urinate, a 1990s term mostly heard in the pub.

Prune

A fool, an idiot. Much like a 'prawn' (qv).

Prune & Plum *Bum*

From one of nature's laxatives comes another term for the breech.

Prussian Guard *Card*

A playing card and also a bingo card. The term was coined when bingo was still called housey-housey.

Ps & Qs *Shoes*

In normal speech, to mind your Ps and Qs is to be careful of what you say and do and not put your foot in it. In RS however, if you don't put your feet in your Ps & Qs it's not worth having 'em.

Psychopathic   *Traffic*   A most appropriate example, which has come into being in the exhaust-fumed wake of the motor car and the problems it engenders, turning normally rational people into would-be killers at the first whiff of a traffic jam. A condition known as road-rage has entered the language and has been used in connection with several well-publicised murders.

Pud/Pudding   The penis, an ancient term based on the original meaning of the word. Puddings were entrails, either human or animal, and the term became associated with sausages because intestine walls make the best sausage skins (hence black pudding). The term is now only ever used in connection with masturbation. Therefore to 'pull one's pudding' is to 'pull one's sausage'.

Pudding/Pudden   a) A second-hand car dealer's term relating to filler in a car's bodywork.
b) A fool, a piece that is often hurled at a numbskull in the form of 'You silly great pudden.'
c) Meat laced with a drug used to put a guard dog to sleep; once accomplished the dog has been 'puddened'. A piece of underworld jargon since the 19th century.

Pudding & Beef   *a) Chief*   An old term for a chief prison officer.
    b) Deaf   A piece that is what it sounds like, Scottish.

Pudding & Gravy   *Navy*   The 'pudden' is one of several terms for the senior service.

Pudding Basin   *Mason*   A 'pudden' is a rare reference to one of the 'funny handshake mob'.

Pudding Chef   *Deaf*   An old piece that seems to have left the kitchen.

Pudding Club   Pregnancy, a well-known term that is more often than not reduced to 'in the club'. An unborn child has long been known as a 'pudding'.

Pudding(s) &   *Eye(s)*   Doesn't appear on the menu as often as 'mince
Pie(s)   pie' (qv), except perhaps in the form of a shiner (qv), a 'black pudding'.

Puddled   Mad, insane or eccentric, an example that's heard mainly 'up north'.

Puddlejumper   A small commercial vehicle, a piece that's used sneeringly by 'big wheels' drivers, i.e. by drivers of heavy goods vehicles.

Puff   a) Breath or wind. When you're breathless you are out of 'puff'. By extension it applies to life, as in:

'I've never exercised in my puff. I believe it should be energetically evaded.'

b) A male homosexual, a variant of 'poof' (qv).

c) Cannabis. A well-known term among those that smoke it: 'I had some puff last night for the first time in years. It knocked me bandy!'

Puffer		An old term for a smoker that is now commonly used of cannabis smokers and crack cocaine users. In more innocent times a puffer was a train.
Puffers		Cigarettes, a term used of fags sold on the black market. 'Is Terry still knocking out puffers?'
Puff & Dart	*Start*	To begin, a term that was used by reluctant workers: 'Better make a puff and dart, I suppose.' In the 19th century the term applied to the heart.
Puff & Drag	*Fag (Cigarette)*	An apt example, it's what factory workers congregate in the lavatory for.
Pug/Pug Away		To stash secretly: 'It wasn't till he died that we found he'd pugged away a fortune in an old shoe box at the back of his coal cupboard.'
Puggy		A name given to someone with an overly upturned nose. Probably a corruption of 'piggy'.
Pugnose		A flattened nose, like one of a 'pug' – a boxer.
Pukka		Genuine, sound, the real thing. A piece often heard spoken by rogue traders. Stand on me, anything they're selling as 'Pukka' won't be!
Pull		a) To pick up a member of the opposite sex, well-known as going 'out on the pull'.
		b) Of the police, to stop or arrest. There seems to be a national sport among the police at the time of writing – giving motorists a pull.
Pull & Push		An act of masturbation based on the action of masturbating.
Pull Down the Shutter	*Butter*	An old example on which the shutters have been well and truly pulled down.
Pull Rank	*Wank*	To masturbate, sounds like one off a military wrist.
Pull-through		A soldier's term for a tall, thin person based on the name of a device used to clean a rifle.
Pump		a) The heart, a piece that's been banging away for the best part of a century.
		b) The penis, and by extension, what it's used for on expansion – sexual intercourse – which is also known as 'pumpage'.
Pump-Out		To urinate, boozer's slang: 'Just going for a pump-out.'
Pump Ship		To urinate, an example of military-style bladder emptying during World War One.
Punaany		The vagina, an example from the West Indies that's

used by black Brits. The word that got the TV comic character Ali G into trouble with the BBC because they had no idea what he was talking about. Also 'puni'.

Punch & Judy *Moody* An example of slang for slang (*see* MOODY & SANKEY), and used in disbelief at an obvious lie: 'Don't give me all that old Punch and Judy.'

Purse The vagina, an 18th-century term that still rates a mention, especially as a bulge in a bikini: 'Look at the purse on that.'

Push in the Truck *Fuck* Applies only to coitus and was seemingly coined in the transport industry.

Push, the Dismissal from work, the sack. Another way of getting the 'shove' (qv).

Pusher Someone who sells or 'pushes' drugs.

Puss A 19th-century term for the face that's heard in expressions like 'Glamour Puss' and 'Sour Puss'.

Pussy a) The vagina, and therefore women in general as sex objects. Boys out on the 'pull' are on the look-out for 'pussy'.

b) An underworld term for a fur coat, a piece that may be connected with (a). *See* FUR.

Pussy/Pussycat Terms that symbolise harmlessness: 'He may look like a beast but he's a pussycat.'

Pussy Willow *Pillow* Sounds like a nice way to drop off to sleep, with your head on a 'pussy'.

Put & Take *Cake* A piece from an early 20th-century caker's shop based on an old gambling game.

Put an Egg in Your Boot! Get lost! Go away! Run! From a Spike Milligan poem which ends 'Put an egg in your boot and beat it.'

Put in the Boot *Shoot* A World War One term that's no longer afoot.

Put It About To be freely available for sex, often said of a promiscuous woman: 'She puts it about.'

Put the Acid In To tell tales about someone in order to cause them harm or to spitefully scupper their chances.

Put the Tin Hat On Put to a complete stop, to end. Variations include 'tin lid' and 'top hat'.

Put the Wind Up To frighten, worry or scare the living daylights out of someone.

Putz The penis, this is the Yiddish version of 'prick' (qv) and like that term, serves as a fool.

Pyramid *Yid (Jew)* A piece that's hardly appropriate given the situation between the Arab and the Jew. Still, the latter is known as a 'pirra'.

Q

Quail		A girl or young woman, seen as prey by predatory males out on the 'pull'.
Quaint		Homosexual, once seen as a nicer word than 'queer'.
Quaker		A hard-baked piece of excrement that will not be passed without a trembling, quaking strain. A 'teeth marks on the lavatory door handle' job.
Quaker Oat	*Coat*	Based on a brand of porridge which, like a coat, is synonymous with warmth.
Quarrel/Row With One's Bread & Butter		To risk one's livelihood, to do something that may lose you your job.
Quarter Past Two	*Jew*	One of a multitude of terms for the non-gentile, this one is a later version of 'quarter to two' (qv). But only by half an hour.
Quarter to Two	*Jew*	An earlier and better-known version of 'quarter past two' (qv).
Quasimodo	*Soda*	Reduced to 'Quasi' or pronounced 'Quasimoda', this is the traditional partner of (Bells?) whisky, and is based on Victor Hugo's *Hunchback of Notre Dame*.
Quatra		The Polari version of the number four based on the Italian *quatro*.
Quean		A homosexual male, an old spelling of 'queen'.

Queen		An effeminate homosexual, especially an older or overt one, like a 'drag queen'.
Queen Mum	*Bum*	The anus, courtesy of Queen Elizabeth the Queen Mother (1900–2002), which was heard as a drunk's put-down of the male members of the acting profession: 'Actors? They all take it up the Queen Mum.'
Queen of Spades		A woman who has been widowed on more than one occasion, one who has buried a number of husbands. A connection with a spade and grave digging.
Queen of the May	*Gay (Homosexual)*	A 1990s term that has to be used in full. 'Queens' are already known as 'queens'.
Queen of the South	*Mouth*	Based on a Scottish football team, which to the English is just a place on a pools coupon.
Queen Vic	*Sick*	Ill or perverted, a 1990s term based on the fictional pub in TV's *EastEnders*.
Queens Park Ranger	*Stranger*	Although employed as a variant of 'Glasgow Ranger' (qv), this has a wider usage. It's the non-regular punter in a betting shop who strikes a large bet, the mysterious face in the pub, the man that children mustn't take sweets from and it's the little star of a happy event.
Queensbury Rules	*Balls*	An ironic piece in that a kick in the 'Queensburys' is totally against the regulations laid down by the Marquis of Queensbury (1844–1900), which govern boxing. Cockney dialect makes a rhyme.
Queer		Homosexual, a derogatory term that has been around since the 1920s. In the 1990s, militant 'queers' turned the term on to themselves, believing the word 'gay' to be too wishy-washy.
Queer Street, in		In trouble, especially financially. A 19th-century term that's still around.
Quid		Once a guinea but now universally known as £1. The term is rarely pluralised; twenty pounds is twenty quid although you can have a 'score of quids' and if you have a good result you could be 'quids in'.
Quiff		a) The vagina and by extension a woman, especially a promiscuous one or a prostitute. b) Sexual intercourse, a 19th-century term, given in a slang dictionary of the period as 'quiffing' – rogering.
Quim		The vagina, a piece that's been on men's lips since the 18th century. 'Quim bush' – female pubic hair.
Quod		Prison, an 18th-century term that's still serving time. 'Quodded' – locked-up.
Quoit		The anus, an alternative to 'ring' (qv).

R

RAF		An ugly or unattractive woman who may be initially as Rough As Fuck.
R G Knowles	*Holes*	An ancient piece that lived and died in the theatre, based on a music-hall comedian who probably did the same. Many times.
Raas		An all-purpose term of abuse from the West Indies, heard in Britain since the 1950s. A corruption of 'up your arse'.
Raasclot		A term of abuse that literally means 'arse cloth'.
Rabbit		To run away or leave in a hurry, to 'do a rabbit'.
Rabbit & Pork	*Talk*	One of the superstars of RS. Always reduced to 'rabbit', it has acquired a piece of slang of it's own. *See* NUN'S HABIT.
Rabbit Food		Green vegetables, especially lettuce. A term that's used sneeringly by the fast food generation and those happy to be fat.
Rabbit Hutch	*Crutch*	A reference to the private parts, which gives a new meaning to a rabbit punch. Also, secondarily, lame people often need the support of a 'rabbit'.
Rabbit's Paw	*Jaw*	With 'rabbit and pork' already established this seems an unecessary term in the sense of to talk, so may be better placed in terms of a telling off, whereby to jaw is to scold.

Racked Off		Annoyed, angry, irritated or generally 'humped-up'.
Racks of Meats	*Tits*	'Racks' for short and more of a rhyme on teats.
Raddie		An Italian, originally one living in London. Not sure why but since many were in the café and restaurant trade, a connection with radish or radicchio (chicory) has been suggested.
Raddled		Drunk, an 18th-century term for being beered-up. 'Raddles' – a name give to a beer lover.
Radio One's	*Runs (Diarrhoea)*	This just has to be based on the verbal outpourings of your average DJ.
Radio Rental	*Mental*	A well-known piece that's based on the high street TV rental company. It describes a crazy, mad person, someone said to 'have his hat on inside out'.
Radish		An idiot or fool, someone who with a bit more brains would rise to the level of daft.
Raffle Ticket	*Ricket (Mistake)*	Often employed by the person who has made the mistake: 'I've made a right raffle. I thought the favourite was in trap 6 and I backed the wrong dog.'
Rag		a) A sanitary towel, an old term that gives rise to 'on the rag' – a period.
		b) The worst horse in a race, the rank outsider. The one you wouldn't back with dodgy money.
Rag & Bone	*Throne*	This is a reference to the lavatory seat and has nothing to do with where Her Majesty sits. At least, not when she's being regal. Strange to think of the queen sitting on the other throne. 'Course she does though, as we've all heard of a royal flush and the royal wee is legendary.
Rag Week		The menstrual period, a 1980s term that's ironically based on the students' week of fun. *See* RAG (a).
Rag, Tag and Bobtail		Anyone who remembers the children's TV programme of this name will be interested to know that it is a 17th-century term meaning the riff-raff, the rabble, the great unwashed.
Rag-Bag		A scruffily dressed person, often a name given to a tramp. 'Rag-Bag Assortment' – an unlikely or ill-matched group of individuals.
Raggedy-Arsed		Descriptive of the poor and needy, a term from a time when 'raggedy-arsed' urchins, kids with the arse hanging out of their trousers, roamed the streets in their thousands.
Raggus		Sugar. The backslang sweetener.
Rag-Head		A Sikh. The term was originally coined by soldiers serving in the desert as a term for an Arab. The modern definition has been around since the 1960s when the turban became a common sight in Britain.

Raging		Students slang for a first-class honours degree, a pun on 'raging thirst'.
Railings		A piece that once saw time as the ribs is now quite a common term for the teeth, especially prominent ones.
Rain & Pour	*Snore*	Always reduced to the first element: 'I hardly slept all night with your raining.'
Rainbow		Any multicoloured pill, a drug user's term.
Rainbow Trout	*Kraut*	A 1990s piece used by the Club Med set when they can't get near the pool for 'rainbows'.
Raincoat		A condom, it keeps a chap dry in wet places.
Rainy Day Woman		Marijuana, seen as something to cheer a man up when he's feeling down. As sung about by American singer Bob Dylan in a hit record from 1965.
Rajputana	*Banana*	An obsolete piece based on a ship that used to commute between the Far East and London's Royal Docks.
Rake		To search thoroughly, as with a fine-tooth comb. *See* RAKE/RAKER.
Rake/Raker		A comb, well-known terms that have been parting the waves for over a century.
Raleigh Bike	*Dyke*	Probably based on a saying that purports to sum up a lesbian: 'I bet her bike's got a crossbar.'
Ralph/Rolf		To vomit, a couple of terms said to echo the sound of someone being sick or 'calling for Ralph'.
Ralph Lynn	*Gin*	This predecessor of namesake Vera (qv), is based on a British actor (1882–1964) who was noted for his performances in farce. The term seems to have died along with the man.
Ram		a) A virile man, one with a well-leaded pencil. b) Of a man, to have sexual intercourse.
Rambo		A name given to a strong, well-built man or ironically to a puny, weak one. Based on the character played by American filmstar Sylvester Stallone.
Rammer/Ramrod		The penis, a couple of terms inspired by 'ram' (qv).
Ramp		a) The bar in a public house: 'Who's up the ramp?' – whose round? b) A swindle, con or racket, especially one that involves selling at exorbitant prices. A 'ramper' does the 'ramping' and the victim gets 'ramped'. c) To rob with violence. An old term that makes a violent thief a 'rampsman'.
Ramped-Up		The price something is set at, especially of second-hand goods: 'The car was ramped-up at two grand but I got it for one and half.'

Ramps		A phoney fight or fracas, orchestrated as a smoke-screen for a swindle or con.
Ramsgate Sand(s)	*Hand(s)*	The 'maulers' are fairly well-known as 'Ramgates'. So if anyone asks for a 'Ramsgate' you now know it's got nothing to do with a scandal involving a minister caught in a compromising position with a couple of male sheep. They just want a hand.
Randolph Scott	*Spot*	The perennial goodie in countless western films (1898–1987) is reborn as a skin eruption and is now starring on the face of a young person near you.
Rangoon	*Prune*	Probably based on the effect that both the place and the fruit are said to have upon the bowel.
Ranjitiki	*Tricky*	An old docker's term for an awkward situation based on a ship that used to berth at London's Royal Albert Dock.
Rantallion		A man whose scrotum is longer than his penis. In the words of Captain Grose, who compiled a slang dictionary in 1811: 'One whose shot pouch is longer than the barrel of his piece.'
Rap		a) The blame for something, famously to 'take the rap'. Maybe from 'rap on the knuckles' – a reprimand. b) A conversation, either a meaningful discussion or witty banter. Also to talk or discuss.
Rape		A pear, a piece of backslang from the market.
Rapid-Fire		Refers to the quick shooting of premature ejaculation. In an effort to combat his own 'rapid-fire', a pal of mine took to thinking of football teams while making love. The method proved successful but the reverse effect means that he can no longer fill in a pools coupon without getting an erection.
Rapiddo		A term used when speed is required. From the Spanish *rapido* and used in the same way as 'lively' (qv).
Raquel Welch	*Belch*	Just goes to show that nothing and no-one is sacred in RS. This glamorous American film star, the sex goddess of her age, lends her name to an expulsion of gas from the stomach.
Rasher & Bubble	*Double*	Mainly applies to a double on a dartboard, sometimes two selections in a bet. The term is a dish of bacon with bubble and squeak.
Raspberry Ripple	*a) Cripple*	An unkind reference to a mentally or physically disabled person. Based on a type of ice-cream, it's also a mock insult directed at someone who didn't

think or act quickly enough: 'What are you, a raspberry?'

	b) *Nipple*	That of a woman, a term used solely by men for whom it's a bit of a mouthful, so it's always a 'raspberry'.
Raspberry Tart	a) *Fart*	A piece that has joined the ranks of mainstream English, but as an oral impression of an anal emission. Raspberries are now blown rather than dropped.
	b) *Heart*	The original meaning of the term but now obsolete in this sense.
Rat		A well-known term for an informer and by extension to 'rat on' is to inform against. And to 'rat someone out' is to betray them. 'King Rat' – a right-royal 'squealer'.
Rat & Mouse	a) *House*	An old piece that's verminously as relevant today in parts of London as it was on it's formation.
	b) *Louse*	Refers to a human louse, an obnoxious person, usually an informer.
Rat Trap	*Jap*	Reduced to a 'rat', this is a World War Two piece that was directed at an enemy and will survive the peace for as long as there remain ex-prisoners of the Japanese.
Rat-Arsed		Drunk. A term that neatly describes the foul anal gases that may accompany a hangover.
Ratbag		A term of mild abuse, often heard raising a giggle-laugh in British comedies of the 1960s.
Ratcatcher's Daughter	*Water*	An old reference to drinking water, a glass of 'rat-catchers'.
Rat-Faced		Drunk, a term from the wine-bar set of the 1980s.
Ratfink		A most unpleasant person, often a backstabber. Originally an American term for a blackleg.
Rathole		A horrible place, a term that takes in anywhere, from a country you wouldn't send your worst enemy to live in, to a pub that employs bouncers to throw people IN.
Rat-Run		A short-cut between two main roads, a cut-through that's handy when only a few people know of it. Once it gets popular the residents complain and the No Entry signs go up.
Rats & Mice	a) *Dice*	A very old term used by gamblers: 'The rats ain't running for me tonight.'
	b) *Rice*	Served up in curry houses, where chicken and 'rats' is a favourite dish.
Rat's Arse		What the useless or inconsequential are said not to be worth.
Rat-Stinker		An obnoxious, despicable person is known as a 'rat-stinking bastard'.

Rat-Stinking		Very drunk. 'Ratted' plus 'stinking' and then some. *See both*.
Ratted		Drunk, 'as rotten as a sewer rat'. *See* ROTTEN.
Rattle		To have sexual intercourse, a 19th-century term for 'bone jumping'.
Rattle & Clank	*Bank*	An onomatopoeic example from the days when the working classes dealt almost exclusively in coins.
Rattle & Hiss	*Piss*	The draining of the tank, another version of 'snake's hiss' (qv). Also refers to alcoholic drink.
Rattle Someone's Cage		To shake someone up, to annoy or to provoke a reaction.
Rattled		Drunk, a 19th-century term for being in a 'right state'.
Rattler		a) A train, a piece from the early days of the railway, before which it referred to a stagecoach. It's also an old term for the London Underground system.
		b) A good example of something. Along the lines of a 'cracker' (qv). An exciting book makes a rattling good read.
		c) A promiscuous woman, maybe the one who famously 'fucks like a rattlesnake'.
Rattlesnakes	*Shakes*	A case of delirium tremens (DTs), whereby the 'rattles' follow the morning after a night on the 'rattle'. *See* RATTLE & HISS.
Raver		a) A male homosexual, a diminishment of 'raving poof'. *See* PRIVATE RYAN.
		b) A sexually experienced and accomplished woman. One who knows her onions.
Ravi Shankar	*Wanker*	An unpleasant or useless person, based on an Indian sitar player who popularised the instrument in the late 1960s by playing at rock venues. It matters not how the name is supposed to be pronounced, in RS it's 'Ravvy Shanker'.
Raw Recruit		An undiluted spirit, a neat whisky for example.
Rawalpindi	*Windy*	Based on the name of a passenger liner that regularly berthed at London's Royal Docks. With the advent of World War Two she was comandeered by the Royal Navy and converted into an armed merchant cruiser. On 23 November 1939 she gallantly but suicidally engaged two of Germany's most powerful battlecruisers, *Gneisenau* and *Scharnhorst*. With the sinking of *Rawalpindi* 265 members of her crew were lost. The term therefore refers to weather conditions, definitely not to cowardice.
Ray-Gun		A hand-held speed-measuring device used by

police officers with nothing better to do than trap motorists.

Rays — Sunshine, especially when sought by holidaymakers.

Razor Blade — *Spade* — An offensive term for a black person that's usually slashed to a 'razor'.

Razzle — A bout of fun and drinking, a spree. You can always tell when someone's been 'on the razzle', he looks awful.

Razzle-Dazzle — Glamorous, glitzy, show-bizzy shenanigans. The Oscars, the razzlinest-dazzlinest night of the year.

Razzmatazz — *Jazz* — Refers to this type of music and the noisy excitement generated by it, especially when played traditionally. The term has been around in America, in one form or another, since the late 19th century, and got hooked on to jazz in the 1920s.

Read & Write — *Fight* — An example that's never truncated, two people having a 'read' doesn't exactly conjure up visions of violence.

Reader — Basically, anything that can be read. Originally a book, then a newspaper and later, especially in prison, a magazine.

Readies — A well-known term for cash money, ready cash. Also known as 'the ready'.

Ready — To bribe, to spread some cash about. 'Ready the rozzers' – to bribe the police.

Ready Wash — A 1980s term for crack cocaine, based on the chemical 'cleaning' required to make the drug.

Ream — To have anal sex, a term from the gay dick 'n' 'arry (qv).

Reamer — Someone who indulges in anal sex, therefore a term for a homosexual. Although heterosexual 'reaming' does go on.

Rear Admiral — A male homosexual, an allusion to sodomy based on a high-ranking sailor.

Rear Ender — *Bender (Homosexual)* — A fitting example, the backside for a backside enthusiast.

Rear Gunner — A male homosexual, an allusion to sodomy based on a back-end shooter.

Rear/Rare Up — To lose one's temper, to confront angrily.

Reckin — £1, a backslang nicker.

Recknaw — A useless or despicable person. A backslang 'wanker'. Said as 'reckner'.

Red — Gold, an old underworld term, hence: 'Red clock' – gold watch. 'Red lot' – gold watch and chain.

Redlush		A shoulder in backslang. 'Redlushes' – a pair of them.
Red Biddy		Cheap red wine fortified with methylated spirit, as swallowed by down-and-outs and winos.
Red Devil	*Level*	A building site term that refers to a spirit level, an important tool of a bricklayer, carpenter, floor layer, etc.
Red Eye		A sore anus that follows a prolonged bout of diarrhoea. *See* JAPANESE FLAG.
Red Flag is Flying/Up		Said when a woman is menstruating and, like the red flag at the seaside, it means no dipping.
Red Flannel/Rag		Old expressions for the tongue: 'Give your red flannel a blow and shut up.'
Red Hots	*Trots (Diarrhoea)*	During a bout of the 'scatters', this aptly describes the muzzle of one's 'scatter gun', the anus.
Red Ink		Cheap and nasty red wine, the worst of which you wouldn't fill your pen with.
Red Rum	*Dumb*	Most commonly used in connection with people who don't speak up for themselves rather than the handicapped: 'Why didn't you say something, you're not red rum.'
Red Sails in the Sunset		Based on a well-known song title, this is generally used by men in reference to a menstrual period.
Red Sea Pedestrian		A Jew, from the biblical story of how the Israelites crossed the Red Sea during their exodus from Egypt without the aid of trick photography.
Red Taper		A government or local government official, a stickler for bureaucracy.
Red, White & Blue	*a) Flu*	Known as the 'red white', a piece that seems apt if red stands for temperature, white for pallor and blue for melancholia.
	b) Shoe	An example from the late 1960s, when psychedelic 'plate holders' (qv) were all the rage and is now relevant to trainers.
Red-Eye		An overnight flight or train journey that arrives at its destination early in the morning, thus depriving the traveller of sleep.
Redraw		A warder. A backslang prison officer.
Redrum		Murder. The 'big job' in backslang.
Reds		The menstrual period, an allusion to blood which has given rise to several other terms within these pages.
Reeb		Beer. A backslang pint. A 'tinnip o' reeb' – a pint of beer.
Reefer		A well-known term for a marijuana cigarette. Based on the Spanish slang for a 'joint' – *grifa*.

Reef Round		*See* WREATH ROUND.
Reelings & Rockings	*Stockings*	A 1950s example that was heard much later when an East End villain walked into the lavatory of a local pub and was stopped in his tracks by the sight of the performing drag act putting on a 'reeling'. 'What's the matter?' asked the performer, 'Never seen a man putting on a stocking before?' 'Only over his head,' came the reply.
Reels of Cotton	*Rotten*	Refers to drunkenness, the putrefication of food and a state of affairs that has gone wrong: 'The job was OK till they stopped the overtime. Now it's all gone reels.'
Reen/Rene		A girl, especially a girlfriend: 'I ain't seen Tommy since he's been with that new reen of his.' From the diminutive of Irene.
Re-Entry		The return to normality after being 'spaced-out' on drugs.
Refill		A convict serving a life sentence. A backslang 'lifer'.
Regal		Lager. A backslang pint. An 'eslag o' regal' – a glass of lager.
Reggie & Ronnie	*Johnny (Condom)*	A case of the brothers Kray still offering protection. Based on the twin kings of the London underworld, Reggie (1933–2000) and Ronnie (1933–95).
Reginald Denny	*Penny*	A term from the 1940s that was probably as well-known as the British actor (1891–1967) it was based on. Didn't make the transition to the modern penny.
Reject		A stupid, useless or hopeless person, one who at birth slipped past quality control.
Rennet		£10, a backslang tenner.
Repap		The backslang term for paper, especially a newspaper. 'Repap posh' – paper shop.
Repock		A policeman. A backslang copper.
Reptile		A thoroughly untrustworthy, unpleasant person. A nasty piece of work, a 'slimeball'. *See* SCALY BACK.
Result		a) A good, favourable or lucrative outcome: 'It was a right result getting that contract, it's a good earner.' Also a stroke of good fortune. 'Ree-sult!' – a cry of success when Lady Luck smiles. b) Police jargon for a successful arrest or conviction, and a criminal's term for an acquittal.
Resworts		Back to front trousers. Backslang strides that is.
Retard		A mentally handicapped person, a common term of abuse for a non-handicapped but thick person, often in the form of 'tard'.

Retirement Age		In bingo, the number 65.
Revd Ronald Knox	*Pox (VD)*	Refers to all types of the disease that this Catholic priest could never have caught, given that he did his job properly. Shortened to 'the Reverend Ronald', it is based on an actual priest (1888–1957), who also wrote detective stories.
Reverse Winston		A V sign, but not the one used by Mr Churchill to symbolise victory. The abusive one.
Revif		£5, a backslang fiver.
Reviver		The first drink of the day following a night of heavy bevvying.
Revlis		The backslang version of silver, especially of coins. The 'revlis' – the silver ring at a racecourse.
Revved Up		Keyed up, excited. 'Revved up and ready to go' – eager to get started.
Rewosh		A shower, a piece of backslang that sounds apt if it's the second one of the day.
Rhino		Money, a piece that's been around since the 17th century. Once on the verge of extinction, the term is now safely back in circulation.
Rhubarb		Nonsense, based on the theatrical term for background babble in a performance, the term now applies to verbal rubbish.
Rhubarb	*Sub*	Always pronounced 'rhubub', this mainly concerns an advance on wages or a loan. To a lesser extent it applies to a substitute: 'Come on Harry (Redknapp), send the rhububs on.' – A disgruntled West Ham fan, 1999.

Rhubarb Pill	*Bill*	Based on a type of purgative for that which must be paid. Heard in a restaurant:
		    Customer: Got the rhubarb, please?
		    Waiter: There's no rhubarb on, sir.
		    Customer: No rhubarb? Lovely-lovely. Fetch me coat then.

Rhubarbs	*Subs*	Applies to subscriptions, as paid by members of social and sports clubs. 'Subs' is also a diminutive of suburbs, for which 'rhububs' is cab drivers slang, London's outer boroughs being part of the knowledge.
Rhythm & Blues	*Shoes*	A 1980s term that leads to 'dancer cases' (qv) being known as 'rhythms'.
Riah		Hair. Backslang 'barnet'. 'Nanti riah' – no hair – bald.
Ribbon & Curl	*Girl*	A term for a little lady that needs no explanation.
Richard/Richie		The penis. Elaborated versions of 'Dick' (qv). 'Wring One's Richard' – to masturbate.

Richard & Judy	*Moody*	Lies and deception may be known as 'a load of old Richard', courtesy of husband-and-wife TV presenters Richard Madeley and Judy Finnegan, an update of 'Punch and Judy' (qv). *See* also MOODY & SANKEY.
Richard Briars	*Pliers*	An electrician's term heard on a building site in the form of 'Richards'. Based on a British actor seen in some of TV's funniest sitcoms.
Richard Burton	*Curtain*	Named after a Welsh actor (1925–84), this relates to a domestic and, more relevantly, a theatre curtain.
Richard Gere	*Queer (Homosexual)*	Based on an American actor that women swoon over. As far as I know the term exists solely because it rhymes.
Richard the Third	a) *Bird*	Originally applied to the feathered variety but is now widely used in connection with a young lady, who is always a 'Richard'. It also refers to the 'bird' as given to second-rate performers; actors dread being given the 'Richard'.
	b) *Turd*	Of secondary usage but quite common, especially when stepped in.
	c) *Word*	A rarely used alternative to 'Dicky bird' (qv). Richard III (1452–85) ruled England from 1483 until his death at Bosworth.
Richard Todd	*Cod*	Based on a British actor, this applies only to a piece of fried cod.
Rick		a) A member of a three-card trick team, one who has a phoney bet and is seen to win, encouraging others to lay down their money in order to lose it. b) A well-known term for a mistake or an error of judgement.
Ricket		A mistake, blunder or error. In general, a cock-up.
Riddle-me-Ree	*Pee/Wee*	A piece that everyone understands, either in full or truncated to 'riddle'.
Ride		Sexual intercourse, a piece that's been in the saddle for generations. 'Ride bareback' – to have sex without a condom.
Riffle		To fondle a man's genitals while they are in a relaxed state in order to arouse him.
Riff-Raff	a) *Caff*	A greasy spoon as represented by the great unwashed.
	b) *Taff*	A Welsh person. A common term based on the common people.
Rifle		Another term for the penis from the weapon store. 'Rifleman' – a womaniser.
Rifle Range	*Change*	Always check your 'rifle', women do, men don't, children spend it and taxi drivers keep it.
Rig		a) The male genitals, an example from the 1950s

whereby a well-endowed man is said to be 'rigged like a donkey'.

b) An articulated lorry, originally an American one. The term also applies to a CB radio.

c) A drug user's term for the equipment needed for an injection.

Right Back   A two in a pack of cards. Footballers in this position wear the number two shirt.

Right Half   A four in a pack of cards. Old-time footballers in this position wore the number four shirt.

Rigid   Drunk, the result of too many stiff drinks.

Rim   To stimulate someone sexually by licking their anus, a literal 'tongue and groove' job.

Rimmer   An anilinguist, a genuine 'arsehole licker'. *See* RIM. Also a term of abuse directed at a toady or crawler. No accident that this was the name of the snide character in the TV comedy *Red Dwarf*.

Ring   A well-known term for the anus since the late 19th century. It had previously applied to the vagina.

Ring/Ring It   To deceive by bending the facts or making up an excuse. To turn things to your advantage by deception. To shift the blame in a roundabout way, women seem particularly adept at this.

Ring Master/ Raider   A couple of examples from the 1990s regarding male homosexuals. *See* RING (a).

Ring Snatcher   Someone who favours anal intercourse, not necessarily a homosexual.

Ringburner   A hot curry, one that, after searing it's way through the digestive system, leaves like molten lava, having a scorching effect on the anus. *See* RING (a). Also called a 'ringstinger'.

Ringer   a) An unregistered player in a team, one who plays under the name of a legitimate team member.

b) A horse or dog entered in a race under another animal's name for gambling purposes.

c) A car that's been spruced up to look better than it actually is, and had it's mileage lowered in order to secure a better price on a used car lot.

d) A stolen car, it's appearances changed and equipped with false number plates.

e) The person who does the 'ringing' at (b), (c) and (d).

f) Someone adept in the art of deception, a quick-thinking maker of excuses. *See* RING/RING IT.

Ringo Starr   *Car*   After writing in *Fresh Rabbit* that I wouldn't be surprised if this term existed, I received a letter saying that it did. Based on the former Beatle, it had a short spell in the RS chart in the 1960s but never got the better of the long-running 'jam-jar' (qv).

Ringpiece
An ancient term for the anus. The circular point of exit. Or entry, for those who are so inclined.

Rinky-Dink — *Pink*
Used in connection with a pink snooker ball and in a sense of well-being, 'in the rinky-dink'.

Rin-Tin-Tins — *Pins (Legs)*
An old term based on a canine star of early western films who was a bit lively on his 'rintys', but never seen to cock one.

Rio
£1000, a play on Rio Grande, the river that flows between Texas and Mexico. No RS connection with current England footballer Rio Ferdinand – it's older than him.

Rip & Tear — *Swear*
A term that has ventured beyond the bounds of RS. To sound off with a barrage of bad language is to 'let rip'.

Rip Off
a) To cheat or swindle. To sell deceptively inferior goods.
b) To copy somebody's work, to plagiarise.

Rip the Piss
A Glaswegian version of 'take the piss' (qv).

Rip Van Winkle — *Sprinkle/ Tinkle*
Known as a 'Rip Van' in relation to urination, tinkle is a juvenile euphemism while sprinkle is the adult version. Based on a character in American writer Washington Irwin's *Sketch Book* (1819).

Ripe
Smelly, often used to describe a person in need of a wash, or the pungent pong that follows a fart.

Rip-Off
a) A fraud, a waste of money, something that doesn't live up to it's publicity. Also overpriced goods.
b) A stolen idea, a piece of blatant plagiarism or any copied work.

Rip-Off Artist/ Merchant
A cheat, swindler, thief, etc. Anyone who will carry out a rip-off.

Ripper
A general term of approval that is generally associated with Australians, but the term was British in the first place.

Ripping
Enjoyable, exciting. An old-fashioned term of approval.

Rip-Rap — *Tap (Borrow)*
Generally known as 'on the rip-rap', which is what scroungers and the perennially skint usually are.

Ripsnorter
A loud emission of wind, a thunderous fart.

Rise
An erection, hence 'rise to the occasion'.

Rise & Shine — *Wine*
Not a particularly apt example, as anyone who's ever woken up with a Bacchanalian hangover will confirm.

Rising Damp — *Cramp*
A 1970s term based on a popular TV sitcom, which

is common among sportsmen and often heard on Hackney Marshes on a Sunday morning when pub football teams are battling it out.

Rispeck/Respect
A greeting used by young black Britons to people held in high regard.

River Lea   *Tea*
A 19th-century term based on East London's other river. What a lousy cuppa is said to taste like.

River Nile   *Smile*
What the 'boat' of an unemployed person breaks into when his 'nightboat to Cairo' (qv) arrives.

River Ouse   *Booze*
A common expression for a drinking session is to be 'on the River Ouse' or just 'on the Ouse'.

River Tyne   *Wine*
Refers to a bottle from the cheaper end of the wine list, it wouldn't do to label a vintage claret a bottle of 'River Tyne'.

Riverina   *Deana (5p)*
A term from the days of our previous currency that survives today. A 'deaner' was a common name for a shilling and is still relevant to it's modern-day equivalent.

Rivets
An old term for money, the metal connection probably makes it coinage. But note 'stiver', an ancient name for a penny. Possibly backslang?

Roach
The butt of a marijuana cigarette, the supposed resemblance between it and a cockroach.

Roach & Dace   *Face*
A rarely used alternative to that other fishy pairing 'kipper and plaice' (qv).

Road Pizza
The flattened corpse of an animal that has been run over and crushed by following traffic.

Road's Up
Said, by men obviously, of a woman when she is menstruating. Therefore the No Entry signs are out.

Roaring
Very drunk. Boisterously, loudly and embarrassingly so.

Roary
A domestic fire, a stunted version of a roaring fire.

Roast
In footballing terms, to beat another player and go past him with ease.

Roast Beef   *Teeth*
An example that's occasionally served instead of the well-known 'Hampstead Heath': 'I'll knock your roast beef so far down your throat, you'll be able to chew your dinner again.'

Roast Joint   *Pint*
Old cockney dialect would have made this rhyme as 'roast jint'.

Roast Pork   *a) Fork*
Applies to cutlery but could conceivably be used to confuse a lost motorist: 'Keep going till you come to a roast pork and chuck an Isle o' White.'

                b) Talk
A rare alternative to 'rabbit', sometimes heard as: 'What're you roasting about?' And a gabby person 'can't half roast pork'.

Roast Potato	*Waiter*	One of several terms rhyming waiters with potaters, this one is generally cut down to a 'roastie'.
Roasted Duck	*Fuck*	A 1930s reference to sexual intercourse which slang users haven't given a roasted duck about since.
Rob Roy	*Boy*	The eponymous hero of Sir Walter Scott's novel entered the RS catalogue at the end of the 19th century, and promptly disappeared at the beginning of the 20th.
Robert E Lee	*a) Key*	Seems to have taken over from its sound-alike version at (d) to take part in one of life's little mysteries. Why are 'Roberts' never where you put them?
	b) Knee	Usually heard in connection with a painful one, famously in the George Formby song 'My Auntie Maggie's Remedy'.
	c) Pee/Wee	Another well-known Lee gets to 'strain the greens'.
	d) Quay	An elderly piece that was coined by London's dock workers, and like the docks seems to have been redeveloped. *See* (a). Based on the commander (1807–70) of the confederate armies in the American Civil War.
Roberta Flack	*Sack*	An American singer comes in to put people out of work, but mostly she represents a bed. The knackered long to 'hit the Roberta'.
Robertson Hare	*Pear*	An old street market term that has long gone to seed. Based on an English comedy actor (1891–1979).
Robin Cooks	*Looks*	An ironic piece based on a Labour cabinet minister, much ridiculed for his not exactly handsome features. Bachelors are advised to get a woman while they've still got their 'Robin Cooks'.
Robin Hood(s)	*a) Good(s)*	Based on the legendary goodie, and seemingly almost as old, this turns up in several guises. It's what children are forever being told to be. It's anything praiseworthy, a second-hand car may be a Robin Hood'un. But mainly it's heard in a sense of anything bad or useless; if it's 'no Robin Hood' or 'no bloody Robin', it's no bloody good. In plural it applies to merchandise, hence 'don't handle the Robins'.
	b) Wood(s)	Fittingly applies to a collection of trees or a chopped-up one. It was also an expression for a Woodbine cigarette, once sold singly as a 'tup'ney one'.
Robinson & Cleaver	*Fever*	A 19th-century term that is now as defunct as the London department store it's based on.

Robinson Crusoe   *Do So*   Used defiantly in response to a threat:

> *'If you don't move your car from in front of my*
> *gate I'll call the police.'*
> *'Well, Robinson Crusoe then.'*

Roby Douglas   The anus, an old term that may allude to a real person who had 'one eye and a stinking breath', to quote Captain Grose in his 1811 book of slang.

Rock   a) An underworld term for a precious stone, especially a diamond.

b) Crack cocaine, well-known among drug users.

Rock 'n' Roll   *a) Dole*   A common term for unemployment, being on the 'rock 'n' roll'. A piece that first signed on in the 1960s.

   b) Hole   What clothes, boots or excuses may be full of. Also applies to having sexual intercourse, i.e., getting one's 'rock and roll'.

Rock of Ages   *Wages*   Often shortened to 'rocks', and based on an old hymn, for what workers originally thanked God it was Friday for.

Rock(s) &   *Shoulder(s)*   Symbolic of strength, the type of 'rocks' on which
Boulder(s)   a friend in need may need to lean.

Rocket   a) A reprimand, a 1940s term with it's roots in the military.

b) The penis, the ultimate phallic symbol, one that 'goes up'.

Rocket Fuel   Strong drink. Make that double-strong drink. Especially vodka.

Rocket Socket   The vagina, that which accepts an inner space explorer. *See* ROCKET (b).

Rockfist   A tightfisted, mean person, someone not easily prised from his money. 'Rockfisted' – tight.

Rockford Files   *Piles*   One of a bunch of terms for haemorrhoids, this one from the 1980s is based on an American TV programme seen in Britain.

Rocking Horse   *Sauce*   Commonly applies to the condiment or ketchup and also to cheek or impertinence: 'You've got some bloody rocking horse.'

Rocking Horse   What anything that's hard to come by is said to be
Manure   as rare as.

Rocks   The testicles, the origin of the famous expression for ejaculation, 'get one's rocks off'.

Rod   a) A pistol, originally a term from the American Roaring Twenties.

b) The penis, especially when erect and ready to go 'fishing'. *See* FISH.

Rod Laver   *Saver*   A bet made to safeguard another, one that insures a win. For example, if, at the start of the football season you back a team at long odds to win the FA Cup and they reach the final, you can back the other side to put yourself in a no-lose situation.

Rodney An upper-class male idiot, a 'chinless wonder' (qv).

Roe Semen, a common old term especially as 'come one's roe'.

Rofe The number four, probably the commonest backslang number, especially among on-course bookmakers. Also applies to £4, odds of 4/1 and a four-year prison sentence.

Rogan Josh *Dosh* A modern term used by young curry-house
(Money) frequenters who trim it down to 'rogan'. Based on the Kashmiri dish of lamb curry and yoghurt.

Roger To have sexual intercourse, a term that's been well to the fore since the 18th century, since when it has also been a term for the penis. The name was commonly given to bulls and rams, hence a connection with stud activities.

Roger Hunt *Cunt* It seems that anyone with this surname comes in for the same treatment in RS, this Liverpool and England footballer of the 1960s is no exception. Refers to a fool, a rat or the vagina.

Roger Moore *Snore* When a woman hasn't slept because of the non-stop 'rogering' of her old man she won't necessarily have a smile on her face in the morning. Based on a British actor who may or may not be prone to noisy 'Bo Peeping' (qv).

Rogering Iron An ancient term for the penis.

Rogue & Villain *Shilling* An old monetary piece that is well and truly spent.

Roland Rat *Pratt* An obnoxious or foolish person is known as a 'Roland', due to a TV puppet.

Roland Young *Tongue* A 1940s term based on a British actor (1887–1953) who made his name in Hollywood and had it hijacked in London's East End. A man with one of those faces whose name is on the tip of your 'Roland'.

Roll/Roll Up A hand-made cigarette, one that may or may not contain drugs.

Roll/Spin/Turn Over Three different ways the police have of searching a place. They 'roll a drum', 'spin a gaff' or 'turn a place over'.

Roll To rob someone, originally a drunk, one who had passed out or was 'sleeping it off'. The hapless victims were literally rolled over so that their pockets could be emptied. The term has evolved so that it now applies to a mugging. 'Queer rolling' – robbing homosexuals.

Roll Me in the Dirt	*Shirt*	Doubtful if anyone has worn a 'roll me' since the 19th century.
Roll Me in the Gutter	*Butter*	A piece from World War One that was probably last heard sometime before World War Two.
Roller		A sticky bogie, one that cannot be easily flicked away and has to be rolled dry.
Rolling		Unable to walk straight through drink, legless.
Rolling Billow	*Pillow*	A piece that has ebbed and flowed for donkey's, but is probably washed up now.
Rolling Stone(s)	*Bone(s)*	An example from the 1970s, before the boys in the band made old 'rollings'. A comment heard after the Queen Mother swallowed a fishbone for the second time: 'The old girl can't eat a lump of Lillian without getting a Rolling Stone in her nanny.' *See* LILLIAN GISH *and* NANNY GOAT.
Rollmops	*Cops*	The police, by way of pickled herrings.
Rollock		To reprimand. To get a 'rollocking' is a polite way of getting a 'bollocking', although it can be just as severe. 'Rollocks' – the testicles, a less offensive version of 'bollocks'.
Rolls Royce	*Voice*	Applies, naturally enough, to a superior singing voice.
Rolly		A coughed-up and spat-out lump of phlegm. What nasty footballers aim at each other.
Roman Candle		A juvenile term for a Roman Catholic.
Roman Candle	*Sandal*	An old piece that fits like a glove for the footwear of the ancients.
Roman Collar		An oversized head on a glass of Guinness, a piece from an Irish pub based on a priest's collar.
Romantic Ballad	*Salad*	Based perhaps on 'The Green Leaves of Summer' or the 'Green Green Cress of Home' maybe.
Ronan Keating	*Meeting*	Business people go from one 'Ronan' to another, courtesy of an Irish singer.
Ronk		A bad smell, a northern term possibly a combination of reek and honk.
Ronnie Barker	*Marker (Pen)*	A piece that was used in betting shops in the 1970s, when this British comedian was at the height of his comic powers and the board-man hadn't been replaced by a wallful of television screens. Results and prices were marked up by hand with a 'Ronnie'.
Ronnie Biggs	*Digs (Lodgings)*	Named after one of the Great Train Robbers of 1963 who, not satisfied with his own living conditions in Wandsworth prison, escaped to find fresh 'Ronnies' in Brazil.
Ronson		A 1950s term for a pimp. Based on a cigarette lighter company and said to be rhyming slang for a 'ponce' (qv).

Ronson Lighter   *Shiter (Anus)*   An example from the 1990s that's responsible for the expression 'up your Ronson!'

Roof   An old term for the head that's still heard in connection with the slightly mad. A person with a 'leaky roof' has a 'couple of slates missing'.

Rookery Nook   *Book*   A 1920s term based on an Aldwych farce of the period. Apart from what you are holding, 'rookerys' were also made at racecourses by 'Joe Rookies' (qv).

Rooster   a) A general reference to a man: 'Who's that rooster staring at?'

b) A predatory and dominant male homosexual, one who preys on 'chickens' (qv, b).

Root   The penis, especially when erect, hence to have a 'Root On' – to have an erection. From this extension, to 'root' – is a well-used term for sexual intercourse.

Rooti   Bread, an example that was brought back by soldiers serving in India, where they would have eaten a loaf called a roti.

Root For   To support, to cheer for, to encourage.

Rope   a) A large penis. Well-endowed men are said to have a lot of 'rope'. Sometimes 'barge rope'.

b) Marijuana, an old drug user's term based on the resemblance of hemp and rope.

Rory O'More   *a) Door*   An ancient entry that's still in constant use. Probably coined by 19th-century Irish navvies employed in London, as it is based on one of the leaders of the Catholic rebels of the Ulster revolt of 1641.

   b) Floor   Apart from what you stand on, drop your dinner on and what lifts stop on, this is often used in a sense of destitution. When you are 'on the Rory' you are as low as you can go. This can be taken as an example of secondary slang, *see* ON THE FLOOR, and so by extension 'Rory O'More' also gets in as 'poor'.

   c) Poor   *See previous definition.*

   d) Whore   From the 19th century and obsolete in this sense.

Rose   A virginal vagina, a piece that's been in existence for 200 years and has long been used in the sense of deflowering. A good girl won't allow her rose to be plucked until she's married.

Roseanne Barr   *Bra*   A 1990s example based on a larger than life American comedienne with the larger than average underwear.

Rosebud   *Spud*   An old term that commonly sees potatoes mashed to 'roses'. Also applies to a hole in the heel of a sock, for which 'spud' is an ancient piece of slang.

Roses Red	*Bed*	Sounds like a painful experience, diving into 'roses'.
Rosie Lee	*Tea*	An evergreen term for the drink with which the English wash down the world's troubles.
Rosie Loader	*Soda*	A piece from the 1950s that generally relates to a whisky and soda.
Rosie O'Grady	*Lady*	From a 1943 film and song title, this oldish term now seems only to relate to the ladies' toilet as the 'Rosie O'Grady's' or 'Rosies'.
Rotcod		A doctor. A backslang sawbones.
Rotgut		Cheap and nasty alcohol, commonly 'rotgut whisky'.
Rotpot		A rascal, an inoffensive and often jocular term for a minor 'baddie'.
Rotten		Very drunk, a common piece that's sometimes embellished to 'rotten as a mouldy pear'.
Rotten Row	a) *Bow*	A 19th-century piece that was probably used ironically about an area of East London. Rotten Row in London's Hyde Park would have been full of swells on horseback and Bow full of scruffbags in barefeet. The term is obsolete in that sense but it has been used in reference to a ribbon and more recently to a bow-tie.
	b) *Blow*	An old reference to a whack, but the police still fetch hefty Rotten Rows to the heads of rioters.
Rotter		A thoroughly bad person, commonly the villain of a film.
Rough Trade		a) A violent or sadistic customer of a prostitute. b) A violent, uncouth or working-class homosexual, a term from the 1930s, when homosexuality was perceived as being an upper-class thing.
Rough-House		a) A pub or club that is known for disorder and violence. b) Boisterous behaviour, often on a sports field, e.g., a football match that is littered with fouls. c) A brawl, what a boxing match will often turn into. Also to 'rough-house' someone is to man-handle them.
Round of Applause		A venereal disease. The 'clap' you can do without after a sexual performance.
Round the Houses	*Trousers*	A very old and well-worn piece that's usually dropped to 'round de's'. Sometimes given as 'Round Me Houses', which gets shortened to 'round me's'.
Round the Twist		Crazy, mad or insane. A play on the well-known 'round the bend'.
Round the World		Prostitute's jargon for oral stimulation of the whole body, including the anus.

Roundeye		The anus, one of several terms to make an anal-optical analogy.
Roundhead		A circumcised penis and also an expression for a man who owns one.
Row In		To allow someone to join or to include them in something, whether they like it or not: 'I've been rowed into a darts match and I couldn't hit the Millennium Dome with a spear.'
Row Out		To bar someone or exclude them from something: 'I wanted to join their lotto syndicate but they rowed me out, so bad luck to 'em.'
Rowton Houses	*Trousers*	A piece that gets tapered to 'Rowtons' after Baron Rowton (1838–1903), and the lodging houses for ragged-arsed men that he founded.
Roy Castle	*Arsehole*	The name of a British entertainer (1932–94) lives on as the 'reeking Roy Castle' of a persistent wind-breaker.
Roy Hudd	*a) Spud*	Baked or boiled, roasted or raw, any potato is a 'Roy Hudd'. Based on a British comedian, actor, writer and life-long devotee of comedy, he now achieves a kind of immortality as a King Edward.
	b) Blood	Only heard this once but the story is worth telling. A less than funny comedian was struggling to get laughs in an East End pub on a Sunday lunchtime. He was heckled, abused and harrassed by an unruly audience and somebody or other would yell out the punch line of every joke he tried to tell. In the end it all became too much for him and, unable to take any more, he held up his handkerchief as a white flag of surrender, which incurred even more derision. With a tear in his eye he pleaded with his tormentors. 'Look,' he said, 'I'm doing my best. What do you want, Roy Hudd?' 'Yes,' replied a wag and promptly launched a light ale bottle in the direction of the funny man's head. He never appeared there again.
Roy Rogers	*Bodgers*	Applies to rogue or inferior tradesmen, suitably based on the name of a western film star who was billed as the King of the Cowboys (1912–98).
Royal Docks	*Pox (VD)*	Apart from the disease this also applies to being irritated by a situation. Long stationary motorists on the M25 may utter 'I've got the right Royal Docks of this.'
Royal Mail	*Bail*	Almost exclusively the property of the criminal fraternity, but then I suppose it would be.
Royal Navy	*Gravy*	An alternative to the more common 'army and navy' (qv) which may be based on the adage 'the navy gets the gravy but the army gets the beans'.

Royal Salute		Twenty-one, a bingo term but also heard in the game of pontoon. Based on the 21 gun salute afforded the queen on her birthday.
Royal, do a		To turn Queens Evidence, an underworld term.
Rozzer		A well-known term for a police officer since the 19th century.
Rub		To masturbate, a well-known euphemism for 'wank' (qv). Commonly heard in connection with anything useless, or 'not worth a rub'.
Rub Down		To search, an underworld term for a police activity.
Rub Out		To murder or assassinate, a task that may be taken on by a 'rubber' – a professional killer.
Rub-a-Dub-Dub(s)	a) *Club(s)*	Refers to any type of club, including a social, a working man's or a nightclub. Also applies to the suit in a deck of cards.
	b) *Pub*	Taken from a nursery rhyme about three men in a boat, this enjoys wide usage, often as a 'rub-a' or a 'rub-a-dub'. Sometimes given as 'Rub-A-Di-Dub' which breaks down to a 'rubbidy'.
	c) *Sub*	A infrequent rival to 'rhubarb' (qv) in regard to an advance on wages or a loan.
Rubber		a) The well-worn term for a condom, itself originally a slang term in the form of a 'cundum', which in the 18th century, was made of the dried gut of a sheep. b) A car tyre, hence to 'burn rubber' – to drive.
Rubber Boot/ Johnny/Jump Suit		A packet of three assorted anti-grief sheaths, i.e., condoms.
Rubber Cheque/ Kite		A worthless cheque, one that bounces. *See* BOUNCER *and* KITE.
Rubber Duck	*Fuck*	Mostly used in a sense of not caring, for 'couldn't give a fuck' read 'couldn't give a rubber duck'. Possibly from 'Convoy', a hit record for American singer C W McCall in 1976 in which the term was the call sign for a truck driver on his CB radio. Occasionally used for the sex act.
Rubber Glove	*Love*	A 1990s term that smacks of fetishism.
Rubber Heel		A sneak, someone who spies on fellow employees. In the police it's a member of the unit that investigates irregularities among its own officers.
Rubik's Cubes	*Pubes*	A famous puzzle from the 1970s finds it's way into peoples underwear as pubic hair. It's awful painful to catch your 'Rubiks' in your zip.
Rub-Off		An act of masturbation: 'He was watching a dirty video with headphones on, having a rub-off. Course, he didn't hear the door open and in walks

his wife, his mother-in-law and two women who'd been invited in for coffee.'

Ruby Murray   *Curry*   Based on the name of an Irish singer (1935–96) who is as famous today as a vindaloo as she was in 1955 when she had five records in the hit parade at the same time.

Ruby Red   *Head*   A World War One term which may have something to do with *vin rouge* and the hangovers it would have given the soldiers who drank it.

Ruby Rose   *Nose*   An old term that's always truncated to 'Ruby', which may be apt in the case of a drinker's bugle (qv).

Ruck   a) A fight or a serious argument, a term that's long been synonymous with football violence. Never mind the ball, get on with the ruck, so to speak.
b) To give someone a severe reprimand, hence, to be rebuked is to receive a 'rucking'.

Ruck & Row   *Cow*   Refers to a disagreeable woman, not the animal. Usually reduced to the first element and prefaced with 'old', as in 'the old ruck next door'.

Rucking   See RUCK (b).

Ructions   Serious consequences of a violent or reproachful nature: 'There'll be ructions when she finds out I've lost half my wages on a pig that was disguised as a bloody greyhound.'

Ruddy   An inoffensive euphemism for 'bloody', often heard, unrealistically, in British films of the pre-permissive era.

Rudolph   A red nose, the result of excessive drinking or pulling sleighs full of toys across the sky on icy winter nights.

Rudolph Hess   *Mess*   A post World War Two term based on the high-ranking Nazi (1894–1987) that is representative of failure. 'He's made right Rudolph of that!' – as Hitler might have bellowed after his deputy's bid for Anglo-German peace ended with Hess being bunged in the Tower.

Rug   A wig or toupee. A well-known piece for a 'skull carpet' as worn by a 'rughead'.

Rug Rat   A small child. A 1970s term for a baby that's at the crawling stage. Also known as a 'rug bug'.

Rugger Ball   Nothing. The spoonerised version of 'bugger all': 'It's got rugger ball to do with you.'

Ruin & Spoil   *Oil*   Fittingly shortened to 'ruin' and probably coined in the wake of the environmental damage caused when an oil tanker runs aground.

Ruined   Very drunk or under the influence of drugs.

Rumble		a) A well-known term for a fight, either a 'one on one go' or a gang fight. b) To find out about, to discover, especially of someone up to no good. 'Rumbled' – found out. c) A fart, a rare term for a common outburst.
Rump		To copulate, an example that's been representing the 'old in and out' for a century or more.
Rumpo		Sex. A euphemism well-known in British comedy with the likes of Sidney James' Rumpo Kid in the film *Carry On Cowboy* and Kenneth Williams' Rambling Sid Rumpo character.
Rumptitum	*Bum*	An old term for the buttocks and known as the 'rumpti', which is probably an extension of rump.
Rumpy-Pumpy		Sex. A piece that's commonly heard on TV and seen in the papers in reports of who has been up to what, and with whom.
Run/Rush		The initial sensation of injecting heroin.
Run of the Green		To drive along a road and have every traffic light in your favour, as opposed to catching them all at red, which is known as a 'bollockache', among other things.
Run Some Off		To urinate, to run some water off.
Runner		An escape, hence the common 'do a runner'. Also applies to an escapee.
Runner & Rider	*Cider*	Sounds as though this could have been formed on a West-Country racecourse.
Run-Off		Urination: 'He won't be long, he's just gone for a run-off.'
Runs		Diarrhoea, from the way the stuff leaves the body and the way we enter the lavatory.
Rupert		A name given to any upper-class male, especially an army officer.
Rupert Bears	*Shares*	A 1980s term that arose after the sell-off of some of the nationalised industries, putting 'Ruperts' in the hands of the general public. Based on the ever-popular children's cartoon character.
Rush		To overcharge or swindle: 'How much did they rush you for that?'
Russell Crowe	*Dough*	A 21st-century term for money based on an award-winning Australian film star who will never be short of 'Russell'.
Russell Harty	*Party*	A knees-up courtesy of an English TV personality (1934–88).
Russian Duck	a) *Fuck* b) *Muck*	A 1950s expression for sexual intercourse. An early 20th-century term for dirt or grime which got scrubbed long before the 21st.

Russians Are Coming		Premenstrual tension, a sign that a period is on the way. For Russians read 'reds' (qv).
Russian-Turk	*Work*	A mid 19th-century term that has long been unemployed.
Rust		Copper coins, a piece that made the change in 1971 from old to new pennies.
Rust Bucket		An old dilapidated car, originally an old ship.
Ruttat/Rettat		A potato, a backslang 'tatur' or 'tater'.
Ruud Gullit	*Bullet (Dismissal)*	A 1990s term which reflects this Dutch international footballer's headline making sacking from his post as Chelsea player-manager in 1998.
Ryach		A chair, somewhere to sit in backslang.
Ryan Giggs	*Digs (Lodgings)*	A 1990s alternative to the older 'Ronnie Biggs' (qv). Based on a Welsh international footballer who will never have to scour the streets in search of a room.
Ryan's Daughter	*Water*	A term that quickly followed the 1970 screening of a film with this title.

S

S & M	Prostitutes and porn merchant's jargon for sado-masochism.
SP	Based on Starting Price, the returned price of a horse or greyhound, 'the SP' has become a popular euphemism for the information, the facts, the situation, etc.: 'How d'you expect me to help you unless you give me the full SP?'
Sab	To sabotage, a piece from the 1980s, a time of much activity by animal rights campaigners and hunt saboteurs or 'sabs'. 'Sabbing' – sabotaging.
Sabu	A 1940s term for an Indian person based on the name of a boy actor (Sabu Dastagir, 1924–63) who became famous as the Elephant Boy, which was the title of his first film.
Saccharino	A false, ingratiating person, one who only 'smiles for the cameras'. Literally someone who, like saccharin, is artificially sweet.
Sack	a) A well-known expression for a bed, the weary have been 'hitting the sack' since the 19th century. b) An ancient term for a pocket, generations of thieves have 'dipped a sack'. 'Sack it' – put something in your pocket.
Sack of Shit	What a scruffy, unwashed person is said to resemble.

Sack Race	*Face*	No nice mooey this, a miserable or angry face may draw the comment: 'Look at the sack on it.'
Sacks of Rice	*Mice*	An old term from the docks, where ships carrying the term would have given passage to stowaway rodents.
Sad		Lonely, pathetic, boring, etc. 'How sad is that Alan? He's reading a book about phone boxes.'
Sad & Sorry	*Lorry*	A rueful-sounding piece that may touch on the loneliness of the long distance driver.
Sad Sack		A thoroughly negative person. A miserable, pessimistic loser. Originally and still largely an American piece that started off in the army as a 'sad sack of shit', referring to a useless soldier.
Saddam Hussein	*Pain*	A 1990s term based on the deposed Iraqi leader who had long been a pain in the arse of the world.
Saddlebags		a) A crude term from the 1990s for the labia majora. b) An over-large scrotum, one that could fit over the back of a pack mule.
Saddo		A lonely, unfashionable, boring person. Someone with a mundane existence who 'should get out more'. A 'sad git'.
Sadie & Maisie		Sado-masochism, more commonly known as 'S & M' (qv).
Safe & Sound	*Ground*	Possibly coined by a nervous air traveller whose only wish was to get his feet back on the 'safe'.
Saffy Eyes		Puffy, baggy or sleepy eyes, especially those belonging to someone suffering with a hangover.
Sailors at Sea	*Tea*	A long-winded piece that's only ever poured as 'sailors'.
Saint & Sinner	*Dinner*	Connotations of Sunday dinner, when the saint cooks it and the sinner goes up the pub, has a skinful, comes home, wolfs his meal then crashes out in the armchair.
Saint Moritz	*Shits*	A 1960s term for diarrhoea which may have something to do with the Cresta Runs.
Salad Dodger		A 1990s expression for a fat person, one who's happy to be so.
Salford Docks	*Rocks*	A piece of nautical slang for those navigational hazards around the coastline.
Salisbury Crag	*Skag (Heroin)*	A 1980s piece based on a landmark outside Edinburgh.
Sally Gunnell	*Tunnel*	Mostly heard in connection with Blackwall Tunnel which runs beneath the Thames between Poplar and Greenwich. Based on a world-beating athlete from Essex who, despite her retirement from the track, will forever run underground.

Salmon & Shrimp	*Pimp*	A version of 'fish and shrimp' (qv) that seems to be based on the flavour of a fish paste. Apt when you consider the 'fishy money boxes' he looks after.
Salmon & Trout	a) *Gout*	In this guise the term is as rare as a tap-dancing sufferer of the disease.
	b) *Snout*	Applies to snout in all it's senses, i.e., the nose, an informer, tobacco or a cigarette.
	c) *Stout*	Refers to this type of beer rather than the waistline that may occur through drinking it.
	d) *Tout*	Originally a racecourse term regarding somebody selling information, it now also applies to those who sell overpriced tickets.
Salome		The biblical dancing girl gives her name to an unhurried, dawdling person. Someone 'too salow to catch a cold': 'Come on Salome, keep up.'
Salt		a) Dandruff, a term from the early 1960s when 'salty shoulders' were a common sight on jackets and blazers.
		b) Heroin, a drug user's term from the 1970s.
		c) An ancient term for a mariner. An old salt is a career sailor.
Salt/Sort		A girl, a piece that's generally used to describe a very attractive one as 'a bit of a salt/sort'. Not sure of the origin or which spelling is correct as they both sound the same in the East End. An informant tells me it's RS, 'Salt Fish' – a dish. But I dunno.
Salt Beef	*Thief*	A sometimes used alternative to 'tea leaf' (qv).
Salt Cellars		The cavity above a woman's collar bone, a term that's famously heard in Tony Hancock's 'The Blood Donor', when he describes models as 'all bones and salt cellars'.
Salt Junk	*Drunk*	Quite well-known in the reduced form of 'salted', which is very old and based on the salted beef fed to soldiers of a previous era.
Salt Water		Tears, hence the prophecy of disaster: 'You watch, it'll all end in salt water.'
Salted		Drunk, an old term along the lines of 'pickled'.
Saltee		The Polari term for a penny, once commonly heard in cockney markets.
Salvadore Dali	*Charlie (Cocaine)*	Based on the Spanish artist (1904–89) and known only as 'Salvadore', this originally went up the noses of arty types before the great unwashed took to snorting it.
Salvation	*Station*	The railway or underground variety. This is an early reference to where the Lord's name is uttered in temper by more people than anywhere else.

Salvation Army	*Barmy*	Nearly always truncated to 'sally army' in regard to someone who may be a brick short of a wall.
Sam Cory	*Story*	An old example from the docks that is based, apparently, on an actual docker who probably had a name for telling whoppers.
Samantha Eggar	*Beggar*	Based on a British actress, this 1990s term relates to the professional beggars who haunt the London Underground. 'Samanthas' are typically woeful-looking foreign women with babe in arm and an outstretched hand.
Samantha Janus	*Anus*	A 'noughties' (qv) term based on a British actress which acts as another example of where the unwanted can be banished to: 'You can stick your job up your Samantha.'
Sambo		A derogatory term for a black person.
Sammo/Sammy/ Sammy Widge/ Sanger		A selection of sandwiches.
Sammy Halls	*Balls (Testicles)*	An old piece based on the eponymous villain of a song from the music-hall era.
Sammy Lee	*Pee/Wee*	Yet another of the clan Lee makes the water ejection connection. This time an England international footballer of the 1980s gets to splash his boots.
Sample		Urine, a term that made a splash on TV. To 'give a sample' is to urinate. To 'take a sample' is to mock in the same way as to 'take the piss'.
Samuel Pepys	*Creeps*	The English diarist (1633–1703) comes in to give a feeling of unease. A place or a person may give you the 'Samuels'.
San Fairy Ann		A World War One term from the French 'Ca ne fait rien', which translates to 'It makes no difference' or it doesn't matter. If it's 'all San Fairy Ann', you can 'forget it'.
San Toy	*Boy*	Based on the name of an early 20th-century play, this specifically relates to a gang member, 'one of the San Toys', who is probably a villain.
Sancho		A homosexual male. A piece that sees the sidekick of Don Quixote, Sancho Panza, become Sancho Pansy.
Sand		Sugar, presumably the brown variety.
Sandras		A 1990s term for the testicles based on the name of an American film actress, Sandra Bullock, who is almost a 'bollock'.
Sandwich		Three-in-a-bed sex. Any combination makes a sandwich but ideally two women and a man.

Sandy McNab	a) *Cab*	A post-war term for a taxi, which is known by the christian name.
	b) *Crab* (Louse)	A piece that's generally known in the plural: 'Stop scratching, you look like you've got Sandy McNabs.' Based on the offspring of Mr and Mrs McNab, a couple famous for having a child in a slang dictionary.
Sandy Powell	a) *Towel*	A 1940s term for a 'drier' based on a northern comedian (1900–82) much heard at the time on the wireless.
	b) *Trowel*	The bricklayer's tool, so rarely heard off the building site.
Santa Claus	*Paws (Hands)*	Mostly used in the warning to 'keep your Santas off'.
Santa's Grotto	*Blotto (Drunk)*	When you go in too heavy on the 'Christmas Cheer' (qv), you'll end up 'Santas'.
Sap		a) A fool or simpleton, originally a 'sapskull' – someone who is soft in the head. An idiot may now be known as a 'saphead' and described as 'sappy'. b) Semen, hence to 'spew one's sap' – to ejaculate.
Sarah Gamp	*Lamp*	A post-war term from the theatre based on a character from Dickens' *Martin Chuzzlewit*, the woman who also gave her name to an umbrella.
Sarnie		A northern term for a sandwich that's now been swallowed up by the rest of the country.
Sass		Originally an American term for cheek, sauce or back-chat. To 'sass' is to answer back. 'Sassy' – saucy. The term arrived in Britain via TV.
Satin & Lace	*Face*	No ugly mug this, it would seem.
Satin & Silk	*Milk*	An ad-man's dream of a term, describing the richness and smoothness of 'cow juice'.
Sauce		a) A well-known term for alcohol. 'On the sauce' – on the booze. b) Semen. To 'pour one's sauce' – to ejaculate: 'I pulled out and poured my sauce down her belly-button.'
Saucepan Lid	a) *Kid*	Children are always known as 'saucepans', be they your own little darlings or the little pests playing 'knock down ginger'. Also employed in the guise of deception, the mock innocent plea of a con man may include: 'Would I try to saucepan you?'
	b) *Quid*	A 'saucepan' is an oft-quoted term for £1.
	c) *Yid*	A not uncommon piece, although one of many for a Jew.
Sausage		An ancient term for the penis that's still cooking.
Sausage & Mash	a) *Cash*	A widely used piece, although most people don't realise they are using truncated RS when they state

		that they 'haven't got a sausage'. To 'sausage a goose's' – to cash a cheque. *See* GOOSE'S NECK.
	b) Crash/ Smash	Cab driver's jargon for a road traffic accident: 'I saw a nasty sausage on the M25 today.'
Sausage Roll	*a) Dole*	Unemployed people have long been 'on the sausage'.
	b) Pole	Applies in all senses of the word, Eastern European athletes excel in the 'sausage vault', enraged people are 'driven up the sausage' and it's also a Polish person.
	c) Poll (Head)	A piece from the early 1990s that chiefly concerned the hated poll tax, or 'sausage tax'. We may also comb our 'sausages'.
Sausage Sandwich		Take a 'sausage' (qv), place between two breasts and, if she knows her onions, 'sauce' (qv) will pour. *See also* TIT-WANK.
Saveloy	*Boy*	Used to describe a small boy but sometimes as a rival gang member to a 'San Toy' (qv).
Saver		A bet placed to safeguard one's money on another bet. If you have a lot riding on the last leg of an accumulator, you can afford to back against the selection so that you can't lose. *See* ROD LAVER.
Savoury Rissole	*Piss Hole*	Refers, naturally enough, to a lavatory, but not exclusively. Any place that can be described as a dump, or a carsey, be it a pub, club, town or even a country, can be a 'savoury'.
Sawbones		A 19th-century term for a surgeon, especially a naval or army doctor for whom amputation during a battle was common practice. The piece is still widely used.
Sawney		Silly, daft or foolish: 'With a bit more sense he'd be sawney.'
Say		Yes, the affirmative in backslang.
Say/Sey		The Polari version of the number 6, from the Italian *sei*.
Say Goodbye	*Die*	As fitting as any term in the book since it's what we'll all do one day.
Say Goodbye/ Goodnight to		To write off, to accept as lost. When your horse is tailed off coming to the last jump you can say goodbye to your money.
Scab		The well-known term for a strike-breaker or someone who refuses to join a trade union. A piece that started out centuries ago as a worthless, good-for-nothing person.
Scabbard		The vagina, an obvious piece when the penis is known as a 'sword' (qv).

S

Scabby Eye	*Pie*	Usually a fat and gristle pie bought from a chip shop.
Scaffold Board		What a person of low intelligence is said to be as thick as. Someone said to have less brains than a shrunken head.
Scaffolding		A recent term among the young for braces, the teeth-straightening device.
Scag/Skag		Heroin, a drug user's term from the 1960s.
Scally		A piece from Liverpool for a young man who may range from a loveable rogue to a hooligan. A dislengthening of the old American term for a rascal, 'scallywag'.
Scalp		a) To sell tickets at above face value, a 19th-century term for what a 'scalper' (ticket-tout) still gets away with. b) A wig, a rare but appropriate piece.
Scalping		A short haircut, a term from the days before skin-heads. Teddy Boys claimed they'd been 'scalped' when their quiffs went under the scissors of National Service barbers.
Scaly-Back		A treacherous, untrustworthy person. A snake. Often extended to 'scaly-backed reptile'.
Scam		Originally an American term for a con-trick, swindle or fraud that is now commonly heard here.
Scapa Flow	*Go*	Meaning a hasty exit, 'scapa' has long held a place in the annals of RS. It is however just as likely to be an example of Polari, the theatrical slang based on Italian, in which *scappare* means to run away. Scapa Flow is a stretch of sea in the Orkney Islands where 71 surrendered German warships were scuttled on 21 June 1919. *See* SCARPER.

Scarborough Fair	*Hair*	A 1970s piece formed on the title of a Simon & Garfunkel song of the period. Two men heard discussing a barmaid:
		  1st Man: 'I like her Scarborough, don't you?'
		  2nd Man: 'Yeah, but I wouldn't want it in my dinner.'

Scarper		To run away, an example of Polari based on the Italian *scappare* – to escape.
Scatter Gun		The anus, especially when its owner has diarrhoea. *See* SCATTERS.
Scatters		A bout of diarrhoea. A sufferer may complain of having 'an arse like the Japanese flag'.
Scavvy		A scaffolder, a term from the building site.
Scene		a) A preference or predilection. But if it's not to your liking, then it's 'not your scene'.

b) The current trend, the in thing, a dated term from the 1960s when a 'scene' was also a party.

Schindler's List *Pissed* A 1990s piece for insobriety following the award-winning film with this title. Usually half cut at 'Schindlers'.

Schlemiel/ Shlemiel A clumsy, unfortunate misfit, a twerp. A Yiddish example of a square peg in a round hole.

Schlemiels on Wheels Bad or reckless drivers, motorcyclists or cyclists. A pun on the Meals on Wheels service.

Schlemozzle/ Shlemozzle A luckless, accident-prone wretch. The type to be butted by a bull while picking a four-leaf clover.

Schlep/Shlep a) A long distance, a run in the parlance of taxi drivers: 'I like a schlep in the country from time to time, it's good to get out of town for a while.'
b) To go, to travel. Often used when sending someone on an errand: 'Schlep over the offie for me and get me some fags.'

Schlepper/ Shlepper An errand boy, a 'gofor' (qv). See SCHLEP (b).

Schlob/Shlob See SCHLUB.

Schlock/Shlock Rubbish, tat, inferior goods. Generally anything that's cheap and nasty or tasteless. 'Schlock Value' – the only value of something is in its total badness. Often said of a film.

Schlong/Shlong The penis, from *schlang*, the Yiddish word for a snake.

Schlub/Shlub A coarse, ill-mannered, uneducated person. Also said as 'schlob', hence 'slob' (qv).

Schluck/Shluck A clumsy, cackhanded, uncoordinated fool. A cross between a 'Schlemozzle' and a 'Shmuck'.

Schmaltz/ Shmaltz Mawkish sentimentality, especially of a film, play, song, etc. 'Schmaltzy' – sickly, oily behaviour. From the Yiddish word for dripping or lard.

Schmeck/Shmeck A taste or flavour, much like the English 'smack'.

Schmecken/ Schmecker Drugs. A 1940s term which saw heroin as 'Schmeck'.

Schmo/Shmo A fool, often used in self-deprecation: 'I suppose Joe Schmo's got to pay the bill as usual.'

Schmock/ Shmock An obnoxious person, or a fool. The Yiddish version of 'prick' (qv).

Schmootz/ Schmutz Dirt, dust, grease or grime, it's all 'schmootz': 'You want me to eat here? A restaurant with wall to wall shmutz?'

Schmooze/ Shmooze To flatter or soft-soap. To give someone a load of 'flannel' (qv). 'Schmoozer' – a flatterer.

Schmuck/ Shmuck The penis, from the Yiddish word for the male member, and like 'schmock' it becomes a fool.

Well-known in the saying: 'You don't have to be Jewish to be a schmuck.'

Schmutter/ Shmutter
From the Yiddish, *shmatte* (a rag), comes this well-known term for clothes. A well-made suit is often termed 'a nice piece of schmutter'.

Schnickel/ Shnickel
The penis, especially when flaccid: 'My old man? He hasn't waved his shnickel in anger for years. Not at me anyway.'

Schnook/Shnook
A fool, a dupe. The sucker who shouldn't be given an even break.

Schnorrer/ Shnorrer
A beggar or scrounger, layabout or loafer. A Yiddish 'mumper' (qv).

Schnozz/ Schnozzle/ Schnozzola
A trio of well-known terms for the nose, generally an ample one. Based on *schnauze* – German for snout. The term is forever associated with the US comedian Jimmy 'Schnozzle' Durante (1893–1980).

School
An old term for prison but now more confined to borstal. *See also* COLLEGE.

Schvartzer/ Shvartzer
A black person, a piece that derives from the German *schwartz*. Sometimes said as 'shvartz'.

Sclerry
An unsympathetic term from the 1990s regarding an alcoholic, one likely to incur sclerosis of the liver.

Sconner
A 1990s term for someone devoid of pubic hair.

Scooby Doo *a) Screw*
A piece of prisoner's slang for one of HM's turnkeys. Based on a cowardly dog from a TV cartoon series.

b) Clue
A modern piece that usually reflects somebody's ineptitude: 'The idiot ain't got a Scooby.'

Scope
The penis, a term from the 1960s that's an abridged periscope, that which goes up.

Scoper
A spastic, a 21st-century term based on the spastic charity SCOPE.

Scorch
To deliberately set fire to something, especially for a bogus insurance claim. 'Scorching' – arson.

Score
a) The most common term for £20, many people never say 'twenty pounds'.
b) To obtain something, especially drugs.
c) To make a sexual conquest, once solely of a man, but nowadays women 'score' too.

Scotch Egg(s) *Leg(s)*
A rival to the well-known 'scotch peg' (qv), the difference being that that this is always used in full.

Scotch Mist *Pissed*
An ultra-familiar piece that's never half cut. Drunks are always 'scotch mist'.

Scotch Peg(s) *Leg(s)*
An example that's been running in the truncated form of 'scotches' since the 19th century.

Scotland the Brave	*Shave*	Always reduced to a 'Scotland', as in the conversation between a barmaid and a customer who has had a severe haircut: *Her: 'Not much 'air about.'* *Him: 'No. You should Scotland more often.'*
Scotsman		£9. A 1930s term used by racecourse bookmakers, Scots would try to pass off nine one-pound notes as a tenner.
Scouring Powder		Cocaine, a term probably only used by those who don't use it.
Scouse		Second rate, inferior, no good to man, beast or plant. A unique piece in that it is reverse rhyming slang. 'Mickey Mouse' in RS is scouse, but in normal slang it means second rate or inferior, so a 'Mickey Mouse' organisation is now a 'scouse' firm.
Scrag		a) The neck, especially the thin, scrawny neck of an old person: 'I had a row with that scraggy-necked old crone next door today.' Elderly actresses tend to wrap scarves round theirs. b) To handle roughly, to beat up. At schoolboy level, first years are 'playfully' scragged as part of their initiation. c) To strangle, a piece that started out as a term for the hangman's noose. The hangman was known as a 'scragger'.
Scraggy Lou	*Flu*	How a woman who normally takes a pride in her appearance may describe herself when riddled with flu germs: 'I've got the scraggy Lou and I look like her.' Based on a lady of scraggy appearance and called Lou.
Scrambled Egg		The gold braid on a senior officer's cap, and therefore the officer himself. Commonly heard of high-ranking policemen.
Scrambled Egg(s)	*Leg(s)*	Typically used in terms of inebriation, when drunks stagger home on 'scrambled eggs'.
Scran		A very old but still common term for food. 'Top scran' – a good meal.
Scrap/Scrap Iron		Loose change. 'Iron' (qv) is an old term for coins, 'scrap iron' is the littlest in value.
Scrap Metal	*Kettle*	An example from the 1950s that's apt in that it's what old kettles ended up as.
Scrape		a) A pre-electric razor term for a shave that's still about. 'Scraper' – a barber. b) Butter, an old and widely spread example, the well-known partner of bread.

Scratch	An old term for money that's now mostly heard in connection with small change, often a tip. 'Leave a bit of scratch for the waitress.'
Scratch House	A cheap hotel or boarding house, one where the bedbugs bite.
Scratcher	A scratch-card, a piece originally heard in Ireland, which caught on in an instant.
Scream	An appeal against a conviction, to 'put in a scream'.
Screamer	An overt or outrageous homosexual, a reduction of 'screaming queen'.
Screaming Abdabs	A well-known expression of extreme nervousness, the horrors or the creeps.
Screeve	A forged document, a 'fakement'. As drawn up by a 'screever' – a forger.
Screever	A pavement artist, a chalker. From the Italian *scrivare* – to write, which is fitting as some of the best 'screevers' ply their trade outside the Duomo in Milan. The term also applies to someone who specialises in begging letters and to a forger, *see* SCREEVE.
Screw	a) Sexual intercourse, a well-known expression that doubles as a partner in sex. He, but more commonly she, may be a 'good screw'.
	b) An old underworld term for a key and also to rob a building by using a key to gain entry.
	c) A prison officer, a piece that derives from (b), which saw a turnkey evolve into a 'turnscrew'.
	d) An income. Anyone earning good wages is said to be on a 'good screw'.
	e) A common euphemism for 'fuck', whereby to 'screw' is to copulate. Also to 'screw up' is to mess or fuck-up and 'screw you!' is a contemptuous dismissal.
	f) To stare at, especially in a provocative manner. Many a fight has followed the question: 'Who are you screwing?'
	g) To break into, originally by use of a key but now a place can be 'screwed' using any means of entry. 'Screwer', 'screwman', 'screwsman' – all appertain to a thief or burglar.
	h) To con, swindle or cheat. Generally, if you've been 'screwed' you've been had over.
Screwball	A mad, zany or eccentric person, originally American but now heard here.
Screwdriver	A prison governor, the person in charge of the 'screws'. See SCREW (c).
Screwdriver *Skiver*	A reference to a person who knows what needs to

		be done and how to get out of doing it. Since the contents of a toolbag are a complete mystery to him, the term doesn't appear to be very apt.
Screws		An old term for rheumatism.
Screwy		Mad, crazy, 'not right'. Also relates to the ambiguous: 'This is screwy this film, I can't make head nor tail of it.'
Scribbins		A replacement word, much like 'gubbins', which is used when the one you are searching for can't be found.
Scribbler		A writer, anyone who makes a living with a pen, from the poet laureate to the crossword compiler with the *Cushion-Stuffer's Monthly*.
Scrike		To cry, a northern term often heard in northern TV dramas. 'Scrikey' – tearful.
Scrimshank		To shirk one's duty, an old military term. 'Scrimshanker' – shirker or slacker.
Scrip/Script		A drug addict's prescription for drugs.
Scroachy		Mouldy, mildewy, covered in anything likely to make you go 'Yeuk!' Presumably the fungal covering itself is known as 'scroach'.
Scrote		An obnoxious, despicable, repellent person. A 1970s term for someone with nothing nice going for him.
Scrubber		A derogatory term for a promiscuous woman that's been hurled abusively at prostitutes and the like for many a moon.
Scruffbag		An untidy, unkempt person. An extension of 'scruff'.
Scruffs		Scruffy clothes for hanging about the house or doing dirty jobs in. Or what slobs go out in.
Scuba Diver	*Fiver*	A fairly recent term for £5 that's happily swimming in the sea of RS.
Scuddy		A 1970s term for anything bad, unpleasant or mouldy. 'Scudbucket' – an obnoxious person.
Scuffer		A police officer, a term that originated in Liverpool and is still mainly heard up north.
Scully & Mulder	*Shoulder*	Something to cry on, courtesy of the partners in TV's *The X Files*, although Mulder scarcely gets a look in.
Scum		Semen, hence to 'come one's scum' – to ejaculate.
Scumbag		a) An odious, repugnant person. The worthless, scum-of-the-Earth type. b) An old term for a condom. *See* SCUM.
Scumsucker		An obnoxious, repellent person, an alternative to 'cocksucker'. *See* SCUM.

Scungy		Dirty, filthy, greasy and horrible. A sort of cross between scummy and gungy.
Sean Connery	*Coronary*	Not sure whether this is admissable as RS, it's more of a pun and is used as a mock warning against getting overexcited and having a heart attack: 'Calm down or you'll have a Sean Connery.' Based on a British actor, famed for his role as James Bond.
Sebastian Coe(s)	*Toe(s)*	Based on a multi-record-breaking British runner, this particularly appropriate example relates to making a swift exit: 'If you see a copper let me know and we'll have it on our Sebastians a bit lively.'
Second-Hand Stamp		A symbol of uselessness: 'You're as much use as a . . .'
See/See Alright		To take care of financially, to tip or bribe. To look after.
Seeing-To		a) Sexual intercourse, an expression used by men to denote a conquest: 'I gave her a good seeing-to or three.'
		b) A beating, a pasting, a thorough bashing.
Seek & Search	*Church*	About as suitable a term as you can get, where man seeks salvation in his search for the Lord.
Seldom Seen	*Queen*	A reference to the present monarch, which seems reasonably apt. Well I've never seen her.
Selina Scott	*Spot*	A pus-filled protuberance, especially on the face of a youth, is a 'Selina'. Based on a British TV personality.
Sell a Dummy		To trick, deceive or lie to. From a rugby player's pretence of passing the ball to fool an opponent, the term has left the pitch and is very common. *See* DUMMY.
Sell a Pup		To con someone by selling them something worthless or faulty. Many a used-car dealer has sold a mongrel as a pedigree.
Seller		A shop. From Harrods to the junk shop by the glue factory, if it flogs things it's a 'seller'.
Semolina	*Cleaner*	Applies to a person who rearranges dust on a professional basis.
Send the Troops In		To ejaculate inside a woman: 'I keep sending the troops in but I can't seem to get her pregnant.'
Sentimental Song	*Pong (Smell)*	Typically used of a young man's living quarters, where unwashed socks, underwear and dishes add to the overall 'sentimental' of the place.
September Morn	*Horn (Erection)*	If your birthday's in June, ask your father about this one.
Septic Tank	*Yank*	If an American is known as a 'septic', is an enemy of Uncle Sam an 'antiseptic'? Cab drivers use the term as 'seppo'.

Sergeant		£3. *See* STRIPE (b).
Setter		The number 7, the lucky number of Polari. Based on the Italian, *sette*.
Settle		To work out a bet. I never realised this was slang, even when I did it for a living, but it's not in the English dictionary so it must be. Now I know why, when I wrote 'settler' as a previous occupation on job applications, I never got a reply. Nobody knew what it was.
Seven & Six	*Fix*	To be in difficulty is to be in a right old 'seven and six', like getting engine trouble and not having the tools to 'seven & six' it.
Seven Dials	*Piles*	An allusion to the painful condition that non-sufferers call 'grapes', based on an area of London close to theatreland, where once dwelled the height of the capital's low-life.
Sex on a Riverbank		Weak beer, especially cheap lager, which is 'fucking near water'.
Sex on a Stick		A sexually attractive but very thin person, usually a female.
Sexton Blake	*a) Cake*	A long-established piece that's based on a fictional detective of comic, book and film fame.
	b) Fake	Refers to a forgery or a copy, especially a painting. Tom Keating, the master copier of old masters, often referred to his works as 'Sexton Blakes'.
Shabba Rank	*Wank*	A 1990s example of masturbation based on the American reggae singer Shabba Ranks.
Shabberoon		A scruffy person, a down-and-out. Sometimes a 'shabberoony'. An extension of shabby.
Shack Up		To live with someone outside marriage, to set up home with.
Shaft		a) An old term for the penis, which doubles as a well-known expression for its procreational function. An incurable romantic will tell you when he's given his girlfriend 'a right good shafting'.
		b) To beat, ruin or swindle. To generally do someone wrong. Commonly used as 'shafted' by those who have been 'fouled'.
Shag		Sexual intercourse, a universal euphemism for 'fuck' that's heard in 'shagging hell', 'shag off', 'shag my old boots', etc.
Shag One's Hand		To masturbate. Or, in the hands of a partner, a 'hand shag'.
Shag-Bag		A prostitute, an old term of military formation.
Shagged Out		Tired, worn out, exhausted. In a word, 'fucked'.
Shaggers Back		A backache, supposedly from too much sex.

Shaggin' Wagon		Same car, different model to the one seen at 'passion wagon' (qv).
Shagnasty		A name given to an unpleasant and unpopular man.
Shake		An ancient term for sexual intercourse, the predecessor of 'shag' (qv). Now only heard in terms of masturbation, as in 'shake oneself' and 'hand shake'. Single men may 'shake hands with the unemployed', while married men 'shake hands with the wife's best friend'.
Shake & Shiver	*River*	A theatrical piece from the 1930s that gets curtailed at 'shake'.
Shakes, the		Delirium tremens, the DTs. The chronic shaking of an alcoholic in need of a drink. To a lesser extent it's also the trembling hands of someone feeling the effects of a heavy drinking session.
Shampoo		A 1950s reference to champagne, which sometimes gets shortened to 'poo'.
Shampoo the Rug		To ejaculate over the pubic hair of a woman. Or, presumably, her wig.
Shampsteads		False teeth. A hybrid of sham (artificial) and the RS version of teeth 'Hampstead Heath' (qv), which in reduced form is 'hampsteads'.
Shank		A knife, especially a makeshift one as made by prisoners. To 'shank' is to stab.
Shanker Mechanic		*See* CHANCRE MECHANIC.
Shant		A drink of alcohol, originally beer.
Sharon		A young working-class woman, seen as unsophisticated and uneducated by the upper and middle classes. The female equivalent of 'Kevin' (qv).
Sharon Stone	*Phone*	A 1990s term that generally refers to a mobile: 'Lost your Sharon? Well, give me the number and if I find it, I'll call you.' Based on an American film actress.
Sharp		To swindle, con or cheat. An old term practiced by a 'sharper'. Con men are typically sharp-witted.
Sharp & Blunt	*Cunt*	Employed only in a vulgar anatomical sense for the vagina.
Sharper's Tool	*Fool*	Given that a sharper is a cardsharp and that cards are his tools, this is a sublimely fitting term for one who will always find the lady when there's no money on it.
Shaun Spadah	*Car*	A 1920s term based on the name of the 1921 Grand National winner. Now a non-runner.
Shaven Haven		A hairless pubic region of a woman, a smooth place for an 'old chap' to take refuge.

Shaver		An ancient term for a man, most commonly heard in relation to a boy, a 'young shaver'.
Shaving Cream		Excrement, a euphemism made famous in a song of this title by Ivor Biggun.
Shed		A promiscuous woman, something men put their tools in. *See* TOOL.
Sheeny		A derogatory term for a Jew. Possibly from 'shayner' – a traditional, old-fashioned Jew.
Sheep-Shagger		A country dweller, a rustic or farm worker. A term often aimed at Welshmen, Scottish Highlanders and Australians, all said to enjoy a wild and woolly sex life.
Sheet		a) £1, a piece that was coined when pound notes existed; out of habit, it still applies. 'Half a sheet' – 50p. b) An old prison term for a cigarette paper.
Shekels/ Sheckles/ Shackles		Money, often coins, a 19th-century term that's still in use. It may be slang here but it's the currency unit in Israel and was a Jewish coin in biblical times.
Shelf		The top of a fat woman's behind, where it juts out from her back.
Shell		a) A caravan, like a shell it's a mobile home. *See* SNAIL. b) An overcoat, an outer covering for the body.
Shell Game		The 'three card trick' with walnut shells, whereby a mark has to guess under which shell a pea is hidden.
Shell Mex	*Sex*	A 1960s term based on the name of an oil company, whereby to have 'blagged a bit of Shell Mex' is to have made a successful pull.
Shellack		To defeat comprehensively, to administer a 'shellacking' is to trounce. Sometimes applied to a severe tongue larruping or 'coating' (*see* COAT). The connection may be that to shellack in standard English is to coat something with varnish.
Shell-Like		An ear, famously: 'A word in your shell-like.'
She-Male/-Man		Both terms apply to bent genders, either a masculine woman or a feminine man.
Shemozzle		A disturbance, brawl or an uproar. A right old shemozzle may follow a scandalous accusation.
Shepherd's Bush	a) *Moosh (Face)* b) *Push*	An area of West London representing an area west of the left ear'ole. Chopped to the 'Shepherds' in reference to dismissal, to get the push.
Shepherd's Pie	*Sky*	Reduced to the first element, this would appear to be connected with the red sky at night.

Shepherd's Plaid	*Bad*	Must be from that terrible day up in the Scottish Highlands when a brothel caught fire and a panicking, tartan-clad shepherd was heard to yell: 'Let's get the flock out of here.'
Sherbet		A drink, an alcoholic one, especially beer: 'Drunk officer? No. I've had a couple of sherbets but I'm not drunk.'
Sherbet Dab	*Cab*	A 1990s term used by taxi drivers in relation to their black money box. It's wise to get a 'sherbet' after a 'sherbet'. *See* SHERBET.
Sherbet Dip	*Tip (Gratuity)*	An appropriate example since in cockney parlance a tip is often referred to as a drink and a drink is known as a 'sherbet' (qv).
Sherman Tank	*a) Wank*	An act of masturbation that's been known in this guise since World War Two, always as a 'Sherman'.
	b) Yank	An appropriate term since the war machine was an American weapon named after one of their Civil War generals. No, not General Tank!
Shice		To cheat, swindle or generally do someone a bad turn. From the German *scheisse* – shit, so literally to 'shit on' (qv). 'Shicer' – a cheat, swindler and all-round bastard.
Shicksa/Shixa		A non-Jewish girl, a Yiddish term that is often derogative.
Shif		A fish, a piece of Billingsgate backslang. 'Eenog shiffing' – gone fishing.
Shill		A member of a team of conmen, especially in a gambling game. The 'shill' pretends to be a winning punter in order to encourage others to lay their money down. Also a casino worker who plays the tables to bring others into a game.
Shillings & Pence	*Sense*	A very old reference to a fool is: 'He ain't got the shillings he was born with.'
Shine		Money, a term from a time when coins were all the working man saw, so really a term for metal money. Also 'shino' and 'shiny'. 'Shiner' – a coin.
Shiner		a) A window cleaner, a good one compared with a 'smears' (qv).
		b) A black eye. An old and somewhat ironic term for a busted 'lamp' (qv).
Shiny & Bright	*Alright*	A state of satisfaction is said to be 'all shiny'.
Shiny Bum Brigade		Office workers, a derogatory term used by manual workers that relates to trouser-wear from continual sitting.
Ship in Full Sail	*Pint of Ale*	The term is as old as it suggests, a pint has long been known as a 'ship'. It's now a museum piece.

Ship under Sail	*Tale*	A very old example, for a line as spun by a con man, that's probably sunk without trace.
Shirley Bassey	*Chassis*	Can apply to the base-frame of a vehicle, whereby a car may be written off if it's got a bent 'Shirley'. Mostly applies to the figure of a shapely female, much like that which was owned by this British singer when this was coined in the 1960s. An overweight woman may have a 'Birley Shassey'.
Shirt & Collar	*Dollar*	An elderly allusion to what is now 25p, which may be responsible for a punter 'losing his shirt' on a horse. Sometimes said as a 'shirt collar'.
Shirtlifter		A well-known term, originally Australian, for a male homosexual.
Shit		a) To defecate and what the act produces, excrement. Obvious but needs to be here I suppose.
		b) A despicable, repellent person. A 'shit of all shits' is an absolute bastard.
		c) Drugs. Originally heroin but during the 60s its main usage was in hashish or marijuana. A potent 'drugfag' is referred to as 'good shit'.
		d) Worthless goods, rubbish. Anything faulty, shoddy or bad: '*The Blair Witch Project?* What a load of old shit. I've seen scarier episodes of *Thunderbirds*.' 'Shitty' – inferior.
		e) Ill treatment, abuse. Commonly heard in expressions like: 'I've taken about as much shit as I'm going to from him.'
		f) Verbal rubbish, lies or boastful talk: 'He's got a mouth like an arsehole. As soon as he opens it you can smell the shit he talks.'
Shit a Brick		To experience extreme fear, to panic. Also to 'shit bricks' and 'shit oneself'.
Shit-Chute		The anus: 'I wish Lady Luck would smile on me for a change instead of keep emptying her shit-chute on me.'
Shit Detail, on		To be engaged in any dirty or unpleasant work. Originally a military term.
Shit from a Rocking Horse		What anything that's extremely difficult or practically impossible to come across is said to be like trying to find. Also 'rocking-horse shit' – something hard to come by.
Shit On		To abuse, take liberties with, betray or generally do wrong to somebody.
Shit Out		To act in a cowardly manner, to avoid a confrontation through fear. Also 'shit it'.
Shit Sack		A nappy, a term from pre-disposable days.

Shit Scared	Terrified, liable to 'shit oneself' through fear, necessitating the need for brown trousers.
Shit Stabber/ Shover	A male homosexual, a brace of terms that need no explanation.
Shit Stirrer	A gossip, someone who makes trouble for others, one who 'stirs the shit'.
Shitbag	An odious, unpleasant person. One on a par with a 'scumbag'. Others include: 'shitface', 'shitarse', 'shit features', 'shithead', 'shitlegs', 'shitpot', 'shitsack', 'shitstain' and 'shitstinker'.
Shitcunt	An absolute no-good, horrible, despicable person. The lowest of all the low, a step down from all the above and even 'manure face'.
Shite	An alternative version of 'Shit' that was commonly heard in the north and in Ireland before catching on in the rest of Great Britain.
Shitfaced	Very drunk, having a physog that forecasts what you will feel like in the morning.
Shit-for-Brains	An abusive term hurled at an idiot or someone who has done something particularly stupid.
Shithead	A habitual marijuana, hashish or cannabis smoker. *See* SHIT (c).
Shit-Hole	a) A lavatory, a piece that's shared the billing with 'pisshole' (qv) since the 19th century. b) The anus, a piece that's probably been about since man stopped using leaves to wipe it. c) An unpleasant or unsavoury place. Anywhere, be it country or town, area or building, if it's not nice it's a 'shit-hole'. d) A dirty or untidy room, usually a young man's bedroom: 'Clean this place up, it's a shit-hole.'
Shit-Hot	Skilful, talented or able. What anyone good at their job is said to be.
Shithouse	a) A lavatory, a piece that only really relates to an outhouse, as it did when it was coined. b) A dirty, untidy, foul place. A slum. c) An overly officious person, a jobsworth. Someone who delights in being obstructive and nasty. Suffering from a touch of the 'Earthas' once, I parked on a yellow line to search for a shithouse and found one in the shape of a traffic warden. *See* EARTHA KITT.
Shits, the	a) Diarrhoea, a well-known and long-running piece. b) Fear or an attack of nerves. A 'touch of the shits'.
Shitstinking	Abhorrent, the most horrible, especially of a place. You really don't want to visit a 'shitstinking

pisshole'. You also wouldn't want to know a 'shitstinking cowson'.

Shitter	a) A well-known term for the anus. 'Shitter-Jitters' – fear.
	b) A derogatory term for a promiscuous girl, a young 'slapper' (qv).
Shitter/Shiter	Whichever way you say it, it's a lavatory.
Shitty	a) How you feel when you're unwell or out of sorts, when you 'feel like shit' (qv).
	b) Frightened or nervous, often in the face of an impending hospital or dental appointment.
Shitty-Helmet	A male homosexual, a piece that relates to sodomy. *See* HELMET.
Shiv	*See* CHIV.
Shiver & Shake *Cake*	An old piece that's usually sliced to a piece of 'shiver'.
Shnide	*See* SNIDE.
Shoes & Socks *Pox (VD)*	The 'shoes' is one of many terms for the sexual blight.
Shonk/Shonker	a) A derogatory term from the 19th century for a Jew, possibly from *shonniker*, a Yiddish word for a pedlar or small trader.
	b) A large nose, a well-known term based on the perceived characteristic of the Jew at (a).
Shonky	Mean, tight-fisted or miserly. Someone said to 'have a mousetrap in his pocket'.
Shoot	a) To ejaculate, a 19th-century term that will probably be about for as long as men 'shoot off'.
	b) To leave. 'Gotta shoot' is a racier version of 'must dash'.
Shoot/Shoot Up	To inject a drug, a user's term.
Shoot One's Bolt/Load/ Milt/Roe	To ejaculate, some of the many terms for the male orgasm.
Shooter	An underworld term for a gun that's universally known because of its popularity with screen writers.
Shooting Gallery	A police and drug user's term for a place where addicts gather to inject themselves.
Shooting Stick	The penis, an old term for that which 'shoots' (qv, a).
Shop	To inform against, a well-known term that started out in the 17th century as a prison. It later became a verb meaning to imprison and, later still, to cause to be imprisoned.
Short	A spirit, originally a measure of gin. Now it's any kind of drink that comes via an optic, although Scotch drinkers claim it refers solely to their tipple.
Short & Curlies	Pubic hairs, most commonly heard in the phrase

'to have by the short and curlies' meaning to have someone under control.

Short Arm
An old term for the penis. In the army, an inspection of the genitals was a 'Short Arm Inspection'.

Short Arms
A name given to a tight-fisted person, one with short arms and long pockets.

Short Eyes
A child molester, a piece that originated in American prisons but is now heard here.

Short of a Sheet
Simple, not all there. Perhaps a reworking of a 'shilling short of a pound'. *See* SHEET (a).

Shortarse
A derogatory term for a small person, especially an unpopular, gabby one.

Shorthouse
A euphemism for 'shortarse' (qv) that was popular in British film comedies of the 1950s and with non commissioned officers (NCOs) in the armed forces.

Shot Down
Infected with a venereal disease. A 1960s term among young men who likened friends who had been 'shot down' to fighter pilots who had been suffered a hit.

Shot Stopper
A condom, a 1960s term that is occasionally euphemistically called a 'goalie'. A goalkeeper stops shots. Well, a good one does.

Shout & Holler *Collar*
A term from the days when they were detachable.

Shove Shit Uphill
To sodomise, a piece that's generally used in regard to male homosexuality.

Shove, the
The push, the sack. In other words dismissal from work.

Shovel
An ancient term, especially among tramps, for a spoon. With which to 'shovel it down'.

Shovel & Broom *Room*
A 'shovel' is a reference to living quarters, not to space.

Shovel & Pick *a) Mick*
Refers to an Irish person, usually a building site worker, which makes the term wholly suitable.

b) Nick
Prison has long been known as 'the shovel'. Also to steal or take: 'Shovel it quick and let's go.'

Shovel & Spade *Blade*
A 1950s term for a knife or a razor as used by gang members.

Shoveller
A labourer on a building site, based on the amount of shovelling that's required on one.

Shovels
Spades, a card player's alternative for the suit. The 'ace of shovels' for example.

Shovels & Spades *AIDS*
Until they find a cure the connection is sadly obvious, shovels dig graves.

Show One's Studs
To be ruthless, brutal or merciless, especially in business. To go in hard, like a footballer committing this foul.

Show Out		Usually of a woman, to let a man know, with a smile or a look, that she is interested in him.
Showboat		To show-off, to appear flash. A piece that's commonly associated with boxers who, when winning comfortably, often resort to crowd-pleasing tactics. Muhummad Ali's 'shuffle', for example.
Shower		A useless bunch of people, originally a sergeant's abuse at inept soldiers. A reduction of 'shower of shit', the term is also used against a single person and was made memorable by English comedian Terry-Thomas in the oft-imitated line: 'You're an absolute shower.'
Shower Bath	*Half*	A term coined on the racecourse originally in reference to ten shillings, which was a half of a pound. Always known as a 'shower' it has made the transition to the present 'half a quid', 50p.
Shrapnel		Originally copper coins but later extended to all small change.
Shreddies		Men's underpants when tattered, worn and stained with various bodily excretions.
Shrimping		An American term for toe-sucking which, since their shrimps are our prawns, should have hit our shores as 'prawning'.
Shrink		The best-known expression for a psychiatrist. A shrunken 'headshrinker'.
Shrubbery		Pubic hair, especially a woman's. To 'spray the shrubbery' is the withdrawal method of contraception.
Shtook		In trouble, often financially: 'I was well in shtook but I backed the last winner.'
Shtum		Quiet. A commonly heard piece of Yiddish: 'Keep shtum' – say nothing.
Shufti		Well-known parlance for a look or a glance. Based on an Arabic word and brought home by serving soldiers during World War Two.
Shut Eye		Constipation. With 'eye' an old term for the anus this speaks for itself.
Shut-Eye		An old and long-serving term for sleep.
Shuvver/Shuffer		A chauffeur, a piece that's not quite as old as the motorcar.
Shyster		A crooked, corrupt or generally dishonest person, originally a bent lawyer. Possibly after an actual one, Eugene Scheuster, a New York lawyer of the 1850s whose dishonesty led to the term 'Scheuster practices'. Could also be a corruption of 'shicer' (qv).
Sick Squid		£6. A pun on six quid that comes from a cringe-making joke.

Sickener		A disappointment, a sad outcome: 'Barnet's relegation from the league has come as a right sickener.'
Sickie		Time off from work for no valid reason except that you may feel a 'wee cough' coming on.
Sickle		A bike, a deliberate mispronunciation of cycle. 'Motor sickle' – motorbike.
Sicko		A pervert or someone with a warped or perverted sense of humour.
Sieve-Head		A forgetful person, someone who allows events to march through his memory without leaving a footprint. One with a 'head like a sieve'.
Sigmund Freuds	*Haemorrhoids*	The Austrian-born grandaddy of psychoanalysis (1856–1939) comes in as 'Sigmunds'.
Sigourney Weaver	*Beaver*	A 1990s example of slang for slang in relation to the pubic region of a woman. Based on a US film actress. *See* BEAVER.
Silas Hockings	*Stockings*	A piece that was formed in the theatre and probably saw its final curtain there. Based on the name of a novelist (1850–1935).
Silent Horror/ Terror		Either way a quiet but pungent fart, one that 'crept out with its boots off'. A 'silent but deadly'.
Silent Night	*Light (Ale)*	A 1950s term for this type of 'Christmas cheer' (qv), which was inspired by the Christmas carol.
Silicon Chip	*Nip (Japanese)*	A component in the electronics industry comes in for someone who helped develop it. Hoist by their own petard. So to speak.
Silly as a Box of Lights		As silly as you can get, completely daft. A box of lights is a box of matches, so perhaps the lack of order inside a matchbox relates to the erratic nature of an idiot's brainbox. Who knows?
Silly Bollocks		A term of abuse aimed at someone considered an idiot or a buffoon.
Silly Boy/Girl Got None		A senseless person, a loon, someone deemed to be as 'daft as a brush'.
Silly Legs		A term of mild abuse aimed at someone behaving like a fool: 'Alright silly legs, that's enough.'
Silly Money		A false or ridiculous price, which could be too low or too high.
Silo/Sylo		An asylum seeker, a piece from the present day that stems from the growing problem of illegal immigration into Britain.
Silver & Gold	*Old*	From the effect that ageing has on the hair and used as: 'I'm getting too silver for this.'
Silver Spoon	*Moon*	The moon was known as 'the silver' long before men stamped their plates all over it.

Silvery Moon	*Coon*	Reduced to the first element, this is an abusive term for a black person.
Simp		A dim-witted or backward person, a reduced form of simpleton.
Simple Simon	*Diamond*	Applies to the precious stone and the not-so-valuable playing card, unless you're holding five of them. Based on the nursery rhyme character who tried to mump a pie off a pieman.
Simpson not Samsom, the name's		A reply when requested to do heavy work or lift something weighty.
Sinbad the Sailor	*Tailor*	A term that was common when most men had their suits made to measure by the local 'Sinbad' but less so now that off-the-peg jobs are so readily available.
Sinex		A name given to an annoying or irritating person, someone who 'gets up your nose'. Sinex is a well-known brand of nasal spray.
Sing		To inform or confess to the police. To 'sing like a canary' – to tell everything.
Singleton		A 1990s term for an unmarried person, someone on their own.
Sip		To urinate. A backslang piss.
Siphon		To urinate, originally an Australian term for the British 'Drain off' (qv).
Sir Alec		A Guinness. A pint of the black stuff down to the British actor Sir Alec Guinness (1914–2000).
Sir Anthony Blunt	*Cunt*	This is the C word at it's most objectionable and applies to a horrible, scaly-backed reptile of a person: 'He's a no-good Sir Anthony and I hate him.' May also give a different slant to the Tony awards. Based on a British traitor (1907–83), whose knighthood was annulled in 1979.
Sir Lancelot		A promiscuous man, a regular user of his 'lance' (qv). A punning 'Sir Lance-a-lot'.
Sir Paul		A condom. A pun on the name of Metropolitan police chief Sir Paul Condon.
Sir Walter Scott	*Pot*	An ancient piece from the world of the drinking classes as this applies to a pint pot, the norm before pint glasses. Based on the Scottish novelist and poet (1771–1832).
Sit Beside 'er	*Spider*	An old example that was common when houses had outside lavatories wherein lurked many an arachnid to keep a person company. Based on the one that gave Little Miss Muffet the horrors.
Sit-Down Job		The act of defecation, especially for a man: 'He's been ages in that carsey, must be a sit-down job.'

Six & Eight   *a) State*   Applies to a state of agitation or nervousness. A less familiar term than 'two and eight' (qv).

   b) Straight   Refers to anything or anyone that can be trusted, if people or goods are not bent or crooked, they're 'six and eight'.

Six Months Hard   *Card*   An out-of-date bingo card based on an equally out-dated prison sentence.

Six Pack   A flat stomach, especially that of an athlete. The muscles resemble beer cans.

Six to Four   *Whore*   Coined between World Wars One and Two, perhaps on the odds against catching something from one.

Sixpenn'orth   An old underworld term for a six-month prison sentence.

Sixty-Nine   Mutual oral sex, based on the shape of two bodies engaged in simultaneous 'noshing' (qv).

Sixty-Eight   Fellatio. A selfishly male play on the well-known term 'Sixty-Nine' (qv): 'You suck me and I'll owe you one.'

Skeeter   A mosquito, possibly the earth's most superfluous creature. In the great scheme of things, what is it good for?

Skein of Thread   *Bed*   A 19th-century term that probably hasn't been slept in since it was stitched-up by 'Uncle Ned' (qv).

Sketchley's Aerial   A wire coathanger used as a makeshift aerial for a car radio after some git has broken the proper one. Based on the dry cleaning company which delivers the goods on such hangers.

Skew-whiff   a) Not straight, twisted or crooked. In tradesman's jargon 'pissed' (qv, b).
b) Drunk, unable to remain in the perpendicular. Again it shares a meaning with 'pissed', so mayhap a connection with 'squiff' – to drink, hence 'squiffy' (qv).

Skid Artist   An underworld term for an expert getaway driver.

Skidlid   A crash helmet, a term from before they became compulsory. Also a 'crash hat'.

Skidmarks   Excrement stains on underpants and knickers. Otherwise known as 'skiddies', they can also be spotted on the sheets of a nude sleeper. Also 'Ginger Marks'.

Skimming   a) Illegally taking details of a credit card by passing it through a special scanner which 'reads' the information contained on the magnetic strip.
b) Stealing a small percentage 'off the top' of the takings of a casino, nightclub, etc. An underworld expression which usually involves crooks creaming

money off their masters and often getting 'creamed' for their misdemeanours. *See* CREAM (b).

Skin
a) A condom, a piece that has kept the cockney population down for generations.

b) A drum. The drummer in the resident rock group in an East End pub during the late 1960s used to make a point of counting his drums before a set. His fourth drum was his 'four-skin'.

c) A cigarette paper, especially one used in the rolling of a 'joint'. To 'skin up' is to roll one.

d) A skinhead, a well-known abbreviation since the 1970s.

e) To swindle or con someone, in a word to fleece them.

f) To separate someone from all his money in a gambling game, the loser ends up 'skinned'.

Skin & Blister   *Sister*
An old and widely used piece. In the jargon of burglars a 'two skins' is a house inhabited by ageing sisters.

Skin & Grief
A painfully thin person, often referred to simply as 'skin'.

Skin Flick
A pornographic film, or at least one that contains a lot of nudity. The porn industry is known as the 'Skin Game'.

Skin Game
Any kind of confidence trick where a mug can be fleeced or 'skinned'. *See* SKIN (e).

Skin-a-Guts
A very thin person, usually said as 'skinny guts'.

Skink
A derogatory term for a white person used by black and Asian youth.

Skinned Rabbit
A flaccid penis, from the appearance of one hanging in a butcher's window. A rabbit that is.

Skinner
For a bookmaker, an excellent result. A race won by a rank outsider and therefore no winning punters. *See* SKIN (f).

Skinny as a Broom   *Groom*
Jokingly dislengthened to a 'skinny', as he stands at the altar with his 'fat and wide' (qv). Both terms come from the comic verse made to fit 'The Wedding March'.

Skinpop
To inject a drug into flesh rather than a vein.

Skint
Having no money, holding 'nuppence'. A very well-known piece that was originally 'skinned'. *See* SKIN (f). When boys have money they think they're men – but when they're skint they're boys again.

Skintitis
A jocular name for the unfunny condition of having no money. *See* SKINT.

Skip & Jump	*Pump (Heart)*	A descriptively accurate allusion to what can do both.
Skipper		Tramp's jargon for a rough shelter, somewhere to doss for a night, hence 'skippering' – sleeping rough.
Skirt		A girl or a woman, generally known as a 'bit of skirt' and relating to women in general, often as sex objects. Men in search of female company go 'skirt hunting'.
Skit		To have a laugh at someone's expense in order to wind them up: 'Don't get rattled. I'm only skitting you.'
Skive		To avoid work or duty, to 'dodge the column' as old soldiers put it. Also to 'skive off'.
Skiver		A malingerer, idler or all-round layabout. A 'dodge-work' is generally 'on a skive'.
Skollobs/ Skowlobs		The testicles. Backslang 'bollocks'.
Skunk/ Skunkweed		A particularly potent variety of marijuana.
Skunky		Evil smelling, a term of abuse often aimed at someone with reeking flatulence.
Sky		To throw or toss something into the air, hence to 'sky a copper' – to toss a coin and in boxing jargon to 'sky a wipe' is to throw in the towel, to submit.
Sky Diver	*Fiver*	A 1980s term for £5 that's in direct competition with 'scuba diver'.
Sky Diver/ Skyman/Skyer		A trio of pickpockets, all based on 'sky rocket' (qv) and all thieving toerags.
Sky Pilot		A clergyman, especially in the military or, when the term was formed, one who escorted a prisoner to the gallows. He supposedly showed the way to Heaven.
Sky Rocket	*Pocket*	A widely used piece, usually solely in the first element. A generous man will willingly put his hand in his 'sky', a mean one will enter his under duress.
Skylark	*Park*	A suitable example since the park is where people go to skylark about. Also used in connection with parking a car: 'Sorry I'm late, I couldn't find anywhere to skylark.'
Skyscraper	*Paper*	Applies to all types of paper, including writing, toilet, news and what chips come wrapped in.
Slabs		The testicles. Backslang 'balls'.
Slack		A prostitute, a 1940s term for a 'loose' woman.
Slack/Slack Off		To urinate, a couple of old terms relating to the loosening of the bladder.
Slack-Jaw		A talkative person, one not to be trusted with

secret information. Someone likely to inform against you.

Slag
a) A prostitute or a promiscuous woman. A 1950s term that is often used by schoolboys about the girl most likely.

b) A worthless or contemptible man, a piece that's used with venom in the underworld where it relates to a coward, an informer and, generally, someone not to be trusted.

Slag/Slag Off
To insult, criticise or generally put someone down. To administer a 'slagging'.

Slagger
A critic or reviewer, someone who 'slags off' for a living.

Slam
To criticise severely. Originally American but now well-known here, successive governments have been 'slammed' over the health service.

Slam Dancing
A craze that developed during the punk era (1970s) which involves people slamming into each other.

Slammer
Prison, a piece that has developed from it's original meaning, that of a door.

Slant/Slant Eye
A derogatory term for an oriental person, especially a Japanese.

Slap
Make-up, especially that used on stage.

Slap & Tickle   *Pickle*
Applies to the edible kind rather than a predicament.

Slap-Head
A bald person, one of nature's skinheads. A 1980s term, possibly from the British comedian Benny Hill's action of regularly slapping the head of Jackie Wright, his bald-headed stooge in the long-running TV show that bore his name.

Slapper
A promiscuous woman or a prostitute, often an ageing one.

Slapsie Maxie   *Taxi*
An example from the 1930s based on American boxer 'Slapsie' Maxie Rosenbloom (1904–76), a world light-heavyweight champion of the period. He later pursued a successful acting career.

Slash
To urinate, a well-known term with many examples of rhyming slang to its name.

Slasher
a) An old term for a violent man, one especially handy with a knife.

b) An excessively violent film, in full a 'slasher movie'.

Slaughter
a) Of clothes, to be much too big for. They overwhelm: 'This shirt slaughters me since my diet.'

b) To drink a whole bottle of spirit in one session, to demolish or kill it: 'He slaughtered a bottle of wine before the second course came up.'

c) To completely destroy someone in an argument, a war of words or a battle of wits. To beat someone down with insults and criticism.

Slaughtered		Extremely drunk, the effect of 'slaughtering' too many pints or bottles.
Slaughtomobile		A car in the hands of a joyrider, a drunk, or one owned by a notoriously mad driver.
Sleazebag/ Sleazeball/ Sleazebucket		A trio of terms for a shabby, immoral, or disgusting person, an all-round squalid individual.
Sledge		To barrack, especially heard in cricket when the fielding side give stick to the batsmen.
Sledgehammer		Anyone lacking in tact or diplomacy, from what they are said to be 'as subtle as'.
Sleeper		In the betting office, a winning bet that remains unclaimed for a long period.
Slice of Ham	*Gam (Fellatio)*	A rare alternative to the widely used 'plate of ham' (qv).
Slice of Toast	*Ghost*	Generally truncated to 'slice' as in the 'slice of Christmas past' and 'Who ya gonna call? Slice-busters.'
Slide & Sluther	*Brother*	Sounds like the slippery member of the family.
Slim Jim		A bootlace tie as worn by country-and-western fans and Teddy Boys.
Slime		a) To behave in a toady, ingratiating way. A crawler may 'slime' his way into a better job. b) An ancient term for semen. 'Slosh one's slime' – ejaculate.
Slimebag/ Slimeball/ Slimebucket		A pick of three terms for an obnoxious, despicable and repugnant person.
Sling Your Hook		A well-known order of dismissal. 'Get lost!' can be dressed as 'Hook it!' or 'Sling it!' The term may come from the docks, where a sling is the rope placed around a set (load) and hung on to the hook of a crane enabling the cargo to be taken away.
Slinger		A workman who 'slings' a rope around a load so that it may be picked up evenly by a crane. The job is usually one step up from a labourer.
Slip a Length		To have sex from a man's standpoint in the same way as to 'give one'.
Slippery Sid	*Yid*	Generally snipped to a 'slippery' and may be based on an actual untrustworthy son of Isra-eel named Sid.
Slit		An ancient term for the vagina that is still with us, especially as a term for a woman in general. There was an all-girl punk group in the 1970s called the Slits.

Slit/Slitty Eye — A derogatory term for an oriental person. On a tour of China, Prince Phillip famously referred to his hosts as 'slitty eyes'.

Slither & Dodge *Lodge* — Applies to the branch of a union or society, especially the Freemasons which is perceived as being somewhat dodgy, making the term apt.

Sloane/Sloane Ranger — A typically upper-class young woman, conventional and traditional in taste, fashion and behaviour. A pun on the Sloane Square area of London and the Lone Ranger.

Slob — A lazy, coarse, scruffy person, typically ignorant, overweight, unclean and having no manners, as described in 'Droppit's Doctrine':

> Slobley Droppit, chips in hand
> Walks along a golden beach
> Shovels in the final tater.
> And over his shoulder goes the paper.
>
> Driving down a country lane
> Fosters four pack at his side
> Down his throat the lagers flow
> The empties out the window go.
>
> Landed gentry shooting pheasant
> City peasant shooting pool
> Trans religion, colour, creed
> Slobley Droppit plants his seed.
>
> In suits from Shell or Savile Row
> In caps for baseball or the hunt
> Slobs across the spectrum thrive
> And Droppit's doctrine will survive.

Slog One's Guts Out — To work very hard, often for little reward: 'I slog my guts out for peanuts.'

Slomvosh *Wash* — An old piece from the East End that was used by mothers when the kids needed a soaping. It's still heard but the origin of the term probably went to the grave with its originator.

Sloop of War *Whore* — An old term for a woman of loose morals and even looser knickers.

Slop — Police in backslang. It works if you see the 'ice' as an 's'.

Slope Off — To sneak away without being seen, especially to avoid working.

Slosh — a) A 1950s term for beer which was originally a 19th-century term for any drink. Also 'sloshy beer'.

b) A tea or coffee stall. An old term for an old meeting place: 'I'll see you at the slosh.'

c) To hit, most commonly heard in a threat: 'I'll slosh you in a minute.'

Slosh & Mud   *Stud*   Originally a collar stud but there's no reason why the modern ear stud shouldn't be known as a 'slosh'.

Sloshed   A well-known term for being drunk from a surfeit of 'slosh' (qv, a).

Slosher   A losing bet, a piece from the early days of betting shops; in fact the first paid work I ever did was filing away 'sloshers' in one.

Sloshmog   A jocular term of abuse to a friend, especially a drinking pal: 'Oi, sloshmog. Fancy a curry?'

Slot   A 1940s term for the vagina that suggests one belonging to a prostitute, one that's coin-activated.

Slowmo   A name given to a person who does everything with an absence of speed, someone who won't be rushed. Short for slow motion.

Sludgegulper   Someone with a huge appetite, a glutton. After the heavy digger used for dredging silt and mud from river beds and harbours.

Slug   An obnoxious, repellent person. A 'slug in the garden of life'. A 'Slimeball'.

Slug & Snail   *Nail*   Applies to the finger and toe variety and is normally trimmed to 'slug', often to an habitual nail biter in the hope of putting him off.

Slugfest   A good boxing contest, one where both fighters give and take a multitude of punches (slugs).

Sluice the Throat   To have a drink of alcohol, especially a pint of beer.

Slummock   A lazy, untidy person, usually a young man.

Slush & Slurry   *Curry*   A recent piece that may often be relevant in appearance.

Smack   a) Heroin. Originally an American term, it arrived here in the 1960s. 'Smacked out' – under its influence.

b) To eat with a noisy, off-putting smacking sound.

Smack in the Eye   *Pie*   Care should be taken when ordering one of these. If the vendor is big and thick, don't.

Smack Off   To masturbate, a 1990s version of 'jack off' (qv).

Smacker   A common term for a loud kiss.

Smackers   Pounds, a well-known piece that's often heard in a gambling sense: 'I drew two hundred smackers on the last race and got out of trouble.' Also called 'smackeroonies'.

Smack-Head   A heroin addict who may also be a 'smack freak'.

Smarmite   A name for a smarmy, ingratiating person: 'OK Smarmite, enough with the crap.'

Smart Money		The money of a shrewd or well-informed gambler: 'The smart money's on Harry Boy in the first race.'
Smart-Arse		A big-headed know-all, the smug 'I told you so' type: 'Don't ask me, ask that smart-arse. He knows everything.'
Smarts		Intelligence, sense, etc. A company in an office block was moving to another part of the building and the staff were told to label their own furnishings. When they arrived the girl with no 'smarts' had labelled her's; 'chair', 'table', 'cup', etc.
Smash & Grab	*Cab*	Either a mini-cab or a black one. Probably most apt in reference to the latter as you need to pull off a robbery just to get in the thing.
Smashed		Very drunk or high on drugs.
Smear & Smudge	*Judge*	One of several terms for the one who'll put a dirty stain on your character.
Smears		A nickname for a window cleaner, a term that doesn't necessarily cast aspersions on his work.
Smeesh		A 19th-century term for a loose-fitting dress, a shift.
Smeg/Smeggy		An abusive term for a scruffy, dirty, cheesy (qv) person. A reduction of smegma that became well used in the 1980s due to it's constant use in the TV comedy *Red Dwarf*, where it was employed as a euphemism for 'fuck', as in 'smegging hell'.
Smeghead		A general term of abuse based on 'smeg'.
Smeller		An old term for the nose that's still alive and sniffing.
Smelly Breath	*Chef*	A 1990s piece aimed at the proliferation of TV chefs. It's probably apt with all the necessary food tasting that goes on.
Smile & Smirk	*Work*	Usually cut to the first element, whereby you may be 'smiling' if you're in work. Unless you're one of natures layabouts of course, in which case you're smiling if you're not.
Smile & Titter	*Bitter (Ale)*	This originally applied to a once popular mix of mild and bitter, but since mild is now rarer than teddy bear's piss it has been transferred to the other partner.
Smoked Haddock	*Paddock*	An example used by the racing fraternity concerning that part of a racecourse.
Smoker		A term employed in the used car trade for an old banger, a jalopy.
Smother		An old term for an overcoat or raincoat: 'Smother weather' – wintry conditions.
Smother Game		Picking pockets with the aid of a concealing overcoat.

Smudger		An old term for a photographer, one that alludes to dodgy developing. 'Smudge' – a photograph.
Smug		To arrest, an occupational hazard for the criminal since the 19th century. 'Smugged' – an old version of 'nicked'.
Snafu		A term used in a chaotic, confused or fouled-up situation. In long hand it would spell Situation Normal, All Fucked Up. A piece from the American military of World War Two.
Snail		A slow driver, especially a motorist towing a caravan who, like the mollusc, is dragging his living quarters around with him. *See* SHELL.
Snake Charmer		An old military term for a bugler.
Snake in the Grass	*Glass*	Originally a looking glass but later, and still, a drinking glass. Always broken at 'snake'. Formed when a mirror was called a 'shiner'.
Snake's Hiss	*Piss*	Applies to urination, the sound you get when you 'siphon the python'.
Snap		Amyl nitrate, the stimulant drug which comes in a glass ampoule that has to be snapped open to enable inhalation.
Snapper		a) A photographer, someone who takes snaps. Also, a 1990s term for the camera that stands by the roadside and 'snaps' the motorist who passes it at speed. b) A young man, especially one who acts younger than his age. A reduction of whippersnapper.
Snatch		a) The vagina, a 19th-century term that's still with us. A way of passing on genital herpes is to snatch a kiss off a girl with a cold sore, then kiss the snatch of a girl who hasn't. The term also applies to women in general. b) An underworld term for a kidnapping and also a robbery, commonly heard in a wages snatch.
Snatch 22		A pun on *Catch 22* regarding a woman who may only be fanciable to a man after he has had a bucketful of alcohol, by which time 'brewer's droop' (qv) will have kicked in, rendering him incapable anyway. *See* SNATCH.
Sneeze		a) An old term for snuff. A 19th-century style of mugging was the 'Sneeze Lurk', where a robber would blow snuff into a victim's face. 'Sneezer' – a snuffbox. b) 'Pass the "sneeze" please.' – the pepper that is. c) Cocaine, a 1980s term for 'nose powder'.
Sneezer		The nose, a 19th-century term that still gets a blow now and then, often on achoosday.

Snide/Shnide a) Counterfeit, phoney or fake. Any imitation, be it money, jewellery or designer clothing is 'snide'.
b) A two-faced, underhand person. Someone who isn't what he seems, a phoney.
c) A nasty remark, a sideswipe. A backstabbing, below-the-belt comment delivered from 'underneath the tongue'.

Sniff a) Any drug for which the point of entry is the nose, be it cocaine or amyl nitrite.
b) Glue or any chemical used for getting high by inhalation.

Sniffer a) A 19th-century term for the nose that's still breathing.
b) A person who inhales drugs or chemicals.

Sniffer & Snorter *Reporter* Conjures up scenes of old Fleet Street, where the intrepid old hack would sniff out a story over a snort of short. Or it may just be a case of someone who gets up people's noses.

Snifter A small measure of alcohol, originally brandy. A snifter being a brandy glass.

Snip a) Something that's easily achieved, a simple task, a doddle.
b) A well-known term for a bargain, when a price is cut.

Snip, the The well-known euphemism for a vasectomy.

Snipcock A 1950s term for a male Jew, the circumcision involved prevents it from being a female.

Snips An old term for scissors, as used by an equally ancient term for a tailor, a 'snip'.

Snitch a) The nose. Folk have had 'snotty snitches' since the 17th century.
b) An informer or to inform against. *See* NARK.

Snog To kiss, well-known because everybody's done it.

Snog & Fuck *Dog & Duck* An inside joke used by workers in the City of London concerning a nearby pub which allegedly had a reputation for being a meeting place for bosses and secretaries. I suppose I should stress meeting place, 'much bunking in the snug' is not suggested.

Snooker To put somebody in a bad position, or an awkward situation. A piece that has escaped the confines of the game and entered the world beyond the doors of the snooker hall. Just as you don't have to be a cricketer to 'bowl someone a googly', so anyone can lay a 'snooker'.

Snooker Player's Pocket		Symbolic of dryness, his waistcoat pocket is where he keeps his chalk. What the thirsty may claim to have a throat like.
Snookered		In an impossible situation or at least in one that's difficult to get out of.
Snoop & Pry	*Cry*	The cause of many a midnight row, a 'snooping' baby.
Snoot		a) The nose, an old variation of 'snout' that is most commonly heard in the word 'snooty', which describes those who look down their noses, or 'cock a snoot' at the hoi polloi.
b) A snob. *See* (a).
Snoozer		A bed, or what passes as a bed, anything you can 'get your nut down' on.
Snoozing & Snoring	*Boring*	An obvious but appropriate offering that is mostly reduced to 'snoozing', and sometimes 'snooze and snoring'.
Snore		a) Sleep, generally said as something to be desired, all an insomniac wants is to get some 'snore'. Also known as 'snoremans'.
b) A bed or a place to sleep, especially a doss-house: 'I'll be glad when I've had enough beer so I can get back to my snore.'
c) A boring or tedious person, thing or experience. A yawn.
Snoregasm		A nightshirt-bulging orgasm reached whilst in the hands of Morpheus. In other words, a wet dream. Or, if it's a somnisexual dream of Trude Mostue, a vet dream.
Snore-Pig		A heavy snorer, one who grunts in his sleep.
Snorky		Well dressed, smart, elegant. The nickname of Al Capone, the one he approved of, no-one called him Scarface to his scarred face.
Snort		An inhaled dose of cocaine or heroin.
Snorter		The nose, especially a large one.
Snot		a) The commonest term there is for nasal mucous, many know it as nothing else. 'Snotty' – having a runny nose.
b) An obnoxious person, often someone young and in a managerial position. Older workers dislike taking a rucking from a 'young snot'. Also known as a 'snotty nose'.
c) A 1980s term for semen. 'Blow one's snot' – to ejaculate. Also known as 'cock snot'.
d) To punch someone on the nose, an order to do so is 'Snot him!'

Snot Groveller   A toady, someone who laps up the drippings of a superior's nose. 'Snot grovelling toe rags' are all too common.

Snot Rag   A vulgar term for a handkerchief that's also a 'nose rag' and a 'snitch rag'.

Snout   a) The nose, so common it's hardly slang.

b) Tobacco, an example that started in prison, when convicts requiring tobacco would touch their 'snouts' (a) as a sign of their need. Having escaped from the nick the term is now at large as cigarettes in general and a single fag is also a 'snout'.

c) A police informer, especially a paid one. Particularly common in TV police dramas where it would appear that every 'pig' (qv) has a 'snout'. *See* Nark *for origin.*

Snoutcast   A smoker, one deemed to be a pariah by non-smokers and banished from a building to indulge in his habit in the street. *See* Snout (b).

Snouter   A tobacconist, a piece that's dated in its original setting of legitimacy. The new 'snouter' brings his wares in from the continent and sells them on the black market to people who refuse to pay exorbitant retail prices.

Snow   a) Cocaine, a common term in the world of drugs which has also applied to heroin and morphine.

b) Silver coins, a piece from pre-decimal days which was commonly heard in public-bar card games, where a kitty with a 'bit of snow' in it was worth winning.

c) A white person through the eyes of a black one. Also 'snowball', 'snowdrop' and 'snowflake'.

d) To confuse with jargon and lies, to deceive or blind someone by covering the truth like a layer of snow. To con: 'Don't try and snow me son, I was a snowman (qv) before you were born.'

Snow & Ice   *Price*   Most commonly applies to a starting price, but a high cost of an article could induce a whining: 'But look at the snow and ice of it.'

Snow Job   A lie, an excuse, or the patter of a con artist.

Snow White   Cocaine. An extension of 'snow' (a).

Snow Whites   *Tights*   The legwear favoured by women but not men, but then men should stick to trousers. Based on the heroine of fairy story, pantomime and film. The pornographic version sees Grumpy watching Snow White undress until he finally comes over bashful; who gets the needle and thumps him.

Snowball		To con, to overwhelm somebody with a lie: 'He was so bloody believable, he snowballed me completely.'
Snowball's Chance in Hell		No chance at all. No-hopers are often told that they 'don't stand a snowball's'.
Snowbird		a) An habitual cocaine user.
		b) A female cocaine dealer.
Snow-Blind		Addicted to cocaine or other white, powdered drugs. As described by the US band Steppenwolf in the song 'Snow-Blind Friend'.
Snowdrop		A military policeman, from the white caps that they wear.
Snowed/Snowed In/Snowed Under		Three ways to be under the influence of cocaine.
Snowflake		A 1980s term for crack cocaine.
Snowman		a) A con man, *see* Snow (d). Also a 'snowballer', *see* Snowball.
		b) A man who deals in cocaine. *Compare* Snowbird.
Snozz/Snozzle		A large nose, the anglicised version of 'Schnozz/schnozzle' (qv).
Snuff		a) One nose powder becomes a euphemism for another – cocaine.
		b) To kill. As the flame of a candle is snuffed out, so is the spark of life. 'Snuff movie' – a film which supposedly ends with the murder of one of the participants.
Snuff It		To die, a common term for the commonest activity. If you can actively die that is.
Snuff-Box		The nose, a term from the time that snuff was commonly sniffed.
Snuffy		Someone who gets sexually aroused by smelling underwear, prostitutes also call such people 'sniffers'.
Snuggle		A bed. Early morning workers can't wait to get back to their 'snuggles'.
Soaked		Very drunk. Anyone seen to have had a 'skinful' is said to be 'soaked to the skin'.
Soap & Flannel	*Panel*	Some people still refer to being out of work as being on the 'soap'. For an explanation *see* English Channel.
Soap & Lather	*Father*	For third-party use when talking about your old man. It also makes the Pope the 'holy soap'.
Soap & Water	*Daughter*	Should be used in full to differentiate it from 'soap and lather' (qv).
Soap Dodger		A dirty, scruffy, smelly person. Often someone who won't bathe, rather than a homeless person who can't. Also a 'soaper'.

Soaper   *See* JOE SOAP.

Soapy   a) A name given to a 'soap dodger' (qv).
b) Crafty, ingratiating, smooth talking. A flatterer, someone free with the 'soft soap' may acquire this nickname.

Soapy Bubble   *Trouble*   Maybe from the story of the sex pest who got into hot water by approaching a plainclothes police woman and inviting her to 'Put it in your palm Olive,' to which she replied, 'Not on your lifebuoy. You're under arrest.'

Soche, the   The Department of Health and Social Security. 'On the Soche' – drawing benefit.

Socket   The vagina, that which gets 'plugged'. *See* PLUG (c). 'Socket money' – money paid for sex.

Sod   a) An unpleasant, bad or mischievous person. A term that takes in a variety of baddies, from the habitual criminal who's been a 'sod' all his life to the naughty child who's a right little 'sod'.
b) A hard, awkward or tricky job. When there's four nuts to undo, one of them has to be a 'sod'.

Sod Off!   Get Lost! The well-known order of dismissal.

Sod-All   Nothing at all. In backslang – 'doss la'.

Sodden   Drunk, an alternative to 'soaked' (qv).

Sodom & Gommorah   *Borrow*   From the biblical cities of sin comes the expression 'on the Sodom', which is fitting because 'sod 'em' is the typical reply of a knocker, when asked when his creditors can expect payment. *See* KNOCKER (b).

Sofa Loafer   A layabout, an idler. Someone content to laze around, a 'do-nothing'.

Soggy   A name given to an inept, feeble or wimpish person. Someone seen as wet.

Soixante Neuf   French for 'sixty-nine' (qv). Often the only piece of French that some people know.

Solar Sex Panel   A man's bald head, the shiny dome that, rumour has it, makes bald men more virile.

Soldier Ants   *Pants*   A reference to underwear, 'soldiers' for short.

Soldier Bold   *Cold*   A 19th-century term for the illness, known as 'catching a soldier'.

Solo Sex Panel   The hand, as used in the solo sex session of masturbation. A recent pun on 'Solar Sex Panel' (qv).

Somerset Maugham   *Warm*   The British writer (1874–1965) comes in for a spell of nice weather. Balmy evenings are said to be 'Somerset'.

Son of a Bitch   A contemptible, no-good person. The term is generally considered American but is originally

British. Also said of a tricky, hard or awkward job. Sometimes abbreviated to SOB.

Song & Dance   *a) Chance*   An example that's used in full for effect when handing out a flat refusal: 'You've got no song and dance.' But not to have a 'song' is the same as not having a hope.

         b) Nance (Homosexual)   An early 20th-century piece from the theatre which is entirely fitting given the sexual leanings generally ascribed to your average male dancer and chorus boy. *See* NANCE/NANCY BOY.

Song of the Thrush   *Brush*   An ancient term for any kind of brush. Also to give someone the 'song of the thrush' is to give them the brush off.

Soot/Sooty   A pair of derogatory terms for a black person.

Sooty & Sweep   *Sleep*   One for use when putting the nippers to bed. Had a slight currency in the 1960s and is based on a pair of TV glove puppets whose creator, Harry Corbett (1918–89), became rich and famous by squirting himself with a water pistol and bashing himself on the turret with a toy hammer. The luckiest man who ever pissed in a pot or what?

Sore-Foot   An Asian person, usually a man. From a manner of walking.

Sorrowful Tale   *Gaol*   An old but still appropriate term when applied to the tales of misfortune as told by convicts. These stories may range from a deprived upbringing to a flat tyre on the getaway car.

Sorry & Sad   *a) Bad*   A very well-known piece, anything in a bad way is said to be in a 'sorry state'.

         b) Dad   It's a wise 'dustbin' who knows his own 'sorry and sad'. A piece from the RS book of proverbs.

Sort   An attractive woman. *See* SALT.

Sort Out   To take care of, usually in a violent way. Resolved problems are said to be 'sorted'.

Sound   First class, excellent or at least very good: 'Sound as a pound'.

Soundo   Sound asleep, out like a light and dead to the world.

Soup & Gravy   *Navy*   Known by sailors as being in the 'soup'.

Soup Strainer   A bushy moustache, a piece that was first grown in the 1930s.

Soup-Up   To modify an engine to obtain maximum performance and speed.

Soused   Drunk, an old version of 'pickled'.

Soush   A house. One down backslang street.

South of France   *Dance*   Applies to both the physical act of dancing and to a social event, an invitation to which sounds irresistible, but when the music ends so must the 'South of France'.

South Pole *Hole (Anus)* Direction wise, being at the bottom, a more fitting variant of 'North Pole' (qv).

Southend Pier(s) *Ear(s)* Known as 'Southends', presumably in relation to the sticking out kind.

Southend-on-Sea *Pee/Wee* A term for 'having one up the wheel' that was probably coined on a beano by a bunch of drunken day-trippers who kept stopping the coach to do just that.

Souvenir a) A venereal disease caught on holiday and brought home for treatment. Souvenirs of Ibiza are are common among the young at present.
b) To steal, a piece that started in World War One when German artifacts were taken as 'souvenirs'. Now, hotel towels and ashtrays are regularly 'souvenired'.

Sov £1, a term that's often heard in the jargon of wide boys, market traders and taxi drivers. Sometimes said as a 'sob'.

Sow A derogatory term for a woman, originally a fat one.

Sozzled One of the many well-known terms for being drunk. 'Sozzle' – to drink alcohol.

Space Cadet A drug addict, one who is permanently high or 'spaced out'.

Spacecake A cake made with the addition of cannabis.

Spaced Out Under the influence of drugs, high, 'in orbit', detached from reality.

Spacker Anything or anybody considered worthless or useless, from a no-hope greyhound to a troublesome car.

Spade A black person, from the colour of that suit of cards.

Spag-Bol Student's and other assorted young people's term for 'spaghetti bollock-naked' or bolognaise.

Spaghetti Bender A fairly common term for an Italian that is sometimes reduced solely to the first element. Also 'spag', 'spaggo' or 'spagaroni', a hybrid of two pastas, the other being macaroni.

Spam Fritter *Shitter (Anus)* A newish term based on an oldish type of junk food.

Spamhead A bald man, especially one with a high forehead, whose head resembles a slice of spam.

Spanish Liquorice. A piece from at least the 1950s, when a penny spanish was a common purchase in the sweet shop.

Spanish Archer		A rejection or dismissal, the elbow or what a 'Don' (qv) fires his arrows with, 'el bow'.
Spanish Guitar	*Cigar*	An old term that's commonly stubbed to a 'Spanish'.
Spanish Main	*Drain*	Money lost or wasted may be regarded as 'money down the Spanish'. Based on the historical name given to the north-east coast of South America between Panama and the Orinoco river, a region regularly plundered by Long John Silver and other TV pirates of the 1950s, when the term was probably coined.
Spanish Onion	*Bunion*	Apt in that both can bring tears to the eyes.
Spanish Waiter	*Potato*	Boil, roast, bake or mash, whichever way you cook it it's still a 'Spanish', although on a Costa holiday it'll probably be chipped.
Spanking		A beating, very often a piece of underworld jargon relating to the punishment meted out to someone considered to deserve it: 'He crossed us so he had to take a spanking.' Also to be well beaten in a sporting contest.
Spanner		A sexually attractive or provocative woman, one who 'tightens the nuts'.
Spare		Unattached women. Boys on the 'pull' gather at pubs where there is 'plenty of spare'. A single female may be condescendingly referred to as a 'bit of spare'.
Spare Prick at a Wedding		How anyone who considers himself to be superfluous to requirements, useless, or standing idle likens himself.
Spare Rib	*Fib*	Fills a hole when a 'pork pie' (qv) is little and white.
Spark		To knock-out, a term from the fight game. A 'sparker' – a knock-out punch.
Spark Out		Unconscious or in a deep sleep, either through exhaustion or a blow, which may render the victim 'sparkers' or 'sparko'.
Sparkle/Sparklers		Jewellery, gems, very often diamonds. A couple of terms from the underworld that have been around for as long as thieves have been leaving the scene of the crime.
Sparks		a) A radio operator, a piece that's been knocking around the military airwaves since a radio was a wireless. b) An electrician, a theatrical term that's now heard on every building site in the land.
Sparrow Brain		A practically brainless person, one who would have to rise in intelligence to become an idiot.
Sparrow-Fart		Dawn, the early bird is up at the 'crack of sparrow-fart'.

Sparrowhawking	Picking up young people, usually runaways, in order to exploit them sexually. The image of small birds and the predatory bastards who prey on them.
Sparrow's Kneecaps	A belittling term for the biceps of a very skinny person.
Spastic	A weak, incompetent, clumsy person. An unkind term that's often reduced to 'spaz' or 'spazzo'. 'Spazzy' – stupid. 'Spazmobile' – an invalid car or wheelchair.
Spat	A 1950s term for a filter tip, a supposed lung protector based on an old-fashioned shoe protector.
Spearchucker	A derogatory term for a black person.
Special K	A 1980s term for the drug ketamine.
Specky/Specky Foureyes	A couple of names given to people who wear glasses.
Speed	An amphetamine drug especially methamphetamine.
Speed Freak	A regular 'speed' (qv) user.
Speed Limit	The number thirty at the bingo hall.
Speedball	A mixture of cocaine with heroin or morphine.
Speeding	The taking of, or under the influence of, 'speed' (qv).
Speedrap	To talk fast and excessively while 'speeding' (qv). When a crowd are on 'speed' everyone talks but nobody listens.
Spending	Money. It you're 'holding spending' you have money to play with. 'Spenders' – coins.
Spend a Penny	To urinate. Coined in the days when the door of a public toilet required an old penny to open it. Now, as we approach monetary union with Europe, will we get the urge to 'euronate'? And if so, will we be 'europeein'?
Spick	To the British, since the 1960s and the package holiday, this is exclusively a Spaniard. To the rest of the world it's any Hispanic person.
Spiel	Patter or the persuasive talk of a salesman or con man. Sometimes said as 'shpiel'.
Spieler	a) A persuasive talker, especially a con man or swindler. b) An illegal gambling club or a big money card game at a private destination. The term is based on the German *spielen* (to play) and sometimes said as 'shpieler'.
Spiffed	Drunk, a 19th-century term that seems to be a reduction of 'spifflicated', which in standard English means 'destroyed', which is also a slang term for being drunk, much like 'wrecked' (qv).
Spifflicated	Drunk. See SPIFFED.

Spike

a) An ancient term for a dosshouse that's still used among those who seek to use one.

b) A drug user's term for a hypodermic needle. To 'spike' or 'spike up' – to inject.

Spill

To disclose information, to 'spill the beans' or 'spill one's guts'.

Spin

To search a property. Jargon of the police and the underworld, to 'spin' someone's drum is to search their house and to 'spin' someone's wheels is to search their vehicle.

Spin on One!

'Up Yours!' 'Get Stuffed!' Or a similar sentiment. 'Spin on This!' (qv) without the finger.

Spin on This!

A comment that accompanies a raised middle finger which roughly translates to 'Up Yours!'

Spinach

Banknotes, another term from the time when pound notes were in existence. *See also* GREENS, LETTUCE *and* CABBAGE. Like the vegetables, nicker notes were also green and crinkly.

Spit & Drag   *Fag (Cigarette)*

An apt example especially where roll-ups are concerned, when bits of tobacco get dragged in and spat out.

Spit & Sawdust

Originally a rough bar where sawdust was strewn on the floor so that any spit, beer and often blood, could be easily soaked up and swept. The term now applies to anywhere basic or unpretentious. A modest hotel or restaurant may be described as 'a bit spit and sawdust'.

Spit Roast

A woman who, while fellating a man is simultaneously being penetrated from the rear.

Spitfire

A cigarette lighter. Perhaps a piece of lost but supremely apt RS on the World War Two aeroplane, the Spitfire fighter.

Spitting Feathers

To be extremely thirsty, having a dry throat.

Splash

a) Water in any form. From a glass of 'splash' to great bodies of 'splash' like rivers, lakes and seas. 'The Splash' – the sea.

b) A swim or a paddle. From an epic 'splash' across the channel to a mess about in a pool.

c) A bath, a shower or a wash. Anything that incorporates soap and water can be a 'splash'.

d) A mineral water as ordered in a pub or restaurant, or the bottled 'splash' from the supermarket.

e) To urinate and what 'splashes one's boots' as a result.

Splash Paper

Toilet paper put into a lavatory prior to sitting on it in order to prevent an anal soaking caused by 'fall-out', which may be double dodgy if there's any Harpic about.

Splash Someone's Throat
To ejaculate into the mouth of a fellator.

Spliff
A cannabis cigarette, a piece that originated in the West Indies but is now commonly smoked in Britain.

Split
a) A detective, a late 19th-century term that's still on the case, which derives from an earlier meaning. *See* (c).

b) The vagina, an example along the lines of 'gash' and 'slit'. *See both.*

c) To inform against, to betray. An example that invokes the unwritten law of the underworld: Never split on a friend. 'Splitter' – an informer.

d) To share, as in 'Come on, I'll split a bottle of scotch with you.' Originally it was a share out of ill-gotten gains, which it still is of course.

e) To leave, a 1950s piece that's left over from the jargon of beatniks.

Split Pea   *Tea*
A piece that was brewed in the 19th century and has all but evaporated.

Splodge/ Splodger
A general term of address to a man: 'How's it going Splodge?'

Splosh
a) Money, a 19th-century term that crossed the currency divide into decimals in 1971.

b) Tea, well-known as a 'cuppa splosh'. 'Splosh wagon' – a mobile canteen. Tea was previously known as 'slops'.

c) The vagina and therefore a general term for a woman as a sex object, i.e., a 'bit of splosh'. From one of the sounds of intercourse.

Spod
An inept, awkward or slow-witted person. A cruel jibe used mainly by teenagers against one of their own age group.

Spondulicks
Money, an old term that's still in circulation.

Sponge
a) A heavy drinker, a 'soak'. Someone who absorbs a lot of liquid.

b) A tough or game boxer, one who soaks up a lot of punishment but still comes forward.

Spook
A derogatory term for a black person used by whites. Strange that a derogatory black term for a white person is a 'ghost' (qv).

Spoon
A measure of heroin, enough to provide one injection. Approximately a teaspoonful.

Sporran
Pubic hair. A furry piece that's used for a purse, comes in for a 'fur-piece' (qv) that covers a 'purse' (qv).

Sporting Life	*Wife*	Either based on an extinct racing paper or the person who coined it had a sexually fulfilling marriage.
Spotted Dick	*Sick*	Not necessarily as nasty as it sounds where men are concerned, any illness can get you booked off as 'spotted dick'. Can also apply to a portion of regurge seen lying on a pavement, perhaps as a result of eating too much of this sweet.
Spotty Dog	*Wog*	Refers to any foreigner, irrespective of colour. Particularly, it would seem, people from Dalmatia.
Sprasi Anna	*Tanner*	A piece that's been consigned to the money box of obscurity. A 'sprasi' (pronounced 'sprarsey') was sixpence in old money, although strangely, around the turn of the millennium, the term (minus Anna) and no longer RS, has made a comeback as £1.
Spray Someone's Tonsils		To ejaculate into a fellator's mouth. To 'coat a throat'.
Spray the Ovaries		To ejaculate inside a woman during unprotected sex, often the moment of passion that ends with a pregnancy: 'If you didn't want the kid you shouldn't have sprayed the ovaries.'
Spring		To contrive the release or escape of a captive, either by direct means or by legal wrangling. 'He got sprung on a technicality.'
Sprinkle		To urinate, the adult version of 'tinkle'.
Sprog		a) A new recruit or novice, an example that originated in the armed forces. b) A child, a piece that has become common since World War Two, often for the product of an unwanted pregnancy. 'Sprogged up' – pregnant. 'Sprog stopper' – a condom.
Sprog Bog		A humorous appellation from the 1990s regarding a child's potty.
Sproot		A pus-filled spot, a yellowhead. One ripe for a squeeze.
Sprout		An old term for a small child, one that, like a sprout, has some growing to do.
Spruce		a) A cheap imitation, a fake. Anything designed to deceive. 'Spruce' perfume for example, may come in the right bottle but it ain't the real McCoy. The term derives from the spruce tree. During prohibition in America, an imitation beer made from spruce needles and twigs, and called spruce beer, was inflicted on thirsty yanks. b) To lie, deceive or con. A swindler will 'spruce' you.
Spud		A hole in the heel of a sock, so called because of it's resemblance to a potato.

Spud Ugly		Descriptive of a homely person, someone who is no vegetable oil painting. 'Spuggly' for short.
Spud-Bashing		A spell of potato peeling, especially as part of a military punishment.
Spunk		a) Probably the best-known term there is for semen. It also comes off as a verb, to 'spunk' is to ejaculate. b) To waste money: 'I spunked my money up the betting shop wall.'
Spunk Bucket		A promiscuous woman, one whose vagina is seen as a receptacle for collecting semen. Also 'spunk pot', which is firstly a term for the vagina and then its owner.
Spunk Stain		A dirty, smelly, all-round repugnant person.
Spunk Stained		An adulterous woman who has been found out, a piece that's been around since the early 1960s. While American singer Connie Francis was singing 'Lipstick on Your Collar' (told a tale on you) at the top of the charts, young men were changing the words to 'Spunk Stains on Your Gusset'. The term may also apply to any promiscuous woman.
Spunker		An old, derogatory term for a promiscuous woman. If she's an 'old spunker' she's well used to semen extraction. Also refers to a prostitute.
Squad Halt	*Salt*	A military piece that stems from World War One, therefore a seasoned campaigner in the service of RS.
Squaddie		A private soldier in the army. A squad member.
Square		An old-fashioned or conventional person, someone out of touch with modern trends.
Square Bashing		A military term for drill on the barrack square or parade ground.
Square Rigger	*Nigger*	A derogatory term that originated long ago, possibly in the docks.
Square-Head		A well-known term for a German, who apparently has a less rounded skull than anyone else.
Squeak		a) A chance, racing jargon. If a horse is 'in with a squeak' it has a good chance of winning. b) A young, naive and impressionable teenager, a boy whose voice hasn't yet broken and a girl just out of the 'teenybopper' stage. c) An informer, an ancient term for one who 'puts the squeak in'. Also to 'squeak' – to inform against, to betray. d) Information that's been given to the police, a tip-off. Also a rumour: 'I've heard a squeak . . .'
Squeaker		An informer, one who divulges secret information, not necessarily to the police.

Squeal		To turn informer, to betray an accomplice to the police, to make the noise of a rat. 'Thou shalt not squeal' – the unwritten law of the underworld.
Squealer/Squeal		A couple of terms for an informer.
Squeegee		A traffic-light windscreen washer, the pest who suds up your screen whether you like it or not.
Squeeze the Lemon		To urinate. Of a man that is.
Squeezer		A yellowhead or any other bustable spot, one which a woman seems to delight in 'getting' or squeezing.
Squid		£1, a play on 'quid' which became popular in the 1990s.
Squiffed/Squiffy		A brace of terms for being slightly drunk or tipsy. Both hail from the 19th century and are still active.
Squiggle		A signature, a term often heard in the courier game: 'Did you get a squiggle for that last job?'
Squire		A general term of address to a man, generally a stranger.
Squirrel-Food		Crazy, zany, mad, eccentric. An assorted variety of 'nuts' get turned into a 'nice one's' (qv) dinner.
Squirt		a) A small, often disagreeable person. An overbearing little bleeder. Also a child, often a precocious one. Sometimes said as 'squit'. b) To urinate, an example often heard in the pub: 'Just going for a squirt.' c) To ejaculate or an ejaculation. Fanciable women are said to be 'worth a squirt'.
Squits/Squitters		Diarrhoea, a pair of terms that have been on the go since the 19th century, so no flash in the pan these.
Sri Lanka	*Wanker*	A useless or worthless individual, an example that was first seen in a national newspaper with a headline which blazed 'What a Bunch of Sri Lankas', an aspersion cast upon our cricket team after it lost a test match to that country.
St Clement	*Lemon*	'An obvious connection with the old nursery rhyme 'Oranges and Lemons'. Based on the patron saint of citrus fruit. Is it?
St George		A name given to a man who likes ugly women, his conquests are always 'dragons' (qv).
St Louis Blues	*Shoes*	A 1960s term that's based on an old jazz song and worn as 'St Louies'.
St Martins-le-Grand(s)	*Hand(s)*	The extended version of 'Martin-le-Grand' (qv). Based on the name of a street in the City of London and always shaken down to 'St Martins'.
Staff of Life		An old and appropriate term for the penis.

Stage Fright	*Light (Ale)*	A theatrical piece hinting at the calming effect a bevvy or two can have on the nerves before a performance.
Stains		An insignificant male, a loner. From the semen stains of a habitual masturbator or someone given to the sheet-soiling dreams of the sexually inactive.
Stair Dancing/ Jumping		Stealing from office blocks, from the nimbleness needed for such an occupation.
Stalk		Impudence, cheek or effrontery. A term that equates a stalk with a neck. *See* NECK.
Stalk/Stalk On		A couple of terms for an erection, both of which are long, and still, standing.
Stallion		A sexually active, virile man. Not necessarily in a stable relationship.
Stammer & Stutter	*Butter*	An old and widely uttered term for bread-spread.
Stamp		The size and build of somebody, often used when describing them: 'I wasn't gonna argue with the bloke, he was about Lennox Lewis's stamp.'
Stan & Ollie	*Brolly*	Famous more for their bowlers, this great pair of clowns would no doubt have placed their new umbrellas under their coats in a shower to stop them from getting wet. *See* LAUREL & HARDY.
Stand/Stand-Up		A brace of terms for an erection, as Prince Phillip did for the Queen on at least four occasions.
Stand at Ease	*Cheese*	Another example that grew out of the trenches during World War One.
Stand from Under	*Thunder*	The term is used by people working at a height as a warning when something is to be dropped to the ground. It's therefore an aptish piece.
Stand In		To cost, as in: 'How much did that round stand you in?'
Stand On		To trust, much heard in the patter of a con man: 'Stand on me, you'll love it.'
Stand One's Corner		To pay for one's share of something, especially a round of drinks.
Stand Still For		To tolerate, suffer or accept. There's a limit to what most people will stand still for before they snap.
Stand the Broads		To be duped, taken in or hoodwinked. Literally to accept what a cardsharp deals you. *See* BROADS.
Stand the Three-Card Trick		To be gullible or easily conned: 'You stand the three-card trick every time. They must see you coming.' The trick is also known as 'find the lady.'
Stand to Attention	*Pension*	Originally referred to an ex-serviceman's pension but has found its way to the post office in civvy street, where pensioners stand in line for their 'stand to'.

Standers		A 19th-century term for the legs which still has a kick left in it.
Stand-Up		A comedian, or comedy itself if it only involves a comic standing at a microphone. A term that came into its own in the 1980s with the boom in comedy clubs.
Stanley Knife	*Wife*	A modern piece based on the tool that seems to play it's part in every trade.
Stardust		Cocaine, due to it's popularity among rock, film and sports stars.
Starkers		In the nude, stark naked or, of a man, 'stark bollock naked'.
Starry Night	*Shite*	Used in connection with rubbish or nonsense. 'What a load of starry night'. How someone who knows nothing about art but knows what he likes may judge a Turner Prize Winner.
Star's Nap	*Tap (Borrow)*	Based on the bet of the day in the *Star* newspaper (the previous *Star*), it wouldn't have been uncommon to tap someone for a nicker to back it. Anyone seeking a loan is 'on the Star's nap'.
Starsky & Hutch	*Crutch/Crotch*	Based on a popular American cops and crooks TV programme from the 1970s, the threat of a 'kick up the Starsky' is a deterrent from that time.
Stash		Drugs, especially cannabis, for personal use. 'Keep your hands off my stash.'
State		An ugly or weird-looking person, someone who dresses scruffily or laughably. Literally a mess. The age-old question: 'How can a state like him pull a tasty bird like that?'
Steak & Bubble	*Trouble*	Steak and bubble and squeak leaves the nosh-up list to give us a spot of bother.
Steak & Kidney	*Sidney*	Shortened to 'steak' to join an elite band of Christian names to have a term of RS. Australians used it as a referrence to Sydney.
Steak & Kidney Pie	*Eye*	A piece that hasn't knocked 'mince pie' (qv) off the menu.
Steam Packet	*Jacket*	Formed on a type of early steamboat, this has been sailing the seas of changing fashions since the 19th century.
Steam Tug	*a) Bug*	With modern hygiene the term 'steamers' is now mainly heard in older people's recollections of the 'good old days'. Although, while unscrupulous landlords exist, don't rule out a comeback.
	b) Mug	A gullible fool, commonly known as a 'steamer', is easily taken in.
Steam Tugs	*Drugs*	A ready-made slogan for keeping kids off drugs –

'Steam Tugs Are for Steamers'. *See* STEAM TUG (b).

Steamboats		Drunk. A 1980s term, possibly an extension of 'steaming' (qv, b).
Steamer		a) A 1960s term for a homosexual based on a steam iron. Also a 'steaming iron'. *See* IRON HOOF.
		b) A racehorse whose odds are drastically cut, a result of punters 'steaming into' it – backing it.
Steaming		a) A mass mugging in a confined space, an underground train compartment for instance, which is rushed by a gang of thieves who rob the passengers in the process.
		b) Drunk. Extremely drunk in fact. Descriptive of someone who sleeps where he falls.
		c) Furious, literally boiling with rage.
Steamroller		Anybody lacking tact or diplomacy, from what they are said to be 'as subtle as'.
Steamroller	*Bowler (Hat)*	A dying piece simply because the headwear of the typical city gent is all but a thing of the past.
Steel, the		A 19th-century term for a prison.
Steffi Graf	*a) Bath*	The German tennis queen comes on court as a modern term for a soak.
	b) Laugh	The 1990s version of 'You must be joking' is 'You're having a Steffi'.
Stenchfoot		An imaginary disease that people with smelly feet are said to suffer from. A play on the real complaint, trench foot.
Stench-Trench		An appropriate term for the anal area.
Stephen Fry	*Pie*	A piece used by young boozers of the 1990s regarding what is frequently bought from the chippy on the way home from the pub. Based on a British actor and writer.
Stephenson's Rocket	*Pocket*	A wise businessman knows that you can't fill your own 'Stephensons' without first lining someone else's. Based on the train built by George Stephenson (1781–1848), which in 1829 zipped along at a breathtaking 29 mph (46 kph).
Sterrika/Sturrika		A strong, hard man, usually a criminal or thug. A corruption of the Yiddish word *schtarka*.
Steve McQueens	*Jeans*	Based on a US filmstar (1930–80) who always had a fashionable image. He lived fast and died young but, unlike a pair of denims, he won't fade.
Stevie Wonder	*Thunder*	A 1990s entry into the RS chart based on an American singer/songwriter. Anything futile may be said to be 'like farting against Stevie Wonder'.

Stew		Alcoholic drink, hence to 'go out on the stew'.
Stewart Granger	*Danger*	A 1980s example that relates to chance, as in the moan of a long-waiting customer of a slow-moving barmaid: 'Any Stewart Granger of getting pissed in here today?' Based on a London-born film star (1913–93).
Stewed		Drunk. 'Stewed as a prune' – very drunk.
Stewed Prune	*Tune*	The job of the rapidly disappearing pub pianist is to hammer out the 'stewed prunes'.
Stick		a) An archaic term for the penis that still gets a shake. 'Stick and bangers' – penis and testicles. b) A cigarette, whether ordinary or one containing cannabis. c) A snooker cue, often when used as a weapon in a pub fight. 'He came at me with a bottle so I broke a stick across his head.' d) To stab, an old piece from gangland. A 'sticker' is a knife or any weapon used for stabbing.
Stick of Chalk	*Walk*	An old piece that's always lagged way behind 'ball of chalk'.
Stick of Rock	*Cock (Penis)*	A piece based on a seaside tradition which seems to have been made for the seaside postcard as a double entendre for oral sex.
Stick One On		To punch, as in 'The Loser's Story' told by Mr S Hubbard, an old East End character: 'I've stuck one on him, he's gone down. He's got up! He's stuck one on me, I've gone down. I didn't get up!'
Stick(s) & Stone(s)	*Bone(s)*	Let's hope we all make old sticks, nobody can ask for more than a long life and a short death.
Sticks		a) Legs, a 19th-century term that is now well used by football pundits: 'He's handy with his left stick.' b) A nickname for a drummer, originally one in a jazz band. c) Goal posts, either on the football or rugby pitch. d) Less than technical jargon for the stumps that make a wicket.
Sticksing		Picking pockets, a piece used by black criminals. 'Sticksman' – a pickpocket.
Sticky		Used to describe a glue sniffer, this is always followed by a name: 'Seen sticky Charlie lately?'
Sticky Bun	*Son*	An uncommon alternative to 'currant bun' for the male offspring.
Sticky Finger		Manual stimulation of a vagina. A term used disappointedly by boys to describe the extent of

a girl's sexual favours: 'Two hours I was trying and all I got was a sticky finger.' Also 'Stinky Finger'.

Sticky Fingers — Said to be the fingers of a thief. Things adhere to his digits.

Sticky-Nose — A glue sniffer, a piece that has recently crept in: 'It's dodgy walking past those garages at night, it's full of sticky-noses up there.'

Sticky Toffee *Coffee* — A cup of 'sticky' as poured from the pen of a TV scriptwriter.

Stiff — a) A well-known term for a corpse, whereby to 'Stiff' someone is to kill them. Also a dull person, the direct opposite of the life and soul of the party. *See* DEAD BODY.

b) An erection, a piece that's been in existence for 300 years and shows no sign of wilting. Also of a man, to have intercourse: 'Sorry I'm late, the wife wanted an early morning stiffing.'

c) A loser, an example that started on the race-course with a bad horse, but now any unfortunate or pitiable individual can be a 'stiff'. 'Stiffs' – in professional football, the reserves.

d) Drunk. 'Stiff as a board' – incapably so.

e) To rob, cheat or short-change: 'A bet's a bet, you lost so pay up. I won't be stiffed.'

f) To knock unconscious, usually with a punch – to 'knock someone stiff' is to 'stiff' him.

Stiffie — A well-known term for an erection. Unromantic wooing: 'Come on luv, I've a stiffie like a baseball bat. Be a shame to waste it.'

Still Shitting Yellow — Young, figuratively still a baby. Usually said of an adolescent in a hurry to grow up.

Stilts — Long legs, especially of a young woman, one whose 'stilts go right up to her bum'.

Sting — a) A complex and well-planned swindle which ends with the victim being 'stung'. As in the famous film of this name from 1973.

b) To borrow money without any intention of paying it back. *See* WASP.

c) To swindle, cheat or short-change. Generally, to dishonestly take money from.

Stinging Nettle *Kettle* — When it's tea-time in the suburbs, they put the 'stinging' on.

Stink — Of a performer or sportsman, to put on a bad performance. An unfunny comedian or a boxer who fights badly may 'stink the place out.'

Stink-/Stinky-Finger		A couple of old names for the middle finger, from it's use in sexual foreplay.
Stinker		a) An objectionable person, a piece from an old-fashioned, upper-class book of insults.
		b) A poor performance by a sportsman, what an off-form footballer may have.
		c) Anything difficult to do. A question in an exam or a crossword puzzle, for instance.
Stinking		a) Drunk as a dozen skunks.
		b) Extremely wealthy, filthy 'stinking' rich. Said by people who aren't.
Stinkpot		A mild term of abuse since the 19th century, probably an extension of 'stinker' (a).
Stinks		Said of anything suspicious, especially of the smell of corruption or sleaze. If it's 'fishy', it stinks like a Billingsgate carsey.
Stink-Weed		Marijuana, from its distinctive smell.
Stir		A well-known term for prison since the 19th century. From the Romany term *sturiben* – a prison. 'Stir crazy' – prison-induced madness, institutionalised.
Stirling Moss	*Toss*	Can be used to signify something of little value, an untrustworthy person may not be worth a 'Stirling'. Also those who don't care 'don't give a Stirling'. After Britain's most famous-ever racing driver.
Stitch Up		a) To con, cheat or generally 'have over'. A victim of a 'stitch-up' may claim to have been 'stitched'.
		b) Of the police, to fabricate evidence to ensure a conviction.
Stiver/Stever		An old penny. Obsolete terms for a vanished coin.
Stocking Fillers		Female legs, especially when long and shapely.
Stocks & Shares	*Stairs*	A lesser-known alternative to the much-quoted 'apples and pears' (qv).
Stoinker		An overweight and smelly person, a cross between a 'stinker' and an 'oinker', or 'pig-stinking'.
Stoke on Trent	*Bent*	A 1970s term for a homosexual which in the 1990s also became an example for stolen goods or 'bent gear'. Anything for sale 'on the cheap' is likely to be 'Stoke on Trent'. (From the Staffordshire town.)
Stoke One's Boiler/Furnace		To masturbate, a couple of ways of letting off steam.
Stomper		A plank used by crop circle hoaxers for flattening a crop.
Stone Bonker/Ginger		A couple of terms that relate to an absolute certainty: 'United have got to be stone bonkers to win the league again.' I don't know about 'bonker' but Stone Ginger was a successful early 20th-century racehorse.

Stone in One's Own Shoe, the		To be one's own worst enemy, to cause oneself unnecessary pain and suffering.
Stone Jug	*Mug*	A rare alternative to 'steam tug' (qv) for someone considered to be the filling for a con man's sandwich.
Stone Me		An exclamation of surprise, a well-known catchphrase of British comic Tony Hancock. Complete surprise comes in the form of 'Stone Me Hooray', a less well-known favourite of British pensioner Bert Puxley, my old man, who has used it for as long as I can remember.
Stone the Crows		A well-known exclamation of surprise.
Stoned		Under the influence of drink or drugs, well-known either way. Drunks and druggies may get 'stoned to the gills', 'eyeballs' or 'out of their minds'.
Stonefaced		Descriptive of a person who never shows any emotion, an unsmiling individual. The nickname of the straight-faced US comedian Buster Keaton (1895–1966).
Stones		An 18th-century term for the testicles that's still rolling.
Stonker		Anything big and impressive or great and good. Large breasts are known as 'stonkers' and it's an erection to be proud of.
Stonkered		Drunk. Well and truly 'stonkered' – tight as a titled layabout.
Stonking		a) Excellent, great. 'The stonking new CD by Malcolm P Barnoldswick and the Fangogglers.' b) Extremely, as in the 'stonking great pay rise' that New Labour MPs voted themselves just after securing a second term in power in 2001.
Stony/Stony Broke		Penniless, entirely without money. Inhabitants of Poverty Row are also said to be 'rocky' and 'pebble beached'.
Stooge		A dominated friend, a lapdog or sidekick: 'If he's happy to be your stooge, good luck to him.'
Stoolie		A police informer, a reduction of the well-known 'stool pigeon'.
Stop & Go	*Toe*	A tootsie term that's often reduced to 'stops', but may be used in full when trouble's afoot, that is when someone's standing on your 'stop and go'.
Stop & Start	*Heart*	An anatomically relevant piece that once it starts should only stop once.
Stop Thief	*Beef*	An ancient piece that may, when it was coined, have been fitting. Food, especially meat, was an oft-stolen commodity among the poor of Victorian London.

Stop Ticking		To die, the image of a stopped clock which is heard in to 'stop someone's clock – to kill them.
Stopper		A hard piece of excrement that causes constipation, much like the one seen at 'bung in the bottle' (qv).
Story		a) An old euphemism for a lie, young children are often told not to 'tell stories'. 'Story teller' – a liar. b) Information, the gen: 'So what's the story?' 'Story teller' – an informer, one who 'tells stories out of school'.
Stotious		Drunk, a term from Scotland from the word 'stot' – to stagger drunkenly.
Stow		To cease from, desist. 'Stow it!' – pack it in! 'Stow your noise!' – be quiet!
Stradivarius		A dishonest way of making money, a good 'fiddle' (qv) based on the up-market violin.
Straight		Someone to be trusted, a term that has bubbled up from the underworld.
Straight & Narrow	*Barrow*	A wheelbarrow, an example heard on a building site for that which is pushed up a straight and narrow scaffold board.
Straighten/ Straighten Up		To bribe, to give a backhander to someone to 'straighten them out'. A 'Straightener' – a bung.
Straighten Out		To put somebody right, to show how to do something the 'right way' even if it's the wrong way, i.e. illegal.
Straightener		A fight that will finally put an end to an argument or long-running feud.
Strain Off		To urinate, to go for a 'strain-off'.
Strain the Greens		To urinate, a colourful expression from the 1950s.
Stramash		A fight or row, generally, an altercation: 'There was a right old stramash down the Skinners last night.'
Strangely Weird	*Beard*	Generally shorn to the first element, a piece from the 1950s, when beatniks typically had 'strangelys' and were considered weird.
Strangler		A necktie, an old term that's still relevant but hardly used today.
Strap		Credit, therefore 'on the strap' – on credit.
Strapadictomy		A humorous euphemism for lesbianism. Say it quickly.
Strap-On		A dildo, one that is worn by lesbians.
Strapped		Short of money, hard-up. Famously 'strapped' for cash.
Strawberry Ripple	*Cripple*	A less-common alternative to the more popular flavoured ice-cream 'Raspberry Ripple' (qv).
Strawberry Tart	*Heart*	Broken to 'strawberry', possibly because of a resemblance.

Street		In racing parlance, a long winning margin: 'It's won by a street.'
Strength, the		The real facts, the information, the gen. In a word, the truth.
Stretch		a) A one-year prison sentence, a 19th-century term that is still serving time. A piece that gets on the end of the number of years given, therefore a five stretch is five years. A long 'stretch' is an unspecified number of years.'
		b) A year, a piece that's escaped the confines of (a) and is commonly used on the outside: 'I haven't had a fag for a stretch now.'
		c) An old term for elastic, which saw men's braces become 'Stretchers' and an elastic band a 'Stretcher'.
Stretched		Hanged, a piece from the days of capital punishment, when murderers had their necks stretched. Still used by the pro-hanging lobby: 'I'd stretch 'em.'
Strides		A common term for trousers, a piece that has seen many changes in fashion since it's formation.
Strike		£1, a piece that may be heard when the hat's passed round for a collection. Day-trippers may throw in a 'strike' for the coach driver.
Strike/Striker		A match, both were quite well used until the cheap disposable lighter hit the scene. A 'box of strikes/strikers'.
Strike Me Dead	*Bread*	Mostly cut to a slice of 'strike me'.
String Beans	*Jeans*	Often shortened to 'strings', which is just as often fitting.
String Vest	*Pest*	A garment, which is worn in full in the company of a nuisance: 'Why do we put up with this string vest?'
Stripe		a) A scar, usually across the face and the result of being slashed with a knife or razor.
		b) £1, a 1950s term used by national servicemen, the boys who turned a 'corporal' into £2 (two stripes) and a 'sergeant' into £3 (three stripes).
		c) A 1990s term for a police car, a white one with a red stripe along the side.
Stripe Up		To con, cheat, short-change or to generally 'have over'. Victims of a 'stripe-up' have been 'striped'.
Stroke		a) To masturbate and also the act of masturbation: 'Talk about embarrassing, his mother caught him having a stroke.' Also a 'stroke-off'.
		b) A liberty, a dirty trick, an underhand or dishonest act. Commonly to 'pull a stroke'.
Stroke Book/Mag		A dirty book or magazine, hard porn or soft. Anything a man can have a 'stroke' by (qv, a).
Strong It		a) To ask one extra favour, or to take one liberty too

many. If you borrow someone's car, you're 'stronging it' if you also want to borrow the petrol money.

b) To behave aggressively or bombastically, to 'come on strong'.

c) To lie extravagantly, to exaggerate, to overdo it.

Stronzer

An unpleasant, repugnant person, from the Italian *stronzo* – a piece of shit.

Strop

a) To masturbate and the act of masturbation, possibly from the action of stropping a razor.

b) A display of bad temper, a sulk, to be in a bad mood: 'She's been in a strop all day.'

Stroppy

Bad tempered, irritable or antagonistic. Many a row has started with the line: 'Don't get stroppy with me, pal.'

Struggle & Strain   *Train*

Originally confined to the railway but in the 1980s came to refer to physical exertion, to train, which seems quite suitable.

Struggle & Strainers   *Trainers*

'Struggles' are the required footwear for 'struggling and straining' (*see previous entry*). They are also the overpriced necessity for fashion-conscious teenagers who have to be seen wearing the right names on their feet.

Struggle & Strife   a) *Life*

If ever there was an appropriate term, this is it. Unless you're one of the silver spoon brigade. Also, a life sentence is a 'struggle'.

b) *Wife*

May be as apt as (a) given the right circumstances, i.e., the wrong woman.

Strum

Of a woman, to masturbate.

Stuff

a) To have sexual intercourse, a euphemism for 'fuck' that's also heard in terms like 'stuff my old boots', 'get stuffed' and the unconcerned can rarely 'give a stuff'.

b) To defeat, either in a sporting battle or a serious one. Also to emerge victorious from a battle of wits or an argument.

c) To get the better of someone with a hoax or a wind-up, where the victim is 'nicely stuffed'.

d) To thwart somebody or ruin their chances, often by foul means.

Stuff!

A general term of approval or delight, short for 'great stuff'.

Stuffed

Beaten, thwarted or ruined. In a word 'fucked'.

Stumble

To break wind in a foul malodorous manner.

Stumer

a) Anything worthless or useless, originally a dud cheque or a counterfeit banknote. Now mainly heard in regard to a flop, which may be a losing

		racehorse or a box office failure at the theatre. To be 'put on a stumer' is to be given a losing tip. b) A blunder, therefore to 'drop a stumer' – make a mistake.
Stumps		The legs, hence 'stir your stumps' – get moving. In the 19th century the term related to a wooden leg, and a peg-legged man was known as 'Stumpy'.
Stung		If you've ever lent money to someone and not got it back, you've been 'stung': 'You stung me for a score last week, you're not getting any more.' Also to be overcharged. *See* WASP.
Stutter & **Stammer**	*Hammer*	Normally banged down to a 'stutter'.
Subby		A sub-contractor, a term heard on every building site in the country.
Suck		A well-known American term that relates to being awful, useless or generally unpleasant. A piece of graffito: Toothless People Suck!
Suck-Arse/Butt		To behave in an obsequious, toadying or grovelling manner. To 'kiss arse in French', i.e., with the tongue well in evidence, as a 'suck-arse' or 'suck-butt' will do.
Suck In		To cheat, con or deceive. To sell a dummy.
Suck Mine!		An exclamation of defiance that's akin to 'Up Yours!' or 'Bollocks!' Also 'Suck Cock!'
Suck Off		To perform fellatio until 'tonsils are sprayed'.
Sucker		a) A gullible fool, someone easily deceived or 'sucked in'. b) A sweet, an old term that's still heard at the pick 'n' mix counter.
Suet		Human fat as worn by the overweight: 'You've put on a bit of suet since I last saw you.'
Sugar		Heroin, morphine and more recently cocaine. In the 1960s it applied to LSD, which was taken on sugar lumps, as in the banned record of the period by the Smoke, 'My Friend Jack' (eats sugar lumps).
Sugar & Honey	*Money*	Very old and widely used in the truncated form of 'sugar', which is a 'sweetener' when used as a bribe.
Sugar & Spice	*a) Ice*	Mainly employed in the sense of a drinks chiller. Too much may draw an admonishing: 'There's enough sugar here to freeze an elephant's arsehole.'
	b) Nice	Always decreased to 'sugar', this doesn't take on the sarcastic aspect of 'apples and rice' (qv).
Sugar Candy	*a) Brandy*	An archaic piece, but one that is still shouted for.
	b) Handy	The major employment for this is in an ironic sense, anything useless may be described as this.

Sugar Stick	*Prick*	A reference to the sex pistol that may loom large at talk of oral sex.
Sugar Up		To bribe, to grease someone's palm, to 'sweeten' them. *See* SWEETENER.
Suit		Somebody who works in management, a piece that's used derogatorily by 'overalls' (qv), often of a faceless bureaucrat, a 'lightender' (qv).
Suitable Case		Mentally unsound, not right. A 'suitable case for treatment', as in the 1966 film *Morgan*.
Suited & Booted		An old term for being dressed in your finest clobber: 'Make sure you're suited and booted. It might make an impression on the magistrate.'
Sumo		A nickname for a fat man, especially one who can punch his weight.
Sumos		Large female nipples. Based on Japanese wrestlers, or 'big nips'. *See* NIP (a).
Sunday Best	*Vest*	Formed when this garment was restricted to underwear and only slobs ventured out in their 'Sunday bests'.
Sunday Morn	*Horn (Erection)*	Seems to be based on the one morning a week that a working couple can take advantage of one.
Sundowner		An early evening drink, an old term that has now effectively been renamed happy hour.
Sunny South	*Mouth*	A largely unsung piece due to the fame of 'north and south' (qv).
Supergrass		a) Very strong marijuana, also known as 'Superweed'. b) An informer who puts the finger on a large number of criminals. A well-known piece that's hardly slang any more.
Surf		To browse leisurely through different web sites on the Internet, known as 'Surfing the Net'.
Surgical Truss	*Bus*	Obviously made up by one who has suffered the bollockache of public transport.
Surrey Docks	*Pox*	Has an identical usage as 'Royal Docks' (qv).
Sus/Suss		a) The abbreviated form of suspicious and suspect, meaning not trustworthy: 'He said he'd had the car five years. Didn't you think it was a little bit sus he didn't know how to open the bonnet?' b) The shortened form of suspicion commonly heard when the 'sus law' was with us, when the police had the power to stop and search people solely on the grounds that they 'looked a bit sus' – suspicious.
Sushi Bar		A 21st-century term for the vagina, for which raw fish is a regular comparison.

Susie Anna	*Tanner*	An old term for sixpence, a piece from the days before decimalisation that's obviously defunct.
Suss		Wisdom, know-how. Anyone 'streetwise' is said to have a lot of 'suss'. Also a shrewd idea or a wise thought: 'I've got a suss for one in the four o'clock at Sandown.'
Suss/Suss Out		To work out, to understand or realise: 'You need a bloody degree in nuclear physics to suss this wiring out.' 'Sussed/sussed out' – understood, worked out.
Suss Out		To investigate, to inspect, to see how the land lies: 'Let's go and suss out the local talent.'
Sussed		Discovered, found out, a common piece of underworld jargon: 'We've been sussed. Scarper.'
Suzi		The number four, a 1970s term based on the American rock singer Suzi Quatro whose surname is Italian for four.
Suzie Wong	a) *Pong*	Formed on the title of the 1960 film *The World of Suzie Wong*, which happens to be set in Hong Kong, a rival term to this in the stink stakes. *See* HONG KONG.
	b) *Song*	With the popularity of karaoke, more people than ever are willing to grab the mike and sing a 'Suzie', making more people than ever more willing to leave a pub before closing time.
Swab		A worthless person, a low-life. An archaic piece often heard in pirate films regarding the lowliest seamen, those who swab the decks. A 'swab' being a mop or washrag.
Swag		Stolen goods, booty. Commonly seen drawn across the sack of a cartoon burglar. 'Swag-shop' – a lock-up where stolen goods are stored.
Swallow		a) A drink of alcohol, the pouring of liquor down the throat: 'Fancy a quick swallow?' Also alcoholic drink itself: 'Got any swallow?' In Scotland it's 'swally'. b) The taking of an illicit pill: 'He's had a good swallow, he hasn't stopped talking all night.' c) To accept a story or excuse without question, especially a false one. d) To back down from an argument or fight, to 'swallow one's pride'.
Swallow & Sigh	*Collar & Tie*	A rare example of a double-word rhyme.
Swallow the Anchor		To give oneself in to the police, to surrender, an underworld example from the 1920s but may be an older, nautical piece.
Swamp		The vagina, especially when damp, hence the disappointed moan of a frustrated man: 'She let me

		dip my fingers in her swamp but that's as far as it went.'
Swamp Donkey		A 1990s term for an ugly, unattractive woman.
Swan Lake	*Cake*	A cup of tea and a slice of 'swan' anybody? Based on Tchaikovsky's 1876 ballet.
Swannee River	*Liver*	Applies to both the living human organ and that of a dead animal reclining on a butcher's slab. Based on the opening line of the song 'The Old Folks at Home': 'Way down upon the Swannee river'.
Swatch		A look in Scotland: 'Gissa swatch at your paper.'
Swave		Smooth, polite and charming, a mispronunciation of suave.
Swear & Cuss	*Bus*	Since millions of people do this every day while waiting for public transport, the term couldn't be more pertinent.
Sweat		A worry, problem or hassle, though most commonly heard when there isn't one, i.e., 'no sweat'.
Sweat On		To wait anxiously for something, especially when gambling: 'I was sweating on all the fours for a full house' – a bingo player's lament.
Sweaty Sock	*Jock (Scot)*	A very common term for the race who seem to be taking over television: 'You can't move for sweaty presenters and commentators these days.'
Swede Basher		A well-known term for a country bumpkin, the yokel in the turnip patch.
Sweeney		A barber, hopefully a better one than Sweeney Todd (qv), the scissor wallah of Fleet Street who had a penchant for making mince-meat out of customers, probably ones who didn't leave a tip.
Sweeney Todd	*Flying Squad*	Named after the fictional? demon barber of Fleet Street, whose contribution to *haute cuisine* was hair raising; he would butcher his clients and sell their bodies to a pie-maker. On entering his premises his customers could have been said to have had one foot in the gravy and ended up having their fingers in many pies.
Sweep One's Chimney		To masturbate, one way of making a mess on the carpet for another.
Sweet		A term of approval for anything or anybody deemed acceptable or OK. Also, when anything goes according to plan and without a hitch. In full 'sweet as a nut'.
Sweet/Sweet Stuff		A couple of terms for sugar: 'Pass the sweet.'
Sweet Fanny Adams/FA		See Fanny Adams.

Sweet Pea	*Tea*	A nice cup of 'sweet pea' is rarely brewed these days.
Sweetener		A bribe or a bung, a payment made in order to 'keep someone sweet'.
Sweetie		a) A derogatory term for an effeminate male homosexual.
		b) An ironic term for a horrible, unpleasant person: 'He's a right sweetie' – he's a charmless git.
Swell-Head		A conceited, self-important person, a 'Bighead'.
Swift		Of the police, to fabricate or plant evidence, therefore 'pull a swift one', a version of 'pull a fast one' – to trick or deceive.
Swiftly Flow	*Go*	Originally an Australian piece that is suitable for it's sense of movement, especially as 'swiftly flowing' where a rapid departure is intimated.
Swill/Swillage		Beer. Bitter, lager or stout. Bottled, canned or draught. If you can swill it, it's 'swillage'.
Swilled		Drunk. 'Pig-swilled' – very drunk.
Swing Both Ways		To be bisexual, neither one way or the other.
Swingers		An appropriate term for the testicles, well it was before tight underpants.
Swiss Army Knife	*Wife*	Said humorously at the approach of the other half: 'Look out, here comes the Swiss army.' Based on the pocket knife with a multitude of attachments.
Switch Off		To close one's mind to, to ignore: 'When he starts talking about work I just switch off.'
Switched On		Fashionable, aware of the latest trends, 'with it'.
Swivel Eyed		Descriptive of an untrustworthy, Machiavellian person. One who changes his personality to match the company he keeps, a bit like a chameleon, hence 'swivel eyed'.
Swizzle		Drunk. 'Bumswizzled' – very drunk. To 'swizzle' – to drink alcohol, a term from the 19th century.
Swoon		To take a dive, especially of a boxer who fakes a KO.
Sword		An 18th-century term for the penis, mostly heard now in 'pork sword'.
Swordsman		a) A sexual athlete, a term from the 1960s. See SWORD. 'Sword swallower' – a fellator.
		b) A receiver of stolen property, a pun on 'fencing' (qv).
Sylvester Stallone	*Alone*	Based on the American filmstar, this is the 1990s version of being alone. Modern youth is more likely to be 'Sylvester' than on his 'Tod'. See TOD SLOANE.
Synogogian		A rare term for a Jew. Sounds like one of the old shul.

Syph/Siff The commonest form of syphilis.

Syrup of Fig   *Wig*   Only ever used as 'syrup', especially in connection with an obvious wig, which may be termed a 'golden syrup'.

T

T Rex	*Sex*	A predatory term from the would-be sexual athlete who goes out on the pull in search of a 'bit of T Rex'. Named after a rock band of the early 1970s.
Ta-Ta Kiss	*Piss*	Only used in the guise of 'taking the piss' or 'taking the tattar'.
Ta-Tas/Tats		A walk, generally said to small children who are to be taken out: 'Coming tats?' From 'ta-ta' – goodbye.
Tab		a) A cigarette, a piece that's been smouldering since the 1920s. 'Tabby' is a condescending name for a smoker.
		b) A tablet, a drug user's term that especially relates to an hallucinogenic drug.
Tablets/Tabs		The testicles, a well-known piece that is derived from 'pills', which itself is a euphemism for 'balls', hence a kick in the 'tabs' is a body blow. *See* PILLOCKS/PILLS.
Tach		A hat. A backslang 'Titfer'.
Tackle		a) A watch chain. Commonly linked with a 'toy' (qv). A 'red toy and tackle' – a gold watch and chain.
		b) *See* WEDDING TACKLE.
Tadger		The penis, a 19th-century term that became popular in the 1980s when TV scriptwriters came across it.

Tadpoles	Those that turn into 'sprogs', i.e., semen, an example that's based on the appearance of sperm. To 'waste tadpoles' is to masturbate and the 'tadpole carrier' or 'taddy bag' is the scrotum.
Taff/Taffy	A Welsh person, a universally known piece that derives from the pronunciation of the name Daffyd, the Welsh version of David. 'Taffia' – a Welsh clique.
Tag	The sprayed signature of a graffiti artist, otherwise known as a 'tagger'.
Tagnuts	Little bits of excrement that get tagged on to the anal hairs.
Taig/Teague	An offensive term for a Roman Catholic that's been used by Irish Protestants for centuries.
Tail	a) An ancient term for the vagina which, down the years, has become synonymous with women in general, especially as sex objects, and is commonly heard in the phrase 'a piece of tail'. b) A prostitute, a 19th-century term that today is better known in its RS form 'brass nail' or 'brass'. c) Sexual intercourse. To 'tail' – to have sex with.
Tail-End Charlie	The last person or vehicle in a queue, a wartime piece that derives from RAF jargon for the last plane in formation. It also applies to a person who is habitually the last one to buy a round of drinks.
Tailor-Made	A prison term for a factory-made cigarette, as opposed to a 'roll-up'.
Take	a) To swindle, con or defraud. A victim may be 'ready for the taking'. b) To accept bribery. Corrupt officials are 'on the take'.
Take a Bath	To suffer a heavy financial loss, mostly heard in the business field but gamblers may also get a soaking.
Take a Day Off!	An expression used to stop someone behaving like a fool. An abridged version of: 'Don't be a cunt all your life, take a day off.'
Take a Powder	To leave, escape or run away. Perhaps based on a laxative – something that makes you go.
Take for a Ride	a) To drive someone to a deserted area before killing them. b) To trick or deceive someone into parting with their money. To swindle.
Take In	To fool, trick or deceive. Everyone gets 'taken in' at one time or another.
Take It Out of the Knocker	What the rent or tally man had to do when they knocked for their money and the people inside

pretended not to be in. A phrase that was later said at the knock of any unwelcome visitor.

Take Odds A sure thing, a phrase that has found its way off the racecourse and into everyday life when a certainty seems likely. You can safely 'take odds' that, when you're in a hurry, you'll catch every red light. To take odds is to bet odds on.

Take On To overcharge, swindle or rip off. If you've ever bought a 'genuine' Wedgwood armchair, it's likely you've been 'took on'.

Take the Mick/ Micky To tease, mock or take a liberty. From the RS 'Micky Bliss' (qv).

Take the Piss To tease, mock or take a liberty. More severe than 'take the Micky', if anyone is trying to gain an unfair advantage, rip you off, etc., they're 'taking the piss'.

Take the Wet Stuff Another version of 'take the piss' (qv). For obvious reasons.

Take up Residence To occupy the bathroom for a while, i.e., a long bout of defecation: 'If you want to clean your teeth, do it now, cos I need to take up residence.'

Take up the Slack To masturbate, to 'pull the rope' till it's rigid. *See* ROPE (a).

Take Your Pick *Thick* An oldish piece for someone who couldn't pass a written spelling test, that may or may not be based on the name of a TV quiz show of the 1950s and 1960s.

Take-On A swindle, swizz or rip-off. Anything overpriced can be a 'take-on'.

Tale of Two Cities *Titties (Breasts)* Dickens' classic novel gets the treatment in the reduced form of 'tale of twos'.

Talk Turkey To perform fellatio, a 1980s slant on the old term 'gobble' (qv).

Talk under Water What a garrulous person is said to be able to do.

Tallywagger The penis, an 18th-century term that is still occasionally brought out in TV comedies.

Tan To beat or thrash, especially as an example of corporal punishment. To 'tan someone's hide'.

Tandoori Two- Step Diarrhoea, the result of a moody Indian, and nothing to do with the eight pints of Guinness.

Tank a) A police van, an example that's used for dramatic effect by 'Old Bill' himself.
b) Of a boxer, to deliberately throw a fight, to 'go in the tank' is wordplay for the well-known 'take a dive'. A bent contest is a 'tank job', and chucking a fight is known as 'tanking'.

c) To crush, overwhelm or bring down, usually figuratively. The Tories, for instance, were 'tanked' in the 2001 election. Based on the trampling nature of the war machine.

d) To behave belligerantly or pugnaciously, also to drive forcefully.

e) The supposed part of a man's anatomy where his sperm is stored:

> 'When your tank be full it must be drained/Lest bedsheets while you sleep get stained.'

Tank Filler — A woman who gets a man sexually aroused but stops short of full sex. A 'prick teaser'. See TANK (e).

Tanked Up — Very drunk, people generally get 'well tanked up'. To 'tank up' – to drink heavily.

Tanker — A heavy drinker, one who 'fills his tank' on a regular basis.

Tanner — A slang term that was more commonly used than the amount in old money which it referred to, hardly anyone said sixpence.

Tap — To borrow, an old and well-known piece. Persistent cadgers – 'tappers' – are usually 'on the tap' so beware their tap on the shoulder. 'Tap City' and 'Tapland' – places the impoverished or the temporarily skint are said to be in: 'Poxy horse! It'a put me in Tapland.'

Tap-Dance — To skilfully get out of trouble, to talk your way out of a dodgy situation. Politicians and criminals tend to make the best 'tap dancers'.

Tape — To size up a situation or get someone's measure. An example of criminal parlance.

Tapioca   *Joker* — That which often runs wild in a pack of cards.

Tap-Out — A cash point, where you tap in your number and out comes the cash.

Tar & Feather   *Leather* — Refers to a leather jacket and worn as a 'tar'. It doesn't necessarily have to be black.

Tart — a) A woman, a 19th-century term that's still used without malice for a girlfriend. Also a commonly heard insult for a man who doesn't behave like one: 'Stop whining you big tart.'

b) A promiscuous woman or prostitute, a piece that branches off from (a) and conjours up visions of vulgarity. 'Tarty' – gaudy or vulgar.

Tartan Banner   *Tanner* — A redundant term from Britain's previous currency.

Tart Up — To decorate, to make something tatty look better than it actually is, usually in order to sell it. Old cars get 'tarted up' on a regular basis.

Tash		An old, clipped moustache. Also a 'muzzy'.
Tasty		An all-purpose term of approbation. Anyone considered attractive, appealing, smart, clever or skilful is said to be 'tasty', as are men who are good with their fists.
Tatah/Tata		A 19th-century term for a hat which appears to be a convoluted piece of backslang.
Tate & Lyle	*Style*	Applies to audacity or guiver (qv). Liberty takers may be told, often admiringly, 'You've got some Tate and Lyle, you have.' Based on the sugar company with long-held East London connections.
Tater		An idiot, another clot from the vegetable patch. *See also* ONION *and* TURNIP.
Tater Trap		The mouth, a century-old piece that's still got a bite left in it.
Taters		Cold, from RS 'potatoes in the mould' (qv).
Tavish		A Scot, a reduced version of the familiar Scottish name McTavish.
Taxi Cab	*Crab*	The seafood traditionally sold outside pubs on Sundays and eaten at teatime.
Taxi Cabs	*Crabs*	Refers to crab-lice, sexually transmitted little nippers known as 'taxis'.
Taxi Rank	a) *Bank*	In the shortened form of 'taxi' this becomes quite fitting, as a London cab is perceived, by those who don't drive them, to be black money boxes. Something vehemently denied by those who do.
	b) *Wank*	A 'taxi' is one of many terms for the act of masturbation, which is like waiting for a cab. One will come eventually.
Tea & Cocoa	*Say So*	Unlike 'coffee and cocoa' (qv), this is used in full: 'If you wanted to borrow the car, why didn't you tea and cocoa?'
Tea & Toast	*Post*	Applies to mail: 'Anything in the tea and toast this morning?'
Tea Caddy	*Paddy*	A 1990s term that may have it's origins in a building site canteen.
Tea for Two	*Jew*	Generally reduced to a 'teafer', possibly after the 1958 hit for the Tommy Dorsey Orchestra 'Tea for Two Char Char'.
Tea for Two & a Bloater	*Motor*	A term that was formed as a condescending allusion to the 'newfangled horseless carriage' and is now obsolete. The inclusion of a 'tea for two' is down to the fact that I like it.
Tea Grout	*(Boy) Scout*	A piece that always rode the crest of the wave behind the one ridden by 'brussels sprout' (qv).
Tea Leaf	*Thief*	The commonest term for the sticky-fingered villain

		and one that is never shortened. Thieves go out 'tea leafing'.
Tea Strainers	*Trainers*	Refers to modern footwear, not necessarily stained and full of holes.
Teabag	*Slag*	A despicable, untrustworthy person. Someone who may land you in hot water.
Team		A criminal gang, one put together for a 'job'.
Teapot		A name given to an excessive tea drinker. If female, she may be a 'teabag'.
Teapot Lid	a) *Kid*	Children have long been known as 'teapots' as a variation on 'saucepans'. *See* SAUCEPAN LID.
	b) *Quid (£1)*	When this was formed a 'teapot' bought a bleedin' sight more than it does today.
	c) *Yid*	A Jew can either be a 'teapot' or 'teapottish' – Yiddish.
Tear-Up		A rough or fierce fight, especially in the boxing ring: 'He may come to box but he'd better be prepared for a tear-up.'
Technicolour Yawn		The act of vomiting, the opening of the mouth to eject the multicoloured contents of the gut.
Teckram		A backslang market. 'Shif teckram' – fish market.
Ted Frazer	*Razor*	Not quite sure if this is in the sense of a tool or a weapon, depends perhaps on whether there's an actual Mr Frazer or not and if he's a shaver or a shivver. My guess is that he doesn't draw blood by accident.
Ted Heath	a) *Beef*	How a British PM of the 1970s later became employed at the meat market. Also called 'Edward', *see* EDWARD HEATH.
	b) *Teeth*	*See* EDWARD HEATH.
	c) *Thief*	A thoroughly bad lot is a 'Ted Heath'. Sometimes known as an 'Edward'. *See* EDWARD HEATH.
Teddy Bear	*Pear*	An old offering from the fruit market.
Tee Off On		In boxing, to land a lot of accurate punches without reply.
Teelas		Salt. A backslang condiment. 'Sap the teelas' – pass the salt.
Teenip		A backslang pint. A 'teenip of rettib' – a pint of bitter.
Teenth		Drug user's talk for a sixteenth of an ounce of whatever they're buying.
Teenuc		The vagina, a fool or an obnoxious person, a backslang 'cunt'. Usually pronounced 'tinnuc'.
Teeve		A television, an abbreviation of TV: 'What's on the teeve?'
Teflon		A football supporters nickname for a bad goalkeeper. The ball never sticks to his hands. Teflon is a brand of non-stick cookwear.

Teflon Brained		Forgetful, nothing sticks in the memory. *See* TEFLON.
Teletubby	*Hubby*	At last a retaliatory piece for the long-suffering wife, who for years has had to put up with having numerous pieces of RS thrown at her. Now her awful wedded husband gets his comeuppance based on the name of a children's TV character.
Tell the Tale		Of a con artist, to deceive or trick with a plausible story. To hoax.
Tellybelly		The large gut associated with the inactivity involved in watching television.
Ten Command-ments		The fingers and thumbs of 'she who must be obeyed' – the wife. A piece that dates back centuries, so it would seem she was ever the boss.
Ten to Two	*Jew*	For whom there are terms in abundance already.
Ten to Twos		Feet that stick out at an angle similar to ten-to-two on a clockface.
Tendencies		A leaning towards homosexuality: 'You'd be blind not to notice he's got tendencies.'
Tennis Racket	*Jacket*	Tailored to the first element, a 'tennis' sounds like it should refer to a sports jacket.
Tent Peg	*Egg*	An eggs-crutiatingly unegg-citing eggsample.
Terence Stamp	*Ramp (Bar)*	Refers to a pub counter: 'Whose turn is it up the Terence?' Based on an East London-born film actor who made good in America.
Terrible Turk	*Work*	Employed by those for whom work is a four letter word, those whose motto is 'If a job's worth doing, it's worth paying somebody to do it properly.'
Terry Waite	*Late*	Based on a Briton who, in 1987, while in Beirut to negotiate the release of hostages of Islamic militants, was himself kidnapped. He was released in 1991, 'Terry Waite' by almost five years.
Teviss		A long-departed term for the long-departed shilling (5p).
Tex Ritter	*a) Bitter*	British beer based on an old-time western filmstar and ordered as a 'pint of Tex'. Born in 1905, Tex's last round-up came in 1974.
	b) Shitter	Refers to a lavatory and, vulgarly, to the anus. In the 1960s the term also applied to a promiscuous girl; 'shitter' is a variation of 'slapper'.
That & This	*Piss*	Only used in connection with water production.
Thatch		Pubic hair. 'Snatch-thatch' – that of a female.
Theg/Taich		Two backslang versions of the number eight.
Thelma Ritter	*Shitter*	Based on an American film actress (1905–69), this has seen service mainly as a lavatory but has sometimes referred to the anus. Either way it's a 'Thelma'.

Thelonius Monk	*Spunk (Semen)*	A 1940s example that comes down to the Christian name of this jazz piannist (1917–82).
There You Are	*a) Bar*	A 19th-century term for a public or saloon bar that fits snugly with relaxation and meeting friends.
	b) Char (Tea)	There you are, a nice cup of 'there you are'.
These & Those	*a) Clothes*	A piece that is never worn short, always put some 'these and those' on.
	b) Toes	A pluralistic term for the 'tootsies'.
Theydon Bois	*Noise*	Named after a village on the edge of Epping Forest in Essex which once constituted a day out for the poor children of London. They would be taken there on school or Sunday school outings and given a taste of life away from the slums. Let loose they would have made a fair bit of 'Theydon'. Incidentally, Bois does rhyme with noise.
Thick & Thin	*a) Chin*	On which a big man is expected to take his punishment.
	b) Gin	The spirit of London revisited, as a 'drop of thicken'.
Thicko/Thickie		A couple of slow-witted fools. Thickheads. Like the dolt who decided to kill his pet goldfish by putting it in a sack and throwing it in the river.
Thimble & Thumb	*Rum*	Always ordered as a 'tot of thimble' as an alternative to the more common 'finger and thumb' (qv).
Thinker		The head, or rather the internal workings of it: 'Use your thinker' – use your brain. Also known as 'thinkbox'.
Third Leg		The penis, another version of the 'middle leg' (qv).
Thirteen and a Bakers		An expression used when there are two ways of doing something and the difference between them is minimal or amounts to the same thing. Thirteen is a baker's dozen.
This & That	*a) Bat*	An ancient schoolboy reference to a cricket bat.
	b) Hat	An example that's always used in full, but is seldom used at all. 'Titfer' rules the headwear department. *See* TIT FOR TAT (b).
Thomas Cook	*Look*	A 1990s advertising campaign for this travel agency suggested we should take a 'Thomas Cook' at their brochure. Mr Cook (1808–92) was a pioneer in the holiday business.
Thomas Tilling	*Shilling*	A defunct term for an extinct sum of money based on the name of the founder of a 19th-century omnibus company. In 1933 Tilling's buses became part of London Transport.

Thora Hird	*a) Bird*	A 1990s term from the suburbs that relates to the feathered variety. Time will tell if this dame of the acting profession (1911–2003) turns back into a young lady.
	b) Turd	A 1980s example of disrespect to a fine actress: 'Mind you don't step in that Thora.'
Thorn in One's Own Side		To be your own worst enemy, the cause of your own trouble.
Thousand Pities	*Titties (Breasts)*	Strange that so much sorrow can apply to things that bring men so much pleasure.
Threads		Clothes, originally American but imported into Britain in the fashion-conscious 1960s.
Three Blind Mice	*Rice*	An order of 'curried chicken and three blind mice' may be a cause of great confusion to an Indian or Chinese waiter. If it isn't, go somewhere else.
Three Parts Gone		Tipsy but not drunk, still in a semblance of control.
Three Sheets to/ in the Wind		Very drunk, a piece that has its origins in the navy of the 19th century.
Three-Wheel Trike	*Dyke*	A 'three-wheeler' is a modern version of a lesbian based on an ancient form of transport.
Threepenny Bits	*a) Shits*	A double dose of the horrors, a piles sufferer with the 'threepennys'.
	b) Tits	A term that still survives, even though this coin died of decimalitis in 1971.
Thrill		An orgasm, a piece used by lads in their early days of masturbation.
Throatsplasher		An act of fellatio that climaxes with ejaculation into the mouth.
Throne		A common term for a lavatory pan. The 'Throne Room' – the lavatory.
Throw One		To become angry. A cut-down version of 'throw a wobbler'. *See* Wobbler/Wobbly.
Thunderbox		A toilet pedestal, from the sound of a noisy 'sit-down job' (qv).
Thunder-Thighs		A fat person, especially an overweight woman.
Tick		A small, irritating person, often a child: 'What an annoying little tick you are sometimes.'
Ticker		a) The heart, an old term that's still on the go, famously as a 'dicky ticker' – a weak heart.
		b) A watch, a 19th-century piece that's still heard even if the modern 'ticker' isn't.
Ticket		The right thing to do, the correct way of doing something. Commonly heard as 'that's the ticket'.
Tickle		Money obtained without working for it. A successful robbery, swindle or gamble is known as a 'nice little tickle.'

Tickle the Ovaries		Of a man, to have sexual intercourse, a pun on the phrase 'tickle the ivories', which is what a pianist does. The term is emphasised by the punning nature of pianist and penis.
Tickle Your Fancy	*Nancy (Homosexual)*	A post World War Two piece that may be a corrupted version of a line in the song 'Billy Boy': 'Did (a) nancy tickle your fancy oh my darling Billy boy'.
Tic-Tac		A signal or sign: 'I'll make my move when you give me the tic-tac.' Based on the racecourse system of hand signals designed to inform bookmakers of fluctuating odds. In the army during World War One a tic-tac was a signaller.
Tic-Tac	*Fact*	When the world and it's brother adopted 'brass tack' (qv), the cockney turned to this and 'tin tack' (qv).
Tiddle		To urinate and also the urine, another version of piddle. Same drink different glass really.
Tiddled/Tiddly		Well-known terms for being slightly drunk. This is to 'tiddle' (qv) what 'pissed' is to 'piss' (qv).
Tiddler		Any low value or small coin, presently the 1p and 5p coins.
Tiddler's Bait	*Late*	Always reduced to the first element, sometimes at the start of an excuse: 'Sorry I'm tiddlers but I met Cyril on the way home from work and he forced me to go for a drink.' This however is not a good excuse and will not prevent the sharp edge of a wife's tongue from tearing her hapless spouse to shreds. Sometimes said as 'tiddley bait', especially when alcohol has control of the tongue.
Tiddlywink	*a) Chink*	A common and usually derogatory term for a Chinese person that's usually curtailed to 'tiddly'.
	b) Drink	Normally reduced to 'tiddly' and widely used in connection with alcohol.
Tiddy		Small. 'Tiddy iddy' – very small. 'Tiddy widdy' – smaller still.
Tide's Out		Said when your glass is empty and it's someone else's round.
Tidy & Neat	*Eat*	Only ever used in the first element: 'Tidy up your dinner first, then you can go out.'
Tie Off		To raise a vein by binding a limb, in order to inject a drug into it.
Tie One On		To drink in order to get drunk. A popular term for a popular pastime.
Tie the Noose		To get married, the cynic's version of 'tie the knot'.
Tiger Tank	*Wank*	An act of masturbation courtesy of a machine of war.

Tight Arse		a) A mean, stingy, rockfisted person. Everybody knows one and they all know what to call him. b) A prude, a fussy, conservative person, one also described as 'anally retentive'. 'Anal' for short.
Tightlip		A person able to be trusted with a secret, someone who won't inform.
Tightwad		A mean, tight-fisted person, one with a vice-like grip on his money.
Tilbury Docks	a) Pox	The 'Tilbury' is an age-old term for a venereal disease.
	b) Socks	A 19th-century term that originated in the navy and is worn as 'Tilburys'.
Tile		An old term for a hat, that which sits on the 'roof' (qv).
Tilt		An erection, from the old joke about the Scotsman who had a 'tilt in his kilt'.
Tim		An old name for telecom's talking clock, which is still used by people who remember dialling TIM before it was changed to 123.
Timber		An old term for the counter in a pub, or a bar in a bar: 'Whose turn up the timber?'
Tin		Money, especially silver coins. A 19th-century term that's still heard.
Tin Bath	Scarf	Sometimes shrunken to 'tin' as a partner to 'titfer': 'It's freezing out so put your titfer and tin on.' *See* TIT FOR TAT (b).
Tin Cupping		Begging. The term stretches from beggars to companies seeking loans.
Tin Hat		A euphemism for an end to something, a full-stop. Heard in the phrase 'That's put the tin hat on that.'
Tin Hat	Pratt (Fool)	Worn in full, it's what may be needed to protect someone who's a bit 'soft in the head'.
Tin Lid	Yid	An expression for a Jew that is often aimed at a supporter of Spurs football club.
Tin Plate	Mate	Would appear to be a less well-off rival to 'china plate' (qv) and is seldom employed.
Tin Tack	a) Fact	Gained popularity when 'brass tack' (qv) stepped out of the boundaries of RS to join mainstream English.
	b) Sack	A common reference to dismissal from work: 'I can see us all getting the tin tack the way things are going.'
Tin Tank	Bank	An inferior version of 'iron tank' (qv), and sounds like it.
Tina Turner	Learner	A learner driver, that is. Male or female, if you're behind someone with L plates you are following a 'Tina'. Based on an American singer.

Tincture		An alcoholic drink, a piece that's been jokingly drunk 'for medicinal purposes' for a century.
Tinfish		A wartime term relating to a torpedo.
Ting-a-Ling	a) King	Applies solely to the playing card.
	b) Ring	No vulgar associations here, it refers exclusively to an item of jewellery. *See* PEARLY KING.
Tinies/Teenies		Little bits of excrement that get stuck to anal hairs. More famously known as 'clinkers' (qv).
Tinkerbell		A derisory term for an effeminate male based on the fairy in *Peter Pan*.
Tinkle		a) A juvenile term for an act of urination.
		b) A telephone call, an example from the time when phones were only equipped with bells and the phrase 'give me a bell' evolved into this.
		c) Money, or more especially coins: 'I always put some tinkle in a poor-box.'
Tins of Beans	Jeans	An alternative to 'baked beans' (qv), which is generally cut down to 'tins'.
Tiny Taters		A trifling amount, one that's too small to be of consequence. A play on 'small potatoes'.
Tiny Tim	Flim (£5)	A flim has been a slang term for this amount since around the time that Dickens was writing about his famous cripple in *A Christmas Carol*.
Tisket		A bastard, a piece from the 1940s based on the song lyric 'A tisket, a tasket. A little yellow basket'. 'Basket' is an old euphemism for bastard and during World War Two it was applied to Japanese soldiers. Little yellow baskets were how they were seen by British troops.
Tiswas		Those who are 'all of a tiswas' are in a state of confusion or in a 'mucking fuddle'.
Tit		a) A piece that has been getting men steamed up for centuries. A breast, of course, and a term that has been used in relation to women in general as 'bits of tit' for just as long.
		b) A fool, often used in embarrassment: 'I feel a right tit in this get-up.'
Tit for Tat	a) Chat	A 1990s example that isn't shortened so as to avoid confusion with (b): 'I just dropped by for a tit for tat.'
	b) Hat	Always shortened to 'titfer', this is one of the few pieces of lowspeak to hit the heady heights of every-day language: 'If you can't fight wear a big titfer.'
Tit in a Trance, like a		In a daydream, miles away. Unable to think straight and therefore likely to draw this comment.
Tit Wank		Sexual gratification gained by placing the penis between a woman's breasts.

Tit Willow	*Pillow*	Based on a Gilbert and Sullivan song, this rarely used term never gets truncated. It doesn't sound seemly to rest your head on a 'tit'. Nice, but not seemly.
Tit-Bag		An old example for a brassiere that's used by men rather than women. The term that is not the garment.
Tithead		a) A policeman, a term that's been common at football grounds since the 1970s due to the shape of a copper's helmet.
		b) A fool, an idiot, a complete doombrain.
Tits Up, go		Originally to die but now applies to failure. When a plan or a business fails it goes 'tits up'.
Titsalina Bumsquash		A juvenile name given to a girl with large breasts, a piece that goes back to, at least, the 1950s.
Tit-Up		A schoolboy term used when the extent of a sexual encounter amounts to a 'bit of tit': 'She let me tit her up and that was it.'
To & Fro	*Snow*	An old term heard when it's been 'to-ing and fro-ing'.
To & From	*Pom*	An Englishman according to Aussie servicemen of World War Two. May now be said of our cricketers, who seem to go to the crease and from it PFQ (qv) against Australia these days.
Toad		A liar or someone who is economical with the truth. A 'lying toad'.
Toasted Bread	*Dead*	A slice of black 1990s humour from the crematorium?
Toblerone	*Phone*	Based on a chocolate bar, this 1990s piece has followed in the wake of the mobile phone boom as a 'Tobler'.
Toby		A police division, the term originally meant a road or highway.
Toby Jug(s)	*a) Lugs (Ears)*	A reasonably well-known piece in relation to ears of the FA Cup handle type that are usually clipped to 'Tobys'.
	b) Mug	A fool by any other name is a 'Toby'.
Tod Sloane	*Alone*	Extensively used in the first element, everyone likes to be on their 'Tod' from time to time. Based on an American jockey (1874–1933) who rode in Britain around the beginning of the 20th century.
Todger		The same as 'tadger' (qv).
Todger Dodger		A lesbian. A member of the club that excludes male members. *See* TODGER.
Toe Rag	*Slag*	In the early 1960s, this was 'lads' talk for a girl of easy virtue. It's also an unpleasant, untrustworthy person of either sex.
Toff		A 19th-century term for a well dressed, upper-class man. A gentleman. 'Toffs' – the upper classes.

Toffee		Flattery, insincerity, flannel. In other words, 'sweet' talk.
Toffee Wrapper	*Napper (Head)*	Napper is an old slang term for the head and here gets reduced to a 'toffee'. I could be accused of nit-picking for insisting that terms should be said in a specific way. But as Confucius would no doubt have said had he come from the Limehouse branch of Chinatown: 'Man who don't pick nits end up with itchy toffee.'
Toffee-Nose		A snobbish, stuck-up person, one whose 'shit doesn't stink'. A well-known term that may have originally been 'toffy nose'. *See* TOFF.
Togged Up		Dressed up, usually in one's finery. Suited and booted in one's best 'togs' (qv).
Togs		An ancient term for clothes that's still in vogue. Fashions may change but they are still 'togs'.
Toilet Roll	*Dole*	May be wistfully employed by the long-term unemployed when asked if he has found a job yet: 'No, still on the toilet.'
Toke		a) Originally a lump of bread doled out in prison, later it referred to food in general. b) A piece from the 1960s relating to a drag on a marijuana cigarette.
Tokyo Rose	*Nose*	Based on a Japanese radio propaganda broadcaster of World War Two, this is always cut to the first element: 'Why do you keep calling me Sinex?' – 'Because you get right up my Tokyo.'
Tom		A well-aired term for a prostitute that once applied to an aggressive, mannish woman of the night. Possibly a backslang version of 'mot' (qv)?
Tom & Dick	*Sick*	Applies to any form of illness, not just the physical act of vomiting. To be on the 'Tom and Dick' is to be off work and drawing benefit.
Tom & Jerry	*Merry*	A reference to being happily drunk, and would appear to be based on the cartoon cat and mouse of TV fame. But in the 19th century a Tom and Jerry was a low drinking house and to 'Tom and Jerry' was to behave riotously.
Tom Cat	*Mat*	Usually a doormat or the one in front of the fire that gets monopolised by the pampered puss.
Tom Cruise	*Booze*	A 1990s piece based on an American film star, one of whose starring roles was as a barman in the 1988 film *Cocktail*. Whether this has any bearing on his inclusion in RS is debatable, I'd say it's just because it rhymes.
Tom Dooleys	*Goolies (Testicles)*	Based on the eponymous hero of a 1958 hit record by Lonnie Donegan, in reference to the spot

where a kick will cause a man to hang down his head and cry.

Tom Finney — *Skinny* — The legendary Preston and England footballer comes in as someone with little meat on their bones. A 1960s put-down of a pencil-like girl was 'nice face, a bit Tom Finney though'.

Tom Hanks — *Thanks* — A 1990s term based on an Oscar-winning American film star. Used by the young as 'Tomanks'.

Tom, Harry & Dick — *Sick* — An extended version of 'Tom and Dick' (qv), that gets pared to 'Tom Harry'.

Tom House — A pub that is well-known for picking up prostitutes. *See* TOM.

Tom Mix — *a) Fix* — In its original form this relates to being in a state of difficulty, in a right 'Tom Mix'. It has now slipped into the world of drug abuse where a fix is an injection of a narcotic. Based on an early star of western films (1880–1940).

b) Six — The number six. A 'Tom Mix' is a common reference to £6. It's also odds of 6/1, a bingo caller's term and a six at cricket.

Tom Noddy — *Body* — Given this example hails from America, this probably applies to a corpse. 'Tom Noddy' is an old term for a simpleton or fool.

Tom Patrol/ Squad — A pair of 1950s underworld terms for the vice squad, especially where prostitution is concerned.

Tom Pepper — A well-known term for a seasoned liar. Based on a mythical sailor who was slung out of hell for telling porkies.

Tom Sawyer — *Lawyer* — Apart from those employed in the legal profession, this often applies to the bar stool know-all, whose freely given advice is seldom needed or heeded. Based on a character of American novelist Mark Twain's imagination.

Tom Thacker — *Tobacco* — Pipe or rolling 'bacca', an archaic piece that probably went up in smoke years ago.

Tom Thumb — *a) Bum* — A piece that's often heard in the mock threat of a kick up the 'Tom Thumb'.

b) Rum — Possibly the term most used by rum drinkers as it fittingly refers to a tot. Based on the three-foot tall 'General' Tom Thumb (real name Charles S Stratton, 1838–83), an American who gained fame when touring the world with Barnum's Circus.

Tom Tit — *Shit* — A very well-known piece that actually means to defecate rather than the resultant mess. Often referred to as a 'Tom' and when pluralised, i.e., 'Tom Tits', it becomes an attack of diarrhoea.

Tom Tug	a) *Bug*	A very old term for a parasite. So sleep tight, don't let the Tom Tugs bite.
	b) *Mug*	A gullible fool, someone easily stitched up. That's a 'Tom Tug'.
Tomato Puree	*Jury*	A 1990s piece which explains how twelve good men and true collectively form, or may be asked to sit on, a 'tomato'.
Tomato Sauce	*Horse*	Usually refers to a racehorse, often the one who is so far behind he'll never ketchup.
Tombstones		Teeth, especially uneven, broken or discoloured ones.
Tomfoolery	*Jewellery*	Mainly an underworld term that's been popularised by countless TV crooks, always in the condensed form of 'Tom'.
Tommy/ Tom Tripe	*Pipe*	Apart from that which is puffed at by a smoker, to 'pipe' means to look at, to observe: 'Tommy the geezer in the dodgy syrup.'
Tommy/ Tommy Atkins		A private soldier in the British army. In the 19th century, the name Thomas Atkins was used on the specimen forms given to new recruits to show them how to fill in their own forms.
Tommy Cooper	*Super*	Based on the legendary British comedian and magician (1922–84). Used as an expression of excellence, this 1970s term was probably inspired by fellow British comedian, Russ Abbot, and his comic creation Cooperman.
Tommy Dodd	a) *God*	A very old euphemism for God that's used as 'Tommy Dodd only knows' or 'if a man is judged by the company he keeps then Tommy Dodd help us all.' 'Tommy Dodd's garden' – a cemetary.
	b) *Odd*	Can be employed in relation to strangeness and with a final 's' it refers to betting odds or the coin-tossing opponent of 'Major Stevens' (qv). In the mid 19th century, a popular song contained the words: 'Heads or tails are sure to win Tommy Dodd, Tommy Dodd.'
	c) *Rod (Gun)*	A piece originally heard in America.
	d) *Sod*	A term of abuse for a 'git' or, less scornfully, for a rascal.
Tommy Farr	*Bar*	Formed on the name of a British heavyweight boxing champion (1913–86) in relation to where drinks are served.
Tommy Fulfiger		A fictitious designer label, said to be the favourite of overweight people. A pun on the Tommy Hilfiger brand of casual wear.
Tommy Guns	*Runs (Diarrhoea)*	Probably inspired by the effect on the faecal factory when staring down the wrong end of one.

Tommy O'Rann	*Scran (Food)*	An old piece of RS for an even older piece of slang for food or provisions.
Tommy Rabbit	*Pomegranate*	A piece from a 19th-century fruit stall.
Tommy Rollocks	*Bollocks*	Used either in relation to a let-down, i.e., a 'kick in the Tommy's', or as an expression of disbelief, politely truncated to: 'What a load of Tommy.' Never used in anger as the word it stands for carries far more venom.
Tommy Roller	*Collar*	A 19th-century term for what originally would have been a detachable one. Now detached from BritSlang.
Tommy Steeles	*Eels*	Applies to the jellied variety, the great cockney delicacy based on a London-born entertainer.
Tommy Trinder	*Window*	Based on a cockney comedian (1909–89) who in his act used aggression tempered with charm. A master ad-libber, he had a reputation for never being stuck for an answer. This would appear, then, to be a perfectly fitting term, as he had all the attributes required to make a blinding double-glazing salesman.
Tommy Tucker	a) *Fucker*	Normally said without malice in reference to a mischievous or spirited person.
	b) *Sucker*	An underworld term for a mug, someone easily sucked in. The type of person who is willingly sold the biggest dummies outside the Land of the Giants branch of Mothercare. *See* DUMMY (b).
Tommy Tupper	*Supper*	A fairly old reference to an evening food intake.
Tommyrot		Nonsense, balderdash. Sometimes reduced to 'Tommy' and has been since the 19th century. So too has the RS term 'Tommy Rollocks' – bollocks. A possible corruption of 'Tommy Roll'?
Tomorrow	*Borrow*	To be on the 'tomorrow' or 'tom' usually means a small loan between friends or neighbours, meant to be paid back the next day. But as we all know, tomorrow never comes because when it does it's today again.
Ton		Relates to 100 in many ways. £100, 100mph, 100 years and 100 runs in cricket, they're all a ton.
Tongue & Groover		A toady, sycophantic crawler. An 'arse licker'.
Tongue Bath		An all-over body licking, including, well, everything.
Tongue Job		An act of oral sex performed by either partner.
Tongue Wrestle		To lock tongues in a passionate kiss.
Tonka Toy	*Boy*	A 1970s term based on a brand of hard-wearing toys which mainly relates to 'the boys' in a gang. A piece that has been around for as long as football violence has been a serious problem.

T

Ton-Up Boy/Kid		A member of a motorcycle gang, a piece from the 1950s that's still on the road. 'Ton-Up' – 100mph.
Tony Benn	*Ten*	A 1970s example from the City of London, where a 'Tony Benner' is £10. Based on a long-standing British MP, born Anthony Wedgwood Benn in 1925.
Tony Blair	*Hair*	The New Labour Prime Minister comes in on a wave from the suburbs and only time will tell if it's to be permanent. Personally I can't see it cutting down on 'Barnet's majority, although a 'Tony' can be a single hair. *See* BARNET FAIR.
Tony Cottee	*Potty*	A 1990s term for a 'nipper's crapper' based on an England international footballer of the period.
Tony Hatch	*Match*	A 1970s term for a 'burner' based on a British composer of many a TV theme.
Tooey		A Jewish expression meaning 'I spit on': 'You call that a sandwich? Tooey on that sandwich. The rabbi threw away more meat after my son was circumcised.'
Tookus/Tochus		The backside, the buttocks. A piece of Yiddish from the word *toches*: 'You call that work? Sat on your tookus all day pushing a pen.'
Tool		a) The penis, a well-known piece that's employed when a man is on the job.
		b) A fool, a term that's used in the same way as other male members 'prick' and 'dick' (qv).
		c) A weapon, usually a knife or a club, although it can be a gun. Carriers are 'tooled up'.
		d) To stab, slash or cut someone with a knife or razor, a piece that's been about since the 1940s.
Tool Along/ Around		To leisurely wander or drive around, to aimlessly poodle about.
Toolbox/Tool Chest		A couple of terms for the vagina, where men put their 'tools'.
Toolkit		The male genitalia, the equipment needed to do the necessary.
Tools		Equipment used by drug users for injection purposes.
Toop		A term from the 1960s regarding a wig or hairpiece, an anglicised version of toupee. A 'patch cover'.
Toot		a) A drinking session, a binge. A piece that's been partying since the 19th century.
		b) Cocaine or any other drug that can be sniffed, an example from the late 1960s. The term also applies to a snort of the stuff.
		c) Rhyming with soot, this applies to shoddy, inferior or second-hand goods. 'Toot sale' – a car boot sale, but then one man's 'toot' is another man's collectables. 'Toot' is a 1960s term for rubbish.

Tooting Bec	*Peck*	Mainly applies to food, for which 'peck' is an old term, but it secondarily relates to a little kiss, as in: 'Give us a little tooting on the hide and seek' (qv).
Top		To kill, originally to execute by hanging. Suicides are said to have 'topped themselves'.
Top Banana		The top man, the chief, the manager. A piece that originated in America where the term applied to the top-of-the-bill comedian, and where slipping on a banana skin is a typical piece of buffoonery.
Top Bollocks		A woman's breasts, large ones, a vulgarism used by drooling men. Also 'Chesticles'.
Top Flat/Floor/ Storey		The head, a trio of old variations on 'attic' (qv). If there's little evidence of grey matter, the 'top flat' is said to be vacant. A 'banging on the top floor' describes a headache or hangover.
Top Gun	*Ton (£100)*	A 1980s term from the City of London based on the title of a 1984 film.
Top Hat	a) *Pratt*	The old term is never shortened and may be based on the annual upper-class pose-in at Royal Ascot. *See* PRAT/PRATT (c).
	b) *Rat*	Applies both to a rodent and to a no-good human 'cows-son'.
Top Job		A murder, especially a professional killing. An old term fron the underworld. *See* TOP.
Top Johnny		The top man, the best performer, the star: 'Manchester United are hard to beat because they've always got eleven top Johnnys on the pitch.'
Top Joint	*Pint*	As with 'roast joint' (qv), this would once have effected a rhyme.
Top Jolly		The main man, the boss, especially a gang leader.
Top of the Form	*Warm*	An old, rarely used term based on an early 1960s TV quiz.
Top Weight		The maximum sentence allowed by law. A piece of prison slang.
Top Whack		The highest estimated amount of money, distance, height, etc.: 'It can't come to eighty quid. Sixty-five top whack.'
Topper		A windbag, a person who 'tops' everything that anybody else has done, seen, knows, owns or has been to. If you've crossed the Himalayas on a yak, he's done it on an elephant. Twice. With a couple of Playboy models for company. Plus he took a photo of a Yeti but lost his camera, which cost £2000 by the way, when he fought off an attack by five bandits in Katmandu.
Toppo		First rate, excellent, the best. A reduced 'top hole'. 'Toppo oppo' – a best mate. *See* OPPO.

Torch	a) An underworld term for a paid arsonist, one who will burn something so that the owner can claim on the insurance. b) To commit arson, often for insurance purposes. Many an unsaleable car has been 'torched'.
Torpedo	A violent thug or a hit-man, an old term for one of gangland's most dangerous individuals.
Torrack	A carrot, an example of greengrocer's backslang.
Tosh	a) Small change, in its time a piece that's gone from a farthing to 5p. In Victorian London a 'tosher' was a slum dweller who made a kind of living searching the sewers for any valuables, usually small coins, which may have fallen through a drain. b) A term of address to a man, akin to 'moosh' and 'nosher'. *See both.* c) Rubbish or nonsense. Anything, from a far-fetched film to the goods for sale at an Oxford Street auction, can be a 'load of old tosh'. d) To paint, a piece from the decorating trade. 'We'll give the lid a quick tosh over and then go to dinner.' 'Toshing' – painting. 'Tosher' – a painter.
Tosheroon	An example that was well-known in its day as a reference to a half-a-crown in old money, or two shillings and sixpence. The coin was also known as a 'Coachwheel'.
Toss	a) Anything worthless, what the uncaring 'couldn't give'. b) To search a premises, an underworld term for what both the cops and the robbers may do. A version of 'spin' (qv). c) To masturbate, commonly to 'toss off'. Also heard in the double entendre about Scotsmen 'tossing their cabers'.
Tosser	A worthless, horrible, no-good person. A well-known version of 'wanker' (qv).
Tosspot	An identical twin of 'tosser': 'I can't have that tosspot at any price.'
Total	To completely wreck or destroy something, a 'totalled' car is a write off. Also to kill someone.
Total Wreck *Cheque*	Perhaps one from an insurance company after writing your car off.
Totter	A well-known term for a rag and bone man, from the term 'tot' – to collect and resell junk for a living.
Tottie/Totty	A sexually attractive young woman, a 19th-century term that's still used, often for women in general. 'Top totty' – upper-class gels.

Touch		a) A piece of good fortune, a 'touch' of good luck: 'That's a touch, no traffic.' b) To borrow, a well-known alternative to 'tap' (qv). 'Toucher' – a persistent borrower.
Touch & Tap	*Cap*	Both elements are slang terms meaning to borrow, so the connection may be in passing the hat round. Old enough not to pertain to a baseball cap.
Touch Me on the Knob	*Bob (Shilling)*	An obsolete piece from the days of previous currency. To 'touch' anyone is to borrow some money from them, so the expression 'Can I touch you for a touch me?' used to be quite common. A touch more colourful than 'five pee', don't you think?
Touch of the Other		A non-specified illness: 'What's a matter, don't you feel well? You look like you've got a touch of the other.'
Touch of the Tarbrush		A derogatory phrase used of someone who looks as though he may have some black ancestry.
Touch Up		To caress someone sexually to cause pleasure. Also to molest or grope someone, causing fear, anger and general displeasure.
Touched by the Moon	*Loon*	Which is precisely what a lunatic is. Said of someone who may have a rafter loose in the 'attic' (qv).
Tough/Toughie		A hard, thuggish person, a 'bruiser'. Someone not to mess with unless you're another tough.
Tough Cookie		A strong, resilient person, both physically and emotionally.
Tough Shit!		Hard luck! Who cares? An uncaring reply to a complaint.
Tough Titty!		Exactly the same as 'tough shit'.
Towel Head		An Arab, a piece from the 1980s that grew in popularity during the Gulf War of 1991.
Tower Bridge	*Fridge*	Always abridged to the first element, whereby cans of beer left over from a party are referred to as 'prisoners' and bunged in the 'tower'.
Tower Hill	*Kill*	Aptly based on the place where executioners once wielded their choppers and royal heads did roll. A warning to a speeding driver: 'Slow down or we'll all be Tower Hilled.'
Town Crier	*Liar*	Everyone knows a 'town crier', a person of whom you disbelieve fifty per cent of what he says and are dubious of the other half.
Town Halls	*Balls (Testicles)*	A piece that doesn't get shortened, dirty fighters aim for the 'town halls'.
Towns & Cities	*Titties*	An old term which was never as popular as it's meaning.

Toy	a) A 19th-century term for a watch that was generally seen in partnership with a 'tackle' (qv). b) An imitator, a phoney. Anyone considered 'not for real'.
Toyboy	The boyfriend of an older woman, a piece that became common in the 1980s when a string of well-known actresses were pictured with younger men.
Tracks	Needle marks and scars along the vein of a drug addict, the result of regular injections.
Trade	Since the 1930s, the clients of a male or female prostitute; since the 1960s, a homosexual lover, whether paid for or not.
Tradesman's Entrance	The anus, an old term that puns on the 'back door'. Often known as the 'tradesmans'.
Trafalgar Square *Chair*	Only sits comfortably when shortened to 'Trafalgar'.
Traff	Anal 'gunfire' (qv). A backslang fart.
Trail Boss	The head of a team of 'cowboy' (qv) builders. Based on the title given to the leader of a cattle drive, as seen in countless western films.
Trainspotter	A boring, nerdy person. The type that takes a pub quiz seriously. Typically someone with a hobby about which he can reel off facts that are of no interest to anyone but a kindred spirit.
Tramp's Neck	What the thirsty may claim to be as dry as, since a tramp's neck never sees water.
Trank	An abbreviated form of tranquilliser used by users. 'Tranked out' – drugged on tranks.
Tranny	a) A 1960s term for a transistor radio. I can still remember my first one, a small Japanese job that was strangely undamaged considering it had fallen off a lorry somewhere in the Royal Docks. Well that's what my old man told me anyway. b) A 1980s term from the gay lexicon for a transvestite or a transexual. c) A Ford Transit van, a familiar term used in the light haulage and courier trades.
Trap	An old and very familiar term for the mouth: 'If he don't watch his trap he's gonna find it full of knuckles and broken teeth.'
Trappy	Descriptive of anybody with a big mouth. A gossip, a boaster, an informer or generally someone with too much to say for himself.
Traps	An oldish term for drums. Used by musicians, it probably has something to do with a 'snare' drum.
Trash	a) To completely destroy something, to vandalise.

In the 1960s it became the norm for rock bands to 'trash' hotel rooms.

b) To criticise severely, to demolish with words: 'The critics raved over *The Blair Witch Project* but everyone I know has trashed it. Must be the emperor's or king's new clothes syndrome.'

Trashed Very drunk or high on drugs. Utterly destroyed.

Travel Agent A supplier of LSD, someone who sends his clients on a trip.

Tray/Trey The number three from the Polari book of numbers. From the Italian *tre*. £3 is a 'tray'.

Treacle Tart *Fart* A 'treacle' wouldn't produce a sweet smell. In and out like a 'treacle' in a colander may describe a brief visit.

Treasure Hunt *Cunt* The next time someone calls you 'treasure', make sure they are smiling. Anatomically speaking it's the booty of a sexual adventurer – the vagina.

Treble Chance *Dance* Refers to a function and what is possibly the biggest waste of energy man has ever invented.

Trendoid A dedicated follower of the latest fads and trends, a slave to fashion.

Trezz The number three, based on the Spanish *tres* – three.

Trick a) The client of a prostitute and also the sexual activity that goes on between them.

b) Any casual sex partner, very often a homosexual.

Trick Cyclist *Psychiatrist* An old and well-known piece although I'm not sure this is RS. But it is slang and it rhymes so here it is.

Trigger A name given to a slow-witted, thick person. Someone seen as being a few hairs short of a wig. Based on the name of just such a character in TV's *Only Fools and Horses*.

Trilby Hat *Pratt* Normally reduced to 'trilby' in regard to a fool.

Trim To cheat, swindle or con somebody out of their money. In other words to 'fleece' them.

Trip A hallucinatory experience caused by taking LSD or some other mind-blowing drug. Also a tablet or dose of LSD. To 'trip out' – to go under the influence.

Trog A put-down aimed at a person of low intelligence, or of primitive ways. A lout. A typical piece of stick the football hooligan has to suffer.

Troll a) An ugsome person. Usually a cruel jibe at an unsightly, overweight and unpleasant woman, about whom the kindest thing you can say is that

		she's slightly effeminate. The complete opposite of a 'doll'. b) An example from the gay world meaning to wander around in search of a sexual partner.
Trolley & Tram	*Ham*	Generally sliced to the first of these two forerunners of the modern bus, as in a 'trolley sandwich'.
Trolley & Truck	*Fuck*	Used in reference to the sexual act since the early 20th century.
Trolley Dolly		An air hostess, or to the homosexual an air steward.
Trolleys		Underpants, a piece that's mainly heard in the north.
Trolleywags	*Bags*	An obsolete piece from the 19th-century which may have some bearing on why the shortened version – 'trolleys' – has come to represent underpants. Then again it may not.
Trombone	*Phone*	People have been making calls on the 'trombone' since the jazz age.
Troops		Semen, seen as individual sperms. 'Pull the troops out' – to ejaculate through masturbation.
Tropical Fish	*Piss*	A Scottish example of a 'drain-off', which they pronounce 'pish'.
Trots		A well-used term for diarrhoea since World War One, a time when fear-induced galloping to the latrines must have been common.
Trotter-Cases		An old term for shoes or boots which should now also include trainers. Whatever the 'trotters' get cased-up in.
Trotters		The feet, an example that's been running for 300 years or so.
Trouble & Fuss	*Bus*	Given the transport problems in London, this is a very appropriate piece and one that's likely to be so forever.
Trouble & Strife	a) *Life*	For many, this is about as apt as RS gets.
	b) *Wife*	By far the best known of all the terms for who, in perfect circumstances, will be wooed, won and wed. Very often though it's a case of bed, bun and brood.
Troubles & Cares	*Stairs*	A seldom climbed version of 'apples and pears'.
Trouser		a) A term from liberated females of the 1980s that relates to men as sex objects. A female answer to the old term 'skirt' (qv). b) To pocket: 'But I gave Smiffy a tenner to give to you. He must've trousered it.'
Trouser Bandit		A derogatory term for a male homosexual, one seen as a predator.
Trouser Trumpet		The penis, a 1980s term for the horn that gets blown.

Trug		A dirty, scruffy person. Someone in need of a good wash and brush-up.
Truggy		Descriptive of the 'scruffbag' at 'trug' (qv), and also a nickname for such a person.
Trump		a) A good, strong, reliable person. Someone to have on your side. *See also* ACE OF TRUMPS.
		b) To break wind with a degree of volume. Trump is archaic English for a trumpet-blast.
Trumpet		A telephone, the old-fashioned type of blower, one that never came with a fifty-page instruction manual.
Truncheon Meat		An old allusion to a victim of police brutality. 'Truncheon fodder' – an unruly mob.
Trunk(s) & **Tree(s)**	*Knee(s)*	An East End term that would seem to have originated in Poplar, London.
Trunker		A lorry driver, a 1950s term for he who cruised the trunk roads.
Tub of Lard		A fat person, an example that first weighed in during the 19th century.
Tube		a) A fool, a Scottish term for someone whose brain is 'on the blink'.
		b) A coward. A tube may be described as a body with a hole at each end with nothing in the middle. It is therefore 'gutless'.
Tuck In With		To go to bed with, to sleep or have an affair with. Read the scandal sheets to see who's 'tucked in' with whom.
Tuck Up		To swindle, cheat or short-change someone. Such an act is a 'tuck-up' and the victims are 'tucked up'.
Tucked Up		Imprisoned, an example of police and underworld jargon: 'That's him nicely tucked up for a few years.'
Tucked Up and **Snuggled**		In bed. A long-winded way of saying it. But that's slang!
Tug		a) An act of masturbation: 'I was having a tug in the shower and my sister walked in. Good job it was steamed up.'
		b) Of the police, an arrest or to be stopped for questioning, another version of a 'pull' (qv). Also used when the law is not involved: 'Give the waiter a tug, I think he's made a rick.'
Tug o' War	*Whore*	A woman who is often pulled.
Tulip		A male homosexual, a piece from the same garden as 'pansy' (qv).
Tumble		a) An act of sexual intercourse, a fairly well-known piece. 'Crumble tumble' – sex between an elderly couple. *See* CRUMBLE.

b) To realise, to fall in, to be aware. An old and well-known piece, but you probably tumbled to that already.

Tumble & Trip *Whip*

Always reduced to a 'tumble' in reference to a whip-round.

Tumble Down the Sink *Drink*

In the decreased form of 'tumble' or 'tumbledown', this is solely connected with drinking alcohol. To go for a 'tumble' is to go to the pub.

Tumblings

An old prisoner's term for loose, rolling tobacco, that which easily falls from a pouch. The partnership between tobacco and cigarette papers is known as 'tumblings and blankets'.

Tunnel

The vagina. What sexually straight men prefer to the 'funnel' (qv).

Tup

To copulate, an ancient term that was used by Shakespeare and is still in use: 'If Big Dave finds out you've been tupping his sister, you've had it.' A tup is male sheep, a ram.

Tupper

A late evening meal, something that comes between teatime and suppertime.

Tuppney Ha'penny

Third-rate, cheap or bordering on the worthless: 'Why am I wasting my time in a tupp'ney ha-penny job like this?' Not worth twopence halfpenny in old money.

Turd

a) A piece of excrement, a term that goes back centuries. Now most commonly associated with dog mess.

b) A horrible, despicable person. A regular 'piece of shit'.

Turd Burglar

A male homosexual, an example of heterosexual mockery for he who 'goes in through the back door'.

Turf

An underworld term for a person's or a gang's sphere of activity, their territory. 'Turf wars' are commonplace.

Turin Shroud *Cloud*

The heavenly sunshield based on the shroud that reputedly covered the body of Christ. Heard as rarely as it's seen.

Turkey

In show business, a flop, an embarrassing failure, especially of a film or show.

Turkey Neck

A post World War Two term for the penis. *See* LAST TURKEY IN THE SHOP.

Turkish Bath *Laugh*

Anyone having a 'Turkish' at your expense is on a wind up or is taking the 'wet stuff' (qv).

Turkish Delight *a) Shite*

Anything considered rubbishy or 'crappy' is deemed to be a 'right load of Turkish'.

	b) *Tight*	A 'Turkish' git is the stingy scrote who 'wouldn't give his shit to the crows'.
Turn Charlie		To come over shy, to 'go the other way', i.e., to be outgoing one minute and suddenly turn coy. Derives from the RS 'Charlie Howard' – coward.
Turn It In/Up		To stop doing something.
Turn Japanese		To masturbate, a 1980s term based on the old joke which ends with the teller squinting his eyes and making his teeth protrude. Supposedly, the contorted face of orgasm is similar to the face of your typical 'Japanese'.
Turn on the Waterworks		To start crying, an old term for what women do to win arguments.
Turn One's Toes Up		To die, an old term that invokes the image of lying in a coffin.
Turn Over		a) To search or ransack a premises, an underworld term for something that's done by the police and criminals.
		b) To cheat, short-change, swindle or rob. An all-purpose term that stretches from welshing on a bet to 'turning over' a bank.
		c) To beat up, especially when robbery is involved. To 'mug', a variation of 'roll' (qv).
Turnip		An incompetent, a fool. An insult levelled at England football manager Graham Taylor in 1993 when his team failed to qualify for the World Cup.
Turn-Off		Anything repellent, disappointing or unerotic. Something that doesn't turn you on.
Turn-On		The opposite of a 'turn-off' (qv).
Turpentine	*Serpentine*	The lake in London's Hyde Park has been known by generations of taxi drivers as 'the Turps'.
Turret		The head, an underworld term that's usually used when violence is involved: 'If he hadn't tried to be a hero, he wouldn't have got a crack on the turret.'
Turtle Dove	*a)* *Glove*	From a lightweight fashion glove to an industrial protector, all gloves are 'turtles'.
	b) *Love*	An old term by romantic balladeers in search of a rhyme, who didn't know they were coining a piece of RS.
Turtle's Head Job		A dire need to defecate. To 'have a turtle's head sticking out' is the picturesque image likened to having a piece of excrement poking out of the anus.
Tush		The buttocks, a piece that derives from the Yiddish *toches*. *See* TOOKUS.
Twat/Twot		a) The vagina, a piece that has been in constant use since the 17th century.

b) A fool, a 'silly bastard'. A term, like 'pratt' (qv), that has become common on TV even though it's directly related to 'cunt'.

Tweedling
Stealing jewellery by substituting a cheap imitation in its place. In a jeweller's shop a 'tweedler' will ask to see an item and with manual dexterity steal it and replace it with something similar. Also known as being 'on the tweedle', when it applies to selling inferior goods, especially perfume, in the guise of expensive brands.

Tweety
A caged bird, normally a budgie or a canary.

Twelve-Inch Rule *Fool*
A pre-metric buffoon.

Twerp/Twirp
A fool, a buffoon. A dullard who wouldn't suss a jockey on TV's *What's My Line?*

Twerpy Legs
A term of mild abuse for anyone acting the fool. *See* SILLY LEGS. Also 'twerpy lemon'.

Twig/Twiglet
To scratch an itchy anus. Disgustingly based on the supposed similarity in appearance of a faecal-stained finger and a Twiglet, a savoury snack.

Twigs
Matches, the easy way of starting a fire based on the hard way.

Twin Set
An unfashionable woman, usually a put-down by other women. 'I haven't seen Emily Twinset for ages.'

Twirl
An underworld term for a key, especially a skeleton key. Also an old term for a prison officer.

Twirly
A name given to someone who, obsessively, has to be on time, someone who gives himself an hour to make a twenty-minute journey. A pun on 'too early'.

Twist & Twirl *Girl*
Descriptive of what a young lady can do to a smitten swain. Round her little finger goes he.

Twisted Eyelash
An old euphemism for an itchy anus. What someone with busily scratching fingers may be asked if he has.

Twit
A silly fool, a cross between a 'twerp' and a 'nit' (*see both*). Often heard on British radio and TV in the 1950s and 1960s. 'Twitty', 'Twitbum' – mildly abusive names given to such a fool.

Two & Eight *State*
Nearly always termed as being in a 'right old two and eight' in reference to being in a state of agitation or on the horns of a dilemma.

Two & Three *Key*
An old term, one which the number may be up on. Reduced to a 'bunch of twos'.

Two by Four *Whore*
An old term for a prostitute that gets truncated to a 'two-be'.

Two Ender
A long-departed term for a florin, or a 'flo', more commonly known as two shillings.

Two Eyes of Blue   *Too True*
See EYES OF BLUE.

**Two Eyes Open &
One Eye Shut**
To be constipated, an old term which likens the anus to a third eye. *See* EYE.

Two Short Planks
What a person of low intelligence is said to be as thick as. A 'brainless wonder'.

Two Thirty   *Dirty*
Refers to uncleanliness: 'His feet were so two thirty you could grow spuds on 'em.'

Two-Bob Bit   *Shit*
Most commonly heard in plural form as an expression for diarrhoea, but may also apply to an emission of wind. In a malodorous atmosphere, the words 'whose dropped a two-bob bit?' may be heard through pinched nasal tones.

Two-Bob Job
Anything or anybody considered to be worthless, inferior or cheap, in other words 'not worth two-bob'. Two-bob was two shillings, now 10p.

Twocker
A car thief, especially a young, so-called joyrider. From TWOC – Taken Without Owner's Consent.

Two'd Up
Prison slang for two convicts sharing a cell. A trio are 'Three'd Up'.

Twoer
Originally racecourse and underworld jargon for £200, now common everywhere.

Two-Foot Rule   *Fool*
Another measure of stupidity, presumably twice the fool referred to at 'twelve-inch rule' (qv).

Twonk/Twonker
A fool, an ignoramus. Someone who may be a card short of a full deck.

Typewriter   *Fighter*
Can apply to a boxer, but mainly refers to strength of character. Anyone who keeps going through adversity is said to be a 'real typewriter'.

Tyrannosaurus Rex   *Sex*
An extension of the older 'T Rex' (qv), that gets reduced to the first element when there's nookie to be had.

Tyrone Power   *Shower*
A 1950s term for a shower of rain that, via the merchant navy, moved into the bathroom. Sweating seamen on passenger ships took regular 'Tyrones'. Based on an American actor (1914–58).

U

US		Useless. Said quickly as 'yewess' normally in regard of broken or inferior goods: 'You're chucking your money away buying cheap gear if it's US.'
Udders		An old term for breasts, human milk-yielders, usually large ones: 'She's got some udders.'
Ugly Sister	*Blister*	That which painfully appears on the hand after a bout of unaccustomed tool usage, or on the foot as a result of wearing a tight shoe or a glass slipper.
Ugsome		Ugly, the type of face that gets an 'ugh' reaction. Used in the antithesis of every woman's dream man, whereby 'tall, dark and handsome' becomes 'short, bald and ugsome'.
U-ie		A U-turn, well-known as 'do a U-ie' – turn around, which may apply to driving or a change of mind.
Umbrella		A euphemism for an erect penis, it also goes up.
Umbrella	*Fella*	Normally used in reference to a boyfriend or husband: 'How's your umbrella these days?' 'He's alright as long as he doesn't leak.'
Una		The Polari version of the number one. From the Italian *una*. Pronounced 'Oona'.
Uncle		An 18th-century term for a pawnbroker that is still in existence. Like a rich relation, he helps out financially. Humorously known as the 'uncle with three balls'.

Uncle & Aunt	*Plant*	As sold at a garden centre, whereby your prize blooms become your 'uncles'.
Uncle Ben	*Ten*	Eyes down, look in. It's another term from a game of bingo.
Uncle Bert	*Shirt*	A rare alternative to the frequently worn 'Dicky dirt' (qv).
Uncle Bertie	*Shirty*	Refers to being annoyed or angry: 'Don't you get Uncle Bertie with me!'
Uncle Bill/Bob/ Nick		Three terms for a policeman, based on 'Old Bill', 'Bobby' and what he may do to you.
Uncle Bob	*a) Job*	The unemployed seek work at the 'Uncle Bob centre'.
	b) Knob (Penis)	Sometimes used vulgarly by a less than smooth operator: 'Come on darlin', come and meet my Uncle Bob.'
Uncle Dick	*a) Prick*	Not to be confused with 'Uncle Bob' (b). Same pipe, different bacca really.
	b) Sick	Very common in relation to being physically sick or in general bad health. Often reduced to the second element, as in 'dicky minces' – bad eyes.
Uncle Fred	*Bread*	A comical example whereby children are encouraged to eat their 'Uncle Fred'.
Uncle Mac	*Smack*	Originally applied to corporal punishment but is now linked with heroin. Based on a children's radio presenter of the 1950s.
Uncle Ned	*Bed*	This enjoys extensive employment, generally in its full extension. Tired people can often hear their 'Uncle Ned' calling.
Uncle Sam	*Lamb*	Applies to lamb as sold by the butcher. A leg of 'Uncle Sam'.
Uncle Wilf	*Filth (Police)*	A 1980s example for the 'narks' that's used derogatorily.
Uncle Willie	*a) Chilly*	A pre-war term that accompanies a shiver and a flapping of the arms as: 'Uncle Willie, innit?'
	b) Silly	An allusion to anyone acting in a manner that suggests substandard mental equipment.
Uncool		The opposite of 'cool' (qv, a, b).
Uncouth	*Youth*	An appropriate piece that has ever related to a boozing, farting, swearing young man.
Under the Arm		Said of anything considered dodgy, fishy or underhand. A situation that may not be quite right, one that 'stinks'. Based on the smell of an untreated armpit.
Under the Cosh		Very busy, up against it or in trouble: 'I'll have to call you back, I'm well under the cosh.' A variation is 'under the hammer'.

Under the Table		Secret, clandestine, especially of a dodgy deal which may be 'all under the table, no questions asked'.
Underkecks		A northern term for underpants: 'You think his shirt's dirty, you should see his underkecks.'
Undershell		An old term for a waistcoat, a third of a 'three piece whistle'.
Unicorn	*Horn (Erection)*	Shortened to 'uni' this is a totally apt example based on a fabled beast with one horn.
Union Jack	*Back*	Anatomically employed, usually in connection with an aching back and it's role in getting you out of any heavy lifting: 'Sorry, I can't lift that, I've got a dodgy union.'
United's at Home		A menstrual period based on the colours, or Manchester United Football Club, known as the Reds. *See* REDS.
Unleaded		An impotent man, one with 'no lead in his pencil'.
Unload		a) To defecate, a fairly widespread term for a 'drop'. b) To ejaculate, sometimes to 'unload the gun'.
Unluck		A jinx. A name given to someone considered to be bad luck: 'Quick, throw a black cat over your shoulder. Here comes unluck.'
Unmugged		To be unknown by the police, they have no 'mug shots' (qv).
Unnecessary		Excited, usually sexually. Elderly woman are often humorously said to 'come over all unnecessary', probably because they are aroused and unable to do anything about it.
Unwrapped		Naked for sex: 'We're both unwrapped and ready when she hears her old man's car pull up.'
Up		To punch, to beat up: 'The geezer was bad-mouthing me bad, but I didn't say anything, I just upped him.'
Up & Down	*Brown*	Used in reference to all things brown, especially brown ale.
Up & Under	*Thunder*	During a violent, middle of the night storm, many nervous people are known to get up and go under the stairs.
Up a Tree	*Three*	Eyes up. Look out. There's another bingo caller about.
Up & Downer		A fight, one that's lasted since the 19th century.
Up Each Other's Arseholes		Not a sexual thing, but said of very close friends.
Up for It		Ready, willing and keen to get on with it.

Up on Blocks On a menstrual period, a chauvinistic piece used by men that compares his partner to a car that's off the road: 'No T Rex for me for a while, she's up on blocks.'

Up One's Own Arsehole Full of self importance, to think a lot of oneself: 'He's up his own arsehole that one.'

Up Shit Creek Without a Paddle In serious trouble with no sign of a get-out. This now-familiar phrase comes originally from a homosexual term for being caught in the act of sodomy.

Up the Duff Pregnant, a play on 'pudding club', duff being a steamed pudding.

Up the Pictures Broken or ruined. Your TV is up the pictures if it's clapped out, as is dinner if you burn the meat. It's also where your money is said to be at the result of a losing gamble. Also 'up the spout'.

Up the Pole Insane, an old term for being mentally off-balance.

Up the Spout a) One of several well-known 'up the . . .' terms regarding pregnancy, including 'Flue', 'Pole' and 'Stick'.

b) Ruined, broken or as said at a loss: 'That's another tenner up the spout.'

Up the Swannee A piece that relates to failure, rejection or a lost opportunity: 'I was late for the interview, so that's my chances up the Swannee.'

Up to Here To be totally fed up with, to have had enough of a situation: 'I've had it up to here with your tantrums.'

Up Top *See* UPSTAIRS (a).

Upchuck To vomit. *See* CHUCK UP (a).

Uphill Gardening Anal intercourse, an example of convicts' slang.

Uphills A 300-year-old term for false dice, the type that always show high numbers. 'Downhills' go the opposite way by only landing on low numbers.

Uppers Amphetamines or other stimulant drugs.

Upstairs a) The head, or rather the internal workings of it. Of a dunce it's claimed that 'there's not much going on upstairs'. Also 'up top'.

b) Heaven, a familiar euphemism for where God, or 'the Man Upstairs' lives.

c) The upper echelons of an organisation or company. A move 'upstairs' is a promotion.

d) Spirits as sold in a pub. The row of bottles being above head height. After a few pints it's common to go upstairs.

Urban Surfing A 1970s term for the stupid craze of riding on the outside of a vehicle.

Urge to Purge The need to defecate, often a dire need.

Uri Geller	*Stella (Artois)*	A French lager based on an Israeli expert on the paranormal. Often on TV, he is commonly known as the spoonbender.
Uriah Heep	*Creep*	An obnoxious, despicable, toady type of person, appropriately inspired by the ever so 'umble creep in the Dickens novel *David Copperfield*. Pluralised, it applies to the feeling such a repellent person may give you, i.e., the creeps.
Used Kleenex		A symbol of uselessness, what a cretin is said to be as much use as.
Uxter		Money, a 19th-century term among rogues and thieves who'd roll a drunk and relieve him of his uxter.

V

VAT

A vodka and tonic, the favourite tipple of Arthur Daley, entrepreneur and all-round dodgy character in the TV series *Minder*.

Vadge

The vagina, a 1990s abbreviation.

Valentine Dyalls   *Piles*

Known as 'Valentines', this is based on a British actor (1908–85), surname Dyall) who was famous as 'the Man in Black' on wartime radio. The term dates from around that time.

Vamoose

To leave in a hurry, to get away. Originally a US term, based on the Spanish *vamos* – let's go, it is safely ensconced in British slang thanks to the Hollywood western.

Vampire

An extortionist, an appropriate term for a 'bloodsucker'.

Vampire's Kiss   *Piss*

To urinate but mainly used in 'taking the vampires', getting a laugh at someone's expense. Often this is light-hearted or jocular (after the well-known Scottish vampire) but usually it's to go for the jugular with a bit of spiteful fun-poking.

Vancouver   *Hoover*

A vacuum cleaner, or the brand name it goes by.

Vanessa Feltz

A heavy dew, when everything is soaking wet and it hasn't been raining. Based on a large Jewish TV presenter whose ambition is to be a thin Jewish TV presenter.

Vanilla Fudge *Judge* An underworld term, criminals go up before the 'vanilla'.

Vanity Fair *Chair* On which people have sat and read the book *Vanity Fair*, by William Thackeray, for many years.

Varda/Vardo To look at, to see. An example of theatrical slang.

Varnish An old term for brown sauce that was common among caff and coffee bar customers: 'I'll have some varnish on that bacon sandwich.'

Vatican Roulette The unreliable and possibly costly rhythm method of contraception, the only form allowed by the Catholic Church. A pun on Russian roulette.

Vegetarian A prostitute who will not perform fellatio, one who won't 'eat meat'.

Vegetarian Lunchbox The testicles, the two veg without the meat.

Velcro A lesbian. Based on the image of female lovers rubbing their pubic areas together, supposedly similar to joining a Velcro fastener.

Venetian Blind *Mind* The workings of the nut gets reduced to the first element of a sunshade: 'You must be out of your tiny Venetian.'

Vera Lynn a) *Gin* Named after the East Ham born songstress who won the hearts of the fighting men of World War Two, this is by far the commonest term in use for the 'spirit of the East End'.

b) *Skin* A modern piece for a cigarette paper used in the making of 'drugfags'.

Verbal To insult or abuse, as a sportsman will do to a rival in a bout of gamesmanship, hence 'give it the verbal'. Also to nag and as 'verbals' – persistent nagging.

Verbal Diarrhoea Said to be the complaint of an excessive talker, someone to whom the phrase 'to cut a long story short' is unknown. The term has been levelled at many a waffling disc jockey.

Veronica Lake *Steak* The tastier version of 'Joe Blake' (qv), based on the Hollywood star of the 1940s (1919–73), who was known as the peek-a-boo girl. Once considered top tottie, 'Veronica' is now top rump.

Vic A name given to an irritating, annoying person. Based on the Vick inhaler, he also gets up your nose.

Vicar A Guinness with an overlarge head, one that looks like a clergyman's dog collar.

Vicar of Bray   *Tray*   The tool of the 'waiting game' but mainly the number three, for which 'tray' is the Polari version. Commonly used for the playing card, it's based on the title of an 18th-century ballad about a popular but Machiavellian vicar. A case of never trusting a man that everyone likes.

Vicious Circle   The vagina of a woman infected with a venereal disease.

Victor Sylvesters   A 1950s term for baggy trousers. Based on the name of a British orchestra leader (1902–78) and presenter of BBC TV's *Dance Club*, the trousers are said to have plenty of ballroom.

Victoria Cross   *Toss*   People who 'don't give a VC', don't give a damn.

Victoria Monk   *Spunk (Semen)*   An example that stretches back to the days of music hall, of which Victoria Monks (1884–1972) was a star.

Victory V   *Pee/Wee*   A sign made by those who were on the point of bladderburst but just made it to the lavatory?

Vin Blong   Cheap white wine, a piece that's been about since World War One. Based on the French *vin blanc*.

Vincent Price   *Ice*   Frozen at 'Vincent' in respect of that which chills a drink, and based on an American filmstar (1911–93) whose film roles chilled many a spine.

Vindaloo   *Poo*   To defecate and also the ejected outcome of it. Based on the curry dish that often generates an 'urge to purge', it's said in full or you may go for a 'vinda': 'I had a vindaloo last night and three vindas this morning.'

Vinegar Strokes   Of masturbation, the final strokes of the penis before ejaculation, or the final thrusts during intercourse.

Vintner's Droop   The effect that too many glasses of wine may have on a man's penis. When the wine is in, the wit is out. As is sex when vintner's droop's about.

Virgin Bride   *Ride*   A rare term for sexual intercourse based on an even bigger rarity, although this was probably not the case when it was formed in the Victorian era in connection with travel. It made the leap into its present meaning during World War Two, if a soldier said, ironically, that he'd just had a 'virgin' it's likely he'd paid to get his end away.

Virginia McKenna   *Tenner*   Based on a British actress, a 'Virginia' comes well down the cast list of terms for £10. Almost unheard of beyond the suburbs.

Vitamin A   Drug user's talk for 'acid' (qv).

Vitamin C   Drug user's talk for cocaine.

Vitamin E   Drug user's talk for ecstasy.

Vivien Leigh	*Pee/Wee*	A 1940s term known as a 'Vivien' and formed on the name of the British actress (1913–67) who found fame as Scarlett O'Hara in the film *Gone with the Wind* (1939).
Vodeodo		Money, an old piece that's a jocular extension of 'dough', i.e., vodeo-dough.
Voker		To speak and understand a language, especially slang and the jargon of the underworld. 'Voker Polari?'; Do you speak Polari?
Volley Off		To give someone a severe telling off, to give them a mouthful: 'I rucked him, and when his old woman joined in I volleyed her off as well.'
Von Trapp	*Crap*	A piece that's always used in full, whereby to have a Von Trapp is to defecate. Based on the name of the family in the film *The Sound of Music* (1965).
Voss		£1. A backslang 'sov'. 'Duey vos' – £2.
Vulcanic		Of a man, to be sexually frustrated, in dire need of an eruption, i.e. to blow his lava (qv).

W

Wack A dirty, scruffy person from a run-down estate or area which may be known as 'Wackville'. *See* DIRTYWACK.

Wack/Wacker Terms of address between men on Merseyside that came to prominence in the 1960s in the wake of the Beatles, when Liverpool was at the centre of the beat music boom.

Wad a) A large roll of banknotes, often produced to impress: 'Flash bastard. The round only came to nine quid and he brought out a massive wad.'
b) Semen, most commonly heard in terms of ejaculation, i.e., to 'shoot one's wad'.
c) The male genitals, another form of 'bundle' (qv, d).
d) A thick sandwich or a bun, something to fill you up, usually during a tea break, hence 'a cup of tea and a wad'.
e) An old term from prison for chewing tobacco.

Wag It To play truant, a reduction of 'hop the wag' (qv).

Wager Wear Outlandish, garish or cheap-looking clothes, the type that prompt the derisive question: 'Are you wearing that for a bet? If so you've won.'

Wait & Linger *Finger* A 'scratcher' (qv). Who knows where points the fickle 'wait' of fate.

Walk		To go free after being arrested, to be found not guilty of a crime.
Walk the Chalk		To live a life of sobriety, to keep off the booze. Before the breathalyser, drivers were deemed unfit to be in control of a vehicle if they couldn't walk a straight, chalk-drawn line. Reformed alcoholics are said to be 'walking the chalk'.
Walkover		An absolute certainty. Based on a one-horse race its use is not confined to the racecourse: 'If you're gonna pay a fiver for a gallon can of wine, it's a walkover it'll make you ill.'
Wallace & Grommit	*Vomit*	The Oscar-winning duo who have made a big splash in the world of animation now make a splash on the pavement. Anything that ever made you sick will now make you 'Wallace'.
Wallace Beery	*Query*	In the betting shop, a dispute over a settler's calculation is a 'Wallace'. Based on an American film actor (1885–1949).
Wallah		A person associated with a particular job or activity, like the well-known 'office wallah' or 'char wallah' – someone in charge of making the tea. From the Hindi word *wala*.
Walloon		A fool or someone acting the fool, a cross between a 'wally' and a 'loon'. In the real world, a Walloon is a French-speaking Belgian from the region of Wallonia.
Wallop		a) A hefty blow, a hard punch: 'For a little bloke he packs a mean wallop.' b) Alcohol, especially beer. What strong drink may pack. c) To beat up, to administer a severe 'walloping'.
Wallopers		The police, a term from the 1950s, when a civilian head was seen as truncheon fodder.
Wally		a) A pickled cucumber, commonly seen on the counter of a fish and chip shop. b) An inept person, a fool. A piece that's been common since the 1970s and may be based on (a) in that a 'dill' (qv) is both a fool and a pickled cucumber, although it could also come from (c). For penis, read 'prick', and a fool and a prick can be one and the same. *See* Pickle. c) Rare East End term for the penis based on the size and shape of (a). Hopefully, not the colour.
Wallybrain		An idiot, a complete fool. Someone who may have 'lost a button'. An extension of 'wally' (b).
Walnut Whip	*a) Kip (Sleep)*	Based on a chocolate sweet, all an insomniac wants is a good night's 'walnut'.

	b) Snip	A vasectomy, laughingly called the 'walnut' by everyone except the one with the sore nuts.
Walter Joyce	*Voice*	An ancient piece that's been long silent.
Wank		The best known act of masturbation that was originally spelt 'whank', which is a dialect word meaning to beat or whack. Also 'wank off'.
Wank Stain		A worthless, insignificant or inadequate person. Someone of less value than a match, i.e., 'not worth a light'. *See* LIGHTS (b).
Wank Your Hairy Crutch		A humorous pun on 'thank you very much'.
Wanker		A useless, worthless or obnoxious person. The original 'tosser' (qv).
Wanking Material		Pornography, in either magazine or video form. 'Wank mag' – a pornographic magazine.
Wanky		Useless, rubbishy or generally 'not worth a rub'.
Wannabe		A person with the ambition and desire to succeed, especially in show business. They 'wanna be' rich and famous. Also, a fan who tries to look and dress like their idol. An imitator.
Wanstead Flats	*Spats*	An obsolete term for a long-departed fashion based on an area of East London.
War & Strife	*Wife*	Another term rhyming her indoors with strife.
Warm		Well off, comfortably rich. Often said in envy: 'I'd like to be as warm as you.'
Warpaint		Make-up, an old term used by men of what's worn by their women: 'Ain't you got your warpaint on yet?'
Warrior Bold	*Cold*	Can refer to the illness, the one that causes you to call in sick with a bad 'warrior', or cold weather, which is often termed 'warriors'.
Washers		Copper coins, a piece that reflects the value of small change.
Wasp		a) A regular borrower of money, a 'tapper'. Someone who will 'sting' you for a few quid and very often forget to pay you back.
		b) A traffic warden, the bane of the motorist who, clad in a black and yellow uniform, may leave a sting under your windscreen wiper.
Waste		To kill, originally a US military term that found its way on to American streets and then British ones.
Waste of Space		A useless, totally incompetent person, one not up to a task and taking up the room of someone who is.
Wasted		High on drugs or 'drunk in fifteen languages'.
Watch		A gullible person, one who is easily 'wound up'. *See* WIND UP.

Watch & Chain	*Brain*	Used in full when castigating someone for not thinking: 'You've got a watch and chain so use it!' Cut to the timepiece, though, when used in the third person. A dullard's watch may be slow, while a 'sharper's will be fast.
Water Rat		An underworld term for an officer of the river police.
Water Sports		Urinating on someone for sexual pleasure, jargon of the sex trade.
Water the Donkey/Horse		To urinate, two ways of 'hosing the yard'.
Water the Garden/ Flowers/Plants		To urinate, three ways of 'sprinkling the lawn'.
Waterbury Watch	*Scotch*	Time was called on this old piece long ago.
Watercress	*Dress*	The garment and the donning of it. To get dressed is to get 'watered'.
Watering Hole		A bar, pub or any establishment that sells alcoholic drinks.
Waterlogged		Very drunk, even more so than those who are merely 'soaked' (qv).
Waterloo	*Stew*	The dish, swallowed as a bowl of 'Waterloo'.
Watford Gap	*Map*	Based on the motorway service area on the M1, which you may need a 'Watford' to find.
Wave When You Get to the Bridge		A phrase used when someone is caught picking his nose.
Wax Cock		A candle used as a dildo. A 'Hampton' with a real 'Wick'. *See* HAMPTON WICK.
Wazz		An act of urination, to go for a 'wazz' is to 'bleed the radiator'.
Wazzered		Drunk. If a 'wazz' (qv) is a 'piss', then this becomes 'pissed'.
Wazzock		A fool, a term commonly heard in TV programmes set in the north: 'Does being a wazzock come natural to you or did you take lessons?'
Weapon		A common euphemism for the penis, a source of double entendres for centuries.
Weasel & Stoat	*Coat*	Commonly cut to the first element. Only in RS can a mink become a 'weasel'.
Wedding Kit		The same accoutrements described in 'wedding tackle' (qv).
Wedding Tackle		A man's genitals, the necessary equipment for postnuptial sport that's often reduced to 'tackle'.
Wedge		Money, originally silver. Criminals in the 18th century used to melt down silver plate into bars

which were known as wedges. Very common in its present form: 'I used to follow Chelsea all over the place but now I ain't got the wedge' – a supporter's view of modern football prices.

Wedge/Wej   A Jew, a backslang descendant of the Israelites.

Wednesday Legs   Known as 'Wednesdays', meaning very thin legs, a juvenile pun on 'When's dey gonna snap?'

Wee/Wee-Wee   Urine, juvenile versions of having a 'sprinkle'.

Wee Cough   Phoney sick leave, a pun on 'week off', said as: 'I feel a wee cough coming on.'

Wee Georgie Wood   *Good*   Formed on the name of a midget British comedian (1897–1979) and generally shortened to 'Wee Georgie', which leads to rubbish being 'no Wee Georgie'.

Wee Willie Winkie   *Chinky*   A Chinese person is known as a 'Wee Willie' as a result of a kid in a nursery rhyme, so Chinese men shouldn't be offended.

Weed   a) Tobacco. Used in relation to the harmful side of smoking, often as 'the dreaded weed', the term is used of a cigarette as a bad thing.
b) Marijuana, a term that's well-known even by those who have never tried it.
c) To steal from an employer, to embezzle, usually in small amounts. Like weeding a garden.

Weedhead   An habitual marijuana smoker.

Weekend   An underworld term for a very short prison sentence.

Weekend Gangster   A law-abiding man who likes to be seen in the company of rogues and villains.

Weekend Pass(es)   *Glass/Glasses*   A military term for a drinking receptacle that doubles up as spectacles.

Weep & Wail   *Tale*   An apposite example that relates to a sob story as told by a beggar.

Weeping Willow   *Pillow*   When you're tired, there's nothing like sinking your nut into a nice soft 'weeping'.

Weetabix   A bad goalkeeper or a piece of bad goalkeeping. Coined in the 1970s in the wake of a TV advert for the cereal, which showed a centre forward who'd had his Weetabix and a goalie who hadn't. When the forward shoots, the keeper dives a couple of feet over the ball.

Weigh Anchor   *Wanker*   Always used in full for a useless or worthless person: 'What a weigh anchor.'

Weigh In   To pay a debt or to pay one's share, to contribute to a collection.

Weighed Off   Sentenced to a term of imprisonment.

Weighed Out   Paid, usually in respect of wages or a winning bet: 'You been weighed out yet?'

Well		a) An old substitute for 'very', a piece that's currently well common with the well youthful.
		b) A pocket. An old piece that was commonly heard when the receiver of a 'bung' (qv) was told to 'Drop this down your well'.
Well Equipped/ Furnished/ Hung/Loaded		Four different examples of being 'well endowed', that's five examples of having large genitals.
Well Hung	*Young*	Sounds like a woman's idea of a perfect toyboy.
Wellington Boot	*a) Root*	A modern term for sexual intercourse, which is about as unromantic as it gets. Unless you're a rubber fetishist.
	b) Fruit	Applies to the wares of a greengrocer and also to a male homosexual, in slang terms also a 'fruit'.
Welly		a) Power or force, commonly heard in the phrase 'Give it some welly' (*See* GIVE IT SOME BOOT/ CLOG/WELLY). From wellington boot, it literally means kick but golfers and snooker players can give their shots some 'welly' as well as footballers.
		b) A substitute word for boot heard in 'welly it' – kick it, and to be dismissed is to 'get the welly'.
West Ham Reserves	*Nerves*	Used in connection with irritation and exasperation, which is apt when you support West Ham. A pest may get right on your 'West Hams'.
Westminster Abbey	*a) Cabbie*	May be derived from the complaint of an American tourist that: 'Whatever journey I made in a London taxi, I went past Westminster Abbey.' Actually it was a Japanese tourist but I can't write in Japanese.
	b) Shabby	A run-down building or a scruffbag of a person may be 'Westminster'.
Wet		a) A drink of alcohol, commonly to 'go for a wet'.
		b) Of a woman, to be sexually aroused: 'Every time we have male strippers here we have to mop the puddles off the chairs' – a club manager after a hen night.
Wet Fart		A breaking of wind that's accompanied by a faecal discharge.
Wetty		A wet dream, the sheet-stiffening dream of youth.
Whack		a) A share, a portion: 'You've had your whack, now let someone else get a look in.'
		b) To kill, especially an underworld execution. A piece heard in countless Mafia films.
Whack Off		To masturbate. There are zillions of terms for a 'strop', having a 'whack-off' is one that comes to hand.
Whack Out		To apportion, to dole: 'Come on whack out the soup, I'm getting hungry.'

Whacko		a) A crazy, mad person, an eccentric. Someone travelling through life with a flat tyre.
		b) Great, marvellous or any other expression of delight or pleasure.
Whacky		Crazy, mad or eccentric. 'Whacky' behaviour is the province of the 'whackpot'.
Whacky Baccy		Marijuana, a piece that's used by non-users.
Wham-Bam-Thank-You-Ma'am		Sexual intercourse that lasts as long as it takes for a man to ejaculate. A chauvinistic piece that sees women as mere objects of male pleasure.
Whang		The penis, a piece that's been about since the early 20th century.
Whanger		An enlarged version of the previous entry.
Wheelie		The riding of a cycle or a motorbike with the front wheel off the ground.
Wheelman		An underworld term for an expert getaway driver.
Wheelnut		A tight-fisted, miserly person. One who is as 'tight as a wheelnut'.
Wheels		A post-World War Two term for a car or other means of transport: 'You got wheels or d'you want a lift?'
Wheels of Steel		A club DJ's term for his record decks.
Wheezy Anna	*Spanner*	A 1950s term that's still used by elderly motor fitters. Based on a song by variety double act the Two Leslies (Sarony and Holmes).
Whigger		A white person who apes the mannerisms, language and culture of blacks. The term is used derogatorily by blacks and whites and is a reduction of 'white nigger'.
Whip		a) A monetary collection, a reduced version of whip-round that's commonly heard in the pub. If the 'whip' is left behind the bar, be sure you can trust the bar staff.
		b) To steal, a 19th-century term that suggests a quick theft: 'While the mug was paying for his petrol I whipped his car.'
Whip & Lash	*Tash*	A moustache, generally shaved to 'whip'.
Whip & Top	*Strop (Masturbate)*	You don't have to be a masochist to 'whip' yourself.
Whip It In, Whip It Out & Wipe It		A brief act of sexual intercourse from a man's point of view. What he does with his penis.
Whip-It-Quick		A name given to a spontaneous or impromptu thief, a sneak-thief. Based on the name of a radio character in the post World War Two radio show, *ITMA*, a pre-PC 'thieving Arab'.

Whiplash	a) *Rash*	Possibly one picked up off a dodgy bird in the pursuit of S & M.
	b) *Slash*	A rare piece but if you wish to popularise it, crack away. It's to 'see a man about a dog' – to urinate.
Whippit Quick	*Prick (Penis)*	Based on a character from an old radio show, and may allude to a swift act of masturbation. *See* WHIP & TOP.
Whisper & Talk	*Walk*	A 19th-century term that's reduced to going for a 'whisper', for which you need soft shhhoes.
Whistle & Flute	*Suit*	A very common piece that's generally cut at the first element, as in a 'three-piece whistle'.
Whistle & Toot	*Loot (Money)*	An old piece that is unusual in that it is most familiar in the second element: 'Got any toot?'
Whistle Blower		An informer, one who 'blows the whistle', especially on misdeeds in the corridors of power.
White		a) An old term for silver, hence a 'white kettle' is a silver watch. Also a silver coin.
		b) Honest, straight, true, etc., hence a 'white man' – a gentleman.
White Cliffs of Dover	*Over*	Known as 'all White Cliffs' meaning the end. A symbolic piece given their position.
White Girl/Lady		A couple of drug users' terms that relate to both cocaine and heroin.
White Knuckle Job/Ride		A very frightening, 'scarifying' ordeal. Anything that makes you grip something, thus exposing the paleness of the knuckles.
White Mice	*Dice*	A post-war term that's used in full: 'The white mice are running for me tonight.'
White Van Man		A mad driver, typically a young man driving a white van, of which there are many.
White Wilfred		A white patch of phlegm gobbed on to the pavement, a pale imitation of 'green gilbert' (qv).
Whitechapel	*Apple*	Named after an infamous area of the East End, famed for its murders, immigrants and, aptly, the fruit and vegetable market at Spitalfields before it transferred to Leyton in 1991.
Whitewash		To have sexual intercourse, the colour of semen, hence to 'whitewash the interior' – to ejaculate inside a woman and to 'whitewash the exterior' – to pull out and 'paint' her stomach.
Whizz		a) Amphetamines, an ongoing term from the 1960s for 'speed', of which it is indicative.
		b) To pick a pocket and also the thief, who may be 'at the whizz', 'whizzing' or one of the 'whizz mob' – a gang of pickpockets.

		c) To steal as a situation arises, to take spontaneously, especially to shoplift.
Whizzer		a) A quick way to do something, often the bodge of a rogue builder. Also a shortcut: 'Look at this traffic. Chuck a left here, we'll do a whizzer.'
		b) A thief, originally a pickpocket but now also an impromptu stealer.
Whodunnit		A mystery baby, one born to a woman known to be having an affair. Is it the husband's or the lover's?
Whooer		A whore, a deliberate mispronunciation for humorous effect.
Whoopsie		A juvenile act of defecation and the resultant mess.
Whopper		Something big, often said of a gigantic lie.
Whore		A pasteboard queen, i.e., one in a deck of cards.
Whore/ **Whorebag/** **Whorebitch**		A trio of terms of abuse, generally for a woman, but can be used against a person of either sex. Also used of anything that causes aggravation: 'This is a whore of a job.'
Whore Hound		A man who regularly seeks sex with prostitutes, a frequenter of massage parlours.
Whore Shop		A 19th-century term for a brothel that's still open for business.
Wicked		Great, excellent and all things good. Part of the modern vogue of youth that sees all things bad as being good.
Wicked Rumours	*Bloomers*	A reference to women's underwear that's now used only in jest.
Wicked Witch	*Bitch*	An obvious piece for a malicious, spiteful woman, often a mother-in-law.
Widdle		An act of urination and the resultant liquid. A cross between a wee and a piddle.
Widdle Chamber		A lavatory, the supposed meaning of WC.
Wide		Descriptive of anyone shrewd, sharp or aware: 'He's wide to what's going on around here.'
Wide Boy		A minor rogue. A streetwise ducker and diver who cocks a deaf eye and turns a blind ear to legality. Alternatively known as a 'Wide-O', he was once also called a 'spiv'.
Widow Twanky	*a) Hanky*	Decreased to the first element, whereby noses are blown on a 'widow'.
	b) Yankee	Based on the pantomime character from Aladdin, this is an elderly theatrical term for an American tourist. A 'widow' is an important bum on a theatre seat. The term has also been used in relation to the bet known as a yankee, which is

four selections in a combination of six doubles, four trebles and an accumulator. So a £1 'widow' will cost £11.

| Widow's Mite | *Light* | A 'widows' is a light for a cigarette. |

| Widow's Wink | *Chink* | A piece from the theatre for a Chinese person. |

Wig — A 1990s term for a barrister which sees the judge as the 'big-wig'.

Wigger — *See* WHIGGER.

Wiggly — A juvenile term for a worm.

Wighead — A wig wearer, especially if the 'gagga' (qv) is an obvious one.

Wilbur Wright *Flight* — A totally suitable example that is always trimmed to the Christian name of this pioneer of aviation (1867–1912): 'What time's your Wilbur?'

Wild West *Vest* — A dated term for underwear that's worn in full.

Wild West Job — Work carried out by Bodge, Fleece & Leggitt, a company of rogue tradesmen, or 'cowboys' (qv).

Wildcat — A mean, vicious, spiteful woman, one who will scratch and bite as she nags and fights.

Wilf — A fool, one who is the equal of 'wally' in the idiocy stakes but not so common.

Wilkie Bard *Card* — Refers to any type of card, but its main usage is in the plural for playing cards, a game of 'Wilkies'. Based on a music-hall entertainer (1874–1944).

Wilkinson Sword *Bald* — A 1990s term that relates to the 'cultivated spamhead' look, i.e., the shaved head. Based on a brand of razor blade, which makes this quite a sharp example.

Will o' the Wisps *Crisps* — Crisps of any flavour, shape or texture are 'willers'. *See* JACK A DANDY.

William — An extension of 'Bill' in various forms. You can pay a 'William', get arrested by 'the William' and it's the penis. *See* BILL (b) *and* OLD BILL (a & b).

William Hague *Vague* — A term from the late 1990s based on the then leader of the conservative party. He resigned after his party lost in the 2001 general election. The piece may survive, it may not. It's all a bit William Hague really.

William Hill *Pill* — A well-known British bookmaker lends his name to a drug, generally an amphetamine.

William Joyce *Voice* — A World War Two example based on the most reviled voice of the conflict, Lord Haw Haw. Joyce was born in 1906 in the US and hanged as a traitor in 1946.

William Pitt *Shit* — Not sure if this is based on Pitt the Elder (1708–78) or his clever dick of a son, Little Pitt (1759–1806). But then who gives a William. As far as RS is concerned, one English statesman is much the same as another, especially when they share the same name. It applies to the act of defecation and the result of it. In plural it's diarrhoea: 'Don't take that out-of-date laxative, it'll give you the William Pitts.'

William Powell *Towel*
A 1940s term for a 'wipe' that has its roots in prison and is based on an American film star (1892–1984).

William Tell *Smell*
How the legendary 14th-century Swiss hero became a 20th-century British stink.

Willie/Willy
An oft-stated reference to the penis. 'Willie waving' – giving it the big macho bit.

Willie Wellie
A condom, a play on the fact that a wellie is a rubber boot.

Wills Whiff *Syph(ilis)*
A term that came to refer to any of the antisocial diseases. Based on a brand of small cigar, a symbol of what's now an antisocial habit.

Willy Wonka *Plonker (Fool)*
A piece heard in a 1980s TV sitcom and based on a Roald Dahl character. The original meaning of the word 'plonker' is the penis, but in this case it's a fool. A 'willy' is already a willy.

Wilson Pickett *Ticket*
Based on an American soul singer, this was valid in the 1970s when a 'Wilson' ranged from a bus ticket to a Cup-final one.

Wiltshire
A penis that's unable to rise to the occasion for whatever reason. A drunken excuse may be 'a touch of the Wiltshires' – wilted, unable to stand erect.

Win
An ancient term for a penny, perhaps because it was a result to find one.

Win Double
A pair of people who are well matched in idiocy. A dopey duo may draw the mocking comment: 'What a right win double.'

Win or Lose *Booze*
An old term from the racecourse, from where comes the rhyme:
> Win or lose we have our booze
> But when we win, we drink gin.

Wind Trap *Flap*
A flap is that piece of hair that semi-bald men pull from one side of their heads to the other in a vain attempt to cover up the bare facts. A totally apt term, as in breezy conditions the wind tends to get under the strategically placed locks causing them to behave in an unruly manner, often like a demented squirrel's tail.

Wind Up
To tease, annoy or deceive, to 'get someone going' by means of a ruse, jibe or story. The golden rule is, disbelieve most of what a 'wind-up merchant'

		tells you and be dubious of the rest. 'On a wind-up' – getting at someone.
Wind-Jammer		A male homosexual, an allusion to anal sex, the blocking of the airway at 'Windpipe' (qv).
Wind-Jammer	*Hammer*	An old, carpenter's term, one that's based on a type of sailing ship.
Window Frames		Spectacle frames. *See* WINDOWS.
Window Licker		An unkind term for a spastic, one often seen on a special coach with his face pressed against a window.
Windows		Spectacles. Go to the bottom of the glass if you haven't heard this one.
Windpipe		Not the one in your throat, the other one, your anus for obvious reasons. Also 'wind tunnel'.
Winds Do Whirl	*Girl*	A 19th-century term that has probably been blown away.
Windsor Castle	*Arsehole*	The 'brown Windsor', as it's sometimes known, is yet again the designated orifice up which the unwanted may be lodged. To confuse even further, try saying: 'Stick it up your Queen's gaff.'
Windy		Cowardly. Descriptive of someone who may easily 'get the wind up'.
Wined/Wined Up		Drunk or tipsy from drinking too much wine, especially at a dinner party.
Wing		a) An arm, an 18th-century term that's still flying, especially when injured, i.e., a 'broken wing'. b) To injure someone by shooting, a term often heard on film.
Wing It		To improvise, to think on one's feet, to fly by the seat of one's pants by playing it by ear. In the theatre, to 'wing' is an old term for learning one's lines at the last minute, often in the wings.
Wingy		A nickname for a one-armed man, once commonly an ex-serviceman seen begging because he'd been 'winged' in the 'wing' and couldn't get work. *See* WING (a & b).
Winkle		A juvenile term for the penis, a source of many a double entendre of a Sunday teatime when a winkle could not be extricated from it's shell: 'Someone get my winkle out.'
Winkle Picker		A pointed-toed shoe or boot, a term and a fashion that started in the late 1950s.
Winklebag	*Fag (Cigarette)*	A 1970s term that's curtailed to a 'winkle' and based on whatever a winklebag is. Perhaps a condom?
Winks		Sleep, famously forty winks, although the number is not limited: 'I've got to get some winks tonight.'

Winnie		To defecate, a 1990s piece based on the children's favourite, Winnie the Pooh. *See* Poo.
Winnit		A piece of excrement stuck to an anal hair, another version of 'clinker' (qv).
Wino		A habitual drinker, an alcoholic, often a tramp.
Winona Ryder	*Cider*	One from the young boozing classes of the 1990s based on an American film actress.
Wipe		A towel, mostly heard in the boxing world where an act of surrender is to throw in the towel or to 'sky the wipe'.
Wipe/Wiper		Old terms for a handkerchief that are still catching a sneeze.
Wipe Out		To murder or assassinate somebody. An alternative to 'rub out'.
Wiped Out		Exhausted, totally shattered, a common term of fatigue.
Wire		a) An electronic listening device used in law enforcement, usually one that is concealed about a person's body.
		b) A signal, a warning to an accomplice to 'send a wire'. Often used between card cheats.
Wired Up		Intoxicated by drugs, getting a 'charge' or a 'buzz' from heroin, cocaine, cannabis or speed.
Wise Monkey	*Dunkie (Condom)*	What's needed to deliver the 'old chap' from evil. Fitting also that condoms traditionally come in threes as do wise monkeys.
Wiss		A euphemism for piss from a time when the word was considered bad language, when a child may have 'wissed' himself and the old man may have come home from the pub a bit 'wissy'.
Wizard of Odds		A top settler, an expert calculator of bets. A piece from within the betting industry.
Wizz		An act of urination, going for a 'wizz' fills the same pot as going for a 'wazz' (qv).
Wobbler/Wobbly		A fit of temper, it has become so familiar to 'throw a wobbler' that it is often abbreviated to 'throw one': 'He's gonna throw one when he sees what you've done to the car.' From the image of trembling with rage.
Wobblychops		A person with a fat face: 'His old woman's become a right wobblychops as she's got older.'
Wog		A derogatory British term for a foreigner, generally considered to be a non-white one, but as the phrase 'wogs begin at Calais' shows, it ain't necessarily so.
Wog Box		Another form of 'Brixton briefcase' (qv).

Wog Gut		An upset stomach suffered by tourists to foreign climes.
Wok Jockey		A Chinese person for obvious reasons. Sometimes shortened to a 'Wock Jock' or a 'Wocky'.
Wolf		a) A predatory male, a pursuant of women for sex since the 19th century.
		b) An immoral, promiscuous, domineering homosexual.
Womble		A fool, a socially inept person since the 1970s, when The Wombles, puppets from Wimbledon, first appeared on children's TV.
Wonga		Money, an old term that became popular in the 1980s, based on the Romany word *wanger* – coal, itself a likely pun on 'cole', a centuries-old term for money. Sometimes said as 'womba'.
Wonk		A crazy, eccentric person. One described as 'wonky' and said to have his 'head on crooked'.
Wonky		Crooked, a well-known term that not only applies to bent objects but also to people: 'This ref's wonky' – a common slight of a football referee. A man suspected of being a homosexual may be referred to as 'a bit wonky'. And it can be levelled at an event suspected of being rigged, a criminal, and the goods he may be 'knocking out on the cheap'.
Wonky Legs		Someone with deformed legs, a cruel old term for a cripple.
Wonkybonce		An idiot, sometimes a nickname for a stupid, thick person. One said to be cutting his vegetables with a blunt knife.
Wood		An erect penis, hence 'to give some wood' – to have sexual intercourse.
Wooden Frying Pan		A symbol of uselessness, although maybe slightly more effective than the cardboard (qv) one.
Wooden Heart	*Fart*	A term that became common for a while after Elvis Presley's hit of this title in 1961: 'Who's wooden hearted?'
Wooden Hill		Stairs, especially those leading to a bedroom. Children are sent up the 'wooden hill to Bedford'.
Wooden Leg	*Egg*	Interesting to see the reaction of a waitress when asked for a 'wooden leg' on toast.
Wooden Overcoat		A coffin, a well-known term associated with fictional villainy, what an intended victim is to be measured for.
Wooden Peg	*Leg*	As old and as outdated as a pegleg.
Wooden Plank	*Yank*	A piece relating to an American tourist. After September 11th 2001, London cabbies were seen

		crying into their cocktails over the lack of 'wooden planks' in town.
Wooden Spoon	a) *Moon*	Heard in prison, where a 'woodener' is a month's 'porridge' (qv).
	b) *Coon*	The prize for coming last is a recent term of abuse for a black person.
Woodentop		a) A fool, someone considered to be an apple short of a fruit salad. A 'plankhead' (qv).
		b) A lay magistrate, an underworld term for one not considered very bright. A 'wooden head'.
Woodentops		Uniformed police, a piece that's based on a children's TV programme of the 1950s and used derogatorily.
Woofter		A male homosexual, a variant of 'poofter' (qv).
Woofy		A familiar name for a dog: 'The best woofy this side of Wooferhampton.'
Wook/Wookie		A nonconformist, a voluntary outsider. A 1980s piece based on a character in the *Star Wars* films.
Woolly Back		A country dweller, a rustic. A comparison to a sheep.
Woolly Mitten	*Kitten*	A baby pussycat but mainly how one feels when illness strikes, as weak as a 'woolly mitten'.
Woolly Vest	*Pest*	Apt in that a nuisance can be as irritating as an itchy undergarment. A grouch may claim that a friend in need is a 'woolly vest'.
Woolly Woofter	*Poofter*	Not really admissable as RS since 'woofter' and 'poofter' have the same meaning and this may just be an extension. Still, it does rhyme and, well, what difference does it make?
Woolwich Ferry	*Sherry*	A fairly common example based on the famous Thames river crossing.
Woolwich Pier(s)	*Ears*	An old term for nature's audio equipment that hails from the docks, where the teeth of the wind get sharp enough to bite your 'Woolwiches' off.
Woolwich & Greenwich	*Spinach*	A couple of boroughs of South-East London give us a piece with its roots in the greengrocery trade.
Wop		A derogatory term for an Italian that originated in America before arriving in Britain. Based on the Sicilian word *guappo* – handsome.
Work One's Ticket		To get out of a chore by feigning illness or injury, a piece that originated in the army.
Work Over		To beat up, to assault and batter.
Working Class(es)	*Glass(es)*	A piece that doubles as a receptacle and spectacles.
Works		A hypodermic needle and other equipment employed by drug users.
Work the Oracle		To successfully perform something through stealth and cunning or with the aid of an outright lie.
Worm Food		A buried corpse: 'Have me cremated, I don't want to end up as worm food.'

Worms & Snails   *Nails*   A useful piece to stop kids from biting their fingernails, which bears a resemblance to the old warning: 'Don't bite your nails you'll get worms.'

Worry & Strife   *Wife*   The 'worry' is an infrequent variation of the oft-mentioned 'trouble'. *See* TROUBLE & STRIFE.

Wossname   An expression used when the name of an object or person has taken leave of one's memory.

Wozzle   A fool, a similar idiot to 'wazzock' (qv), who is often dismissed as a 'wozz'.

Wrap   a) A very small quantity of a drug wrapped in paper or foil.

b) To tie up. An underworld way of incapacitating a victim.

Wrap Up!   Be quiet! A well-known order of silence that isn't used by monks in silent orders.

Wreathe Round   To caress or fondle someone sexually: 'She let me have a wreathe round but that was it.'

Wreck of the Hesperus   What an untidy, unkempt or dishevelled person or place is said to resemble. A piece from the early part of the 20th century, when schoolchildren learned Longfellow's ballad of this title. The schooner *Hesperus* was wrecked off the coast of Massachusetts in 1839.

Wrecked   Very drunk or smashed on drugs.

Wrigley's Gum   *Bum*   A shapely backside may be known as a 'Wrigleys' due to the well-known chewing gum firm.

Wrinkly   An old person or anyone over thirty to an early teenager, or a 'pimply'. Ha! That's one back on them.

Wrong 'Un   A criminal, a thoroughly bad person, someone not to be trusted. To the criminal, however, a wrong 'un is an informer.

Wul/Wulbert   A couple of recent terms for a fool based on 'wally' (qv). Wul is the diminutive of the name and Wulbert an extension of that.

Wyatt Earp   *Burp*   A 1960s term based on the famed American lawman (1848–1929) who may or may not have suffered with indigestion.

Wylet   A television, a backslang telly.

X

X Files   *Piles*   Based on the cult TV series about a team of FBI agents who try to get to the bottom of paranormal activity and the horrors of the supernatural. Unfortunately for the sufferer, the pain of the anus horribilis is only too real.

X-Ray Specs   *Sex*   A piece, shortened to 'X-Ray', that had a brief currency in the late 1970s when a British group of this name had a few hits.

XTC   A piece of 1980s youthspeak for the drug ecstasy.

Y

Yab/Yabber		Idle, tedious chatter: 'Cab yab' – shop talk between taxi drivers.
Yack		Idle chatter, endless trivial talk: 'He was yacking away for ages, Gawd knows what he was on about. I switched off after the initial hello.' Often extended to 'yackety-yak'.
Yag		Gay, a recent piece of backslang. 'Yag rab' – gay bar.
Yadnarb		Brandy. A backslang tipple. An 'eltob of yadnarb' – a bottle of brandy.
Yankee Doodles	*Noodles*	Confuse a Chinese waiter by asking for crispy 'yankees' with 'Goldie Hawns' (qv).
Yappy		Overly talkative, gabby. Another version of 'trappy' (qv).
Yard of Tripe	*Pipe*	Not exactly an ad-man's dream of a term. Live in peace with your yard of tripe? I don't think so.
Yarmouth Bloater	*Motor*	A piece that harks back to the days when only toffs had cars.
Yates not Gates, the name's		A reply given when asked to pay an exorbitant amount for something: 'You're having a laugh! The name's Yates not Gates.' A reference to Bill Gates, the billionaire American entrepreneur.
Yawn		Anything considered boring or tedious, such as a dinner party when you are the only non-golfer present.

Yawn Cocktail

Extreme dullness. How a group of uninteresting people, or a series of boring events or tedious acts may be described. Also an uninspiring night's TV viewing: 'What a yawn cocktail on the box tonight.' A pun on that least interesting starter, the prawn cocktail.

Yeckrut

A turkey, a slice of backslang from the meat market. The traditional Christmas 'Rennid' – dinner.

Yellow Pages   *Wages*

A modern update of 'greengages' (qv), whereby 'greens' turn into 'yellows'.

Yellow Pages Job

Of a woman, to masturbate. To let her fingers do the walking.

Yellow Silk   *Milk*

A piece that was used by milkmen of a century ago, who would substitute the word 'pint' with 'yard', hence a 'yard of yellow silk' was a pint of milk.

Yennep

A backslang penny. Pluralised, 'yenneps' once meant money. The term harks back to the old 'yennep-a-pint' days of the 19th century, when a pocketful of pennies meant you were holding 'spenders'.

Yennum/Yenom

Money. Backslang dough.

Yer Actual

An intensifier that signifies the unrivalled, the one and only, the peerless: 'His prized possession is a fag packet signed by yer actual Muhammad Ali.'

Yet to Be   *Free*

An elderly piece that refers to all senses of the word, but mainly to free of charge.

Yewess

Useless. *See* US.

Yid

a) An old and well-known term for a Jew. 'Yiddisher' – Jewish.

b) A supporter of Tottenham Hotspur, a name given by fans of other London clubs. The area has a large Jewish population.

Yiddisher Dodgem

A London taxi-cab, a term from the time when the feet on a taxi's pedals were predominately Jewish.

Yiddisher Mama   *Bummer*

A disappointment or let-down based either on a Jewish mother or the song about her, 'My Yiddisher Mama'. Either way, it's a 'Yiddisher'.

Yips

A condition suffered by golf and darts players, which takes the form of an inadvertent hand movement at a crucial time, causing a missed putt or shot.

Yob

A boy, a backslang lad that became famous as a tearaway. 'Worrab yob' – barrow boy.

Yobbo

A thug, lout or hooligan. A well-known extension of 'yob'.

Yob Hat

A baseball cap, headwear commonly associated with the young. Therefore an old git's term.

Yocks		The eyes, a piece of Polari based on the Italian *occhio* – eye.
Yog		A juvenile term for an egg. 'Geg' – a scrambled egg.
Yogi Bear	*Chair*	A 1960s term based on a popular cartoon character; for a while people were 'pulling up a Yogi' to watch him on TV.
Yomp		A military term for a long march carrying a heavy load, a piece that came to the fore during the Falklands War in 1981.
Yonks		A long, but unspecified, time. A long-lost friend hasn't been seen in 'yonks'.
Yorkshire Rippers	*Slippers*	A 1980s example based on the media nickname for the mass murderer Peter Sutcliffe.
Yorkshire Tyke	*Mike*	Referring to a microphone, the term had its beginnings in the entertainment industry and was picked up by those doing a turn down the pub.
You & Me	a) *Flea*	An old piece that may still be scratching around somewhere, at the vets perhaps.
	b) *Pea*	Fresh, frozen, tinned or dried and blown through shooter. They're all 'you and me's'.
	c) *Pee/Wee*	'Let's you and me go for a you and me'. Sounds like one for the ladies, who tend to 'water the plants' in tandem.
	d) *Tea*	An elderly piece that's still on the boil as 'a nice cup of you and me'.
You Couldn't Make it Up		A phrase popularised by journalist Richard Littlejohn in his newspaper column, which highlights the ridiculous and the unbelievable news items.
You Know	*Snow (Cocaine)*	The term 'snow' for cocaine has been around for about a century, and this rhyming equivalent for almost as long. RS at its most secretive.
You Must	*(Bread) Crust*	A term used by parents when trying to get their offspring to eat all of their bread.
You Sure?		A quizzical term of disbelief said with raised eyebrows. Short for, 'Are you sure you know what you're talking about?/doing?'
Young & Frisky	*Whisky*	One that's occasionally included in a round of drinks.
Young Fogey		An old-fashioned young person, one who behaves, dresses and effects the mannerisms of someone much older.
Young Shaver		A boy or young man, a well-known piece that's based on the Romany *chavo*. See CHAVVY.
Yours & Mine	*Nine*	Eyes down for another piece from the bingo hall.
Yours & Ours	*Flowers*	A piece that grew in the flower market.
Yowie		A cat, a piece that's based on a reduction of the miaowie sound it makes.

Yuck

A juvenile term for excrement or an act of defecation: 'I wanna do a yuck.' 'Yucksack' – a nappy.

Yucky

Descriptive of anything repellent, unpleasant, messy or disgusting. Also anything oversentimental or sickly.

Yul Brynner *Dinner*

A 1960s piece that's never shortened, you always break for your 'Yul Brynner'. Based on a famously bald Hollywood actor (1915–85).

Yuletide Log *Dog*

An unusual alternative to 'Christmas log' (qv) in reference to a greyhound, although both are left in the traps by 'cherry hog' (qv).

Yumyums

Anything that gives pleasure, often used in regard to sex. 'Yumyums' are out when the 'painters are in'.

Yuppie Puppie

The child of a yuppie couple. A term from the 1980s, the day of the 'Young Urban Professional'.

Z

Zachary Scotts	*Trots* *(Diarrhoea)*	Shortened to the 'Zacharys' and based on an American film star (1914–65).
Zaftig		A buxom, attractive woman, from the Yiddish word for juicy.
Zap		To kill, to destroy. A 1930s term from the word seen to accompany the firing of a comic-book space gun. Hence to wipe anything out, from germs to garden pests, from dandruff to spots, is to 'zap' them.
Zapper		A TV remote control, a well-known example with the same root as 'zap' (qv).
Zasu Pitts	*Shits* *(Diarrhoea)*	Another term for the 'squitters' based on a Hollywood film star (1898–1963). Suffered as the 'zasus'.
Zeds		Sleep, from the cartoon image of a sleeping man and the Zs seen to be coming from his head.
Zeppelin		A drugfag of large proportions, a giant joint.
Zero		An insignificant person, a nobody. Often a jobsworth who considers himself to be important but isn't. Or a 'wannabe' whose tenet is 'It's better to be a small somebody than a big zero.'
Zigzag/Zigzagged		Drunk. Whichever way you slur it, unable to walk straight.

Zilch		Nothing. Originally an American term but often heard here, especially in regard to having no money: 'I've got zilch.'
Zip Your Lip		A shouted instruction to be quiet, often reduced to 'zip it!' – 'shut up!'
Zit		A spot, a well-known term for a yellowhead or pimple. 'Zits' – acne.
Zola Budd	*Spud*	A 1980s term for a potato based on a South African runner. Heard down the market as 'a pound of Zolas'.
Zombie		a) A humourless, disagreeable prison officer as seen by convicts.
		b) A dolt, an easily led numbskull. Someone with a vacancy in his brain cavity.
		c) An inactive, lifeless individual. One not given to sudden bursts of energy, and at the merest hint of hard work will ask: 'What're you trying to do, kill me?' To which the reply is: 'How can you kill a zombie?'
		d) Someone out of his skull on drugs, in a zombie-like state, brain-dead.
Zonk		To hit or strike, especially to bash someone over the head.
Zonked/Zonked Out		a) Rendered unconscious by being bashed over the head. Also said as 'zonko'.
		b) Senseless due to an excess of drink or drugs. Out of one's skull. Also said as 'zonko'.
		c) Exhausted, and also sleep brought on by exhaustion. Also said as 'zonko'.
Zonz		A juvenile term for a sausage.
Zoom		Indicative of speed, it's a term for that type of drug, amphetamines.
Zorba		A Greek person, a common example since the film *Zorba the Greek* hit the screens in 1964.
Zorba the Greek	*Leak (Urinate)*	A 1960s term that is always cut to a 'Zorba' and is based on the 1964 film of this title.
Zsa Zsa Gabor	*Whore*	A 1960s term based on an oft-married Hungarian film actress. If she wants to sue, she should know I'm a compiler not a composer.
Zulu		A derogatory term for a black person, especially an African. A piece of racist graffito on a toilet wall in London – NAZIS – Not A Zulu In Sight.

Like time, language never stands still. It's continually regenerated, updated and reinvented to suit the changing world in which we live, evolving and expanding to reflect current affairs, trends and personalities of the day. Most terms make it into conventional dictionaries, but the rest, the more interesting, entertaining and least likely to be found in crossword puzzles, make their mark on history by sneaking in through the back door into books on slang.

The following pages contain terms that have been added to catalogue of low-speak in the past year.

Welcome to The Back Door.

Ackdov	Vodka, back slang Russian wine. Ackdov and Emil – vodka and lime.
Ackwa/Aggwa	Water, 'polari' versions of 'splash' (qv) based on the Italian *aqua* or Spanish *agua*. *See* POLARI.
Alfalfa	A 1950s term for a piece of hair at the crown of the head that won't lie down. Named after a member of The Little Rascals who had just such an unruly tuft of 'barnet'. The Rascals were the TV version of the *Our Gang* comedies of the 1930s about a gang of American kids.
Asparagus Veins	The silly version of the not-so-funny complaint, varicose veins, or 'vellicky veins', as some would have it.
Bantling	Ancient term for a small child, probably a junior version of bantam. A small person.

Bargain Hunt	*Cunt*	Not necessarily one for sale in a cheap brothel, this mainly applies to a fool or a despicable person. Therefore, if someone tells you that you are a 'bargain', make sure it's in jest. An early 'noughties' (qv) term based on a popular TV series of the period.
Barkey		From the Italian word for boat, *barca*, we get the polari (qv) and therefore gay term for a sailor.
Barnacle		A sedentary, inactive person, a sluggard. Someone who, as this little crustacean clings to a rock, is seemingly stuck to his chair. The one most likely to enrol on an Inward Bound Course.
Batsman		A piece of excrement stuck to an anal hair, so-called because it occupies the 'Crease' (qv), obviously not an English batsman. Among the many terms for the faecal hanger-on are 'Bumberry', 'Clagnut' and 'Conker'.
Belinda Carlisles	*Piles*	An example of 'popney rhyming slang' (qv) that may actually catch on. Based on a late 20th–century American singer, which sees the haemorrhoidally afflicted suffering with 'Belindas'.
Big-Up		To praise highly or lavishly, a piece from the lexicon of black youth of the 1990s that has become commonplace.
Bill Murray	*Curry*	An American comedy actor makes an entrance as a rival to his well established namesake 'Ruby' (qv), but has so far failed to upstage her.
Bishop of Norwich	*Porridge*	I am informed that people in the Shoreditch area of London once breakfasted on 'bishop' and that the term is derived from the name of a pub that once existed in the area.
Bob Dylan	*Villain*	Based on the legendary American singer, whose biggest act of villainy is impersonating a singer. Love the songs, though, Bob.
Bogatory		A toilet, a hybrid of 'bog' and a lav-less lavatory. A 'site for sore eyes' – a 'bogatory' in a dysentery ward. *See* EYE.
Bonecruncher/ Crunchbones		An osteopath or chiropractor, a medic of the 'no pain, no gain' persuasion.
Bouncy Castle	*Parcel*	Dropped to a 'bouncy' by some careless workers in the parcel delivery industry where 'Bounce the Bouncy' would appear to be a popular game, especially if the package is labelled 'Handle With Care'.
Boutros-Ghali	*Charlie (Cocaine)*	A late 1990s term based on the Egyptian diplomat, Boutros Boutros-Ghali, who served as General Secretary of the UN (1992–96). An upper class 'sniff' (qv) is 'Boutros'.

Breeder		A gay reference to a heterosexual; someone whose sexual proclivity is of the productive kind.
Bride		A wife or live-in girlfriend, no matter how long the relationship may have endured. A pal of mine has been battling his 'bride' for years.
Brown Starfish/ Star		The anus, from a supposed resemblance. A crudism from the 1990s, as is 'Tea Towel Holder' meaning the same thing and based on a plastic or rubber kitchen accessory.
Carrot & Onions		Man's genitalia, the vegetarian version of 'meat and two veg' (qv).
Charley Chase	*Race*	Originally an Australian term for a contest but occasionally heard here. A withdrawn horse is said to be 'out of the Charley'. Based on an early American film comedian (1893–1940).
Cheapjack		A mean, stingy individual. Someone who wears his poppy with pride but only pays a penny for it – the British version of the American 'Cheapskate'.
Cheddar Gorge	*George*	'Cheddar' is a rare appellation given to men and boys of this name. Named after the deep gorge in the Mendip Hills, Somerset.
Chicken Fillets		Gel-filled pads that are inserted into the bras of women who seek to create the curves that nature has denied them. An out-of-body boob job for those who don't want intrusive surgery.
Civil Servant		Heard at the beginning of the 2003 war with Iraq, this is squaddie's slang for a useless gun – one that doesn't work and never gets fired.
Clampett		An idiot, a gullible fool or, at best, a naive simpleton. A piece that's based on the family name of the archetypal 'innocents abroad' in the TV series, *The Beverly Hillbillies*, an American sitcom from the early 1960s.
Clunker		A useless, clumsy, incompetent person from the 1950s, often a hopeless soldier on National Service. The one most likely to end up 'Spud-Bashing' (peeling potatoes) or 'Square-Bashing' (doing drill) – the British version of the American 'Clunkhead'.
Coal-Hole		The dark, sun-less place that is the anus. In the days when coal fires were the norm, house-proud people would emulsion their coal cellars. Now 'whitewashing a coal-hole' takes on an altogether different meaning. *See* WHITEWASH.
Cod-Latin		A make-it-up-as-you-go-along language, which, with the addition of 'us', 'icus' 'imus', etc, English words sound ridiculously ancient Roman, e.g.

		'boilingus hoticus' – boiling hot. 'Nippicus nippicus' – double nippy (very cold). 'Grabbus a taximus' – grab a taxi. See COD.
Cooking Fat	*Cat*	I'm not sure if this is RS or a Brummy spoonerism for a mog that got under someone's feet.
Cracked		Crazy, mad, insane. Someone said to have 'sneaked past the quality controller in the head department'.
Crease		The gap between the buttocks wherein dwells our anal equipment.
Crumbum		A contemptible, despicable person, someone considered to be 'lower than a worm's arsehole'.
Deloc		Cold, a backslang drop in temperature, as opposed to 'Toh' or 'Toe' (hot). You may also catch a 'deloc'.
Densa		An imaginary society for the unintelligent or dense, a jocular reverse of Mensa.
Devil's Dandruff		A late 20th–century term for cocaine, which likens the white 'nose-powder' with Old Nick's scalp-scurf.
Didgeridoo	*Clue*	Used in the sense of cluelessness. Those with no idea of what's going on or the terminally thick are said 'not to have a didgeri'. Or they didgeri-don't have a didgeridoo. Based on an Australian musical instrument of sorts.
Dinarli/Dinari		Money, 'polari' versions of 'spending' (qv) based on the Italian dinaro.
Dinge		A derogatory term for a person of mixed black-and-white parentage. A piece of abuse since the late 19th century.
Dirty Whore	*Four*	Once, but no longer, a reference to £4 and an example from a coarse bingo caller.
Dixie Dean(s)	*Bean(s)*	Most commonly baked beans, whereby beans on toast becomes 'Dixies on Holy Ghost'. Based on the legendary William (Dixie) Dean (1907–80), freescoring Everton and England footballer of the 1920s–30s.
Dogging		Exhibitionist sex in a public place for the voyeuristic pleasure of onlookers. Doing what dogs do with a careless abandon but not necessarily in the same fashion.
Dooey Bit		An early 21st–century term for a £2 coin, a piece with its roots in polari (qv). See DEWEY.
Drench the French		To urinate. A piece heard in a pub 'piddler' in 2003 during the war with Iraq, a time of more antagonism than usual towards France and her people.
Edgar Allan		A chamberpot (more commonly known as a 'po'). Coined in the 1930s by touring variety artistes who would have had first-hand knowledge of every Edgar

Allan in every boarding house, from Bournemouth to Blackpool. *See* EDGAR ALLAN POE.

Edge of Darkness
A sexually inactive man is said to be on the Edge of Darkness. Such a man is likely to take his sex life in his own hands, and a well-known warning against habitual masturbation is that it makes you go blind. *Edge of Darkness* was the title of an award winning TV drama from 1985, so presumably the term has been around since then.

Eeosh
A back-slang shoe pronounced ee-osh it's what you wear on your 'toof' (foot), or if in a pair you case your 'teef' (feet) in 'eeoshes'. Unless you favour 'toobs' (boots) of course.

Eesenich
A backslang Chinese. Once common in Limehouse, when London's Chinatown was situated there. Now used for a Chinese meal, whereby a few 'teenips' (pints) up the 'bup' (pub) followed by an 'eesenich' is a typical boys' night out.

Eighty-Six   *a) Fix*
To kill, an underworld term for a murder, often a revenge 'hit', whereby a rival is 'eighty-sixed'.

       b) Nix (Nothing/None)
A piece from the restaurant trade that was used of a commodity that had run out, i.e. there was none left. Also if a customer was not to be served he got 'eighty-six' – nothing. *See* NIX.

Elm Street
A bad dream – if a sweet dream occurs while you are in Dreamland, then you'll have a nightmare on 'Elm Street'. *Nightmare on Elm Street* was a 1984 horror film that spawned several sequels.

Fatboy/Fatgirl Dim
An overweight and none too bright male or female. A rotund retard whose neck size in inches tends to be higher than his or her IQ. A pun on British DJ Fatboy Slim.

Filter Tip(s)   *Lip(s)*
Based on the end of a fag that smokers put between their 'filters'.

Fleetwood Mac   *Back*
A 1980s term based on an enduring British/US rock band. Its main use is anatomical but you'll always find the tradesman's entrance round the 'Fleetwood'.

Frank Swift   *Lift*
A 1950s term for an elevator heard in the aftermath of World War Two, when the bomb-ravaged streets of London were cleared to make way for high-rise flats. Based on an England international goalkeeper of the period (1914–58). Heard in a Poplar tower block: 'The Frank Swift's stuck? That's out of order.'

Fraught Thought
A thought that leaves you cold with fear, distress or anxiety, often a 'what if?' scenario that's best not

dwelt upon. Or it could be a nightmarish vision that pops into your mind's eye, like that fat, greasy, middle-aged politician having his nipple sucked through his string vest by a bulldog.

Fuzzy-Wuzzy Originally a 19th–century soldiers name for a wild-haired Sudanese warrior. It later became an offensive term for black people in general and is still heard.

Gag-Up Of a horse or greyhound, to win easily: 'I had an even ton on the favourite and it's gagged-up.'

Gammy Brain A completely stupid or slow-witted person considered handicapped by a disabled brain. Like the 'diddlo' who would only play draughts for money if his superior opponent played left-handed.

Garlicky *See* SMELL GARLICK.

Geek Originally a socially inept American but now a universally studious, unfashionable and generally 'uncool' person. 'Geeky' – descriptive of such a person.

Give the Cat Some Milk Of a man, to have sexual intercourse. A term that makes sense when you see separate entries for 'Milk' (a) and 'Pussy' (a).

Grinch A grumpy, grouchy person, a killjoy. Based on the meanie who stole Christmas in a 2000 film.

Groper Ancient term for a blind person, especially a sightless beggar – the image of such a person groping their way around.

Grote An untrustworthy person, an informer – the kind of 'rat' who would shop his granny for four pence and has been doing so since the 19th century, when a groat was a coin for just that amount; a connection.

Grubber A term of respect for a good wife and mother, one who doesn't scrimp on food for her family.

Haggis-Head Semi-abusive term for a Scot, that may also be offensive to the haggis.

Hairy Ape *Rape* A modern piece, heard in a TV crime series. A term that demeans apes.

Half a Scissor A symbol of ineptness, what the usefulness of a 'feather-brained' person is compared to.

Hammer & File *Style* A serviceman's term from World War Two, when a slick, smart or smooth operator was said to have 'had some hammer'. (Probably responsible for 'Hammer' (f).)

Hand Over Fist *Pissed* An extension of hand and fist (qv), which sees the stupefied drunk as 'well hand over'. Probably from the way he crawls home.

Handball In the haulage industry, to unload a lorry without the aid of a fork lift truck, to do the work by hand.

Hedge-Muncher		A sarcastic term for a vegetarian, someone who would rather munch his way through a hedge of blackberries or any other wild growing fruit, than a meat feast. 'Hedge Munchies' – blackberries or similar fruits.
Henhouse		A home that's ruled over by a dominant wife, where the rooster gets his feathers ruffled by the boiler – the tough old bird. An 18th–century term that later came to include a woman's prison or hostel.
Hook, Line & Sinker	*Clinker*	Probably the commonest term for a piece of dried excrement attached to an anal hair gets itself a piece of RS in the reduced form of a 'hook-line'. *See* CLINKER.
Igg Layer		A Hindu, a piece that's based on the old joke: What's a Hindu? It lays iggs.
Incurable Romantic		A cruel jibe at someone who has caught genital herpes as a result of a sexual encounter.
Incy		A juvenile term for a spider, any size, any species. Sometimes an 'Incy Wincy', as in the nursery rhyme.
Insaniac		This hybrid of insane and maniac describes someone who has totally lost their senses, either temporarily or permanently, a wild-eyed individual who may be described as a 'map of the loony bin'. *See* MAP.
Ironed		Said of someone who has undergone cosmetic surgery. Most of the American acting profession has had their wrinkles and creases 'ironed'.
J Edgar		A vacuum cleaner, a play on the name of the former director of the FBI J Edgar Hoover (1895–1972), which is one in the eye for James M Spangler, the man who invented it. 'Hoover' is the only word most of us use for a 'suckdirt'. Oh, there's another . . .
James		A name given to anyone who habitually hangs back from the bar until everyone else has bought a round of drinks in the hope that the last round is the cheapest. Therefore James Last, the German band-leader becomes James last up the ramp (qv, a).
Jelly Tot	*Spot*	Based on a kiddie's confectionery, this is how acne sufferers get to be covered in 'jellies'.
Jerk		To stab or slash with a knife, a term used by football hoolies who are not averse to 'jerking' rival fans.
Jethroes		A term from the 1960s, given to a pair of trousers worn at 'Half Mast', i.e. too short. Jethro was an uncouth character in the American TV show, *The*

Beverly Hillbillies, whose strides always appeared to have had a row with his boots.

Jordan
A chamberpot, that which sits discreetly beneath the bed. This is an ancient term and has nothing to do with the British pin-up (who seems to do nothing discreetly, beneath the bed or otherwise).

Joyful Eyeful
Something pleasing to look at, a nice view, a sight to cheer the soul. Alternatively, used with an ironic slant at an unpleasant or appalling sight. Heard during the Iraqi conflict: 'Did you see that little kid on the news last night with his arms blown off? What a right joyful eyeful that was at tea-time!'

Kaiser
The penis, a piece that's based on the only German emperor most of us have ever heard of, Kaiser Wilhelm II (1859–1941), or Kaiser Bill as he was known during World War One. The connection is the name and the well-known penile terms 'Willie', 'William' and 'Old Bill', all to be seen within these pages.

Kaylew
A whelk, a back slang portion of the seafood much loved by generations of East Enders.

Kaynich
A Chinese person, a back slang 'Chink' (qv).

Kermit
A road, a derivation of RS 'frog & toad' (qv), which sees pedestrians crossing the 'Kermit'. *See* KERMIT THE FROG.

King Kong   *Pong*
Based on cinema's greatest ape, this is an example that never gets shortened. A nasty niff is always a bad 'King Kong'.

Kissers
See RUBBERLIPS.

Klingon
A piece of dried excrement that clings to an anal hair. Based on a barbarous alien, the sworn enemy of Starfleet in TV's *Star Trek*. The scourge of the Starship now hangs around the dark recesses of the Starfish. *See* BROWN STARFISH.

Lace
To bash, thrash or thoroughly beat up; a mid-20th–century gangland term whereby the victim is 'laced' or 'laced up'.

Lady from Hitchen   *Kitchen*
A piece from the theatre based on the famous limerick. It refers to the room where the crab-riddled Hertfordshire lass named Rose was caught scratching herself.

Lashed
Drunk, a piece that derives from 'lash', to urinate, which mirrors piss and pissed.

Laters
An example of early 20th–century 'yoofspeak' meaning goodbye or 'see you later'.

Lazyboots/ Lazylegs		A couple of expressions for an idle, slothful person. Pieces of BritSlang since the 19th century when 'Lazybones' left to join mainstream English. A male waster may also be known as 'Lazybollocks'.
Lazy Money		A substantial amount of money not stashed away in a savings account, cash that is lying around the house in a 'safe place'. So-called because it's not working for you, not earning interest. May also be called 'Lazy Dough', 'Lazy Dosh' or 'Lazy . . .' whatever else you call money.
Lecky		A common term for electricity heard mainly in the North. People now receive 'lecky bills', where they used to have 'lecky meters'.
Leek/Leekie		A person from Wales or 'Leekshire' as it was known in the 18th century. A 'cocky Leekie' is a flash Taff and a 'cheeky Leekie' a saucy one. The leek is the Welsh national emblem.
Light-Minded		Unintelligent, slow of thought, stupid. Said of someone whose brain is outweighed by his cap. Such a person is known as a 'Light-mind'.
Loaf		A lot of money. Anyone 'holding a loaf' is carrying a large amount of 'bread' (qv).
Low Tide		A situation that arises when the beer content of a glass falls below an inch. When it's empty the 'Tide's Out'.
Madonna	*Sconner*	A recent piece of 'popney' (qv) which sees the American singer as a person with a shaved pubic area. See SCONNER.
Mamsahib		An old, upper-class reference to a wife, the lady of the house. Pronounced 'mamsaab' after 'she who must be obeyed' in India.
Man Upstairs		An often used reference to God. If Heaven's above then that's where 'The Man' is.
Meat & Two Veg		A well-known euphemism for man's genitalia. A piece that is often aimed at the bulge in a ballet dancer's tights and it's what wives threaten to cut off as a deterrent to straying spouses.
Meldrew		A miserable, moaning, cynical man. One who will view a field of buttercups and see only the cowpats. Based on Victor Meldrew, the main character in the British sitcom, *One Foot in the Grave*.
Merry Monk	*Spunk (Semen)*	A Johnny-come-lately rival to the long known 'Harry Monk' (qv). Based on the jolly friar who, given his vows of abstinence, may wake up with a messy habit.

Metal Mickie	*Sickie*	A moody (qv) day off work since the 1980s, when this robot first appeared in a TV series that bore his name. It's also down to him that any male deemed to be a bit on the 'wrong side of right' may be known as 'Mental Mickey'. *See* Sickie.
Minerals		Physical courage, hardness, 'bottle' (qv). See also Balls (c) and note the mineral based terms 'rocks', 'pebbles' and 'stones' within these pages, which relate to testicles.
Minger		An ugly, repellant, unpleasant person or thing, a popular piece of abuse or criticism since the 1990s that seems likely to cause offence for years to come. So 'mingers' beware!
Minging		Extremely drunk. Rotten, stinking, rolling so. An early 21st–century term that is derived from 'Ming' (qv b). *See also* Rotten.
Mingy		Tight, mean or stingy. Possibly a hybrid of the last two. A well known description of the niggardly type, who is said to have hermetically sealed pockets.
Mobile Throne		A commode, a recently coined pun on mobile phone heard in the geriatric ward of an Essex hospital. *See* Throne.
Molly		One of the oldest terms for a homosexual or sodomite. This 18th–century term was frequently used of scandalous men and it later evolved into a verb, whereby 'to molly' was to have anal intercourse and 'mollying' is buggery. 'Miss Molly' – an effeminate man.
Mondayitis		A non-specific condition, not dissimilar to 'lazyitis' (qv), which only occurs on Monday mornings and afflicts the sufferer with a chronic aversion to work or school, resulting in a day off with a moody excuse. Also known as a 'Touch of the Bob Geldhofs' after the Irish singer whose group, The Boomtown Rats, hit the charts with the song 'I Don't Like Mondays' in 1979.
Mont		An ugly, unattractive person. One barred from haunted houses for fear of frightening the ghosts. A reduced form of monster.
Mopsqueezer		A condescending term for a henpecked husband, otherwise known as a 'Mouse'. Someone seen to be forced into doing the housework by a domineering wife. A man who willingly does the chores is known as a 'self made mouse'. The original 'mopsqueezer' was a 19th–century housemaid.

Mort	Centuries old term for a woman, originally a prostitute, still in occasional use, mostly in the underworld where she is seen on the arm of a villain.
Mortar	The vagina, a 19th–century term for that which accepts a 'pestle' (qv).
Mullet	A condescending way to describe a man's hair-style, a long back and short sides. The look was widely seen at the back-end of the 20th century and considered old fashioned by the beginning of the 21st century. Especially, it seems, by 'green-eyed', bald, young men.
Munter	A piece of late 20th–century 'ladguage' for a promiscuous but unattractive woman; an 'abandoned dog', so to speak.
Narrow-Guts	A gaunt, skinny person. One said to be 'in need of a few meat puddens'. 'Narrow-gutted' – thin.
Nazy	Drunk, a centuries-old piece based on the equally ancient term 'Nase' – a red nose.
Nellie Pledge, do a	To make a verbal gaffe or malapropism, as this character in the British TV sitcom, *Nearest and Dearest* was prone to do. 'Our Nellie', who was played by English comedienne Hylda Baker (1908–86), would, for example, turn an ombudsman into an omnibusman, cook with desecrated coconut and give an octopus testicles.
Nipper-Crapper	A child's potty, otherwise known as a 'toddler's piddler'. For use when baby outgrows the 'cack-sack'.
Obliterated	One of many terms of destruction used to represent the extreme effects of drink or drugs. Others include 'Wiped Out', 'Destroyed', 'Knocked Out' and 'Kayoed'. Drunken punsters get 'Oblottorated'.
Off the Road	Anything broken, out of action or in need of repair draws comparison with a broken down vehicle that cannot be used until it is fixed. Crude, insensitive men also use the term in relation to women who may be on a menstrual period.
Old Iron	An old term for a watch and chain heard famously in the music-hall song 'Any Old Iron' as sung by Harry Champion (1866–1942) and a hit record for British actor/comedian Peter Sellers (1925–80) in 1957. If you want to cause offence, use it about someone's Rolex.

Pestle		A 19th–century term for the penis that also sees action as a verb for the sexual act from a man's standpoint. *See* MORTAR.
Pimply		A teenager, a spotty little erk to whom anyone over 30 is a 'wrinkly'.
Piss-Pipe/ Piddle Pipe		A couple of terms for the penis in call of nature mode, whereby incontinent men suffer from 'leaking pipes'.
Pit Stench		The condition also known as 'reeking armpits', which is easily cured with an effective under-arm destencher.
Plaster/ Bandage/ on a Wooden Leg		Three symbols of the inept. Useless articles may be deemed to be 'about as much use as a bandage on a wooden leg'.
Polish & Spit	*Shit*	This is the word in 'rubbish mode. Anything considered 'crappy' (qv) is said to be 'polish': 'This referee's polish.' – a disgruntled Crystal Palace supporter.
Popney		A form of slang invented by young people around the turn of the millennium. Known as Popney Rhyming Slang, the idea is to make up a piece of RS on the name of a celebrity of the day. Some catch on, but many don't.
Poppet		A 60s term for a piece of dried faecal matter attached to an anal hair takes the name of a chocolate sweet, a Payne's Poppet, from a supposed similarity in appearance. Has anyone actually made a comparison? Another confectionery, 'Chocolate Raisin', has been used for the same reason.
Poshney		The direct opposite of a 'mockney' (qv), which sees the cockney putting on a more eloquent voice. Or going all la-di-da and putting on 'hairs' and graces as they say in Wapping.
Postman Pat	*Pratt*	A complete fool becomes a 'prize postman', thanks to mail deliverer from kiddies TV.
Potato Chip	*Zip*	Only ever used as 'tater' and most commonly in relation to a fly. Most men know the agony of catching an unsuspecting willie in a 'tater'.
Prannet		A fool, an idiot from the 1970s. One deemed to be a wise man short of a Nativity scene.
Pushpencil		An office worker or loosely, anyone who makes a living with a 'scribbling stick', from the tally clerk

at the docks to the columnist with the Candle Makers' Wickly.

Pussy-Whipped Of a man, to be dominated by his wife. The American version of henpecked has landed on these shores, exposing the British 'mouse' to a pubic flogging. *See* MOPSQUEEZER.

Racky An Iraqi, a term that became popular in the wake of the hostilities in Iraq 2003.

Ready Steady Go *Po* A chamber pot from the 1960s based on a TV music show of the time. Also known as a PP (Piss Pot), it was standard issue in the basic chalets at Holiday Camps, so if you needed a middle of the night 'pee pee' in the PP, you'd grab the 'ready steady' and go.

Recky The anus, an abbreviated rectum, whereby a 'drecky recky' warrants no pondering over. *See* DRECK.

Rikki Tikki Tavi *Lavvy* A toilet courtesy of the snake killing mongoose in Rudyard Kipling's *Jungle Book*. The 'Rikki Tikki' sounds like the ideal place for men with 'tendencies' (qv) to get their 'trouser snakes' 'eaten'.

Ring-Rot An unspecified disease of the anus, what heterosexuals consider homosexuals to be prone to. Also a good curse for use against people who do you a bad turn, an inconsiderate motorist, for example, may sit uncomfortably after 'I hope you get ring-rot' has been aimed at them.

Roasting Taking advantage of women for group sex, likening them to poultry, whereby a man 'pulls a bird' and has sex with her, after which they are joined by his friends, who take it in turns to 'stuff the chicken'. The term hit the headlines in 2003 when some footballers were accused of taking part in the gang rape of a young woman in a London hotel.

Robert Money, the Spanish word for which is *dinero*, so therefore a pun on the name of American actor, Robert De Niro. Used by young Brits on Spanish holidays, much to the bewilderment of the locals.

Rolf Australian entertainer and artist Rolf Harris gets cockneyfied to 'Aris' to become a term for the backside. *See* ARISTOTLE.

Roy Race *Face* A 60s term for the ultimate English hero, the cleaner than soap footballer Roy of the Rovers of Tiger comic fame. Never take an honest 'Roy Race' on trust, it may house a dishonest mouth.

Rubberhead		A thick person, a dimwit. One who couldn't pass a maths test with a calculator. Someone whose head is likened to an eraser, i.e. a solid lump.
Rubberlips		An unkind name hurled at someone with prominent 'kissers'. Another is 'Linolips', which is aimed at those said to have lips like rolls of lino. Although the 'kisser' is a well-known term for the mouth, the pluralised 'kissers' are lips. Guess why.
Rut		To indulge in sexual intercourse. In standard English, 'rutting' is the sexual activity of deer but has found its way into BritSlang as a course description of human coupling. I'm told a lot of it goes on at stag shows.
Saga Lout		An elderly scoundrel or troublemaker, especially when drunk. The senior citizen version of 'lager lout' (qv). SAGA is an organisation that caters for the over-50s.
Sailor		In the 1960s all things nautical were seen, by comedians of the day, as a source of humour involving homosexuality and a gay man became a 'sailor'. Men with that particular bent was said to be 'a bit Ahoy' and 'Hello sailor' said in a camp way became a national catchphrase.
Salmon & Prawn	*Horn (Erection)*	A couple of swimmers represent a show of excitement at the merest whiff of a 'fish shop'. See FISH (a).
Sandbag/ Sandwitch		A pair of unpleasant or unattractive Arabic woman. A piece brought back by soldiers of the North Africa campaign of World War Two.
Sand Wog		An Arab, especially one who is hostile towards the West. A piece that's been used against terrorist bombers in the wake of the Iraq invasion of 2003.
Scaffold Poles		A late 19th–century term for chips, which most likely hasn't been served up for a century or so. Probably descriptive, which means spuds must have been bloody big back then!
Scratchers		The fingers. Yours if you've got an itchy bum, someone else's if the itch is a bit higher.
Scribe		To sign and also a signature. You may 'scribe' a cheque or put your 'scribe' on it.
Second-Hand Dartboard		A term used to describe a promiscuous woman who, like an old target, will have had many pricks. As the saying goes: She's had more pricks than a second-hand dartboard. See PRICK (a).
Seig Heils	*Piles*	Another case of haemorrhoids, where a nasty 'chute' (qv) becomes a Nazi salute.

Sex Up		To exaggerate something to make it more attractive or appealing. Infamously, the government dossier of Iraq's weapons capabilities in 2003 was said to have been 'sexed up' to make an unpopular war seem necessary and unavoidable.
Shania Twain	*Stain*	Another piece of 'popney' (qv) that turns a beautiful Canadian songstress into soiled goods. Clothes, mattresses, carpets, gussets, etc can all get 'Shania'd'. Wonder if this will impress her much?
Silly as a Bunch of Lights		A direct rival to the 'light minded' (qv) one who is as 'silly as a box of lights' (qv). I have yet to find out what a bunch of lights are and what's so silly about them. Possibly connected to 'Lights', a 19th–century term for a fool.
Sir Oswald		A piece recently heard in a Stepney supermarket regarding muesli (or as it's said in the area, 'moosli'). Pun on British fascist Sir Oswald Mosley (1896–1980). Coincidentally, Mosley, along with his followers, came unstuck in Stepney in the so-called Battle of Cable Street (1936).
Slightly		An ironic example from the late 1960s that mirrors the older, 'Not Much', 'Not Many', 'Not Half', etc, meaning a great amount. Do I like the Stones? Slightly.
Smell Garlic		To be suspicious, a 19th–century version of 'smell a rat' that seems to imply that if anything untoward is going on, there must be a foreigner in the vicinity. 'Garlicky' – highly suspect. Like the telephone call informing you that you've won a prize when you didn't enter a competition.
Sneak		a) To steal, to lift something in a casual, opportunist manner. Sneak thieves have been going 'On the Sneak' since the 19th century when it mainly involved entering houses whose doors had been left open. b) A lower than your average thief, a light-fingered lowlife who will 'nick anything that ain't nailed down'. c) An informer, mainly in the form of a tell-tale or snitch. One who will go behind your back and 'offer you up' to authority and 'drop you in the shit'.
Sneaksby		A very low, untrustworthy person. A grade 1, listed 'littleworth' (qv) of whom it would be a pleasure to 'shit in his hat and punch it'.
Spadework		An unskilled or menial job. A piece from the 1950s when West Indian immigrants began arriving in

	Britain, mainly getting employment in the low paid public sector, usually in cleaning or labouring positions. *See* SPADE.
Spanner	An incompetent, weak person – a jibe from the 1990s that's probably a corruption of 'Spazzer'. *See* SPASTIC.
Spice	To rob. A piece of 18th–century 'rogue speak' pertaining to a street or highway robbery, whereby the victim is 'Spiced' – robbed, and the robber is a 'Spicer'. Back then a street robber was a footpad, the forerunner of today's mugger.
Spliced	Married – so common that it's easy to forget that it's slang for a bipartisan union!
Squeeze	A good result, a slice of good fortune that's slightly sweeter than a 'touch' (qv a).
Squirch	Television or radio interference – an onomato-poeic term for static. Without a decent aerial, all you'll pick up is a load of 'squirch' or your picture may be 'squirchy'.
Sticker	A knife used as a weapon, a piece that's been doing damage since carving out a name in 19th–century gang-slang. Other 'Scarmakers' include 'Stabber' and 'Striper'. There is a story of an old knifeman who named his trusty weapon 'Old Glory', after the American flag. This alluded to the scars and stripes it had inflicted. *See* STRIPE (a).
Stewdle-oo	A stew, an example from days gone by, when the stew pot was continually on the go.
Suckdirt	A vacuum cleaner, a rival to hoover that's unlikely make much of a challenge.
Take to Sketchleys	To strip someone of their money or assets by way of a gamble or con. Another version of 'taking someone to the cleaners', Sketchley's being a well-known High-street dry cleaning company.
Testicular Toe-Punt	A setback, letdown or major disappointment, literally a boot in the gonads. There are many ways of expressing a kick to this part of man's anatomy: this is the least offensive:

> *One Knockback Too Many*
> *Many's the night I've lain in the dark*
> *Thinking. Pondering.*
> *Wondering.*
> *Who builds all these barriers*

That curb my ambitions?
And who puts up all these no-entry signs
That prevent me from making any right turns
Into the roads I long to travel?
Who owns that giant invisible hand
That keeps me treading this laborious,
Tedious, deeply rutted path
Towards my eventual inglorious end?
Is it God? Is it fate? Or is it I?

Thingamabobs		Everyone's used this for something they can't put a name to, but how many realise it originally referred to the testicles?
Three & Fourpence	*Reinforcements*	An old army term based on three shillings and fourpence in old money. The story goes that by the time the message, 'Send reinforcements we are going to advance' got down the line, it became 'Send three and four pence, we are going to a dance'.
Tilbury Forts	*Shorts*	'Tilburys' were the khaki leg revealers worn by soldiers engaged in desert warfare in World War Two. Based on a Thamesside fortification built at Tilbury, Essex in 1682.
Timberhead		A stupid person, a dunce. Someone said to 'have sawdust for brains'. Also 'Timbernut' and 'Woodnut'.
Timber Toes		An old, unkind reference to someone with a wooden leg, generally an ex-serviceman who had lost a limb in battle. Before the welfare state such men were reduced to begging or busking. A land fit for heroes?
Toe Jam		Dirt and other gunk that accumulates between the toes of unwashed feet: 'Go and grow some taters in you toe jam.' A piece of abuse aimed at a 'dirtywack' (qv).
Toodles		An irritating way of saying goodbye in the 'noughties' (qv). A cut-down version of 'Toodle-oo' or 'Toodle-pip'. An overheard piece of banter in a London wine bar:

    1st man: I'll say toodle-oo then.
    2nd man: Where are you going?
    1st man: To der loo. Ha ha!
    2nd man: It's where you belong. Stay there!
    1st man: Toodles.

Trout Pout		A currently well-known term for the fishy-mouthed appearance of someone who has gone a bit too far with a lip enlargement operation. Such a person may be tagged 'Cod lips'.

Tyre Kicker		A mug, someone a slick salesman or a conman 'sees coming'. Based on the type of person who, when buying a second-hand car, kicks the tyres as a test of its roadworthiness.
Under the Arm'ole		A decidedly strange way of saying 'let's go', possibly polari (qv) since it is based on the Italian '*andiamo*' meaning precisely that.
Unzipped		Mad, mentally 'cut adrift without a lifebelt'. Somebody said to 'have a button hanging off'. The BritSlang version of 'Unhinged'.
Vincent Van Gogh	*Cough*	Based on the Dutch painter (1853–90), there are two ways of shortening this. You either have a 'Vincent' or a 'Van Gogh' – never the Full Monty.
Waste of Space/ Air/Oxygen		What a totally useless, stupid or inept person is said be. In effect the space could be better occupied and the air breathed by someone more reliable.
Water the Wurzels		To urinate, how the countryman has 'one up the wall'. He may also 'Water the 'Weeds' or 'Water the Bushes'.
Wee Room/ Office		A toilet or public urinal, any 'little chamber' where water is discharged.
Weeble		A pear shaped person, a narrow shouldered, fat bottomed endomorph. Much like the similarly shaped toy that was famously advertised: 'Weebles wobble but they don't fall down'.
Wonderloaf		A name given to a supremely idle person, a loafer of international standard. Also known as a 'Superslob'.
Wyruc		A curry. If you fancy a backslang vindaloo, this is what it looks like. 'Neckich wyruc' – chicken curry.
Yoghurt		A gullible fool, someone who may be soft, thick and decidedly lemonish. *See* LEMON (a).
Zedland		One of the places we visit when asleep, along with Dreamland, the Land of Nod, Snorefolk or on Elm Street (qv). *See* ZEDS. The term once referred to the West Country, where local dialect turns the letter S to Z as in 'Zomerzet'.
Zip/Zippo/ Zip-All		Three Stateside terms for nothing, which are now used here due to TV and film usage. American dunces know 'zip-all'. British ones know 'fuck-all' or 'kaycuff la' in backslang.
Zoes		A turn of the millennium term for the testicles, a play on the name of Zoe Ball, a famous woman of the time.

EXTRA EXTRAS

Eli Wallach(s) *Bollock(s)* A testicle or two from the 1960s based on the American actor who famously 'dropped a major Eli' when taking on the original Magnificent Seven. *See* DROP A BOLLOCK.

Handshagger Someone known not to have any sex life other than masturbation. A member of the Wet Dream Prevention Society. Also an unpleasant person of the 'wanker' and 'tosser' variety.

Nugget A fool, someone considered to be a nut short of a nougat, which in the East End is pronounced 'nugget'.

Rory McGrath *Laugh* The 'noughties' version of 'Steffi Graf' (qv), whereby piss takers, wind-up merchants and practical jokers are said to be 'having a Rory'. Based on a British comedian.

Smelly Perfume, aftershave, etc. Heard on the radio during the run-up to Christmas 2003: Men are lucky really – if they get stuck for a present for their wives they can always buy them a bottle of smelly.

State of the Ark Technologically out of date, old fashioned or antiquated – typically, an early mobile phone. 'State of the Art' technology in reverse can take in anything deemed to be 'straight out of the ark'.

Tonto Crazy, mad, mental. Not sure how the red Indian sidekick of The Lone Ranger got involved here, but if he ever went 'tonto', he lost his sanity either on a permanent or temporary basis. An insulting term for the mentally ill.

You're Having a Laugh/Chuckle/ Giggle Three terms of disbelief that have been commonly employed since the 1990s. They translate to 'You can't be serious' or 'You're whipping the widdle'.